THE SECRET WAR

The Story of International Espionage

Since World War II

Ted Morgan
alias

Sanche de Gramont

The Story of International Espionage

THE SECRET WAR

Since World War II

G. P. PUTNAM'S SONS : New York

TO MY MOTHER

Acknowledgments

I would like to thank the following persons whose kind assistance and advice were indispensable to the writing of this book in New York, Washington, London, Paris, East and West Germany, and other places: David Dallin, James B. Donovan, Alan Winston, Franz Felix, John T. Dublynn, J. D. Panizza, Albert H. Socolov, Archibald Palmer, Abraham Pomerantz, Dr. Gunther Nollau, Jacques Bergier, Georgi Okolovich, Albert Hamilton, Roger Mennevee, Don Cook, Tom Lambert, Benjamin Mandel, Rear Admiral George B. Thomson, Charles Huber, John Austin, Donald Davies, Dr. Clarence Schilt, and Nancy Suydam.

Contents

Contents

I. Total Espionage

IN 1955, anxiety over the United States' "intelligence gap" led to the investigation of the Central Intelligence Agency by a Hoover Commission task force. The task force recommended "greater boldness at the policy level." The contrast was made between Soviet intelligence, which had gone about "the collection of vital secrets in this country with relative ease" and America's fumbling intelligence. The task force suggested greater "willingness to accept certain calculated political and diplomatic risks and full use of technological capabilities."

It can safely be said that these recommendations were in the next six years carried out beyond the task force's greatest expectations. After the Cuban adventure and the U-2 overflights, no one can accuse the CIA of timidity. These days it is fashionable to describe the agency as a monster on the rampage. Fred Cook, who wrote an "exposé" of the CIA in *The Nation* (June 24, 1961), summed up:

> The President speaks peace; but the CIA overthrows regimes, plots internal sabotage and revolution, foists opium-growers on friendly nations, directs military invasions, backs right-wing militarists. These are not the actions of a democratic, peace-loving nation devoted to the high ideals we profess. These are the actions of the Comintern in right-wing robes.

13

Cook expressed the shock that many must have felt upon learning that the United States, while basing its foreign policy on the preservation of peace, was working in the shadows to subsidize wars.

There is something equally unexpected, however, in the fact that it took only six years for this reversal. In 1955, the problem was how to unleash the CIA, which was not providing adequate intelligence, particularly behind the Iron Curtain. In 1961, the problem was how to curb the CIA to prevent giving the United States yet another black eye with another Cuban fiasco. The power and aggressiveness of American intelligence is all the more surprising when one recalls that the CIA is a recent arrival to the intelligence field. It was founded in 1947 but did not really get started until 1950, when Allen Dulles joined it.

In that short time, which significantly coincides with the Cold War, it had grown like a delicate child who in adolescence becomes the bully on the block.

In the meantime, Soviet intelligence had not exactly been lazing, and as Dulles himself once noted: "Since I have been with the CIA a mountain of hard evidence on Communist intrigue has passed over my desk." Soviet spies have been operating in the United States for more than forty years and the apparats all over the world went into high gear for the Cold War.

Cuba and the U-2 have made public opinion dimly aware of this basic fact: the United States, like the Soviet Union and because of the Soviet Union, is practicing total espionage. It is matching the Soviet Union in the secret warfare of intelligence just as it is matching it (or trying to) in the construction of missiles. There are few techniques used by Soviet espionage that American intelligence cannot duplicate. The intelligence organizations of the two blocs are monolithic and powerful, and work in a climate of secrecy and ruthlessness.

Soviet and American intelligence communities trade charges; each accuses the other of being the largest. A. N. Shelepin, former chairman of the Committee of State Security (KGB) who was Allen Dulles' opposite number, wrote in *Pravda* early in 1959 that "the espionage apparatus in the capitalistic countries, above all the United States, is constantly growing. The CIA alone, for example, now employs more than 20,000 persons and spends more than $1,500,000,-000 a year. The scale of U.S. counterintelligence has increased twelvefold in the past few years as compared with the first postwar years." Dulles said in the only on-the-record interview he ever gave (*U.S. News and World Report,* March 19, 1954): "Certainly the Soviet intelligence leads the field in this respect [number of agent networks]. They recruit and run agents in all important countries of the world, and through their 'front organizations' they control a great many more." He said again, in another speech:

> The Soviet has the largest number of trained agents for espionage and secret political action that any country has even assembled. In Moscow, Prague, Peiping, and other Communist centers, they are training agents recruited from scores of other countries to go out as missionaries of Communism into the troubled areas of the world. Much of the Middle East and Southeast Asia, and Black Africa are high on their target list. They do not neglect this hemisphere as recent disclosures of Communist plotting in Mexico show us.

There is also a similarity of tone in charges about the villainy of espionage services. The Soviet Information Bureau's brochure "Caught In the Act" (a 160-page denunciation of the CIA published in 1960 and given to this writer by a United States intelligence official who commented: "This isn't the Bible, but it's got some good stuff") states that "espionage and subversion conducted by the United States have indeed become total and global in character. This activity ranges from the tapping of telephone conversations and the decoding of foreign government correspondence to the insolent and overt violation of the sovereignty of other states by sending agents and spy planes into them and the hatching of plots and *coups d'état*."

The booklet "Patterns of Communist Espionage," prepared by the House Committee on Un-American Activities, states:

> Communist embassies, consulates, U.N. delegations, trade and other missions have been, and are presently, used as legal covers for international Communist spy rings. . . . The personnel of Communist diplomatic, trade, and similar missions is made up to a considerable degree of trained MVD (Ministry of Internal Affairs) and military intelligence operatives. . . . Communist diplomats . . . resort to blackmail, terror, and other reprehensible techniques . . . there is also some evidence that the Soviet Union is using the exchange program to assist its espionage objectives.

J. Edgar Hoover, whose Federal Bureau of Investigation is in charge of thwarting Soviet espionage activities in the United States, said in his 1960 appropriations request before the House subcommittee on appropriations that "there has been no letup in Red subversion . . . our investigations have clearly disclosed an over-all expansion of Soviet bloc intelligence activities against the United States."

Soviet espionage in the United States is nothing new. The first organized apparats came under the cover of Amtorg, the Soviet trade agency which set up New York offices in 1924. The FBI has had nearly forty years' experience in dealing with Communist spies. Penetration of the Soviet Union by American intelligence, however, is a recent development. Vladimir Petrov, an MVD agent who defected in 1954, could make this remarkable statement based on his own experience: "In all my twenty-one years as a professional state security officer I never came across one authentic case of foreign espionage in the Soviet Union in peacetime. Thousands were accused of espionage and shot without a shred of evidence being produced. . . . I never heard of a case in Russia comparable to those of Fuchs and Nunn May, Greenglass or Golos in America, Andersson and Enhom in Sweden, or Richard Sorge in Japan. Yet according to the ceaseless warnings of the Soviet authorities, Russia is so riddled from top to bottom with agents of foreign intelligence that only perpetual and relentless vigilance saves it from destruction."

Before the last decade, the United States was spied upon but not spying, whereas the Soviet Union was spying but not spied upon. But thanks to the pressures of the Cold War, the United States did some catching up, and in doing so strained some of the elementary principles of a democratic society. Dulles' statement that "if you believe in a program, you may have to break a little crockery to put it into effect" is rather chilling now that the public has been given a glimpse of the CIA's closet full of broken dishes.

The revelation that the United States was waging an intelligence war with as much vigor and determination as the Soviet Union shattered the illusion of a "moral" cold war, a crusade fought against "godless Communism." Part of public disenchantment with the CIA came when it was learned that hitting below the belt was not exclusively a Soviet tactic. The CIA's record of duplicity and "dirty tricks" put it in the same league as Soviet espionage. In shattering the illusion, however, the problems of an effective intelligence organization in a free society were laid bare. Can a society that believes in government by the people, in the people's right to know, and in noninterference in the affairs of other nations send agents to spy on foreign governments, subvert Soviet officials, and sanction the professional spy's arsenal of villainy?

The central problem, as statesmen from Pericles to President John F. Kennedy have pointed out, is the opposition between closed and open societies. When Pericles forged a free Athenian society, he little expected that fourteen years later it would be entombed under the might of the Spartan military state, which embodied the antithesis of his words:

> Ours is a free state both in politics and daily life—we are superior to our enemies, too, in our preparations for war. Our city is open to the world. We are not always expelling foreigners for fear of their learning or seeing something of military importance. We live freely and yet we face the same dangers quite as readily as they . . . those men surely should be deemed bravest who know most clearly what danger is and what pleasure is and are not made thereby to flinch.

It is for historians to judge whether Athens crumbled because it was an open society and allowed spies to operate unhindered.

United States policy in the Cold War has been to recognize the dangers of an open society and try to achieve a balance between national security, the basic freedoms, foreign policy and intelligence operations. This sometimes places the Executive in embarrassing postures. The last two Presidents have found themselves publicly condoning espionage, something no chief of state in history had been known to do before. President Eisenhower admitted after the U-2 was shot down that he had personally approved a policy of pursuing intelligence by every possible means. President Kennedy was twice embarrassed by the Cuban incident. On April 13, 1961, five days before the invasion, he walked the thin line that separates declaration from intent with the pledge that the United States would not intervene "under any conditions" to help bring about the downfall of Castro, that he would do everything possible "to make sure there are no Americans involved in anti-Castro actions around Cuba," and that he "would be opposed to mounting an offensive" against Castro from this country. The President did not lie—there were no Americans among the rebel forces that landed in the Bay of Pigs on April 18. The offensive was not launched from the United States but from islands off the coast of Nicaragua, which were leased in 1916 by the United States for 99 years. Mr. Kennedy was in the position of the driver who was stopped by police for going eighty miles an hour and who replied in all candor: "But Officer, I haven't been driving for an hour."

When the CIA's preponderant role in the adventure was unmasked, the young President took the blame, as his predecessor had done in the U-2 incident. But his faith in the superiority of an open society was so shaken that he suggested voluntary censorship to newspaper publishers.

On April 27, still smarting from the Cuban experience, Mr. Kennedy told the American Newspaper Publishers Association:

> The facts of the matter are that this nation's foes have openly boasted of acquiring through our newspapers information they would otherwise hire agents to acquire through theft, bribery, or camouflage; that details of this nation's covert preparations to counter the enemy's operations have been available to every newspaper reader. That the size, the strength, the location and the nature of our forces and weapons, and our plans and strategy for their use, have all been pinpointed in the press in a degree to satisfy any foreign power. And that in at least one case, the publication of details concerning a secret mechanism in our possession required its alteration at the expense of considerable time and money.
>
> Every newspaper now asks itself, with respect to every story: Is it news? All I suggest is that you add the question: Is it in the national interest?

An intelligence official told this writer that the President had been particularly annoyed by a story that appeared January 9, 1961, in *The New York Times* with the unlikely dateline of Retalhuleu, Guatemala. *Times* correspondent Paul P. Kennedy (no relation), blew the whistle on CIA training of Cuban rebels for the forthcoming offensive. He said: "Commando-like forces are being drilled in guerrilla warfare tactics by foreign personnel, mostly from the United States," in a camp and hidden airstrip in the Cordillera foothills a few miles from the Pacific. They were being trained, he said, "for what Guatemalans consider will be an almost inevitable clash with Cuba." This was the kind of news the President clearly did not deem fit to print.

The Soviets have tried to debunk the problems posed by an "open" society. According to "Caught In the Act," the theory "advanced by the U.S. statesmen to justify the activities of American intelligence is nothing more than a crude trick of propaganda beneath criticism. It is common knowledge that all the governments take necessary measures to protect their state secrets. And the United States is no exception in this respect."

The Soviet argument here is weak when one considers the present clamor from responsible sources against the CIA, and the personnel and organization changes which have come about as an aftermath of the Cuban washout, including the replacement of Allen Dulles at the head of the organization. Because of the open society, intelligence and counterintelligence services in the West are beset by two permanent sets of problems:

1. The availability of Western information and the unavailability of Soviet bloc information. Allen Dulles, who won his varsity letters in espionage against the Nazis, has remarked that "Germany was a pipe dream compared with what we have to meet now." Mr. Dulles has also pointed out that "it's much easier for the Russians, it's all under one umbrella. All they have to do is bend over and pick it up."

Soviet defectors have estimated that a Soviet military attaché in the United States is able to obtain 95 per cent of the material he needs simply by asking for it. The Government Printing Office supplies at a nominal cost such items as harbor installations of the United States, dimensions and locations of airfields, lists of United States mineral resources, registers of retired officers; in short, practically everything from "how to drive a nail" to "how to build an atom bomb." The Map Information Office of the U.S. Geological Survey, Department of the Interior, is another favorite source, and provides topographic maps of the entire United States. Subscriptions to technical magazines such as *Aviation Week* and *Bulletin of Atomic Scientists* are never allowed to lapse. Soviet diplomats also attend industrial conventions. At the Western Electric convention in Los Angeles in 1959, two Russian diplomats collected so much literature they could not carry it and had to hire a station wagon. It was estimated they left with about 250 pounds of literature. Publications such as *The Pilot's Handbook* or the eighteen-volume edition on port facilities put out by the Army Engineers would certainly be restricted in the Soviet Union—in the United States they are available to anyone.

In April, 1960, Vice-Admiral Hyman G. Rickover told Congress's Joint Atomic Energy subcommittee that a toy manufacturer had produced a model of the Polaris atomic submarine so accurate that "a good ship designer can spend one hour on that model and tell he has millions of dollars' worth of free information."

The notice that came with the $2.98 toy said:

> This ballistic missile firing nuclear submarine is another of a series of models built in strict accordance with specifications contained in offical U.S. Navy Blueprints. We wish to take this opportunity to express our sincere gratitude to the Electric Boat Division of General Dynamics Corporation for generously furnishing complete and accurate data. Without this cooperation, the development of a completely authentic model would not have been possible. This model incorporates all the interior details of the submarine including atomic reactor, control room galley, crew's quarters and two Polaris missiles. Your model is authentic in every detail and is accurately scaled to 1 foot = 300 feet.

Admiral Rickover said he was "aghast" that the model had been placed on the market and that "if I were a Russian, I would be most grateful to the United States for its generosity in supplying such information for $2.98." The admiral, known as "the father of the atomic submarine," said the model provided accurate data on the size of the reactor compartment and the size of the crew needed to operate the vessel. A European scientist, when asked about Admiral Rickover's protests, however, said: "Even if the Russians could get the blueprints for the atomic submarine they would not be worth stealing; they are so voluminous it takes a three-story building to house them. And once you have them, it would cost you so much to convert the specifications to the metric system it would be quicker and less expensive to build your own."

This same scientist, who recently returned from a trip to the Soviet Union, claimed that the Russians were releasing more scientific information than the United States. He said developments on atomic sites and missiles were freely available and that the Soviets had even put out a brochure the approximate title of which was: "The American Vanguard Missile, Why It Doesn't Work and How to Make It Work."

Other scientists, however, have noted that the Soviets are morbidly secretive about their atomic plants. They hide atomic installations under cover names. The Soviet equivalent to the Atomic Energy Commission, for instance, has been given the title of "Ministry of Medium Machine Building."

Meanwhile, Soviet scientists come to the United States to visit U.S. atomic installations. A group led by V. S. Emelyanov, head of the Central Directorate for the use of atomic energy, recently spent twenty-one days touring U.S. atomic installations. Admiral Rickover himself showed them the Shippingport atomic power station near Pittsburgh. The Enrico Fermi power station near Erie, Pa., was the next stop, and then the Argonne national laboratory, where the Russians examined the reactors and studied processes for producing plutonium fuel elements. Mr. Emelyanov noted with awe that "work is carried on through portholes with gloves." The Soviets visited Oak Ridge, Berkeley, Los Alamos, and were given details on a new method for injection of plasma and maintaining it in a magnetic trap. One scientist on the tour said cheerfully, "We locate our atomic reactors in rectangular buildings whereas you use circular buildings —but everything else is the same." American scientists would have to take his word for it, for they were never given such a blanket tour of Soviet installations.

Peter Axel, a professor of physics at the University of Illinois, who was asked by the Government to organize an exchange of Soviet and American scientists in 1959, emerged from the experience perplexed. The Soviets had no regulations for exchanges, he said, "and despite my efforts I could never learn from whom in the Soviet Union a reciprocal invitation should come." On the American side, he noted "suspicion, based on past Soviet performances, that the Soviets are trying to circumvent reciprocity in certain technical and scientific fields."

Edward Teller, the Hungarian-born physicist who played a key role in the development of the hydrogen bomb, wrote in a magazine article that there was much to be said for an open society and lack of secrecy in scientific achievement. "In America, people do not like to work in secret," he pointed out. "Secrecy has tended to shunt away some of our best men and best minds from work which is badly needed for our defense. Most of us prefer to work in a field where the free interchanges of ideas is encouraged and where we can become known to our colleagues.

"Secrecy is contagious. It erects barriers between friends. It causes suspicion between strangers. And it obscures needed public discussion on the national and world-wide scene. Openness will certainly help the free world to obtain the initiative in the great task of world organization." On the other hand, he added, "in Russia, secrecy is a way of life. Even scientists outside the nuclear field are restricted and regimented."

Thus, on the problem of availability of information, we are divided between the demands of elementary security and the belief that secrecy is inherently unrewarding in a free society. We complain that the Russians are finding out too much from open sources, but the complaints would be even louder if there was any attempt to censor these sources:

2. The question: how can intelligence and counterintelligence organizations exist and be effective within a democratic framework? The two American organizations affected by this problem are the Federal Bureau of Investigation, in charge of counterintelligence and internal security operations, and the Central Intelligence Agency, in charge of foreign intelligence.

J. Edgar Hoover has long been the favorite of Congressional committees and other government bodies that scrutinize the agency he heads. The 1955 Hoover Commission report on intelligence said: "We found the director of the FBI, through his forcefulness, initiative and managerial ability, to have developed the agency into a model organization of its kind. We are confident that in the FBI we have a most effective counterintelligence service."

Despite his notable record of convictions, Mr. Hoover has complained long and loud that in espionage cases he is hamstrung by "antiquated" U.S. legal methods. The four most painful thorns in the FBI's side are listed as:

a) The requirement of a public trial, which makes the government reluctant to prosecute because it will have to put confidential information on the record. In Britain, for instance, the sensitive case of Soviet agent George Blake was tried *in camera* in 1961. In the United States, the technique is to convince the defendant he will profit by pleading guilty. A light sentence is bartered for the lack of public trial. Thus in 1957, Jack Soble was sentenced to seven years in prison after pleading guilty to espionage. In 1961 his brother, Dr. Robert Soblen—a far less important espionage figure—was given a life sentence after pleading not guilty to similar charges.

b) The statute of limitations often prevents prosecution. This situation has been altered with the so-called Rosenberg law, which rules out statutes of limitation in cases affecting national security.

c) Existing statutes are not applicable to the kind of offenses committed in the Cold War. The statutes are directed against wartime espionage and sabotage. As a result, prosecutors have fallen back on conspiracy statutes, where it is enough to prove that a conspiracy to commit a crime exists without showing that a crime has been committed. The vast majority of Cold War espionage cases in the United States have been conspiracy cases.

d) Diplomatic immunity is an obstacle to detection and punishment. The FBI has handled this problem by turning the findings of its investigations over to the State Department, which declares the diplomat *persona non grata*.

Sometimes, the FBI is able to have a law tailored to its needs. In 1934, Congress granted the FBI the power to make arrests on condition that it obtain a warrant or written permission from a judge. Reasonable grounds for suspicion had to be shown, to protect the innocent from summary arrest. In 1949, when FBI agents arrested Judy Coplon, they somehow neglected to obtain a warrant, and thanks partly to this, her conviction was reversed by a court of appeals. Within a month of the reversal, Congress had passed a new law that a warrant was no longer required in cases involving national security. The feeling was, and this is one instance where the democratic process is strained in the name of security, that it is preferable to legalize police conduct presently unlawful than let spies go unpunished.

The FBI does many ungentlemanly things—it taps phones, goes through people's trash and garbage, opens mail, interviews maids about the failings of their employers, invites relatives and friends of suspects to spy on them, uses decoys, arrests people without telling them why, traps them into confessing, and occasionally has been known to use a little muscle.

But it tries to do these things in a gentlemanly way. No one can sound more respectable than Hoover explaining to Congress the FBI's wire-tap activities. In February, 1960, he said: "The FBI presently has only 78 wire taps in operation throughout the entire United States and its possessions, all of which are being used on security investigations. . . . The policy which the FBI follows is most restrictive and we know of no other agency which must first secure the written approval of the head of its department to use a wire tap. That the Attorney General, the highest legal officer of the nation, should authorize every wire tap which we use, after considering the facts involved, is a proper and just safeguard. . . . It is interesting to note that far too often the most vociferous critics of our restricted use of wire tapping are those engaged in criminal activity or attorneys who defend the notorious criminal element."

In the general view, Hoover has managed to make the FBI a highly effective counterespionage organization in spite of his complaints that he is "hamstrung by technicalities." He has achieved this while sidestepping the pitfalls the CIA has fallen prey to. He has never been publicly accused of interfering in policy matters. He has sometimes been criticized for autocracy, secrecy and remoteness but has never come under the hail of scorn that is the CIA's present lot.

With respect to policy making, Hoover has stated that "the FBI does not make policy, recommendations, conclusions or rulings based upon our investigations. The FBI, since I became its director in 1924, has adhered strictly to the premise that it is a fact-finding agency."

Secrecy in the FBI is mainly operational. Files cannot be made public and case histories cannot be disclosed until all possible ramifications have been untangled. There is also a great deal of secrecy about what goes on within the agency, attributable perhaps to Hoover's position as the "Robespierre" of the law-enforcement world—an incorruptible man at the head of an incorruptible organization. Most of the criticism against the FBI's so-called "secret police" methods comes from the extreme right and left.

Hoover was called a "little Hitler" by the Harry Bridges defense committee in 1940. In 1939, an anti-Semitic publication put out by the Pelley publishers in North Carolina charged that "a definite effort is afoot to make the reading or distributing of anti-Semitic literature a felony—as in Soviet Yiddish Russia. . . . The G-man force of the FBI has taken its first step toward functioning as an American OGPU, putting crime on the shelf while Judah's enemies get the G-man heat."

Hoover's indestructibility in office is a sign that he has been able to find a common ground between the demands of his profession and the checks and balances of an open society.

One may deplore the fences that protect this common ground. They have been built with the help of the most effective public relations campaign ever conducted. Many Americans believe that only Hoover stands between them and Communism. As many others are convinced that he has personally wiped out organized crime in the United States. A relentless advertising campaign has created the image of an ideal and infallible FBI. While it is far from that, it is no closer to a Soviet-style secret police. The FBI does not solve the problem of an effective police force in an open society. Rather, it is the product of a given society, dependent on its myths and failings. There is a wide breach between the FBI's public image and its reality.

The CIA, on the other hand, has reaped derision from all sides, from members of Congress to Soviet writer Ilya Ehrenberg, who once wrote in *Pravda* that "even if the spy Allen Dulles should arrive in heaven through somebody's absent-mindedness, he would begin to blow up the clouds, mine the stars, and slaughter the angels." Daily, Moscow radio refers to "Foggy Bottom, where the black octopus, CIA, has its lair." A Tass dispatch of a Dulles speech before a veteran's group said: "He was full of a wild mixture of lies, impotent rage, and half-helpless fury. We don't know how superspy Allen Dulles will end his life, but it is already evident that there are symptoms of Forrestal's disease on his face."

In the United States, the CIA is criticized in the press and in Congress for three main reasons: its secrecy and freedom from government control, its tendency to influence policy, and its backing of reactionary groups in foreign countries.

Unlike the FBI, the CIA does not have to make public its budget, the number of its employees, or its operations. As it states in a pamphlet for the press, "Because of this secrecy—required by law and by considerations of national safety—the CIA does not confirm or deny published reports, whether good or bad; never alibis; never explains its organization; never identifies its personnel (except for the few in the top echelons); and will not discuss its budget, its methods of operations, or its source of information."

Although it does not have the powers of subpoena and arrest granted to the FBI, it has other, far more extraordinary powers that add to its reputation as an occult force. These powers were granted in the Central Intelligence Agency Act of 1949, and specified:

1. Whenever the Director, the Attorney General, and the Commissioner of Immigration shall determine that the entry of a particular alien into the United States for permanent residence is in the interest of national security or essential to the furtherance of the national intelligence mission, such alien and his immediate family shall be given entry into the United States for permanent residence without regard to their inadmissibility under the immigration or any other laws and regulations, or to the failure to comply with such laws and regulations pertaining to admissibility: Providing that the number of aliens and members of their immediate families entering the United States under the authority of this section shall in no case exceed one hundred persons in any one fiscal year.

2. The sums made available to the agency may be expended without regard to the provisions of law and regulations relating to the expenditure of government funds; and for objects of a confidential, extraordinary, or emergency nature, such expenditures are to be accounted for solely on the certificate of the Director and every such certificate shall be deemed a sufficient voucher for the amount therein certified.

With this kind of extra-legal power helping to shroud its activities, the CIA has largely escaped Congressional scrutiny. Congress has made repeated efforts to appoint a watchdog committee over the CIA. A joint committee called in 1956 for this purpose said that "once secrecy becomes sacrosanct, it invites abuse. Secrecy now beclouds everything about CIA . . . our form of government . . . is based on a system of checks and balances. If this system gets seriously out of balance at any point, the whole system is jeopardized and the way is open for the growth of tyranny."

Allen Dulles had already replied to this objection in his 1954 interview in *U.S. News and World Report*. He said:

Any investigation, whether by a Congressional committee or any other body, which results in a disclosure of our secret activities and operations or uncovers our personnel would help a potential enemy just as if the enemy were able to infiltrate their agents right into our shop.

If it were necessary to go into the details of operations before any committees anywhere—the security of our operations would quickly be broken. You couldn't run an intelligence agency on that basis. No intelligence agency in the world is run on that basis. In intelligence you have to take certain things on faith. You have to look to the man who is directing the organization and the result he achieves. If you haven't got someone who can be trusted, or who doesn't get results, you'd better throw him out and get somebody else.

In fact, the CIA is working under multiple government controls. It is responsible first, of course, to the President, who checks on the CIA through a board of consultants on foreign intelligence activities. The board, on which President Kennedy's father has served, travels all over the world looking into the CIA's clandestine operations and reports its findings to the President. Next the CIA is responsible to the National Security Council (made up of the President, Vice-President, CIA director, Secretaries of State, Defense, and Treasury, and director of the Office of Defense Mobilization), which has a subcommittee on CIA operations. The CIA acts on directives which it has been given by the President and the National Security Council. The CIA is also responsible to four Congressional committees, the House and Senate Armed Forces and appropriations committees. These all have CIA subcommittees. CIA representatives have appeared before other committees, including the Senate Committee on the Judiciary and House Un-American Activities and Foreign Relations committees. Admittedly, however, the number of Congressmen who are "in" on CIA secrets is kept at a minimum. Lieutenant General C. P. Cabell, deputy director of the CIA, wrote in a letter to Senator Mike Mansfield (Dem., Montana) that "the CIA appropriations figure is very tightly held and is known to not more than five or six members in each house."

One of the Senators in the know, Richard Russell of Georgia, testified that relations between favored Congressmen and Dulles were cordial but sometimes frightening. "Although we have asked him very searching questions about some activities which it almost chills the marrow of a man to hear about," Russell said, "he has never failed to answer us forthrightly and frankly in response to any question we have ever asked him."

Some Congressmen have said privately they would rather not know what the CIA is doing, for the knowledge might identify them, to their constituents, with CIA fiascos. It can be said on good authority that when the U-2 incident broke, there was not a single member of Congress who had a clear picture of the program or its true purpose.

The charge that the CIA influences policy was dealt with by Dulles with words that have a hollow ring today in the light of recent events. His own appointment to the CIA was due largely to a memorandum he submitted in 1947 when Congress was considering the National Security Act, and to his service on a committee in 1948 which recommended improvements to the Act. The late General Walter Bedell Smith, who then headed the CIA, called Dulles and told him: "Now that you've written this damn report, it's up to you to put it in effect."

In his memorandum, Dulles wrote:

> The Central Intelligence Agency should have nothing to do with policy. It should try to get at the hard facts on which others must determine policy. The warnings which might well have pointed to the attack on Pearl Harbor were largely discounted by those who had already concluded that the Japanese must inevitably strike elsewhere. The warnings which reportedly came to Hitler of our invasion of North Africa were laughed aside. Hitler thought he knew we didn't have the ships to do it. It is impossible to provide any system which will be proof against the human frailty of intellectual stubbornness. Every individual suffers from that. All we can do is to see that we have created the best possible mechanism to get the unvarnished facts before the policy makers, and to get it there in time [sic].

One example of a chief of state who did not trust his intelligence service for this very reason was Sir Winston Churchill, who preferred raw intelligence reports to the "collective wisdom" of his agencies. He saw that Panzer divisions were being transferred from Greece to Poland in the spring of 1941 and advised Stalin that he would be attacked in the summer. Stalin decided the advice was "English provocation" and was unprepared when the invasion came in June.

Churchill's principle in these matters, as expressed before the House of Commons in 1939, was: "It seems to me that Ministers run the most tremendous risks if they allow the information collected by the Intelligence Department and sent to them, I am sure, in good time, to be shifted and colored and reduced in consequence and importance, and if they ever get themselves into a mood of attaching weight only to those pieces of information which accord with their earnest and honorable desire that the peace of the world should remain unbroken."

It would seem from the outcome of the Cuban invasion that President Kennedy and his advisers attached weight only to those pieces of information which accorded with their "earnest and honorable" desire to remove the Castro regime.

The CIA has in fact become as direct a policy-maker as the State Department through its political forays. It is much more than an intelligence agency and serves to counter the spread of Communism throughout the world. In the Soviet Union, proselytizing is a party not an intelligence function—it is up to the party to support leftist regimes, workers' groups and the like. Since 1956, when the Cominform was dissolved, there has been no specific Soviet agency directing the operations of international Communism. Yet, under the party's Central Committee, these operations are still an essential branch of Soviet foreign policy. They have never been the function of Soviet intelligence. Yet they are fought in every theatre of world tension by American intelligence. How can the CIA avoid being right at the heart of policy, when it selects anti-Communist regimes to support in trouble spots such as Laos, Iran, and Guatemala?

It is hard to see how Dulles himself could reconcile his repeated stand that he had nothing to do with policy and his admission as far back as 1954 that the CIA was the *"éminence grise"* of half a dozen stalwartly anti-Communist regimes.

Part of the unique interview in *U.S. News and World Report* is worth quoting to show that the CIA was vested from the start with the powers of an anti-Cominform:

> Q. Is that part of your function—to stir up revolutions in these countries?

A. Let me answer in this way: the Soviet Union is mounting a "Cold War" on the free world, and is using all the techniques that Communist inventiveness can supply. They have built up a whole series of "front organizations"—associations of youths, lawyers, women, and Cominform. They penetrate and control the major labor unions in France, Italy, Indonesia, and many other countries of the world.

Q. And some of ours—

A. In many countries of the world they have very vigorous political parties spearheaded by a hard core of Communists, and they use these political parties for their own ends in order to try to bring about Communist revolutions. That whole movement constitutes a threat to the stability of the free world. It constitutes a threat behind our North Atlantic Treaty Organization lines. We would be foolish if we did not co-operate with our friends abroad to help them to do everything they can to explore and counter the Communist subversive movement.

We were later to learn that "it's all in choosing your friends."

The interesting thing is that in the postwar period in which the CIA launched its secret political offensive in various parts of the world, the Soviet ceased to use its international Communist organization for espionage purposes. The Comintern, which had been a hotbed for intelligence agents and which was riddled with Stalin's secret police, was dissolved in 1943 and replaced in 1947 by the Cominform.

As Dr. Gunther Nollau (a West German intelligence official) writes in his book *International Communism and World Revolution:**

> During the nine years of the Cominform's existence not a single Cominform agent was arrested in the free world. Not a single passport was impounded that could be shown to have been "fixed up" by the Cominform. Is one to assume that the Cominform worked in such complete secrecy that its activities could remain undiscovered? If so, it must be the only intelligence service to have achieved this feat so long. Between 1947 and 1956, hundreds of Soviet, Polish, Czech or Hungarian agents were caught in Western Europe, but never a Cominform agent. Why was this? The answer is because there were no Cominform agents.

* Gunther Nollau, *International Communism and World Revolution* (London: Hollis & Carter, 1961).

Even though the chiefs of the Soviet intelligence organizations (KGB and MVD) are high up in the party organization, qualified sources believe that the policy-making role of the Soviet espionage and counterespionage organizations is a minor one. The shadow of Beria, who tried to use his post as head of the MVD to plot a coup after Stalin's death, still lingers. Beria had been given great political power as one of four First Deputy Chairmen of the Council of Ministers and his was an important voice in policy matters. Under his aegis, for instance, the criminal code was revised and certain political prisoners were set free. Beria's fall from grace, however, led to the divorce of espionage and secret police from policy.

Soviet espionage, for all its ubiquity and iniquity, would have trouble matching the CIA's record in the last ten years of meddling in the affairs of other countries. Based on published reports, the most glaring examples are:

1950: The CIA established a cover organization on Formosa called Western Enterprises Inc., which armed, trained and equipped Nationalist Chinese guerrillas that raided the Red Chinese mainland from the offshore islands.

1951: The CIA supported a guerrilla force of Chinese Nationalists that had fled to Northern Burma after the Communist take-over of China.

1952: The CIA supported the coup that ousted King Farouk from Egypt and brought Gamal Abdel Nasser to power.

1953: The CIA plotted the coup that ousted Premier Mohammed Mossadegh from Iran and brought back the Shah Mohammed Reza Pahlevi.

1953: The CIA set up an independent intelligence organization in West Germany under Reinhard Gehlen, an intelligence chief under Hitler. Gehlen sent agents into East Germany during the 1953 riots.

1954: The CIA supported Colonel Carlos Castillo Armas in his successful overthrow of the pro-Communist regime of Jacobo Arbenz Guzman.

1955: The CIA built an underground tunnel into East Berlin and tapped the Soviet East sector's telephone lines.

1956: During the Hungarian uprising, arms were supplied by the CIA and by Gehlen agents to the Hungarian patriots.

1958: The CIA urged military intervention in Lebanon and was instrumental in the decision to order the Sixth Fleet there and land Marines.

1960: The CIA backed General Phoumi Nosavan in Laos. Phoumi turned out to be little more than an unpopular and ineffective war lord and the United States was burdened with another losing proposition.

1961: Cuba.

In this brief chronicle of a busy decade, it is apparent that the CIA has gone far beyond its stated functions of:

1. Advising the National Security Council with respect to governmental intelligence activities related to the national security;

2. Correlating and evaluating intelligence related to the national security;

3. Performing services of common concern for the benefit of existing intelligence agencies.

Indeed, a fourth function seems to have been added as a kind of escape clause that gives the CIA the right to do anything from assassinating Khrushchev to decorating Mao Tse-tung. It states that the CIA shall "perform other functions and duties as directed by the National Security Council."

Considering that the CIA has had a finger in every major upheaval of the last ten years, it can hardly be considered, in the words of Dulles' euphemism, "a fact-finding agency." The FBI is a fact-finding agency: it investigates an individual or a situation and makes a report to the Justice Department. The CIA does much more than this since it acts on its own recommendations—with the agreement of the President and the National Security Council.

The disasters to which this privilege can lead were especially glaring in the Cuban escapade. On April 18 the landing force reached the swampland in the Bay of Pigs and established a beachhead. Two days later Castro announced that the operation had been crushed. Failure was attributed to four major reasons: the Cuban population did not rise against Castro after the landing had taken place; the swampy beachhead was a strategic failure; United States air support with unmarked planes was withdrawn at the last minute by Presidential order; the ship carrying all the rebels' communications equipment was sunk. In the Cuban post-mortem, it came out that the CIA had favored right-wing Cuban exile groups to the detriment of more powerful groups, that it had picked its own leaders, and that it had purged the striking force of what it considered undesirable elements.

Dulles told *Newsweek* Magazine in May, 1961, that he conceded Cuba was a defeat. By way of explanation, he said: "They were determined to fight Castro. Were we to say no? Were we to tell them 'it's too soon' or 'it's too late'? Were we to tell them 'it's no use'?"

Privately, CIA officials refuse to take all the blame for the Cuba failure, and point to what they call "executive lapses." As one CIA official told this writer:

"Our intelligence reports did not say that the population would rise against Castro, but that the masses would remain indifferent, waiting to see if there was a real struggle before making up their minds.

"Among the anti-Castro groups we were training, there were conflicting factions and a great deal of quarreling. We had to create a homogeneous striking force and to do this we had to restrain certain elements and give the nod to others.

"The plan called for unmarked planes, jet fighter and interception planes, to support the landing and neutralize Castro's artillery and tank groups. Kennedy decided at the last minute this was too bald a step to take and the air support was called off.

"There was poor military planning. All communications equipment was sent on the same boat, and it was sunk, so the landing parties couldn't communicate. When Ike heard about that he said he had learned at West Point and again on D-Day that you always split your radio equipment among several vessels so you could at least get one through. The military planners chose the Bay of Pigs because a small landing party could not be flanked in the swamps. As it turned out, there was only a dirt path and a railroad track out of the swamp, and Castro was waiting for them at the exit. We don't deny our role, but we don't like being made the scapegoat for the mistakes of half a dozen other groups."

Because the CIA has been involved in so many intrigues, it has automatically become the suspect in every international upheaval. Anywhere in the world, when a minister resigns or a military junta takes over, the handwriting on the wall immediately spells CIA. Communist plants and forgeries, the systematic attacks of Tass (the Soviet press agency), the willing subservience of the Communist press in France, Italy, and Great Britain, and the credulity of a public opinion trained like Pavlov's dog to drool whenever the CIA is mentioned, have made political fodder of the most farfetched rumors.

The day after President Jano Quadros announced his resignation in Brazil, in August 1961, a Tass dispatch put the finger on the CIA for masterminding the move. The Lavon affair in Israel was another dark plot of the CIA, according to the same quarters. Perhaps the most damaging allegation of this kind concerned the CIA's part in the April 1961 generals' revolt in Algeria. Partly because of the boorish reluctance of the French Government to deny the rumors and partly because the campaign was better planned and many-pronged, uneasiness still persists that it was only after assurances of support from the CIA that General Maurice Challe and his three starry-eyed cohorts attempted to overthrow President Charles de Gaulle.

On April 25, in the midst of the *Putsch,* the rumor made its appearance in *Pravda.* That newspaper's regular front-page column, signed "The Observer," charged in virulent tones that the Algiers coup had received support from the CIA and "the unholy triumvirate of Dulles-Salazar-Franco."

The *Pravda* article quoted as a source the fellow-traveling Rome newspaper *Paese,* which is often used for anti-American plants. This was enough to give the rumor a healthy push. The *Pravda* piece was picked up by Tass. Havana radio and Cairo radio broadcast it over Latin America and the Middle East. On April 26, the fellow-traveling Paris newspaper *Libération* echoed the charge. In Washington, the correspondent of the Tunisian weekly *Afrique-Action,* pointed up the speculation in his dispatch. In three days, the rumor had gained enough currency to alarm responsible press organs.

On April 28, the respected Paris newspaper *Le Monde,* which has eminently close contacts with the French foreign office, asked the Quai d'Orsay for a denial. This was a time when General de Gaulle was peeved with President Kennedy for offering to help out in the *Putsch,* a French internal matter. Also, the Quai knew there had been some low-level contacts between CIA agents and the insurgents. The CIA in this case had no ax to grind. It was simply doing its job of intelligence-gathering and had accurately predicted that a *Putsch* would take place. U.S. commanders in France had been warned that insurgent forces might try to take over American installations and were told to oppose them. If trouble started, American airfields were to be strewn with obstacles to prevent paratroop landings. Thus, the foreign office, although it knew there had been no CIA encouragement of the *putschists,* failed to gauge the importance of the rumor and refused to deny it.

The April 28 issue of *Le Monde* said in a front-page editorial that "the behavior of the United States during the recent crisis was not particularly skillful. It seems established that American agents more or less encouraged Challe, whose experience with NATO would normally have acted as a warning against the acts of irresponsible mutineers. . . . President Kennedy, of course, knew nothing of all this."

Le Monde's support of the rumor was like canonizing a heretic. Communist diplomats and the Communist press could quote it as a source. Diplomats in Paris claimed at dinner parties to have documents proving the CIA's interference. Reports from Washington said that rightist Jacques Soustelle once had lunch with Richard Bissell Jr. of the CIA. *The New York Times* lent credence to a completely unfounded fabrication charging that "at a meeting in Madrid on April 12 or 13, a United States agent is said to have told General Raoul Salan, one of the mutineers, that the United States would recognize a new government in France within forty-eight hours after its successful establishment if there were no attack on Tunisia or Morocco."

To compound the difficulty, it was learned that two naval attachés from the Washington Embassy had been in Algiers at the time of the *Putsch.* Advisers to Challe? The truth was far more simple.

A new naval attaché had arrived in Paris and had been taken to Algiers by the man he was replacing as a "breaking in." Had they known the date of the *Putsch* they would undoubtedly have gone to great lengths to cancel their trip.

Few French newspapers kept their heads in the mounting wave of innuendo. *Le Figaro* said wisely: "American secret services? Challe has exercised high enough commands to know that they are created to be disavowed, and knew enough not to base his hopes on assurances of this kind. . . . What could they offer Challe other than verbal encouragement? At the most, to help the insurgents through their influence in certain sectors."

The French Government, meanwhile, continued to behave like a sulking child. Foreign Minister Maurice Couve de Murville himself gave the rumor substance in an off-the-record talk with an American columnist. When the U.S. Embassy in Paris lodged "a very strong protest," the French began backing away. Walter Lippmann, who had seen General de Gaulle in Paris just before the *Putsch,* wrote that "the reason why the French Government has not really exculpated the CIA of encouraging the Algerian rebel generals is that it was already so angry with the CIA for meddling in French internal politics. The French grievance, justified or not, has to do with recent French legislation for the French nuclear weapon, and the alleged effort of CIA agents to interfere with that legislation." The French, like so many others, were acting on the principle of guilt by association.

The New York Times did not know what to do with the rumor. Its columnists were divided. James Reston wrote from Washington that the CIA was "involved in an embarrassing liaison with the anti-Gaullist officers who staged [the] insurrection." On the same page but on a different day, C. L. Sulzberger wrote under the headline A TIME TO SQUASH SORDID RUMORS:

> No American in Algeria had to do with any insurrectional leader. General Smith, Paris military attaché, was in Algiers on a routine trip. He withdrew to the Sahara. No consular employee saw any rebel. The only contact was indirect, through the Swiss dean of the Corps, who demanded diplomatic transmission facilities.
> Nor did any CIA agents see the junta. Like the French Government, the CIA knew another plot was brewing to prevent Algerian peace negotiations. But, like French security services, it knew nothing of the timing. The CIA co-operated with the French—when they solicited this. Apart from that, it stuck to its task of informing Washington.

This, as even the French foreign office grudgingly admitted in private, was the substance behind the rumor. For once, the CIA had not taken sides and had done its intelligence work well. But rumors have a way of lingering, and two months after the event this one was still alive. Fred Cook, in his exposé of the CIA in *The Nation* wrote that "the highest French sources . . . have called the Algerian incident closed—but they have not, pointedly they have not, given a full and clean bill of health to the CIA. It is a sequence that leaves a foul taste in the mouth. It is also, for once, a sequence that provides its own mouthwash."

The final criticism of the CIA is based on that agency's consistent support of reactionary regimes. Walter Lippmann has argued that far from helping the West win the Cold War, the shoring-up of crumbling right-wing regimes helps to keep the West on the defensive. He wrote:

> I venture to argue that the reason we are on the defensive in so many places is that for some ten years we have been doing exactly what Mr. Khrushchev expects us to do. We have used money and arms in a long, losing attempt to stabilize native governments, which, in the name of anti-Communism, are opposed to all important social change. This has been exactly what Mr. K.'s dogma calls for—that Communism should be the only alternative to the status quo with its immemorial poverty and privilege.

The *New Yorker* noted a consistency in backing the wrong horse that ranged from the Mensheviks in 1919 to pro-Batista Cubans in 1961. In 1919, it wrote, "Intelligence, having talked to a reliable source in a tearoom, expected the muzhiks to rise up bearing gifts of shashlik for the returning masters they had booted out." In World War II this venerable tradition was maintained when the OSS favored General Henri Giraud over General Charles de Gaulle as the savior of France. The *New Yorker* concluded that all these years American intelligence has been masterminded by an "Old Man in the Crypt," who sends out orders from a secret hiding place. As an afterthought on Cuba, the magazine observed: "It used to be said that you would never need an enemy if you had a Hungarian for a friend, and Señor Castro has probably by now concluded that you will never need a friend if you have the CIA for an enemy."

Because the CIA is operating in an open society, its flaws are all too apparent. It has gone so far to meet the Soviet threat that it is now tagged as an "invisible government" operating without mandate from the people and without check of any kind. Soviet intelligence, on the other hand, is never publicly berated for its failures or excesses; even when they are gutted by purges, the secret police organizations retain their power. Soviet intelligence operates at the heart of a system where secrecy is the air you breathe and conspiracy is the ground you walk on. It could no more be criticized for going too far than the Communist Party could be criticized for being the only party. The tradition of an all-powerful Soviet secret police and intelligence net reaches back to the czars, while the United States intelligence apparatus is a child of the Cold War.

II. A Look Backward

TODAY the United States and the Soviet Union consider powerful espionage agencies vital to national security. In Russia, secret police and espionage organizations have thrived for centuries and on them the survival of the Soviet regime has largely been based. As the czars needed the Okhrana (Czarist secret police) for survival, Mr. Khrushchev needs his State Security Police. An aura of Byzantine conspiracy and governments within governments, like Chinese boxes, have been the stigmata of every Russian regime since Peter the Great. The United States, on the other hand, managed very well without a comprehensive intelligence organization until 1947, when the CIA was created.

One of the most curious results of the Cold War is that the two traditions, almost diametrically opposed across the centuries, have finally bred offspring which have what the French call *"un air de famille."*

The Russian tradition considers espionage, subversion, and conspiracy as essential branches of government; secrecy and ruthlessness as essential methods. The American tradition is marked by distaste for espionage and secrecy and a nagging conviction that government measures not enacted in the glare of publicity have something immoral about them. Stalin thought it perfectly normal to tell the eighteenth Congress of the Communist Party in 1939: "Our punitive organs and intelligence service no longer have their sharp edge turned to the inside of the country, but to the outside against external enemies." And he bragged that his agents were so effective that military victory depended only on "several spies somewhere on the [enemy] army staff, or even divisional staff, and capable of stealing the operative plans."

It was only eleven years before this vote of confidence in espionage that Secretary of State Henry L. Stimson learned to his horror that the State Department had a cryptographic bureau. He ordered all State Department funds removed from the code-breaking agency, fired its founder and director, Herbert O. Yardley, and is reported to have said in pious outrage: "Gentlemen don't read other people's mail."

Mr. Stimson possibly did not know and certainly did not care that Russian security police have always considered reading other people's mail as natural as reading their own. A. T. Vasilyev, who served as head of the Okhrana in the early 1900's, stated the case for indiscriminate mail censorship in peacetime. "I should like to point out," he wrote in his memoirs "that this censorship of letters many a time enabled the Russian police to prevent robberies, murders, and terrorist crimes. The advantages of the system were therefore undoubtedly very real, and I do not believe that the disadvantages were ever worthy of serious consideration. The right-minded citizen never had any reason to fear the censorship, for private business was on principle completely ignored."

This heartfelt defense could only be made in a country where a succession of police states has not allowed the concept of legal and individual rights to emerge. A country where barbarity and the fetishism of secrecy are so ingrained that today, if two security policemen were to arrest an individual on Gorki Street in Moscow in broad daylight it would cause no surprise.

The man the street was named after acknowledged bitterly that "cruelty is the national characteristic of the Russian people." Even cruelty can be institutionalized. Peter the Great, who consolidated the Russian state and introduced many Western reforms among his people, included a device he had seen in Prussia—a technique for executing criminals by breaking them on the wheel. Today in the Soviet Union, official barbarism has been renounced. The relics of a violent and obsolete age are on view in a room hung with black crepe in Moscow's

Museum of the Revolution. The exhibit, as elaborate an object of pride as the crown jewels in the Tower of London, includes knouts, cat o' nine tails, leaded clubs, whips with lashes studded with nails, a collection of fetters in many styles and sizes, and tools that gleam like surgical instruments and were used for prying open nostrils and tearing out finger- and toenails.

The implication is that humanitarianism came to the Communist regime like a vision. Those recently released from Soviet prisons can testify that the disuse of torture instruments is not an abolition but a refinement of methods. Erica Glaser Wallach, who spent five years (1950-1955) in Soviet jails and work camps on espionage charges, gave the following description of the treatment of prisoners:

> One of their main methods is not to let you sleep. I would be called out at 10:30 or 11 [for interrogation] and it would last until 4 or 5 in the morning. . . . I had to stand hours and hours because of something I had said which did not please them . . . during the day I was guarded with special instructions not to let me sleep one second. The guards would watch me and come in and make me walk in the cell. I would walk until I used to bang my head against the wall and then I would simply sit down again, and they would get me up again, and that is the way the day would pass. . . . I could not wash. I had been in that prison fifteen or sixteen days and I was never allowed to wash, and I was absolutely filthy. . . . They put me in a special punishment cell for sixteen days where I was naked except for a man's undershirt and man's underpants, barefoot and naked. Everybody could look in from all sides; I was lying on a stone floor and handcuffed in the back with heavy iron handcuffs. I was fed every fourth day and it was icy cold.

This kind of treatment over an extended period of time is designed to break down resistance as effectively as czarist torture instruments.

There have been other refinements to old secret police methods, but the tradition has endured despite the 1917 revolution. Regimes could be overthrown, societies galvanized into revolution, amorphous masses forged into a self-concious proletariat, but the one indispensable chain that linked Bolshevism to Czarism like an unwanted umbilical cord was the secret police.

It was Nicholas I who set up early in the nineteenth century a so-called corps of gendarmerie to watch over the Russian citizenry. Under the czars, the techniques and traditions of espionage were directed essentially against their own people. The third section of this czarist secret police was as notorious as the Gestapo in Nazi Germany, and had the power to make mandatory arrests and hold prisoners without trial. In 1890, the Okhrana replaced this ruthless gendarmerie— the change was the first of many in the secret police. Like a criminal with aliases, these organizations regularly change names to shake off the reek of their excesses. The czarist Okhrana gave way to the Communist Cheka (1917-1922); the Cheka became the GPU and OGPU (State Political Administration); in 1934 the OGPU was renamed NKVD (People's Commissariat of Internal Affairs); and in 1941 a separate People's Commissariat of State Security was created (NKGB). These two People's Commissariats were made ministries in 1946 (MVD and MGB).

After Stalin's death in 1953, Lavrenti Beria became head of the MVD but was liquidated for trying to set the police above the Party and the Government. The MVD saw many of its functions given to other government agencies. A new title was devised for the MGB to show that it was completely separated from the MVD. In 1954 it became the KGB (Committee for State Security) in charge of all Soviet espionage except military espionage, still under the control of the Red Army's GRU (Chief Intelligence Directorate of the Soviet General Staff).

These rather fastidious enumerations cover up the unending conspiracy and cycle of purge and renewal that is the very fabric of the system. But in each new agency there are dregs of the old. The Okhrana police had blue uniforms and blue became the symbol of their terror for the Russian populace. It remains so today thanks to the blue uniforms of the MVD internal security police. Today political prisoners are incarcerated in Lubyanka Prison, a gilded former office building on Dzerzhinski Square. The six-story gray stone building is across from the Detskymir, a toy emporium. Former prisoners of Lubyanka (which had had some distinguished guests, among them U-2 pilot Francis Gary Powers) report that the solitary cells in the cellars are dank and windowless, but that the regular cells are almost as comfortable as a doctor's waiting room, with bed, table, and chair, and a large barred and screened window. Since Lubyanka is for political prisoners, different colored lights shine on and off in the corridors to announce the passage of a prisoner so that he will not encounter a fellow inmate and tell his friends when and if he is released: "Guess who I saw in Lubyanka?" The czars had a fetid dungeon in Peter and Paul fortress for their political prisoners, known as Trubetskoy bastion. And the ill-famed Siberian camp of Vorkuta is a direct descendant of the camp at Katorga which the czars had set up for citizens out of favor.

The 1917 revolution did not retard the growth of the Soviet secret police. When the February revolution brought Kerensky to power, he decided to keep the Okhrana, with its vast quantity of dossiers, but to staff it with men of revolutionary conviction. He had the names of Okhrana agents published in the press, but when his position grew shaky, he contacted some of these very agents. Orders were sent out to recruit experienced Okhrana men for the provisional government, for even Kerensky realized that you could no more govern Russia without a secret police than you could make blinis without flour.

The October revolution saw the demise of Kerensky and the replacement of the Okhrana by the Cheka (Extraordinary Commission for Combating Counterrevolution and Sabotage). Felix Dzerzhinski, an implacable, pale-eyed Pole with the angular profile of a grand inquisitor, headed this new terrorist group and promptly adopted Okhrana methods, bringing back into use the black cabinets and the surveillance of the secret police by secret-secret police. In the chaos of early revolutionary days, the Cheka flourished with unlimited power as the fourth branch of government—the punitive branch. From its headquarters in Moscow's Smolny Institute, a former finishing school for young women of means, the Cheka revived in Soviet hearts the deadly fear of the Okhrana. The techniques were the same and many sources insist that a number of Chekists were former Okhrana agents. At the core of the new proletarian regime lay the worm of medieval despotism. Victor Serge, a well-known October revolutionary, wrote in his memoirs: "I consider the creation of the Chekas one of the gravest and most inconceivable mistakes the Bolshevik Government made when plots, embargoes, and foreign intervention made it lose its head."

The terrorism inherited from the czars was no accident. It had approval in the highest quarters. Leon Trotsky had told the Central Executive Committee less than two months after the October revolution that "in not more than a month's time terror will assume very violent forms, after the example of the great French Revolution. The guillotine and not merely jail will be ready for our enemies." Lenin himself had said before the Congress of Soviets that "when violence is exercised by the toilers, by the masses of the exploited against the exploiters—then we are for it."

They were for it with a vengeance, as Victor Serge testifies in his description of the wave of Chekist terror that followed the August 1918 attempt on Lenin's life:

> The suspects were taken by cartloads outside the city and shot in the fields. How many? In Petrograd, between 100 and 150, in Moscow between 200 and 300. The following days, at dawn, the families of the victims walked through the fields picking up relics of the dead, buttons, bits of cloth. Later, I met one of the authors of the Petrograd massacre. "We thought," he told me, "that if the People's Commissioners wanted to be humanitarians, that was their business. Ours was to cut down the counterrevolution."

A sample of the extent of the cutting down is given in a report by a Chekist leader, Martin Latsis, which stated that for the first nineteen months of the Cheka's operations (January 1918 to July 1919), "344 uprisings were suppressed in which 3,057 were killed; 412 counter-revolutionary organizations were uncovered; 8,389 persons were executed; 9,496 persons were sent to concentration camps; 34,334 were imprisoned. The total number of arrests was 86,893."

This helps to explain why the following proverb of czarist times survived the regime: "Russia is divided into three parts—those who have been in prison, those who are in prison, and those who are waiting their turn."

Through its excesses the Cheka became such a symbol of terror that even the leaders of the regime denounced it, and in 1922 a government decree stated that "the All-Russian Extraordinary Committee (Cheka) and its local agencies are to be abolished." All that was really abolished was the name Cheka, for arrests and executions continued unchecked under the GPU, successor to the secret police's scepter of abusive power.

In 1926 Felix Dzerzhinski died of a heart attack. The death was notable because it was natural. In some countries, secret police chiefs entrench themselves behind a fortress of dossiers and confidential information on political leaders and survive regime changes because of their knowledge. Joseph Fouché performed the feat of serving as police chief in four successive regimes during the most troubled period of France's history: the French Revolution under Robespierre, the *Directoire* under Paul Barras, the Empire under Napoleon, and the Monarchy under Louis XVIII. He died a natural death at the age of sixty-one, not a bad life expectancy for his time and his function.

More recently, we have the example of Reinhard Gehlen, a professional soldier who became an intelligence chief of the German Army in 1942. A general at forty-three, Gehlen was captured by the Americans at war's end and had the foresight to bring his files with him. His grasp of the intelligence situation in Germany led to his being put in charge of an autonomous espionage ring under the personal tutelage of the CIA and later brought under the control of the West German Government. One can wonder what Gehlen's fate would be if a Russian regime were installed in West Germany. Would he, like another Fouché, survive a Soviet take-over with his files intact and his judgment unshaken?

In the Soviet Union, however, police chiefs are not known for their durability. The slow beast of the secret police setup slouches on through history impervious to political change, but its leaders are usually the victims, like the doctor who invented Frankenstein. Comparison can be made, for example, between the men who headed the Soviet secret police and the men who headed the Federal Bureau of Investigation.

Soviet heads of secret police and time of service:
Felix Dzerzhinski (1918-1926): Died of a heart attack in 1926.
Genrikh Yagoda (1926-1936): Liquidated in a purge trial in 1938.
Nikolai Yezhov (1936-1938): Liquidated in the purge to which he gave his name (Yezhovschina) in 1939.
Lavrenti Beria (1938-1953): Executed in 1953.
Sergey N. Kruglov (1953-1956): Disappeared in 1956.
Ivan A. Serov (1956-1959): Serov, a former Chekist, is one of the two men since Dzerzhinski to have survived removal from office. He is said today to have an important intelligence post and has been mentioned as chief of the GRU, in which case his transfer in 1959 should be interpreted as a promotion.
Alexsandr N. Shelepin (1959-1961): Shelepin is the other fortunate secret police chief to have left the job after a promotion. He was elected a secretary of the Communist Party Central Committee

during the 22d Congress in Moscow in October 1961. Mr. Shelepin, a protégé of Khrushchev, seems destined to a bright political future with his admission to the Party's leadership.

Vladimir V. Semichastny (1961-   ): Semichastny, in his mid-thirties, is the youngest holder of the difficult post. He is his predecessor's protégé, and like Shelepin, came to the secret police by way of the Young Communist League.

FBI heads and time of service:

Stanley W. Finch (1908-1912): Died a natural death.

A. Bruce Bielaski (1912-1919): Retired, still alive.

William J. Flynn (1919-1921): Died of heart disease.

William J. Burns (1921-1924): Died of a heart attack.

J. Edgar Hoover (1924-   ): An outstanding example of survival. Mr. Hoover, although in his seventies, is still serving in the post to which he acceded thirty-seven years ago. He has served under six presidents, three of them Republicans (Coolidge, Hoover, and Eisenhower), three of them Democrats (Roosevelt, Truman, and Kennedy).

Considering the risk involved in accepting promotion it is surprising the Soviet secret police has no recruiting problems. Actually, one of the charges often made against it by Communist Party organs is that it attracts the most unsavory elements of society. Party bulletins under the Cheka complained that "sadists, criminals, and degenerates filled its ranks," and that the taste of unlimited power and sanguinary methods finally corrupted the "honest" elements. Lenin himself admitted there were "strange elements in the Chekist ranks."

The Bolshevik regime hardly waited for its own consolidation before launching foreign espionage operations. The espionage networks were set up mainly in capitals which had received the flow of White Russian *émigrés,* such as Paris and Berlin. Dzerzhinski founded a foreign department for the Cheka in 1921 (the INO). Cheka agents were sent to spy on Russian *émigrés* rather than foreign governments and to dislocate the anti-Bolshevik movements that were starting up. This early period was, as David Dallin points out in his authoritative book, *Soviet Espionage,* "a basically defensive operation—the fight against counterrevolution," which had to be carried beyond Soviet borders.

Soon, however, there was a proliferation of intelligence services directed against foreign soil. The foreign office inaugurated "legal" networks, with diplomatic officials doubling as agents and collecting secret information. Leon Trotsky set up another espionage network under the People's Commissariat for War. As early as 1921 there existed in embryonic form the parallel and often competing espionage networks that still operate today under other names.

The swift evolution from a specific counterrevolutionary function to a general offensive espionage function is shown by the attempts in the 1920's to infiltrate the United States, which had no large *émigré* group.

Gregory Besedovsky, a former Soviet agent, wrote that in 1926 he was sent to the United States as a representative for the Soviet trade agency Amtorg (which even today operates in New York City). His boss at Amtorg was a member of the GRU who told him there were two illegal networks in the United States, with headquarters in New York. The resident, he said, was a man named Filin, with a Polish passport and an herb-importing business as a cover. Said Besedovsky:

> Representatives of the Soviet War Department came to the U.S.A. with lists of products and techniques necessary for the military organization of the Soviet Union. They gave Filin the instructions of the Centre and brought back to Moscow the information obtained by him and his agents. Berzine [then chief of the GRU] spoke with contempt of the American police, which allowed the luggage of military representatives to pass customs without being opened.

Berzine's contempt is a persistent factor in Russian thinking, which opposes the realism, guile and tenacity of Soviet totalitarianism with the naïveté, slackness and liberalism of American democracy. Soviet espionage networks, created almost simultaneously with the Communist regime, proliferated through the world like toadstools. They developed unchecked despite wars and alliances and because of the apathy of the countries where they operated. Stalin is said to have been dumfounded by the news that a foreigner could come to the United States and obtain citizenship after five years of residence. "If this is the case," he reportedly exclaimed, "why don't we send five thousand men and women over there and let them sit until we need them?"

The Red Army field manual states that "intelligence will be conducted permanently and ceaselessly." This has certainly been the case in the forty-four years of Soviet history. Espionage has been a thread of continuity, oblivious to internal and international changes. It continued during the years of the New Economic Plan as it did during the Nazi-Soviet pact and World War II. It was directed indiscriminately against enemies and allies, unclouded by the sentimental deterrent that one does not spy on one's friends.

It was continued even while purges shook the foundations of the secret police organizations and prompted defections of agents abroad who knew that obeying orders to come home meant arrest and execution.

This then is the Soviet tradition. Secrecy, subversion, and espionage are basic principles of the regime. By comparison the history of American intelligence-gathering may at first glance give the impression of a wishful Pollyanna trying to counter the Svengali-like plottings of the Soviet Union.

A society based on individual rights and the Jeffersonian principle that the best government is the least government has a profound loathing for any kind of secret police. In the United States, moreover, the policy of isolationism codified by the Monroe Doctrine and maintained through one world war had no need for spies in foreign lands. The main current of American thought before World War II held espionage to be an immoral and unnecessary practice. (There was a strong cross-current which we will discuss later.)

The United States is, curiously enough, a nation convinced of the fundamental immorality of spying and also the only nation that boasts a spy as one of its national heroes. Yet even in the story of Nathan Hale we can find the traditional distaste for espionage. Nathan Hale is admired for his death, not his profession. As historians have since noted, soldiers could refuse espionage assignments because of their "disgraceful" nature. One historian wrote: "Who respects the character of a spy?"

John Bakeless, in his book *Turncoats, Traitors, and Heroes*, explained that Nathan Hale was picked to spy behind the British lines after Lieutenant James Sprague refused the assignment, saying, "I am willing to go and fight them but as far as going among them and being taken and hung up like a dog, I will not do it." Hale's last words did much to redeem the reputation of a tarnished calling but did not prompt a rush of spy volunteers in Washington's army.

Spies in the Anglo-Saxon tradition did not have the right to an honorable death. Soldiers died in combat or before a firing squad; spies were hanged. Major John André, the British spy who negotiated the betrayal of West Point with Benedict Arnold, pleaded, after his capture, not for his life, but for the form of his death. In a letter to George Washington, he wrote:

> Buoy'd above the terror of death, by the consciousness of a life devoted to honorable pursuits, and stained with no action that can give me remorse, I trust that the request I make to your Excellency at this serious period, and which is to soften my last moments will not be rejected.
>
> Sympathy towards a soldier will surely induce your Excellency and a military tribunal to adopt the mode of my death to the feelings of a man of honor.
>
> Let me hope, Sir, that if ought in my character impresses you with esteem towards me, if ought in my misfortunes marks me as the victim of policy and not of resentment, I shall experience the operation of these feelings in your breast, by being informed that I am not to die on a gibbet.

The request was denied. André was hanged two days after penning his eloquent plea. Charles Thomson, Secretary of Congress, wrote for the record:

> . . . the time which elapsed between the capture of Major André, which was on the morning of the 23rd of September, and his execution which did not take place till 12 o'clock on the 3rd of October; the mode of trying him—his letter to Sir Henry Clinton on the 29th of September, in which he said "I receive the greatest attention from his Excellency General Washington and from every person under whose charge I happen to be placed"; not to mention many other acknowledgments which he made of the good treatment he received —must evince that the proceedings against him were not guided by passion or resentment. The practice and usage of war were against his request, and made the indulgence he solicited, circumstanced as he was, inadmissible.

Perhaps an even more graphic example of the little indulgence Americans have always held for spies is a letter from General Israel Putnam to the British Governor, William Tryon:

Sir:

Natham Palmer, a Lieutenant in your King's service was taken in my camp as a Spy—he was tried as a Spy—he was condemned as a Spy—and you may rest assured Sir, he shall be hanged as a Spy.

I have the honor to be, etc.

ISRAEL PUTNAM

P.S. Afternoon. He is hanged.

Through the years, this almost Calvinistic horror of the spy was matched by an almost total lack of interest in building up espionage and counterespionage services. To be sure, a Secret Service division of the Treasury Department was established in 1869, but it was mainly concerned with guarding the President and hunting counterfeiters. There was also the Department of Justice's division of investigation, which became the FBI. But most of its efforts were consumed by the rise of gangsterism that followed prohibition.

Public and official apathy to the entire area of intelligence and espionage were such that Lieutenant General Hoyt S. Vandenberg, first director of the Central Intelligence Agency, could say before the Senate Armed Services Committee on April 29, 1947, "I think it can be said without successful challenge that before Pearl Harbor we did not have an intelligence service in this country comparable to that of Great Britain, or France, or Russia, or Germany, or Japan. We did not have one because the people of the United States would not accept it. It was felt there was something un-American about espionage and even about intelligence generally. There was a feeling that all that was necessary to win a war—if there was going to be another war—was an ability to shoot straight. One of the great prewar fallacies was that if the Japanese should challenge us in the Pacific, our armed services would be able to handle the problem in a matter of a few months at most. All intelligence is not sinister, nor is it an invidious type of work."

Like a soldier in the field who suddenly discovers that his rifle has no bayonet, American military leaders were shocked to find after the United States entered World War II that there was no intelligence service. Military intelligence in the three branches was so bad it was reduced to "little more than what a military attaché could learn at a dinner, more or less, over the coffee cups" (General George C. Marshall before the Senate Committee on Military Affairs).

Instead of being trained intelligence officers, military attachés tended to be a self-perpetuating clique of well-to-do officers who formed the Army's most exclusive club. As a result there was general contempt for whatever information they did come up with and military intelligence was sorely neglected. This neglect necessarily bred misunderstanding of the intelligence function. The late Ellis M. Zacharias, a naval intelligence pioneer, asked a flag officer during World War II: "How is the intelligence work in your force, sir?" The officer replied: "We don't need any intelligence work. There are no Communists on our ships."

Zacharias recalled that military intelligence during World War II was so bad that he was told in 1942 by Rear Admiral Oscar Badge, who was in charge of maintenance of port facilities after landings were made: "Do you know that I have $180,000,000 worth of material waiting to go to Oran and I don't know whether they have a single damned crane with which to take it from the ships?"

The few who tried to buck the apathy were defeated. Herbert O. Yardley was a brilliant cryptographer who worked during World War I in the State Department's amateurish and understaffed code room. He went to a high-ranking officer at the War College with suggestions for a complete revamping of the code room and was told: "That's a lot of nonsense. Whoever heard of going to all that trouble? During the Spanish-American War we didn't do all those things. We just added the figure 1898 to all our figure code words and the Spaniards never did find out about it."

Through sheer doggedness, Yardley was able after the war to set up MI-8, the cryptographic bureau of military intelligence, but this precursor of the National Security Agency (which broke allied codes just as the NSA does today) was scuttled by Secretary of State Stimson.

Mr. Stimson's hostility ruled out any progress in intelligence-gathering under his department, to such a point that a more broad-minded successor to the post, Dean Acheson, could tell Congress in 1945 that until World War II, the State Department's "technique of gathering information differed only by reason of the typewriter and telegraph from the techniques which John Quincy Adams was using in St. Petersburg and Benjamin Franklin was using in Paris."

American defenses against Soviet espionage were equally deficient. Although J. Edgar Hoover could boast that he had recognized the

Communist menace since its earliest days, there were few who shared his perception. The FBI, when he took it over, was practically unknown. When Hoover appeared one year before a Senate appropriations committee, one of the Senators thought he represented the Secret Service, which had made its budget bid a few days before. As Hoover began to speak, the angry Senator rose and shouted: "What, are you back again asking for more money?"

The first espionage law was passed by Congress on June 15, 1917, under the impetus of American intervention in World War I. Under the law, the maximum sentence for peacetime espionage was two years in prison and/or a $10,000 fine. Today, under the so-called Rosenberg law, peacetime espionage is punishable by death.

Actually, the Rosenbergs, convicted of stealing atomic secrets for Russia, were sentenced to death under the old law because it was proved their offenses were committed in wartime—a nice legal point, since the Soviet Union was then our ally. The Rosenberg law also eliminated the ten-year statute of limitations in espionage cases. The Rosenberg case was to counterespionage what Pearl Harbor was to military intelligence—it shocked the nation into an awareness that threatened to become a phobia.

The period of awareness came only after more than twenty years of untrammeled Soviet espionage during which phalanxes of agents stole information as easily as if they had been shopping in a supermarket. The United States only gave diplomatic recognition to the Soviet Union in 1933, but the commercial agency Amtorg had set up offices in New York as early as 1924 and provided the first espionage base. The first Soviet spy to be prosecuted in the United States was Mikhail Gorin, a Red Army intelligence agent who was arrested in 1939. Between those years, the Soviet espionage network went about its business without hindrance.

Soviet agents came into the United States on false passports, set up their apparatus, recruited Americans, received unlimited assistance from the American Communist Party, and infiltrated all sectors of economic and political life. Hede Massing, a Soviet agent of the thirties, wrote that "during the four years of my operation I was not once questioned by the American authorities. Not one of the members of the apparatus was ever interfered with."

No other country made life for spies so satisfyingly easy. Was a false passport needed? All one had to do was apply for birth certificates for people whose names appeared in newspaper death notices—a passport could be obtained with the birth certificate. Were agents needed? The powerful American Communist Party of the thirties was always ready to release members for "special duty." As Mrs. Massing testified before the Senate Internal Security Committee: "They didn't consider themselves agents and would have been surprised if they had been called spies. They were Communists on special duty. They were soldiers of the revolution. They were Communists that had been chosen for a particularly difficult task and they were proud to have been chosen. They never considered themselves agents, of course not."

Were state secrets needed? There were, according to Whittaker Chambers, at least seventy-five government officials involved in Soviet espionage in the period from 1936 to 1938. One of these, Nathan Gregory Silvermaster, a long-time employee of the Department of Agriculture, allegedly headed one of the most successful espionage cells. Elizabeth Bentley, confessed Soviet espionage agent, wrote that "the Silvermaster group managed to collect a fabulous amount of confidential information which he photographed and passed on to the Russian secret police." The Silvermaster group, reports Miss Bentley, had such excellent contacts in the Office of Strategic Services that it knew the date of D-Day four days in advance. The only cloud in the bright sky of Soviet espionage activity was the arrest of Gorin. The arrest was not the result of counterintelligence work but of a staggering blunder on Gorin's part.

Under the cover of Intourist manager for Los Angeles, Mikhail Gorin was GPU resident for the West Coast. He had been successful enough to subvert a United States naval intelligence officer with relatives in the Soviet Union, Hafis Salich. In December, 1938, Gorin left some secret papers Salich had given him in a suit that was sent to the cleaners. The cleaner can claim a niche as a pioneer in American counterintelligence, for he had the good sense to turn over the pants and its contents to the police.

Gorin and Salich were arrested, found guilty of espionage, and sentenced to six and four years in prison respectively. The verdicts were appealed and affirmed by the Supreme Court in 1941. Gorin could still appeal to the laxity of a government which recognized neither the threat of Soviet espionage nor the contempt with which the Russians receive benevolence. Following pressures from Constantin

Oumansky, then acting Soviet Ambassador, the State Department recommended to the Los Angeles court that Gorin's sentence be suspended. He was placed on probation and told that he would be freed on condition that he pay a $10,000 fine (part of his sentence), court costs, and that he leave within forty-eight hours. He sailed the next day for Vladivostok. Salich stayed behind and served his sentence.

This first arrest of a Soviet agent thus created a precedent for giving convicted spies suspended sentence. Gorin had no claim to diplomatic immunity. In two later cases involving Soviet members of the United Nations Secretariat staff, claims of diplomatic immunity were overruled, arrests were made, but the spies were released on recommendation of the State Department. The defendants in these cases were Valentin Gubitchev, courier for Judith Coplon, and Igor Melkh, accused of trying to obtain aerial photographs in 1961.

Paradoxically, in the pre-World War II years when foreign espionage thrived unhindered, it was the very freedom from prosecution and accessibility of information that provided built-in safeguards. The words of an unidentified German spy, as quoted by Ellis Zacharias in *Secret Missions,** are worth repeating in this connection:

> On the surface, the United States had no secrets which an efficient and alert foreign operative could not procure. A trip to the United States Printing Office in Washington usually yielded data at a normal price which agents elsewhere would have had immense difficulties in obtaining. Most of the Army's and Navy's manuals were offered for sale. The document rooms of the Senate and House were other sources of information. Very often we had to pay thousands of dollars for blueprints of a new airplane design in France and Britain while we obtained all the necessary data for the price of a daily paper or a periodical in the United States.

Despite this wealth of free information, the agent continued, the United States presented an insoluble problem for intelligence gatherers.

First, because "the United States is too vast a continent by itself, with developments going on simultaneously at distances of thousands of miles, interrelated as they are and requiring simultaneous observations by operatives. But how can any foreign power station the great

* Ellis Zacharias, *Secret Mission* (New York: G. P. Putnam's Sons, 1946).

number of spies in the United States required to carry out this observation . . . no intelligence service can afford to concentrate such a huge army of qualified agents in any one country."

Second, because of "the improvised character of America's defense system, for the system used in war is entirely different from the system maintained in peace. The nucleus of forces maintained in peacetime have no similarity to or relation with the vast people's army and navy which the United States puts into the field or sends to sea when the emergency rises. Plans change fast."

And finally, "the abundance of material which America provides intelligence services. Thousands of sheets of paper pour in every day to intelligence organizations abroad, all revealing some seemingly secret information. But who can sift this data and weed out the bad from the good?

"We usually discover that while we have too much information, we can make very little of it, since a co-ordination of the incoming material overtaxes the usually limited facilities of any intelligence agency."

Here we are given a provocative vision of a United States able to confound foreign intelligence agencies thanks to an embarrassment of riches and a determination not to keep secrets. All this is far less true today, particularly the improvised character of defense. The Cold War has placed the United States on a war-preparedness footing. Permanent military installations and progress in armament are an essential part of the Soviet agent's quest.

During World War II, however, there was a veritable boom in Soviet espionage in the United States. As David Dallin observed:

> No one in Soviet intelligence could have expected to find the American gates as wide open and the American security agencies as agreeable as they were after the start of the German-Soviet war. For the Soviet apparatus these were golden days. With each passing month the heads of these agencies in this country as well as in Moscow centers increased the tasks and the personnel of their services.

The golden era of lend-lease brought hundreds of Soviet technical experts and government officials streaming into Washington. They went on an orgy of intelligence-gathering, and few doors were closed to them. The policy then was to go to any extent to give the Russian allies what they needed in the way of goods, blueprints, and technical information. The effort was so thorough that the United States found itself manufacturing Russian boots, called *Vitiajnye,* for Russian soldiers. These are high and watertight felt-lined leather boots that have been made by hand in Russia for hundreds of years. Snowy winters and muddy springs make them an essential part of the Russian soldier's equipment. In Washington, a Russian *émigré* was found who had once headed the czar's boot factory and knew how to make them. Soon a machine process was developed and the boots were turned out by the thousands and sent to the Soviet Union.

It was the same with information as it was with the boots. There was no limit to what the Russians could obtain. After the war, Congressional hearings were conducted on the amount of atomic material the Soviets obtained during the war years. It came out that in 1943 and 1944 the Soviet Union was able to purchase 700 pounds of uranium oxide, 720 pounds of uranium nitrate, and 75 pounds of uranium metal through American and Canadian firms. As Victor Kravshenko, an official with the Soviet Purchasing Commission who defected after the war, explained: "We transferred to the Soviet Union not just this one package [of uranium oxide]. We transferred dozens of tons of material, not just by airplane. We also were using Soviet ships that came from lend-lease for the Soviet Union, and they called this material super lend-lease. Who cared what we took? Had we taken the Empire State Building and put it on a ship, no one would have cared. I saw dozens of times how Soviet boats were loaded and I know what I am talking about."

A more vivid example of the systematic plunder of information was given in Congressional testimony by George Racey Jordan, who was contact officer between the Army and the Soviet Purchasing Commission at Great Falls, Montana, first point of an air route to Fairbanks, Alaska, and Siberia. Major Jordan took his job seriously, and inspected outgoing luggage if it did not have diplomatic immunity. His assiduity finally led to Soviet threats that they would apply pressure to have him transferred.

"The Russians are very close with their money," Jordan related. "They don't spend anything they don't have to. I used to have to pick up their checks at the officers' club where I ate with them. In fact, we assigned three slot machines where the profits went to pay the checks of the Russians. This particular night the Russians, much to my surprise, invited me to Great Falls for a chicken dinner. There was a lot of vodka. It happened I didn't drink. They suggested a toast to Stalin, Molotov, Roosevelt, and everybody else. I was suspicious but I had left word at the control tower that if a plane came in to call me at the restaurant, and a call came and I went to the field and two armed Russians were standing over the suitcases. One of them tried to keep me out of the plane. The suitcases were black, cheap patent leather, with white rope sash cord tied around them and gobs of red sealing wax over the knots. They screamed diplomatic immunity and I said: 'That doesn't look diplomatic to me.'

"I ripped the cords off and opened about one third of them. I had one of our own guards stand with a rifle on his shoulder so they would know I had some protection."

In the suitcase, Jordan found some material from the Oak Ridge atomic testing site, which included the words *Manhattan Engineering Department, uranium 92, neutrons, protons, energy produced by fission,* and *cyclotron.* There was also a memo from the White House that said: *Had a hell of a time getting these away from Groves* [General Leslie Groves, commanding general of the armed forces special weapons (atom bomb) project]. The memo was signed H. H.

Major Jordan also noticed some engineering maps where the place for the label *Secret* had been cut out. "If I had found the word 'Secret' I would have grounded the plane," he said. There were also "automobile maps, the kind you can get at automobile stations. They had been trimmed and cut, and on the maps were marked the locations of our industrial plants." Major Jordan also had a strong suspicion, which he could never prove, that the Russians were stealing morphine from Army first aid kits, which were kept in the same stockrooms as the Soviet luggage in transit.

Things were so chummy that in late 1943, Major General William J. Donovan, founder of OSS, went to Moscow to discuss a joint intelligence project with the Soviets that involved training Soviet agents in the United States with modern American equipment. The plan was to start with an exchange of OSS and NKVD missions. Thanks partly to the objections of J. Edgar Hoover and Admiral William Leahy, General Donovan's ebullient experiment in spy exchanges never materialized.

The halo of friendship did not pale after the war was over. It seemed that the Government, in order to keep Soviet-American friendship untroubled, was willing to shut its eyes to palpable instances of treason deep within its ranks. This is the only explanation one can consider for the lack of action taken when J. Edgar Hoover in 1945 sent President Roosevelt a confidential report on twelve government officials suspected of being Soviet agents. Among them was Harry Dexter White, assistant to the Secretary of the Treasury. The only action taken against Mr. White was his promotion the following year to an even more important post, in the International Monetary Fund.

This was the zenith of nearly thirty years of misunderstanding of the Communist threat and of espionage in general. A high government official accused of treason was raised to greater prominence, where he had access to more confidential information and had a broader role in shaping postwar policy.

Five jolting incidents were instrumental in bringing American intelligence and counterintelligence out of centuries of somnolence: the aftermath of Pearl Harbor, the exposure of the Canadian spy ring, the Hiss-Chambers confrontation, the case of Judy Coplon and the Rosenberg atom spy ring. Each of these had the impact to mold public opinion in a certain way, and government agencies were in turn forced to face dangers they could no longer overlook.

The painful post-mortem of Pearl Harbor showed that the glaring weakness was not so much lack of intelligence as lack of an agency to evaluate that intelligence. It came out all too clearly in the 25,000-page transcript of hearings on the naval disaster that intelligence reports of a Japanese attack and advance notice given by radar and by Navy destroyer *Ward* were ignored. Responsible officials, including Secretary of the Navy Frank Knox, simply did not believe the Japanese would stage a mass attack on Pearl Harbor, and disregarded whatever signs pointed in that direction. The lesson of Pearl Harbor was most clearly stated by the 1955 Hoover Commission, which said:

> The Central Intelligence Agency may well attribute its existence to the surprise attack on Pearl Harbor and to the postwar investigations into the part intelligence or lack of intelligence played in the failure of our military to receive adequate and prompt warning of the impending Japanese attack.

On September 5, 1945, Igor Gouzenko, a cipher clerk at the Soviet embassy in Ottawa, defected to the West with more than 100 documents. The documents constituted a description of the vast Soviet espionage network in Canada and provided the Western world with its first comprehensive insight on the working of the apparats. Gouzenko's documents provided the basis for the arrest of twenty-six accused Soviet agents (sixteen were acquitted). A Royal Commission on espionage made a final report on the basis of hearings that was 733 pages long. The June 27, 1946, report said:

> While holding forth at international conferences with voluble statements about peace and security, the Soviet Government is preparing secretly for the third world war. To meet this war, the Soviet Government is creating in democratic countries including Canada, a fifth column, in the organization of which even diplomatic representatives of the Soviet Government take part. . . . Instead of gratitude for the help rendered during the war, the Soviet Government is developing espionage activities in Canada, preparing to deliver a stab in the back of Canada—all this without the knowledge of the Russian people.

(It is significant that espionage cases involving Russians go largely unreported in the Soviet press.)

The Canadian spy ring case sounded another warning knell—the first case involving the theft of atomic secrets. Gouzenko's documents led to an unusual arrest. On March 4, 1946, a distinguished scientist was arrested in England as he was leaving Kings College where he had just delivered a lecture. The nickname he had been given by the spy ring was "Alek." His real name was Alan Nunn May. He confessed to having given the Soviet Union its first uranium samples and was sentenced to ten years in prison under the Official Secrets Act (he served six and a half years).

Dr. May's confession said in part: "I took the very painful decision that it was necessary to convey general information on atomic energy and make sure it was taken seriously. For this reason I decided to entertain a proposition made to me by the individual who called on me. After this preliminary meeting I met the individual on several subsequent occasions while in Canada. He made specific requests for information, which were just nonsense to me. He did request samples of uranium from me and information generally on atomic energy. At one meeting I gave the man microscopic amounts of U.233 and U.235 (one of each)—I also gave the man a written report on atomic research as known to me."

The Canadian alarums swiftly crossed the border and led to increased vigilance in the United States and greater attention in government quarters to cases the FBI had on file.

Alger Hiss was one of the names involved. Specific information on the brilliant State Department officer had first come from Elizabeth Bentley, who in 1945 went to the FBI with a story of nearly ten years of espionage. It was not until 1948, however, that the Hiss case came to light through the good offices of another reformed Communist, the late Whittaker Chambers. Public opinion was startled to learn that Hiss, who advised President Roosevelt at Yalta and was Secretary-General of the San Francisco Conference where the United Nations was born, was implicated in a Soviet espionage network. After Hiss's perjury trial and the publicity given to Chambers' revelations, it became apparent that it could happen in the United States as well as in Canada.

Indifference turned to vigilance, and vigilance soured into apprehension. A growing public hysteria ushered in the "spy scare" period, of which McCarthyism was a by-product. 1949 was the turning point, the end of apathy to espionage at home, the beginning of an imaginative and aggressive espionage policy abroad.

At home, it was a banner year for espionage cases. Judy Coplon was arrested and tried for using her job in the Justice Department as a listening post for the Russians. She was the first American civilian ever tried for espionage and her case is studied in detail in later pages. Atomic scientist Klaus Fuchs was arrested in England and confessed to having given atomic secrets to the Russians. Like the chain reaction Fuchs knew so much about, his arrest led to eight others, all in 1950: Harry Gold, Alfred Dean Slack, David Greenglass, Abraham Brothman, Miriam Moskowitz, Morton Sobel, and the Rosenbergs.

The case of Julius and Ethel Rosenberg is the last of the quintet cited as having shaken the American public from insouciance in espionage matters. The Rosenbergs, although proven guilty, suffered from having to ride the wave of a public opinion swelling into outrage and hysteria. In the public eye, they will always be remembered either as "spies who stole the atom bomb and gave it to the Russians," or "innocent martyrs who were persecuted in a period of witch hunts." They were neither.

That they were in charge of a ring that stole atomic information was proven beyond cavil. That they stole the atom bomb was shown to be manifestly absurd by a variety of sources. Yet Judge Irving R. Kaufman, who sentenced the couple to death, emphasized that "your conduct in putting into the hands of the Russians the atom bomb years before our scientists predicted Russia would perfect the bomb has already caused, in my opinion, the Communist aggression in Korea."

The gravest result of the combined activity of the atom spies (May, Fuchs, Pontecorvo, and the Rosenbergs) was that "it may have advanced the Soviet atomic energy program by eighteen months," according to a 1951 report of the Joint Congressional Committee on Atomic Energy. This, while far from a negligible offense, is not quite the same as stealing the atom bomb as one steals "a recipe for corn bread." And the committee report specified that the advance gained by the Soviet, thanks to the spies "is not to imply that Russia could never have broken the American atomic monopoly through her own unaided labors." (It will be remembered that the first American test bomb was exploded in July 1945 and the first Soviet bomb in September 1949).

Nobel Prize winner Dr. Harold Urey was another who denounced the myth of a stealable atom bomb. "It would require eighty to ninety volumes of close print which only a scientist or an engineer could read," he said. "Any spies capable of picking up this information will get information more rapidly by staying at home and working in their own laboratories."

Dr. Edward Teller, who played a key role in the development of the hydrogen bomb, wrote in *The New York Times* magazine section on November 13, 1960:

> I believe that Russian scientists could have produced an atomic bomb explosion without information from spies. The Russians are fully capable of unraveling the secrets of nature and putting them to effective use; there is probably no major scientific development of which the Russians are ignorant . . . the relevant principles [of the bomb] were published in the Smyth Report as early as 1945. . . . At the 1955 conference on the peaceful uses of atomic energy in Geneva, we ourselves took the initiative in revealing essential portions of reactor technology. There is little reason to believe that even a small nation willing to spend the time and money would be unable to trigger a nuclear explosion.

The Rosenbergs were guilty, but they were guilty at the wrong time. In a way, they were the victims of a catharsis—their death sentences served as atonement for thirty years of official neglect. Only four years earlier, in a little-known case, a Soviet naval lieutenant was arrested and tried in Portland, Washington, for trying to obtain secret atomic data in connection with the Bikini atom bomb tests. Lieutenant Nicolai G. Redin had been tailed by FBI agents who observed him receiving information from an American contact. At the trial, the contact admitted selling Lieutenant Redin information but said it was information that could be obtained at the public library. The prosecutor warned the jury, "If you come back with a verdict of not guilty, you will be branding the FBI witnesses as perjurers. That would have a more far-reaching effect than anything that could happen in this case." The jury of seven men and five women stayed out ten hours and returned a verdict of not guilty. That was in 1946.

It took only four years to advance from a conception of espionage as a farfetched farce to the belief that it is the most serious possible crime. At Redin's trial, Judge Lloyd L. Black refused to take the proceedings seriously. "There is not a syllable of evidence presented that the Kremlin instructed Lieutenant Redin to secure the secret information at issue here. Or, that the Kremlin even knew he was in America. . . . I am sorry that the dignity of this trial has been threatened by such extravagant claims." There was no more evidence that "the Kremlin," or "Joe Stalin himself" had ordered the Rosenbergs to steal the atom bomb, but that did not help them get a stay of execution. Extreme severity in espionage cases continues to be the rule in United States courts. On August 7, 1961, Robert A. Soblen was given a life sentence on espionage charges. Dr. Soblen, the brother of another convicted spy, Jack Soble, was sixty-one years old at the time and was suffering from lymphatic leukemia. The sentence had an ironic quality since doctors had given him less than a year to live. It was not made clear in the trial exactly what secrets Dr. Soblen had transmitted to the Soviet Union during World War II, more than fifteen years before he was tried (under the Rosenberg law, the ten-year statute of limitations was rescinded for espionage cases). Federal Judge William B. Herlands explained that "the severity of the defendant's sentence must be consonant with the obvious character of the defendant's crime. A conspiracy to obtain and transmit American national defense secrets may imperil the lives of all Americans. Such a crime is analogous to a conspiracy to commit mass murder."

It was a sign of this new approach that the Justice Department leaned heavily on conspiracy indictments to nail suspected spies. The Rosenbergs, Judy Coplon, Rudolf Abel, and Dr. Soblen were all found guilty of conspiracy. As D. N. Pritt, a well-known British criminal lawyer, has pointed out:

> The crime of conspiracy is complete as soon as two or more persons have agreed in any way whatsoever, whether formally or informally, by words or by conduct, to commit some crime; it is not necessary for the prosecution to prove the commission of the ultimate crime nor even of acts amounting to an attempt to commit it. It is thus in general easier to secure a conviction for conspiracy than for any other offense, for less has actually to be proved against the defendants; and prejudices or excitement may lead a jury to convict parties on a mere allegation that they agreed or arranged together to do something under circumstances where, if it were necessary to prove some positive criminal act, the jury would have to acquit because there would be no evidence of any such acts.
>
> It is little wonder, in the circumstances, that in all periods of tension, in all countries, charges of conspiracy have been frequently made, and many defendants have been found guilty and sentenced to imprisonment, although little has been proved against them and no other crime could plausibly even be charged.*

From laxity in security, government agencies became overcautious. Scientists working on atom bomb projects told hundreds of anecdotes about security measures they considered absurd and ineffective. According to one story, security officers in a supersecret laboratory in Savannah, Georgia, that was working on the hydrogen bomb were told to censor any references to hydrogen in outgoing mail. The following letter from a scientist reached his wife intact: *Darling, we are involved in work so secret here that I can't tell you anything about it. I can't even mention the ingredient, although when you add two parts of it to one part of oxygen it makes water.*

The CIA, founded in 1947, was eager to find a historical tradition as a bed for its anchor. The first paragraph of its brochure states

---

* Denis Nowell Pritt, *Spies and Informers in the Witness Box* (London: Bernard Harrison, Ltd., 1958).

that "the United States has carried on intelligence activities since the days of George Washington, but only since World War II has this work been systematized on a government-wide basis."

General Washington little knew he was giving the CIA a mandate when he wrote John Hancock on July 26, 1777:

> The necessity of procuring good intelligence is apparent and need not be further argued. All that remains for me to add is that you keep the whole matter as secret as possible. For upon secrecy, success depends in most enterprises of this kind, and for want of it they are generally defeated, however well planned and promising a favorable issue.

This and seven other letters are on exhibit in the CIA main hall.

Shifting from the onus of being "un-American," as General Vandenberg put it, espionage now had the benediction of the founding fathers. General Washington had a network of spies behind the British lines. He received no pay as general in chief of the armies and kept his own books so that he could be reimbursed for his expenses out of pocket. One can find among his cash paid accounts this notation: *Five guineas for expenses and rewards obliged to employ to carry out a correspondence with Jersey residents behind the enemy lines.*

The CIA of necessity had to turn its back on the tradition that considers espionage dishonest, the tradition exemplified by Addison's charge that "a man capable of so infamous a calling as that of spy will be more industrious to carry out that which is grateful than that which is true."

It rejoined a far older tradition which considers espionage essential to the survival of a great power and makes moral objections superfluous. Secrecy, treachery, bribery, a well-stocked vocabulary of malevolence and guile, were stamped APPROVED and necessary for the service of the state. By a different path, the CIA arrived at the philosophy of its Soviet counterpart, the KGB-GRU. Possibly both American and Soviet espionage chiefs would accept as their spiritual ancestor the Chinese military theorist Sun Tzu, who wrote in 500 B.C. an ageless treatise on the spy in a book called *Roots of Strategy —Art of War*. He said:

> Knowledge of the enemy's disposition can only be obtained from other men. Hence the use of spies, of whom there are five classes: Local, inward, converted, doomed, surviving.

When these five kinds of spy are all at work, none can discover the secret system. This is called "diverse manipulation of the threads." It is the sovereign's most precious faculty.

Local spies means employing the services of the inhabitants of a district. [The Russians have been fortunate with local Communist parties.]

Inward spies is making use of officials of the enemy. [As the Russians used Harry Dexter White or as we used Polish officials who leaked the secret Khrushchev 20th Party Congress speech to the CIA.]

Converted spies, getting hold of the enemy's spies and using them for our own purposes. [Martin and Mitchell, Peter Deriabin, and all the other defectors who are induced to go from the West to East or East to West, are contemporary examples.]

Doomed spies, doing certain things openly for purposes of deception, and allowing our own spies to know of them and report them to the enemy. [Known by Departments of Dirty Tricks all over the world as decoys.]

Surviving spies, those who bring back the news from the enemy's camp. [Francis Gary Powers was a surviving spy who did not survive.]

Hence it is that with none in the whole army are more intimate relations to be maintained than with spies. None should be more liberally rewarded. [Cicero, the butler who spied on the British Ambassador in Ankara for the Germans, was paid 300,000 pounds—in counterfeit bills.]

In no other business should greater secrecy be preserved. Spies cannot be usefully employed without certain intuitive sagacity. The end and aim of spying in all its five varieties is knowledge of the enemy. And this knowledge can only be derived in the first instance from the converted spy. Hence it is only the enlightened ruler and the wise general who will use the highest intelligence of the army for purposes of spying, and thereby they achieve great results.

How successful American and Soviet intelligence systems have been in the application of Sun Tzu's advice and an examination of the people involved in contemporary espionage is our next field of inquiry.

III. Judy Coplon: A Spy in the House of Love

ALBERT H. SOCOLOV is a forty-one-year-old lawyer with a prosperous general practice. A tall, pleasant-faced man with an engaging manner, Socolov has offices on lower Broadway. On his desk, there is a photograph of his wife. She is not pretty, but has one of those old-young faces that wear their ravages well.

The Socolovs were married in May, 1950, according to orthodox Jewish rite. As part of the ceremony, the bridegroom broke a wineglass with his heel, succeeding on the first attempt. This was a sign that the marriage would be blessed with good luck. The couple has four children: a nine-year-old daughter, and three sons aged eight, six, and one. The youngest was born on the fourth of July.

The couple lives in a hundred-and-thirty-year-old brownstone in downtown Brooklyn. There is nothing exceptional about their lives. They are interested in the arts, enjoy the theatre, museums, and concerts. The school-age children go to public school. Mrs. Socolov, according to her husband, "is preoccupied with raising four kids and does some charitable work. She has a serious interest in writing and one of these days she will do some writing."

Mrs. Socolov likes to travel. Not long after the war, she went on a tour of France and Italy. But in the last ten years she has been restricted to the Eastern seaboard. Also, for the last ten years, the couple has had a nagging financial problem.

Mrs. Socolov's maiden name is Judith Coplon. On March 4, 1949, she was arrested in New York City in the company of Valentin A. Gubitchev, a United Nations Secretariat member. She was working in a highly security-conscious branch of the Justice Department at the time. The FBI men who arrested her searched her purse and found it bulging with secret material obtained from Department of Justice files and dealing almost exclusively with Communist espionage and counterespionage activities in the United States.

She was convicted in a 1949 Washington trial of stealing secret documents with intent to transmit them to a foreign power. In a 1950 New York trial, she was convicted of conspiring with Gubitchev to transmit the documents to the Soviet Union. She never served her Washington sentence because, in 1952, the Supreme Court refused to review a motion for retrial, in effect invalidating the initial conviction. She never served her New York sentence because the second circuit court of appeals reversed her conviction in December, 1950.

The appeals court did not dismiss the indictment, which still stands. Judy Coplon Socolov is technically still under the four-count conspiracy indictment and still owes her physical freedom to the $50,000 she put up for bail. That sum is frozen in the clerk's office of the United States District Court Building in Foley Square, New York City, and the conditions of her bail forbid her to leave the Eastern seaboard. The Justice Department let it be known in 1958, however, that the Coplon case would never be retried. As far as anyone connected with it is concerned, the case is closed.

This interpretation is vigorously endorsed by Mr. and Mrs. Socolov. They were married at a time when Miss Coplon had already been sentenced to serve from forty months to ten years in jail as a result of her Washington conviction and was in the midst of her New York trial, in which she faced a thirty-five-year jail sentence and a $20,000 fine. Persons close to Socolov have noted that he displayed more of the crusading spirit than the average man in marrying a woman whom he might only see on prison visiting days for many years to come. Al Socolov had met Judy while working as a clerk in the office of a law firm that was handling the Coplon case, Neuberger, Shapiro, Rabinowitz, and Boudin. A law office is not usually thought of as the setting for a romance, but the two met in January while poring over trial records, and were married in May. (SHE MARRIED HER MOUTHPIECE, a headline read.) The first year was the most trying.

Judy was notorious, her face had appeared regularly on the front pages of newspapers, and every day she had to go through the experience of being recognized in public; sometimes the reaction was curiosity, more often it was animosity. The Socolovs began their married life with Judy's mother on Ocean Parkway, Brooklyn, moved to Morningside Heights, then came back to Brooklyn. They made no attempt at secrecy.

Asked about their life today, Al Socolov says that "the affairs of ten years ago are completely forgotten. New York is a funny town, a fellow sees his picture in the papers and thinks his life is shattered forever. But ask the average man about it a few months later, and he doesn't even know what you're talking about. We have been able to live a normal private life. We have been involved with the job of living and surviving and all the things everybody else does."

Forgotten though it may be by the public, the Coplon case remains one of the most important and most baffling American espionage cases. Judith Coplon was the first American civilian to be tried and convicted of spying for Russia. Her trial marked the beginning of a decade heavy with Cold War espionage. Earlier trials had involved Communists in government, but not espionage. Alger Hiss and William Remington were both convicted for perjury, a much less serious offense.

The case also was crucial for the FBI. About eighty agents worked on the investigation, but were apparently unfamiliar with this type of case for they bungled it badly. Some of the evidence came from wire taps that were maintained on the telephones of the defendants while the trial was in progress. Wire-tap evidence is not admissible in a Federal Court, and FBI agents committed perjury to keep the issue out of the Washington trial. The fifty-odd records made of the tapped conversations "disappeared" following an FBI memorandum from Howard Fletcher, who was in charge of the case, to D. M. Ladd, Assistant FBI Director.

The memorandum read: *The above named informant* [Tiger, the code name of the tap] *has been furnishing information concerning the activities of Miss Coplon. In view of the imminency of her trial, it is recommended that this informant* [the wire tap] *be discontinued and that all administrative records in the New York office covering operations of this informant be destroyed.* The agent who destroyed the records testified that he peeled the wax surface off the discs by dropping them in hot water, cut the surfaces into strips and burned the strips in an incinerator.

Worse than that, the FBI arrested Miss Coplon and her Russian co-defendant without a warrant. The law at that time stated that flight must be suspected before the FBI can act without a warrant. If a suspect is arrested as he is boarding a plane for Mexico, no warrant is needed. But Coplon and Gubitchev had just gotten off the subway and were walking slowly down Third Avenue when they were arrested, and the FBI failed to convince the court that they were fleeing. Why the FBI, which had been trailing Miss Coplon for months, failed to get a warrant was never explained.

It proved a blessing in disguise, however, since on December 21, 1950, Congress passed legislation to empower federal agents to make arrests without warrants in cases involving espionage, sabotage, or other major crimes. Critics charged that the FBI's unlawful conduct was being legalized and that due process was going out the window. Those in favor of the change argued that it was better to extend the framework of the law than let spies go unpunished.

The two Coplon trials also opened a window on the FBI's investigative techniques. In Miss Coplon's handbag at the time of her arrest were found thirty-four data slips she had typed up herself. The information on these slips was taken from FBI reports to which Miss Coplon had access in her job with the Justice Department. The issue of whether the data slips should be allowed as evidence was brought up at the Washington trial, with the prosecution contending that national security would be affected if the cases referred to were made public. But Federal Judge Albert L. Reeves said that "justice must be done though the heavens should fall" and allowed them to be introduced. The data slips demonstrated the FBI's "vacuum-cleaner technique," in which the wheat and the chaff of intelligence are gathered up together and sorted out later. Thus, some of Miss Coplon's data slips were based on unfounded rumors, others on cases that had been followed through.

Two other sensational revelations were made in the Coplon trials:

1. Abraham L. Pomerantz, Gubitchev's shrewd lawyer, while cross-examining an FBI agent at the New York trial elicited the information that the FBI was tapping the phones of U.N. Secretariat personnel in their offices.

2. The following exchange occurred between Archibald Palmer,

attorney for Miss Coplon, and another FBI agent: Q.—Has the United States counterespionage agents working in embassies, consulates, and United Nations delegations of other nations including Russia? A.—Yes.

A State Department denial was released the next day but the damage had been done.

J. Edgar Hoover was evidently displeased with the way his men had handled the Coplon case. Shortly after the end of the trials, Howard Fletcher, agent in charge of internal security for the United States and directly responsible for the investigation, was shunted to an administrative assistant's job in the Washington office.

Another unusual element in the case involved Miss Coplon's relationship with Archie Palmer, her lawyer, which deteriorated so badly that she fired him in the middle of the New York trial. The three court-appointed lawyers who succeeded Palmer were unfamiliar with the case and could not do much to help her.

The last and possibly most publicized sensation of the case was the love angle. Miss Coplon's defense was based on an alleged romance with Gubitchev, the Soviet engineer who worked for the United Nations. But the prosecution showed that at the time her romance with the Russian was supposed to have been flourishing, she was spending weekends in Baltimore and Philadelphia hotels with Harold Shapiro, a young lawyer in the Justice Department. This made for some juicy testimony and raised an interesting psychological point: whether a woman in love with one man could simultaneously be having an affair with another. The jury was evidently shocked at the suggestion, to the disgust of Archie Palmer, who claimed that the Coplon Washington trial had been transformed from "an espionage case to a sex case."

Judy Coplon, the young lady responsible for all these developments, has since been consecrated in a book entitled *The World's Great Women Spies*,* where she is depicted as following the majestic tradition of Mata Hari. And yet, if one word can be used to sum her up, that word is *unassuming*. In high school, she was a wallflower and a drudge who piled up an academic average in the 90's. In college, she was a permanent library fixture and an editor of the weekly *Barnard Bulletin*. She dressed badly, did her hair badly, and went to

* Kurt D. Singer, *The World's Great Women Spies* (London: W. H. Allen, 1951).

concerts alone. One person who knew her well says she was a *nebbisch,* a Yiddish word for some one who is unimportant and unimpressive. A college friend remembers her as "the typical bright college girl from a middle-class Jewish background. You'd see her walking briskly across the Barnard campus with a copy of *P.M.* rolled under her arm."

Physically, she was not impressive. A shade under five feet tall, weighing about ninety pounds, she had that quality often observed in men who need to compensate for lack of height: drive fed by nervous energy. She also showed aggressive self-confidence in intellectual matters and vulnerability in emotional matters.

At the time of her arrest in 1949, she was twenty-eight. She had black curly hair, thick brows, a heavy, petulant mouth, and expressive brown eyes, her best feature. Her figure was boyish, her legs athletic. She had taken ballet lessons in college and her favorite exercise was cycling.

Judy was a young lady accustomed to praise. Up to the time of her arrest, there was never an unkind word written about her by her teachers or her bosses. In addition, she was an obedient and a dutiful child who did not overtly revolt from the strict family ties of her Jewish family household. She got along well with her brother Bertram, who was five years older than she. She was brought up in a one-family stucco house in the East Flatbush section of Brooklyn. Her family, of Polish extraction, was rooted in American tradition. Her grandfather, a union sympathizer, was jailed in Georgia during the Civil War. Her father, Samuel Coplon, was a member of a liberal Masonic lodge. Mr. Coplon was a jobber in toys. He never made much money, but each Christmas he sent toys to needy children in Warrensburg, near Lake George, where he had lived as a young man. He came to be called the "Santa Claus of the Adirondacks." Mr. Coplon, who had been ill for a long time, died of a cerebral hemorrhage less than a month after his daughter's arrest.

Judy went to the local high school, James Madison, and had a 90 plus average for the four-year period. Displaying her first interest in journalism, she was on the staff of the school magazine, *The Highwayman.*

Granted a scholarship after obtaining a 97 average in the New York State regents examinations, she matriculated at Barnard College in 1939, majoring in history. Dean Millicent McIntosh summed up her college career by saying when she graduated in 1943 that "Miss Coplon has a brilliant record as a student and a personality rating higher than any I have ever seen."

The personality rating was a result of Judy's throwing herself into extracurricular activities with a kind of desperate energy that made up for her lack of social life. She was on half a dozen committees and was a member of Arista, the Honor Society. There was hardly a student activity at Barnard that she did not have a hand in. Senior year saw her become one of three managing editors of the *Bulletin*, a weekly newspaper for the girl's college.

From her student advisers to her bosses in the Department of Justice, Judy's passage brought one long train of praise. According to them, she possessed all the virtues. Her faculty adviser at Barnard wrote that "she is a most generous and unselfish young woman, always industrious and extremely capable and dependable, but withal so exceedingly modest and unassuming about what she does that she could easily be overlooked."

The Barnard Placement Bureau listed her "in the top category in the following qualities—natural ability, application, originality, integrity, straightforwardness, modesty, fair play, public spirit, enthusiasm, leadership, good breeding." With that kind of recommendation, she had no trouble getting a government job.

Her bosses in Washington found her equally deserving of high praise. Her first chief, Laurence A. Knapp, said, "I found that she had superior talent which she coupled with a distinctly co-operative and friendly personality. Her judgment had a scope and dependability not usually found in persons of equal age and experience."

Her next boss, Jesse M. MacKnight, wrote her in 1946 to "express my personal appreciation for your work on my staff and to tell you that you have been an able and valuable colleague. . . . . Please feel free to use my name as a reference when applying for a position in Washington or elsewhere."

Even Tom Clark, Attorney General at the time, praised Miss Coplon's record. When she was promoted in 1948 from civil service grade P-2 to P-3, he wrote:

Dear Miss Judith:
    P-3 is really an accomplishment and I congratulate you on it. I did not know we had political analysts in the criminal division, but

on checking I find that you are in the Foreign Agents Registration Section. Keep up the good work.

It was one of her teachers at Barnard who made the prophetic appraisal that Judy "takes a keen interest in national affairs."

In this connection, Judy's articles in the Barnard weekly cast some light on her frame of mind during her college years, which coincided with the first four years of World War II. Her last school year, '42-'43, started at about the same time as the battle of Stalingrad. Judy's reactions were those of many Americans; she did not disguise her admiration for the Russian stand before the Nazi invaders and she was horrified that the Allies did not do more to help Russia. In signed editorials (which meant that they did not necessarily reflect the opinion of a majority of the eleven members of the weekly's managing board), she urged a second front. Stalin had been complaining bitterly that Churchill and Roosevelt had not kept their promise to open a second front in Europe in 1942 and engage some of the German troops then fighting in Russia. Miss Coplon, in her editorial called "The Politics of War," indicated that opposition to the second front came from shameful political motives, from those who wanted the Germans to bleed Russia white before the Allies won the war.

In another editorial, she charged that the United States was skimping in its lend-lease to Russia. "There is no acceptable answer in the flat statement that we have sent enough to Russia," she wrote. "That is the stargazer's attitude. We need realism now. We must realize that Russia is at this moment the heart of the war and that our obligation is to keep that heart beating."

Judy was active in exchange programs between Russian and American youths. In October, 1942, she helped with arrangements for Soviet Union delegates to the International Student Assembly, including a twenty-six-year-old girl guerrilla "who has killed 309 Germans," according to a Barnard *Bulletin* interview.

Judy's usual editorial position was that American values could be best preserved through an attitude of dissent and criticism. In one editorial, she wrote:

The American tradition, he could tell them what it is, he who has reveled in the backwash of all the filthy waters of America. We're not deluding ourselves. We know about the factory hand in

Bayonne who makes $5 a week. And the migrant farmer with the dust in his eyes. And the Negro whose only way to go is through the servant's entrance. It's dirty, smelly, and bad.

But, she added, there was still some hope, and she pointed to "the people who wouldn't accept a constitution without a bill of rights. And we're talking about those abolitionists who would be heard. And we're talking about the growth of a democratic labor movement in the United States as in England."

What comes out most strongly from Miss Coplon's writings is that at an age where most girls are concerned with harvest hops and heavy dates, she was concerned with Russian war relief, the opening of a second front, and America's downtrodden.

Her reputation as a crusader was well established, and in a farewell editorial, one of her successors wrote: "The fiery eye is typical of the Coplon temperament. A born crusader, Judy is never happier than when she is putting her whole heart into something, whether a cause, a course, or a *Bulletin*." Whether Judy simply had a strong case of youthful radicalism and whether her interest in Russian affairs was limited to the war effort remained to be seen.

She underwent routine security investigations when she started working for the Government as well as an intensive FBI probe when she was under surveillance, but was never found to have been even remotely connected with any Communist organization. In her government work, she was zealously anti-Communistic. She once prepared a list of fifteen groups for inclusion on the Attorney General's list of subversive organizations, based on material she had prepared.

Nathan Lenvin, a Justice Department attorney who shared an office with Miss Coplon, said the day after her arrest: "She was a wonderful actress; she would sit down and read the *Daily Worker* and laugh at its comments and editorials." Her brother Bertram had the following exchange with newsmen:

Q. Does your sister have any radical connections?

A. My sister has never had any radical connections.

Q. Have you ever had any radical connections?

A. Only if you call the Republican Party radical.

John M. Kelley Jr., a prosecutor in the Coplon case, believed but never proved that Miss Coplon had formed Communist associations early in life but was considered such a valuable asset that she was not allowed to join the Party. Kelley, who died of cancer in 1958, held that Judy was considered an ideal agent to infiltrate the Government. She had a brilliant academic record, had never signed any peace pacts or attended any study groups or meetings. In this view, Judy graduated from college as a full-fledged Soviet agent. She was told to get a government job, to work her way into a department where she would see secret documents and could leak information to a Soviet courier. Since her usefulness as an agent could only last as long as her security clearance, she was ordered to avoid contact with known Communists.

Whatever her reasons, Miss Coplon did not pursue the writing career she had so eagerly looked forward to in college. Five days after she had graduated *cum laude,* she went to work in the Economic Warfare Section of the War Division in the Justice Department's New York office. She was an assiduous worker and was transferred in January, 1945, to a far more interesting Washington assignment. The Justice Department was not her first choice. She had applied for a job with the CIA and been turned down in the preliminary weeding-out.

Her new position was assistant political analyst in the Foreign Agents Registration Section of the Justice Department's Criminal Division. Any agent for a foreign government must register with the Justice Department or face imprisonment up to five years or a fine up to $10,000 or both. During the war, when a hunt was on for Nazi front groups, the Foreign Agents Registration Section grew in size and importance. By 1945, there was a general cutback in the Justice Department, and the staff in the F.A.R. section was progressively reduced to six: a head of department, two lawyers, two clerical workers, and a political analyst.

Judy Coplon started working in the section when the cutback was in process. At first, she was assigned to French and Belgian agent registrations. But by 1946, she was the only political analyst left and she took on greater responsibilities. She moved into her own office, Room 2220 of the main Justice Department building. It was a large room with unlocked file cabinets, a library-type table where records and dossiers were kept before they were filed, and Judy's desk. She had the office to herself until the start of 1949, when, to her annoyance, a new lawyer for the section, Nathan Lenvin, moved in with her.

She began to specialize in agent registrations from the Soviet Union and Iron Curtain countries. She had access to FBI reports forwarded to the Department of Justice because they disclosed violations of various statutes. There were many reports on Soviet diplomats, for instance.

In a government office used to handling a steady flow of confidential and secret documents, a certain amount of negligence can almost be taken for granted. Employees grow accustomed to seeing the label TOP SECRET, leave file cabinets unlocked, and misplace documents. A secretary in Judy's section once left a confidential report in the ladies' room. Judy found it there and brought it back to her. This nonchalance extended to other departments, and Judy was able to obtain classified State Department reports simply by asking an acquaintance for them.

Miss Coplon's own contempt for the secrecy label was expressed when she took the stand in her Washington trial and said, "A lot of this confidential material was a laughing matter. The day before, we would hear about the Un-American Activities Committee having hearings and having someone like Miss Bentley testify, or the breaking of an espionage case. We would get a confidential memo the next day from the FBI where we would see the same information."

Nonetheless, she displayed a keen interest in confidential FBI memos. When she was arrested, hundreds were found in her desk. Judy's thirst for knowledge made her the ideal employee for certain assignments. Thus, Raymond P. Whearty, who was boss of the section in 1947, asked her to go through a backlog of thousands of data slips dealing with internal security and see which ones could be thrown out for storage space. Whearty turned up again in the Coplon case, as the assistant U.S. attorney who prosecuted her with Kelley.

Miss Coplon did so well in internal security work that in October, 1948, she was assigned specifically to process FBI reports on Communist investigations. She became the Justice Department's specialist on Communist affairs. It was about the time she got this new assignment that Judy met Gubitchev.

It was also about this time that the FBI started worrying about a leak. In the words of a 1952 House Un-American Activities report, "The Shameful Years":

> Highly confidential investigative reports being conducted by the FBI concerning Soviet and Russian satellite diplomats were finding their way back to these individuals.

It did not appear that the information was coming from any American contacts and therefore must have been coming directly from Moscow. This then was the pattern . . . someone having access to FBI files was channeling the information to some person who in turn was furnishing it directly to Moscow. Once there, the Kremlin examined the material and then, through courier and pouch, was notifying the Soviet embassy and the various consulates.

The FBI's concern about this roundabout espionage network first centered on itself. But the possibility that an FBI agent might be responsible for the leak was discounted after a security check.

The Justice Department then came in for some scrutiny, since all the reports in question had been forwarded to the criminal division. How suspicion came to center on Miss Coplon remains a mystery. According to FBI testimony, a confidential informant implicated her in December, 1948. In FBI parlance, a confidential informant often means a wire tap. It is possible that taps were put on all the employees in Miss Coplon's section toward the end of 1948. There were only five. Another explanation is that a tap on Gubitchev's United Nations phone led to Miss Coplon. She admitted calling him at his office at least once.

The best cloak-and-dagger interpretation came from a retired counterspy for the FBI, Matt Cvetic, who posed as a Communist for many years. In a recent address to a patriotic group in Philadelphia, Cvetic claimed he had blown the whistle on the Coplon case. "I got a tip from a not too clever female Communist agent," he said. "We were having coffee in a restaurant when she started bragging about the accomplishments of women Communists."

Cvetic said the woman told him: "Why, we have one of our own girl comrades working as a clerk in the Department of Justice in Washington right now and the FBI doesn't know a thing about it. She's one of our best agents and she's doing a fine job for the revolution." Appealing as this account may be, the FBI quickly discounted it as "naïve."

In the first week of 1949, William E. Foley, a portly, backslapping sort who had succeeded Whearty as head of the F.A.R. section, walked into Judy's office and saw her reading a report on Soviet espionage. Glancing at the report, he told her: "I've got a new one."

"Could I see it?" Judy asked.

"I don't know," he replied, "it's top secret."

The following day, Foley got the surprise of his government career. He was called into the office of Peyton Ford, assistant Attorney General, and told that Judith Coplon, his specialist on Communist affairs, his praiseworthy political analyst, was suspected of leaking confidential reports and was "running around with some Russian."

Foley was instructed to remove her from internal security work without arousing her suspicions. At the same time, a microphone was installed in Miss Coplon's office telephone which recorded her conversations in the office as well as her phone calls. The telephone in her small Washington apartment was also tapped, as was her mother's phone in Brooklyn.

The FBI had twenty wire-tap monitors working on the Coplon case in Washington and another twenty in New York. After Gubitchev had been identified as the Russian Judy was seeing, his home phone was monitored by Russian-speaking FBI men. The taps continued long after the arrests. Conversations between Judy and her lawyer were monitored in New York at a time when pre-trial hearings were going on.

Annoyed by the news that the leak was in his department, Foley stormed into Miss Coplon's office, pulled out the internal security drawer from her desk, and told her: "This is one drawer you won't be using any more." When Miss Coplon demanded an explanation, her chief said that she was being taken off internal security so that she could devote herself exclusively to foreign registrations. The internal security work, he said, would be taken care of by a newcomer, Mrs. Ruth Rosson.

Judy felt slighted by the change. She thought it was a criticism of her abilities. She did not for a moment suspect that she was under surveillance. Several days later, she told Foley: "Taking me off this work is a reflection on me. I wonder if I've got any future in this department." Foley replied, "You can be fired any day. If any big shot reads over the assignment list of the Foreign Agents Registration Section and comes across the term 'political analyst,' he may decide 'maybe we don't need a political analyst' and he can dismiss you [snapping his fingers] like that."

"You know, I am taking a civil service exam," Judy replied, "and I may come out a P-4." (Judy did not have regular civil service status; she had been hired under special provisions.)

Although she seemed to be under a cloud, Judy continued to ask for reports that were now outside her jurisdiction. The next time she saw Foley she said offhandedly, "When am I going to see that top secret report?"

"I don't think you can see it," Foley answered.

A month later she asked a third time to see it, and Foley dismissed the report as "just a lot of old stuff."

Judy was showing Mrs. Rosson the ropes on the internal security material. Conveniently, Mrs. Rosson was in an adjoining office, and Judy made a point of asking her to send over all reports dealing with internal security R (for Russia).

She also went in to see Foley's chubby, red-haired secretary, Margaret McKinney, and told her: "Sometimes I might need some information out of the files and there won't be anyone around. Would you mind telling me where Mr. Foley keeps the keys?" The secretary showed her how to unlock the file cabinet, which included secret reports for the internal security section.

Miss Coplon continued to feel she had been treated unfairly. In mid-February she asked Foley whether his attitude toward her had changed. An FBI activity (wire-tap) record for February 18 shows that she called her friend Harold Shapiro and told him that she was not getting along with Foley because he criticized her work. "What in the hell, you can't win," she added.

She was dissatisfied enough to inquire about courses at the Columbia Graduate School of Journalism. She was told that no one was admitted in mid-year, and that she would have to apply for the '49-'50 year of study, which began in September.

Miss Coplon was in the habit of spending about one weekend out of three in New York. Her first New York weekend of 1949 started January 14. By that time the FBI surveillance was operating, and she was followed from the time she left her apartment for Washington's Union Station, suitcase in hand. She arrived at Pennsylvania Station at 5 P.M., but instead of going to her family's home in Brooklyn she took a subway to the Washington Heights part of the Bronx, near the Cloisters and Fort Tryon Park. She stood on the corner of Broadway and 193rd Street and after a ten-minute wait, Gubitchev showed up. The pair went to the De Luxe Restaurant, 143 Dyckman Street, and had dinner, while in the next booth, some FBI agents were having theirs. Judy seemed relaxed and fed nickels into the jukebox. When they walked back to the Eighth Avenue subway, the four agents tailing them testified that they were having an argument, that Judy was raising her voice and poking at Gubitchev with a rolled-up newspaper. This detail of the meeting was magnified during the trial, for it indicated some sort of emotional involvement between the two, and bolstered the defense argument that this was simply a case of "a man meeting a maid." Judy and "Val," as she said she called Gubitchev, took the subway downtown together, and at the 125th Street stop the Russian bolted out just as the doors were closing, thereby eluding his surveillants.

Coplon and Gubitchev employed this bus and subway technique at all three of the meetings that the FBI observed. It corresponds closely to what Hede Massing, a confessed Soviet agent in the United States, described as the "techniques of an *apparatchik* [member of a Soviet spy network, or apparat]" in her book, *This Deception*:

> The person who was being trailed sat relaxed and seemingly unconcerned to the very last split-second before the train was about to move and the doors shut tight, and then he jumped out for all he was worth. The trick is to put the surveillor at ease, make him feel that everything is well in hand and then, when he least expects it, to disappear.

This was the way Coplon and Gubitchev regularly behaved when using the city transit system. On February 18, Judy was back on the same corner, waiting for her Russian. She was late this time because she had broken the ankle strap on her shoe while getting off the train. She had taken a different subway uptown, and used a subway elevator to get to Broadway. It was a cold evening, and the only other persons on the elevator with her were two FBI men and an FBI matron.

Judy wasn't sure how to reach Broadway and asked one of the FBI men. He grumbled an incoherent reply. She found herself in a dead-end street, turned around, and almost collided with the second FBI man and the matron. "Which way is Broadway?" she asked. "We're lost too," they replied. "Oh God," Judy said, "this is awful, I had a seven P.M. dinner date." "We're late for dinner too," the FBI couple rejoined, and the man added gallantly: "My, you really are a brave little girl being out in all this darkness alone."

Gubitchev, meanwhile, had come and gone, true to another espionage rule: when your contact is late at a "treff," you leave and return in an hour. Judy arrived at the corner, stood there five minutes, then went into a shop to have her shoe fixed. At 7:58 P.M., Gubitchev showed up again, looking nervous.

Judy opened her purse, and Gubitchev reached for it but instead of removing something from it, he closed the clasp. On this tender note, the pair separated.

The FBI thought things were going a bit slowly, even for a romance, and decided to do a little prodding. One of its agents prepared two "decoy" memorandums containing a hodgepodge of true and untrue information which was to be made available to Judy on the theory that she would try to pass it to Gubitchev. Judy had told her boss she was planning to go to New York for the March 4th weekend. Foley got the decoy messages from the Attorney General's office, and plunked them on Judy's desk the morning of March 4. The conversation that then transpired is one of the enigmas of the case. In the Washington trial, Foley denied knowing the memos were decoys, but he went back on this testimony in the New York trial, thereby implicitly admitting perjury. Although Judy's office was still "bugged," this particular conversation was not recorded. According to the FBI, there was some technical problem with the mike, although everything before or after came through clearly.

In any case, as Foley finally admitted, he gave the decoys to Judy and told her, "This is very hot and interesting. Give it to Lenvin when he comes in." That afternoon, Lenvin brought the memos back into Foley's office and said that since they were confidential, he would rather have them locked up.

Judy's somewhat different version of the conversation goes like this: Foley came in and said, "This is very hot and interesting, I want you to make a note of this and give it to Lenvin." Later that morning, he came back and said: "Did you make a note of this?" She said she had. "Let me see it," Foley said. He looked her notes over, then said: "I would like you to work on this over the weekend."

"You know I'm going to New York," Judy complained. "I want you to take this note to New York and think about the matter," Foley insisted. Judy was annoyed and commented, "I must say I have been getting a lot of odd information and a lot of odd requests have been made of me these last few weeks."

She took the decoys and put them in her purse. "What do you want me to do, put it in like this?" "Oh, no," said Foley, "put a wrapping around it, or something."

When Lenvin came into the office later that morning, Judy told him she was going to New York again, and he teased her about having a "beau." Judy says she answered: "Yes, I'm seeing someone at the United Nations, an engineer."

Judy took an early train and got to Penn Station at 5:30 P.M. The weather was brisk and she was wearing a black coat and skirt, a tan sweater and a pearl choker. The FBI had its troops out in force. There were twenty-seven agents and six unmarked radio cars patrolling Washington Heights. The evening was like one of those cliché-ridden movie scenarios where the audience is always a step ahead of the protagonists. Judy kept looking back to see if she was being followed, but like an experimental mouse in a labyrinth, she again took the subway to Washington Heights. Gubitchev was waiting at 183rd Street and Broadway but did not acknowledge her arrival. The pair went into complicated maneuvers obviously intended to shake off surveillance. Judy took one subway and Gubitchev took another. They met at Times Square, with the tail still on them. Walking west, Gubitchev spotted a Ninth Avenue southbound bus and broke into a run. He held the bus for Judy, and they sat in different seats. The FBI lost them at that point, but another radio car picked up the bus farther down. The pair got off at 14th Street and promptly boarded a BMT Canarsie Line subway. There were about fifteen persons in the car, five of them FBI agents. But again Coplon and Gubitchev pulled the trick of bolting before the doors closed and again they lost their surveillance, at the Third Avenue stop.

It was 8:30 P.M. when Judy and Val emerged from the subway at Third Avenue and 16th Street, convinced that they had shaken their tails. They stood talking under the El, then Gubitchev went into a candy store and made a phone call while Judy stood outside.

Meanwhile the FBI was scouting the area, inspecting side streets as discreetly as possible and setting up a security cordon to prevent the couple's escape. Making a routine check of Third Avenue at 8:45 P.M., they were astounded to find that their quarry was less than a block away from the subway station.

The FBI decided to move in for the arrest, even though they had no warrant, estimating that:

1. Coplon and Gubitchev might otherwise seek sanctuary in the Soviet consulate. Gubitchev's telephone call was later seen as a plea to the Russians for help. The FBI believed that when the two were arrested, they were waiting to be picked up by a Soviet diplomatic vehicle that would have taken them to safety.

2. If Judy had anything to pass to Gubitchev, she would have done so by then.

3. There might not be another chance to arrest them together and establish solid grounds for a conspiracy indictment.

"This is ridiculous," Judy said when FBI agents seized her in the shadow of the El between 15th and 16th Streets. The short, balding Gubitchev did not say anything. He just looked glum. On the way to the FBI offices, Judy's small frame was squeezed between two husky agents in the radio car. One of them noticed her chewing, remembered his training about agents swallowing poison capsules and asked her what it was. Judy spat the remains of a lime Lifesaver into his hand.

After going through the fingerprinting and photographing departments, Judy and Gubitchev were separated. An indignant Judy was searched by FBI matrons. "They undressed me," she testified, "poked all over my body, made me open my mouth to see whether there was anything in it. I don't know what they expected to find."

She was noncommittal under questioning. Part of the FBI report reads:

> Q. What is your name?
> A. No comment.
> Q. Where do you work?
> A. No comment.
> Q. Did you come from Washington?
> A. No comment.
> Q. Do you recognize this picture of the Department of Justice?
> A. No comment, no comment, no comment, no comment, no comment.

An angry FBI agent hovered over her and barked: "What do you mean by answering no comment? Who do you think you are? You are just a piece of trash. I have had all kinds of trash in this chair. I have had racketeers, white slavers, all kinds of crooks and low forms of life in that chair. What gave you the idea you could answer no comment?"

Gubitchev had also been stripped and searched, and was equally unresponsive. "Who was that woman we saw you with?" the FBI asked. "I don't know that woman," he replied. "Would it make any difference if I told you that fifteen FBI men had seen you in her company?" Gubitchev shrugged.

The questioning lasted about four hours, during which time neither was told the charges against them nor allowed to communicate with lawyers. After her initial stubbornness, Judy began to co-operate with her questioners, giving them the background information they requested and joking with them. But Gubitchev, in an affidavit filed in pre-trial hearings, charged that he had been "subjected to many hours of examination by the FBI in order to get from me information about Soviet industrial and military affairs as well as state matters of my fatherland."

Searching Gubitchev was not much help to the FBI. True, he had $125 in an envelope in his inside suit pocket that could have been a payoff to Coplon. On the other hand, $125 was the amount of his weekly United Nations pay check. He said the money was for the purchase of household goods. The search failed to find that Judy had passed anything to Gubitchev. There was nothing on him except the money and the trivia usually carried in pockets, including a package of Aspragum and some dental floss.

Judy's search proved more rewarding. In her handbag, along with her powder, her "Irresistible" brand lipstick and $20 in bills and loose change, there was a wealth of information taken from Justice Department files, including the two decoy memos foisted upon her earlier in the day by Foley.

The main decoy memo had been copied in its entirety and the paper had been folded into a small square. The edges had been sealed with Scotch tape and an arrow had been inked in a corner to indicate where to separate the tape. The second memo had been summed up in two pages of handwritten notes.

In addition, Judy's purse contained thirty-four typewritten data slips referring to current FBI investigations; three biographical sketches of friends, noting their pro-Communist sympathies; some information about herself; and the highly incriminating "Michael" note. All this documentation was in plain envelopes which had been sealed in a Belle Sharmeer ("leg-size stockings for leg-wise women") hosiery wrapper. It had about the same thickness and weight as a pair of stockings, and was carefully taped.

Judy explained that Foley had told her to study the decoy memos over the weekend, and the other material was connected with a book she was writing called *Government Girl*.

In her trial testimony, Judy explained that some of the material in her purse was written in the first person because "the heroine of the book was myself."

> "I was going to write it in the first person. I wanted to tell the story of how I came to Washington, how it felt that first day when the weather was warm and springlike and how the trees looked down by the river. I wanted to put into it the hopes and excitement that Washington means to a new government girl.
>
> "And I made notes about people I knew and figured to put them into the book, developing them, of course. But I made a mistake in putting down the real names in my notes. And then, as I got the feel of the place, and came to realize what those buildings were, I wanted to picture Washington as a great big mausoleum with all the fretting workers, policed, probed, fingerprinted, running in and out—like the cockroaches."

Why did she concern herself so single-mindedly with Communist investigations?

> "One of the chapters was on what I call this hysteria, this witch hunt about loyalty, espionage, etc. . . . I had written a part on this espionage and this witch hunt in which I had used, not by name but ideas which I had gotten myself from FBI reports . . . there were thousands and thousands of reports. . . . Every day, I could get this whole impression, this whole fabric of people, these wives who would go through their husband's pockets and report to the FBI what they found, these daughters that report on their mothers. . . . You get this whole impression of spy and counterspy, irrespective of family, irrespective of religion; everyone is reporting on everyone else."

Judy explained that she could not show the court her manuscript. She had thrown it in the incinerator because she did not want it read at the trial.

It is hard to see how the "Michael" note could have fitted into the pattern of such a book. The note said:

> I have not been able (and don't think I will) to get the top secret FBI report which I described to Michael on Soviet and Communist intelligence activities in the U.S. When the moment was favorable, I asked Foley where the report was (he'd previously remarked that he had such a report). He said that some departmental official had it and he didn't expect to get it back. Foley remarked there was nothing new in it. When I saw the report for a minute, I breezed through it rapidly, remember very little. It was about 115 pages in length; summarized first Soviet intelligence activities, including Martens, Poyntz, Altschuler, Silvermaster et al. It had a heading on the Soviet United Nations delegation but that was all I remember. The rest of the report I think was on Polish, Yugoslav, etc. activities and possibly some information on the CP in the United States.

Judy's Bible-quoting lawyer, Archie Palmer, gave the most far-fetched explanation of the trials when he said that Michael was simply Michael the Archangel, who slew a great red dragon with seven heads and ten horns, one of the seven signs mentioned in the Apocalypse chapter of the New Testament. The FBI held that Michael was the code name for the head of a Soviet espionage network operating in New York, possibly Yuri Novikov, the Soviet Embassy second secretary who was at Gubitchev's side during the trial and who was expelled from the U.S. in 1953 for his part in another espionage case.

On the same sheet of paper as the Michael note, Judy had typed some information about graduate work she was doing after office hours. "Beginning with the spring semester of 1946, I attended the American University, Washington, D.C., until the time I completed my class credits for an M.A. in international organizations and international relations. All I need for my degree is the completion of a thesis by summer. My subject will deal with certain aspects of international propaganda and control." To the FBI, this meant that Judy had been asked to submit up-to-date biographical information in connection with a promotion on the Soviet intelligence ladder.

The next items in her purse-sized research library concerned a former high school friend, the friend's husband, and a young man Judy had met at the American University. These were character sketches in the manner of Somerset Maugham, Judy explained. They took the basic traits of an individual and after some adding and subtracting, came out fictionalized.

The high school friend was Lorraine Elkin, who had married Alvin Sinderbrand. The couple was living in New York. Judy wrote of Lorraine that "she remembers me as a Communist, and I think she is confused as to whether I am still a C, and if so why I continue to work for the government in Washington or if I've sold out. I think her opinion is somewhere between the two, that is, that I'm just a neurotic." She said Lorraine's husband had pro-Communist leanings. When the Sinderbrands were asked about Judy's sketches, they said they had not seen her in years and were completely mystified.

The third sketch, dealing with Alfred Boynton Stevenson, said: "I met Steve, as he is known, in the summer of 1946. I would characterize Steve as pro-Communist, albeit a bit wishy-washy idealist and politically naïve."

The interesting thing about the sketches is that they followed the outline in use for reports on possible spy recruits, as disclosed in the exposure of the Canadian spy ring in 1946 and other cases. In the established format of these reports, there are six headings. 1. Where the writer met the subject. 2. Description of the subject (age, job, origin, family, etc.). 3. Friendliness to Communism. 4. Political affiliations. 5. Close friends. 6. Subject's personality and flaws. All three of Judy's sketches adhered closely to these headings.

Judy had collected a variety of information on the thirty-four typed data slips, all dated March 3, 1949, the day before her arrest. Each data slip referred to an FBI case report, but Judy had in most instances picked out one or two points in the report that interested her. However, over the strenuous objections of the prosecution at the trial, the entire reports were introduced as evidence. As an example, data slip No. 11 said only: *Stuart Legg—possible Russian espionage agent.* Judy had taken this information out of an unconfirmed report on alleged Communist sympathies of such entertainment figures as Fredric March, Edward G. Robinson, Dorothy Parker, Paul Muni, John Garfield, Melvyn Douglas, Canada Lee, Donald Ogden Stewart, and others. The report at that point had not gone beyond the rumor-mongering stage, but when it was aired at the trial it created a sensation.

In another data slip, Judy mentioned that Morton E. Kent, a Russian-born Harvard graduate who had spent ten years in government service, had tried to establish contact with the Soviet secret police. Shortly after the report on Kent was made public, he cut his throat and his body was recovered floating in the Potomac River.

In general, the data slips showed that the FBI overlooks no one and that suspicions may be initially cast on an individual for the most indirect or remote reasons. Referring to a report on a suspected Soviet agent, Judy wrote: "In March, 1946, the subject had in her address book the name of Ruth Gruber. Gruber has been reported to have been a contact of F. A. Garanin of the Soviet embassy in Washington. Gruber was secretary to Harold Ickes, Secretary of the Interior." Disclosure of this data slip at the trial brought the following rejoinder from Mr. Ickes: "If that's a test of the accuracy of the FBI, they had better disband. Some fool writes her name on a slip of paper and they try to smear her. If she's a red, I'm a hottentot."

One was a report on a San Francisco man, Mario Joseph Pezzola, who was called into the FBI office because he had written several friends, bragging that he belonged to secret intelligence organizations. Pezzola sheepishly admitted that the letters were fabrications to impress his friends.

Suspicion had also fallen on a William J. Ragin because of his "possession of expensive photographic equipment, signs of unusual affluence, and references to contacts with the Russian Embassy." Ragin turned out to be a megalomaniac who sported an impressive diamond ring that he said he obtained "for a number of slabs of bacon" during the war in Europe. He enjoyed displaying a thousand-dollar bill he always carried on his person, yet claimed that "the American dollar is worthless." He spoke German, Russian and Polish, and had held an incredible number and variety of jobs in defense plants. He had worked for the American Ordnance Engineers and when questioned by the FBI, he readily admitted that his knowledge of ordnance equipment was far superior, and bragged about how he smuggled classified information from defense plants. He was the very essence of a harmless braggart, and hardly an effective spy.

Another investigation had uncovered that a Communist barber was working at the guided missile proving grounds in White Sands, New Mexico, and was reportedly extracting information from his customers in the barber's chair. The FBI informant reported that the barber, Eugenio Chavez, had asked his Communist friends not to visit him at the base so as not to arouse suspicion. The informant said "it was expected that the subject would be able to get photos, cipher information on the activity of the White Sands proving ground and that it would be transmitted to the Russian Embassy in Mexico City."

Some reports were conjectural to the point of absurdity: *Philip Levy's brother met with an individual who looks like a Russian general. The brother, Jacob Levy, came back from abroad with $5,000 in twenties. It is noted that this denomination has often been used in Soviet espionage payoffs.*

Other reports showed the FBI was keeping a careful check on the movements and associations of Soviet diplomatic and United Nations officials in the United States: *George Dimitri Sotirov, a Bulgarian in the United Nations department of social affairs, is suspected of working for the Bulgarian or Russian intelligence. He obtained a United Nations position to have freedom of movement in the United States.*

Perhaps the most substantial report was one showing that shipments of "atomic implements" had been made to Russia from 1947 to 1949 without export licenses. The implements had been bought by the Amtorg Trading Corp., the Soviet Government's official trading firm in the United States, from the Cyclotron Specialties Co. The first shipment reached the Soviet Union aboard the steamship *Mihail Kutuzov* in August, 1947, and another shipment was found on September 2, 1948, aboard the steamship *Murmansk* in New York harbor, but was removed. A third shipment was seized at the dock in Claremont, New Jersey, in January, 1949. What these secret atomic instruments were was not disclosed, except that the shipments included geophones, a device for measuring atomic blasts that was developed years ago and is commercially manufactured.

The data slips provided an intimate glimpse into FBI investigations never afforded the public before or since. One reason the Justice Department has declined to re-try Miss Coplon is that the FBI strongly opposes being placed under this type of scrutiny again.

Mention of the Amtorg Corp. brings us to the two decoy memos, the final items in Judy's purse. The memo from which Judy made notes was marked strictly confidential and addressed, from: Director FBI, to: Mr. Peyton Ford, Assistant to the Attorney General. Subject: Amtorg Trading Corp.

The memo, actually composed by an FBI agent, stated that "we are presently using, on a confidential basis, two highly placed officials of the Amtorg Trading Corp. One of these is Isidore Gibley Needleman, the Amtorg legal representative, with whom we have been maintaining a rather indirect contact through an intermediary. We have not been entirely satisfied with this arrangement, as to the extent of information supplied by Needleman, and for that reason, in order to check his sincerity, we desire to obtain from him more complete information on a variety of matters."

Those "secret" atomic implements, geophones, were again mentioned in the memo, which went on: "I have previously furnished you with information concerning the efforts of the Amtorg Trading Corp. to obtain equipment relative to atomic research developments. In this connection, the Bureau has recently learned through an informant that Amtorg Trading Corp. must have some knowledge of the use of these instruments. The above represents another example of the security risk present in the activities of this corporation."

The second memo, addressed to Foley and marked TOP SECRET, dealt with three FBI men posing as officials of Amtorg who were about to undergo a new loyalty test to make sure "they were still on our side."

In connection with the memo handwritten by Judy, this writer conducted the following test—a photostat was shown to Dorothy Sara, former president of the American Graphological Society and a handwriting analyst highly regarded in her profession. Miss Sara was told only that the writer of the note was a young woman. Here are excerpts of her findings:

> The writer's attitude toward life and her emotions are no more mature than a teen-age schoolgirl's. She may "put on an act" of being a mature person, but actually she is very young emotionally. She is a pseudo-intellectual, who wants to do something important, who wants to be applauded as doing something outstanding, and she can fall for any adulation that is tendered to her. She has very poor judgment in appraising other people, in evaluating true situations as they occur. She has a dramatic flair, and she is always "playing a role" and sees herself as the great star.

Whatever role Judy was playing, she had been in Washington a year and a half when Gubitchev arrived in the United States. Valentin Alekseevich Gubitchev was born June 24, 1916, in Orlovsky province in the Ural Mountains. He was trained as an engineer and was graduated from the Moscow School of Construction with a master's degree. In 1946, for no apparent reason, he was given the diplomatic rank of third secretary in the Ministry of Foreign Affairs in Moscow, although he had had no previous diplomatic training. Things moved fast for the short, blond, and balding Russian, and he arrived in New York on July 20 with an appointment to work as a construction engineer on the United Nations building that was then going up at 44th Street and First Avenue. He was attached to the Department of Conferences and General Services of the United Nations Secretariat with a salary of $6,600 a year, tax free.

According to "The Shameful Years," "the Soviets were aware that a close scrutiny was being made on embassy and consulate personnel. For this reason they went outside the official diplomatic ranks for this particular contact," and placed their man in the U.N.

In his U.N. application, Gubitchev emphasized that he would not be willing to travel or accept a job outside New York. He noted that his speaking English was fair, his reading good, and his writing excellent.

According to "The Shameful Years," "the Soviets were aware that standard Secretariat oath, in which he pledged his allegiance to that international civil service: "I solemnly swear to exercise in all loyalty, discretion, and conscience the functions intrusted to me as a member of the international service of the United Nations, to discharge these functions and regulate my conduct with the interests of the United Nations only in view and not to seek or accept instructions in regard to the performance of my duties from any other authority external to the organization."

With his wife, Lidija, who was a year older than he was, and his ten-year-old daughter Violetta, Gubitchev settled in a comfortable apartment on West 108th Street, from which he commuted to his office at 1270 Avenue of the Americas. Perhaps he thought the construction of the U.N. building was dull work, for in January, 1947, he applied for a transfer. He wanted work in either the U.N. security office or the headquarters planning office.

The Soviet Government had not revoked Gubitchev's diplomatic status, although the U.N. charter clearly states that Secretariat members are not to hold diplomatic rank. Gubitchev had entered the country on a diplomatic passport with the rank of third secretary, and the Russians evidently meant to see to it that he did not lose his diplomatic immunity. The reason for this became apparent when Gubitchev became the second Russian national to be arrested for espionage in the United States. The first had been Mikhail Nicholas Gorin.

The day after Gubitchev's arrest with Judy on March 4, 1949, an exchange of notes began between the Russian Embassy in Washington and the State Department. Soviet Ambassador Alexander S. Panyushkin expressed his shock and surprise that a Russian national protected by diplomatic immunity could be arrested like a common criminal. The State Department replied that under the rules of the United Nations, a Secretariat member could hold no official position with his government. Gubitchev had automatically given up his diplomatic rank when he signed the U.N. oath.

While these exchanges were going on, a first secretary of the Russian Embassy, Lev S. Tolokonnikov, was dispatched to New York to give Gubitchev instructions. He told the defendant, who was in the Men's Federal Prison at 427 West Street, not to accept the sovereignty of the court. In this way, Gubitchev was told, he might avoid trial.

This explains his contentious and arrogant behavior at a time when he faced serious charges. After his first visit with Tolokonnikov, Gubitchev appeared before reporters, wearing a pair of faded blue denim trousers, and complained that "they have me associating with common criminals. There are two others in my cell. I think they are income tax evaders."

Several days later, Gubitchev and Coplon met again in United States district court for a hearing on bail. Standing before Federal Judge Simon H. Rifkind, observers noticed that Gubitchev was the same height as Judy in her two-and-a-half-inch heels. He was handcuffed, fingered his brown felt hat and gazed at the ground. She looked directly at the judge. They did not speak or even look at each other.

Gubitchev moved Judge Rifkind to anger when he said he did not want counsel because "these proceedings are a comedy played from start to finish with the sole aim of firing the passions of enmity against my country. It makes me wonder whether there is any use for me to bring into this comedy one more person by having a defense counsel. I consider my rights violated, rights normally held in somewhat civilized countries. I don't know your laws or your constitution, but I do know my laws, and we don't deal with foreign diplomats the way I'm being dealt with here. I know we're in a backward country, but these are inquisition methods."

Judge Rifkind found Gubitchev's belligerent sarcasm hard to take and replied, "If you can tell me there are nations in the world reputed to be civilized who give greater protection to the accused and afford him a better opportunity to defend himself, I have not found it on any map or atlas of the world. There is no comedy involved; it would be a grave mistake on your part not to treat it with gravity and seriousness." Judge Rifkind gave Gubitchev more time to make up his mind because "maybe the habits and customs and traditions that make up our freedom are unknown to you."

This further period of reflection did nothing to change Gubitchev's attitude, for when he appeared in a pre-trial hearing he refused to speak a word of English, to the annoyance of Judge William Bondy. "You ready to go to trial?" Gubitchev shook his head. "How did you understand what I said if you don't know English?" Gubitchev shrugged. "You understand English?" *"Nyet."* "You understand my question?" *"Nyet."* "How did you understand what I said?" *"Nyet."*

"I don't know what he's saying, I'm going to assign counsel," the exasperated judge said.

Under this threat and because the State Department had thrown out the Soviet Embassy's immunity claim, a lawyer was found for Gubitchev. Meanwhile, the Russian Embassy had put up $100,000 in bail, for no bondsman would touch the case. Judge Rifkind had asked Judy: "Miss Coplon, are you entertaining any ideas that this world is so big that you can run away?" Judy shook her head and was granted the lower bail.

As counsel for Gubitchev, the Soviet Embassy secured the services of the very able Abraham Pomerantz. This was one of the few criminal cases Pomerantz ever tried. He specializes in arguing suits on behalf of small stockholders against corporation executives suspected of fast deals. In this unusual legal specialty, he estimates that he has made corporation heads pay back a total of $20,000,000 to their companies. For defending Gubitchev, he received one of the largest fees on record in a criminal case—$50,000. At the same time, he lost several clients, who fled association with a man defending a Russian in an espionage case.

Judy's problem was just the opposite—she wanted a lawyer but couldn't pay for one. After shopping around unsuccessfully between those whose fees she couldn't pay and those who wanted no part of her case at any price, she found Archibald Palmer, a specialist in bankruptcy cases, who assumed her defense "as a thank-you job"; that is, without a fee.

Palmer, a roly-poly five-footer who favors a flamboyant legal manner, did not have much time to prepare the first trial in Washington. Judy was charged with stealing secret documents to transmit them to a foreign power, and Gubitchev was not involved and did not appear. Palmer and Judy prepared the now-famous "romance" defense, which attributed all of Judy's aberrations to love. In this version, Judy had been guilty only of loving a Russian; her mistakes were mistakes of the heart.

The trial moved quickly after a squabble over the legality of the arrest. Judge Reeves ruled that "with all her glaring indiscretions in her associations with a Russian national, with her pocketbook bulging with government secrets, with all the things she had done before, it was the duty of the officers to make the arrest."

The climax came when Judy took the stand. The jury of eight men and four women, half white, half Negro, many of whom were government workers themselves, awoke from their summer torpor to hear Judy's classic tale of romantic involvement. Demure in a chartreuse blouse and black skirt, Judy recounted that the romance had begun when Gubitchev picked her up in the Museum of Modern Art on Saturday, Sept. 4, Labor Day weekend of 1948. Her exchange with Palmer:

Q. Tell me under what circumstances Mr. Gubitchev came upon you and to your attention.

A. Well, it happened this way. I was standing looking at a picture. They have a whole gallery of cubistic art.

Q. Cubistic art? Is that the kind of art which is supposed to depict something in the future and you are supposed to think out what the picture means, more or less?

A. That is more surrealistic—cubistic is when it is all broken planes.

Q. You are looking at the picture . . .

A. There was a small group in front of this picture. A man, as if addressing the group, said "What do you make of that?" I happened to be standing right next to him, and I said, "Not much, it is rather confusing." That turned out to be Mr. Gubitchev.

Gubitchev made a strong first impression on Judy, she testified. He was attractive, spoke English well, had a wry sense of humor. At this initial meeting, she said, they discussed literary and artistic purges in Russia, and Gubitchev opined that the purges were "inane." He asked Judy to call him "Val."

Thereafter, Judy continued, they met half a dozen times until the January 14 meeting chaperoned by the FBI. They met in public places and practiced the innocent ritual of platonic love. At the end of September, Gubitchev had called Judy's Washington office and asked, "When are you coming in?" She came in that weekend and they went rowing in Central Park. "He did the rowing," Judy added.

In October, they had a Saturday night dinner in Greenwich Village, at Charles' French restaurant, Sixth Avenue and 10th Street. Again in October, they met in the south hall of the Butler Library at Columbia University and walked all the way to the Cloisters. Gubitchev was always gentlemanly, never even attempted a kiss. They discussed music and literature.

Judy was "amazed to find out that he was some sort of authority on Milton. He had done some papers . . . we also discussed Shakespeare and Shelley . . . he was particularly fond of Shelley."

Palmer, always quick to seize the slightest implication, rejoined: "Shelley—he wrote about love in every shape, manner, and form?"

Judy had fallen in love at some point during these brief autumn and winter outdoor meetings, she testified, and wanted Val to meet her family in Brooklyn.

At Christmastime, "we met at Rockefeller Center right near the skating rink. It was rather a cold day. We went into a little store on Sixth Avenue and had some coffee. I saw him for a short time on Christmas Day because he had been operated on during the month of December and he did not feel well. He got ill. Again I asked him whether he could come over the next day and meet my family."

At this Christmas meeting, Gubitchev arrived bearing flowers, and Judy had a box of chocolate chip cookies and a brown striped tie she had bought in Washington. ("The tie that bound," Palmer quipped.)

At the January 14 meeting, Judy said, she wondered why Gubitchev had made the date in Washington Heights. "It's freezing, why go up there?" she asked. Gubitchev insisted because he had a friend to see in the neighborhood. Palmer elaborated that the neighborhood was "a quiet place that might be selected by lovers who wanted to whisper sweet nothings." But this meeting turned out to be a crisis for the "lovers," Judy testified. In her best Victorian manner she told how, as they were leaving the De Luxe Restaurant, Val grabbed her arm and said, "There's something I have to tell you. I can't withhold it any longer. I'm a married man and I'm miserable with my wife."

Judy was shocked, she was angry, she was "so astounded and furious—I felt so imposed on—I let loose and started to cry. I had a newspaper and I suppose I was brandishing it."

Gubitchev tried to kiss and embrace her to quiet her down. "Don't be provincial, like so many other American women," he said. "I am only trying to explain how miserable I am, and you're not even listening." They took the subway together, Gubitchev presumably explaining all the while, until he leaped out at 125th Street. Judy had promised herself not to see him again, but when he called offering further explanations, she agreed to a February meeting.

This was the abortive meeting in which the FBI also took part. They stayed together less than a minute on the Washington Heights sidewalk. Judy explained that Gubitchev was afraid he was being followed by detectives hired by his Russian wife.

They made plans to meet again March 4, their final meeting, the meeting Judy later described as "like a Walpurgian night, everything was working against me." When they were arrested, Judy said, Gubitchev had just been telling her he thought he might have been followed by members of the Russian Secret police, the NKVD. He had confided to Judy that he was against the Stalinist regime and was planning to defect to the United States. Judy said she was terribly frightened by the thought of being trailed by the Russian police. At the same time, they were in the Third Avenue neighborhood on the way to a quiet dinner at Luchow's, the German restaurant at 14th Street off Third Avenue.

The arrest was a complete surprise, she said. Now, Judy fervently told the jury, she no longer knew what to think. She felt betrayed by a man "I thought I was in love with."

Palmer chimed in that "love knows no bounds," and went on in the same vein, depicting Judy as a hard-working government girl who had fallen for the wrong man. "You started with the glamour of a job," he concluded with a flourish, "and ended with the dirt and degradation of a trial. Your witness, Mr. Kelley."

Prosecutor John M. Kelley Jr., a former actor and the man who tried Axis Sally, led Judy gently along the path of cross-examination. With a clear voice and a forthright manner, Judy told about her duties at the Justice Department, her life in Washington, her family, and her meeting Gubitchev. Kelley was sympathetic, almost cajoling, when he asked Judy: "You loved him very deeply, then, didn't you?" Judy, her voice trembling, replied that she had.

But Kelley's manner changed. His tone became menacing as he began the exchange in which, in the words of the pamphlet "The Shameful Years," "he discredited the love angle by showing that Judith was obviously bestowing her favors in other quarters."

Despite the hot and humid Washington weather, there had been standing room only in the courtroom since Judy had taken the stand. Judge Reeves had threatened to have the courtroom cleared several times after commotions usually involving Palmer or the defendant, whom the magazines referred to as "Little Miss Giggles." Palmer had been fined $100 twice for contempt of court and had been called a "buffoon" by the judge in front of the jury. But as Prosecutor Kelley took on his cold, incisive tone, the proverbial hush fell over the courtroom.

Q. Isn't it true, Miss Coplon, that you and Gubitchev never were in love whatsoever in the slightest degree?

A. As far as I know, I was very deeply in love with him. From what he said to me, I thought he was very deeply in love with me.

Q. And that is how you felt right up to January 14, the moment before he told you he was a married man?

A. I did.

Q. Is it not the truth that one week prior to that date, prior to January 14, which would be the night of January 7, you spent the night in Room 12 in the Southern Hotel in Baltimore, Maryland, while registered with a man under the name of Mr. and Mrs H. H. Shapiro, from 122 Burnside Avenue, East Hartford, Connecticut?

(*At this point, Judy jumped up from the witness chair and screamed out her answer.*)

A. That's a damn lie. Why are you doing this in front of my mother?

Q. Did you not spend New Year's Eve of this year with Mr. Shapiro in fornication in an apartment of a friend of his in this city?

A. I did not.

Judy was caught short by Kelley's attack. She improvised an explanation. Shapiro, a young Justice Department attorney who worked on the floor above her, was "a sweet friend, a platonic friend—someone to confide in." She had met him in the summer of 1948 and had seen him often since.

Judy admitted spending one night in Baltimore and the next night in Philadelphia with Shapiro, but insisted she had been "fully clothed" and that nothing had transpired. On neither of those nights did she sleep, she said, because of the soul-searching discussions she was having with Shapiro.

"Did you have breakfast in bed in Philadelphia?" Kelley asked.

"I did not."

Kelley produced a hotel room service bill for $2.35 for two breakfasts. "It was served in the room, not in bed," Judy explained lamely.

As Kelley continued probing her personal life and disclosed that the FBI had witnessed and recorded her trysts, Judy lost her composure and blurted: "You have branded me as a spy and now you are trying to brand me as a harlot."

The court was recessed, and when Judy took the stand the next day she had a different explanation for the weekend. She had gone shopping with Shapiro "because I wanted to buy a suit, I felt that Washington was a bit limited." Shapiro never slept in her room, he had his own room. Shapiro paid for the rooms, she admitted, but as a "gracious gesture. He made more money than I did."

As for the New Year's Eve spent in a friend's apartment in "fornication," Judy explained she had drunk too much champagne and had fallen asleep on a couch. "I'm not a drinker," she added.

Kelley wound up his cross-examination before a goggle-eyed jury by brandishing an FBI report under Judy's nose and asking, "Does this refresh your memory?" Judy shook her head violently, but flushed. The report, accompanied by photographs apparently taken through a transom in the best private-eye tradition, were a compendium of the awkward poses and the phrases to which a man and a woman are committed when they spend the night together.

Kelley's excursion into Judy's private affairs had nothing to do with espionage. It did not directly have anything to do with Gubitchev. It relied on the principle that a woman in love with one man does not have an affair with another. As many a sophisticate can testify, this principle is sometimes breached. But since sophistication is not the key to the average American jury, Kelley was able to brand Judy a liar by the standards of conventional morality.

Judy was a sophisticated young woman who had lived alone in Washington for four years, who was twenty-eight and single. That she was no paragon of virtue she would have been the first to admit. Those who knew her said that "she took her fun where she found it." The list of her paramours grew by leaps and bounds after the Shapiro testimony. On the basis of rumor-mongering that followed the Washington trial, she acquired an undeserved reputation for nymphomania.

The Shapiro incident marked the first major breach between Judy and her hyperbolic lawyer. Palmer had wanted to put Shapiro himself on the stand. His reasoning was that Shapiro had taken Judy across two state lines for the purpose of fornication, had reported the entire business to his superiors, and that no action had been taken against him. Ergo, by a superb legal twist, there had been no wrongdoing and Judy remained legally speaking "as pure as the driven snow." Judy, however, did not want to be "dragged through the mud."

Judy remained unswayed by her lawyer's rhetoric, and Palmer agreed to disregard the Shapiro incident. He then assured Judy that the prosecution would never bring up the incident, for he would object to it as not pertinent. As it happened, Palmer's objections were overruled and Judy had to improvise on the stand.

Judy's angry charge that Shapiro was part of a conspiracy to frame her appears unlikely. The FBI wire tap of her office records that on the day following her arrest, Nathan E. Lenvin, the attorney who shared the office, told a co-worker over the phone that "Shapiro is completely dissolved," and added "It was a wonderful act, you would have to crawl inside her to figure out her mind."

After Kelley's cross-examination, Judy's anger had gone to the point where she intimated that Gubitchev himself was in on the frame-up. "This case is so fishy it smells to high heaven," she said. "Was Gubitchev some sort of plant you were using?"

Kelley further angered Judy by countering Palmer's efforts to make a romantic heroine out of her. He called her "a tough little baby" with a "Swiss watch mind," and made much of her cleverness on the stand. "You'd ask a one-cent question and get a thirty-cent answer," he said.

The jury went out June 29 and returned a verdict of guilty after deliberating for twenty hours. Judge Reeves sentenced her to serve from three years and four months to ten years on the first count of the indictment, which charged that she tried to obtain documents vital to the national defense for the benefit of a foreign nation; and from one to three years on the second count, charging theft of government papers—both counts to be served concurrently.

He recommended that Judy be imprisoned in the Women's Reformatory at Alderson, West Virginia. Shaking his head, he commented: "Here is a young woman with infinite prospects, a great future in front of her, yet she attempted to betray her country. What prompted her to do it, I do not know." The judge added in a cryptic aside that "Benedict Arnold was one of the bravest men who fought in the Revolution—a brave and fearless soldier . . . yet who in the end became a traitor to his country."

Judy had the last word, saying, "They would have me jailed in lieu of a ten-thousand-dollar bond for my trial in New York. They know I'm a person of limited means and they want to break me by keeping me in jail. But I'll never break. The newspapers said I broke on the stand and became hysterical. I never broke then and I never will. I will never be hysterical. I believe I was deprived of a fair trial in this loyalty-ridden town." In addition, Judy charged that the press had reported the trial in a "filthy sort of way, a horrible sort of way," and that the prosecution might "gloat in the glory of their Pyrrhic victory."

To use another image derived from the Greeks, Judy was now going from Charybdis to Scylla. Her Washington trial was over, but her New York trial with Gubitchev as co-defendant was to begin soon. She returned to the family home on Ocean Parkway and faced the additional ordeal of notoriety. Reporters hounded her for interviews, a press service offered $5,000 (and was refused) for exclusive rights to her story.

Everywhere she went she was recognized, and she told her brother Bertram, "I'm ready to shoot myself because I can get no peace." Within the Coplon family other clouds hovered. Bertram's wife, Shirley Seidman Coplon, was not fond of her sister-in-law. FBI phone taps revealed that Shirley had told Bertram when they learned of Judy's arrest that "it must be true or they wouldn't have arrested her." At this, Bertram called his wife a "loud-mouth." She was calling from Florida, and Bertram told her, "You might as well stay there."

Judy refused to discuss the case with members of her family, and the discussions she held over the telephone with her lawyer were dutifully recorded by the FBI monitors, who were still tapping her home phone. The New York trial was not to start before January 24, 1950, but Palmer was involved in lengthy pre-trial hearings on whether the prosecution's evidence was based on wire taps and was therefore illegal.

Palmer called the wire-tap evidence "poison fruit" and quoted J. Edgar Hoover as writing in a 1940 letter to the Harvard Law Review that wire tapping was "an archaic and inefficient practice," which "has proved a definite handicap or barrier in the development of ethical, scientific and sound investigative techniques."

Palmer was very upset when it came out that thirty FBI men had been assigned to monitor Judy's telephones. "I want the names of all the thirty agents who did this dastardly thing," he said. He was even more upset when testimony about some of his conversations came out at the trial. An FBI monitor testified primly that Palmer "had called the FBI an obscene name." In another conversation, Palmer told Judy: "You'll never get a fair trial from that s.o.b. of a judge" (referring to Federal Judge Sylvester Ryan, who presided at the New York trial).

After the sensational proceedings in Washington, the New York trial was an anticlimax. There was the added attraction of Gubitchev, of course, but he never took the stand. Pomerantz, a former U.S. counsel who helped obtain indictments against Nazi war criminals in the 1946 Nuremberg trials, defended Gubitchev brilliantly, but was limited by the supervision of Soviet officials. Gubitchev, like Colonel Abel in his 1957 trial, never said a word in court. At his side sat Yuri V. Novikov, Second Secretary at the Soviet Embassy in Washington. Pomerantz wanted Gubitchev to take the stand, mindful of the implications of guilt created in the jury's mind when a defendant does not reply to the accusations made against him. Pomerantz also felt that Gubitchev, with his handsome face and quick, responsive manner, would make an appealing witness. Novikov vetoed these arguments and told Pomerantz to concentrate on questioning the FBI men on their investigative techniques.

Gubitchev himself was by turn jocular and dour. On March 4, 1950, he asked if there was going to be a party to celebrate his first anniversary under arrest. Another time, when a deputy marshal asked him what he had in a package, he replied, "A bomb." But as Pomerantz fought to re-establish the love angle, Gubitchev remarked smugly: "You are a good lawyer, but you are too naïve. Do you think there is any justice in America?"

The most dramatic aspect of the New York trial was not in the testimony, much of which was a rehash of Washington testimony, but in the client-lawyer conflict. Friction is not unknown between lawyers for codefendants in conspiracy trials. But in this instance, there arose what was described as "a deep and pathological animosity" between the two counsels. Even at the pre-trial hearings, Palmer had said that he and Pomerantz were "poles apart." Pomerantz, annoyed by Palmer's laborious examination of witnesses, would say: "You are making an ass of yourself." Palmer would retort: "You are the front and the rear." This kind of bickering continued through the trial, and certainly did the defense no good.

Far more harmful to Judy, however, were the deteriorating relations between herself and her lawyer that caused her to fire Palmer in February. Soon after the trial had begun, Judy, nervous because she was facing a stiffer prison sentence this time, had argued with Palmer over the way he was conducting her defense. The two were not on speaking terms. Palmer defended Judy as though she was not even in the courtroom, and Judy ignored Palmer.

Judge Ryan held hearings in chambers to try to reconcile the defendant and her lawyer, but in an emotional scene Judy accused Palmer of using profane language in the presence of reporters, of striking her, and throwing her across his office.

Judy was referring in part to a press conference held five days after the start of the New York trial. She told reporters that her present feeling for Gubitchev "was certainly not one of love. I don't think he's a spy, though." Palmer snapped: "That's a sarcastic answer. Don't get sarcastic with these people."

"I didn't answer," Judy said.

"I heard you. It was a sarcastic ridiculous statement. I always told you you were a damn fool at times." Then he told her to shut up.

Palmer told Judge Ryan that Judy was trying to tell him how to run her defense and that he was not about to begin accepting a client's domination. He added that he had taken the case without a fee, had spent a year working on it, and was ready to continue. But Judy was adamant. Judge Ryan warned her that a change of lawyers in mid-trial would not constitute grounds for a mistrial. After lengthy discussion, three new lawyers were appointed to defend Judy. They were Leonard B. Boudin, Samuel A. Neuberger, and Sidney J. Berman.

Judge Ryan gave them a week to catch up on the background of the case (the Washington trial transcript alone constituted forty-five bound volumes). Staggered by the task, the three lawyers moved for a mistrial, stating in their brief that Judy had suffered, in effect, from incompetent counsel. They described the reaction in the courtroom to the lack of co-operation between counsel and defendant, Palmer's insistence that Judy take the stand again, his efforts to bring the Shapiro incident up again, and his refusal to consult with Pomerantz. From that point on, the three lawyers took a back seat, reserving themselves for action in the higher courts and declining to deliver a summation on behalf of their client.

Pomerantz had to carry the ball for Coplon as well as Gubitchev. In his summation, he held that "only lunatic spies, only musical comedy spies, would have done what these people did." His argument was that if Judy and Gubitchev were spies, they were pretty poor ones. Instead of using a drop to transmit information they met three times in the same neighborhood. Judy's animated conversation and striking at Gubitchev with a newspaper at the January 14 meeting was "hardly spy-like," Pomerantz pointed out. Both had "the frantic behavior of those pursued" during their final meeting and yet they waited around to be arrested under the Third Avenue El "like clay pigeons in a shooting gallery." Judy had plenty of opportunity to unload the incriminating material in her purse while she and Gubitchev were being followed, but she held on to it.

That Judy and Gubitchev departed from the behavior pattern of conventional spies is certain. But in the eyes of espionage experts they acted foolishly, not guiltlessly. Judy, it is held, was overconfident. She knew she and Gubitchev were being followed, but she was convinced they had shaken their tail by the time they reached Third Avenue. Moreover, there had been no time to set up an elaborate drop where the documents could be planted. This was information the Soviet needed quickly, and Judy had assured them she was above suspicion. Gubitchev thought he was beyond the law's purview because of his diplomatic immunity. They took risks no *apparatchik* ordinarily takes.

The jury stayed out forty-eight hours in the New York trial.

According to Pomerantz, the first ballot was eight to four for conviction. The jury deliberations were marked by confusion over an error in the copy of an indictment the jurors had been given. The indictment had four counts, the first count in six parts detailing the charges. Part four of the first count stated that Judy, "*lawfully* having possession of, access to, and being intrusted with documents, writings and notes relating to the national defense as aforesaid, would willfully communicate and transmit and attempt to communicate and transmit the same to persons not entitled to receive them."

The second count of the indictment, however, read that "on March 4, defendant *unlawfully* having possession of, access to, and being intrusted with documents, writings, and notes relating to national defense, did willfully attempt to communicate and transmit said documents to Gubitchev."

The jury foreman came out in the midst of deliberations, visibly disturbed, and asked Judge Ryan whether "in count two of the indictment the word appearing on line three should be 'lawfully' or 'unlawfully'?"

Judge Ryan sent for the original copy of the indictment and declared: "There is a small pencil marking through two letters of 'unlawfully' so that it reads with the correction in pencil 'lawfully.' The original indictment, which is the indictment which you must consider, reads: 'lawfully.' "

Judge Ryan pointed out that the error in the indictment did not make much difference, since the statute reads that whoever "lawfully or unlawfully" possesses documents and tries to transmit them is guilty of violation. In other words, Judy's possession of the documents was not questioned, only whether she had attempted to transmit them to the representatives of a foreign power.

Pomerantz argued that the error in the indictment had given the jury an erroneous impression and one of Judy's attorneys asked for a mistrial, which was denied. Then Pomerantz asked that the jury be recalled and instructed that all the papers found in Judy's pocketbook were legally in her possession. This motion was also rejected, and the jury returned a guilty verdict. Since it was the jury who first discovered a glaring contradiction in the indictment which the defense had not noticed after supposedly close scrutiny of that document, it is reasonable to assume that the jurors realized what was involved.

Nonetheless, the verdict was confusing. It found Judy guilty on count one (a six-part summary of the conspiracy with Gubitchev) and count four (attempting to communicate documents to the advantage of a foreign nation on March 4), but it found her not guilty on count two (attempting to communicate and transmit documents to Gubitchev). It found Gubitchev guilty on count three (unlawfully attempting to receive documents from Judy).

The jury appeared to contradict itself by finding Judy innocent of attempting to communicate information in count two which it found Gubitchev guilty of receiving in count four. Pomerantz pounced on this inconsistency, asking that the verdict be set aside because "it is a logical and physical impossibility for Gubitchev to receive documents which Coplon did not attempt to pass him."

By a sort of perverse logic, the jury had apparently elected not to convict Judy of a count which had been typographically misrepresented to them. The substance of that count, however, was covered in count four and part four of count one. The one thing that permeated the indictment was that Judy had unlawfully attempted to pass documents, whether they were in her lawful possession or not. There can be little doubt that this was the understanding of the jury.

Pomerantz still feels he was dealt with unfairly in the trial. He says that recently a woman came up to him on the bus and asked, "Don't you recognize me? I was on the Coplon jury." Pomerantz asked the woman if she had really believed Judy guilty of trying to pass secret information to Gubitchev. "I don't believe she did," the woman allegedly said. "But we were dealing with a Russian and we were going to give that Russian the same kind of justice Russia would have given an American."

On the day of sentencing, Judge Ryan scathingly denounced both defendants. Sentencing Judy to a total of twenty years in prison, he said: "You have brought dishonor upon the name you bear. You have brought disgrace and even tragedy upon your family. You have been disloyal to the country which has nourished you, helped you acquire an education, and placed you in high trust and confidence. You have proved yourself an ungrateful daughter. My observation of you during the trial convinces me that the seeds of disloyalty still find root within you."

Turning to a smirking Gubitchev, Judge Ryan sentenced him to a total of fifteen years in prison and remarked: "You came here as an emissary of peace, you were accepted among us in the role of a friend; you violated your oath of office to the Secretariat of the United Nations of the world . . . you stand convicted before the world of betrayal of all mankind . . . and you do that with arrogance on your lips, and with a smile on your face as you stand here before me for sentence in defiance of all humanity."

Then, bitterly, Judge Ryan announced that he had been asked by Secretary of State Dean Acheson to suspend Gubitchev's sentence on the condition that he leave the country and give up his right to appeal. The trial had moved from the confines of a New York Federal Court to the chessboard of foreign policy. The State Department memorandum expressed concern for American citizens in Eastern Europe. Reprisals were feared if Gubitchev was made to serve a prison term.

Regretfully, Judge Ryan said that "it is beyond my province to question the reasons for or the wisdom of this recommendation," but he told Gubitchev in parting that "your treacherous actions to the cause of peace will bring down on you the maledictions of mankind."

Gubitchev and his wife lost no time packing their bags (his daughter had been sent back to Moscow, before the case broke, to attend a boarding school run by the Soviet Ministry of Foreign Affairs). The Russian remained arrogant to the last. On March 20, he sailed with his wife aboard the Polish ship *Batory*. The couple's first-class fare, amounting to $585, was paid by the United Nations. Technically, he was still a secretariat employee and had in fact been receiving his full salary during the trial. As a bonus, he took home about $2,000 in severance pay from the U.N.

With his ten pieces of luggage, he had a large-screen television set which, he said, "I bought with my own money." Asked by reporters if the Russians had television, he replied, "Why, the Russians invented television. That's why I'm taking it back with me." For reading matter, Gubitchev took aboard the 6,000-page transcript of the New York trial. He was also asked if he had any parting words for his co-conspirator. "I wish her luck," he said lightly. The *Batory* docked at Gdynia in Poland on April 3, and from there Gubitchev was whisked to Moscow. He has not been heard from since.

Pomerantz claims that Gubitchev and his wife were divorced soon after. The divorce would bolster the theory that there really was a romance between Judy and Val.

Palmer was recently asked what he thought had happened to Gubitchev. He replied, in an apparent slip of the tongue, "I would think he's probably in Siberia after having failed in his mission."

In December, 1950, Judge Learned Hand and two other court of appeals judges ruled that the arrest of Coplon and Gubitchev had been illegal, that the Government had failed to show its case was not based on illegal wire-tap evidence, and that the trial judge erred in not showing the defense certain documents. Judges Jerome N. Frank and Thomas W. Swan concurred in an opinion that said in conclusion: "The conviction must be reversed but we will not dismiss the indictment because the guilt was plain."

The real epilogue to the Coplon case, however, did not come until 1954, when two MVD officers defected to the West. They brought information as a proof of good intentions, and each shed new light on the Coplon case.

Yuri Rastorov, second secretary of the Russian Mission in Japan and a lieutenant colonel in the MVD, disclosed that he had been in Moscow in 1951 when Gubitchev returned with his family. Gubitchev was not, like himself, in the MVD. He was a captain in the GRU, the overseas intelligence branch of the Red Army. He was put on the carpet for failing in his mission, lost his rank and was discharged from espionage service. In testimony before the Senate Internal Security Subcommittee in February, 1956, Rastorov was asked: "Did you know Gubitchev?"

"Yes, I know him," he replied. "I saw him when he came from this country after unsuccessful operation against Coplon as everybody knows. She was recruited by him, and because of unsuccessful operation he was recalled and later fired from the service. He was arrested himself. This is practically one of the reasons why he was fired, because they couldn't trust him any more. They have a very definite policy about this, that people who have once been arrested by counterintelligence service of a local government, they never trust you any more."

As for Alexander Panyushkin, the Soviet Ambassador to Washington who had fought to have Gubitchev's diplomatic immunity recognized, he had originally arranged for Gubitchev to be brought in as a U.N. Secretariat member. Panyushkin was one of the highest-ranking officers in the MVD, a major general, and one of the few to weather the purges that followed Beria's removal from office. He left the United States in 1952, spent a year in Red China as chief of mission, and returned to Moscow in 1953 to assume a command post in the newly formed KGB, where he still is.

Panyushkin's role was confirmed by the second defector, Nikolai Khokhlov, a captain in the MVD who defected in West Germany where he had been sent to assassinate an anti-Communist Russian leader. Khokhlov told American intelligence that one day in 1953 he came to KGB headquarters in Dzerzhinski Street and learned about the new boss. "Panyushkin is a man of colossal experience," he was told. "He's an expert in all our work. Now he's in charge of the entire intelligence service. We have few professional intelligence officers with a diplomatic background."

The Coplon-Gubitchev case ended with each of the two principals submitting to the justice of their respective nations. Gubitchev was purged and probably sent with his family to a labor camp. Judy profited from a judicial system which, while recognizing her guilt, prevented her conviction because her rights were violated, even though she was working to overthrow the system that created those rights.

IV. Harry Gold's *Mea Culpa*

"Just as in mythology, in the case of Cadmus, when he planted the dragon teeth, and the soldiers sprang up full grown and all armed and ready to fight, I didn't evolve in that way. There were events that happened over a period of seventeen years." (Harry Gold before a Senate subcommittee in 1956.)

PERHAPS even more revealing than the Coplon case is the story of Harry Gold. In a profession sometimes referred to as the "silent service," Harry Gold will go down as one of the most garrulous specimens. His arrest in 1950 opened the floodgates after years of secrecy. He talked to the FBI, he talked at his trial, he talked to newspaper reporters. He lovingly described how he transmitted atomic secrets from Klaus Fuchs and Julius Rosenberg to Soviet contacts in New York. After he had been sent to Lewisburg Prison to serve a sentence of thirty years, he agreed to appear before a Senate subcommittee to talk some more. His volubility did nothing to mitigate his sentence—on October 26, 1960, a parole board turned him down.

The Senate session developed into a unique *examen de conscience,* a benign inquisition into the life of one already branded a heretic. The Senators were groping to explain Harry's misdeeds in the familiar terms of the American way of life. They tried to make him say he had erred because he had not really known what he was doing. A spell had been cast, and he had been hexed into treason. Harry stubbornly insisted on his own responsibility, on the free choice he had made, on his refusal to accept payment, and on his clear understanding of acts and motives. The Senators were consternated to find themselves before a man who had acted out of strength, not weakness, of character.

This small, dumpy man with the kind of face one sees on Egyptian medallions (long-lashed feminine eyes, curiously pointed ears, and receding chin) held off attempts to measure his remoteness from the American dream. That was not the answer, he patiently explained. Senator Herman Welker of Idaho asked Harry: "In the early part of your espionage, you actually had an inferiority complex. Could that be true?"

"I don't think I have ever had what is called an inferiority complex," Gold replied. "I have, I think, a lot of drive. I like to get things done. And I have a sort of one-track mind, that once I get started on something, I go right ahead to the finish of it. It takes something to stop me."

The Senator persisted: "You have never had much happiness, I take it, in your life?"

"That is something I would like to hammer and nail down. There has been an incredible amount, a whole mountain range of trash that has appeared—anywhere from saying that I got into this because I was disappointed in love—well, I haven't been uniformly successful, but anyhow, I didn't get into it for that reason—through reasons that I felt inferior, and wanted the adulation of people. It would take months to refute it, and it is sheer balderdash."

Harry was no self-deceiver. He knew what his trouble was. "My only trouble was that I was always sure I was doing the right thing." Harry was more Faust than Walter Mitty, and his devil understood him better than did the perplexed Senators at the hearing.

The Russians, Harry said, "operated with me in the very manner that a virtuoso would play a violin. They did a superb job on me, now that I come to think of it. They knew what would appeal to me and what I would be repelled by. I was not a paid agent, and they would continually commend me in indirect fashion and would low-rate the people who were accepting money."

Here then is the story of Harry Gold's thralldom to the Soviet Union from 1935 to his arrest in 1950, corrected and annotated by him. His parents were Russian Jews named Golodnitsky who fled their home town of Kiev in 1907 and sought refuge in Switzerland. Harry was born December 12, 1910, in Bern, an undersized and delicate baby. The family emigrated to the United States when World War I broke out, and became American citizens in 1922. On the advice of an immigration official who had trouble pronouncing their name they shortened it to Gold during entrance formalities at Ellis Island.

Mr. Gold was a cabinetmaker and found work in Philadelphia in a budding industry—he made cabinets for the Victor Talking Machine Company. One of Harry's earliest memories was the trouble his father had at work because he was a Jew. Mr. Gold carried the burden of his race with stoicism. Mrs. Gold was more expansive, and her sense of outrage was often communicated to Harry and his younger brother, Joseph.

After 1920, there was a mass influx of Irish and Italian labor, and Mr. Gold was the butt of factory humor. They stole his chisels, poured glue in his toolbox and in the pockets of his good suit, which he carefully hung in his locker every day. The Irish foreman was openly anti-Semitic and told him: "You Jew son of a bitch, I'm going to make you quit."

Production techniques had changed by then. The old-world artisan cabinetmaking had given way to an assembly line, and the foreman put Mr. Gold on the line to hand-sand cabinets. The old man could not keep up with the pace of work and came home at night with his fingers raw and bleeding. He wore gloves so his children could not see his injured hands.

Harry did not have to wait long for his own experiences with anti-Semitism. The Golds lived on the fringe of a respectable neighborhood, in the 2600 block of Phillip Street. The street was paved but beyond it extended a slum known as The Neck, a marshy section of the city dump. The inhabitants were mainly Irish immigrants who raised pigs and produce in the mosquito-infested slough. Jews, with their striving for respectability and cleanliness, were the object of their special hatred, and a gang of young toughs called the "Neckers" made periodic forays into the "Jew territory" on Phillip Street, armed with bricks, sticks and insults. "When I was twelve," Harry recalls, "I made regular trips to the public library at Broad and Porter streets, two miles from home. Coming back one day, I was seized by about fifteen gentile boys at 12th and Shunk streets and badly beaten. Two others with me fled— My father after that convoyed me from the library and back and would wait outside while I got my books. I was ashamed of this protection and sought to conceal it. Later I lost my fear and made the trip alone."

When the Soviet spies who recruited Harry struck the chord of anti-Semitism, they found a willing listener. On this topic he responded emotionally. His critical faculties were numbed by his memories. "The Soviet Union is the only country where anti-Semitism is a crime against the state," he was told, and believed.

Even the Nazi-Soviet pact failed to sway him. He was indignant when he heard of the alliance and asked his contact for an explanation. "What in the world goes on here?" he asked.

"We need time," was the reply. "We will buy time from the devil, if we have to, and the devil in this case is Adolf Hitler. When we are ready we will strike, and then we will wipe Nazism from the face of the earth."

This argument convinced Harry, who continued to believe that the Soviet Union was the only power fighting Nazism, and therefore anti-Semitism. "To me," he explained, "Nazism and fascism and anti-Semitism were identical. This was the ages-old enemy, the evil, bloody stench of the Roman arena, of the medieval ghetto, of the inquisition, of pogroms, and now, of the concentration camp. Anything that was against anti-Semitism I was for."

Other factors of his early social condition did not leave a mark on Harry. His family was poor, but he was never grasping about money. Indeed, he refused to be paid for his espionage work, and estimated that over the years he had spent $7,000 in his travels as courier and that half that amount came out of his own pocket. In 1930, when the depression hit the Gold family, Harry gave $1,000 of his $2,500 savings to his mother, even though he had himself lost his job.

Harry's years in South Philadelphia public schools were another gantlet to run. The weak and spindly youth was banned from the neighborhood sports and nicknamed "Goldie" by his classmates. When they kept him on the sidelines in the sandlot football games, he spent long hours devising a complicated parlor football game made up of two checkerboards. This admiration and envy for what he could not conquer stayed with Harry, who became a fanatic devotee of spectator sports.

The recollection of his last meeting with a Soviet agent on October 23, 1949, provides a pathetic insight into the workings of his mind. "The reason I feel precise about the date," he explained, "is that after I left Sarytchev [his Russian contact], I bought a newspaper, the New York *Daily News,* which contained on the sport page an account of a professional football game between the New York Yankees of the league which is no longer in existence, and the San Francisco Forty-Niners, and I remember particularly a couple of phrases from that account, to the effect that New York's two, the Yankees' huge tackles, one of whom was Arnie Weinmeister, these two tackles had kept breaking through the San Francisco line and spilling Joe Perry, the San Francisco halfback, and Frankie Albert, the quarterback, for consistent losses. Perry, before he could get started running and Albert before he could start his fancy hipper-dipper stuff."

There was a "dreams-of-glory" side to Harry's character that may have been partly satisfied by his clandestine activities, although he described espionage as the worst drudgery he had ever known.

At the South Philadelphia High School for Boys, Harry was so brilliant in chemistry that he at last won respect from his classmates. They came to him with their homework and no longer called him "Goldie." His high school nickname was "Silent Visage." Harry never played hookie and never talked back to his teachers. His self-effacing manner had none of the exuberant revolt and lack of discipline that stamps the American teen-ager. He was the quiet, hard-working, trustworthy Harry Gold, the honor student the teachers could count on.

Yet there was already ingrained in his character what he described as "an almost suicidal impulse to take drastic and if need be illegal action when I believed a situation required it."

In his senior year Dr. Farbish, the English teacher, asked Harry to grade some papers for him. "I took them home," Harry recalls, "and I sat up until five in the morning filling in the answers, erasing wrong ones, and substituting the correct ones, and even faking some twenty-five different types of handwriting. And when I had finished, everyone had passed, every single boy. That morning I handed the papers in to Dr. Farbish; and that afternoon he met me in one of the school's halls. He merely said, with a gentle sarcasm that still rankles and burns: 'The class did very well, did they not, Harry?' "

Harry did well too, so that when he graduated from high school in 1928, he took courses in chemical engineering at the University of Pennsylvania. But he couldn't afford the tuition and went to work for the Pennsylvania Sugar Company, attending night classes at the Drexel Institute of Technology.

When Harry began to feel the effects of the depression, he sought the answer in the possibilities of a political system that could guarantee economic security. In 1932 he publicly praised Socialism and Norman Thomas to a group of pipe fitters. He was laid off that December for his troubles. Through an acquaintance named Tom Black, Harry heard about a job with a soap manufacturer in Jersey City and was hired. Harry had spent six jobless weeks and was vulnerable to new ideas. Black, a bluff Irishman with carrot hair and freckles, told Harry the first week at the factory: "I am a Communist and I am going to make a Communist out of you."

Partly out of boredom, partly out of a sense of obligation to Black, partly out of need for companionship (the foreman at the soap factory had told Harry good-naturedly that "all the Jews in America should be put on ships and the goddam boats sunk in the middle of the ocean"), Harry went to his first Communist meeting.

He was revolted by what he saw. The Party members were what he considered "distasteful types—strong-arm hoodlums, bohemians who prattled of free love, lazy bums who would never work under any economic system, others who are called in Swiss dialect 'plodersacken,' endless boring talkers." Even his friendship with Tom Black was strained when Black jumped up one night after a long evening of Marxist dialectic and dago red and yelled, "To hell with this, give me six good men and I'll take Journal Square by storm." It all seemed futile and juvenile to Harry, who steadfastly refused Black's demands that he become a Party member.

In September, 1933, there was an opening at the sugar refinery where he had previously been employed and he left Jersey City with relief. Harry was happy at the refinery because he had found a mentor. Dr. Gustave Reich, the research director, took Harry under his wing. "He sort of raised me from a pup. I started to work in the lab, cleaning spittoons, and when I finally left the company I was a capable chemist."

It was not long after Harry had been back in Philadelphia that he again heard from Tom Black. Black gave him a lecture on the industrial backwardness of the Soviet Union. "These people are still in the eighteenth century," he said. "They eat off rough, bare boards. You can help them live a little better, a little more as humans should."

Blac , whom Harry described as "a two-hundred-year throwback to his Irish peasant ancestors," unflaggingly pressed his case. He wanted Harry to obtain some of the sugar company's processes on industrial solvents, materials used in various finishes and lacquers. "The people of the Soviet Union need these processes," he said.

This was Harry's first espionage assignment. He accepted with open eyes and a clear mind. His reasons were that he still felt he owed Black something for getting him a job in a depression year; that by helping Black he got out of the disagreeable prospect of joining the Communist Party; that he had a genuine sympathy for the people of the Soviet Union; and that if he thought something was right, he waved aside moral concepts. This he recognized as a dangerous hallmark of the scientists: "I have seen it repeated in other people," he said, "particularly those who are in scientific fields. They get to know their own particular field and think, Well, if we are right in this, we are right in all other decisions."

Harry started looting the files of Dr. Reich, one of the few men who had shown him kindness. He duplicated blueprints and reports, taking the material home at night and replacing it in the morning. He was wrapped up in the technical side of his clandestine work—how to get the material in and out, how to copy the voluminous dossiers, how to loot the files without anyone catching on.

He had keys made so that he could get into the files, and volunteered for night work to make his looting easier. As Harry said, "We started off in a very innocent fashion. What are chemical solvents, after all? But then, step by step, they advanced the tempo."

He continued turning over material to Black until 1935, and Black told him how delighted the Russians were with his work. He said one of the Russians wanted to meet him personally to thank him.

The meeting was arranged one afternoon near Penn Station in New York. A short, stocky man with a round face and flaring nostrils introduced himself as Paul Smith and peremptorily told Black to leave. The Russian said he wanted a complete dossier on Harry and his family and that Harry would be given new, more important tasks. The sugar company was dry as a source, he was told, and he would have to get a new job. Meanwhile he would be put to work checking suspected Trotskyites in Philadelphia. This time there was no ambiguity. Harry knew he was working for the Russians. Still he accepted. He accepted because "I had lost faith in the democratic process and I had an inborn desire to do something about a disheartening set of circumstances. Once I dropped a desiccator containing twenty-two crucibles and a week's work. I did not sit down and cry, nor did I go out and get drunk—I just worked all that night and most of the following two days and nights and repeated the analyses."

Harry embarked on what he called "eleven very active years" for the Russians, from 1934 to 1945. He had three different Soviet contacts, all of whom were working for Amtorg as a cover. A courier usually keeps the same contact for a year and a half, but Harry worked with Semen (Sam) Semenov for four years (1940 through 1943). Semenov posed as a mechanical engineer who bought oil refinery equipment from American firms. He was a swarthy, "Almost Mexican-looking man with black dancing eyes and a warm smile," Harry recalled.

Semenov had entered the United States in 1938 and attended the Massachusetts Institute of Technology, where he obtained a master's degree in science in 1940. He left the United States in 1944.

Semenov confided in Harry that the espionage work they were doing was a necessary unpleasantness that was far beneath them. "Look," he said, "I am a chemical engineer and a mathematician. You are a chemist. You know, we don't belong in this business. What are we doing running around begging people for information, cajoling them and threatening them? I want to design things. You want to work in a lab. Oh boy, someday the happy day will come when you can do just that. Because inevitably you are going to get caught. You know, you can't stay in this forever. The trick is to get out before they do catch you." Harry was completely won over by Semenov's mixture of commiseration and promise. When he was told, as he often was, that "after the revolution, we'll put you in a laboratory to do research," his critical faculties melted.

At this time, Harry was carrying out a variety of courier assignments for the Russians, none of them of great importance. He was being shaped for the future, and at the same time, the glamour was wearing off. Harry said himself that "it was a dreary, monotonous drudgery. If anyone has an idea that there is anything glamorous or exciting about this, let them be disabused of it right now.

"It is nothing but dreary drudgery. You work for years trying to get information. Sometimes you are unsuccessful, you spend long hours waiting on street corners. The success, the amount of success actually in the work, is very small in proportion to the effort you put into it. And what becomes even more important, I was gradually losing my identity and my desire to be an individual. I was becoming someone who could be told what to do and would do it."

Harry was still living with his family in Philadelphia, and his frequent, unexplained absences and irregular hours convinced his mother that he was leading a wild life and conducting a large number of love affairs. The truth was that Harry had fallen in love with several girls but was unable to sustain the relationship because of the devouring demands of his underground work. One girl took this to be a lack of ardor on Harry's part.

By the time he was given his first important assignment, the requirements of an espionage courier "had become deeply ingrained in me—the lies I had to tell at home, and to my friends, to explain my absences, the weary hours waiting on street corners, waiting dubiously and fearfully in strange towns where I had no business to be and the uneasy killing of time in cheap movies, gazing unseeingly at the screen while my mind was fretting about how affairs were proceeding outside."

Harry had also fallen into the little subterfuges of espionage. In 1938, his contact told him the Soviet Government wanted him to continue his interrupted studies and would pay for his tuition. He enrolled at Xavier University and graduated in 1940 as a Bachelor of Science *summa cum laude*.

He began to invent a network he had allegedly recruited at the university to show his mentors that their money was not being wasted. He sent confidential reports on fellow students with Communist sympathies. He obtained technical information from the college library. Perfectly conscious of his mythomania, Harry said that "sometimes I lied so much I could almost feel the steam coming out of my ears."

In 1942, Harry reported to his draft board, but to the relief of his Soviet superiors he was classified 4F because of hypertension. His brother Joseph was drafted and came back three years later from the South Pacific with three Bronze Stars.

Harry also won a medal, in 1943—the Red Star, which allows the holder to travel on the Moscow trolley gratis, a privilege Harry never had the chance to exercise. Harry's most celebrated mission involved handling atomic secrets which Klaus Fuchs gave the Russians. In Harry's opinion, however, he carried out another far more important assignment, even though it was less dramatic. In 1940, his Soviet contact told him to get in touch with Alfred Dean Slack, a research chemist for Eastman Kodak in Syracuse. From 1940 to 1942, Slack furnished Gold information on color film processes developed by Kodak. These processes were such a highly guarded industrial secret that Kodak had not taken out patents for them. The formulas for the sensitizers and developers used in the process could only have been obtained by the Russians by setting up a vast organization with trained chemists to rival Eastman Kodak—or by stealing them.

For this reason, Harry said, "I considered this more damaging [than the atom bomb] because it could not be duplicated . . . once it was known that the atom could be split, anyone could do it with sufficient technical and industrial potential. Given the time and the potential and the equipment and the industrial background for it, it could be done eventually: it would be done eventually. There is no question about it, because the theory was known. Everything had been published in theoretical journals. But this was something where there was no theory. It was just a matter of know-how, a matter of very, very specialized know-how on minutiae, very little things, but things which might take two or three years to find out. It might take a man two or three years to develop a particular sensitizer. And the process of making some of these photographic emulsions, I understood from Slack, some of these emulsions had six or seven layers of colored emulsions."

Slack also gave Harry information on the manufacture of nylon. He was arrested after the exposure of the Rosenberg ring and sentenced to a fifteen-year prison term.

Harry's meetings with Slack were interrupted in late 1943 by an urgent message from Semenov, who told him: "Something has come up. And it is so big and so tremendous that you have got to exert your complete efforts to carrying it through successfully. You have got to concentrate on it completely. Before you make a single move, think, think twice, think three times. You cannot make any mistakes in connection with this. It must be carried through. This is an extremely dangerous assignment. Are you sure you want to go through with it?"

Harry felt intrigued and self-important and said he would do his best.

"There is a man coming to this country from England," Semenov continued. "He is going to work with a group of American scientists in New York City. This man will have information on a new type of weapon, completely new and devastating and your job is to meet this man and get the information from him."

The meeting with the "man from England," whose name Harry did not know, took place in early February, 1944, in a lower East Side neighborhood in New York City where tenements were being torn down and replaced by a housing settlement. Walking across an empty playground from opposite directions came a squat figure with a rumpled fedora pulled low over his brow, and a tall, gaunt man with pale features and thick-rimmed glasses. The tall man was incongruously carrying a tennis ball. The short man wore one pair of gloves, carried another in his left hand, and had a book under his arm.

The two went to Manny Wolf's restaurant, a midtown steak house. Fuchs introduced himself and rebuked Harry for picking a public place for the meeting. "I'm working around the Wall Street area with a group of scientists—it's the Manhattan Project," Fuchs said.

At their next meeting, Fuchs was going north on Lexington Avenue and Gold came up behind him as he turned toward Park Avenue and took a large bundle of papers from him. He turned the bundle over to his new Soviet contact, "John." The contact was a clerk in the Soviet consulate named Anatoli A. Yakovlev.

He directed Harry's work with Fuchs from 1944 through late 1945. His superiors were so pleased with the results that in July, 1946, on his return from a two-month trip to Moscow, he was promoted from clerk to vice-consul. Yakovlev wisely left the United States in 1946 when he realized that members of the Rosenberg ring were being investigated, and he was named codefendant in the Rosenberg trial in 1950. Since he never returned to the United States, he was never tried.

Harry arranged his schedule at the sugar refinery, where he had continued to work after his graduation from Xavier, so that he stayed on overtime and then took several days off. "I took my whole life," he said, "and I didn't realize at the time I was taking my whole personality, my entire soul, and I was turning it over to these people."

In 1944, Harry and Fuchs met six or seven times in New York City, and Harry dutifully turned over bundles of information to Yakovlev. Harry, as he grew to know Fuchs, developed a strong admiration for him. "The word that sums him up is 'noble,' " he said. After his arrest, Fuchs was depicted as a victim of controlled schizophrenia, a Jekyll and Hyde personality; by Harry's standards, he was a perfectly balanced and lucid individual. Fuchs also took a liking to Harry and shared some of his problems with him. He was worried that the scientists with whom he was working would find out about his Communist background because the British were planning to bring his father to join him in the United States. "If they do," he said, "he is bound to prattle about my background, and once they begin to pry, you know what will happen. How am I going to keep them from doing this presumed kindness without arousing suspicion?"

Harry couldn't answer that one, and thereafter lost contact with Fuchs for nearly a year. On the first of January, 1945, Harry got an "urgent" from Yakovlev that he was to pick up information from Fuchs in Cambridge, Massachusetts. Fuchs had a married sister living there, Mrs. Crystal Heinemann, and it was at her home that the turncoat scientist and his courier renewed their acquaintance. Fuchs explained he had left the Manhattan Project for the Southwest, where research on the bomb was going on at a converted private school for boys called Los Alamos. In Cambridge, Harry said, "I received a huge bundle of information."

In June, 1945, Yakovlev summoned Harry and told him he was to go to Santa Fe, New Mexico, fifty miles away from Los Alamos, for more information. He also wanted Harry to make a side trip to Albuquerque to see another man who was working at Los Alamos. Harry complained bitterly about this added risk. He was tense and overworked, living on his nerves, and "just for once I got up on my hind legs and almost flatly refused to go to Albuquerque."

In Santa Fe, Fuchs delivered "fifty, sixty, a hundred pages of very close writing on yellow pads, sometimes white. And he had a very small crabbed hand—it not only contained a tremendous amount of theoretical mathematics, it contained the practical setup. I think that as much as any one man knew about the progress of the atom bomb, except possibly those at the very top of the Project, Fuchs knew, and was in a position to give . . . possibly he knew even more than those, because he was in intimate contact with it, in daily contact with it."

Harry's understanding of the material he received was limited, he admitted. "As a chemist, I had a very vague knowledge of the subject of nuclear fission. I mean, I knew some of the fundamentals. But I am no nuclear physicist."

From Santa Fe, Harry went to his Albuquerque meeting with David

Greenglass, who was a member of the Rosenberg network and the brother-in-law of Julius Rosenberg. As the FBI's "Exposé of Soviet Espionage" (May, 1960) pointed out, in asking Harry to contact Greenglass "the Soviet disregarded one of their cardinal rules prohibiting contacts between members of separate espionage networks. This error that cost them an espionage network was realized by Rosenberg, the head of the network. When he learned of Gold's arrest, he gave Greenglass and his wife $5,000 and instructions to go to Mexico where arrangements would be made for false passports with which they could travel to Czechoslovakia."

It was thanks to this one meeting, the report continues, that the Soviet espionage network headed by Julius Rosenberg was uncovered (Fuchs' arrest and confession in Britain had led to the arrest of Harry Gold, who led to Greenglass and the others).

When Harry got to Albuquerque, there was no one at the Greenglass home, and he spent an uneasy night in a hotel room, clutching the "huge mass of information I received from Fuchs." The next day he returned to the small apartment in a run-down house: "I walked up this steep flight of stairs and I knocked on the door and this young man answered, a dark-haired young man. And I almost fell down the steps, because I was shocked. He was wearing army pants and I could see behind him on the wall there was hanging an army sergeant's uniform. I had expected a civilian. I had never dealt with an army man or a military man before."

"I bear greetings from Julius," Harry said, and pulled out one half of a Jello box top from a pocket. Greenglass matched the box top with a half he pulled from his wife's handbag. Harry also gave Greenglass $500, and was told to return in the afternoon, because the information "needs some finishing touches."

Harry was consternated by Greenglass' airiness. "What upset me quite greatly," he said, "was his extreme naïveté." Harry trembled in fear and anger when Greenglass said, "You know, there are several men at Los Alamos who might give information. Why don't I ask them?"

"The devil you can," answered Harry. "You just don't approach people like that and say: 'Say, can you get me information on the atom bomb?'" Greenglass sulked like a petulant child at Harry's rebuke and Harry wondered: "Whoever in the world got this guy into this business? Does this poor baby [Greenglass was then twenty-three and was stationed as a mechanic at Los Alamos] know what the hell he is fooling with? Does he know what he is doing, even?" Harry felt that to Greenglass, it was like playing with toys.

Back in New York, Harry met Yakovlev in a deserted area in Flushing and gave him Fuchs' material in a folder labeled *Doctor* and the Greenglass data in a folder labeled *Other*. Greenglass had made a crude drawing of the atom bomb after eavesdropping on scientists talking shop at Los Alamos.

Yakovlev, a tall and bulky man with a lock of hair he kept pushing back in a characteristic manner, told Harry to go to Cambridge to find out "when Klaus is coming our way again." Harry saw Fuchs in Cambridge and the atomic scientist predicted that the Americans would never finish the atom bomb in time to use it in World War II. Fuchs later admitted that he had sadly underestimated American potential and ability to get the job done. As Harry explained, Fuchs' data "was very complete as far as his own work went, but his knowledge of the Manhattan Project was far from so. Originally he knew of the existence of neither Los Alamos nor Oak Ridge and he had no conception of U.S. industrial potential."

The Cambridge meeting was the last time Harry saw Fuchs, who went back to England in June, 1946. Fuchs saw Harry again on film, when the British M15 asked him to identfy his courier after Fuchs had been arrested in England.

In 1946, Harry was quietly dropped by the Russians after committing what was considered a breach in security. Harry had left the sugar refinery in Philadelphia and come to live in New York. He got a job with Abe Brothman, a research chemist who dabbled in giving information to the Russians for a price. Brothman was already on the FBI's list as a result of the disclosures of Elizabeth Bentley. Miss Bentley said she had been introduced to Brothman by Jacob Golos, a high-ranking Soviet agent of the thirties.

Yakovlev told Harry to give up the job immediately. "I think I can arrange to leave as soon as the pressure of work at Abe Brothman's has eased a bit," Harry replied. Yakovlev was furious because he knew the FBI was watching Brothman. Harry's new job led Yakovlev to leave the United States as soon as departure became feasible.

Things at the Brothman laboratory were far from rosy. Brothman and his secretary, Miriam Moskowitz, treated Harry like dirt. Harry made himself appear important with a complicated fabrication that involved a wife, two children (twins), wealthy relatives, and offers to work in secret research from numerous and famous laboratories. Brothman's business was flagging and one week out of two he could not pay his employees. When Harry complained about back pay, Miriam Moskowitz told him, "Get back to the laboratory where you belong, you worm." As Harry saw the swiftly changing situation at Brothman's: "When there was no money I was a partner and when there was money I was an employee."

Another example of Harry's extravagant imagination came when his mother died of a heart attack in 1947. The death was a severe blow and caused him to have a fit in the Brothman office in front of another employee. Harry accused Brothman of having influenced him to leave home when his mother needed him. "I killed my mother," he screamed, "did you hear, I killed my mother!"

"Is that so?" an employee asked noncommittally.

Things reached the point where Harry pressed suit for $4,000 in back pay, quit, and was accused by Brothman of stealing a $600 refractor and other equipment. Harry went back to Philadelphia and got a job at $4,000 a year with the Philadelphia General Hospital as a research assistant. In 1947, both Gold and Brothman were called to testify before a grand jury investigating Communism. They spent hours together before testifying so they could get their stories straight and gave false testimonies. Brothman said he had met Harry through Jacob Golos, who could not be asked to confirm the testimony, since he had died several years before. As a result of their appearance before the grand jury, Brothman and Miss Moskowitz were indicted on a charge of conspiracy to obstruct the administration of justice. Both received two-year sentences and heavy fines.

Harry emerged unscathed from his experience with the grand jury, but in January, 1950, Fuchs was arrested and confessed. Questioned at Wormwood Scrubbs Prison in London, Fuchs described his courier in the United States as a fat, foreign-looking American about forty years old who wore a blue pin-stripe suit. The courier was not a nuclear physicist, he said, but someone with a knowledge of chemistry and engineering. Fuchs was shown photographs of Gold but did not recognize them. The FBI showed him films which he did recognize, and Harry was arrested May 22, 1950, in a now-famous scene: under questioning, Harry claimed he had never been west of the Mississippi

—the FBI men searching his apartment found an annotated travel folder from Santa Fe, New Mexico, and Harry broke down when faced with the evidence.

At his trial he was a co-operative witness who admitted that for a period of eleven years "I lied desperately." Although he provided insights into his own motives through his articulate and probing confessions, there remains a mystery in the Harry Gold case. The mystery was hinted at when Harry appeared before the Senators in 1956.

At the end of the session Senator Welker said, "I know you to be a very capable chemist in a very great profession. You have sinned wrongfully against your country, your fellow man, and as I said at the outset of this concluding remark, time alone will show the extent of the terrible criminal—which is a minor name for people that have done things like you—that you really are and maybe after you have passed away, maybe after I have gone away from the Senate, there will be a shaft of light thrown on the life of Harry Gold. I know that you know what I am referring to and I know that you know I am going to respect the confidence that you have placed in me, not anything that you have asked for. It is something that you have asked me not to say, I am concluding my remarks with that statement."

Whatever it was that Harry Gold asked Senator Welker not to say, the secret was sealed when the Senator died in late 1957.

If we consider Judy Coplon and Harry Gold as "amateur" spies, it is necessary to consider in some detail the organizations of international espionage and their methods of operation before going on to the "professionals."

V. Clash by Night:
The CIA and the KGB

SHIELD: Argent, with a compass of sixteen-point gules. Crest: On a wreath argent and gules an American bald eagle's head. Below the shield on a gold scroll, the inscription United States of America in red letters, and encircling the shield and crest at the top, the inscription Central Intelligence Agency in white letters. All in a circular blue background with a narrow gold edge. The eagle is a symbol of strength and alertness—the radiating spokes of the compass depict the coverage of intelligence data from all over the world to a central point.

If heraldry is a symbol of accepted worth, the CIA's escutcheon testifies that it is here to stay. In the past, American intelligence organizations were hastily formed in times of emergency, then disbanded as unnecessary when the emergency abated. Although replaced by John A. McCone as Director of the Central Intelligence Agency in November, 1961, it was Allen Dulles who made the CIA what it is today, gave it a sense of permanence, a mellow patina that makes it seem far more ancient than its fourteen years.

CIA's acknowledged founding father is Major General William J. (Wild Bill) Donovan. This remarkable man, who blended recklessness with unusual foresight, headed the wartime Office of Strategic Services and in 1944 proposed the creation of a permanent intelligence agency.

125

Donovan is said to have been given his nickname in World War I, while in France with the "Fighting 69th" of the Rainbow Division. One day he ran his regiment five miles with full packs to limber them up. When his men grumbled, he told them he was ten years older than they were and also had a full pack.

"But we ain't as wild as you, Bill," one replied.

In 1940, after a fact-finding mission to England, the Balkans, and the Middle East, Donovan returned to President Roosevelt with three conclusions that had a major effect on United States policy. He said he was convinced the British could hold, that the Germans would strike at Suez through North Africa, and that the United States should prepare for a global war.

He stressed the need for a service to gather wartime intelligence and conduct clandestine operations behind enemy lines. Roosevelt reportedly told him to set up such a service and said: "You'll have to start from scratch. We don't have an intelligence service." In July, 1941, Donovan became head of the Office of the Co-ordination of Information, but in 1942 this was split into two groups, the Office of Strategic Services, which Donovan headed and which conducted intelligence and unorthodox warfare work; and the Office of War Information.

The OSS has left behind an aura of romance and unbelievability that clouds its true value. It probably was, as once charged, a clubbish amalgam of scholars and socialites, of businessmen and peacetime idlers, who found under Donovan's mercurial leadership limitless outlet for their dreams of glory. Carpers claim that if the OSS had supplied one-third the intelligence that it did anecdotes, the war would have been over sooner.

Ambassador David Bruce, a close OSS associate of Donovan's, wrote that "his imagination was unlimited. Ideas were his playthings. Excitement made him snort like a race horse. Woe to the officer who turned down a project because, on its face, it seemed ridiculous, or at least unusual." For several painful weeks an officer under his command tested the possibility of using bats taken from concentrations in western caves to carry delayed action incendiary bombs to destroy Tokyo. The general, backed by the intrigued President Roosevelt, was only dissuaded from further experiments in this field when it appeared probable that the cave bats would not survive a transpacific flight at high altitudes.

Donovan dealt out foreign intelligence assignments as though they were trips to the corner grocery. This is the account of a retired colonel's first mission for the OSS: "Wild Bill called me in, put his arm around me and said: 'Do you know anything about Spain? We don't know what's going on over there. Why don't you go and see what you can find out?' That's how I wound up in Lisbon on my way to Spain. I hadn't gone to any espionage school, I went in cold. My orders were to follow the streetcar tracks on Santa Anna Street to a fork in the road and continue until I was in front of a new building.

"I went to the end of the line in Santa Anna Street and saw the new building in front of me. I walked in and as I stepped inside, two krauts in uniform blocked the door and a third asked me what I was doing there. 'You're in the German Embassy,' he told me. I knew I wasn't because I'd passed the German Embassy on the way. I apologized and calmly walked out the door, which opened before I touched it. I went back to the fork, took the other road, and wound up in front of another modern building. This was the American headquarters, and I recounted my adventure to the man in charge, who said: 'Do you know you're the first person to go into Gestapo headquarters and come out on his own?' "

Not all OSS operations were that unrehearsed, and for every picaresque hero there was a valuable agent working quietly behind enemy lines and a researcher in Washington providing essential data.

In late 1944, Donovan wrote a memorandum to President Roosevelt:

> I have given consideration to the organization of our intelligence service for the postwar period.
>
> Once our enemies are defeated the demand will be equally pressing for information that will aid in solving the problems of peace.
>
> This requires two things:
>
> 1. That intelligence control be returned to the supervision of the President.
>
> 2. The establishment of a central authority reporting directly to you.

On April 5, 1945, a week before his death and with the strength already ebbing from his body, Roosevelt replied:

> Apropos of your memo of November 18, 1944, relative to the establishment of a central intelligence service, I should appreciate

your getting together the chiefs of the foreign intelligence and internal security in the various executive agencies, so that a consensus of opinion can be secured.

It appears to me that of the ten executive departments, as well as the Foreign Economic Administration and the Federal Communications Commission, I have a direct interest in the proposed venture. They should all be asked to contribute their suggestions to the proposed central intelligence service.

Roosevelt did not live to see the project take shape. On September 20, 1945, President Truman by executive order disbanded the OSS, transferring its functions to the State Department and the Department of War. He was acting under pressure from the armed services, the FBI, the Department of State, and the Bureau of the Budget, and from his own conviction that a cloak-and-dagger outfit in peacetime was anomalous.

The need for some form of intelligence was so apparent, however, that in January, 1946, Truman issued an order establishing the Central Intelligence Group, precursor of the CIA. He now received a daily intelligence summary and wrote in his memoirs: "Here at last, a co-ordinated method had been worked out, and a practical way had been found for keeping the President informed as to what was known and what was going on."

The Central Intelligence Group existed twenty months under three different directors: Rear Admiral Sidney W. Souers, General Hoyt S. Vandenberg, and Rear Admiral Roscoe H. Hillenkoetter. It was General Vandenberg who disclosed the high percentage of intelligence that is as available as flowers in a field if only you find somebody to pick them. "Before the second World War," he told the Senate Armed Services Committee in April, 1947, "our intelligence services had left largely untapped the great open sources of information upon which roughly eighty per cent of intelligence should normally be based. I mean such things as books, magazines, technical and scientific surveys, photographs, commercial analyses, newspaper and radio broadcasts, and general information from people with a knowledge of affairs abroad.

"What weakened our position further was that those of our intelligence services which did dabble in any of these sources failed to co-ordinate their results with each other. . . . I am talking now of the failure to exploit obvious sources."

The National Security Act of 1947 replaced the Central Intelligence Group with the Central Intelligence Agency, a far more powerful body. From the hearings on the National Security Act it is evident that no one knew exactly what the nature of the beast would be. Representative Fred Busby made a prophetic remark: "I wonder," he said, "if there is any foundation for the rumors that have come to me to the effect that through this Central Intelligence Agency, they are contemplating operational activities."

Allen Dulles in his memorandum to the Senate before the National Security Act was passed, stressed a certain number of points which he did not fully adhere to once he became director of the CIA.

1. In apparent allusion to the swift turnover of chiefs in the Central Intelligence Group, he urged that "service in the Agency should not be viewed merely as a steppingstone to promotion in one of the armed services or other branches of the Government. It should be directed by a relatively small but elite corps of men with a passion for anonymity and a willingness to stick at that particular job."

Dulles applied the first half of his statement when he became head of the CIA. He stayed on the job as director for more than eight years, and developed professionalism within the organization's ranks to an unprecedented degree. He made intelligence work a career rather than a stopgap assignment for civil servants at loose ends. His own passion for anonymity, however, was questionable. Although he was supposed to be sequestered from the press, articles about him kept appearing. His benevolently cheerful pipe-smoking countenance, with its mustache and spectacles, was reproduced in magazines almost as often as the glamorous profiles of some of our movie stars. He was certainly the best-known American "master spy" since Pinkerton. He encouraged his legend as the unassuming wizard of intelligence with often-quoted statements such as "I've never been shot at and no one's ever tried to kidnap me."

2. Dulles insisted that "because of its glamor and mystery, overemphasis is generally placed on what is called secret intelligence, namely the intelligence that is obtained by secret means and secret agents." He noted that 80 per cent of intelligence could be obtained through the press, the radio, and "the many thousands of Americans, business and professional men and American residents of foreign countries, who are naturally brought in touch with what is going on in those countries."

A review of the CIA's activities abroad, however, gives the impression that most of its resources are devoted not to the collection of "White" research, but to the clandestine activity which agents refer to as "magic." The use, as part-time agents, of Americans abroad is a twilight zone that might be called "Gray" research. It can be argued that the CIA would have done better to emphasize open research and that the reliance on secret operations is self-defeating. This was the point of view one of Joseph Conrad's characters took in *The Secret Agent,* saying: "I should lay it down that the existence of secret agents should not be tolerated, as tending to augment the positive dangers of the evil against which they are used. That the spy will fabricate his information is a mere commonplace. But in the sphere of political and revolutionary action, relying on violence, the professional spy has every facility to fabricate the facts themselves, and will spread the double evil of emulation in one direction, and of panic, hasty legislation, unreflecting hate, in the other. However, this is an imperfect world. . . ."

3. Dulles pointed to the British system as a successful example of intelligence. "The British system," he said, "has behind it a long history of quiet and effective performance, based on a highly trained personnel with years of service and great technical ability. In this country we have the raw material for building the greatest intelligence service in the world. But to accomplish this we must make it a respected, continuing, and adequately remunerated career. The personnel need not be very numerous. The operation of the service must be neither flamboyant nor overshrouded with the mystery and abracadabra which the amateur detective likes to assume."

The British system which Dulles praised has always held to the strict principle of separating intelligence-gathering from operational functions, the one being relegated to MI6 and the other to the Special Operations Executive. This precludes suiting facts to policy. As for the "not very numerous" personnel, it is generally supposed that today the CIA has more people working for it than the State Department, which has become a rather parochial organization by comparison with the mushrooming intelligence community.

And the flamboyance of CIA deputy director, Robert Amory Jr., who reportedly appeared three months before the Cuban invasion at a Washington "New Frontier" costume party dressed like a Castro *barbudo,* would be hard to match.

The CIA, through the necessities of the Cold War and the energy of its director, has strayed from the precepts Dulles drafted in 1947. In its pre-Dulles days, however, most of its sins were sins of omission.

In 1948, less than a year after the agency was founded, the first of many inquiries on intelligence failures was held. Admiral Hillenkoetter was called before a Congressional committee to explain why the CIA had not given warning about a revolution that was taking place in Bogotá, Colombia. It was particularly embarrassing for the United States since Secretary of State Dean Acheson was in the Latin-American country attending a conference and was caught in the middle of the upheaval. During the admiral's tenure, from 1947 to 1950, the CIA missed on two other major events: the Soviet explosion of the atom bomb in 1949 and the start of the Korean war. But the CIA quickly became active in Korea. It launched "Operation Bluebell," in which literally thousands of Korean refugees were sent behind North Korean lines and told to make their way back as best they could. Those who returned were able to supply intelligence on enemy movements. The CIA reportedly found that the best intelligence came from children. When a decision had to be taken whether Allied forces should cross the 38th parallel into North Korea, the CIA estimate was that there would be no massive Red Chinese retaliation.

President Truman wrote in his memoirs that "on October 20 [1950], the CIA delivered a memorandum to me which said that they had reports that the Chinese Communists would move in far enough to safeguard the Suiho electric plant and other installations along the Yalu River which provided them with power." The Chinese hordes did not stop at the Yalu, routed the United Nations forces under General MacArthur and made his "you'll be out of the trenches by Christmas" promise an empty boast.

Admittedly, the early CIA years were faltering and hesitant. The poor record of U.S. intelligence in the Korean war led to the appointment of the late General Walter Bedell Smith as director in 1950. In his three years as director, this hard-boiled career soldier ran the organization as though it were a barracks full of green recruits. Smith, who had served as Eisenhower's European chief of staff and Ambassador to Moscow, gave the CIA three years of tightening up.

In the words of an associate, he "kicked out the misfits, the Martini set, and the OSS leftovers." He was quoted as deploring the complexity of his task: "America's people expect you to be on a communing level with God and Joe Stalin . . . they expect you to be able to say that a war will start next Tuesday at 5:32 P.M."

The general's most startling estimate dealt not with foreign intelligence but with his own organization. With characteristic bluntness, he acknowledged that there were Communists in the CIA. His testimony was given before the House Un-American Activities Committee on October 13, 1952. Asked if he thought there were Communists in the State Department, he replied:

"I do. I do. I believe there are Communists in my own organization. In the past we have discovered from time to time one or two, and I believe that in the future we will from time to time discover them, but as I said, none in the United States, no Americans, and none within the scope and responsibility of this committee.

"You will remember that I have no internal security responsibility inside the United States and am prohibited from exercising any of these functions."

Asked if he knew the Communists, the general said, "I do not. I wish I did. I do everything I can to detect them, but I am morally certain, since you are asking the questions, that there are. I believe that they are so adroit and adept that they have infiltrated every security organization of government in one way or another. . . . I from time to time discover them in my own activities in various places, which I would prefer not to discuss in open hearings."

Aside from this admission that the CIA, because it employed a large number of foreign agents, could not be security-proof, Bedell Smith's most important accomplishment in the CIA was perhaps bringing in Allen Dulles as his deputy. When the general left the agency in 1953, Dulles took over, the first civilian to head it. In a total of eleven years in the CIA, Dulles left his strong personal stamp on the organization, on his country and on the first Cold War decade.

As he once remarked, "There is something about intelligence that seems to get into the blood." Few people can claim a more precocious aptitude for intelligence than Allen Welsh Dulles. In 1902, when he was eight years old, he wrote a history of the Boer war in which he indicated the careful preparations of British intelligence in its use of native spies to reconnoiter the terrain. "In the battle of Dundee," the young Dulles wrote, "the British left various things behind them and among them was an iron box and on top, it said 'not to be left behind,' and they opened it and found maps and it showed every footpath, how they were going to get the land from the Boers three years before the war.

"The British were sly enough to go and get in the land when the Dutch were being killed by the smallpox," Dulles added. The thirty-one page pamphlet, which was privately printed in a limited edition, concluded that Britain "is all the time picking into little countries . . . the Boers want peace but England has to have the gold and so she goes around fighting all the little countries, but she never dares to fight either China or Russia. I hope that the Boers will win for the Boers are in the wright [sic] and the British in the wrong in the war."

High office was a tradition in the Dulles family before the time of Allen and his brother John Foster. Their maternal grandfather, General John Watson Foster, became Secretary of State in 1893, the year before Allen Dulles was born. An uncle by marriage was Robert Lansing, who was Secretary of State under Woodrow Wilson. Both John Foster and Allen chose diplomacy rather than the calling of their father, Allen Macy Dulles, who was a Presbyterian minister.

At the age of twenty-three Allen Dulles was tall and gangling with a toothbrush mustache, a Phi Beta Kappa key on his watchchain, and the carefully groomed air of a Princeton graduate. His first diplomatic assignment under the aegis of his uncle, Mr. Lansing, was Vienna. This turned out to be an intelligence assignment as well. Through his friendship with Dr. Heinrich Lammasch, tutor of the Emperor Charles of Austria, Dulles was instrumental in setting up in Bern in 1918 a secret meeting to discuss the future of the Austro-Hungarian empire in the postwar period.

The secret talks between a representative of President Wilson and a representative of the House of the Hapsburgs were intended to sound out the possibility of maintaining the monarchy. Dr. Lammasch tried to sell the idea that the best interest of the United States was to keep the emperor on his throne. He reportedly suggested that there should be "a bridge of gold between Vienna and Washington" (whether he meant the gold in the emperor's crown or in the United States Treasury he did not clearly explain). When asked whether the United States would be allowed a voice in the regime, he replied: "We shall not only allow it, we shall be delighted." Thanks largely to British skepticism, President Wilson did not openly back the emperor, who soon after abdicated his throne. The incident, though fruitless, had given Allen Dulles the first example of how real power is wielded— behind the scenes.

At the Versailles conference, Dulles was the assistant of Ellis Dressel, an expert on German affairs. He followed Dressel on a mission to Germany, served two years in Constantinople, and went back to Washington as head of the Near East Affairs section of the State Department. In 1926, Dulles received his law degree at George Washington University and resigned from the State Department to join the law firm where his brother was a member—Sullivan and Cromwell. The firm had important German clients, and critics of the Dulles brothers have charged that they favored German interests in World War II.

A violently anti-Dulles pamphlet written in 1961 by Bob Edwards, a British member of Parliament, and Kenneth Dunne, charged that the Dulles brothers were "agents" for the German firm of Robert Bosch:

> Bosch had a branch in the United States called the American Bosch Corporation. At the beginning of the second world war, this firm found itself in danger of being black-listed. Its owners in Stuttgart took immediate action. They reached an agreement with the famous Swedish bankers, the Wallenberg Brothers, that their bank should take nominal control of the American Bosch Corporation with the obligation of returning it after the war. The Wallenbergs consented. But they needed an American contractor to execute the formalities. This was the role assigned to the Dulles brothers, who undertook to bluff the American authorities and conceal Nazi property under the Swedish flag. The brothers handled the deal neatly but some years later it was discovered. In 1948 there were even court proceedings. We have never discovered the verdict, but the very fact of what had happened is enough to make us skeptical about the ability of Allen Dulles to place American interests before those of Germany.

The pamphlet also said Allen Dulles was a director of the Schroeder Banking House, a German-run firm that helped finance the Nazi movement.

Dulles took time out from his business interests to run unsuccessfully for Congress and helped organize the Wendell Willkie campaign in 1939. In 1942 his cloak-and-dagger days began. He was appointed

OSS chief in Switzerland by Wild Bill Donovan. Considerable controversy surrounds Dulles' role in the war years.

On the one hand, he achieved feats that hastened the end of the war. On the other hand, he has been accused of holding secret talks to discuss "a soft peace" with the Germans at a time when Churchill and Roosevelt, at Casablanca, had vowed they would seek nothing less than "unconditional surrender." Although those in a position to know have cited Dulles for doing "the best single intelligence job of the war," his activities are shrouded in mystery even today and cannot be made public. It is common knowledge, however, that Dulles had a pipeline into the German Abwehr and, as a result, American counterespionage people knew the activities of German agents.

The best available appraisal of Dulles' wartime role can be made by comparing the glowing citations he received with excerpts from alleged "secret documents" dealing with his meetings with the Germans in 1943.

The citation for the Medal of Merit praises Dulles for building up

> . . . an intelligence network employing hundreds of informants and operatives, reaching into Germany, Yugoslavia, Czechoslovakia, Bulgaria, Hungary, Spain, Portugal, and North Africa, and completely covering France, Italy, and Austria. He assisted in the formation of various Maquis groups in France and supported the Italian partisan groups both financially and by pin-pointing airdrops for supplies. The exceptional worth of his reports on bombing targets and troop movements both by land and sea was recognized by diplomatic, military, and naval agencies of the United States Government. Particularly notable achievements by Mr. Dulles were first reports, as early as May 1943, of the existence of a German experimental laboratory at Peenemunde for the testing of a rocket bomb, his report on the flooding of the Belgian and Dutch coastal areas long before similar information came in from other sources, his report on rocket bomb installations in the Pas de Calais, and his reports on damage inflicted by the Allied Air Forces as a result of raids on Berlin and other German, Italian, and Balkan cities, which were forwarded within two or three days of the operations. Mr. Dulles, by his superior diplomacy and efficiency, built up for the United States enormous prestige among leading figures of occupied nations taking refuge in Switzerland. He carried out his assignments in extremely hazardous conditions, despite the constant observations of enemy agents.

The secret documents were made public in the pamphlet by Mr. Edwards and Mr. Dunne. They are alleged reports from SS agents on talks in February, 1943, between Dulles and German emissaries. In the report, Dulles is referred to as "Mr. Bull" and the German emissary, Prince Maximilian Hohenloh, as "Herr Pauls." The talks were held in Geneva. "Herr Pauls" was Himmler's envoy. According to the report:

> Mr. Bull is the most influential White House man in Europe and the Swiss believe he is in direct telegraphic contact with the American President, by-passing the State Department. . . . He has been given the mission of exploring European, and especially East-European problems. . . . He is a tall, powerfully built sporting man of about 45, with a healthy appearance, good teeth, and a lively, unaffected, and gracious manner. Assuredly a man of civic courage. . . .
>
> [Mr. Bull said] he was fed up with listening all the time to out-dated politicians, *émigrés* and prejudiced Jews. In his view a peace had to be made in Europe in the preservation of which all concerned would have a real interest. There must not again be a division into victors and vanquished; that is, contented and discontented; never again must nations like Germany be driven by want and injustice to desperate experiments and heroism. The German state must continue to exist, as a factor of order and progress; there could be no question of its partition or the separation of Austria.
>
> Herr Pauls intimated that he sometimes actually felt the Americans were only going on with the war so as to be able to get rid of the Jews and send them back again. To this Mr. Bull, who in the course of the conversation had clearly evinced anti-Semitic tendencies, replied that in America things had not quite got to that point yet and that it was in general a question of whether the Jews wanted to go back. . . .
>
> Mr. Bull turned to the subject of National Socialism and the person of Adolph Hitler and declared that with all respect to the historical importance of Adolph Hitler and his work it was hardly conceivable that the Anglo-Saxons' worked-up public opinion could accept Hitler as the unchallenged master of Greater Germany. People had no confidence in the durability and dependability of agreements with him.
>
> He agreed more or less to a Europe organized politically and industrially on the basis of large territories, and considered that a Federal Greater Germany, with an associated Danube Confederation, would be the best guarantee of order and progress in Central and

Eastern Europe. He does not reject National Socialism in its basic ideas and deeds so much as the "inwardly unbalanced, inferiority-complex-ridden" Prussian militarism.

This view of an anti-Semitic, pro-Nazi Dulles promising that Germany would emerge from defeat practically intact is the view of a German agent reporting to his superiors. It reflects a wish for approval. Dulles, on the other hand, was playing the intelligence game of cat and mouse rather than making statements of principle. For these reasons, the documents cannot be accepted as indicating that Dulles was "soft" on Nazism; they show, if they are legitimate, simply that Dulles conferred with Nazi envoys on the possibilities of a surrender. He was not in Switzerland to make policy, and President Roosevelt repeatedly made it clear that unconditional surrender was the only acceptable end for the war.

One of Dulles' accomplishments when he became CIA chief was changing intelligence work from a shadowy and unpopular pursuit to a highly respectable professional career. A visitor to the CIA buildings in Washington could almost expect to find a sign reading: LEAVE YOUR DAGGER AT THE DOOR. The climate is similar to that in any large office building. There are suggestion boxes and notices on bulletin boards. In an office, a CIA official told his secretary, "I'm afraid I'll have to keep you on overtime tonight." In the cafeteria, there is the same bad food, easy mingling, and trivial conversation that mark any large corporation. The CIA's corporate manner is betrayed by only a few details. Armed guards at the entrance ask visitors to fill out time sheets. Visitors are escorted at all times in the building and taken through in elevators that are to be unlocked with special keys.

The mundane, open atmosphere goes only as far as security allows. The CIA is listed in the telephone book, but CIA operators are instructed to accept only calls asking for an extension. If you ask for someone by name you won't get him, as the wife who forgot her husband's extension discovered. CIA employees have what is known as a "shallow cover" to hide their real work. Secretarial and clerical staff are told simply to say they work for the Government. Above that level, CIA men have semifictitious teaching assignments or business connections. The "shallow cover," however, is often entirely forgotten, and a recent copy of the George Washington University alumni magazine had this item in its notes: "Betty Jean Smith (name fictitious) is now working with the Central Intelligence Agency doing economic research. Good luck, Betty Jean."

Even operatives abroad seem to make little effort at hiding their CIA role. Thayer Waldo of the San Francisco *Chronicle* wrote that while in Cuba the names of eight CIA men at the American Embassy were made known to him by other correspondents or embassy employees. In all the important capitals, correspondents know the identities of the CIA men with embassy covers. This can sometimes be a source of embarrassment to the operative. In Paris, a CIA man has been put on the spot several times by correspondents who, seeing him at a restaurant, would call out something like "Hi, Ed, still stringing for the CIA?" or "How's the spook business these days?" The CIA man's face would blanch, and the person he was with would give him a quizzical look.

Under Dulles, the CIA has emphasized intelligence as a career, like teaching or medicine. There is a Junior Officer Training program which selects outstanding students in the best colleges, approaching them with vague offers (how would you like to work for the Government?) several months before they graduate. The JOTs, who receive special training, form the cadres for the organization, which now promotes from the inside. Employees are in the civil service ranks, but here as in the exterior appearance of the CIA plant, however, there are aspects that remind one of the agency's function. There is no job security. "The director can walk in this office and fire me any time he feels like it," a high official said. There is no appeal to civil service control, as other government workers have. In addition, there is a three-year probationary period before becoming eligible for the "career" plan.

Dulles foisted a spirit of "togetherness" in his organization, has encouraged inter-CIA marriages (one advantage is that both have been checked for security), and bridge clubs. The CIA appeals to the patriotism of its recruits. "The Old Man won't have anyone who's in it for the money," is a frequent statement at CIA. After a number of years, however, quite a few CIA higher-ups get out for the money and cash in on their *sub rosa* experience with private industry. In the lower echelons, the secretaries get married or drift to other jobs. Some of the intelligence people leave because they dislike working in secrecy, where their accomplishments get no recognition. Others suffer nervous breakdowns, or leave in protest of CIA methods.

Despite all these problems, the CIA claims to have the highest-quality personnel of any government department, including the State Department. It boasts that it has never had a defector or a security leak. But it also has a high rate of turnover in its personnel. The CIA stoutly defends itself against being ivory-towerish. Roger Hillsman, in his book *Strategic Intelligence and National Decision,* quoted one official who opposed the recruitment of university professors because "they're useless—I don't like the adulation of the printed word you get on campus—and I don't like the kind of fellow who's spent all his life on one minute of the Battle of Gettysburg."

The congeniality of working conditions at the CIA is matched by strict security procedures. The "need-to-know" principle and compartmentalization of work prevail. Work groups (set up by subject and geographical desks) are tightly knit and know nothing about other work being done. Only the director of the Central Intelligence Agency has an over-all view of his agency's accomplishments. Even his three chief assistants tend their respective bubbling caldrons: Air Force General Charles P. Cabell,* deputy director since 1953 and the guiding spirit of the U-2 overflights; Robert Amory Jr., deputy director for intelligence, a former professor of business law and accounting at the Harvard Business School; and Richard M. Bissell Jr.,* who as deputy director for operations co-ordinated the Cuban disaster (known in Washington as the "Bissell gap").

Colonel Stanley Grogan, a former professor of military science at Lafayette College, supervises the information released to the press and the public. He has no information to give, since the CIA "neither confirms nor denies" published reports and allows rumors and defamations to go unchallenged and glowing praise to go unthanked. It is one of Colonel Grogan's duties to receive the press and explain patiently why the CIA must remain beyond the public's right to know. "If we talked, we'd be out of business," he says cheerfully. Although the CIA doesn't talk it occasionally whispers when it feels the need to bolster itself in the public eye. Thus in late 1954, Richard and Gladys Harkness, personal friends of Dulles, wrote a three-part series in the *Saturday Evening Post* called "The Mysterious

* No longer with the CIA.

Doings of CIA." The articles contained a blow-by-blow description of the CIA's role in unseating Premier Mossadegh in Iran.

Other well-informed articles have appeared from time to time with hints of CIA successes. *Newsweek* Magazine seems to have one of the best pipelines into the intelligence network. The only official interview ever granted by Dulles was the 1954 question-and-answer session with *U.S. News and World Report*. The interview was done at Dulles' request. He wanted to clear up some misconceptions about the CIA and state once and for all why his was a secret organization and why "I can't advertise my wares." Seven years later, CIA men tell you that the interview is "still good," there is nothing to add to it.

A favorite Washington guessing game involves the budget and number of employees of the CIA. Grogan, when asked the question point-blank, takes on a mock horror expression and exclaims, "Why, I can't tell you that—I'd go to jail." Estimates vary enormously and the only clue Dulles ever gave was in this exchange in the 1954 interview.

Q. Has it ever been published how much appropriations you have?
A. No, but I have seen some speculation in the press with figures which were several times exaggerated.

Press estimates cover a wide range. *The New York Times* over the years has published at least five different sets of figures, the latest of which is 12,000 to 18,000 U.S. citizens as employees, with additional thousands of foreign agents, and a budget of $1,000,000,000 a year. Ransom, in his work on central intelligence and national security, put the figures at 8,000 to 10,000 agents in the United States and a budget of "several hundred millions of dollars annually." The British pamphlet "Study of a Master Spy" said the CIA has 40,000 officials. This is an even more generous figure than the official Soviet estimate, which allows the CIA 20,000 agents.

Construction of the new CIA building in Langley, Virginia, ten miles outside Washington, has given amateur sleuths new clues. The $42,000,000 building has exactly 1,135,000 square feet. An enterprising Senator learned from an architect that every worker in a large office needs 98.5 square feet and came up with the answer that the CIA has exactly 11,523 employees in Washington. It was also noted that the sprawling two-story building with five connecting six-floor towers would have parking lots with a capacity of 3,000 cars (actually many employees will use bus service); a cafeteria that can seat 1,000; and an auditorium with room for 500.

The building is in a wooded area overlooking the Potomac and features continuous glass windows for the two main floors, making the CIA architecturally the most transparent intelligence organization in the world. Inscribed on the wall of the main entrance are words that bear witness both to the agency's aims and its shortcomings: YE SHALL KNOW THE TRUTH AND THE TRUTH SHALL MAKE YOU FREE (Gospel according to St. John). Some of the items in the construction budget approved by Congress were $105,000 for incinerators to burn classified material and $50,000 for radio antennas.

The building was due to be ready for occupation in the spring of 1962, and the CIA began to move its voluminous files and equipment from the "Foggy Bottom" compound in January, 1961. Critics have viewed the move with alarm, noting C. Northcote Parkingson's celebrated law that the architectural magnificence of an organization grows to a point where symptoms of decline appear.

In 1955 there was a test of power between the CIA and the Pentagon that pitted Dulles against the Secretary of Defense, the Joint Chiefs of Staff, and other high military personnel. At stake was the authority of the CIA over the intelligence branches of the armed services, which it is meant by statute to cap.

The test involved Lieutenant General Arthur Gilbert Trudeau, then head of Army intelligence (G-2). In 1954, General Trudeau was guest at a dinner given at the German Embassy in Washington in honor of Chancellor Adenauer. He sought out the German chief of state and expressed his misgivings about the CIA backing of a West German intelligence network under Reinhold Gehlen. Trudeau said he doubted Gehlen's reliability and the political advantage of a "spook outfit" backed by American intelligence and headed by a former Nazi officer. Apparently, Adenauer was impressed. Trudeau was invited back to the Embassy for longer talks.

When Dulles learned of the conversations, he had one of his rare accesses of anger. He took the case directly to President Eisenhower, charging that Trudeau had bypassed normal channels in going directly to Adenauer and had undermined the policy interests of the United States. Important figures in the defense community, including the

Joint Chiefs of Staff and Defense Secretary Charles (Engine Charlie) Wilson, took up Trudeau's defense. To no avail, for soon after, the general was unceremoniously fired from G-2 and kicked upstairs as deputy chief to General Lyman Lemnitzer in the U.S. Far Eastern command.

A visit to CIA offices gives some idea of the agency at work and the vast amount of information at its finger tips. A high-ranking officer pushes a button, and a balding scholar with watery eyes and a rumpled suit appears. "How many trains a day between Archangel and Sverdlovsk?" he asks. "Eight," the scholar replies. Another button is pushed and the scholar gives way to an Ivy Leaguer with carefully brushed hair and Brooks Brothers clothes. "What is the address of Lubyanka Prison and how many political prisoners are interned there at present?" The Ivy Leaguer answers, "Two Dzerzhinski Street and one hundred and eighty-six."

This kind of exercise gives the impression that the CIA does its intelligence research with rare know-how, that one piece of military intelligence sometimes depends on a dozen or more factors that the agency alone is in a position to fit together.

It was an odd coincidence that in the same month of the same year, November, 1961, the chiefs of the Soviet and American intelligence services were replaced. Allen Dulles, who survived the exposure of the U-2 program, could not continue in his job after the failure of the Cuba invasion. He turned over the burdensome mantle of America's master spy to John A. McCone on November 29 after these parting words from President Kennedy: "Your successes are unheralded, your failures trumpeted."

A reported who saw Dulles a month before his retirement said that "he looked like a beaten man. His buoyancy, his enthusiasm, and the vigor that belied his age had vanished. He complained about his gout and spent a good part of his working day in a reclining chair. It was obvious that events had worn him. He joked about his retirement, but the jokes were hollow." This depressing picture of the man who more than any other had shaped American intelligence was only momentary, however. Far from seeking the privacy of retirement, Dulles gave newspaper interviews and appeared on television. The public image of confident strength was restored. Far from apologizing for the Cuban coup, he said on television:

"I think that Latin America is far more alerted to the dangers of Castroism and Communism, as a danger to their system, than they were, let's say, a year ago, or last April. Many countries in Latin America have now broken diplomatic relations with Cuba, and I think therefore that the impact of Castroism has decreased in many Latin-American countries over the last six months because of what has taken place in Cuba, and their apprehension of what might take place in their own countries."

And he announced that in his retirement he would be "of counsel" to his old law firm of Sullivan & Cromwell in New York and to President Kennedy in Washington. He is also planning a book on intelligence (without giving away any of the secrets which he is bound by statute to keep) and a book on international Communism.

Only sixteen days before Dulles retired, the replacement of his Soviet vis-à-vis was announced in Moscow. Aleksandr N. Shelepin was as little known as Dulles was notorious. He was promoted to head the KGB in 1958 and his appointment was considered unusual by Soviet specialists for several reasons. Shelepin represented a new generation of Communists, the generation born after the revolution. He was born in 1918 in Voronezh, on the banks of the Don. Shelepin had no previous secret service experience. He rose through the Party and became a protégé of Khrushchev. Thus he passed from head of the Komsomol (Young Communist League), where he won a reputation as a talented propagandist, to the leadership of an organization competing with the CIA for the title "biggest spy network in the world."

As head of the Komsomol, Shelepin controlled 19,000,000 members and was cited for his success in quelling the disillusionment among Soviet youth that followed Stalin's death in 1953. Although he came from a *petite bourgeoisie* background (his father was an office worker) one of Shelepin's tasks in his Komsomol role was to denounce the softness of a white-collar career and to encourage youth to go to the farm and factory. In his new job, he turned his flair for propaganda to attacks on American intelligence, and is said to have personally supervised the publication of the anti-CIA booklet "Caught In the Act."

Under Shelepin's leadership, the KGB made efforts to shake off its reputation as a ruthless and powerful state within the state and present itself as simply another government agency. Thus, shortly before his replacement, Shelepin told the 1961 Communist Party Congress in one of his rare public addresses:

> "We are happy to report that the state security organs have fully liquidated distortions in their work and violations of Socialist legality. Decisive measures of the Party's Central Committee and the Soviet Government have finished with this, finished forever. The state security organs have reorganized, greatly reduced in number, been deprived of their improper functions and freed of careerist elements. Many party, government and youth officials have been assigned to work in the police organs."

Further attesting to the rehabilitation of the KGB, Shelepin left the secret police not under sentence of death or imprisonment as so many of his predecessors had done, but for a prominent job as one of the nine national party secretaries serving directly under Khrushchev.

His replacement, Vladimir Y. Semichastny, came as he did from the ranks of the Young Communist League. Semichastny, in his mid-thirties, is the youngest man ever to have bossed the huge KGB network.

His career has closely paralleled Shelepin's. He rose in the Komsomol until he replaced Shelepin as First Secretary in 1958. A year later he was appointed to a high party post in Azerbaijan, the Soviet Caucasian Republic. In anticipation of his KGB promotion, Semichastny was made an alternate member of the Central Committee during the Party Congress. The most obvious implication of his appointment was that the KGB, which in the days of Beria rivaled the Party in power, was now firmly under Party control and has even become something of a sinecure for Khrushchev protégés. It would be naïve, however, to conclude that because of its subservience to the Party, the KGB has been whitewashed and has given up the infamous methods for which it has become known. Shelepin's comforting assertion that the KGB is greatly reduced in numbers remains to be proved.

The comparative size of Soviet and United States intelligence nets defies analysis. The CIA is the funnel for half a dozen intelligence groups, all with staffs and budgets of their own, and in addition the FBI handles counterintelligence work within the United States. A review of United States and Soviet intelligence communities shows the following agencies:

For the United States: The Central Intelligence Agency, with a minimum of 15,000 employees at home and abroad.

The National Security Agency (dealt with in a separate chapter), with at least 10,000 employees in the United States charged with the increasingly important mission of communications intelligence.

Army intelligence (G-2), which includes sixty-nine military attaché posts and the Counterintelligence Corps, with its vast West German network. To obtain military intelligence, which is then transmitted to the CIA, Army intelligence today has a yearly budget well over the $100,000,000 mark ($125,000,000 in 1958) and its staff has been beefed up to about 5,000, according to recent unofficial reports. In the 1958 budget, the next to largest single item was for "secret activity" ($27,000,000).

Navy intelligence (Office of Naval Intelligence), which maintains naval attachés and collects information on the navies of the world, harbor installations, and the Soviet fleet. The budget and personnel of Navy's intelligence are much smaller than the Army's.

There is the Air Force's intelligence, which performs varied intelligence functions dealing with the air strength of foreign nations. One of its prime tasks is the analysis of potential targets through its Targets Directorate. The Air Force has its own counterintelligence, the Office of Special Investigations.

The State Department has its Bureau of Intelligence and Research, which receives information from embassies and consulates and is often useful for spot intelligence when an unexpected foreign crisis breaks. With a small budget and staff the State Department intelligence service seems to have a diminishing role in proportion to the growth of the CIA.

The Atomic Energy Commission has a division of intelligence which is responsible for producing intelligence on Soviet atomic tests and achievements. It receives intelligence from the other agencies and helps process it.

The Federal Bureau of Investigation, with its 6,000 agents and $100,000,000 budget (1960 fiscal year), is hard after spies and saboteurs within the United States.

All these agencies furnish intelligence and keep their files open to the CIA—with the exception of the FBI, which has with characteristic standoffishness established a system whereby the CIA may obtain specific information upon request. It is the CIA's main responsibility to use all the intelligence available from these multiple sources in the preparation of intelligence estimates.

Thus, an enlightened guess on the size and budget of the intelligence community would be: CIA, 15,000 and $1,000,000,000; NSA, 10,000 and $500,000,000; FBI, 6,000 and $100,000,000; Navy and Air Force, 2,000 and $50,000,000; G-2, 5,000 and $125,000,000; and other, 1,000 and $1,000,000. For a grand total of 39,000 and $1,776,-000,000.

The vastness of the Soviet intelligence community is even more difficult to determine. In contrast to the centralization of the American intelligence community with its all-knowing CIA reporting directly to the President, the Soviet intelligence agencies run parallel systems with a salmagundi of functions that on the surface have nothing to do with intelligence.

There are three major agencies, all operating directly under the Communist Party's Central Committee and the Council of Ministers. Of the three, only the GRU (Glavnoe Razdevyvatelnoe Upravlenie or Chief Military Intelligence Directorate of the Ministry of the Armed Forces) performs a pure intelligence function. It can be compared with G-2, since it is the Red Army intelligence and has existed as long as the Red Army itself.

The effective head of the GRU is the Minister of Defense. The GRU has a "legal" network in the presence of its enterprising attaché staffs who work like beavers to collect essential data about a country's armed forces, military installations, and prime targets. It also has a thriving "illegal" network, and many of the top spies caught since the end of World War II were GRU men. The list would include Klaus Fuchs, the Rosenberg ring, Valentin Gubitchev, Rudolf Abel (a colonel in the GRU), and Gordon Lonsdale (a major in the GRU). The notorious prewar agent Richard Sorge was also in the GRU.

GRU headquarters is a baroque palace in downtown Moscow, at 19 Znamensky Street. There an estimated staff of 5,000 work in four main divisions—operations, information, training, and auxiliary—the most important of which controls the operations of agents abroad. To these agents, the GRU is referred to only as "The Center."

In 1953, a Soviet defector, Ismail (Ege) Akhmedoff, described the operations division of the GRU as comprising eight sections: Western Europe; the Middle East; the United States and Far East; technically advanced countries (U.S., Germany, Great Britain, France, etc.); terrorism (responsible for kidnaping, sabotage, and political assassination); false passports and other documents; direction of intelligence from Red Army districts; and cipher.

Because of its role in World War II, the GRU has grown in prestige and importance. It was unaffected by the post-Beria purges and profited from the onus that fell on its sister organization and bitter rival, the KGB.

The KGB (Komissariat Gosudarstvennoi Bezopastnotsi or Commissariat of State Security) is a direct descendant of the Cheka, and has one distinct advantage over the GRU. It has its men planted in military intelligence, while the reverse is not true. Like the GRU, the KGB has an important foreign intelligence network. Besides that, however, it handles counterintelligence, border troops, communications intelligence, the Kremlin guard, wire taps and censorship, forgeries, and security investigations.

In a compound of buildings near the Kremlin, on Dzerzhinski, Kuznetsky Most and Ogareva streets, the KGB's employees work. There is none of the openness that prevails at "Foggy Bottom." This heart of Moscow where a secret world pulses is heavily policed. Loitering in the area is not recommended, and even passing through is grounds for suspicion.

The most important branch of the KGB is its foreign intelligence administration (INU), which controls networks of "legal" and "illegal" agents that operate independently from the GRU networks. The other branches are the Special Political Administration (SPU), the Economic Administration (EKU), the Counterintelligence Administration (KRU), and Counterintelligence (GUKR).

The differences between state security and military intelligence was described in *Soviet Espionage** by David Dallin:

> Rivalry and antagonism between the Army and GB are almost as old as the Soviet State itself. The GB is the agency of coercion and terror, feared by all and hated by most; the Army is the institution for the defense of the country. The activity of the GB is directed at the

* David Y. Dallin, *Soviet Espionage* (New Haven: Yale University Press, 1956).

Russian foe of the dictatorship, that of the Army against the foreign enemy. The Army, based on universal conscription, embraces all persons of military age; the personnel of the GB are selected in accordance with special requirements. The Army is the mass; the better paid GB is the privileged group. Even under its Communist leadership, the Army embraces the people; the GB is the stern whip held over the people. The Army, which is recruited mainly from the Russian peasantry, has a better understanding of mass needs than any other agency, has always resented the police apparatus, and has never felt enthusiasm for the unpopular collective farms.

Like the GRU, the KGB has its "special" terrorist section (Spetsburo), which has taken credit for the assassinations of Leon Trotsky in 1940 and Walter Krivitsky in 1941, among others.

According to defector Peter Deriabin, a former KGB official, the network in 1952 had 3,000 persons in foreign intelligence alone and 15,000 agents abroad. The essential result of the 1954 post-Beria shakeup was the administrative split of state security into two district organizations, the KGB and the MVD. The division of functions would seem haphazard and filled with duplications to an untrained observer. The MVD (Ministerstvo Vnutrennikh Del or Ministry of Internal Affairs) lost its internal and foreign intelligence functions, with the exception of a small counterintelligence section. The KGB was brought within the party's fold through the choice of two Khrushchev men (Ivan Serov and Aleksandr Shelepin) to head it.

The MVD today has a variety of duties which in the United States would be handled by half a dozen or more government bodies. It seems somehow to have been given the residue of tasks not already allotted. These duties are of the following types:

Police: It controls the police (militia) and the special internal troops and it is in charge of prisons. The control of border troops was given to the KGB in the shakeup.

Public Works: It is in charge of the nation's highways.

Immigration: It handles deportations.

Treasury: It is responsible for the safeguarding of the Soviet Union's gold reserve.

Transportation: It directs railroad construction.

Defense: It controls mobilization, antiaircraft defenses, and prisoners of war.

Last but not least, it heads the Soviet Union's fire departments.

These two vast intelligence communities (United States and Soviet) have their own built-in strengths and weaknesses. Responsible officials of the two blocs seldom have a chance to compare the merits of their respective intelligence systems. Allen Dulles recalls that he "got a good laugh" from an exchange with Khrushchev when the latter visited Washington in September, 1959.

"You, Mr. Chairman, may have seen some of my intelligence reports from time to time," Dulles said.

Khrushchev: "I believe we get the same reports, and probably from the same people."

Dulles: "Maybe we should pool our efforts."

Khrushchev: "Yes, we should buy our intelligence data together and save money. We'd have to pay the people only once."

Again in Los Angeles, Khrushchev hammered away at the CIA and said: "You're wasting your money. You might as well send it direct to us instead of middlemen because we get most of it anyway. Your agents give us the code books and then we send false information back to you through your code. Then we send cables asking for money and you send it to us." Khrushchev said he had in his desk a copy of a telegram sent by the Shah of Iran to President Eisenhower asking for assistance.

If the Soviet networks can saturate the world with thousands of agents, it is at heavy cost to their intelligence product. The officials at the Center who use these agents hold them in derision and call them *"shavki"*—homeless, hungry mongrels who go sniffing in back alleys and garbage pails. The Soviet policy is one of mass penetration. With a trained Resident to control their reports, the *shavki* are used at comparatively little cost. At best, they can obtain valuable information. At worst, they have undoubted nuisance value for counterintelligence services. The lower-echelon agents are told nothing that could incriminate the Resident or the Soviet Union. They need no special training, and their capture creates no problem. At the same time, their reports are usually misleading, full of lies and extravagances. This creates a strong sense of suspicion in the case officer at the Center, who is likely to dismiss a true report as "Western provocation" and accept a false report he knows will find approval in higher quarters.

Ismail (Ege) Akhmedoff told how the Center failed to believe a reliable Czech source who warned in 1941 that the Germans were concentrating troops along Soviet borders. Akhmedoff, then a major in the GRU, said "the source reported that in the second half of June, 1941, the Germans are going to declare war against the USSR. . . . That was one of the most important informations received by the GRU since it began . . . it was sent immediately to the members of the Politburo, including Stalin . . . that night I was shown the cablegram with the resolution of Stalin which was written and signed by Stalin in red ink, and it read: 'This information is English provocation, find out who is making this provocation and punish him.' "

In this major error in appraisal, the work of a foreign agent was botched by the Center. The feeling that the Center is inept has often been expressed by agents. Alexander Foot, an Englishman who was GRU resident in Switzerland during World War II, wrote in his diverting *Handbook for Spies*:

> The inefficiency of the Russian intelligence service was a perpetual source of amazement to me. It would seem impossible to an ordinary person that a service run on such inefficient lines could ever achieve any results. Any ordinary intelligence service would have fiddled itself into inanition long ago. That the Red Army (GRU) intelligence continues to function and to function efficiently is due, I feel, far more to the efficiency of its agents and organisers in the field and to the facilities offered by the local Communist parties than to the driving and organizing power of the Centre.

One of the major postwar blunders of Soviet intelligence was the failure to predict Tito's 1948 break with Stalin. In this instance, observers have found both agents and the Center at fault. Brigadier C. H. Dewhurst, who was the British Military Attaché in Belgrade at the time, observed:

> . . . I would blame it [failure to predict the break] on their intelligence service, which is far less expert than is commonly held—their security service is second to none, because suspicion is part of the Russian character and they are more "apt" for the work. Moreover they have not demobilized their specialist personnel, as we did after the war, for they believe the war to be still in progress. But they are not good at the acquisition of intelligence, which requires a great insight into foreign character and psychology.[*]

* Brigadier C. H. Dewhurst, *Close Contact* (London: Allen & Unwin, 1954).

Because there was a Soviet apparat working close to Tito, however, Stalin called for a probe of the intelligence failure and found that regular reports had been sent to the Central Committee of the CPSU about the forthcoming break and were ignored. Members of the Central Committee were afraid to report Tito's deviation to Stalin.

Brigadier Dewhurst's remark about the Soviet agent's lack of insight into foreign character and psychology seems less valid today. Residents such as Colonel Abel and Gordon Lonsdale played their parts well enough to avoid detection over a period of years. In the past, however, important Soviet agents have behaved with open contempt for the country they were in. Vasili Zubilin operated in the United States off and on for fifteen years, sometimes with embassy cover, sometimes without. He was a bibulous, loud-mouthed vulgarian, who bragged to counterspy Boris Morros: "I am head of the NKVD in this country and I feel as free here to do exactly as I want as anywhere in the world."

Zubilin had told Morros not to attend any functions at which other Russians might be on hand. Once, at a large party where some Russians were present, a drunken Zubilin staggered up to Morros and began to shout in Russian, "What's happened to your memory, my good Boris—didn't I tell you not to be seen with Russians at affairs like this? Do you want the whole world to know that your sympathies are with us?"

"He seized me by the lapels," Morros wrote, "and slammed me against a wall. Then he shoved a gun that he had in his pocket against my stomach . . . he was drunk and in a rage."

"You will be of no use to me, you fool, if you become known as a man who openly associates with Russians," Zubilin warned.

Elizabeth Bentley had a Soviet contact remarkably like Zubilin, who bragged: "No one can kill me, I'm indestructible." Once, when invited to dinner, he said: "I hope the food is good. Americans are such stupid people that even when it comes to as simple a matter as cooking a meal, they do very badly." This was an unusual tack to take with American Communists who had been recruited into the Soviet apparats with loving tact.

Miss Bentley reported that another constant among Soviet agents was rivalry and lack of co-operation. "They never worked as a team," she wrote. "Under the merciless discipline and inhuman competition, each agent was out for himself, trying to claw his way up the ladder. He would disparage his fellow workers and even spread vicious gossip about them."

Competition is an inevitable result of the proliferation of services, with parallel networks operating in the embassies and in the field. It is no wonder that contradictory reports filter into the KGB and GRU "Centers" and that the mass of true and false information is sifted and checked and then prepared into four kinds of intelligence reports, with different degrees of validity. According to defector Peter Deriabin, special reports are written for: all the members of the Praesidium; the seven most powerful members of the Praesidium; the three most important members of government; and the secretary of the Communist Party Central Committee.

The other side of the coin in multiple networks is duplication. The classic answer to the threat of duplication was given by a G-2 officer appearing before appropriations hearings in 1957 before the Senate. Asked if there was duplication between the CIA and Army intelligence, he replied: "There may be a minor overlapping, sir, but we feel that a lap of small proportion is better than a gap." This seems to be the Soviet attitude as well.

One sphere in which U.S. and Soviet intelligence may be contrasted is the place in society of the intelligence officer. In the Soviet Union, he is the fair-haired boy, an aristocrat of the regime with a high standard of living, special apartments, cars, luxuries, a private telephone, and tremendous prestige. KGB men have a magnificent club on Dzerzhinski Street, they can get tickets to the Bolshoi without waiting in line, they have no trouble finding servants or *dachas* in Moscow's most pleasant suburbs. A position with the KGB is much sought after, despite the fear of purges. As E. A. Andreevich wrote in *The Soviet Secret Police*:

Those who survived [the purges] . . . were lavishly rewarded and appointed to high executive posts which in ordinary times would have been far beyond their expectations. Those who had been, or were in the process of being, liquidated were replaced by a new generation of young Chekists. Coarsely and unceremoniously these young men elbowed their way up the promotion ladder, pushing aside everyone and everything that stood in their way. They did not care what means or methods they used to further their own careers. There were no moral principles, standards or bounds in this internecine struggle for promotion to higher posts in the organs of state security. Attractive posts, including the highest, had become accessible to many, but the candidates by far outnumbered the vacancies. As soon as any post became vacant in the NKVD system it was filled with dizzying speed. Success went to those who possessed the characteristics of a Chekist in the highest degree—determination, impetuousness, intransigence toward enemies, devotion to the Leader, and cruelty.

In the United States, intelligence was never the plum. Often it was considered a blind alley for the military and a storage bin for incompetents and misfits in civil service. In May, 1956, Major General Robert A. Schow, Deputy Assistant Chief of Staff for Intelligence, told a Congressional committee that his assignment to G-2 was "almost the kiss of death" as far as his own career was concerned. Only since the Dulles era has intelligence risen from the mire of neglect and opprobrium to attract the kind of brains and character the work requires.

Like an overtight corset, the centralization of the Soviet foreign intelligence often prevents it from breathing properly. The thousands of desk men in Moscow control everything down to the color of the car an agent buys and the "drops" where messages are to be concealed. After scrupulously training its resident agents in espionage techniques, the Center does its best to deprive them of initiative. This ironclad control was never more clearly shown than in the so-called Moscow letters released by the Australian Royal Commission on Espionage in late 1955. The letters comprise a day-to-day account of the operation of a "legal" network working through the Soviet Embassy in Canberra and were turned over to Australian authorities by Vladimir Petrov when he defected in 1954.

The report of the Royal Commission said that "administrative control from the Moscow Center was intensely strict and very little discretion was given to the local Resident. Instructions were required to be carried out to the letter in the manner directed and no deviation from the directions were permitted, save with the Center's approval. For example, the tasks for each worker on the Resident's staff were set not by him but by the Center, and neither the Resident nor any other member of his staff could interfere in the performance of those tasks without its specific permission."

When an agent obtained permission to buy a car, the Center snapped back a note saying:

> We request you to communicate to us in the next mail a brief description of the motorcar which has been acquired, under what cover story it has been purchased, what is the cover story for its presence in the garage of the Embassy, and what are your proposals for its further use. Point out to Pakhomov [the Tass representative and KGB agent] that he failed to observe our directions concerning maintenance of the motorcar [perhaps he did not use the kind of oil prescribed by the Center]. We authorize Pakhomov to use the car for operational purposes only in Canberra. He must not travel in this car to Sydney.

No detail was too slight for the Center to overlook. The Residents were not even allowed to pick their hiding places for documents. A critical note from the Center said:

> The secret hiding places for documents selected by you have a number of defects. They are all located in one and the same area, which facilitates their detection by the counterintelligence, even if you move from one secret hiding place to another.
>
> The description of the secret hiding places for documents was not accompanied by sketches which would give a clear idea of the advantages and defects of the selected places, and of their exact location.
>
> In our opinion, a crack between the boards supporting the railroad bridge embankment cannot be used as a secret hiding place for documents, because the railway bridge is probably regularly inspected by the appropriate persons, and in exceptional circumstances might be guarded.

The Center enclosed a long covering note describing what sort of secret hiding places should be sought and detailing the defects and advantages of secret messages. The Center roundly reprimanded poor espionage work. It wrote:

> The reports sent by you concerning meetings with agents and with persons who are of interest to us are basically deficient in their formulation. The reports are compiled negligently, they are badly related to the code book, and are not photographed. All this is an infringement of the elemental rules of secrecy. We request you to

take note of these observations, and, in future, to send reports in negatives together with the letter, as enclosures to the corresponding paragraphs.

The Center also kept close tabs on new agents, some of whom had no previous intelligence training. A note concerning Nicolai Kovaliev, a KGB man posted to Canberra under the cover of Commercial Attaché, said:

> In view of the fact that Kovaliev has no experience of intelligence work, it is essential that you should hold discussions with him for the purpose of teaching him ways and means of conducting intelligence work and that you should render him timely assistance in the purposeful study of the acquired contacts.
>
> In three months' time after the arrival of Kovaliev in the country we request you to send us information as to how he is engaging in our work.
>
> For establishing contact with him the following pattern has been agreed:
>
> Our worker turns to him: "Regards to you from Moscow from Vladimir Pavlovich."
>
> Kovaliev's reply: "What progress in studies?"
>
> Our worker replies: "Good," and names his code name.

This almost maniacal centralization is generally absent from CIA procedures. The CIA, however, does not delegate powers very far, and any big case is certain to be handled from Washington. When KGB captain Nikolai Khokhlov defected to West Berlin in 1954, the CIA immediately dispatched several top Washington men to oversee the defection. In 1953, Allen Dulles flew to the Swiss Alps, ostensibly on a vacation but actually to supervise the coup that was to overthrow Premier Mossadegh of Iran. Richard Bissell, deputy director of the CIA, was in charge of the Cuban operation. On important operations, there is a direct chain of command from the agent in the field to one of the directors of the agency.

The Moscow letters also provided a close look at the Soviet intelligence product. The Center was eager for reports on Australians who might prove friendly to the cause of the Soviet Union. The reports were to be as complete as possible, indicating the subject's background, interests, affiliations, and personal quirks and weaknesses.

Agents did so well to satisfy the Center that the general tone of the reports was "a farrago of fact, falsity, and filth," according to a counsel for the Royal Commission.

Some of the reports in the hands of the Royal Commission were so scandalous they were never made public. One such document was a series of short reports on forty-five Canberra journalists, prepared by Fergan O'Sullivan (code name "Zemliak") in 1951, when he was working for the Sydney *Morning Herald*.

Details included, according to the Commission:

> The subject's religion—whether it was Roman Catholic or Protestant; whether he was radical or conservative, left-wing labor or right-wing labor; whether he drank or was talkative; his financial position, his marital status and the number of his children; and of one it was said that he was "promiscuous." . . . Of a certain person O'Sullivan wrote: "Fierce Catholic, probably Catholic Actionist, also probably helps Security." Of another he wrote: "Believed to be a security agent."

From O'Sullivan's raw report, the "legal" network delivered its own version to the Center. The man O'Sullivan described as a possible security agent came out in the report to the Center as "reactionary, insolent and debauched. He has intimate relations with ——. [He] is a collaborator of the counterintelligence, and, possibly, the leader of a group of counterintelligence people in the press. He sometimes experiences financial difficulties."

Another report, thirty-seven pages long, was given to the Soviet Embassy in May, 1953, by Rupert Lockwood (code name "Voron"), a journalist and admitted Communist. The Commission said that "amongst many other matters, the document contains personality reports on a great number of persons—politicians of every color, newspaper proprietors and journalists, businessmen, etc. Many of the reports are scurrilous and grossly defamatory (some of the allegations are of a filthy nature), in some cases pointlessly so, since they refer to persons long dead."

Intelligence services acknowledge that raw reports are untrustworthy and often defamatory. The FBI reports found in Judy Coplon's purse the night of her arrest were no more elevated in tone than those sent to the Moscow Center. Indeed, they might almost be interchanged.

Soviet intelligence has been building up its "farrago of fact, falsity and filth" for more than forty years and is said to have the bulkiest and most complete name file in the world. Files were gathered from Communist parties in more than fifty countries, from the web of agents working parallel to the parties, and from recent acquisitions such as the Abwehr files captured by the Soviets in 1945. To compete with this occult fund of knowledge, the CIA has concentrated on modern filing and indexing techniques. In 1960, the Senate Committee on Government Operations praised CIA files as "the most comprehensive information system now in operation."

The system includes more than 40,000,000 punch cards, and machine translation computers that can translate Russian texts into English at 30,000 words an hour. The new translation machines CIA specialists are working on will be able, they claim, to translate *Gone With the Wind* into Russian in five minutes.

Like its Soviet counterpart, the CIA's intelligence product is a mixed bag. General Bedell Smith explained, when he was director of the CIA, the checks and controls that are in place to prevent false information from influencing policy. "There are two sorts of evaluation of intelligence," he said. "First is the evaluation of the source and the authenticity of information. That is done by people who secure it, and I don't know myself what the sources of information are, and it is done on a code basis. But let us take, for instance, what I am now saying to you, if I am speaking about the CIA and using a hypothetical code, it would be evaluated let us say as X-100. That means it was said by a responsible official who was in charge, that it was not a document. Beyond that only the source and the person who receives it and who deals with the source knows who the individual is and what type he is.

"There is another form of evaluation which means in fact the assessment of all information which flows into government and the boiling of it down into estimates of what may be the most probable intentions or the capabilities of our enemies. That is done by a committee which consists of the heads of all of the intelligence services of the Government acting under my chairmanship."

Allen Dulles once said he would like to write a book on history's outstanding intelligence successes and failures. "One might start with the Trojan Horse in 1200 B.C., when no one would listen to Cassandra, and with the fatal campaign of the Athenians against Syracuse," he proposed. "Coming down to more modern times, one could debate the consequences of the miscalculations of the Kaiser in 1914, and of Hitler in World War II, and not overlook our own Pearl Harbor.

"Then there are the spectacular successes, like those of the highly competent spies of Joshua, who found shelter in Jericho with Rahah the harlot, and the much more recent feat of British intelligence in deciphering the Zimmermann telegram in 1917, and the American intelligence prelude to the great victory in the Battle of Midway."

The last chapter of this hypothetical book could chronicle the successes and failures of Dulles' own organization. A feat to match the deciphering of the Zimmermann telegram was the publication of Khrushchev's secret speech at the 20th Communist Party Congress in Moscow in 1956. The Congress was held from February 14 to 25. The speech, smuggled out of Poland by a CIA agent, was published by the State Department on June 4. Publication of the speech, according to Dr. Gunther Nollau, "was followed by a wave of discussion unparalleled in the history of Bolshevism during the previous thirty years."

The speech was a denunciation of Stalin and included typical examples of Khrushchev humor, such as: "In those days, I often used to have conversations with Bulganin. One day we were driving together in a car, he said: 'It sometimes happens that a man goes to visit Stalin as his friend and at his invitation. And when he is sitting together with Stalin, he does not know where he will go when he leaves—home or in gaol.' "

Khrushchev was furious at the leak. Not long after, when the publisher of *The New York Times* asked him whether the State Department text was authentic, he replied angrily, "I don't know what you mean by the text of my speech. There was one text which was apparently concocted by the American intelligence service. This publishing firm, led by Allen Dulles, enjoys no very high reputation with us. I am not interested in what it publishes."

But even Khrushchev indicated that the text was accurate when he said at the 1959 Writer's Congress "Did anyone force us to make our statement at the 20th Party Congress on the cult of the personality and its consequences?"

Other CIA coups reportedly include: forecasts of the Anglo-French excursion to Suez in 1956, although John Foster Dulles piously pretended the United States knew nothing of the plans; a semi-accurate appraisal of unrest in Hungary and Poland in 1956 (the CIA believed uprisings would come first in Poland); information well in advance of events about the May, 1958, coup in Algiers that brought General de Gaulle back to power; information about Soviet orbital flight launchings, with the possible exception of Sputnik I.

The CIA also delights in telling anecdotes about Soviet leaders. Two that circulated in 1959 were:

That Khrushchev lobbied in the Nobel Prize Committee to have the Peace Prize awarded to him for his untiring and earnest efforts toward world disarmament.

That when Khrushchev visited the United States exhibit in Moscow in 1959, he inspected an American kitchen and said airily, "We have all these things in the Soviet Union, only our styles are more attractive." He then pointed to a gadget, a can opener common to nearly all American kitchens, and asked, "By the way, what's that?"

In 1957, in a speech at San Francisco, Dulles predicted that Marshal Georgi Zhukov's star was on the rise. Dulles saw the Soviet Minister of Defense instrumental in the formation of a military dictatorship and the ouster of Khrushchev. The speech was delivered September 20. On October 26, Moscow announced that Zhukov had been "relieved" as Defense Minister. Many other successes and failures of the CIA remain shrouded in secrecy. It does not seem, however, that the CIA's record of misses is much worse than in the Soviet services. And the day when an infallible intelligence service is created will be the day, to borrow one of Khrushchev's pithy sayings, when "the shrimp learns to whistle."

Another problem common to intelligence services on both sides of the Iron Curtain is security. Security begins with recruitment. The KGB, like the Knights of Malta, insists on three untainted generations. The purges attest to the obsessive security once a recruit has passed the admission tests. One Soviet defector noted that caution was so inbred that KGB men would look up their fiancées and lady friends in the files to make sure there was nothing on them. These stringent precautions, however, do not prevent Soviet intelligence officers from defecting. Rather, the purges encourage defection, and the westward flow of Soviet spies bearing precious information is perhaps the gravest problem of their secret service today.

The CIA boasts that it has never had a defection. Generally, the filtering at the recruiting level is effective. In 1952, General Walter Bedell Smith testified before a Congressional committee that "of the applications which we receive, eighty per cent are screened out by our personnel people. Let us take the arbitrary figure of one thousand. Of every thousand applications, eighty per cent or a little more are eliminated by our personnel people. The remaining twenty per cent are turned over to our security agencies for investigation, our own and the FBI's.

"Of the remaining twenty per cent, eleven per cent are eliminated as a result of security investigations. That does not mean the individuals themselves are suspects. It does mean that security considerations of one kind or another are considered and they include a very wide spectrum, from those individuals who may have relatives behind the Iron Curtain and who are susceptible to pressure to those individuals who may drink a little bit or talk a little bit.

"Eleven per cent are screened out, and of that eleven per cent, four per cent are screened out for really genuine security reasons; that is, people who have contacts which we consider render them undesirable for a sensitive service. You can see what the residue is. Those are the people we employ."

This proportion of refusals holds true today, and the only change since General Bedell Smith testified is that the FBI no longer has anything to do with CIA investigations. Yet even though only 90 out of 1,000 applicants are admitted to the CIA's house of secrets, there are from time to time incidents reported in the press that show all is not right among the chosen few. CIA men in Washington are sometimes picked up for petty thefts or morals charges. They plead mental stress and are usually released. In one such recent case, a CIA analyst was caught after he had stolen a butcher knife from an elderly lady. In another case, a veteran analyst just back from a two-year tour of duty in Frankfurt am Main in West Germany sealed a suicide pact with his wife. The analyst, James A. Woodbury, jumped into the Potomac River at Great Falls, Virginia, with his wife Dorothy. She was swept into an eddy and foundered on a rocky ledge, while he was caught in a whirlpool. Both drowned. Witnesses said they saw the couple jump hand in hand into the rapids. In a note left in his Arlington apartment, the thirty-two-year-old agent said the pressure of his work was too great and the CIA would not release him from unwanted duty. The CIA said it realized Woodbury was under mental strain and had planned to put him in a mental hospital.

The closest case to defection was probably the bizarre suicide of Nick Clark Wallen. Wallen lived in an apartment in Arlington Towers, a fashionable residential hotel in Arlington, Virginia, with his English-born wife. She was a working girl and left as usual for her job on the morning of April 25, 1956. She called her husband at home at 1 P.M. and he seemed in good spirits. When she came home at 5 that evening, she found the chain on the inside of the front door locked. She called the maintenance man to cut it open and found her husband dead in the kitchen. Wallen had killed himself by so elaborate a system that police reasoned it must have taken him at least an hour to rig it. He had cut the tip from the middle finger of a rubber kitchen glove and taped the open finger to the main gas jet of the kitchen stove. He then taped the wrist opening of the glove to the nozzle of a vacuum-cleaner hose. He placed the other end of the hose down the neck opening of a cloth and plastic bag and taped the tops closed. He unzipped the side of the garment bag and slipped it over his head. He zipped the bag up again and stuck the ends into his belt as though he were tucking in his shirt. He turned on the gas jet and sat down in a kitchen chair, where his wife found him. On the telephone table in the hall, Wallen had left a neatly written note, declaring his love for his wife, his lack of success in life, and the existence of a conspiracy against him.

Wallen had been hired by the CIA in January, 1955, as a research specialist. He showed signs of instability and was "released" in December of the same year. The CIA does its own housecleaning. As a security measure, a CIA surveillance was kept on Wallen. He was observed holding meetings with a military attaché from the Soviet Embassy, Lieutenant Colonel Anatoli A. Popov. Wallen was bitter about being fired, and tentatively agreed to work for the Russians. Popov suggested he find work in the Defense Department. As a result of the investigation that followed the suicide, Popov left the United States.

In the world of Soviet intelligence, murder is more common than suicide. The mystery that usualy surrounds the demise of an intelligence chief is symptomatic of a regime where political crises can only be solved through intrigue and conspiracy. The power struggle that followed Stalin's death in March, 1953, and led to the arrest and execution of Secret Police Chief Lavrenti Beria has never been fully explained. All existing accounts, however, plunge us back twenty centuries to the sanguinary days of imperial Rome where murder plots were customary instruments of political succession. Confronted with the stories of Beria's downfall, we ask: Are we talking about a modern state, one of the world's great powers? Are we talking about chiefs of state in a twentieth-century government?

Several versions of Beria's death have circulated in the West and continue to circulate eight years after the event. The official version released by the Soviet Government was that Beria was ousted from the Praesidium in June after trying to seize power. His arrest and those of five other high-ranking State Security officers were announced July 10. He was tried in a six-day closed trial and his death sentence was announced Christmas Eve 1953 and carried out immediately. The official account left many questions unanswered and rumors soon began to spread. The most tenacious rumor was that Beria had been shot and killed after a stormy Praesidium session with the help of high-ranking Army officers.

In 1956, Khrushchev lent credence to another version during the visit to Moscow of a delegation of French Socialist Party leaders. Pointing to Trade Minister Mikoyan, he told the delegates half-jokingly: "You are sitting next to the man who killed Beria." He then explained that Beria had admitted his anti-State plot at a tense four-hour meeting of the Praesidium. As Beria left the meeting hall and walked down an adjoining circular corridor, Mikoyan came up from behind and shot him in the back.

This was not to be Khrushchev's last word on the subject. At the 22nd Party Congress in October, 1961, he gave what was apparently intended to be a definitive version of Beria's death in a secret speech to the 1,000 Soviet and foreign delegates. The substance of the speech, which was leaked to Western journalists in Warsaw in mid-November, sounds like a showdown between two rival gangs. Dramatic high points feature Beria and Khrushchev grappling over an automatic pistol and Beria being gunned down (or arrested at gunpoint; the Warsaw informants here seem to have been of two minds) by a Soviet general.

Accounts of the secret speech quote Khrushchev as saying that Beria had used the NKVD troops under his command to surround the Kremlin and have the Praesidium members hostile to his bid for power constantly watched. They were searched each time they entered the Kremlin. At the same time, Beria was placing his men in key Party and Government posts. The plot to liquidate Beria was initiated by Khrushchev with the support of Molotov, Malenkov, and Bulganin. The scene for the showdown was a special meeting of the eleven Praesidium members called to discuss military matters. The reason for the meeting justified the presence in the Kremlin of three Army generals loyal to the anti-Beria group: Georgi Zhukov, World War II hero who had been forced into obscurity by Stalin; Rodon Malinovsky, who was later to become Minister of Defense; and Kirill Moskalenko, the "hatchet man" of the plot, who was rewarded for his decisive role with the rank of Marshal in 1956 and with the post of Deputy Defense Minister in charge of Soviet rocket forces in 1960.

Zhukov and Malinovsky were admitted to the conference room when the evening meeting started. Moskalenko, who had smuggled a submachine gun past Beria guards, was in an adjoining room with about six men. He was to act when summoned by a buzzer under Malenkov's foot. When Beria arrived at the meeting, Khrushchev questioned his right to be there. He charged that Beria had never been admitted as a Communist Party member.

This charge was patently false, as Beria had been named secretary of the Caucasian Communist Party in 1939 and had been a Politburo member since 1946. As Beria protested, Khrushchev assailed him with another extravagant charge—that in 1934 he had been accused of having been a British agent in 1918. Beria replied that he had been vindicated of this charge by Stalin himself. Realizing that the Praesidium meeting had been called to trap him, Beria reached into his attaché case and pulled out an automatic. Khrushchev said he lunged at Beria and wrestled with him for the weapon. Malenkov pushed the buzzer. Moskalenko burst into the room and (here is where accounts differ) either cut down Beria with a submachine-gun burst or arrested him at gunpoint for subsequent execution.

Perhaps this account could be discounted as too fantastic to be true were it not for the fact that a month after the Warsaw leak a prominent Polish journalist committed suicide two days after his arrest in connection with the leak. The journalist, Henryk Holland, was a former editor of the Polish Press Agency and was well known for his liberal views and his opposition to the Gomulka regime. Soviet demands that the leak be investigated were an indirect admission that the secret speech was genuine. The investigation led to Holland's arrest. On December 21, the forty-one-year-old journalist accompanied Polish security police as they searched his fifth-floor apartment. As the security police busied themselves opening closets and drawers, Holland jumped out a window to his death.

Whatever the exact circumstances that surrounded Beria's liquidation, it marked the start of a troubled era in Soviet intelligence.

Inside Russia, the cadres were replaced and state security was placed under tight Party control. Outside Russia, the defection of the Petrovs, Yuri Rastorov, Peter Deriabin, and others weakened the Soviet net of apparats. Many other legal and illegal agents who did not defect were recalled. The arrests of Colonel Abel in New York and George Blake and Gordon Lonsdale in London showed that vigilant counterintelligence could thwart the Soviet apparats. Increased surveillance of local Communist parties led the Center to sever its connections with these traditional allies. Former agents linked with Communism have been discarded. The use of International Communism for espionage, which was so common in the United States in the thirties, now proves too dangerous to be worth while. The old-style agents were recruited out of Communist Party ranks and went underground, like Elizabeth Bentley. The new-style agent has no overt Communist ties and is recruited by more subtle channels, like Judy Coplon. It used to be that senior members of Communist parties served as "spotters" for new espionage talent, but this is no longer the case, particularly in the United States. Some of the favorite themes for Soviet recruitment are no longer valid.

The "Help the Russians" slogan so potent during World War II and the second front is meaningless today. So is the theme that "facism is the greatest enemy and must be fought at all costs." A review of the reasons given by atom spies for giving information to Russia seems completely outdated:

Klaus Fuchs: "I had complete confidence in Russian policy and I believed the Western Allies deliberately allowed Germany and Russia to fight each other to the death."

Harry Gold: "I felt that as an ally I was helping the Soviet Union obtain certain information that I thought it was entitled to."

David Greenglass: "I felt it was gross negligence on the part of the United States not to give Russia the information about the atom bomb, because she was an ally."

Julius Rosenberg: "I wanted to do the work I felt I was slated for and I wanted to do something to directly help Russia."

Abraham Brothman: "The Soviet Union is the only country conducting a real fight against fascism."

Another atomic scientist, Alan Nunn May, gave a motive that is still being used: "I only embarked on it [espionage]," he said, "because I felt this was a contribution I could make to the safety of mankind." The idea that science has no national boundaries and that progress should be made available to everyone still seduces. One example of a scientist who saw through the blandishments was J. Robert Oppenheimer. In 1943, Peter Ivanov, vice-consul of the Soviet consulate in San Francisco, contacted Charles Eltenton and asked him for help in obtaining atom bomb information. Eltenton got to Oppenheimer through Haakon Chevalier. But, as Chevalier recounted, when Oppenheimer was approached, "he made some strong remark to the effect that this sounds terribly wrong to me." Oppenheimer later advised security people that "Eltenton bears watching," and after some vacillation also implicated his friend Chevalier.

Thus, today, the Russians find they can no longer count on Communist parties for espionage, nor do they find so many willing idealists to help them. The Cold War is not World War II, and Berlin is not Stalingrad. Today the non-Communists who do not have pangs about "helping Russia" are few. Still, Soviet intelligence continues to use non-Russians in espionage work, such as the Englishman George Blake, whose sudden conversion to Communism baffled the Foreign Office. The CIA, in like fashion, uses non-Americans, and claims that only non-American agents penetrate the Soviet Union. The agent is still a commodity to be bought and sold, and the trading is brisk. Soviet intelligence has in many key spots installed residents who are superbly trained in the customs and language of the country. In some cases they are "sleepers" who will wait for an emergency to begin their operational work. Others are already at work rebuilding apparats shattered by counterintelligence or going about the day-to-day task of recruitment and information-gathering. Crude hooligans like Zubilin have been replaced. Controlled from Washington and Moscow with limitless funds of dollars and rubles and an armlock on foreign policy, the vast networks are in place and cover the world. Their methods range from reading the morning newspaper to assassinations and *coups d'état*.

VI. NSA: The CIA's Silent Partner

THE National Security Agency has been far more successful than its fellow "silent service" in keeping out of the limelight. Its functions are as obscure as those of the CIA have become notorious. It is described laconically by the Defense Department as "a facility concerned with specialized research and training activities."

Yet the NSA matches the CIA in size and importance. It reportedly has more than 10,000 employees working in a vast three-story steel and concrete building second in size only to the Pentagon. The building in Fort George Meade, Maryland, is larger than the CIA's new headquarters (1,400,000 against 1,135,000 square feet). Like the CIA building, it is a monument to planned intelligence, and authorized visitors to the U-shaped structure are shown these marvels of modern intelligence-gathering: the longest unobstructed corridor in the United States (980 feet long and 560 wide); a double barbed-wire fence ten feet high, with four gatehouses manned by guards armed with machine guns; a basement full of electronic computers (reportedly including the new Whirlwind computer built in co-operation with IBM and Remington Rand, and said to be able to break any code); conveyer belts that run through the basement and carry documents on trays to substations at the rate of 100 feet a minute; pneumatic tubes for interoffice transmission of documents; more electric wiring than any other building in the world; wastebaskets with paper linings specially marked for each office—these are stapled at the end of the day and stored for a given period to make sure nothing has been mistakenly discarded.

The NSA also is said to have 8,000 armed forces personnel working for it abroad to man radio intercept and radar stations. This gives it a total of close to 20,000 persons under its command, which matches the CIA personnel figure. Its budget, according to reliable sources, approaches the half-billion-dollar mark, with about $380,000,000 earmarked for the maintenance of its foreign network and another $100,000,000 for the home base. This great lump of money is concealed in the Defense Department budget and must tax the imagination of those responsible for planting it among other items.

Such gigantic means should have a commensurate aim. The NSA is engaged in "communications intelligence." This innocuous term means in everyday language that:

1. It breaks the codes of every foreign government that has a code worth breaking.

2. It designs the United States codes and changes them as it learns they are broken by other powers.

3. With more than 2,000 radio intercept stations spotted around the world (some located in ships or planes), it monitors communications in foreign countries.

4. It locates the radar defenses of Iron Curtain countries.

A source familiar with NSA methods explained that it "records every Communist electronic emission and scrap of communications traffic that it's possible to commit to tape. It's a fantastic task that staggers the imagination. Much of the monitoring is of voice traffic in the clear, but most of it of course is coded and the tapes are used to break Communist codes. We rely on intercepts between Soviet military, naval, and air headquarters and units for early warning of any Communist build-up for surprise attack."

The primary aim of this prodigious eavesdropping mission is, according to a former NSA employee, "to be able to pinpoint the location of every military regiment in the world, on both sides of the Iron Curtain. The NSA claims to have this information at its finger tips—it says it can give the location of military units in every army in the world, because these armies have to communicate, and their coded messages are monitored by NSA computers."

Thanks to NSA monitors, it could be ascertained that U-2 pilot Francis Gary Powers lost altitude because of engine trouble and dropped to 36,000 feet before he was fired upon by Soviet antiaircraft crews—the monitors taped the voices of the gun crews reporting the plane's maneuvers.

Thanks to NSA tracking stations, the United States learned in the Korean war that Soviet pilots were flying with the North Korean Air Force—the tracking stations recorded the pilots speaking in Russian on the plane radios.

Thanks to NSA intercepts, the West learned of unannounced Soviet failures in missile launchings—the NSA had tapes of the Red countdowns.

These NSA successes come out inadvertently, never through the agency, which is so publicity-shy it makes the CIA look like an advertising agency. Allen Dulles, partly through campaigns in the Communist press but also partly through his own subtle form of public relations, became the incarnation of the master spy. But who outside the intelligence community has ever heard of Admiral Laurence H. Frost, present head of NSA (intelligence chiefs of the three armed services are rotated in this sensitive position). The chiefs of NSA never speak to the press, either on or off the record.

The NSA was born with the CIA through the National Security Act of 1947. The Act consolidated the cipher agencies of the armed services, the most important of which was the Army Security Agency. It was first housed in Arlington Hall, a former girl's school in Virginia, and was moved to Fort Meade after Congress approved a $30,000,000 appropriation for its new building.

That it has been less successful in keeping some of its own secrets than in collecting those of others is not its fault. The law of human probability is one that makes scientists at NSA shudder. With manpower in the tens of thousands, no security filter is fine enough to bar an occasional misfit. On two occasions, NSA has come into public notoriety through the misbehavior of its employees. The most recent and most important example was the August, 1960, defection of two junior mathematicians, William Martin and Bernon Mitchell. Their case is dealt with in another chapter, but it should be pointed out that they were not stingy with details about their former employer.

In a Moscow press conference, Martin and Mitchell gave the Russians information which NSA had successfully concealed from the American public and most American officials for thirteen years.

It was learned for the first time (and never denied) that NSA headquarters is divided into four main offices.

1. PROD (office of production) receives intercept material from the outstations, performs cryptanalysis and traffic analysis, and analyzes information. PROD subdivisions are ADVA, which studies advanced Soviet cipher systems and diplomatic codes; GENS, which studies Soviet code systems and medium level systems; ACOM, which looks into the codes and ciphers of Asian Communist nations; ALLO, which keeps tabs on the codes of allies, neutrals, and some Communist nations; and MPRO, which provides electronic digital computing and data processing services to other divisions.

2. R/D (research and development), with the following subdivisions: REMP, which conducts cryptanalytical research and works on applied cryptanalytic problems without restrictions as to country, provides consultation to other divisions, and researches computer componentry; RADE, which designs radio receivers and transmitters, radio direction finders, fingerprint apparatus, and studies unknown communications systems; STED, which studies possible weakness of cipher machines in general and theoretical problems such as that of enciphering speech.

3. COMSEC, which is responsible for the production and security of the U.S. cipher system.

4. SEC, the personnel department, which investigates applications and conducts lie-detector tests on loyalty and integrity.

NSA is one of the most assiduous users of the lie detector, but Martin and Mitchell are unpleasant proofs that it can be beaten. There has been criticism of the lie detector on two levels: First, that it is ineffective (J. Edgar Hoover once said, "I personally would not want to accept solely what the operator of a lie detector says the instrument shows in proving that a man was or was not a sex deviate"); second, that it is offensive—recruits are told that the test is optional, but that without it their security clearance will take much longer. Operators are often rough-and-ready ex-policemen rather than specialists. The test itself is unsettling. The examiner wraps a blood-pressure gadget around the subject's arm, hooks a pneumograph around his chest, attaches an electrode to his hand, and the pens begin tracing their jagged lines on graph paper. Questions are embarrassingly personal.

Since the Martin and Mitchell defection, the agency is relying more heavily on psychiatric interviews and has reportedly weeded out eight other suspected homosexuals in intensive post-defection security checks.

The investigation of the defections by Congressional committees led to the resignation on November 10, 1961, of Maurice H. Klein, personnel director of NSA. Klein resigned under pressure after it was found that he had falsified his own job application when he joined NSA in 1949. He forfeited his pension rights and is under threat of perjury indictment for tampering with Federal documents. Klein's alterations in his job application seem harmless enough on the surface: He said he was a graduate of Harvard Law School while in fact he obtained his law degree at the New Jersey College of Law; he said his mother had been born in the United States, whereas she was born in Russia; and he gave his name as Maurice Harold Klein, while it was listed in other records as Morriss Harry Klein. These minor irregularities became important because they had been committed by a man with one of the most sensitive jobs in the nation's most sensitive government agency, and also the man who ultimately was responsible for hiring Martin and Mitchell. Klein's demise came as the result of his testimony in a closed session before the House Un-American Activities Committee, which was investigating security gaps at NSA. At the time, committee investigators hinted that there had been grave security breaches and that heads would roll. Klein's resignation seems to have climaxed a shake-up in which at least a dozen employees found to be poor security risks were involved.

Martin and Mitchell made no secret of the fact that the NSA had been eminently successful in spying on the allies of the United States and "reading the codes of forty nations." This success, they said, is due partly to the skillfulness of cryptanalysts and also to the fact that the United States provides other nations with machines of which they know the construction and wiring; also because it subverts code clerks in friendly embassies.

Of all intelligence work, ciphering and deciphering is acknowledged to be the most difficult. A high percentage of NSA employees resign because of strain and overwork. Despite the emphasis on electronic computers, there are vestiges of the kind of nervous disorders described by Herbert O. Yardley, who headed the "American Black Chamber," a State Department code agency that flourished briefly after World War I.

Yardley wrote that he had to let go two women cryptographers because "one dreamed constantly that a bulldog was loose in her room. For hours she chased it under and over the bed, behind the chair, under the dresser, and finally when she caught it, she found written on its side the word CODE. The other girl dreamed each night of walking along a lonely beach, weighed down by an enormous sack of pebbles. She struggled along for miles with this heavy burden on her back, searching for pebbles that matched those in her bag. When she found one that exactly matched she would take the duplicate from the bag and cast it into the sea. This was her only method of lightening the burden that weighed so heavily on her shoulders."

The other occasion when NSA, to its horror, found itself in the headlines was the arrest and trial of one of its cryptographers in 1954. Joseph Sydney Petersen was charged with stealing classified documents from the NSA and transmitting some of them to another power. The other power was the Netherlands and what Petersen had done in effect was to give the Dutch back their code, which the NSA had cracked. The prosecution impressed upon Petersen how sticky it would be if the case went to trial, and NSA was forced to unveil itself publicly in a courtroom. A guilty plea, on the other hand, would be almost sure to lead to a suspended sentence. Petersen pleaded guilty but was sentenced to seven years.

Some information on NSA came out in the pre-trial hearings through the testimony of Dr. Lawrence W. Shirm, deputy director, who described the tight security of his establishment:

> The buildings are surrounded by double barbed-wire fences which are patrolled night and day. The interiors of the building are, for the large part, patrolled night and day. Individuals who are cleared to work in the agency undergo a very thorough check. Their backgrounds are thoroughly explored. Classified documents which are within the confines of the agency must be kept under safe storage

even while within the building and within the double barbed-wire fences. There are roughly three types of areas. In one area no classified material may be held at any time, or at least overnight, unless it is under three-tumbler-lock storage. These areas are also patrolled.

In certain large areas where there are insufficient three-tumbler-lock storage facilities, arrangements are made whereby documents may be left in ordinary file cabinets or unlocked file cabinets, or in some instances desks, but these areas themselves are locked and under armed guard at all times, when they are not occupied by working personnel.

Certain designated personnel, who have cause to take classified documents from the agency for the purpose of transmitting them to another agency, or to a meeting at which they will be employed, are provided with property passes and are permitted to become custodians for these documents for the periods in question. They, for example, if they travel in their private car, must travel in pairs. They are not allowed to travel singly if they are conveying classified documents.

The documents are normally transmitted in a locked brief case of the type which I have here today, and at the end of the meeting they must be placed in safe storage either in another agency or returned to the parent agency and there secured for the night. They may not be taken home by the person.

As for security consciousness among employees, "there is their entrance indoctrination in which they have special training in security. There are periodic rebriefings by security division personnel, and there is, in addition, a requirement to sign periodically a statement that you have reread the pertinent part of the regulation."

Despite this plethora of precautions, security officers learned that no quantity of "three-tumbler locks" could control a man's mind. The case of Joseph Sydney Petersen, a spy who was not a spy, is an example of the complex and fragile human equation caught in the unyielding rigor of security requirements.

Petersen is a tall, sallow-faced man, mild and myopic. He was born in New Orleans in 1914 and went to school at Loyola University and then at St. Louis University, where he obtained his Master of Science degree. He taught for a time at Loyola and was then appointed physics teacher at Riceland College in New Orleans. His health was poor—

he had a perforated eardrum and suffered tuberculosis in 1938—so he took the teaching job that was nearest his home.

In 1940, he received a circumspect letter from a Colonel Aiken, who was in charge of Signal Corps intelligence for the Army. The letter offered him a free correspondence course in cryptanalysis with a possible job in the offing. The correspondence course began coming in and Petersen noted with surprise that the lessons were classified. After a year of studiously solving the problems that came weekly in the mail, he was offered a job in May, 1941, and started work in July for the Army's cipher agency, which was under the command of the Signal Corps.

During the war years, Petersen made friends with Colonel J. A. Verkuyl, who was stationed in Washington as liaison officer between Dutch and American armies. The two men worked closely on technical aspects of cipher work. After the war, Colonel Verkuyl went home, but Petersen kept in touch with other Dutch friends. He joined NSA when it was created in 1947 and was assigned to the training program. Senator Eugene McCarthy, who worked with him in those early years, testified that "his reputation was very good. He was, I think, considered one of the top or very nearly the top people working in the agency."

Another colleague testified that "Mr. Petersen has carried on, often under difficult and trying circumstances, a task that really needed doing and has acquitted himself extremely well. He has done an excellent job. He is an excellent technician and an outstanding instructor."

Petersen was one of the founders of the training program. He compiled and conducted classes and, at the time of his arrest, had twenty-two hours a week of lectures, aside from his regular cipher work.

Petersen himself said that "the work was very soul-trying at times." His only diversion seemed to be amateur theatricals. He was an active member of the theatrical guild at Arlington Hall. But his consuming interest was the agency, its operation and development.

In 1948, Petersen did a curious thing. He took a Chinese commercial code used in courses at NSA from his office to his Arlington apartment. He wrapped the code in a newspaper and spirited it past security guards. The code, which reduces 10,000 Chinese characters to sets of four digit numbers, was available commercially at a cost of $15. Questioned later, Petersen said he used the code at home to devise problems for his courses. At other times he brought home other NSA classified documents. One included material on a cryptograph machine called the Hagelin, which has been in use since 1939 and which can be bought from a Swedish manufacturer as war surplus. Another was an analysis of NSA monitoring of Communist transmissions during the Korean war. This document was dated February 20, 1951, and was called "Routing of North Korean Security Traffic."

Also, between 1948 and 1952, Petersen held meetings with Giacomo Stuydt, communications officer at the Dutch Embassy, and provided him with information. He told Stuydt that NSA had cracked the Dutch diplomatic code and was monitoring communications between the Embassy and the Dutch foreign office.

There was no money exchanged. Petersen acted out of friendship with his Dutch friends. About this time Petersen showed what is sometimes considered a sure sign of mental strain—he began to write letters to the editor. On August 29, 1950, the Washington *Post* published one of his letters which said that "today our government agencies are accused of everything short of treason by irresponsible persons. The faith of the American people in the Government is being undermined by vilifiers seeking self-aggrandizement. In order to restore this waning faith of the people, agencies are forced to sacrifice all upon whom the breath of suspicion falls."

Perhaps it was this letter that led to a security check-up on Petersen. Perhaps it was the discovery that classified material to which he had access was missing. Perhaps it was his mysterious absences at the office which led his superior to give him a "satisfactory" rather than an "outstanding" rating.

Whatever the reason, on September 28, 1954, Petersen was called from his classroom in the NSA building and turned over to two FBI men. They questioned him in a friendly and general way. The following Saturday, the men came to his Arlington apartment. He was in the living room and his wife was dressing in the bedroom. "They pushed me into a chair, searched me to see if I had any gun on me, took me out and handcuffed me," he said. They allowed him to knock on his bedroom door and tell his wife: "I'm going out with these men for a little while."

"Overnight?" she asked.

"Most likely," he said. "You'd better get my toilet articles for me."
Petersen was taken to the Alexandria courthouse and locked up.

"Before that," he said, "I had co-operated with the agents, answered all their questions. I had no idea whatsoever of what they were after." He had co-operated to the extent of signing a waiver so that they did not need a search warrant to go through his apartment.

The FBI had no trouble finding the compromising material. It was in the same closet, on the same shelf, where Petersen had kept it for years. Yet he had been given plenty of time to dispose of it since his first questioning.

When the FBI told Petersen what they had found, he made the following statement: "I neglected to return these documents to Arlington Hall because I was emotionally disturbed as I realized the gravity of my actions to my country in illegally furnishing information from secret U.S. Government documents to unauthorized foreign nationalities. This emotional disturbance resulted in complete inaction on my part which is typical of me in times of stress."

Petersen's trial began in January, 1955. He could not have been a more willing defendant. And he finally discovered what he was being charged with when the defense asked for a bill of particulars. The Justice Department indictment said that he "copied and made notes from classified documents indicating the United States' success in breaking codes utilized by the Netherlands." He made a deal with the prosecution: two of the three counts in the indictment would be dropped if he pleaded guilty to a third, which charged that he used classified information in a manner prejudicial to the best interests of the United States.

The Justice Department's generosity was based on the fact that a not guilty plea would have obliged NSA officials to make public some of the agency's operations. Petersen's lawyer indicated strongly that a guilty plea was tantamount to a suspended sentence.

One interesting point that came up in the hearings was the classification of the documents Petersen had in his possession. The defense said they were grossly overclassified, since the Chinese code and the Hagelin cryptograph machine were commercially available.

A member of the director's staff at NSA patiently explained the meaning of the classifications. *Top secret,* he said, meant that disclosure could lead to grave damage to national security, a definite break in diplomatic relations, armed attack, war, or compromised defense plans. *Secret* meant that disclosure could lead to serious damage to national security, or jeopardy to diplomatic relations or defense plans. *Confidential* was for information that would be prejudicial if leaked.

The Chinese code, he said, "was published and prepared by this agency. It identified it with the agency, and therefore it implies the work of the agency." Moreover, he said, it contained material above and beyond the code itself. It was a device created by Far Eastern people whose language consists of ideographs, not adaptable to electric transmission. The device simply catalogued ideographs in language and number. The code was used throughout China and may still be in use.

Instead of a suspended sentence, Petersen was given seven years. The man who never had "so much as a parking ticket against him" was pictured as a dangerous spy who had committed an offense that "could have—may have, for all we know—led to very very serious consequences to the security of the United States," as the presiding judge said.

Petersen's guilty plea had saved the Government from dwelling on an embarrassing fact that could easily have compromised diplomatic relations with the Dutch—namely, that NSA systematically spies on its Allies. The Dutch smoothed things over by saying they thought Petersen had the authority to give their man information. The good faith of the Dutch was not questioned.

Petersen was jailed at the Federal Medical Center in Springfield, Missouri, because of his failing health. From his prison, he wrote the trial judge in February, 1955, that "now that the first shock is wearing off I am beginning to realize the extreme severity of the sentence—seven years in a federal prison." He said he had discovered there was no appeal from the guilty plea but that the sentencing judge could alter his sentence for a legitimate reason. Petersen also said he had learned that he could make a change of plea if it could be shown that the guilty plea was based on bad advice or inexperienced counsel. Petersen said that when he was arrested he had no counsel. The jailer called in a friend, David B. Kinney, whose first words were, "My fee is three thousand dollars in advance." Petersen said his savings were depleted by the lawyer's fee and that his wife had trouble finding a job because she had a speech defect. There was no action taken on the basis of the letter.

The Government had been virulent in its prosecution of Petersen, although for once Communism was not an issue in an espionage case. "There is no way we can appraise the damage that has been done to security of the United States," said Attorney John F. Reilly of the Internal Security Division. Petersen's actions were labeled "near treason." If his case showed anything at all, it was that "near treason," like "near beer," can fall pretty flat.

VII. American and Russian "Magic"

JOHN T. DOWNEY has been with the CIA more than ten years, but nine of those years have been spent in Tsao Lan-Tze (Grass Basket) Prison in Peiping. The first two years he was in solitary confinement awaiting trial on espionage charges. After being sentenced to life imprisonment, he received good treatment. He gets three meals a day, with rice, vegetables and meat. He is allowed to walk in the prison yard an hour a day and smoke his ten Chinese cigarettes. Through the Chinese Red Cross he gets his mail and his favorite magazines and newspapers. Over the years, he has received nearly 1,000 letters, many from unknown sympathizers, some from lonely hearts. His mother, Mrs. Mary Downey, a schoolteacher in New Britain, Connecticut, sends him the sports pages from the local papers. She was allowed to visit him in 1960, when he had just turned thirty. She brought him books and American cigarettes and saw him five times, for two hours each time. She found him looking well, and wearing the Chinese "uniform" of blue cotton, a blue padded jacket, and felt shoes.

Another CIA man in Grass Basket Prison is Richard Fecteau, a native of Boston. Fecteau has twin daughters he has never seen. His wife died after the Government announced that he and Downey had been lost at sea, and his daughters live with relatives. For a while, Fecteau shared a cell with Downey, but now he has a Chinese cellmate who speaks English. "He got fifteen years for espionage," Fecteau says about his cellmate. "He worked for the Kuomintang. He's about fifty years old and he was wealthy. Two pieces of property, a brand-new Buick. Now, he's lost everything. You'd expect that he'd be sore, but he's very objective about it."

Fecteau and Downey asked the prison administrator, Chi Ch'ao, for permission to share a cell again and were told it would be possible if they kept up their good behavior, but the application has not gone through.

For Downey, the CIA was a first job. He was recruited for "a civilian job with the Defense Department" when he graduated from Yale in 1951. This was the year the CIA recruited its largest batch of college graduates, because of its operations in connection with the Korean war. After training in Washington, he was sent to Atsugi, a small town about fifty miles southwest of Tokyo. There the CIA ran a camp for Chinese nationalist volunteers who were dropped into Manchuria on guerrilla missions. The camp was opened with the agreement of the Japanese Government in July, 1951, as a result of the Korean war. It was reportedly shut down recently. The Chinese agents were airdropped into Manchuria, supplied and, if need be, evacuated by U.S. Air Force planes. The planes were equipped with special devices for picking up personnel and matériel without landing. The "cover" for the flights into Manchuria was a military air transport service from Seoul to Yokohama.

One of the planes that left Seoul on November 29, 1952, with Downey, Fecteau, and nine Chinese guerrillas on board never reached Yokohama. It was brought down over Red Chinese territory.

Fecteau happened to be on the plane because he felt that his chosen profession of football coach did not pay enough. He came to the CIA by way of the merchant marine, and a Boston University football scholarship. After deciding there was no money in coaching, he went to work for the CIA.

Downey and Fecteau had been told their Manchurian overflights were a prelude to conquest of the Chinese mainland by Chiang Kai-shek. Downey was not convinced. "I couldn't believe Chiang could win back the mainland," he said. "I suppressed these thoughts because I thought the Korean war was the prelude to World War III. Since China would be on the side of Russia, the U.S.A. had to try and hang on to what little she had."

At their trial in 1954, Downey was amused to hear himself described as "the arch-criminal of all the American prisoners." He is an easy-going, almost lethargic type whose physical strength is not apparent. At Yale, he was a member of the wrestling team, but he had been considerably weakened by two years of solitary. Fecteau, husky and broad-shouldered, had lost twenty pounds and developed a nervous tic during the period of harsh confinement.

The only news of the trial came from Peiping broadcasts monitored by Reuters, the British news agency. According to the broadcasts, "The United States spies admitted they received specialist training in espionage and guerrilla warfare." Their tasks, it was charged, were "besides psychological warfare missions, the introduction, supply, resupply, evacuation and recovery of underground personnel . . . the airdropping, maintenance, and evacuation of underground agents." Exhibits at the trial included firearms, secret code books, gold ingots, and Chinese currency. Peiping radio said Downey admitted to the chief judge that he and Fecteau had been trained as CIA agents.

The trial was given as big a propaganda splash as the Soviets gave the Powers trial. It was held in the grandiose Palace of Culture. Pieces of the plane wreckage were shown, as well as maps, arms, and canned food found on Downey and Fecteau. There was a photograph of an American major with a shin wound from a parachute jump being treated by a Chinese male nurse.

Of nine Chinese guerrillas tried with the two Americans, four were sentenced to death. A few weeks after the sentencing, Downey and Fecteau had some company in prison. The crew of a B-29 that had been shot down over Manchuria was awaiting trial. The plane's pilot, Colonel John Knox Arnold Jr., was quoted by Peiping radio as admitting that his air wing worked for the CIA to "airdrop special agents, resupply and maintain liaison with and evacuate special agents on the ground." Fecteau recalls that the three weeks the crew spent at the prison were "beautiful."

A high point of their captivity was a guided tour in 1956 that included Shanghai, Hangchow, Harbin, Chenyang, Nanking, and Wuhan. Fecteau had already been to Shanghai as a merchant sea-man, and he was impressed by the change. "Shanghai before was full of beggars and prostitutes," he said. "When you landed in Shanghai, about two hundred kids would follow you with tomato cans, begging.

And if you refused them, they had some beautiful American swear words for you. If you notice the kids now, they look well taken care of. Their clothes are not from Kennedy's [a clothing store in Boston], but they all have clothes. Shanghai makes the Communists look good."

The tour also impressed Downey, who said: "I've never been an all-glory-to-free-enterprise boy anyway. Now I'm convinced that some sort of planned economy is the answer for China, India, and the rest of the world as well." Downey has come to the conclusion that the United States should recognize Red China. He believes that since "the United States has minimum relations with the Soviet Union . . . it should maintain at least the same with Red China." Also, recognition might lead to freedom for himself and for Fecteau. Both men deny they have been brainwashed.

In 1957, a visiting group of students who defied the State Department and accepted an invitation to visit Red China were granted interviews with Downey and Fecteau. It is from their reports that the previous quotations have been taken. They saw the two men separately and were not allowed to take notes or photograph them. They were not allowed to discuss the trial or the charges against them. After the meetings they got together to compile a written report. After the report was out, there was some quarreling about its editorial content. Some in the group of forty-one were obvious fellow travelers and attempted to describe treatment in Chinese prisons in a too favorable light. Larry Moyer, one of the group, issued a minority statement that "Downey's hands trembled and he spoke in short, sometimes incoherent sentences."

Another American interviewed by the group was Morris R. Wills, one of the twenty-one turncoats of the Korean war. Wills, a native of Fort Ann, New York, was taken prisoner in 1951 and is now a student of Chinese at Peiping University. The gangling, six-foot defector proudly told his interviewers that he was the star of the Peiping University basketball team and that he had married the daughter of a Communist general.

The accuracy of the report as a whole has been confirmed by Reverend Warren McKenna, a member of the group and now with St. John's Episcopal Mission in Holbrook, Massachusetts. In a letter to this writer Reverend McKenna said the controversy over the report started because Moyer was reporting the China trip for a news service.

It had been previously agreed by all those interviewing the prisoners that no word would be divulged until the group involved had written its report. We were aware of the news value and hoped by this method to be as fair and accurate as possible. Immediately following the interviews we secreted ourselves to compile the report and then asked the Chinese to make copies for us. We left this project for a scheduled meeting with Chou En-lai and a supper following. The result was a delay until the next morning before the Chinese had provided us the copies. Meanwhile, Moyer kept his promise and would not reveal any news to his man in Moscow, who grew impatient and finally fired him. Moyer became upset naturally and there was a long session with the whole delegation in which there were some intimations and charges that the report had been purposely delayed. Meanwhile . . . one of the less desirable and dishonest members of the group had filed a report on the basis of some of the things said at the delegation meeting. Later Moyer disowned the ideas and words attributed to him by this person. The whole situation arose from the extreme pressures of our itinerary and the news value of what we were reporting.

However, the two reports are quite accurate and I believe would not be repudiated by any who were at the interviews and who also made the written reports.

Added support for the accuracy of the reports came from the mothers who subsequently visited their sons.

Before closing this report on Downey and Fecteau it should be noted that the American government has never acknowledged that they were CIA agents. The only governmental statement regarding Downey and Fecteau lists them as civilian employees of the Department of the Army.

Just as the Soviet spy network infiltrates the United States and other Western countries with apparats, the CIA penetrates Communist territory. The case of Downey and Fecteau shows how it has been done in the Far East. In penetrating the Soviet Union with "illegal" networks, the CIA is more careful. It does not send native-born Americans on secret missions into the Soviet Union. No matter how well such agents could be trained in language and custom, no matter how authentic their forged papers looked, they would have very little chance of surviving in the hermetic Soviet society. A Soviet agent can land in New York with an immigrant's visa, a cardboard suitcase and an accent you can cut with a knife, and still blend with the scenery. But an American agent in Russia would need a daily miracle to get by. In 1949, Lieutenant General Wedemeyer, then director of psychological warfare for the Army, admitted that "the life of an agent in Russia today would not be worth very much. We do have a few. That is something that has to be generated very slowly, an intelligence organization within Russia. We do not get from Russia very good intelligence reports, but they are improving."

Since 1949, the CIA has perfected the technique of sending *émigré* Russians into the Soviet Union. There is nothing on the surface to link these agents with American intelligence. Ostensibly, most of them are members of the NTS (Union of Russian Solidarists), an *émigré* organization based in Frankfurt that has been sending agents into the Soviet Union since the thirties and "knows the ropes." Through the NTS and other *émigré* organizations, the CIA has effective control of these agents, however, and supervises their training and their penetration missions. The agents either go on a specific intelligence mission and then return or they integrate Soviet society as "sleepers" or active agents. The usual route is through West Berlin, East Germany, and into one of the satellites. The borders between the Soviet Union and Poland and Czechoslovakia are not tightly guarded. There are also long unguarded stretches in the Soviet Union's common border with Iran and Afghanistan. Other methods of getting agents in are by parachute or by boat to one of the Baltic states.

The Soviet booklet "Caught In the Act" lists 23 agents captured trying to penetrate the Soviet Union between 1951 and 1961. It adds that "only an insignificant fraction of cases can be listed here. The same lot is in store for all who may still be undergoing training for spy assignments at the intelligence schools."

The booklet at the same time reveals that the number of agents who have not been caught has the regime worried. In January, 1960, an astonishing amendment to the Soviet criminal code was passed to the effect that agents giving themselves up would not be prosecuted. The amendment reads:

> A citizen of the U.S.S.R. enlisted by a foreign intelligence service to conduct hostile activities against the U.S.S.R. shall not be liable

to criminal prosecution if he has committed no acts in pursuance of the criminal assignment given to him and has voluntarily reported to the authorities about his connections with a foreign intelligence service.

Not even the far-reaching Soviet police network can saturate a land mass twice the size of the United States (more than 6,000,000 square miles). Also working on the agent's side is the amount of inner migration in the Soviet Union. The thousands each year who are released from prisons and labor camps form the nucleus of this itinerant society. The migrants are welcomed in sparsely populated regions, in factories and collective farms, where authorities sometimes look the other way if papers are not in order, because they are grateful to get a new pair of arms. The man with a police record is part of the Soviet scene; he may benefit from multiple complicities or he may be turned in by his neighbor. It is more difficult to settle in cities like Leningrad and Moscow. The needed right of residence is hard to obtain in these crowded urban centers for someone who does not have a job waiting for him.

The agents sent in from Germany have all the right papers— Komsomol card, former residence card, army service card, and working papers. They find it easy to settle and obtain work once they are over the border. Often they go to towns where agent cells or NTS cells already operate. A new arrival in a Soviet town or village creates no commotion. It is an everyday event.

The accounts of "blown agents" in the booklet "Caught In the Act" are filled with inaccuracies and exaggerations, but they are fairly typical, according to American intelligence officers.

N. I. Yakuta served in the Red Army on the German front and was wounded and captured in 1941. Prisoners of war were given the option of joining the German Army—Yakuta joined. He found himself at war's end in a displaced person camp in Munich. He and others were put to work repairing an airfield and were given token payment. In 1946, he met a long-established Russian émigré in Munich who was recruiting labor for South America and Africa and promised "a prosperous life." It could not be worse than the camp, and Yakuta signed up. He was sent to Casablanca, where he worked as a laborer for five years at low wages. With the assistance of another Russian émigré, he made his way back to Germany in 1951. In Frankfurt he met Georgi

Okolovich, a leader of the NTS, and joined the NTS annex—The Institute for Russian Studies. From there, he was sent to an American-controlled camp where he spent nine months in "advanced" training, including the use of radio transmitters, cryptography, small arms practice, and intelligence-gathering missions.

Yakuta was caught crossing the border into the Soviet Union and surrendered. In February, 1957, he gave a press conferenece at the Central Journalists Club in Moscow that was carried *in toto* in *Pravda* the next day. In this clumsy propaganda effort, Yakuta claimed that "American intelligence corrupted us, encouraging hard drinking even during classes, cards, etc. We were taken to brothels in Munich. It was disgusting and deliberate corruption of Soviet citizens from among the displaced persons. . . .

"It should be added that the Americans kept telling us that in the event of the danger of detention in Soviet territory we should commit suicide rather than surrender. Ampoules of hydrocyanic acid were sewn into our shirt collars by an American intelligence agent for this purpose before we took off from Greece, and we were told that the poison acted instantaneously and painlessly. Among ourselves we called these ampoules the 'friendly gift' from Allen Dulles."

A. M. Novikov was seventeen when German troops occupied his native Byelorussia. He was sent to Germany and put to work on a farm. In 1945, he found odd jobs with an American food center and with the Munich-Rome airfield.

He too was recruited by Okolovich and worked for a time at the Institute for Russian Studies in Frankfurt. In 1949, he went to the advanced training camp at Bad Wiesse. In April, 1953, he was sent into the Soviet Union, equipped with a radio transmitter. He turned himself in and said at his press conference:

> American officers had foreseen much in training us to be their agents. In case I was detained by Soviet security authorities I should commit suicide with the poison given to me. I should categorically deny my connection with the Americans and say that I was connected with the French intelligence service, which had allegedly trained me in West Germany.
>
> I was hiding for some time in the woods, and then began venturing among people. I was deeply impressed by all that I saw in my wanderings through Byelorussia, and realized that the Soviet people

had recovered rapidly from the ravages of war and that living conditions in the Soviet Union were far removed from the picture painted by American intelligence.

I mastered my fears and gave myself up to the state security authorities. After I had given detailed information about myself, I spent a long time with security officers looking for equipment I had buried in different places. Then I was sentenced to five years of exile. When my appeal for a pardon was met last year, I could go to any place I liked in the Soviet Union, but I chose to stay and work on a state farm in Krasnoyarsk Territory. I married there and expect to be a father soon.

This poignant tale of love for the land and patriotism in the face of evil blandishments is calculated to stir the readers of *Pravda* and offer a similar solution to other misguided Russian *émigrés*. Nonetheless, these accounts contain kernels of truth. It is common knowledge in West Germany that Russians are trained in CIA camps and sent into the Soviet Union on espionage missions.

The Soviet accounts are amusingly naïve. The self-confessed agents mention their American trainers by name, and almost always mention the same ones. Thus, according to these accounts, a certain Captain Holliday must be the most overworked CIA man in West Germany. His name crops up again and again. "Captain Holliday warned me sternly that I should commit suicide," said Novikov. "Spy techniques were taught by Captain Holliday and other secret service agents," said Yakuta. "Under the guidance of Captain Holliday . . . I was trained to be a spy and saboteur," said M. P. Kudryavtsev, who "gave himself up" in 1953 to Soviet authorities. *The New York Times,* reporting the arrest in November, 1960, of Mikhail S. Platovsky, described as a CIA agent, wrote that he was "said to have been trained in spy schools in West Germany by three United States instructors whose names have become well known to readers of the Soviet press." One of the three was the ubiquitous Captain Holliday.

The agents almost invariably turn themselves in, according to "Caught In the Act." They realize the error of their ways, and the great strides forward the Soviet Union has made since they were last there. They all have spy kits including portable radio receivers, cameras, morphine, poison needles, firearms, radio beacons to guide planes to landing spots, collapsible bicycles, frogmen suits, compasses, munitions—in short, an endless inventory of equipment that must make the spy look like an itinerant tinker. The combat fatigues that certain agents allegedly wore were U.S. Government issue, with the Army insignia painted over. Some agents were found loaded down with stereotype blocks for printing anti-Soviet leaflets.

Training camps for these agents are reportedly spread all over the globe. In West Germany there are highly specialized camps. In Kaufbeuren, fifty miles west of Munich, there is a small airfield where prospective agents practice parachute jumps. In Landsberg, ten miles north of Kaufbeuren, there is a sabotage school where, according to one captured agent, "We were taught to derail trains, wreck railway tracks, blow bridges, sabotage arms industry buildings. We were taught to use Bockford fuses, blasting cartridges, electrical detonators. . . . We practiced the exploding of pipes, self-combustibles in metal boxes resembling cigarette cases. We saw a special instruction film on how to set fire to enterprises of the arms industry and office buildings."

Penetration is the most direct and most dangerous of clandestine methods which intelligence organizations refer to as "magic." There are a number of others in the repertoire of United States and Soviet spy networks. The most important among these are the use of tourists and students; the use of forged documents; approaching Soviet visitors to the United States and vice versa; bribery, blackmail and sex; subversion and front groups.

Allen Dulles once said that "if you can get an official to give you important information, that's intelligence. If he leaves a classified document on his desk and you steal it, that's espionage." This definition effectively separates white research from "magic."

The main task of intelligence agencies is to piece together scattered "white research" and make some sense out of it. For instance, a researcher might come across a letter to the editor in a local Soviet newspaper from a factory foreman complaining about slow raw-material deliveries. News from a military attaché about altered train schedules comes in. *Pravda* launches a campaign to recruit workers in a region near Siberia. Several days later, a satellite official makes a speech praising renewed industrial activity in the same region and includes a cryptic paragraph about the peaceful uses of atomic energy.

From these scraps, the intelligence specialist is able to discover the locations of two new Soviet atomic plants.

This is the daily work of the intelligence beehive in Washington and Moscow. Behind the scenes, however, agents are occupied with a multitude of clandestine tasks.

One of these is the use of amateurs for intelligence-gathering. The CIA calls this the "patriotic informant" technique. Students, school-teachers, businessmen—or tourists on their way to the Soviet Union—are contacted by the CIA and asked to "help out." In the Soviet Union, every visitor to the United States is told that one of his duties as a patriotic citizen is to pick up information and report what he has seen.

Robert Berlin, a twenty-eight-year-old vice-president of sales for a manufacturing company, decided in August, 1960, to go on a ten-day visit to the Soviet Union. Berlin said in an interview with the Chicago *American* that a CIA agent approached him and "asked me if I would consider making certain mental observations while I was traveling in Russia and if I would submit a copy of my itinerary for the trip." The CIA man had obtained Berlin's name through Maupintour Associates, a travel agency in New York that specializes in handling trips to the Soviet Union.

Berlin said he was not offered money for the job "but that would probably come up if I had accepted the job. I found out later that someone who identified himself as being from the CIA questioned my neighbors about my background and reputation. I also heard they tried to check my high school record." He considered the CIA request for two days and turned it down. He heard no more from the agent. Commenting on Berlin's disclosures, a CIA spokesman in Washington said, "It's our business to seek information wherever we can get it, just as the Russians try to get information. And it is a lot easier for them to get it."

In the summer of 1960, Mark I. Kaminsky, a graduate student from Cass County, Michigan, was sentenced to seven years in prison by a Soviet court on charges of entering a forbidden zone of the Soviet Union and engaging in military espionage. He was expelled after Soviet authorities claimed he had confessed his guilt. Shortly after his return to the United States, a column by Drew Pearson drew attention to the number of tourists who were being booted out of the Soviet Union on spy charges. The column came to the attention of Senator William J. Fulbright, chairman of the Senate Foreign Relations Committee, who queried Allen Dulles about the advisability of using "patriotic informants" untrained in espionage techniques. He in effect asked Dulles to "go easy" on the use of tourists and students.

The use of tourists to the Soviet Union is particularly delicate because security regulations are so stringent. A tourist comes under suspicion simply because he has a Brownie Kodak around his neck. He can be arrested for photographing a railroad station or a number of other innocuous objects that violate Soviet security regulations. If a tourist is given directives by the CIA, as is often the case, he is being exposed to dangers of which he is unaware, and a possible prison term.

One of the most recent cases of this type involves a Fullbright scholar at the Free University in West Berlin, Marvin William Makinen. In an obvious propaganda move tied to the Berlin crisis, Makinen was tried for espionage on September 5, 1961, and sentenced to eight years' imprisonment. The State Department filed no protest with the Soviet Government. The arrest was followed by a strongly worded Soviet statement to the American Embassy calling for an end to the use of tourist travel for espionage purposes.

The Soviets were obviously holding the case for a time when it could be used to the greatest propaganda advantage. Makinen was arrested in Kiev on July 27 and was held incommunicado for more than a month. U.S. authorities in West Germany did not announce his disappearance. Finally, on September 4, Radio Moscow disclosed his arrest.

Makinen, a twenty-two-year-old graduate of the University of Pennsylvania, who spoke fluent German and halting Russian, was on a car tour of the Ukraine when he was picked up by MVD security police. According to lengthy accounts in the Moscow press, Makinen hired a cab in Kiev and asked to go to an out-of-the-way address. The driver, Victor Daniluk, said, "When I brought the tourist to that street, he was uneasy. He squirmed in his seat, turning his head in all directions and scrutinizing every building. He was interested in military installations on the street but pretended he was interested in street repairs."

The cabbie, faithful to the Soviet anti-spy vigilance campaign launched after the U-2 incident, reported his nervous fare to security police. Two MVD men and a Soviet Army officer arrested Makinen as "with trembling hands the spy aimed his camera and clicked away rapidly." Found in Makinen's body belt were eight rolls of film, road maps, and some notebooks. The film was processed and Makinen was quoted as saying when he saw the prints: "Yes, these are certainly not tourist photographs."

He allegedly confessed that his trip through East Germany, Poland, and Southern Russia had been organized by the CIA. Two agents named "Jim" and "Dyer" had given him a green sunroof Volkswagen and expense money. He was to take notes on military installations using an elementary code. In his reported confession he said: "When I saw soldiers I wrote that I saw peasants and when I saw military barracks I wrote that it was raining. When I came across military cars I used the expression 'big traffic.' "

G. Z. Klemov, the prosecutor at his two-day trial before a military tribunal, charged that Makinen had received a six-week course in photography, codes, and map work under CIA mentors, and that he had been assigned a list of military installations to check. The Soviet press made much of the fact that Makinen's journey had started in West Berlin and continued through East Germany and Poland into the Soviet Union. *Izvestia* published photographs of his car with its West German plates. It also published some of his notes, written in the code shorthand.

Although the trial was held in camera, *Izvestia* reported that Makinen said: "I fully realize now the nature of my deeds and that I am subject to severe punishment under the laws of the Soviet Union." Severe punishment is what he got—eight years' detention, just two years less than U-2 pilot Francis Gary Powers. Whether one wanted to accuse the Soviet Government for manufacturing spies to add fuel to the Berlin crisis, or the United States for sending tourists with intelligence missions into the Soviet Union out of West Berlin, the real victim was Makinen, who had hoped to return to the University of Pennsylvania for his medical degree and who now was going to spend three years in a prison and several more on a prison farm for getting involved in something he knew little about.

Soviet intelligence, on the other hand, does not rely only on the information of tourists. It goes one better by always planting a KGB or MVD man with tourist groups or cultural or sports delegations. There was one of those rare moments of levity in Senate hearings when defector Yuri Rastorov explained that a colonel in the KGB accompanied a skating team that went to Japan. "But can the man skate?" Senator Herman Welker of Idaho wanted to know.

That is possibly one way to recognize the ringers. At the Rome Olympics, the KGB agent was the slim, attractive young woman who couldn't throw the discus. When the Moiseyev folk dancers triumphed in New York, the clumsy member of the corps de ballet in peasant garb whose *jetées* were heavy-footed hops gave himself away. Defector Peter Deriabin recognized him as KGB Colonel Aleksandr A. Kudryavtsev, a long-time intelligence officer. Be it at the Brussels Fair, at the Soviet exhibit in New York, on a tour of U.S. atomic installations, or on a student exchange mission, there is always an intelligence officer along with a double mission: To supervise the collection of intelligence and to keep an eye out for possible defectors.

When Rudolf Noureev of the Leningrad Ballet defected in Paris in the summer of 1961, he was being tailed by two KGB men assigned to the troupe, heavy cloddish types barely capable of playing hunters in *Swan Lake*. Noureev had to shake himself free of his two guards and seek asylum at Orly Airport minutes before he was to be packed off of a plane for Moscow.

The intelligence services also make attempts to subvert visitors. American tourists or members of delegations are arrested in Moscow on phony charges, and promised release if they will co-operate. Other ways of enlisting their services are mentioned in the chapter on defectors. The CIA, no slouch in this department, gets in touch with Soviet officials who are in the West, some of whom may have given indications in the past that they would like to defect if given the opportunity. This is the way defections are often arranged. Sometimes the defection backfires or is clumsily handled. In 1955, a second secretary at the Soviet Embassy in Vienna let it be known that he would like to flee to the West with his wife and daughter. Things moved to the point where an authorization for special entry and permanent residence in the United States was made out for the potential defector, B. Y. Nalivaiko. The authorization came from the Department of State and was signed by a special assistant to the Secretary of State.

On February 5, 1955, two CIA men met Nalivaiko in Vienna's Gartenbau Café to arrange details. They showed Nalivaiko the authorization, which he promptly pocketed after rebuffing the agents. They tried to keep him from leaving the café with the document. Nalivaiko threw what was left of his beer in the face of one CIA man. This was a signal for Soviet officers in uniform to block the café exits. The CIA men, realizing they had fallen into a trap, retreated to a back room and tried to get out through a window. The Austrian police arrived, but the Soviet officers would not let them make arrests until the tripartite military police had come.

When they did, the Russians left with their man, and the Americans with theirs. The U.S. agents were identified as Robert Gray (a pseudonym) and Colonel Francis R. Manning. Soviet or American trap? A little of both.

At the Soviet exhibit in New York in 1960, anti-Communist Russian *émigrés* were used to strike up conversations with the exhibit personnel and see if any were ripe for defection. Job offers and promises of permanent residence were made, the "prospect" was wined and dined, and told to think it over. If the "prospect" had a family, it was suggested that he talk it over with his wife when he got back to the Soviet Union. Families of touring Soviets are kept home as hostages, and often with good reason. Many a Soviet visitor to the West would gladly defect if it did not mean leaving a wife and children exposed to certain prison terms.

Forged documents are another of the established "magic" techniques. In West Germany, the CIA uses the Ullstein Publishing House to publish forged copies of East German newspapers such as *Neues Deutschland*. The NTS in Frankfurt puts out forgeries of *Pravda* and *Izvestia*. The Soviets are expert in the "big lie" in forgery. In January, purported "secret documents" were leaked to London's sensational *Daily Express* (circulation circa 4,000,000). One of the documents was a single sheet of instructions from former Secretary of State Christian A. Herter to officials in the British Embassy to speed up the defection of Communist-bloc nationals. The other was a five-page memorandum from Secretary of the Army Wilbur M. Brucker dealing with the same topic. The documents looked official, with their seals and file numbers, but an embassy spokesman said, "Investigation has failed to reveal the existence of either document referred to in press reports this morning."

The common Soviet technique is to plant forgeries with a Western power about one of its allies, to create confusion and discord. Over the years, the most blatant forgeries coming from the false document factory in the East Berlin suburb of Oberschoneweide have been: a note from Secretary of State John Foster Dulles on undermining Egyptian prestige in the Arab world; a report from Assistant Secretary of Defense Dr. Frank B. Berry that 67 per cent of U.S. Air Force personnel were "psychoneurotic, involved in sexual excesses, and drug taking"; a diplomatic note advising the U.S. Embassy in Bonn to back fascist groups in West Germany; and a memorandum from Admiral Laurence Frost, then chief of Naval Intelligence, suggesting that the U.S. back antigovernment rebels in Indonesia.

Another Soviet forte is the use of blackmail and sex for espionage. It is generally conceded that the days of Mata Hari are over. As Allen Dulles once said, "It is much easier to put a listening device in someone's room than a lady spy in his bed." As for one-time KGB boss Lavrenti Beria, his contempt for women was such that he said a man's success depended on how effectively he was able to eliminate them from his life. However, Beria, as he once confided in an interview, was not above using women agents.

"I don't like to employ women in the secret service," he said. "But sometimes they are useful as decoys. One would hardly believe how small the great men are in bed, and what they are prepared to tell their women. I have sometimes got information from a tart whose lover was one of the big boys in the Politburo, but which was too secret to discuss at meetings."

U.S. officials believe that the Soviets no longer systematically use prostitutes or "permitted girls" on espionage missions. Boris Morros, however, said in 1958 that when he was in Moscow, "I was given a tour of a School for Seduction, where floor after floor was devoted to training pretty girls and attractive women in the ways of securing secrets and brainwashing their men." According to other former Soviet agents, even men are given seduction classes.

Anatoli Granovsky, who defected in 1946 from a Soviet ship anchored in Stockholm, described in his book *All Pity Choked** the clinical interest in sex at the GRU training camp near Bykovo, forty miles from Moscow. Along with courses in map reading, cryptography, and sabotage, the curriculum included a course in seduction. The teacher of this novel instruction insisted that his students call him "Rasputin." He said in his lecture:

"Now here is a very important point. Let a woman know that you love her, that you want her and are excited by her. But if you are unsuccessful in the sexual expression of your love, the more you love her personally without this cardinal success the more you arouse in

---

* Anatoli Granovsky, *All Pity Choked: The Memoirs of a Soviet Secret Agent* (London: W. Kimber, 1955).

her contempt and boredom. You become tedious and even hated, at best tolerated. But, be eminently successful in satisfying a woman sexually and even if you do not love her, she will love you, and a woman's love is more passionate and less selfish than a man's in all its manifestations. . . . I am going to teach you how to produce this effect in women, in any woman, whether they attract you personally or not. Furthermore, I am going to show you how, with a little training, you can do this a number of times and be none the worse for it."

Rasputin followed his opening remarks with a lesson in human anatomy in which he described the primary and secondary erotic zones with the help of charts.

Passing from theory to practice, Rasputin took the class to a house on Leningrad Road, where a stocky peasant girl was brought in. "She is no beauty, as you can see, and she does not attract me in the least. But I am going to make love to her and make sure that she is richly satisfied. . . . I am still not in the least excited, although she is already naked beside me. But obviously, I must become excited. Now, in cases like this, it is best to look deeply in a woman's eyes, for it is surprising how the eyes of a woman are so seldom properly noticed and yet with their message, their desire or their challenge, they can, coupled with the contact of the flesh with the flesh, arouse a man. Once you have achieved a certain excitement and are in actual physical contact with a woman like this you must fill your mind with a vision of the most satisfying sexual experience you have ever had, one that you would like to repeat. Conversely, if the girl with whom you are lying does attract you but circumstances do not permit you to reach an orgasm, when you feel you are in danger of going too far, you must concentrate your mind on anything that repels you."

Granovsky wrote that Rasputin "then started with a full use of primary and secondary zones of excitation to make love to the girl. She seemed to respond with an elephantine sluggishness, but then quite suddenly she arched her back, pressing the back of her head down into the divan, and cried out—a cry that any man will recognize. Soon she cried out again, and then she lay back relaxed and kissed Rasputin. In the course of the next eight hours we spent there, Rasputin took five women, and it was quite clear that each one was abundantly satisfied. He himself appeared no more tired than if he had spent a day at the beach."

There are indications that American intelligence organizations do not always sneer at the use of women in espionage. Herbert O. Yardley, who headed the "American Black Chamber" wrote that "a captain working for intelligence (in the twenties) had been commissioned for intelligence for no other reason than that when a woman agent was required for espionage to tear a secret from some poor devil, he could on a moment's notice find any woman to fit any requirement. Old or young, fat or thin, beautiful or homely, blonde or brunette, it made no difference."

A more recent case, charged in "Caught In the Act" but unconfirmed, deals with A, "a professional intelligence officer who worked in Potsdam from the beginning of 1958 until May, 1960, under the guise of the Soviet Army group in Germany, instructed his young wife to entice Comrade B, a Soviet citizen who had stayed a long time in Berlin without his family, and then to become intimate with him for the purpose of blackmail.

"A created an appropriate environment for his wife to become intimate with Comrade B and then to blackmail him. [She] followed her husband's advice and subsequently tried to get B to betray his country and go to the United States. But this intrigue of the American intelligence failed: Comrade B declined the criminal offer and reported the case to the Embassy of the USSR in the German Democratic Republic in May, 1960. Fearing a public scandal over this failure, the U.S. intelligence had to urgently recall its ill-starred agent and his wife at the end of May, 1960."

There are always cases where the old-fashioned seduction techniques succeed where all else fails, even if seduction is not established CIA policy. The Soviets use sex with particular ruthlessness, however. Defector Yuri Rastorov explained how the KGB exploited a Japanese agent's weakness for Soviet women. "In the summer of 1946," he said, "one of the oldest, most reliable, and faithful agents of the MVD, Takemore Shigezu, made his appearance at the Soviet mission in Tokyo. Takemore spent considerable time in the Soviet Union as an official representative of the Japanese Government, representing a Japanese commercial firm with concessions in the northern part of Sakhalin Island.

"He was recruited by the MVD intelligence service through the exploitation of a known weakness on his part. Having learned that his weakness was Russian women, the MVD arranged for Takemore to meet an attractive Moscow prostitute who was an MVD agent. The MVD-sponsored romance soon blossomed out into a secret marriage that eventually resulted in the recruitment of Takemore as a full-fledged agent of the MVD. As payment for his espionage activities, Takemore was given infrequent opportunities to meet his wife in North Sakhalin, where she was brought from Moscow under escort of two MVD colonels. These meetings between Takemore and his wife were usually held in a house assigned for this purpose by the MVD. The colonels were assigned to this duty because of the importance attributed to Takemore by the MVD. Takemore honestly and faithfully worked for the Soviet intelligence, transmitting great amounts of valuable classified information and numerous secret documents from the Japanese Ministry of Foreign Affairs. He continued his activities through 1954."

Along with sexual and other types of blackmail, huge sums are expended by intelligence services for bribes. A Soviet agent in Iran who defected said that bribes in the millions of dollars were given to Irani politicians each year to further Soviet interests. And thanks to the CIA, there is a general of the Indo-Chinese terrorist sect Binh Xuyen now living in comfortable retirement in Paris, after $1,000,000 was reportedly deposited to his account in a Swiss bank. The only condition—that he stay in France to spend it.

The use of fronts for espionage is as old as the Trojan Horse. For years, the Soviets had a ready-made, all-purpose front in the local Communist parties, which were able to supply agents, false papers, funds, and other valuable assistance to underground agents. Today in the United States, the Communist Party is not powerful enough and too closely watched to be useful. Other private Russian groups, however, have emerged as new front organizations. One of the least known is the Russian Orthodox Church, whose patriarchate in North America is in close collaboration with the Soviet Government. A dissident anti-Communist orthodox faction seeking control of St. Nicholas Cathedral in New York City filed a suit in 1945 and it is still in appeal. The New York State court of appeals ruled in its favor, stating that "the record is replete with instances of political diatribes by the patriarchate in the furtherance of the interests of the Soviet state." The state supreme court, however, reversed the ruling in June,

1960. Through the Orthodox Church and other Russian groups, the Soviets conduct a relentless campaign in the United States to enlist *émigré* Russians as agents and to engineer redefections.

In the next four chapters, spies are shown at work, using some of the techniques elaborated by their chiefs in Moscow and Washington to gather intelligence and avoid detection. In contrast to these underhanded and often violent methods, the effective spy is rarely a swashbuckling type who craves excitement. The demands of his métier require, above all, patience to endure implacable monotony. The successful spy is not a master of disguises, but a man who needs no disguises because he passes unnoticed. He needs an infinite capacity for detail far more than boldness and daring. He is more craftsman than genius, more painstaking than adventurous. Romantic misconceptions dissolve in the face of unpleasant facts: the hours are long, the work is dirty, the pay is not generous considering the risks, there is no job security, and the only excitement is usually that of being caught.

VIII. Rudolf Abel: Portrait
of the Artist

AT seven o'clock on the morning of June 21, 1957, three FBI men walked into the lobby of the Hotel Latham, 4 E. 28th Street, New York City, and took the elevator to the eighth floor. They knocked on the door of Room 839, whose occupant had registered under the name of Martin Collins. Collins, a tall man in his late middle age with the air of fading distinction that clings to many residents of third-rate hotels, paid $29 a week for his room. He was thought of by the management as a good tenant because he paid his rent on time, received no visitors, and required little service.

A muffled voice replied "just a moment" to the knock, and Collins, scantily clad because of the warm June weather (the temperature was in the mid-80's), opened the door as far as decency would allow. The FBI men pushed in and allowed Collins hastily to put on a pair of shorts. One of the agents noticed false teeth in the soap dish of the washbasin and handed them to the nearly bald, thin-faced man.

"We hope you're going to co-operate with us, Colonel," one of the FBI men said. Collins showed no surprise at being granted a high military rank. His interrogators asked if he had ever rented an artist's studio in Brooklyn under the name Emil Goldfus. He rather wearily admitted that he had.

At 7:30 P.M., Immigration Investigator Robert E. Schoenberger entered Room 839. He questioned Collins about still another name. "Did you enter the United States from Canada in 1948 as Andrew Kayotis?" he asked. Collins nodded. He was told he was under arrest for entering the country illegally as an alien.

The FBI men continued their attempts to make Collins admit what they had shown him they already knew: that under the aliases, he was Rudolf Ivanovich Abel, and that he held his rank in the KGB, a corps not noted for giving snap promotions. The FBI later learned that although the rank was real, the name Abel was simply another *nom de guerre,* one known to have been used in the twenties by several Soviet agents in France. Abel was also known by the code name of Mark to his fellow agents. His real name has never been learned.

At that moment in the hotel room, as Martin Collins alias Emil Goldfus alias Andrew Kayotis alias Colonel Abel alias Mark sat on the bed with his elbows on his knees and his hands cupping his head, it was hard to imagine him wearing the stiff cloth and heavy braid of a Russian officer.

Yet, in nearly ten years of undercover work as the top Soviet agent in the United States, who could say he had not earned the rank? Certainly not Allen Dulles, head of the Central Intelligence Agency, who is reported to have commented admiringly: "I wish we had a couple like him in Moscow."

The FBI acknowledged that Abel was the biggest spy catch they had ever made. Bigger than the Rosenbergs, the Sobels, or Gubitchev and Coplon. They ranked Abel as the master Soviet spy of the twentieth century. Superior to Richard Sorge, who posed in Japan as a Nazi foreign correspondent and became the confidant of the German Ambassador; superior to Rudolf Rossler, the Czech Communist who gave Russia daily reports on German troop movements in World War II and had a pipeline to the German General Staff.

Abel had the title of "Resident" Soviet agent, with headquarters in New York. Today, the FBI believes that his bailiwick extended far beyond the New York area, that he was the Resident for all of North America and even for Mexico and Central America. He acted as a sort of team captain for the Soviet spy network. It was not his job to develop sources of information himself. He called the plays, edited the information he received, sent it to Moscow over a communications system he controlled, and kept track of finances. He was known by sight only to one or two "cutouts" who acted as his links with the network of couriers, agents, and sources.

Abel's duties were described as those of the executive vice-president in charge of personnel for a large corporation. In time of peace or cold war, he saw to it that the network was operating smoothly and was kept intact. In time of hot war, he was prepared to launch sabotage operations.

Abel seemed to accept the fact of his capture as though he had lived through it often in his own mind. His conscience was clear. As a professional, contemptuous of slipshod work, he knew he had been caught through no fault of his own. The FBI had been handed the case on a platter when one of his assistants, Reino Hayhanen, defected and turned him in. Abel had joined Soviet intelligence in 1927 and the year of his capture marked his 30th anniversary as a spy.

"Get dressed," Mr. Schoenberger said. Abel rose, went to the closet across from his bed, and selected a gray tweed herringbone suit. Another immigration agent had started throwing his personal effects into a suitcase, but Abel objected that they were not being properly packed, and asked to do the packing himself.

He folded each item of clothing carefully before placing it in the suitcase. As he packed he began discarding certain objects and throwing them into a wastebasket in the corner. The room was littered with paints, brushes, paper and pencils. On a night table lay a Hallicrafter short-wave radio, its green antenna trained along the wall and out the bathroom window. On another table were a number of books, including *Nights of Love and Laughter, The Ribald Reader, A Time to Love and a Time to Die,* and *Paintings from the São Paulo Museum.*

When the wastebasket was filled and Abel had packed, he put on his tweed jacket, and Mr. Schoenberger saw him slipping a piece of paper up his sleeve. He removed it. The graph paper had five digit numbers arranged in neat rows. It was a coded message. An FBI man snapped handcuffs on the prisoner, and he was led out of the hotel. Agents who remained behind went through the wastebasket and found a block of wood covered with sandpaper—the block came apart, and contained a 250-page booklet with a series of numbers, all in five-digit groups, on each page. It was a cipher pad, an aid to writing coded messages.

The tiny booklet, its pages bound with glue, contained the key to Abel's personal code, printed in neat columns in black and red. The code was simple; it replaced the letters of a message's text by numbers.

At the same time, it was unbreakable. To each number group a digit was added at random so that the final coded message showed neither regularities nor frequencies. The random numbers might be population figures from an Atlas or corporation tax returns from a company report.

A stubby pencil with an eraser that concealed a cavity was also found. Inside the cavity were eighteen microfilms, several of them letters from Colonel Abel's wife and daughter. One was his time schedule for broadcasts to Moscow.

On Abel's person, the agents found two birth certificates, $6,000 in cash, a bankbook, a safe deposit box key, and an international certificate of vaccination that showed the colonel was contemplating a trip abroad. One birth certificate was made out to Emil Robert Goldfus, born August 2, 1902, in New York. This was the same year and exactly one month later than Colonel Abel's real birth date. His real birthplace was Moscow. A check with Department of Health records showed that the real Emil Robert Goldfus had died on October 9, 1903, at the age of one year and two months. The other birth certificate, made out to Martin Collins, born July 15, 1897, turned out to be completely phony. The bankbook from the East River Savings Bank showed a balance of $1,386 and entries from June 12, 1950, to April 5, 1957.

The safe deposit box, which he kept in the name of a friend at the Manufacturers Trust, contained $15,000. In accounting for his wealth, Abel displayed for the first time some of the romantic imagination with which spies are by tradition endowed. "I had found a large sum of American money in a ruined blockhouse in Russia," he explained. "I then bought a forged American passport in Denmark, and with this passport I entered the United States from Canada in 1948."

The FBI agents were surprised that Abel had so much evidence, including the fake pencils and coded messages, on his person. "Anyone so skilled would not be expected to leave items of evidence around," one said. From his hotel room, Abel was taken to immigration headquarters, then at 70 Columbus Avenue. He was questioned briefly and at 4:15 P.M., the same afternoon, he was flown to McAllen, Texas, for an immigration hearing.

Before leaving for Texas, however, the traditional mug shots were taken of the prisoner. In these photographs, Abel looks something like an unfrocked monk who has been caught blaspheming. A scowl clouds his ascetic face, and the sparse fringe of brownish-gray hair around his ears and the back of his head is disarranged. He is looking down an aquiline nose with tired eyes, and his receding chin is darkened by a one-day growth of beard. The collar of his white shirt is unbuttoned, and his striped tie is askew. Looking at this face, one might think immediately of a clerk who has worked too long in the same department. The photograph brings to mind an observer's remark: "He had a genius for the inconspicuous," and the surprise of the foreman of the Abel jury, John T. Dublynn, who exclaimed when he first saw the defendant: "He could be walking down the street and he could be anybody."

In repose, his face had a mild, birdlike quality. He was about five feet ten inches tall, lanky, and dressed with what has been termed "unobtrusive bad taste." He wore black straw hats with dashing bands. Those who, like the superintendent of the building where Abel had his artist's studio, tend to judge men by their physical presence, wrote him off as "seedy-looking."

His flawless English, like his appearance, had aroused no suspicions during his stay in this country. Abel had been a language teacher in Moscow before turning to the less didactic profession of spying, and he speaks and writes five or six languages fluently, among them German, Polish and Yiddish.

In retrospect, those who knew him have detected accents described variously as "a Scottish burr," "a touch of Dublin," and "Oxonian." One gentleman who had a studio in the same Brooklyn building insists that after several months in the neighborhood, he developed a Brooklyn twang. In any case, he stayed in parts of the city where accents are the rule rather than the exception, and his English was colloquial. During the trial, when the prosecution lost a point he would turn to his court-assigned counsel and whisper, "He sure struck out on that one."

In the McAllen prison, Abel was segregated from the other inmates and given his choice of food and a private bath. In contrast to the comfort of his accommodations, he was subjected to arduous periods of interrogation, during which he admitted his identity and that he was a Soviet citizen posing as an American with the help of false documents. He was told that he was subject to deportation proceedings and was asked if he would fight them. "I would say that I would accept deportation," Abel replied laconically. Discreet inquiries from the Soviet Embassy in Washington about expediting the colonel's deportation lent further proof that this solution was viewed with favor by both Abel and the Soviet Government.

Some of Abel's countrymen, before and since his capture, have come to the United States holding diplomatic or consular rank only to attract the attention of the Federal Government by breaking Talleyrand's basic precept for young diplomats: *"Surtout pas de zèle."* Yet however blatantly they spied, their only punishment was to be sent home. Unfortunately for him, Abel did not have the cover of diplomatic rank. He could draw comfort only from the legal rights of the ordinary citizens he had been impersonating for such a long time.

He was told that deportation was doubtful, and that he would be tried as a spy. It was pointed out that if he was found guilty he could be sentenced to death. In the next breath, however, the FBI described a rosier solution to his troubles. "They told me they would get me good food, liquor, and an air-conditioned room in a Texas hotel," Abel said in an affidavit exhibited at his trial. When he remained impervious to these blandishments, the FBI borrowed a technique known in the business world as piracy—hiring away a talented executive from a rival firm, so that he will bring his accounts along. Abel was offered a job "with a Federal agency" at a starting salary of $10,000 a year.

The FBI, mindful of the standard of living in the Soviet Union, may have thought this was a pretty sum to offer the colonel. It came out later, however, that with salary and expenses, he was doing better working for the Soviets here. In fact, as one of his New York friends remarked: "He could have lived at the Waldorf." Unlike ordinary citizens, Abel did not have to worry about financial security. He knew that he would never be overdrawn at the bank. Money arrived as though by magic in unlimited amounts from mysterious sources. This prosperity extended to his wife and daughter, who lived in their *dacha* outside Moscow in a style that many a capitalist would envy. They had a summer home in the north of Russia, several servants, and a car. Abel's wife, in her microfilmed letters, complains about the servant problem in Russia.

Abel politely turned down the job offer, and on August 7, 1957, about a month and a half after his arrest, a Federal Grand Jury in the Eastern District of New York (Brooklyn) indicted him on three counts. It first charged him with conspiracy to transmit military information to the Soviet Union; this carried the death penalty as the maximum sentence. In the second count, he was accused of entering a conspiracy to gather such military information; this was punishable by a maximum of ten years' imprisonment. He had already admitted his guilt to the third count, which charged him with being in the United States illegally and without registering as a foreign agent with the State Department. The maximum penalty for this count was five years.

Abel was brought back to New York and given a cell in the Federal Detention House on West and 11th Streets. His most urgent business was to find a lawyer to defend him. John J. Abt, counsel for the Communist Party, had declined Abel's request that he handle the case, claiming "prior commitments." With this in mind, Abel appeared in Federal Court in Brooklyn on August 13 before Judge Matthew T. Abruzzo.

"It is very difficult, your Honor, to choose one lawyer out of the several thousands that there are," Abel said. Judge Abruzzo explained that he could not allow too much time for the selection, since the trial had to start soon. "Do you think a week would be exorbitant?" the colonel asked. A week was granted, and then Abel made the move that was to assure him the best legal talent he could have obtained at any price. "There is another alternative," he said. "I understand a request can be made to the Bar Association." Judge Abruzzo told him he understood correctly, and Abel's request was transmitted to the Brooklyn Bar Association. Abel then asked to see the indictment. "I have not yet received a copy."

"I direct that you give him one copy of the indictment, which you can keep and read at your leisure," the judge told the clerk and Colonel Abel, adding: "You have plenty of leisure, I take it?"

"I have another request," the colonel said. "Would it be possible to have a certain small sum of moneys taken from me allotted to me?"

"How much do you want?" Mr. Abruzzo asked.

"Well, I don't need very much, perhaps about fifty dollars, I imagine."

"Give him two hundred and fifty dollars," the court generously told the clerk. "He might want to buy cigarettes." (Abel was in fact a heavy smoker.)

Then, assuming the benign tone of a schoolmaster in civics class, the judge peered down at Abel and said, "You see, you are in a democracy here, sir. This is the way we do things here. I hope you appreciate that. You will before we are through. We will see if we can't make you as comfortable as we know how to do in jail."

By his own admission, Abel did appreciate the fact that he received a fair trial and an excellent defense. This did nothing to change his basic viewpoint, however. When his counsel asked him after the trial to imagine the fate of an American spy caught in the Soviet Union under similar circumstances, Abel replied complacently, "I didn't write your Constitution."

As for his comfort in jail, Abel's time of detention in the West Street jail surprised veteran observers. Convicts are a notoriously patriotic lot. Whatever crime they may commit against the law of the land, they are always the first to wave the flag when that law is threatened. Politically, as a group, they are probably far to the right of Old Guard Republicans. Whatever shady practices may have brought them behind bars, convicts are fervent crusaders where patriotic ideals are concerned.

There is nothing they hate worse than a Communist. William Remington, the government economist jailed for perjury, was beaten to death by two convicts in his unlocked honor cell in Lewisburg Federal Penitentiary in November, 1954. David Greenglass was subjected to unflagging abuse at the hands of his fellow prisoners in Lewisburg.

It was with some apprehension that federal authorities viewed Abel's stay in the Manhattan prison. He was put in a cell with a Brahmin of the prison population, Vincent J. Squillante, dues-paying member of the Mafia and godson of the late Albert Anastasia. Mr. Anastasia had been known as king of the rackets before he was gunned to death in his barber chair several years back. Squillante was making a brief appearance in the West Street establishment for extortion as "king of the garbage collectors." He was indignant to find that his cellmate was a foreigner and a Communist. He asked Warden Alex Krimsky to be released into the general prison population. When this request was denied, he launched a campaign of passive resistance to express his distaste. Every morning, he asked for soap, water, a bucket and a mop, got down on all fours, and scrubbed his cell. He scrubbed for hours, like a man obsessed, wiping away the stench of Communism like Lady Macbeth washing the blood off her hands.

Whether Squillante lacked the perseverance of a Gandhi, or whether he decided his cellmate was not such a bad guy after all, is not known, but the hoodlum soon became friendly with the spy, and the other convicts followed Squillante's example.

They treated Abel with the deference provided for high-ranking prisoners of war in the Geneva Convention; they addressed him as "Colonel." Responding in the best way he knew, Abel offered to give Squillante French lessons, and the warden agreed to provide the cellmates with a primer. When Squillante left West Street to serve a one-year sentence in Lewisburg, he displayed his linguistic ability by telling the warden *"à bientôt,"* which he probably meant more as a casual form of farewell than as a commitment for the future.

Left to himself, Abel proved to be a voracious reader. His counsel, James Britt Donovan, decided he might like some literature on his chosen profession, and selected a work on German wartime espionage. But he ran afoul of a prison rule that no prisoner shall be allowed any reading matter that could tend to lead him back to his path of crime. Donovan observed that a colonel in the KGB was not likely to be influenced by romanticized accounts of espionage, and the warden allowed the book to go through after some good-natured grumbling. One of the books Abel enjoyed most during this period was *I Willie Sutton,* an "as-told" book by Quentin Reynolds about the celebrated robber. It described the loneliness of a hunted man who could not even sit on a park bench and hear the leaves rustling behind him without turning instantly in fear.

The date of the trial, October 14, was drawing near, and Abel's counsel was closeted daily with the prisoner to prepare his defense. Counselor Donovan had been chosen by a three-member panel of the Brooklyn Bar Association following Abel's request in Federal Court. Then forty-one years old, the Harvard Law School graduate had been singled out primarily because of his trial experience and background in counterespionage work. He had served as counsel to Vannevar Bush's highly secret Office of Scientific Research and Development. As a naval officer, he had been general counsel for Major General William J. (Wild Bill) Donovan's Office of Strategic Services during World War II. Later, he was a principal assistant to Supreme Court Justice Robert H. Jackson in establishing the Nuremberg trials.

Donovan, a successful partner in a New York law firm, did not need the publicity of the Abel case to drum up business. The case, in fact, caused him many hardships, and the time he spent on it could have been more profitably employed. By his associates' estimate, he gave his notorious client the kind of attention for three years that a private client could not have received for less than $250,000. It had been impressed upon Donovan by the Bar Association that if the case fell into the wrong hands it could be a disgrace to the bar and the judiciary. He agreed to defend Abel as a "public service in the national interest."

As his fee, Donovan received $10,000, paid through a correspondent of the Chase bank in Leipzig. Ostensibly, the money came from Mrs. Abel and arrived in the form of two checks, one for $3,500, the other for $6,500. Donovan redistributed these two checks three ways, giving $5,000 to Fordham, his undergraduate alma mater, and $2,500 each to Harvard and Columbia law schools, which he and the two young lawyers who helped prepare his defense had attended. Explaining this largesse, Donovan said: "It is my belief that in a land of plenty such as the United States, the most effective means of combating totalitarianism lies in the furtherance of sound moral training and true understanding of justice under law." Of $21,406 that Abel had in his possession at the time of his capture and that had been put on deposit with the clerk of the court, Donovan used $11,043 for expenses during the trial and the period of appeal. Another $3,000 went to pay the fine that was part of his sentence. Abel kept the balance for pin money.

If Donovan's hair had not already been prematurely white, the Abel case could easily have done the trick. In 1957, the reverberations of the McCarthy hearings still echoed in the public imagination, and guilt by association—even in the case of a lawyer defending a client—remained fashionable in certain sectors. Thus it was that Donovan, a Brooklyn resident, had to cut off his telephone service when the crank calls started coming in. His three daughters and one son had their mettle tested daily by the taunts of their schoolmates. His associates in the law firm felt that his court-assigned legal work was bad for business.

Donovan, a cheerful, stocky man with the build of an ex-football player, was surprised at such hostility, but carefully wore his Legion of Merit decoration, won in World War II, through the trial. He attributed the hostility philosophically to "people's viewpoint today—it's just a question of whose ox is being gored." Aside from the personal attacks, there were professional hardships. The trial was involved and difficult to prepare, since the defendant was unwilling to discuss with his lawyer what he had refused to tell the FBI. After the trial was over, and Abel had been sentenced, the case was in appeal for three years.

Unlike most convicted defendants, Abel bore his defense lawyers no grudge. In a statement to the press at the end of the trial, he said: "I would like to take this opportunity of expressing my appreciation of the way in which my court-appointed attorneys conducted my defense. I wish to express my thanks to them for the tremendous amount of work they put into their efforts on my behalf and for the skill and ability they have shown in doing so." Abel further expressed his gratitude by giving Donovan one of his paintings, a seascape that is hanging today in the lawyer's home on Prospect Park West. Donovan has remained Abel's closest contact with the outside world. Where Abel was first stiff and formal, the two men are now on a "dear Rudolf" and "dear Jim" basis in their correspondence. Abel, who sometimes displays haughtiness toward those he considers his intellectual inferiors, cottoned to his lawyer upon learning of his OSS background. "He treated me like an understanding colleague," Donovan recalls.

For those who wonder that there should have been any trial at all in the case of a Soviet spy caught in *flagrante delicto,* and who would rather see such a man shot on the dawn following the day of his capture, Donovan had this reply in his summation: "Abel is an alien charged with the capital offense of Soviet espionage. It may seem anomalous that our constitutional guarantee protects such a man. The unthinking may view America's adherence to the principles of free society as altruism so scrupulous that self-destruction might result. Yet our principles are engraved in the history and the law of this land. If the free world is not faithful to its own moral code, there remains no society for which others may hunger."

A panel of nine men and three women was speedily selected. On the bench sat veteran Federal Judge Mortimer W. Byers. This was not Judge Byer's first espionage case. In 1943, he had judged two Nazi spies and had sentenced both to prison terms, although he could have invoked the death penalty against them as members of a country with which we were at war. In Abel's corner, besides Donovan, were two young lawyers with experience as assistant U.S. attorneys. Arnold Fraiman, now in law practice in New York, and Thomas Debevoise

III, who in 1960 became Attorney General for the State of Vermont at the tender age of thirty. The prosecution was handled by United States Attorney William Tompkins and three assistants—Kevin T. Maroney, James J. Featherstone, and Anthony R. Palermo—all special attorneys for the Department of Justice.

It was a unique trial. First, as Donovan pointed out, it was the first time in American history that a Soviet national was tried and sentenced under United States law as a spy. Valentin Gubitchev, the Soviet United Nations official who was accused with Judith Coplon, was brought to trial in 1950 but was allowed to leave the country with a suspended sentence. Abel's case was also the first time an alien was being tried under the Rosenberg law, which provides, in effect, that a man is subject to the death sentence on the charge that he acted as a spy for a foreign nation with which we are legally at peace.

The trial also had an unusual geographical aspect. The Brooklyn artist's studio which Abel had rented at 252 Fulton Street was two blocks away from the impressive turreted structure that houses Brooklyn Federal Court at 271 Washington Street. Like those news stories that tell of successful holdups committed next door to a police station in broad daylight, Abel's brazenness had a piquant quality. There were wild rumors that he had led the antenna of his short-wave set from his window to the Gothic tower of the federal building for better reception. The ancient, six-story brick building, known as the Ovington Studios, and the castlelike federal building were in plain sight of each other. Judge Byers took the trouble to point out to the jury that from the trial room they could easily see the fifth-floor room where Abel worked on his paintings and other activities.

Another intriguing point was that Abel did not utter a single word in his own defense during the trial. He had told Donovan that he did not expect any help "from the outside," and appeared resigned to his fate. He did not take the stand, and Donovan in fact called no witnesses. Several who testified for the government were turned by cross-examination into character witnesses, men who had known Abel as a painter and who testified that his work was "interesting" and that his reputation in the community was "beyond reproach." Donovan made his points in cross-examination by questioning the veracity of the key prosecution witnesses. Abel did not wish to testify, for he knew that the capital sin for a spy is to draw attention to himself—

even after he has been caught. And Donovan agreed that to expose his client to cross-examination would do far more harm than the favorable impression he might create on the stand would do good.

With all this to play with, the press had a field day. The trial was front page news all the way to China, and special correspondents from countless publications crowded the courtroom. A barrister who defends criminals in the Old Bailey was sent by a London newspaper. Two FBI agents sat in as observers, and *Life* Magazine dispatched a battery of earnest young lady researchers and commissioned an artist to sketch trial scenes, since photographers were barred from the courtroom. One of these sketches shows Donovan and Tompkins pleading a point before the judge's bench, while in the background, a haggard-looking Abel, seated at the defendant's table, is cupping a hand over his right ear and cocking it in their direction. He was hard of hearing and showed visible irritation when some part of the trial was conducted out of his earshot.

The trial performed the feat of upstaging the world series in most of the nation's newspapers, and the only country where it did not get front-page play was the Soviet Union, which did not acknowledge Abel's existence until November 14, after his conviction. On that date, the semi-official *Literary Gazette* branded the trial "a hoax" and denied that Abel was a Soviet citizen. Readers of the literary weekly were told that "the bouncing young Pinkertons from the FBI discovered among the contents of his studio coded reports and other objects without which no detective book is worth its salt. The authors of this crime fiction have made the photographer into the brains of a spy ring which quite naturally exists on 'Moscow gold.' "

Abel's initial appearance led to descriptions of him in the press as "seedy-looking" and "arty." This dismayed Donovan, who saw to it that his client thereafter had his hair trimmed, his nails cleaned, and wore a dark suit of Ivy League cut. The next day, when Abel appeared, smiling and confident in his new finery, the press epithets changed to "nattily dressed." He took great interest in the trial, peering through his bifocals at the judge and scribbling notes for Donovan. He also made ink sketches of trial scenes, less accomplished but more expressive than those of the *Life* artist.

The Government unveiled its star witness, the mysterious Reino Hayhanen, at the start of the trial. Hayhanen was the man who had put the finger on Abel. He had been sent to the United States in 1952 by the KGB to serve as an assistant resident to the colonel, who, presumably, had too much of a work load for one man to carry. Hayhanen did not meet Abel's exacting standards of excellence, however, and in April, 1957, he was sent back to Russia for a "vacation." Realizing that he would probably spend his vacation in the salt mines, Hayhanen went as far as Paris, where he turned himself in to the American Embassy. He returned to New York on May 4, and gave the FBI its biggest break since John Dillinger's girl friend let it be known what movie she planned to attend with the gunman on the night of July 22, 1934.

Hayhanen arrived in court wearing dark glasses, his hair and mustache dyed. He looked like the classic movie heavy, thickset, furtive, and nervous. In a heavy accent, he described his and Abel's espionage activities, their use of microfilm messages, secret "drops," and their executions of orders from Moscow. The most damning part of his testimony involved the so-called "Quebec message," an order to follow up the recruitment of a U.S. Army sergeant for espionage work. The Quebec message was found in Hayhanen's home in Peekskill, hidden in the cavity of a "special" bolt. It read:

> Roy A. Rhodes [code name—Quebec] Born in 1917 in Oiltown, Okla. A senior sergeant in the War Ministry, former employee of the U.S. military attaché staff in our country. He was a chief of the garage of the U.S. Embassy. He was recruited to our service in January 1952 in our country. He left in June 1953. He was recruited on the basis of compromising materials, but he is tied to us with his receipts and the information he had given in his own handwriting. He had been trained in code work at the Ministry before he went to work at the Embassy but as a code worker he was not used by the Embassy. After he left our country he was sent to the School of Communications of the Army CI services at the city of San Luis, Calif. He was to be trained as a mechanic of the coding machines. He fully agreed to co-operate with us in the states or in any other country. It was agreed that he was to have written to our embassy here special letters but we have received none during the last year. It has been recently learned that he is in Red Bank, N.J., where he owns three garages. The garage work is being done by his wife. His father, Mr. W. A. Rhodes, resides in the United States. His brother works as an engineer at an atomic plant in Camp Georgia.

The fact that Abel and his subordinates had been ordered to subvert an Army sergeant who was supposed to have a brother with access to atomic information weighed heavily in determining his guilt. In Rhodes' case, however, the KGB was on the wrong track. Rhodes had given the Russians a heady mixture of truth and lies. He had no brother working in an atomic plant, either in Georgia or anywhere else, and he himself was not in Red Bank but in Arizona, when Abel and Hayhanen went looking for him. He later was assigned to Fort Monmouth in New Jersey.

Rhodes had collected large sums of money from the Russians in Moscow, and it is evident that he exaggerated and embellished his information to make himself look important. The Russians seem to have taken his ramblings at face value.

After the prosecution had guided Hayhanen through an elaborate account of his five years as Abel's "right arm," Donovan attempted to invalidate his testimony in cross-examination. Before the trial, Donovan had availed himself of the defense's right in a capital case to look over the prosecution witnesses, and had asked to see Hayhanen. The FBI took him to a "secret hideout" they had rented for the day, where they had Hayhanen under wraps. Hayhanen was uncommunicative, but Donovan, adroit with a pad and a pencil, sketched him on the way back to the office. He gave the sketch to a private detective, who managed to pick up Hayhanen's traces in Newark, N.J., and who unearthed quite a bit of unsavory material showing that Abel had good reason to be dissatisfied with his associate's conduct.

Donovan attacked Hayhanen's character and his competence as a spy. He also brought out a major contradiction in Hayhanen's testimony. As a trial witness who had apparently made a deal with the FBI after "defecting to the West," Hayhanen said he had spied for Russia in the United States for five years. But in a thirty-seven-page deposition to the FBI in May, 1957, just after he got back to this country, he said: "I resided and worked in Finland from July 1949 to October 1952. There I received my American passport and arrived in New York in October of 1952. I did not engage in espionage activities, and did not receive any espionage or secret information from anyone during my stay abroad, neither in Finland nor in the United States of America." This variance in his statements was never cleared up, and Hayhanen was never tried for his part in the spy plot. After the trial, Hayhanen disappeared. In the winter of 1961, he was interviewed on a New York television program. Some reports say he is still working for the Government.

Donovan summed up Hayhanen's predicament as that of a man caught between two stools, scorned by both Russia and the United States, whose "only hope of clemency is not only to implicate as many as he can in his crimes, but that he make as important as possible the information he has."

After Hayhanen's sensational testimony, the rest of the trial seemed an anticlimax. Sergeant Rhodes testified that he indeed had given "some true, some false" information to the Russians while he was in Moscow with the American Embassy. Donovan denounced Rhodes, describing him as "the only soldier in American history who has ever confessed to selling out his country for money." Rhodes, a tall, raw-boned man—then thirty-nine—smirked throughout his trial appearance as though he was highly pleased with what he had done. His behavior led observers to express wonder that he had risen to the rank of master sergeant. He was convicted on February 21, 1958, given a dishonorable discharge and five years at hard labor by an Army court-martial, and is serving his sentence in Leavenworth Prison. The prosecution also marshaled platoons of FBI men to the stand, and the federal agents described at length how they had kept Abel under surveillance for several months prior to his arrest, how they had arrested him, and what they had found on his person, in his hotel room, and in his Brooklyn studio.

Toward the end of the trial, the defense asked permission to read into the record some letters written by Abel's family and found on microfilm in the Hotel Latham. The letters from his wife Ilya and daughter Evelyn marked the first time in the trial that Abel was given a dimension as a human being. He had been portrayed as a master spy who manufactured new identities and personalities like paper dolls. After such a long and successful masquerade, it was difficult to think of him as one thinks of other men with families, homes, and only one life to lead.

His wife showed deep concern for his health and safety, while his daughter, then twenty-five, told him of her marriage and her new job, and betrayed her adoration for her father by admitting that her husband could not match him. It seemed somehow incongruous to learn that the resident spy for the Soviet Union in the United States was getting letters from his wife asking about his digestion and telling him that the dog was fine—just as it would seem odd to find out, for instance, that a mass murderer collected butterflies for a hobby. The letters read in court were made more moving because the feeling was that it would be a long time before Abel would see his family again. Members of the jury say that the only time Abel betrayed any emotion was after the reading of the letters; they thought they saw his glasses cloud.

Aside from their intimate glimpses into Abel's home life, the letters showed that the Russian agent had visited his homeland in 1955-56, then returned to the United States. He had left for Moscow on June 10, 1955, via Paris and Austria.

In a letter dated February 20, 1956, Evelyn writes:

DEAR DAD:

It's almost three months since you went away. Although it's not so much to compare with eternity, still it is a long time and the more so as there is a great quantity of news to tell you. First of all, I am going to marry. Please don't be astounded. I am much surprised myself, and still it is a fact to be taken for granted. My future husband seems to be a good guy. He is thirty-four and a radio engineer. Mother likes him very much. We met at the birthday of our friend who lives in the bungalow. On Feb. 25, we shall celebrate our wedding. I hope you will like him when you get back. I think you will have much to talk about.

News number two—We are to get a new flat of two rooms—it is not what we're supposed to get but it is a flat for ourselves and much better than what we have now. News number three—I found a job, engineer referrent in aviation, so now I shall be somewhat closer to you. [Evelyn here apparently refers to her father's ability as an electrical engineer.] The job seems to be a decent one. They promised to pay me well and my future boss seems to be an intellectual and polite guy. I did some odd jobs there and received a pretty sum of money. My future husband and I both are deeply interested in photography, especially in color photography.

He has an Olympia car and we both enjoy meddling with it. We received both your letters and the key from the suitcase, but the latter is still wandering somewhere. Our childhood friend writes regularly and sends you his and his family's best regards and wishes. All our friends wish you health and happiness and a happy and quick way home. Well, this is all I have to say.

Yours,
EVELYN

The second letter from Evelyn, written in English to impress her father, seems to be a birthday greeting (Abel's birthday was July 2). At the same time, she complains that her marriage is not working out:

> Dear Dad, many happy returns. Daddy dear, I am missing you so much. You just cannot imagine how much I need you. It is about four months now since I have married and to me it seems like an eternity, so dull it sometimes is. In general, he is a good chap, but he isn't you. I have got a job. My boss . . . is a bit like you though not so broadminded and not a very great erudite. Though very clever. I am in a great hurry now as I have to go to work.
>
> Yours,
> EVELYN

The silver cord manifest in Evelyn's correspondence shows up in the third and last letter, in which she indicates her dissatisfaction with her husband because he fails to measure up to her father:

> DEAR DAD:
> We liked your presents very much—we planted the hyacinths that survived and by now three of them have sprouted. You say you want more particulars about my husband. I shall try to give you a better picture of him. He is short, green-eyed, rather handsome. He is rather gay and talkative when the conversation considers cars or football. He works as an engineer—he is capable though rather lazy. . . . You ask me whether I am happy with him. As one of our greatest poets once said, there is no happiness in life but there is peace and free will.
> The only thing that troubles me is that I find him boring sometimes. Now about my in-laws. They are awful. I do wish you were with us. Everything would be much easier for us then. I am missing you very much. I thought at first that my husband could substitute you in some respects, but I now see that I was mistaken. Now about my work. I like it fine. I have a splendid boss. He is a very interesting man, clever, talented, tolerant, and handsome. We like each other and spend much time talking about various things. He is forty-four, single and rather unhappy. I wish you could see him and talk to him. My health is okay. P.S. I have started writing poetry in this language. Next time I shall send you a sample.

Aug. 21, 1956

The letters from Abel's wife are an exercise in feminine resignation. She seems to have some knowledge of the nature of her husband's work, and finds it hard to accept the enforced separations. She keeps him up to date on her household problems, but behind the news from home runs a strain of sadness based on the conviction that her husband has been wrongfully taken away. "I want to live with you for ourselves," as she writes at one point, is the perennial plea of the army wife.

The first letter found on Abel seems to have been written shortly after he returned from his 1955-56 vacation in the Soviet Union. Suffering the pangs of separation once more, his wife writes:

> After your departure, I certainly was ill. There was a hardening of the arteries of the heart. I sleep poorly and I do not go out on the street. I walk on the balcony. Sometimes I approach your instrument [Abel played the guitar] and look at it and want to again hear you play and I become sad. For the remaining money I asked them basically to have them send it all to you. Evelyn has married (in late February) and she, after getting married, always says there are no such men as her papa and therefore she is not too much in love with her husband. You are the best of all for us. And don't frown, everyone says this who knows you.
>
> If you look at things with a philosophical point of view, then taking hair from your head doesn't pay. I kiss you firmly and congratulate you. Try to arrange everything so that you do not delay the period of our meeting. Years and age will not wait for us. How are you there? How is your stomach? Take care of yourself—I want to live together with you for ourselves.

The next letter, dated April 6, indicates that Abel has not lost a daughter, but gained a son. Evelyn's husband is concerned about the impression he will make on his father-in-law:

> MY DEAR:
> I am writing a second letter—up till now I only heard from you from the trip [Abel's trip back to the United States]. I want very much to find out how are you. How is your health? I am gradually beginning to come to myself. I could go for a rest, but I am afraid to travel alone, so that I have not yet decided, although I passed the medical board. How necessary you could be to me now. And how

good it is that you do not yet feel the need of being with us. [Abel did feel his family's absence deeply, but his resignation was more Spartan and less voluble than his wife's.]

Evelyn works part time and on her free time from her husband and work she took me to the doctor and at the same time she herself had a check-up. Spring here will again be late. Up till now, it has been cold, damp and snow. The winter was simply horrible. And I am worried about my flowers. Evernya [an affectionate diminutive for Evelyn] says the plum trees froze and it's hard to get the plums. Your father-in-law . . . is awaiting your earliest return, and I, although I know it is silly, I am counting off the days of the known period. I have not received your package yet . . . A childhood friend visited us . . . we talked a lot, reminisced, and most all day, dreamed. Don't let us down. In general, our whole life, constant waiting. That's the way it is, dear. Write as often as possible.

The children, there are two now, send greetings. Son is very disturbed what kind of impression he will make on you. He might not appeal to you at once. I kiss you firmly. I wish you luck, health, and most of all a speedy return.

On June 21, Abel's wife finds cause to rejoice in a package from her husband containing some hyacinth bulbs (ostensibly sent from the United States through the Soviet diplomatic pouch). She also illustrates that the Abel family enjoys a standard of living far superior to the average Russian's:

MY DEAR:

At last we received your small package. Everything pleased us very much, and as usual, whatever you do, with care and attention. We were glad to receive a letter from you and to learn that everything is fine with you. It is a pity you have not had letters from us [Abel received the letters in bunches]—such a long time. I sent you several. Congratulations on your birthday. We will drink a toast to your well-being and your early promised return.

We are at the summer place. In many respects our garden has suffered. On the best apple trees, from which last year you culled a plentiful harvest, only now have the leaves started to appear. I am still fighting with the house servant and do not have a new one. . . . The television works but I seldom look at it. The dog behaves very well—she too awaits her master, and I also wait. It is desirable to have a husband at home; at the present time I feel your absence more, especially since I have been with you and remember what you promised me before your departure. [Perhaps Abel had promised his wife to quit espionage after his current assignment.] Our new chef is wonderful, attentive, and tactful.

On August 20, Mrs. Abel acknowledges a letter she has finally received from her husband in which he asks if the package he sent had arrived:

MY DEAR:

How glad I was to learn you had received one of my letters. We received the package in May. It is a shame the hyacinths traveled long and two of them perished altogether. The rest are planted and already have rooted. This is a live greeting from you. Next year they will bloom. We count every month that passes and you remember this.

In his summation for the state, Tompkins dwelt on the fact that Abel was good in his job. "This was a master spy, a real pro," he said. "This was his chosen profession, he knows the rules of the game and so do his family." Abel did indeed know the rules, the first of which is that once you are caught you are on your own. There was sudden amnesia in Moscow when his name was mentioned.

One of the ironies of the trial was that Donovan used this same argument of professionalism, but for a different purpose. The defense and the prosecution were of one mind that if Abel was a spy, he was an outstanding one.

"Let's assume," argued Donovan, "let's assume for the moment that the man is what the Government says he is. In the first place, it means that such a man was serving his country on an extraordinarily dangerous mission. We in our armed forces only send on such missions the bravest, most intelligent men one can find." Donovan made the assumption to question the validity of the Rhodes and Hayhanen testimonies. Abel, a man of extraordinary talents, had been brought low by two confessed liars and "bums," he said.

Tompkins made the same assumption to discredit the defense's character witnesses and letters from home. Abel was not being judged on his virtues as a family man, Tompkins said, but on his misdeeds as a spy. Donovan maintained, however, that "it's not so much that an international spy is against the law. He's outside it."

On October 23, the jury withdrew into a high-ceilinged court chamber at 12:15 P.M. John T. Dublynn, a thirty-six-year-old Brooklynite employed in a New York City sewage treatment plant, was foreman. "It was no open-and-shut case," he recalls. The members of the panel were in general sympathetic to Abel as a man.

"If I had to choose a spy," one commented, "that's the kind of spy I would choose." Yet they felt that the burden of evidence against him was overwhelming. Dublynn, realizing that balloting by show of hands might keep some timid persons from expressing their true convictions, suggested unsigned paper ballots for the first vote. As he opened the folded slips in front of him, he came to one that read: "Not guilty." When he had opened them all, the count was eleven to one for conviction. The same situation was the topic of a recent play and movie entitled *Twelve Angry Men,* in which the one dissident on a murder jury manages to swing the eleven others around and engineers an acquittal practically single-handed. There was no such tour de force on the Abel jury.

The man who had voted not guilty was uncertain that the prosecution had proven the first count of the indictment, conspiracy to transmit military information to the Soviet Union. He asked to examine further several exhibits, among them the Quebec message. By then it was lunch, and the jurors took an hour and five minutes to satisfy their appetites. They returned at 2:20 P.M. and examined the Quebec message until the dissident juror was satisfied. Again there were words of compassion for the defendant, but they could not shake the jury's deep conviction that they were dealing with a professional spy. The jurors had unanimous contempt for Hayhanen and Rhodes, but they nonetheless believed that the two told the truth on the stand.

The government witnesses who testified to Abel's character and reputation failed to impress, for as Dublynn points out, the witnesses were testifying about another man. They had known a shy, benign, and engaging painter named Goldfus. They were being asked to testify about a calculating and clever spy named Abel. The whole thing was like a painful case of mistaken identity.

The jury felt the defense had done its best, but that it had not had much of a case. In the panel's opinion, Judge Byers bent over backwards to be fair, and all the lawyers concerned were capable. There had been none of those flashes of melodramatic eloquence that television has taught juries to expect. "They were no Perry Masons," says Dublynn.

At 4:50 P.M., after three and a half hours of deliberation, the jury came in with its verdict: Guilty on all counts. Abel stood to hear it. In the bustle that followed, he quickly left the courtroom, walking with his head up and his back straight. Nothing about him indicated defeat.

Sentencing did not take place until November 15, but in the meantime Donovan sent Judge Byers a letter which, in the light of later events, now takes on the aura of a prophecy. Assuming the correctness of the jury verdict, Donovan listed the arguments against giving Abel the death penalty. The normal justification of the death penalty, he wrote, is its possible effect as a deterrent, but it would be absurd to believe that the execution of Abel would deter the Russian military forces. Again, the effect of imposing the death penalty should be weighed by the Government with respect to the activities of our citizens abroad. Here Donovan apparently referred to any U.S. agents that might be inside Soviet territory, or to U.S. citizens already in Soviet jails for various reasons.

Although the Government has received no co-operation from the defendant, Donovan continued, it is still in the national interest to keep the man available for a reasonable period of time. (In other words, he might yet talk.)

It was in his next argument that the former OSS general counsel showed prophetic foresight. "It is possible," he wrote, "that in the foreseeable future, an American of equivalent rank will be captured by Soviet Russia or an ally—at such a time an exchange of prisoners through diplomatic channels would be considered to be in the best national interest of the United States." In May, 1960, Francis Gary Powers and his U-2 plane crashed into the heart of Russia and bore out Donovan's enlightened guess. And less than two years later, thanks to Donovan's drive and determination, the exchange became a reality.

As to the time Abel should serve, Donovan pointed out that in the 1920's, the average sentence given by French courts to Soviet spies was three years. In a last argument, the lawyer examined Abel's age and motives. "Abel is a man fifty-five years old [in 1957]," he wrote. "He has faithfully served his country, and whether that country is right or wrong, it is his country. I ask only that the court consider that we are legally at peace with that country."

On the day of sentencing, Judge Byers acknowledged Donovan's plea, though only he can say to what extent it moved him. "The court knows next to nothing about this man's personal life or his true character," the judge said. "Lacking insight into the man known as Abel, the evidence requires that he be dealt with as one who chose his career with knowledge of its hazards and the price that he would have to pay in event of detection and conviction."

Translated into years and dollars, this meant thirty years and a $5,000 fine on the first count, ten years and a $2,000 fine on the second, and five years and a $1,000 fine on the third. The sentences were to be served concurrently, which meant a maximum of thirty years in jail.

It was pointed out to the judge that the first count, though it provided for the death penalty, had no provision for a fine, so the $5,000 fine was rescinded. Abel was removed to the Federal Penitentiary in Atlanta, Georgia, to begin serving his sentence.

The trial was over for Abel, but not for Donovan, who began the fastidious legal work involved in appeals. On the grounds that some of Abel's belongings had been illegally seized at the time of his arrest by the FBI and had been illegally introduced as evidence at the trial, the case went to the U.S. Court of Appeals, where the judgment was affirmed in July, 1958. From there, Donovan took the case to the Supreme Court, where, after five hours of oral argument and reargument, he drew an unusual five to four decision on March 28, 1960. Justice William O. Douglas wrote the dissenting opinion. The question at hand, he said, was whether seven items were properly admitted into evidence, adding: "Cases of notorious criminals, like cases of small miserable ones, are apt to make bad law. When guilt permeates a record, even judges sometimes relax and let the police take short cuts not sanctioned by constitutional practice." Donovan's last legal move, a petition for rehearing, was denied by the Supreme Court, and the case was officially closed in June, 1960, at which time Abel paid off his fine, drawing from funds in the East River Savings Bank branch at 743 Amsterdam Avenue.

In Atlanta, Abel was officially registered as prisoner No. 80016-A. The Bureau of Prisons was reluctant to discuss what they call his "institutional adjustment." D. M. Heritage, the warden, said that "it is a long-standing policy of the Federal Prison Service not to furnish information" on the prisoner's life. "This," he said, "is protection to the inmate and also serves to keep from 'glamorizing' any individual inmate. You can be sure that we attempt to accord each inmate the same treatment. 'Name' prisoners are not accorded any privileges not available to the other men. Neither are restrictions imposed arbitrarily."

From unofficial sources it has been learned that Abel was one of the institution's most popular prisoners and that his adjustment was splendid. He was respected as a military man who suffered a reverse in the fortunes of war. He shared a maximum security cell with three other men whom he taught to play bridge. He had a position of responsibility in the prison's commercial art department, where he taught and supervised the other inmates interested in art. The prison population numbers forgers, counterfeiters, and bad-check artists, all of whom have a natural propensity for fine arts. Abel helped provide a healthy outlet for their creative urges. He invented a silk-screen process which is used to turn out the prison's institutional Christmas cards, sent to the friends and relatives of the inmates. In 1958 and 1959, he also designed the card. The first one was a Russian winter scene with snow flurries whipping across the steppes. In 1960, he switched to the standard theme of shepherds watching over Bethlehem.

This model prisoner kept up with the outside world by subscribing to *The New York Times* and the *Scientific American*. He was also interested in anything that was written about him in other publications, and continued to receive art books and other works through the good offices of Donovan.

The lawyer visited his client in Atlanta and found him in good spirits. When he mentioned that he was stopping in Washington on his way back to New York, Abel's eyes lit up and he asked, "Have you ever been in the FBI museum in Washington?" Donovan said he had not.

"I understand they have a new exhibit on my case," Abel explained earnestly. "I wish you would stop in and look it over. They may have made some mistakes."

Donovan was amazed that Abel, in his maximum security cell, could be so well informed about the FBI's activities, but he promised to check the exhibit. Guided by an unsuspecting agent, he took one of the regular museum tours, which recount the most glorious hours of the FBI in word and picture. The last room was not unfamiliar to Donovan—it held a complete layout on the Abel case—it was all there, from pictures of the artist's studio and the Federal Court building to the hollowed-out coins and pencils. Donovan wrote Abel that the FBI had compiled the exhibit with customary thoroughness.

*   *   *

The man known as Rudolf Ivanovich Abel was born in Moscow on July 2, 1902. He was the only child of a good family from southern Russia. His grandfather had been a minor public official under the czars. Abel's father traveled a good deal, and the only child acquired an extensive knowledge of his country at an early age. He was studious and intelligent and decided to become a teacher. He showed an unusual gift for languages, and taught English, German, and Polish in a secondary school in Moscow in his early twenties. When he was twenty-five, he made the two most important decisions in his life: he married and he joined what was then the OGPU, the Soviet secret police. He was assigned to the foreign espionage branch.

At first, he taught English to espionage trainees, but in the thirties his knowledge of German won him his first assignment abroad. He was cited for distinguished action during the second World War as an intelligence officer on the German front, and by the time the war was over, he was a major in the NKVD. In 1954, the NKVD was split into several branches, and Abel was attached to the KGB (Komtet Gosudarstvennoi Bezopasnosti).

After the war, the Soviets intensified their espionage efforts in the Western Hemisphere. The favorite route for U.S.-bound Soviet spies was Canada, which screened immigrants less carefully and boasted a more generous immigration quota. In 1946, Abel was planted in a displaced persons camp in Germany under the name Andrew Kayotis.

He applied for entry to Canada as a D.P. and arrived there some time in 1947. With his Canadian papers he entered the United States the next year. Before going to New York, he wanted to see the rest of the country. He traveled through the Northwest and down the West Coast. Perhaps his trip was a sort of inspector's tour of regional offices, and he contacted the Soviet agents under his command. He later told a friend that he had been a lumberjack in the Northwest and that it was there he had learned to play the guitar. His descriptions of the area were precise, as were his recollections of Los Angeles, San Francisco, and Chicago.

His arrival in New York can be traced back to June, 1950, the time of his first deposit at the East River Savings Bank. He lived in hotels on upper Broadway, in the West 80's and 90's, moving frequently. It was at this time that he made one of his two or three close friendships. Abel has been described as a man with "a mind like a steel trap," and "without a nerve in his body." In prison tests, he was given an I.Q. rating close to the genius level. For a man alone in an alien land on a dangerous mission, his self-control was exemplary. But he was not completely the machine man the job demanded. Spying is a lonely business where a man must forego the warmth of ordinary human relationships to protect himself. Even Abel, a man whose soul was discipline, could not tolerate absolute loneliness. He made friends. He chose them carefully, men considerably younger than himself, painters like himself, and above all, men supremely unconcerned with politics or the world as it is described in newspapers.

Alan Winston fitted the picture well. He was a student at Columbia University who had rebelled against wealthy parents and wanted to be a painter. He became Abel's only close friend until 1954, when the colonel met Burt Silverman, another painter, in the Brooklyn building where both had studios.

In a bankbook for the National City Bank, under the heading "in case of emergency, please notify," Abel had listed Burt Silverman, 252 Fulton Street, Brooklyn. He had complete confidence in Silverman and Winston, to whom he gave $15,000 to be put in a safe deposit box under Winston's name. He explained that the money was his life savings as a photo finisher. He and Winston shared a passion for art and music, and went to museums, concerts, and movies together. They ate together on many occasions, with Abel doing the cooking and selecting the wines. With his usual competence, he was an excellent chef and sommelier.

Quite aside from his social life, Abel was continuing the patient labors of a spy, but in 1952 he decided he needed some help, an assistant resident, and he asked Moscow to send him a likely candidate. The KGB looked over the crop of spies the Russians had planted in neutral European countries for just such emergencies, and picked Reino Hayhanen, a thirty-two-year-old lieutenant in the KGB.

Born in Leningrad of peasant parents, Hayhanen had been an honor student with Finnish as his second language. In November, 1939, a month after receiving his teacher's certificate, Hayhanen was drafted into the NKVD as an interpreter on the Finno-Russian front. In the

226 THE SECRET WAR

next eight years, he singled himself out in intelligence work in the Soviet Union and Finland. In 1948, he was sent to a high-echelon spy school, and a year later he went back to Finland with a new identity.

Hayhanen had been sent to Finland to establish a "legend" that would enable him to enter the United States quickly when the need arose. He had papers in the name of Eugene Nicolo Maki, ostensibly an American born in Enaville, Idaho, who had spent most of his life in Finland. He worked in Finland as a blacksmith's helper and an automobile mechanic, all the while building up the legend. When Moscow was certain his background would hold up, they told him to apply for a United States passport in Helsinki. The American legation, a model of efficiency, had the passport ready in a matter of days. He only had to show his Idaho birth certificate and proof that Maki had never voted or served in the Finnish army. In August, 1952, not long after Abel's request, Hayhanen was called to Moscow for a three-week training program for his new assignment. He crossed the border concealed in the trunk of a car and spent three weeks in a refresher course in English, and courses in microdot, soft film, and cipher techniques. He received the code name Vik and was told that his boss in New York had the code name Mark.

His instructions were to contact Mark, help him recruit agents, and keep in touch with Soviet officials in New York. He was given a lump sum of $5,000 to set himself up in a "cover" and his salary was set at $400 a month with $100 a month for expenses. Another salary paid to him in Russia was sent directly to his wife.

In Moscow, he met another superior, the man he worked with in New York until he was turned over to Mark in 1954. This man he knew only as Mikhail; later, he identified him from FBI pictures as Mikhail Nikolaevich Svirin, First Secretary of the Soviet United Nations delegation in New York from August 1952 to April 1954. He also met the assistant chief of the American section of the KGB, a man he knew only as Pavlov, who gave him a pep talk on the eve of his departure. "In espionage we are always at war," Hayhanen was told. "If real war comes, either total war or war between several countries, spies must remain at their posts. Even if you no longer hear from us, continue to carry out your espionage work in the country where you are assigned. After the war, everyone will be asked what part he played."

Pavlov explained that espionage information comes from a wide variety of sources. He included "all the information you can get from newspapers or any other official sources, either by asking or obtaining pamphlets or written information. Illegal or secret information involving national security, military installations, or atomic secrets."

After his three-week espionage primer, Hayhanen went back to Finland via the car trunk. His wife remained in Russia, but as part of his cover in Finland, he had married a Finnish woman, Hanna Kurikka, and she accompanied him. The two left Finland for England in early October as Mr. and Mrs. Maki, boarded the *Queen Mary,* and arrived in New York on October 21. Their first night in New York was spent in the Chesterfield Hotel (they later lived in furnished rooms in Harlem and Brooklyn) and the next day Hayhanen went for a walk in Central Park. Near the Tavern on the Green restaurant there is a bridle path crossing with a sign that reads BE CAREFUL OF RIDERS. He placed a red thumbtack under a beam in the fence near the sign. This spot was one of several signal areas he had been assigned in Moscow. The tack was simply to let his superiors know that he had arrived safely.

Hayhanen later learned that the signal areas had to be checked daily to determine whether he had to pick up any messages. Other signal areas were park fences or subway stations marked with blue chalk. A horizontal mark meant that a message had been placed in the drop; a vertical mark meant that a message had been retrieved. In five years of working in New York, Hayhanen had occasion to use more than half a dozen drops in New York City. One was in a crack in a cement wall that runs from 165th Street to 167th Street along Jerome Avenue in the Bronx; one was behind a loose brick under a bridge that spans a bridle path near the Central Park reservoir; one was near the Soldiers and Sailors Monument at Riverside Drive and 89th Street. Others were under lampposts in Prospect and Fort Tryon Parks. There was a special drop for magnetic containers, under metal mailboxes between 74th and 79th Streets on Central Park West.

On one occasion, Hayhanen and Abel used a hole in a flight of stairs in Prospect Park as a drop. Park employees had noticed the hole, and when Hayhanen arrived to pick up a message one night, he saw that maintenance men had cemented it. They had not found the message, however, because years later the FBI dug it out from behind the cement. It was a tiny strip of microfilm in a hollow bolt asking Hay-hanen why he had missed two meetings.

These elaborate precautions may appear excessive when we see the kind of messages that were passed back and forth. In a city the size of New York, anyone can meet on the street and talk for hours without attracting attention. Hayhanen had made special excursions to see if he was being trailed and was justly convinced that he had entered the country undetected. What then was the purpose of using a complicated system of signals and drops to transmit what were for the most part innocuous messages and letters from home, all in code?

The answer is that for Abel, spying was a matter of "good habits." He felt that the greatest degree of caution had to be exercised in the most trivial matters. He had to keep the same rigorous standards in every detail of his operation, no matter how time-consuming and im-practical the methods. Abel lived with the conviction that his first mistake would be fatal. He and Hayhanen also had spent most of their lives in a police state, and probably exaggerated the degree of surveillance that they would come under in the United States.

Abel's precautions, like a knight's armor, were so cumbersome that they eventually helped lead to his downfall. Part of his spy parapher-nalia was an assortment of hollowed-out pencils, bolts, and flashlight batteries that were not, as the prosecution pointed out, "the kind that Boy Scouts use." These were used as containers for microfilm mes-sages and left in the drops, where, even if they were found by accident, they were unlikely to attract suspicion. He also had some fake coins, nickels and pennies that looked like the real article. The coins were perforated on one side, and by inserting a pin, they could be opened in two to disclose a space on the inside.

Abel replied with a written message that he coded, microfilmed, and placed inside one of his fake coins, a 1948 Jefferson nickel. He wrapped the coin in one of the drops. The message, written in English, detailed Abel's first orders to his new assistant.

> We congratulate you on a safe arrival. We confirm the receipt of your letter, to the address V repeat V and the reading of the letter no. 1. For organization or cover, we gave instructions to transmit to you $3,000 in local currency. Consult with us prior to investing it in any kind of business, advising the character of the business.
>
> According to your request, we will transmit the formula for the preparation of soft film [Hayhanen was supposed to have learned this

in his Moscow training], together with your mother's letter. It is too early to send you the Gammas [what the "Gammas" were is anybody's guess]. Encipher short letters, but the longer ones make with insertions. All the data about yourself, place of work, address, etc., must not be transmitted in one cipher message. Transmit insertions separately. The package was delivered to your wife personally. Everything is all right with the family. We wish you success. Greetings from the comrades. December 3 [a month and a half after Hayhanen's arrival].

What happened next is one of the case's unexplained mysteries. Hayhanen claims he never got the message. Perhaps a passer-by, attracted by the glint of metal behind a loose brick, simply pocketed the nickel. Perhaps Abel was guilty of an aberration, spent the fake nickel and put a real one in the drop. In some manner, the nickel entered the national economy.

One hot morning in the summer of 1953, James Bozart, a fourteen-year-old newspaper delivery boy, had just received fifty cents in change from a customer at 3403 Foster Avenue, an apartment building in Brooklyn. With a quarter and five nickels clutched tightly in his hands, he said, "I was walking down the stairs, and the change slipped from my hand and it dropped on the staircase, and when I picked it up, one of the nickels had split in half. I picked up the pieces—one of them had a piece of microfilm in it. It was a picture of a file card, or an index card. There seemed to be a row of numbers on it."

James turned the coin over to the police and was commended for his acumen. If he had not stumbled on the stairs, the nickel might be buying newspapers yet. The New York Police gave it to the FBI, and the FBI gave it to its cipher experts, who were unable to crack the code. From the summer of 1953 to the spring of 1957, when Hayhanen turned himself in, the nickel remained an enigma to the FBI. Hayhanen gave them the key to the code.

It was based on four easy-to-remember keys: the Russian word for snowfall, stanzas of Russian folk songs, a patriotic date, and the number thirteen. First in the system of substitutions came the seven-letter word *Snegopa,* or snowfall; the date was 3/9/45, Russia's victory over Japan, written continental-style; the first twenty letters of the Russian folk songs and number thirteen were used for further transpositions. This was Hayhanen's personal code, used only by him and his superiors. Unlike Abel's personal code, discovered in his tiny cipher booklet, it was not unbreakable (even though the FBI had no luck with it). But it had the advantage of providing perfect security, for all the keys could be remembered by rote and there was no need for an incriminating cipher pad to be carried around. In his five years in the United States, Hayhanen sent about thirty ciphered messages and received about twenty-five.

"No man could ever break that code," exclaimed Donovan when it was explained by an FBI cipher expert at the trial. Involved as it was, it could have been broken, and in 1956 some of its elements were changed for security. Hayhanen continued to exchange messages with Abel, but did not meet him in person until nearly two years after his arrival. In the meantime, he was in contact with Mikhail (Svirin), whom he had already met in Moscow.

At his first *treff* (secret meeting) with Svirin, at the Lincoln Road exit of the BMT subway at the Prospect Park stop, Hayhanen was wearing a blue tie with red stripes and was smoking a pipe, although he is a nonsmoker. Svirin gave him a microfilm container with some letters from his family and wished him continued success in his new post. Svirin left the United States abruptly in April, 1954, just as the Government was getting interested in him.

In the spring of 1953, Hayhanen was given his first job. He contacted a Finnish sailor known as Asko, whose ship had landed in Hoboken. They arranged a *treff* at the Seventh Avenue exit of the BMT Brighton Line subway, and Hayhanen received and paid for several messages. They used the underside of a seat in a phone booth in a bar on Amsterdam Avenue as a drop.

After Mikhail's departure, Hayhanen was placed under Mark's (Abel's) personal command. On a day in August, 1954, he received word to be in the men's room of the RKO-Flushing movie theater at 8 P.M., wearing his blue tie with red stripes and smoking his pipe. He had a password ready, but the thin, unassuming man who came up to him said: "Never mind about the password, I know you're the right man. Let's go outside and talk." They went into a coffee shop down the street and Abel sized up his confederate. He did not like what he saw, a small, squat man with the pasty face and thick lips of one concerned too much with food and drink. He gave an overwhelming impression of softness. Hayhanen could sense his superior's contempt from the start, and grew to hate Abel. "He treated me like a chauffeur," he said.

The first assignment Abel gave Hayhanen was quite literally that of a chauffeur. Hayhanen had bought a car and a house in Peekskill, N.Y., where he had prudently buried his fake birth certificate and other incriminating evidence in the cellar. Hayhanen drove his boss to the Croton Reservoir in Westchester, where Abel was looking for a likely spot to set up his short-wave radio.

He had a converter from 6 to 100 volts that he plugged into the car lighter to make the short-wave set work. He put the antenna in a tree, but couldn't get much of anything. The two later went to Hopewell Junction up the Taconic Parkway, shopping for a house where they could set up a radio station, but couldn't find anything for less than $15,000, more than even the Soviet Government was willing to pay.

Abel got his first jolt about the new man during the auto trip when he asked Hayhanen to jot down something coming over the radio in Morse code. Hayhanen rather sheepishly admitted he had never learned Morse. Abel was shocked. "In illegal espionage work, everyone has to know Morse code," he told his associate sternly. "What did they teach you in Moscow?"

In November, 1954, Abel got the Quebec message and told Hayhanen they would have to go to New Jersey to look for Sergeant Rhodes. "He would make a good agent," Abel remarked, "because he and some of his relatives are working on military lands." The two went snooping around in Red Bank, but at the time, Rhodes was in Fort Huachuca, Tucson, Arizona. Abel found out that Rhodes had relatives in Colorado and sent Hayhanen to try and get a line on him. Hayhanen, unlike Abel, had trouble with his English. (In fact, during the trial he complained that the lawyers were going too fast, and Judge Byers cautioned that "we have a witness who is not as conversant with the English language as the rest of us.") He called up Rhodes' married sister in Salida, Colorado, and frightened her with his thick accent and inarticulate speech, but she nonetheless gave him her brother's address. Nothing ever came of trying to reach Rhodes, however.

There followed for Hayhanen two other brief missions, a trip to Boston to contact Olaf Carlson, a Swedish ships engineer, and a sortie to Arleigh, New Jersey, to recruit an agent. In both cases, he was unable to find his man. Abel began to wonder whether Hayhanen was much good at finding things, and as a test, he sent him to Bear Mountain to hunt for buried treasure. Abel had buried a total of $5,000 in the state park that he intended to use as payment for Mrs. Helen

Sobell, wife of Morton Sobell, who was convicted with the Rosenbergs in 1951. Sobell is serving a thirty-year sentence in the same prison where Abel is serving his thirty-year sentence, Atlanta Federal Penitentiary.

Map in hand, Hayhanen dug around Bear Mountain Park and found the hiding places and the paper parcels, one containing $3,000, the other $2,000. It is sad to record that there is no more honor among spies than among thieves. Hayhanen, instead of paying Mrs. Sobell, pocketed the money. He reported to Abel the next day: "I gave her the money and told her to spend it carefully." For once Abel was satisfied with his assistant's work. "That's good," he replied. "We like to recruit husband and wife together as agents."

In May, 1955, Abel decided it was time for Hayhanen to set up a photographic shop in Newark, New Jersey, as a cover. He soon discovered that his assistant knew little about photography, but set about helping him when Hayhanen rented a store and apartment in a run-down section of town, on Bergen Street.

Carried away by his good intentions, Abel made the mistake that cost him his freedom. He disobeyed the first rule of an espionage network—that agents must never know their superiors' names and addresses—and took Hayhanen to his studio on Fulton Street to give him some photographic material and a spare short-wave radio he had in a storeroom. It was this one carelessness on Abel's part that allowed Hayhanen to lead the FBI to the resident spy.

Abel showed Hayhanen how to build a special table suited for photographic material. He wrote pamphlets to explain the use of a vacuum board for making matrices and how to make separation negatives for color photography. He told Hayhanen what chemicals to use to make soft films. The chemical removes the stiff film base, leaving the soft emulsion, or top layer, which is pliable and can be easily fitted into a small container after the backing has been dissolved.

Stressing that he should have learned all this in Moscow, Abel also helped his assistant improve his microdot technique. This is a method for photographically reducing a document; an eight-by-ten-inch photograph can be reduced to the size of a period on a typewriter.

A thirty-five-millimeter negative is reduced by using a lens with a very short focal length and the light from a projector. Abel used spectroscopic film for his microdots. This film, which is available at any Kodak store, has what is called "high resolving power." It can record

1,000 lines per millimeter and keeps distinct the white and black lines of the microdot, whereas ordinary film would show no more than a black smudge. Hayhanen was getting poor results even with spectroscopic film, and Abel showed him how to achieve higher contrast so that every word of the message would be clear when it was enlarged to natural size. He showed Hayhanen how to send microdot messages to Moscow. He undid the stapling of thick magazines like *American Home* and *Better Homes and Gardens,* inserted the thin strips of microdots, and glued the stapling back together. Then he mailed the magazines to a prearranged poste restante number in Paris.

Only a month after Hayhanen had moved to Newark, Abel got a welcome surprise. His superiors, pleased with his work, promoted him to full colonel and granted him a six-month leave with his family. He left on June 10, by way of Paris and Vienna. With Abel gone, Hayhanen could breathe a bit more freely. He did not have to check the signal areas daily, or drive out into the suburbs looking for sites for radio stations, and he did not have to take lessons in spying from his didactic boss. Instead of opening his photography shop, he put Glasswax in the windows to make sure no one would think he was open for business. And he began behaving in a strange way for a spy.

As Donovan said later at the trial, "If Hayhanen was an undercover agent in Newark, he made every mistake possible. A spy must be faceless in a crowd. Hayhanen did all he could to attract attention." His behavior came to the attention of his neighbors, his landlord, and finally the police. If Abel had known what Hayhanen was up to in Newark, it would have spoiled his first vacation in six years.

Hayhanen liked vodka and, for the first time in his life, found himself in a financial position to buy as much as he could drink. He went on mammoth drunks, throwing the empty bottles in the trash can behind his store-apartment until he was notorious in the neighborhood. Following the classic pattern, he began to berate his woman companion in public. The proprietor of a bakery recalls that Hayhanen came into his establishment with his "wife" one day, roaring drunk, and bought a loaf of bread. He took the bread, threw it on the ground, and ordered his wife to pick it up. He let out a mighty roar of laughter when the woman got down on all fours to retrieve the bread.

In his next public scrape, however, he came out a poor second. He was making such a racket one night that neighbors notified his landlord, who came in to see what the fuss was about. The landlord found Hayhanen bleeding from a knife wound in the left leg and his wife sobbing in a corner. A police ambulance was summoned and Hayhanen told police he had cut himself while wrapping packages. Hayhanen kept on drinking, unhappy over his assignment as Abel's assistant. He brooded over the fact that he had been promised a soft job in the "legal" branch of Soviet espionage, where he could be sent somewhere as an embassy attaché. Instead, he had drawn a "hardship" assignment.

When Abel came back from his vacation in early 1956, he tried to contact Hayhanen but found that he was missing signals and drops. He finally reached him and asked how the photography studio was coming. "Newark is too wet, it's impossible to open here," Hayhanen explained. Abel was not satisfied with this explanation and scolded his assistant for falling down on the job. Then his tone changed, he said he realized Hayhanen was under a strain, and that it might be better if he went on a vacation to Moscow to see his family. It took a few months for a message from Moscow to arrive, granting the leave and promoting Hayhanen from major to lieutenant colonel. Abel organized his trip. He was to leave by way of Paris and travel under the name Lauri Arnold Ermas. Ever thorough, Abel showed Hayhanen how to use the Paris dial phone to call the Soviet Embassy. This sudden vacation and promotion unsettled Hayhanen. He realized Moscow did not want to see him to praise his good work. Stalling for time, he told Abel he was getting a ticket on the *Queen Elizabeth,* sailing in January, 1957. He accepted $200 for trip expenses, but he never took the boat.

In a February 14 message, he made up a story about being questioned by the FBI and taken off the ship. In complete panic by this time at the thought of going home, he also claimed he was being tailed. Abel was adamant, and Hayhanen left on the *Liberté* on April 24. He landed at Le Havre and called the number Abel had given him, KLEber 3341. The password was "Can I send through your office two parcels with Meri Company?" A Soviet official met Hayhanen in the street and gave him some francs and $200. Having milked the Russians for all he could, Hayhanen reported to the American Legation in Paris the next day and turned himself in. The story he told flabbergasted legation officials, but he did display a hollowed-out coin and, on the outside chance he might be telling the truth, he was sent back to New York and turned over to the FBI.

In New York, Hayhanen was kept incognito at the U.S. Quarantine station in Staten Island, where psychiatrists gave him tests to see whether he was a psychopath whose story could be discounted. The tests revealed that he was an alcoholic with suicidal tendencies, but when he told the FBI how to crack the "Vic" code they began to take him seriously. Abel, who sensed that something had gone wrong, was arrested in June in the midst of departure plans.

No two spies could have been more dissimilar than Abel and Hayhanen. Abel was brilliant and methodical, Hayhanen was dull and careless. One was dedicated, the other an opportunist. One was tall and thin, the other short and squat. One was ascetic, the other a sybarite. They remind one of the classic rivalry in Soviet literature between the corrupt and the honest civil servant. Hayhanen is the provincial subprefect who thrives on graft, vodka and housemaids. Abel is the municipal judge, whose bearing indicates an almost religious devotion to duty.

At the trial, Donovan said of Hayhanen: "If that man was a spy, history will record that he was the most fumbling, self-defeating, indifferent spy that any country ever sent on any conceivable mission. It is incredible to believe that this is a lieutenant colonel in the Russian military intelligence sent here to obtain our highest defense secrets. That bum wouldn't have private first class stripes in the American Army." These were harsh words, considering that Rhodes was a master sergeant.

When the news of Abel's capture was made public, most surprised of all was his small group of friends and acquaintances. It would be reassuring to report that Abel, like Hayhanen, aroused suspicions among the inhabitants of the rather run-down block where he kept his artist's studio: that the building superintendent complained about strange visitors at late hours and wondered why he received so many letters from remote lands; that the delicatessen down the street kept large-grain beluga caviar in stock specially for him; that the barmaid in the local tavern thought he was a riot because after downing a shot of vodka, he would smash the glass on the floor and dance the Kazatska.

Alas, such was not the case, and Abel never committed an action or uttered a word that people who knew him thought singular. He was Emil Goldfus, a mild, rather insignificant painter of German origin. It was only when his true identity came to light that commonplace remarks and banal details began to take on a new shape. A television repairman with a shop in the same building as Abel's studio recalled, on reading about the short-wave transmissions, that there had been complaints of strange interferences from TV owners in the neighborhood. One of the artists in the building used to meet Abel coming up the stairs at 10 P.M. for his nightly conversations with Moscow. "Why are you painting so late?" he asked, to which Abel replied, "I'm so busy during the day." Another tenant, a sculptor whose sixth-floor studio was directly above Abel's room, remembers that in the winter of 1956 there was a violent snowstorm. Water began to drip into his studio from a leak in the skylight, and he rolled in an empty trash can from the hall. Abel came dashing up to help, as the water must have been coming into his room also, and when they had the situation under control the sculptor thought, What a nice man that is.

The Ovington Studios is a massively ugly structure built by the Ovington brothers, Brooklyn giftware merchants, in 1863. They used it to manufacture pottery and later sold it. The six-story brick building has a mansard roof with skylights, well suited to artists' needs. Abel had a $35-a-month studio, a dingy, irregular room, and a storage room at $20 a month, both on the fifth floor. He did not live in the studio, but commuted there almost every day from his Broadway hotels.

Those who knew him in the building remember a friendly but not overbearing man. He made a conscious effort at being "in good" with everybody, even the superintendent and elevator man, Harry McMullen, whom he invited out for drinks. Once, when the elevator was on the blink, he offered to repair it, using his own equipment, and had it working again in record time.

He had several reasons for choosing the Ovington Studios as his headquarters. The rent was low, he could get reasonably good reception on his Hallicrafter from his fifth-floor room, with the antenna fixed to the roof, and the building was removed from his residences, making detection less likely. But above all, the masquerade as an artist afforded him an excellent cover. Masquerade is perhaps the wrong word, for critics admit that he was a talented painter whose work could pass for professional. A man of Abel's varied talents could have posed as a language teacher, a photographer, an electrician, and a number of other professions. His interest in painting was genuine. At the same time, the pose was expedient; it explained his irregular hours, and he knew that artists are not inquisitive about each other's personal lives. He could talk shop with another painter for days on end without ever being asked where he lived, whether he had a family, and where he came from. Respect for privacy is part of an artist's credo, or as Nathanael Kaz, a painter in the building, put it: "Artists' creative drives make them unaware of their surroundings."

This indifference to surroundings was such that one day Burt Silverman, who had become a close friend of Abel's, burst into his studio as Abel was receiving a broadcast in Russian from Moscow. Abel nervously turned the set off and followed Silverman into his studio across the hall. The phone rang, and Silverman answered and said, "I'm here with Emil, and we're listening to Moscow on his short-wave set." Abel blanched and said slowly, "Don't ever say anything like that again." Silverman thought nothing of the incident. The notion that an affable artist in the Ovington Studios was a Soviet spy was so remote that only an outright confession could have given Abel away. Franz Felix, a painter who met Abel through Silverman, said that on the day when Mr. McMullen "shoved a newspaper under my nose with the story, it was like believing you are living in a republic, but then someone tells you, didn't you know, this is a monarchy?"

Silverman was shocked by the news. His friend Goldfus had disappeared in a cloud of smoke, and a Soviet spy had risen from his ashes. Was Abel the man who had attended his wedding in early 1957 and given the couple a rosewood jewelry box with silver hinges and a clasp with a silver medallion that he had made himself? Was it Abel who posed for Silverman for a portrait entitled "The Amateur" that brings out the quiet intensity and patrician modeling of the subject's face? Was it with Abel that he had gone on expeditions to the lower East Side, where his companion, a Leica strung around his neck, took the photographs he used as a basis for his paintings? Silverman's sense of loss was difficult to describe. "To lose a friend by death is one thing," he said. "But to lose one through the discovery that he is really someone else is not merely sad but strangely dislocating."

With a mind as orderly as a filing cabinet, Abel had effectively compartmentalized his life. He had sought out the three men who became his friends, Burt Silverman, Alan Winston, and David Levine.

He had met them on their own level as painters, and he had been genuinely fond of them. He had demonstrated his kindness and generosity on several occasions. For instance, he had set up a darkroom where he developed and printed his friends' snapshots. He was considerate of their feelings. When he left on his mysterious trips, he always let them know, pleading the need for a change of climate to cure his sinus trouble. His explanations were always plausible. He did have sinus trouble. His voice often had a congested, nasal sound and he was forever sniffing at a nose inhalator that he carried in his pocket. The man they knew was a part of the real man. They were astounded by the identity of the real man, like the blind men who, feeling different parts of an elephant, take it to be a snake or a donkey.

Abel told them all the same story—that he was of German origin, had lived in New York and Boston as a photofinisher, and was using his savings to devote himself to painting. He said he had no family, and when Silverman asked him why he had never married, he replied that "women are always after something." His friends noticed on several occasions that although he expressed his distrust of women, he was fond of them.

Silverman took him to parties in Brooklyn where more than one woman commented on the perception and intelligence of the balding painter with the slight British accent and European formality. And Winston recalls Abel's bursts of enthusiasm upon seeing an unusually pretty girl on the street. *"Fantastisch,"* he would exclaim in German, turning his head to follow her fleeting figure. His own relationships with women during the long years of separation from his wife were of an anonymous or first-name variety. A postcard found in his studio bears the greeting *Hello Emil* from *Gladys*.

Essentially, however, Abel was a conservative, almost prudish man. He scolded the ebullient Winston for telling off-color stories and for taking him to see "risqué" foreign films, the way a father would scold his son (Abel was twice Winston's age). The two discussed sex freely, but Abel was shocked that Winston was carrying on several concurrent affairs and lectured him on fidelity and against the evils of libertinage.

Despite his vast culture, he claimed to be self-taught. His friends remarked that "he was a very intelligent man who read a great deal," and that "there was nothing he didn't know." What he didn't know he was anxious to learn. "He was the kind of man who would ask you to teach him to play chess and would be beating you at the game within two weeks," one of his friends said. When Winston showed him how to use lacquer on paintings, he bought a book on the subject and became an expert at it. When they were walking in Central Park one evening, Winston commented on the green of the trees under the artificial light and Abel went into a discourse on the psychology of color. His interest in mathematics was far above the heads of his artist friends, who pleaded they had trouble keeping their bank accounts straight. Abel insisted on lending them books like *The Philosophy of Mathematics* and *Calculus for Pleasure,* which they politely kept several days, gave back, and insisted they had enjoyed.

That he talked and acted like a European caused no concern among his friends, some of whom had heavy accents themselves and were of European origin. Mr. Felix, who describes himself as "of the old school" and might be mistaken for a retired colonel in the Austrian imperial guard, with his mustache and liquid blue eyes, liked Abel's "excellent manners," and remembers that "his painting was not painful."

Abel was eager for advice on painting but was sensitive to criticism. Winston, whose own work is in sympathy with the German Expressionist school of the thirties, feels that Abel's painting grew cold and realistic after he met Silverman, a precise, academic painter. An art critic who saw the more than fifty canvases Abel left in his studio, said the style smacked of Soviet social realism. Silverman felt that Abel had a good sense of color and composition, but that his drawings were distorted and lacked clarity. Felix, whose specialty is portraiture, once told Abel to try some still lifes and portraits instead of always using photographs as a starting point. Several days later, he walked in to find Abel gazing searchingly into a small mirror, brush in hand.

The title Silverman gave to Abel's portrait, "The Amateur," could not have been a worse misnomer. Abel never dabbled. If he was not quite professional in his painting, that was only a matter of time. One day he heard Bach played by Andrés Segovia, the classical guitarist, and decided to take up the guitar. He bought all available Segovia records, the sheet music and a tape recorder. Then he bought a guitar and practiced until he could play Bach and Villa-Lobos.

Even with his close friends, he was modest and self-effacing. When he came back from Florida in May, 1957, and told Silverman that

"I may be going away very suddenly," Silverman asked why he had not written. "Why bother you with my problems?" Abel replied.

He usually avoided arguments and did not discuss politics. "Leave politics to the politicians," he said. Only when art was discussed did he show any fervor. His masters were Rembrandt and Vermeer, and abstract paintings did not appeal to him. He scorned painters who "paint a tree and make it look like something else," explaining that "if you want your watch fixed you don't go to a shoemaker." Walking on Madison Avenue with Winston, he would stop in front of a gallery, spot an abstract painting, stoop in apparent fascination until his nose was against the window, and say with a mock serious tone, *"Unglaublich, unglaublich."*

This clownish side of his personality came out periodically. Winston remembers that he would show up at his apartment with a bottle of Liebfraumilch and the ingredients for Eintopf. They would wind up the evening singing buffoon German songs, with Abel complaining loudly that Winston was off-key.

It was Levine, another Ovington Studio painter, who noticed in Abel a chameleon quality, an ability to fade into the background. He noticed also the strained self-control of a deeply lonely man, and this led him to believe that "Emil must have been on the bum once." This was not a bad guess, for there was about as much stability in Abel's life as in a bum's. Furthermore, Abel brought out in conversation that he had traveled extensively, had worked at odd jobs, and had known periods of penury. It was during one of these periods, he said, that he had learned to make "jungle coffee," boiling the coffee directly in the water and adding an eggshell to help the grounds settle.

Abel was not demanding with his friends, but in retrospect, he had the leper's touch. When his true identity became known, they were hounded by the press and had television cameras trained on them whenever they left their apartments. Everyone who had had even a remote connection with Abel was questioned at length by the FBI and had the burden of disclaiming any guilt by association. The Ovington Studios became "the place where that spy lives," a building marked as though by a stigma. Visitors arriving by taxi were asked ominously by the driver: "What do you want to go there for?" Levine, Silverman, and Felix, besieged by all manner of intrusions, regretfully left the building and sought studios elsewhere. The landlord had trouble finding new tenants. Winston too was forced to move from his Manhattan apartment.

Despite the trouble he caused his friends, they cannot stifle their admiration for the man, even knowing that he is a Soviet spy and deserved his punishment. Abel represents a rare type of individual, a contemporary version of the Renaissance man, a man equally at home in the arts and the sciences. He was a gifted painter, a practiced musician, an excellent photographer, an accomplished linguist, and an outstanding mathematician, chemist, and physicist. For relaxation he read Einstein, solved calculus problems, and did the *Sunday Times* crossword puzzle in an hour.

Dozens of books were found in his studio and storage room, ranging from detective stories to *Elements of Symbolic Logic, Book Cryptoanalysis—a Study of Ciphers and Their Solution, Numbers, the Language of Science,* and *How to Run a Lathe.* He was the author of a pamphlet entitled "You Cannot Mix Art and Politics."

He knew carpentry and made bookshelves and tables for his friends. He made some of the containers discovered in his studio, such as a tie clasp with a wooden ornament that came off to reveal a small cavity. He told Donovan he got the idea for the hollow coins from reading Victor Hugo's *Les Miserables,* where the hero, Jean Valjean, escapes from prison thanks to a coin with a file inside it. Like the men of the Renaissance, he made knowledge an ideal. We can only deplore, with Allen Dulles, that he was not a product of the United States intelligence service. In reality, like all truly remarkable men, he went far beyond the constrictions of any system.

Donovan insists that he is not a doctrinaire Marxist, perhaps not even a Communist Party member. (Hayhanen had been a Party member since the end of World War II.) "Leave politics to the politicians" was a statement of Goldfus the painter, who felt the artist was removed from the political obligations of ordinary men. It was also a firm conviction of Abel, the professional spy who probably viewed the policy changes and court intrigues in his own country with contempt. In that case, one may ask, why did he serve a government whose failings he recognized? The answer is disarmingly simple—he served because his country needed him. We tend to think of other reasons, as many of those connected with the case did. Donovan feels that it is a sad commentary on a smug civilization that the only reasons

advanced were "he did it for his family" or "he did it for the money,"
"the adventure," or "the glory."

The belief that Abel sacrificed his life to help his family can only
spring from minds whose loftiest ideals extend no further than the
concept of togetherness. Two other ideals, money and prestige, appeared to many of those questioned sufficiently worthy to justify Abel's
mission. No one asked to explain Abel's motives replied: "He did
it for his country."

Donovan laments that "we've lost so much of our burning patriotism that we look for reasons we can explain." Practical, sensible
reasons not involving intangibles like love of country, or outdated
maxims like "my country right or wrong." Donovan, the man who was
closest to Abel, is convinced that it was precisely this mysterious bond
with his country, this almost mystical identification with "Mother
Russia," that made Abel accept a dangerous assignment and refuse to
talk after he had been caught. Russia has given other examples of men
who dedicated their considerable talents to their country, even though
they were not directly concerned with furthering the cause of Communism. (It is likely that Abel's vocation would have been the same
under the czars.)

Boris Pasternak was such a man. He refused to accept a Nobel
prize in literature that would have meant exile. He had spoken out
against the rulers of the land, but he could not leave it. He equated
exile with death and declared that "love of country is one of the highest
and most stirring human emotions. Patriotism must not be blind. The
mother corrects her child and the son sees the weakness of his father.
But love does not turn aside from ugliness and error. Loyalty to the
land where you were born and the people from whose loins you
sprang is the beginning, not the end, of internationalism."

Pasternak elected to remain in Russia, after explaining wearily that
the great majority of us are required to live "a life of constant, systematic duplicity." Abel's duplicity was a professional necessity. It was
his burden that he could best serve his country by being away from
it. It would be interesting to know how that country has repaid him
now that he has been returned to Russia in exchange for Powers. The
usual retribution for agents who have been caught, no matter how
estimable their conduct, does not leave him a very promising future.

IX. Clipped Wings for the U-2

THE United States has admitted employing the services of a spy exactly twice. There was Nathan Hale, who spied behind British lines in the War of Independence disguised as a schoolteacher and was hanged without a trial in 1776, at the age of twenty-one. His last words, "I regret that I have but one life to give for my country," are printed in every American History textbook and engraved in the Yale University quadrangle.

And there was Francis Gary Powers. Powers' "last words" were a plea for mercy at his Moscow trial; he claimed he was "a human being who is not a personal enemy of the Russian people, who has never had any charges brought against him in any court, and who is deeply resentful and profoundly sorry for what he has done." He was speaking as a practical man trying to get out of a difficult situation. He escaped death but lost his chance for a patriot's treatment in history books.

There are many who found Powers' attitude of co-operation with his captors shocking. Here was a man who could have emulated Nathan Hale but turned state's evidence instead. Powers also compared poorly with Abel, who said only seven words at his New York trial, pleaded not guilty, and was sentenced to thirty years to Powers' ten.

To describe the case against Powers at its blackest, the U-2 incident embarrassed the Eisenhower Administration, scuttled the Summit Conference, put an end to the CIA's most successful intelligence-gathering operation (in Washington, CIA was said to mean *caught in the act*), and handed the Russians their biggest propaganda break since the start of the Cold War. These discouraging developments were indirectly due to Powers' failure to do one of three things:

1 Push the "explosion" button on his instrument panel, which would have set a time bomb mechanism working to blow up his plane after he had been ejected.

2 Use the curare-filled needle he had been given for use in case he was tortured.

3 Obey the first commandment of espionage—silence.

The fact that Powers did none of these three things was viewed with scorn in some parts and with understanding in others. Khrushchev explained that "living things want to go on living." Some of Powers' former Air Force friends agreed in interviews that he "did the right thing. What else could he do?"

The case against Powers was most eloquently stated by William Faulkner, who seldom comments on current affairs but who wrote from Oxford, Mississippi, not long after the trial:

> Now the Russians will parade him about the non-Western world for the next ten years like a monkey in a cage, as a living example of the sort of courage and fidelity and endurance on which the United States must now desperately depend. Or better still, set him free at once in contemptuous implication that a nation so desperately reduced is not worth anyone's respect or fear, the agent of its desperation no longer dangerous enough to be worth the honor of martyrdom for even the cost of feeding them.

Who was the pilot who applied the average man's "don't stick your neck out" rationale to a matter so vital to his country? To begin with, he was no spy. He was not trained in the techniques of espionage, nor was he conditioned for the experience he underwent. He was an experienced pilot who had been singled out by the Central Intelligence Agency because his record was one of colorless competence. The CIA was not after brilliant men for the "overflight" program, it was after men who knew military discipline and could fly a plane. Solid, reliable men of sober habits who had never stood out either for their faults or their accomplishments.

Francis Gary Powers went on trial in Moscow on August 17, 1960, the day of his thirty-first birthday; in those thirty-one years, he had seldom been singled out for anything. He was born in the Kentucky coal country where his father, Oliver, was a miner. When Oliver was injured in a mining accident, the family moved to a small farm in Pound, Virginia, near the Kentucky border. Oliver bought a small shoe repair shop in nearby Norton. The family, which grew to include Francis and four sisters, was never prosperous, but the elder Powers saved enough money to give his only son a good education. He wanted Francis to be a doctor.

Francis, a shy, curly-haired youth, went to Grundy High School not far from his home in Pound, and the main impression he left on his former teachers and classmates was that of "a nice boy who never got into trouble" and who "didn't say much." He graduated somewhere in the middle of his high school class and went on to Tennessee's Milligan College where, on his father's advice, he took pre-med courses. His roommates at Milligan recall that he was painfully shy with girls and did not once go on a date in four years of college life. He graduated in 1951, 22nd in a class of 59, and told his father he had changed his mind about being a doctor.

Pre-med had shown him, he said, that he "couldn't measure up to it—it took too much time and effort." Instead, Powers took a job as a life guard in a swimming pool in Johnson City, Tennessee. When the summer season was over, he joined the Air Force. Flying was the first thing this introverted, lethargic youth had ever taken pride in. He had been up in a plane once, when he was fourteen years old—a $2.50 ride in a two-seater barnstorming crate in Princeton, West Virginia— and had never forgotten the excitement of flying.

Powers became a first lieutenant and in 1954 was stationed as a jet pilot at Turner Field, the Strategic Air Command base near Albany, Georgia. At the base he became friendly with a Mrs. Brown who worked in the cafeteria, and who invited him one day to try her home cooking instead of the cafeteria steam tables. Mrs. Brown was a widow who lived in Milledgeville, a small town not far from the base, with her eighteen-year-old daughter Barbara. Barbara, with her soft southern charm and quiet good looks, managed to turn Powers' shyness into a whirlwind courtship. They were married the same year.

In 1956, Powers decided to leave the Air Force and his $700 a month first lieutenancy and try something else. He and Barbara wanted to settle down and open a filling station, but they lacked the capital. Powers tried to get a pilot's job with commercial airlines, but they told him that at twenty-seven he was too old.

At the time Powers was shopping around for a new job, the Lockheed people in Burbank, California, were shopping around for pilots in connection with a new program. The program was the brainchild of C. L. Johnson, Lockheed's chief engineer.

In 1954, Johnson had wanted to test airplane engines and electrical systems at high altitudes. He also wanted to gather data for Lockheed's prize fighter plane, the F-104 Starfighter. To carry out this program, he designed a plane that could stay at high altitudes for long periods of time. He called the plane the "Utility 2," or U-2. Like the man who invented the magnifying glass because he wanted to be able to see the barbs on pepper grains, Johnson designed the U-2 for a completely different purpose than the one which brought it notoriety.

The U-2 is essentially a glider or sailplane with a turbojet engine. Thanks to its long wings, light frame, and special fuel, it is able to reach altitudes close to 100,000 feet and cruise along for hours at 70,000 feet at a speed of 500 miles per hour. The plane is so light that its wings flap like a giant insect's when it is close to the ground, and the main landing gear is no more than a strut with two wheels. The U-2 was a costly plane to build; special attention had to be paid to joints and riveting to insure a smooth surface and keep friction down at high altitudes.

The first models, tested in early 1955 and hand-built in Lockheed's experimental department, weighed 17,720 pounds, including fuel tanks with a thousand-gallon capacity, and had a wingspan of eighty feet. The range of these early models, with extra fuel tanks under the wings, was about 2,600 miles.

The U-2 was powered by a single Pratt and Whitney turbojet engine and used a specially refined kerosene fuel. This fuel, outrageously expensive to distill, has a boiling point of 330° Fahrenheit, about twice that of normal jet fuels. The high boiling point is essential for long flights at high altitudes, for it keeps evaporation losses at a minimum.

Equipped with these special features, the plane could continue to climb until the air grew so thin it could no longer sustain the giant wings. This combination of thin air that slows the plane down and increasing drag of the critical Mach number* (the closest the plane can get to Mach 1, at which point it breaks the sound barrier) is known as the "coffin corner." Another danger at high altitude is the flame-out, as Powers was to learn. The thinner the air, the likelier the turbojet engine is to stall, because it is not getting an adequate supply of oxygen. Flame-outs were not infrequent at 90,000 feet when the U-2 was being tested, and the pilot would have to glide to a lower altitude to restart the engine. The disadvantage of the special U-2 fuel, known under the designation of MIL-F-255524A, is poor altitude restart. In case of a flame-out, the pilot had to drop 30,000 or 40,000 feet before he could start the engine. This turned out to be the U-2's major hazard.

When the Lockheed people saw how successful the high-flying jet glider was, they told the Air Force about it, and the Air Force bought several U-2s in the summer of 1955 for joint research it was carrying out with the Atomic Energy Commission. In August, 1955, the Air Force released photographs of golf links taken at 50,000 feet, probably from a U-2; on one link, two golf balls could clearly be seen.

In 1955, President Eisenhower came back from the Geneva Conference discouraged by the rejection of his "open skies" policy. The policy, in effect, would have allowed planes to collect reconnaissance data over foreign countries. The plan was offered as a kind of inspection system that could lead to disarmament and further the cause of world peace. But the Russians would have none of it, reasoning that they had nothing to gain by it. They could get data from their spies on location and had been well supplied over the years with aerial photographs of military installations and key industrial and urban centers. The open skies plan would have been a boon to the United States, which has a much tougher job of collecting data in the Russian police state, 40 per cent of which is closed to foreigners, and many parts of which are off limit even to Soviet citizens.

The Joint Chiefs of Staff were like three blind men when it came to Soviet targets. If a war broke out they would not know what to bomb, other than the large cities, and even there, they had little

* Mach numbers relate to the speed of sound under various conditions; Mach 1 is rated at 759 mph at sea level, but in thinner atmosphere it is somewhat less than that.

information about the new cities behind the Urals. Aerial reconnaissance was as essential to them as it had been to Noah when he "sent forth the dove to see if the waters were abated from the face of the ground."

Not that the Western countries had been inactive in the field of aerial reconnaissance—on the contrary. Ever since the end of World War II, planes have skirted the fringes of the Soviet border, sounding out radar installations and picking up whatever information they could. When they were shot down by Soviet antiaircraft crews, the newspapers were told that the plane had gone off course and wandered across the Soviet border. This sort of activity was carried on wholesale by the British, who called it "spoofing."

In February, 1958, two Oxford undergraduates gave the game away in a student magazine called *Isis*. In one of the most sensational articles ever written for a college monthly, Paul Thompson and William Miller, who had served in the Royal Navy from 1953 to 1955, wrote:

> . . . frontier incidents are almost invariably reported as ferocious and unjust attacks by Russian fighters on innocent Western aircraft cruising well within their own frontiers. Sometimes it is conceded that the victim has lost its way. This is British understatement at its best. All along the frontier between East and West from Iraq to the Baltic, perhaps farther, are monitoring stations manned by national servicemen trained in Morse or Russian, avidly recording the least squeak from Russian transmitters—ships, tanks, airplanes, troops, and control stations.
>
> Since the Russians do not always provide the required messages, they are sometimes provoked. A plane "loses its way" while behind a frontier. Tape recorders excitedly record the irritated exchanges of Russian pilots and when the latter sometimes force an airplane to land, an international incident is created. It is believed, perhaps rightly, that this flagrant breach of the Geneva Convention can provide accurate estimates of the size and type of Russian armaments and troops and the nature of their tactical methods. In a moment, irresponsibility of this kind could well frighten the Russians into war.

That these revelations were no Oxonian hoax was proven shortly afterward when the two writers were arrested and charged with violating the Official Secrets Act. Their trial was held *in camera* and in July, the student editors were sentenced to three months in jail.

"Spoofing," however, was limited to flying across the border and back, and reconnaissance into the heart of the Soviet Union was still despairingly inadequate.

The U-2 was the answer to the failure of the "open skies" proposal and our appalling lack of data. Someone at CIA recognized its extraordinary reconnaissance potential. Here was a plane that could fly over the Soviet Union's huge land mass at an altitude where fighters could not reach it and antiaircraft missiles would be useless against it. The possibility of using the U-2 as a "spy plane" was considered and adopted at high-level policy meetings in late 1955.

U-2 reconnaissance flights into Russia were launched in 1956 and for four years continued unhindered. They were considered one of CIA's most brilliant and successful coups. Secretary of Defense Thomas S. Gates admitted to a Senate Foreign Relations Committee hearing in 1960 that, with the end of the flights, "we have lost . . . an important source of information" and that "we will have to augment other methods toward obtaining this information." The kind of information obtained, he said, was "on airfields, aircraft, missiles, missile testing and training, special weapons storage, submarine production, atomic production and aircraft deployment and things like these. The results were considered in formulating our military programs."

Gates further indicated that the U-2 flights were a deterrent against the threat of a Soviet surprise attack. "The flights built up a story that gives you a judgment for surprise attacks," he said. "It gives you a judgment on important installations, it gives you some judgment on production. It gives you some judgment on logistic backlog, actual military sites, so that I would say it gave you a very definite look-see at their military position. It gave the impression that they were better armed than advertised."

Gates admitted that the overflights were "our best information." To guard the secrecy of the operation, it was given the cover of an inoffensive weather-research program conducted by the National Advisory Committee for Aeronautics. The U-2s were bought from Lockheed by the Air Force and presented to NACA for its weather flights. Allen Dulles met with two members of the House of Representatives at about this time to tip them off about the hidden appropriations for the program.

The first U-2 squadron, with only three planes, was formed in January, 1956, at Watertown Strip, Nevada, and was dubbed the

Weather Reconnaissance Squadron, Provisional (1st). The squadron carried out legitimate meteorological tests, measuring air turbulence at high altitudes. From time to time, NACA published unclassified reports on the findings of the weather flights.

In May, 1956, NACA announced that it was spreading its weather tests to Europe and would base U-2s at USAF bases in Lakenheath, England, and Wiesbaden, Germany. There was no announcement about two other bases set up for U-2s, one at the Incirlik base near the bustling commercial center of Adana in Turkey, the other at Atsugi Airport near Tokyo.

This was the pioneer period of the U-2 reconnaissance mission, and considering the small number of planes involved, casualties ran high. Two of the initial seven CIA-hired pilots, ostensibly civilians loaned to NACA by Lockheed, were killed in the first year of the program and another escaped death when his U-2 crashed. The first accident occurred in February 1956. A U-2 undergoing tests at the Nevada base was flying over Arizona when a fire started in the cockpit. The pilot, Robert J. Everett, dropped to 30,000 feet and bailed out. On September 17, pilot Howard Carey was killed when his U-2 crashed near Kaiserslautern, West Germany, about sixty miles south of the U-2 base in Wiesbaden. In April, 1957, Lockheed test pilot Robert L. Sieker was killed when his U-2 crashed in a barren region of Nevada. Another of the original seven, Bruce Grant, suffered damage to his brain as the result of an oxygen deficiency while he was flying the U-2 at 100,000 feet.

The U-2s that were sent on weather missions in Europe, Turkey, and Japan, were an improvement on the original design. They had a more powerful engine, the Pratt and Whitney J75. Range and altitude had been improved. (Powers' flight route was about 3,400 miles at 70,000 feet.) Seven camera windows had been built into the plane's underside for the operation of wide-angle cameras able to take continuous pictures at high altitude thanks to a continuously rotating prism instead of a conventional shutter. The camera was preset, entirely automatic, and the movement of the film was synchronized with the plane's speed to freeze the motion and deliver a clear picture. All the pilot had to do was push a button over designated points. The new U-2 also was provided with a tape recorder that could register radar signals in its flight area. Last but not least, behind the cockpit there was a destructor unit with a three-pound explosive charge and an electric detonator, operated from the pilot's instrument panel. A timing mechanism made it possible for the pilot to push the "explosion" button and get out of the plane safely before it blew up. The charge was powerful enough to destroy the entire aircraft.

Armed with these improvements, the squadrons of U-2s began to go on missions that had little to do with the weather. At the Incirlik Military Air Base on a bleak plain near Adana, Turkey, a mysterious detachment called "10/10" arrived in early 1956. The pilots were aloof and had separate quarters from the others on the base, and little was known about the unmarked, dark gray planes they flew.

When the pilots were asked whom they worked for, they said they were civilians employed by Lockheed and lent to the NACA. Strangely enough, the planes only flew when the weather was good, although the NACA was ostensibly collecting data on air turbulence in all weather conditions. The unmarked planes with their outsize wings and dark coloring soon became a familiar sight in the Adana region, but all questions about their design or their purpose were discouraged.

Despite these elaborate attempts at secrecy, Russian radar picked up the planes as they flew over the border. The route for the Incirlik U-2s in the early days was due east about 400 miles to a lake near the Turkish-Iran border, Lake Van, then southeast another 400 miles until the U-2 was over Teheran. From Teheran, it would continue east about 500 miles until it reached the Meshed region, where Afghanistan, Iran, and the Soviet Union have a common border. The plane skirted the 600-mile Soviet-Afghan border, never penetrating deeply into the Soviet Union, then returned to its base over the same route.

These timid incursions were good training for the overflights to come, and were duly recorded by Soviet radar. Meanwhile, the U-2s based in Lakenheath and Wiesbaden were observing "weather conditions" in the Baltic Sea area. One flight was sent out the day after the departure from Moscow of Nathan F. Twining, Chief of Staff of the U.S. Air Force and an enthusiastic promoter of the U-2 reconnaissance program. Twining left Moscow June 30 after witnessing displays of Soviet air might and forcing his tact to the point where he raised his glass to a toast offered by a Red Chinese air marshal. Ten days later, an angry Soviet note protested that American planes had flown over Soviet territory in the Baltic Sea area.

The State Department, splitting hairs, insisted that no "military" planes had been on mission over Soviet territory and that the note was a plot to hinder the improvement of international relations. The writer of an article in *Sovietsky Flot,* one of the Russian Defense Ministry's two daily newspapers, was grieved because "these flagrant violations coincided with General Twining's stay in West Berlin."

Khrushchev echoed this grief in a speech at the Czechoslovak Embassy on May 9, 1960. He said that "when Twining was here, we welcomed him as a guest, and wined and dined him. He left our country by air and next day sent a plane flying over our country at a great altitude. This plane flew as far as Kiev." Khrushchev then gave vent to the type of scatological jest he seems to favor. "All that Twining may be compared to is an animal that does its dirty doings right where it eats," he said.

Thus, the Russians knew almost from the start of the U-2 program that their air space was being violated, but did not connect the overflights with the weather planes until two years later. A May 1958 article in the Soviet Air Force Newspaper, *Soviet Aviation,* indicated that the GRU was looking into the operations of the U-2 because the plane "lacks all identification marks indicating its mission." The article suggested that strategic reconnaissance was included in the versatile plane's mission.

There was a healthy curiosity about the planes in countries where they were based. In England, *Flight Magazine* published an alleged photograph of the mystery plane in 1956 which was no more than a black blob with wings traveling through the sky. The Japanese were luckier and it was a Japanese editor who "broke" the story of the U-2.

In March, 1958, the Japanese magazine *Air Review* published photographs of U-2s landing in Japan, reportedly taken by a sixteen-year-old aviation bug who was standing at the end of the runway and escaped the security check. And in September, 1959, some members of a Japanese glider club unwittingly became part of the secret. They were photographing landings at Fugisawa field, a light-plane strip forty miles south of Tokyo, when an unmarked black turbojet made an emergency belly-landing only a foot away from them. They approached the plane, shutters clicking, but the pilot instead of emerging pulled the cockpit shut. Fifteen minutes later, a Navy helicopter full of civilians landed at the field. The pilot opened his canopy and got out, saying, "I'm O.K." The Japanese noticed that he had no markings on his uniform and wore a pistol at his waist. The civilians who had arrived in the helicopter surrounded the plane and ordered the glider club members away at gunpoint.

The following day, Eiichiro Sekigawa, editor of *Air Review,* was given a description of the crash landing and put U-2 and U-2 together. He noted in an article that the plane probably had a far greater range than that indicated by its fuel supply, since it seemed to be able to coast for miles like a glider.

There were six U-2s based in Japan and daily flights were reported. The Japanese expressed gratitude at the valuable weather data the U-2s were producing in tracking hurricanes. Other flights, unmentioned in official dispatches, went north into the Sea of Okhotsk and to the eastern seaboard of the Soviet Union and south to the Yellow Sea and over Red China, whose radar installations are primitive in comparison with the Soviet Union's. Only five months before Powers crashed near Sverdlovsk, another article in *Soviet Aviation* gave design details of the U-2 and said flatly that they were being used for strategic reconnaissance.

Getting back to Powers, after two interviews in May, 1956, he had filled out a questionnaire to the satisfaction of the CIA and signed a two-year contract in which he pledged to keep his enlistment secret, even from his wife. In the routine security clause of the contract, he was warned that divulging any information about the CIA and its activities could lead to ten years' imprisonment and/or a $10,000 fine. He was told that once he was sent on missions, his salary would be $2,500 a month, with $1,000 held back until successful completion of the mission. His main job, as he understood it, would be to fly U-2s along the Soviet border to pick up radar and radio information. If all went well, he might get other duties.

Once he had signed the contract, Powers was sent to the Watertown Strip base in Nevada for high-altitude flight training. He was given a special flight suit that had been tested in an altitude chamber. For two and a half months, registered under the cover name of Palmer, he flew a U-2, studying its special equipment for intercepting radio and radar signals. In August, 1956, after having flown the U-2 successfully over California and Texas, Powers was sent to the Incirlik base to join the 10/10 group, which had six other pilots. He was told that his overseas tour would last eighteen months and that his wife could not accompany him because there were no accommodations for her.

Barbara Powers was not prepared to accept prolonged separation from her husband, and when he left for Turkey, she made plans to join him on her own. She followed him to Europe and got a job in Greece as secretary in a U.S. Air Force office. Powers managed to fly to Greece once or twice a month to visit her.

Early in 1958, not long before Powers' first contract was up, the Lockheed people made arrangements for the couple to live in a small brick house in downtown Adana. Since he had his wife with him, was making more money than he could ever dream of making elsewhere, and since the flights were so routine they had become known as "milk runs," he signed up for another hitch. Soon after that, the entire 10/10 detachment was moved to a trailer colony near the Incirlik base following requests from the other pilots to have their families join them. The Powers had trailer 1356, at the end of the row with a view of the Toros Mountains. The 10/10 families were secluded from the rest of the base like some Hindu caste, and life for Barbara Powers became a mixture of bridge and boredom while her husband made his regular incursions behind Soviet borders. She thought, as did the other U-2 wives, that her husband was flying T-33 jet trainers for service and overhaul to Germany. The fact that he often flew to "Germany" and back in the same day did not perturb her. From time to time, the monotony was broken by a visiting dignitary. Several Congressmen, General Frank F. Everest, head of the Air Force in Europe, General Thomas D. White, Chief of Staff of the U.S. Air Force in Europe, and Francis Cardinal Spellman were among the notables who came to inspect the 10/10 group, which was commanded by Colonel William Shelton.

The U-2 "spoofing" continued for Powers until August, 1958, when he was ordered to fly a U-2 from Incirlik to the field at Bodoe, a small Norwegian fishing village, without going over Soviet territory. This was to acquaint Powers with the Bodoe approaches in the event of future flights. The route for the legitimate Incirlik-Bodoe flight was over Athens, Rome, Frankfurt, and Stavanger (Norway), a shorter and less perturbed itinerary than the one he was later to take.

In June, 1959, Powers was given the cover role in a U-2 flight. When an overflight was scheduled, two U-2s were flown from Incirlik to Peshawar in Pakistan. One of the U-2s left Peshawar for a legitimate weather mission in the Lake Van region while the other crossed the Soviet Union on its reconnaissance mission, landing at the Bodoe base. On this occasion, Powers piloted the cover plane, and another pilot made the 3,000-mile trip across the Soviet Union.

The flights were intensified in 1960, and were apparently made at one-month intervals with the start of spring bringing longer days and the promise of good weather. In April, 1960, a month before Powers crashed, a U-2 made a successful flight across the Soviet Union. Khrushchev, referring to the April flight, said that "we should have shot down the reconnaissance plane on April ninth as well. But our military men muffed it, to put it mildly, and we gave them, so to speak, a dressing down for it."

As far as Barbara Powers was concerned, it was all part of the Incirlik routine when at 6 P.M. on April 27, 1960, Powers came into the trailer and asked his wife to fix him "a good-sized lunch." She knew that meant another flight, and prepared a thermos of hot potato soup, another with coffee, sugar, and cream, six sandwiches, pickles, olives and cookies.

The same night, Powers flew from Incirlik to Peshawar in a U.S. Air Force transport plane that also carried Colonel Shelton and about twenty members of the U-2 ground crews. The specially equipped U-2 was flown to Peshawar by another Lockheed pilot.

When Powers arrived in Peshawar, a Pakistani border town near the Khyber Pass, he did not know he was to fly over Russia. Two pilots were being prepared for the flight, and it was only two hours before the actual take-off that he was told he had been picked. Final orders came from the CIA in Washington, based on long-range weather forecasts and strategic considerations. After it was over, the Administration was criticized for timing the flight so close to the Summit Conference. This factor had not been overlooked by the U-2 planners, and it had been decided that other considerations were more important than the proximity of the Summit talks. Secretary of State Herter told the Senate Foreign Relations Committee: "Conditions at a later season would have prevented obtaining very important information. There is never a good time for a failure of an intelligence mission. We believe it unwise to lower our vigilance because of these political negotiations."

There were three decisive factors in picking the May 1 flight date:

1 Clear skies had been forecast (actually, Powers had cloudy weather during his flight) which meant clear pictures.

2 May 1 for the Russians is something like the Fourth of July for Americans. It is a national holiday that honors the solidarity of the working class. In Moscow it is the occasion for a display of armed might in a mammoth parade that winds past the Kremlin where high Soviet officials, including Khrushchev, watch the troops and matériel go by from a reviewing stand. It was felt in Washington that the Soviet vigilance might be relaxed on May 1 because of the holiday, that perhaps radar and antiaircraft crews would be celebrating to the detriment of their duties.

3 The CIA had intelligence that a new Soviet rocket, twice as large as anything produced by the United States (our largest rocket is the 108-foot-long Centaur), would be on its launching pad for a May Day test. The launching pad, it was known, was at a new missile base near Sverdlovsk. Vice-President Nixon, in his 1959 visit to Russia, reported seeing the new missile installations in the Sverdlovsk industrial complex and noted that the launch points were domed rather than following the herringbone pattern of the older Russian ground-to-air-missile sites.

On the morning of May first, at about 2 A.M. Moscow time, Powers was summoned by Colonel Shelton and told that he was to fly that day. Another pilot was awakened at the same time and the two were given breakfast and sent to breathe oxygen, an essential preliminary to high-altitude flights. Soon after that, Powers was told he had been picked for the overflight, while the other pilot would make a weather flight in the Lake Van area as a cover.

Powers was given his flight maps and told that his specific reconnaissance mission was the mammoth rocket on its Sverdlovsk launching pad. Other main checkpoints he was briefed on were a rocket launching site east of the Aral Sea and the Navy and Air Force bases in Archangel and Murmansk, which Powers never reached. Colonel Shelton also pointed out a spot on the map where, he said, "I think there's something but I don't know what it is." Powers' duties were simple. He had to follow the course plotted on his maps in red and blue pencil, over the Aral Sea, Sverdlovsk, Kirov, Archangel, Murmansk, and Bodoe. At the points indicated on the map, he had to turn the camera controls on and off.

Powers was given the standard survival material, a pneumatic rubber boat, a set of topographical maps of the European part of the Soviet Union, means for making a fire, signal cartridges, a flashlight, compasses, a saw, fishing tackle, a dagger, and a semiautomatic .22 pistol with a silencer and about 200 cartridges.

After he had donned his heavy flight suit and his white helmet with the number 29 on it, Colonel Shelton gave him several other items "in case anything should happen."

These were: 7,500 rubles which were stuffed into the pockets of his flying suit, some French gold Louis wrapped in cellophane, which Khrushchev described as "neat American packaging," and West German and Italian currency; two gold watches and seven ladies' gold rings. ("What possible use could he make of all this in the upper strata of the atmosphere?" Khrushchev asked later with heavy irony. "Perhaps he was to have flown still higher, to Mars, and meant to seduce the Martian ladies [laughter and applause from the members of the Supreme Soviet].")

As a final note of precaution, Colonel Shelton gave Powers a silver dollar that concealed a needle containing a poison of the curare group. "There isn't any danger because no Russian plane or rocket can get to your altitude," Colonel Shelton told him, "but in case something happens and you're captured, the needle contains poison and if you're tortured and can't stand it, you can use it."

Powers was also briefed about the destructor unit which he was to set before bailing out in case anything happened. As to what he should do if he fell into Soviet hands, there does not seem to have been any hard and fast directive. "Suicide was optional," a laconic State Department note announced after his capture, and Powers exercised his option.

As a radio call signal, Powers was given *Puppy 68* and told to use radio contact only in case of emergency while he was over the Soviet Union. Once over Norway, the *Puppy 68* signal would alert ground crews in Bodoe to stand by for his landing. Allied tracking stations near the Soviet border would be able to follow his route at all times, he was told, and the tapes of Soviet radar signals he made would also be relayed to allied control points.

As day broke in Peshawar on the morning of May 1 at 4.30 Moscow time, Francis Gary Powers, feeling "scared and nervous," flew northward into a troubled sky on what had been described to him as a "routine" mission and was to develop into one of the Cold War's most sensational chapters. The 3,400-mile trip was to take a little over eight hours and he expected to have lunch in Norway.

The first lap of his trip, the 300-mile run from Peshawar to the Soviet border, took the U-2 pilot about an hour flying at his cruising altitude of more than 60,000 feet. As the plane crossed over the Soviet-Afghan border at 5:36 A.M., its trail was picked up by NSA tracking units and followed thereafter as it penetrated deeper into the Soviet heartland. The U-2 trail was also picked up by Soviet radar. Antiaircraft and fighter plane units along the plane's presumed route were alerted. As he flew over his first reconnaissance targets Powers found that he had trouble keeping on course and using the cameras over the designated points, because of bad weather. Most of his route was masked by clouds and he could not orient himself from the ground.

Flying over the Urals and nearing Sverdlovsk, the plane was jarred violently, as though something had struck it, and the glow from an orange flash at the tail of the plane alerted Powers that he had fallen victim to the U-2 pilot's main hazard, a flame-out. The flame-out was accompanied by a hollow explosive sound, similar to a gas stove blow-out.

Powers gave his emergency *Puppy 68* call to Bodoe, explaining his predicament. The U-2's single engine had stalled at a particularly awkward time, when he was nearing his main reconnaissance target. He glided the plane downward, hoping that air richer in oxygen would bring his engine back to life. By this time, he was about twenty miles southeast of Sverdlovsk, an industrial region with antiaircraft missile installations. Still the engine refused to start, and he dropped as low as 30,000 feet when Soviet missiles began to burst about the plane. At this altitude, the U.S. tracking stations lost the U-2 and it is believed that one of the Soviet rockets damaged the plane, although the state of the wreckage indicated that no direct hits were made.

This was not the first time a U-2 pilot had faced the moment of truth. There are persistent but unconfirmed reports that at least one other pilot whose plane had been detected in unfriendly skies pushed the "explosion" button and blew his plane and himself up in mid-air. These reports tend to suggest that the timing mechanism on the destruction device was not operating and that destruction of the plane meant destruction of the pilot. A Russian expert testifying at Powers' trial said that "it was impossible to establish the time lag of the explosion since no timing mechanism was found in the wreckage."

In his appearance before the Senate Foreign Relations Committee, Secretary of State Herter's comments on U-2 losses were deleted from the heavily censored committee report. (Q: Were any other planes lost on these same ventures prior to May 1? Herter: [Deleted] Not over Soviet territory.)

In any case, Powers had received specific instructions to blow the plane up if he was detected, and he disobeyed those orders and bailed out. As he explained at his trial, "I was unable to use the ejection seat because of the pressure arising from the falling plane. I remember that I was at a height of thirty thousand feet and I realized I could not use the ejection seat. So I opened the canopy and loosened the straps. The centrifugal force pressed half of me against the instrument panel while the other half hung outside. I had forgotten to disconnect the oxygen hoses and they held me in. I had to struggle to get out. The parachute opened automatically immediately after I left the airplane. By that time I was at an altitude of fourteen thousand feet." Powers said the reason he knew the altitude was 14,000 feet was that the parachute was set to open at that altitude.

The Soviets insisted they had shot down Powers at his cruising altitude of 68,000 feet. Again and again Khrushchev hammered away at this point, and at the Moscow trial, Roman Rudenko, the Soviet Union's chief prosecutor and a man known for his shrewdness at interrogation, strove to establish the Soviet version firmly in the public mind. In his testimony, Powers remained purposely vague. He did not antagonize the Soviet prosecutor to the extent of stating that he had been shot down at a lower altitude, nor did he ever say himself that a Soviet rocket had struck the U-2 at 68,000 feet.

"At what altitude was your plane when it was struck by a rocket?" Rudenko asked.

"It was at the maximum altitude, sixty-eight thousand feet," Powers replied.

There is a vital difference between direct statement and inference. When Rudenko asked the same question again "for clarification," Powers' answer was different.

> Q. It was at that altitude of sixty-eight thousand feet that you were struck down by a Soviet rocket?
> A. It was at that altitude that I was struck down by something.
> Q. You say you were struck down by something?
> A. Why, I had no idea what it was. I didn't see it.
> Q. But it was at that altitude?
> A. Yes.

Rudenko then had read into the record the report of Major Voronov, commander of the rocket unit that shot down the U-2. "As the plane entered the firing range at an altitude of over twenty thousand meters [about 68,000 feet]," Major Voronov said, "one rocket was fired and its explosion destroyed the target. The hitting of the target was observed by instruments and after a short interval, visual observation posts recorded falling plane fragments and the parachuting down of the pilot, who bailed out of the crashed plane. The results of the shot have been reported by me to the superior command and measures have been taken to apprehend the flyer who came down by parachute."

The major's report coupled with Rudenko's emphasis were effective propaganda to flaunt the might of Soviet rocketry, capable of felling a plane at 68,000 feet with one shot. Rocketry experts, however, scoff at the one-shot theory, pointing out that rockets are not fired singly but in battery. Technically, it is not impossible that the U-2 was struck down at its cruising altitude. The United States has antiaircraft missiles that can reach targets traveling at 100,000 feet, such as the Nike-Hercules. The older Nike-Ajax can hit targets at 70,000 feet. The Soviet Union also has rockets that can reach those altitudes and presumably could have shot down the U-2. The fact remains that Powers did report a flame-out to his base, that his plane was tracked to 30,000 feet before it was hit, and that the wreckage of the plane was in such good shape that the Russians were afraid to show it at first.

The fake U-2 wreckage initially displayed by the Soviets was the mangled wreck of an Aeroflot TU-104 jet transport that had crashed three months earlier near Sverdlovsk, killing Chinese members of an official delegation to Moscow. "Kelly" Johnson, the U-2 designer, spotted the photographs as fakes and pointed out the difference between the heavy structure of the wreck and the light U-2 structure. Later, the Russians showed the real U-2 wreckage in Moscow's Gorki Park. Much of the reconnaissance equipment was intact, as was the tail section except for a missing rudder tab. Most of the damage was in the wings. American experts who saw the wreckage said the wings had been dismantled from the plane on the ground.

The Soviet's eagerness to prove that Powers was shot down at 68,000 feet was again demonstrated after his trial. The pilot's father, Oliver Powers, who attended the trial, said back in New York that he understood his son had not been shot down at all. Several weeks later, *The New York Times* published a letter ostensibly written by Powers and refuting his father's statement:

> Apparently my father misunderstood the answers I gave to questions put to me during the trial. I would like to make clear this misunderstanding by saying that even though I did not see what it was that caused the explosion, I feel sure that it was not the aircraft which exploded. All of my engine instruments were normal up to the time of the explosion which I both felt and heard. I also saw an orange flash or glow when I looked out. I cannot be sure but I think the explosion came from behind and maybe to the right of the aircraft. I felt no impact of anything against the airplane itself, therefore I think the shock wave from the explosion caused the damage.

It can be assumed that the letter was not Powers' idea, and that he simply signed his name to a document prepared in the best interests of Soviet propaganda.

What is closer to the truth is that at about 8:30 that morning, Major Voronov and his eight-man crew were lounging in the ready room of the Sverdlovsk antiaircraft base when the battle alarm sounded. The U-2 had been sighted, and the order to fire came from the Kremlin. At 8:53 the rocket crew opened fire, and one of the rockets apparently exploded close to the plummeting plane, inflicting some damage. The crew was later decorated with the Order of the Red Banner for its good work.

When Powers bailed out at 14,000 feet, he was making his first non-practice parachute jump, and inexpertly landed on his back at the edge of a small stream after narrowly missing some high-voltage lines.

He was about twenty miles southeast of Sverdlovsk, near a state farm. Some farm workers who had heard the rockets and the plane crashing saw Powers floating down and picked him up when he landed.

One of them, Vladimir Surin, said he was having breakfast when he heard the noise. He saw some white smoke in the sky and spotted "a white circle coming down lower and ever lower, a white umbrella with a black figure under it." Leonid Chuzhakin, a driver at the state farm, joined Surin, and the two drove to the spot where Powers would land. "In the area there are fields, a forest and a river," Surin said. "We were worried he might land in some electric wires." About seven other workers were at the scene when Powers landed. One of them, an Air Force veteran, held on to Powers to prevent him from being dragged by the parachute, and helped him spill the air from the parachute. Others helped the shaken pilot get to his feet, and removed his bulky helmet. Powers had a black eye and a skinned ankle but was otherwise all right.

Part of his equipment was a silk scarf with phrases printed in fourteen languages, including Russian, by which he could express such pithy thoughts as "You will be rewarded if you help me." He also had his supply of rubles, his gun, his dagger, and his poison needle. He used none of these, however, and instead, according to one of the Russian workers, "said something in a language we did not understand."

"We asked him who he was, but he made no reply. Then we realized that he was a foreigner. This put us on the alert and then Anatoly Cheremisin removed the long-barreled pistol in the leather holster that was hanging from his belt. We asked him by using signs whether he was alone. He replied also by signs that he was alone. Seeing that the parachutist was alone we decided to detain him." Surin later said in his report that "when we learned who he was, we were startled by the effrontery of the imperialist."

The workers bundled the dazed Powers in their car and took him to the state farm office a few miles away. Powers gestured to indicate thirst and his captors obligingly stopped at a farmhouse and asked a housewife for some water. Two officers at the state farm questioned Powers in German, but he could not understand them and shook his head. None of the Russians could speak English, and Powers was flown that day to Moscow, about 1,000 miles west of Sverdlovsk, and questioned in Lubyanka Prison. At the same time, the U-2 wreckage, which was reportedly scattered over an area of about twelve square miles, was gathered and sent to Moscow for Powers to identify.

In Moscow, the May Day holiday—that great international celebration of the worker's rise through socialism—was in full swing. Across the cobblestones in Red Square, the four-hour parade was proceeding. On a dais atop the Lenin-Stalin mausoleum, Khrushchev waved his astrakhan hat in vigorous approval as thousands of uniformed men and women stepped smartly by. He applauded when rockets on wheeled launchers passed the reviewing stand and he laughed when thousands of small balloons with pennants inscribed PEACE were sent aloft.

At Khrushchev's side were Marshal Rodion V. Malinovsky, Soviet Minister of Defense, President Klementi E. Voroshilov, and a guest of honor, East German Premier Otto Grotewohl. Malinovsky had arrived late, but made up for his tardiness with news he could not hold back. An American U-2 had been shot down, he told Khrushchev, the wreckage had been recovered and the pilot was alive. Malinovsky then made his scheduled May Day speech, on the theme of vigilance.

Powers admitted his guilt. In the wordy indictment personally drawn up by KGB boss Aleksandr Shelepin, Powers was quoted as saying, "I plead guilty to the fact that I have flown over Soviet territory and over the points indicated on the chart, and turned on and off the necessary controls of the special equipment mounted aboard my plane. This, I believe, was done with the aim of collecting intelligence information about the Soviet Union."

In Bodoe, members of the 10/10 detachment knew that Powers was in trouble, but they waited until midafternoon, when his fuel supply would have been exhausted, before notifying Washington. Because of the time lag, Dulles received the news that the plane had not landed at Bodoe or any of the alternate bases in Finland and Sweden at about the same time (local time) as Khrushchev got the news in Moscow. As far as the CIA was concerned, Powers was a "blown agent" who had outlived his usefulness. No search was instituted for the missing plane, and no news about the flight was released.

In Washington, the news spread among the departments concerned.

It was Sunday, and there was some trouble locating department heads. Dulles, Gates, and Hugh L. Dryden, Deputy Administrator of the National Aeronautics and Space Administration, were among the first to know.

They decided on a policy of "wait and see" and took the prearranged cover story out of the moth balls just in case. President Eisenhower was at his Gettysburg farm. Secretary of State Herter was in Istanbul, at the other end of Turkey from Incirlik, attending a NATO meeting. He had troubles of his own, for student rioting in the streets of the city had grown to the point where martial law was declared on May 3.

At 5:30 A.M. on May 2, Barbara Powers, asleep in her comfortable trailer, was awakened by friends who told her: "We have bad news for you. Gary is missing. We have search planes out but they haven't found him." Mrs. Powers fainted and was treated by the doctor at Incirlik base. She was advised to go back to the United States, and she was home in Milledgeville, Georgia, when the story broke.

The week that followed was the setting for an extraordinary chess game played before world public opinion between the chiefs of state of the world's two most powerful nations. In this classic example of Kriegspiel chess, Khrushchev opened with a Fianchetto attack, a vigorous deployment of pieces to hold the key center squares of the board. Eisenhower started the game with the handicap of an open file since the Russians had the plane and the pilot and the U.S. did not know it. Once installed in a strong position, Khrushchev set his trap. He announced on May 5 that the Russians had shot down a U.S. plane over Soviet territory but purposely omitted giving the plane's location or the fate of the pilot. His long and rambling accusations against the "warmongering imperialists" veiled his omissions.

The President moved too fast and fell into the trap. Releasing the palpably false cover story had the effect of castling too soon, when you put yourself in a vulnerable position to protect your king.

It was decided to let the State Department move the pieces when the U-2 developed into an international incident. State Department spokesman Lincoln White repeated the NASA cover story released May 3, which maintained that a weather research plane based in Adana was missing, that the pilot had reported oxygen trouble, and that the plane may have "accidentally violated Soviet air space." At the same time, NASA released data about the weather flight program, the number of U-2s in use, the instrumentation, and the flight routes followed over Turkey. This bit of candor was designed to allay suspicions and remove the stigma of secrecy from the U-2 program.

On Thursday, May 5, word came from American Ambassador Llewellyn Thompson in Moscow that gave the State Department reason for a policy shift. Cocktail party chatter, said Thompson, had the pilot of the U-2 captured and in good health. Even after this news, however, the United States clung to its cover story like a shipwrecked sailor to a waterlogged buoy.

On May 7, Khrushchev moved in for the checkmate. He told a meeting of the Supreme Soviet: "Comrades, I must let you in on a secret. When I made my report I deliberately refrained from mentioning that the pilot was alive and safe and that we had the remnants of the plane. We did this deliberately, because had we given out the whole story, the Americans would have thought up another version." Khrushchev then exposed the U-2 story in all its detail, as Powers had told it to his Soviet interrogators.

But in the midst of his diatribe, Khrushchev did a curious thing— he refrained from delivering the *coup de grâce* to an opponent in an awkward position, and kept the game alive by offering President Eisenhower an escape hatch. Was Khrushchev thinking of the Summit Meeting being prepared at that very moment in Paris' Elysée Palace? Was he trying to discredit Eisenhower by proving that military cliques were acting independently of the Presidential mandate? Whatever the reason, he acknowledged that the President may not have known about the overflights.

"I am prepared to grant that the President had no knowledge of a plane being dispatched to the Soviet Union and failing to return," he said. "But that should alert us still more."

This magnanimity left the way open for an Eisenhower gambit. In chess, the player in a poor strategic position often sacrifices one of his men, usually a pawn or a knight, to gain a better position. Khrushchev had invited Eisenhower to say that he had not known about the overflights, which would have allowed him to leave for the Summit Conference without the embarrassing wreckage of the U-2 in his luggage. But the price of such an admission was great, and this is perhaps the underlying reason for Khrushchev's seeming generosity.

The price was the resignation of Allen Dulles, the knight who would be lost in the gambit, allowing the game to continue. For if President

Eisenhower did not know about such a vital intelligence activity as the overflights, and if Dulles had been acting on his own, then Dulles had to go.

Dulles offered to be the scapegoat in the U-2 affair, but the President refused to expend him. The decision was a courageous one, for it made the President the first chief of state in the history of the world to assume direct responsibility for espionage.

It lay him open to savage attack from Khrushchev and to perplexed questions from Congressmen who could not see the need for associating the executive head of government with a shabby spy fiasco.

The President's responsibility in the overflight program was stated twice, just so there would be no equivocation. Herter in a May 9 statement explained that "in accordance with the National Security Act of 1947, the President has put into effect since the beginning of his administration directives to gather by every possible means information required to protect the United States and the free world against surprise attack and to enable them to make effective preparations for their defense. Under these directives, programs have been developed and put into operation which have included extensive aerial surveillance by unarmed civilian aircraft, normally of a peripheral character, but occasionally by penetration."

The President himself said two days later: "As the Secretary of State pointed out in his recent statement, ever since the beginning of my administration I have issued directives to gather, in every feasible way, the information required to protect the United States and the free world against surprise attack and to enable them to make effective preparations for defense."

The President was saying, in effect, that espionage had become a national policy, albeit a "distasteful one." It is paradoxical that the United States, the country which came latest and most reticently to accept espionage as a necessity, became through Eisenhower's candor the first country to legitimize what has always been the bastard offspring of foreign policy.

The same day as the President's conference, May 11, Khrushchev addressed the press in Gorki Park, where the remains of the U-2 were being shown in an elaborate exhibit. He was furious at the President's admission. "This plan had the President's approval," he fumed. "It's simply unheard of! And after that they expect me to say: Oh, what nice fellows you all are! To do such a thing would mean to have no self-respect. I would say that Mr. Herter has stripped off all the veils with which U.S. imperialistic policy was masked, prettified and rouged up, so to speak. In his statement, he [Herter] was displaying the horrible fangs of militarism."

In Congress, there was bewilderment that the United States had so bluntly accepted responsibility for spying. Senator Fulbright, chairman of the Senate Foreign Relations Committee, had trouble swallowing the bitter pill when he questioned Herter at the end of May:

Q. Is the public assumption of responsibility for espionage by the head of a state the usual and customary practice among nations?

A. No, the general practice has been, I think, for a long period of time, to deny any responsibility whatsoever.

Q. Do you know of any precedent in our history or in the history of any great nation in which the head of a state has assumed personal responsibility for espionage activities?

A. No, I do not know of any firsthand. It may be that there have been some. On the other hand, I would point out, Mr. Chairman, that this particular incident was of a very unusual nature.

The public too was confused about the President's willingness to take the blame. Perhaps the best story illustrating public reaction is the following, which circulated in Washington in the summer of 1960:

A sixteen-year-old high school girl came home from school one evening and told her father: "We were discussing the U-2 incident today in class, but no one could explain why the President took the blame for it."

Her father, a plain-spoken man, replied, "Look at it this way. Suppose you live in a nice neighborhood and a few blocks away in the same neighborhood there's a man you don't get along with. You don't see eye to eye on anything. Nothing he does is right. He makes you so mad that from time to time you go and water on his lawn. One night you're over there with your pants down when he turns on the light and catches you. Now, you could pull your pants up and pretend you just happened to pass by, or you could run off. But instead you say, 'I am watering on your lawn and I will continue to water on your lawn whenever I feel like it.'"

The daughter took it all in and said, "That's a good story, Daddy, but I still can't explain it to the class."

If we draw up a balance sheet of the U-2 incident, we find that on the credit side of the ledger, the CIA survived its first great crisis intact. Allen Dulles did not say a single word for publication on the U-2 and his entire testimony before the Senate Foreign Relations Committee was censored. Six months after the U-2, he was maintained in his job by the incoming Kennedy Administration. His eventual departure from the CIA had little or nothing to do with the U-2 incident. The Russians were also served notice that the United States had no intention of sitting idly by while its own state secrets were being bought and filched by an army of espionage agents restricted only by their own initiative in freedom of movement.

On the debit side, the U-2 was held responsible as the major factor in scuttling the Summit Conference. President Eisenhower acknowledged the hostile climate created by the U-2 as early as May 6, when, in response to a newsman's question about a proposed visit to the Soviet Union, he said: "If I go." As it turned out, he did not.

Macmillan, de Gaulle, and Eisenhower went to the Summit as men of good will but little hope. The atmosphere was poisoned from the start. Khrushchev had the U-2 in his pocket and lost no time in taking it out and brandishing it. In a preliminary statement on May 16, his first words were: "As everyone knows, a provocative act has been committed recently against the Soviet Union by the American Air Force." He then demanded that Eisenhower "condemn the impermissible provocative acts of the U.S. Air Force" and promise to "renounce such actions" for the future. "It goes without saying," he added, "that if the U.S. Government does so, it cannot fail to call to strict account those directly responsible for the deliberate violation of the state boundaries of the USSR by American aircraft." It also went without saying that no responsible head of state could accede to such demands, and the Summit Conference ended then and there.

A few days later, Charles E. Bohlen, the President's special adviser on Soviet affairs, conducted a post-mortem for a specially selected group of newsmen. He conceded that the U-2 had been one of three main reasons for the failure of the Summit talks. The other factors, he said, were controversy in Moscow over Khrushchev's conduct of foreign relations—which led the roly-poly premier to take a firm stand—and the belief that there would be no hope of settling the Berlin question to his advantage, which made him feel that sinking the Summit would be no great loss.

The Summit Conference failure ended the first phase of the U-2 incident, leaving Russia piously triumphant and America licking her wounds. The Russians, anxious to squeeze every drop of propaganda value out of Powers, prepared a grandiose trial designed for world consumption.

Powers, in Lubyanka Prison, was receiving preferred treatment. In letters to his wife marked with the return address 2 Dzerzhinsky St. (MVD headquarters, which includes Lubyanka Prison, usually reserved for political prisoners), Powers said he had been treated "much better than I expected." From his letters, it appears he was treated more like a tourist than a jailbird. "On May 2 I was taken for a tour of Moscow which I enjoyed very much," he wrote. "These people are real proud of their capital city and it is beautiful."

As for the material things, he said, "I get more than I can eat and plenty of sleep. . . . I am still smoking too much. By the way, these cigarettes here are pretty good. . . . I also get to walk in the fresh air every day that it doesn't rain. One day I even took a sun bath. It has been too cold to do that every day."

Powers was also let out of prison to view the wreckage of his plane. The exhibit at the Gorki Central Recreation Park in Moscow opened May 11 to high fanfare, including Khrushchev's press conference, and was replete with the careful staging that marks large-scale Soviet propaganda efforts. It was adjacent to a Finnish display of agricultural machines, paints, and furniture, and the Russians made much of the contrast between the "peaceful" Finnish exhibition and the U-2 display. "Comparisons suggested themselves," wrote *Pravda* smugly, "and they were in no way to the credit of the American exhibition."

As some 500 newsmen pushed into the pavilion, they were stopped at the entrance by an elderly man who just happened to be wearing a row of decorations across his civilian jacket. "My name is Alexander Sergeichuk," he proclaimed. "I, an old man who knows what war is, cannot understand how the Americans can cry peace at every step and speak of sincerity when they send bandits like Powers to us. I mean Herter. I am an ordinary Soviet citizen and I can't for the life of me understand how these people could have fallen so low and what their morals are worth."

The display showed the torn and unmarked wings of the plane, Powers' nylon altitude suit, his pressurized helmet, the tape recorder which a Soviet technician turned on for spectators who listened enthralled to the "bleep-bleeps." Maps, other documents and photographs were set up on stands. The .22 pistol, the poison needle, the foreign currency, nothing had been left out.

The "American Exhibit," as it came to be known, remained open until July 5, when it was moved to Moscow's imposing House of Trade Unions, where the trial was to be held. In Gorki Park, some 10,000 persons had seen it daily. Classes of school children were taken to see the *"Amerikanski Samelot"* (American airplane). In a comment and signature book for visitors, there were few kind words for the pilot and the plane. Typical remarks were "death to imperialism," "what kind of a friend are you?" and "wolf in sheep's clothing."

On July 18, two and a half months after his capture, Powers was ordered to stand trial on espionage charges and a trial date of August 17 was set. He pleaded guilty to the long and detailed indictment on August 9 and wrote his wife: "I have a Russian defense counsel assigned to me and feel sure he will do his best and that is all I can ask of anyone.

"I am still taking walks every day and am getting a pretty good sun tan," the letter continued. "I am reading *Gone With the Wind* now and I like it very much. I don't know why I never read it before. I have also been given a Bible, which I read every day. I like to see night come because that means one less day to wait. Always before I hated to see each day pass, for that meant one day older."

When the trial started on August 17, coincidentally the date of Powers' thirty-first birthday, it was more like an opening night at the opera than a courtroom proceeding. Holding the trial in the extravagant House of Trade Unions, whose proletarian title belies its magnificence, was as though the United States had held the Abel spy trial in Carnegie Hall.

The House of Trade Unions is an eighteenth-century palace in the heart of Moscow, a block away from the Bolshoi. It was built by the czars as a concert hall and Liszt, Rachmaninoff, and Tchaikovsky played there. The revolution put an end to the czar's concerts and the building was used for state functions, such as the Moscow University student's annual masked ball. It was also used as a memorial building for the Soviet great, and Lenin and Stalin both lay in state there after their deaths.

The most ornate chamber in the two-story building is the Hall of Columns, with forty-foot ceilings, crystal chandeliers hanging in two tiers between each column, and hundreds of candle-shaped lights mounted near the ceiling. At the end of the Hall of Columns, the three judges sat in high-backed chairs on a four-foot raised stage. Above them, a ten-foot red and gold hammer and sickle hung like a sword of Damocles. Powers, who made his entrances and exits through a side door between two guards, sat in the raised prisoner's dock to the left of his judges. On the stage with the judges were six large black cases full of exhibits selected from the Gorki display, including Powers' bright orange parachute.

In the orchestra, the press and selected spectators sat. No complaints from newsmen were heard during the trial. Each press seat was equipped with headsets for translation from Russian into French, English, and German. Outside the courtroom, telephone booths, cable desks and typewriters were available. The trial was on the second floor, and on the main floor a buffet provided champagne and Coca-Cola, caviar, and ham sandwiches. In the main lobby, books and magazines were sold and a checkroom operated with unusual efficiency. Huge crowds pressed to attend the performances in a *panem et circenses* atmosphere and were kept back by guards in blue uniforms who cordoned the building with iron piping. Soviet television did the crowd scenes. When the trial started, and after every recess, a warning bell sounded, like an intermission buzzer.

Some of the "first nighters" arrived in limousines. On the first day, Powers' wife stepped out of an Intourist limousine with her party, including two lawyers, a doctor, and her mother. Powers' parents, traveling separately, arrived in another black limousine. Wife and parents were brought together in the Hall of Column's royal box, a raised marble affair with the best view in the house.

The trial had a short run, from August 17 through 19, and each day was S.R.O. There were some spectators of note among the audience of 2,200—newsmen spotted Guy Burgess, the British defector, dressed in flannels and a tweed jacket. It was presumed that he had a hand in drawing up the voluminous accounts of the trial put out in English by Moscow's Foreign Language Publishing House.

Although the trial was predetermined (the only surprise was the lightness of Powers' sentence), there was a curious sense of drama about it.

The vastness of the décor probably had something to do with it. And Roman Rudenko, who reminded spectators of a nervous Charles

Laughton, squeezed what suspense he could out of his examination and summation. But the real drama was in the presence of Powers, dressed in a Russian-model blue double-breasted suit two sizes too big for him and answering Rudenko's shouted charges in soft Virginia tones.

For here was an individual who represented to the Russians the "aggressive policies" of a great nation they have been taught to fear. It has been said many times in many places that the Russians were putting the United States on trial and that Powers was an unfortunate instrument and victim of the Cold War. The man in the prisoner's dock who answered questions through an interpreter and into a microphone was perhaps ill-equipped to assume such a vital role. It was his frailty that was most impressive. In spite of himself, he had his moments of nobility from the very fact that he was an individual being prosecuted in a land where the individual is normally of no importance. To use the Powers incident for propaganda purposes, the Russians were forced to grant a tremendous importance to Powers the individual, were forced to take into account the personal drama of a man caught in a crisis he but dimly grasped. In the Powers trial, the Russians found themselves in the paradoxical position of glorifying the individual by ostensibly giving the defendant the choice to decide his fate. That Powers made what many feel to have been the wrong choice does not dismiss the embryonic struggle of man against the state that was a part of his trial.

Powers' voice was neutral as he answered Rudenko's questions, and his answers were neutral too. The tactics drawn up by his defense attorney, Mikhail Griniev, called for Powers to be responsive but to disassociate himself as much as possible from the reconnaissance aspects of his mission. He was to picture himself as a robot whose role was to push buttons and pilot the plane, and not to reason why. Rudenko asked him what instructions he had been given for the aerial reconnaissance photographic equipment:

A. I was not given any specific instructions to operate the equipment. I was to turn switches on and off as indicated on the map.

Q. With what aim did you switch on the equipment?

A. I was instructed to do so. It was indicated on the map where the equipment was to be turned on.

Q. Defendant Powers, you probably know the purpose for which you had to turn on and off the equipment?

A. I could very well guess the purpose for which I turned on and off the equipment. If I was to be very exact, I would say no.

Q. On your plane, radio intelligence equipment and tape recordings of various Soviet radar stations were found. Is that correct?

A. I have been told so, but I don't know. In any case, I do not know what much of the general equipment looks like except what I have seen here.

Powers' docile indifference came out again in questioning about his instructions:

Q. You stated here and during the investigation that you switched the equipment on and off at definite points?

A. I did what the chart indicated.

Q. Not knowing what the special apparatus was?

A. I never saw the apparatus.

Q. With the same ease you could have pulled a switch to release an atom bomb?

A. It could have been done, but this is not the type of plane for carrying and dropping such bombs. [The transcript reads at this point: *These words, which Powers lets drop with amazing indifference, are received with indignation in the courtroom.*]

Powers bristled mildly once during the examination, when Rudenko attempted to implicate Francis Cardinal Spellman in the espionage flights. It came out in the testimony that Cardinal Spellman had visited the 10/10 detachment at Incirlik, to which Rudenko asked, "Is the Cardinal also interested in military bases?"

"He is a church dignitary," Powers replied. "I would say he is interested in military personnel, not bases."

"The very same personnel that carries out spy flights," Rudenko observed.

Under examination by his defense counsel, Powers strove to divorce himself from his job and his country.

Q. Did you take part in political life in your country and did you belong to any party?

A. No, I never belonged to a political party. I never took part in political life, I never even voted. [Animation in the hall. Lack of political affiliation was a sure sign of disaffection to the Russians.]

Q. What were the reasons that prompted you to work for the

Central Intelligence Agency? Did you take this place on your initiative?

A. No, I was approached first. When my period of service in the Air Force was finished, I wanted to get a job in civil aviation, but I was too old when my term was over to be acceptable. And so when I was approached and offered this job with the same pay as that of a senior pilot of a commercial airliner, I thought I was lucky to get such a job.

Powers insisted he did not know what special apparatus had been placed on the U-2, that he was never told the results of his flights, and that he was obeying orders in going on the flight.

Q. Could you refuse to go on this mission?

A. No, I could not refuse. It was an order. I would have been considered a coward by all of my associates and it would have been also an unsuccessful completion of my contract.

Powers then made amends for his sins:

Q. What is your attitude now to your job in the Central Intelligence Agency? [Animation in the hall.] And do you understand how dangerous your first flight was?

A. Yes, I understand a lot more now than before. At first I had hesitations in renewing the contract; I did not want to prolong it. If I could have found another job, I would have never renewed the contract—and now I know a little of the consequence of such flights.

Q. Why are you sorry now, as you say, that you prolonged the contract?

A. The situation I am in now is not too good. I understand that because of the direct result of my flight the Summit Conference did not take place. There has been a great increase in world tension. I am sincerely sorry I had anything to do with this.

Powers' attitude paid off when Rudenko summed up. After laboriously recounting the U-2 incident, Rudenko concluded, "I have every reason to ask the court to pronounce the supreme penalty on the defendant Powers. But, taking into account the defendant Powers' sincere repentance before the Soviet court of the crime which he committed, I do not insist on the death sentence being passed on him and ask the court to sentence the defendant Powers to fifteen years' imprisonment."

The most vituperative denunciations of the United States and its foreign policy did not come from Rudenko but from Griniev. The balding defense counsel, shaking his horn-rimmed glasses in wrath and pulling on his goatee as he paced the Hall of Columns, defended Powers by indicting the United States. He was probably protecting himself at the same time from charges that he was a "lackey of the imperialists" in defending Powers.

"There should sit and invisibly be present here," Rudenko said, "in the prisoner's dock, his masters, namely, the Central Intelligence Agency headed by Allen Dulles and the American military and with them all those sinister aggressive forces which strive to unleash another world war."

Griniev pictured Powers as a victim of "the almighty dollar . . . which in reality corrupts the conscience and morally debases the so-called average American, one of whom my client Powers is." He praised Powers for bailing out of the U-2 instead of destroying it and urged that "in determining the punishment for Powers you will have to take into account this breach of Colonel Shelton's order on his part."

Griniev noted the "truthfulness and sincerity" of Powers' testimony and pointed out that "the divulgence of state secrets in the United States is punishable by ten years' imprisonment, or a fine of ten thousand dollars, or both. Despite this, Powers gave truthful testimony and thus entered into a sharp conflict with his employer. It is not accidental that in testimony given at the preliminary investigation defendant Powers said: 'I know that I shall be tried in your court, but if I happen to return home I shall be tried there as well. But this worries me little because I am not likely to return home.' "

Griniev asked for a verdict that would "add one more example to the numerous instances of the humaneness of the Soviet court, and will offer a sharp contrast to the attitude to Man on the part of the masters of Powers—the Central Intelligence Agency, the ruling reactionary forces of the United States who sent him to certain death and wanted his death."

The judges, a lieutenant general and two major generals, reached a swift verdict. Presiding Judge V. V. Borisoglebsky noted that "Powers' sincere confession of his guilt and his sincere repentance proceeding from the principles of socialist humaneness" had been taken into account. He was sentenced to ten years' confinement with only the first three years to be served in prison, and with the term of punishment counting from May 1, 1960.

Powers' concessions had paid off. He escaped the death sentence that is the traditional lot of spies, and his ten-year term was only a third the sentence given to Abel in New York City in 1957.

Griniev explained to his relieved client that under the Soviet penal code, he would be sent to what is called an "assigned residence" after his three years in jail. The "assigned residence" is usually a loosely supervised labor camp where he would be given work according to his capabilities. With an unblemished record, he would be liable to time off for good behavior after three and a half years in the work camp. Under the Soviet code, his wife could join him there.

Shortly after his trial, Powers was transferred to Vladimir, the Soviet Union's model prison. Vladimir is 150 miles east of Moscow, a massive gray structure that stands alongside the Trans-Siberian railroad track. The cells are spacious, and inmates can supplement the prison diet with food purchased at the commissary. Powers was given menial duties in the prison mail room while he waited to become eligible for transfer to a labor camp.

Powers was pleased with the sentence but distressed by his counsel's savage attack on the United States. The next day, the Russians organized a family reunion at which the airman told his father and mother that he did not want to associate himself with Griniev's remarks. He added, with the candor of revelation: "After all, I AM an American."

The family reunion, held in a cozy anteroom of Lubyanka Prison under the eyes of six guards and the cameras of twice as many Soviet photographers, was a bit forced. There was bad blood between Powers' parents and his wife. Powers senior had long been pictured as the aggrieved father who would spare no sacrifice to help his son, and his "from one father to another" appeals to Khrushchev found a sympathetic reception. When the parents were invited to attend the trial, a financial problem arose. Mr. Powers was far from wealthy and could not afford the trip. He accepted an offer from *Life* Magazine for an exclusive story and was paid $5,000 plus the trip expenses. To Barbara Powers, who refused several lucrative offers and made the trip to Moscow on her own, the conduct of her in-laws was deplorable.

In a case already tarnished by the supremacy of material values over patriotism, there were indications that even a father's grief was for sale. In turn, Barbara was criticized for releasing several of her husband's letters to *Newsweek* Magazine, but *Newsweek* denied it had paid for the letters. A family conflict about who was acting in the best interests of the stricken pilot arose, and relations were strained long before departure for Moscow. Finally, the parents left on their own, with their own team of advisers, lawyers, and doctors, and Barbara followed soon after with her entourage.

Barbara was able to see her husband several times, but never alone. She reported that he had lost weight and seemed nervous. He did not appear to have a clear idea of the proportions the U-2 incident had reached in the United States. At their last meeting in late August, she brought him heavy shoes and underwear, a fur hat, and other items to brave the Russian winter. A snack of tea, coffee, and caviar was set for the couple as the inevitable photographers took the final pictures. Francis told Barbara that she was entitled to mail him 17.6-pound shipments of food and clothing every month and asked that books be included in the packages.

The end of the trial did not mark a pause for the Soviet propaganda machine. A week later, the rocket crew that supposedly downed the U-2 was quoted as saying, "We are greatly satisfied with the ten-year sentence—as before, we are vigilantly manning our posts and shall continue to perfect our combat readiness."

In September, excerpts from the trial were as common on Soviet television screens as weather forecasts, and the following month the uncut version of the trial made the rounds of what corresponds to the neighborhood-theater circuit in the Soviet Union. If there is a man, woman, or child in Russia today who has never been exposed to the U-2, he or she is probably lacking all of the five senses.

For months after the trial, mass meetings continued to be held in the Soviet Union at which the mention of the U-2 was enough to whip the audience into a frenzy of anti-American slogans. *Pravda* often quoted participants of these rallies whose opinions were not notable for variety. The quotes ran to "the warmongers have to be curbed" (Smekalin, turner at the dynamo plant, Moscow); "the imperialists won't cease rattling the saber" (Lomov, seaman, Pacific submarine fleet); "every honest person experiences a sense of indignation at the foul act of the American brass hats" (Ivan Topor, tractor driver at the Michurin kolkhoz, Tiraspol district, Moldavian, S.S.R.).

One can only wonder why the Russians, who had a pretty airtight case to begin with, felt the need to bolster it with a multitude of propaganda techniques. Their handling of the U-2 case finally fell victim to the faults of an overwritten scenario—bombast and bathos.

Another chapter in the U-2 story came with little-noticed items in aviation magazines, reading: "All remaining U-2s in Turkey have been grounded," and "Three NASA U-2s shipped to the U.S. from their base in Atsugi, Japan, are now in hangar storage at Edwards Air Force Base, Calif."

Even Khrushchev's vociferous rancor had dissolved by the time he reached New York City in September, 1960, to attend the United Nations General Assembly. In a relaxed, jocular sidewalk interview, he shrugged off the U-2 incident with the remark that "there have always been spies and there always will be spies. We treated Powers leniently. You electrocuted the Rosenbergs and they never pleaded guilty. Powers got ten years and he'll be out in three."

Khrushchev was better than his word. After less than two years of imprisonment, Powers was released and sent home on February 10, 1962, in exchange for Colonel Abel.*

* The Abel-Powers exchange occurred just as this book was going to press. See the Epilogue for the background of this unprecedented exchange and the highly dramatic events of February 10th.

X. A Bad Year for England

THE British security services will long remember 1961 as a year which saw them often where they hate most to be—on the daily newspapers' front pages. In January, an espionage ring that was stealing classified documents from the Portland Naval Base was discovered. Its exposure was also the exposure of a slovenly security setup in the Royal Navy and an inadequate British counterspy network. In May, George Blake, an agent for British intelligence abroad, was convicted for nine undetected years of espionage for the Soviet Union. Blake had been posted two years in Berlin, and had access to information which helped shape the present Soviet threat to that city, according to Western intelligence sources. He systematically betrayed Western agents and Western secrets to the Russians through East German contacts. His years of deliberate and unrepentant treason in the service of Communism were the most severe blow to British intelligence since the Burgess-Maclean defections in 1956.

These two cases shook the foundations of British security. Commissions were formed to find ways to strengthen the traditionally infiltration-proof intelligence services. After six months in session, the Radliffe committee recommended drastic revisions including trained psychologists for all sensitive government departments, periodic security checks, detailed personal files on all government employees who handle classified material, and greater care in hiring naturalized

Britons and Britons with mixed parentage for security work (Blake did not have a drop of English blood).

Public opinion in England was awakened to the fact that espionage is not a fiction manufactured for paperback books with bloody daggers and roses on the cover. Professional agents from the Soviet Union had been operating unperturbed in London over a period of years, using the same techniques of violence and intimidation to recruit weak-willed persons that they use in their own country.

Also, the famed British "silent services," the marvelously thorough and discreet intelligence units which engineered coup after brilliant coup in World War II and served as a model for many another intelligence organization, had been caught resting on their laurels.

Worse, British subjects had been enlisted to collect information for the Soviet Union. In a country that bows to no other for civic pride and a quietly stubborn patriotism, this was the unkindest cut of all.

The capture of the Portland ring came at a particularly bad time for the Government, which was negotiating with the United States for increased sharing of atomic secrets and atomic weapons through the North Atlantic Treaty Organization. The Portland case did personal injury to Prime Minister Harold Macmillan ("this is a terrible blow to me," he said in the House of Commons) in weakening his position on NATO with the United States.

Mr. Macmillan probably was reminded of the original U.S.-British pact made in 1956 for the sharing of nuclear secrets. The executive agreement was signed by President Eisenhower over the objections of the Senate and called for giving the British all the blueprints and designs of the atomic-powered *Nautilus* power plant. Thanks to this information, the British started working on their *Dreadnought*.

While the agreement was before the Senate, Thomas Murray, then a member of the Atomic Energy Commission, said he was withdrawing his approval "on the basis of information I have received reflecting inadequacies of British security procedures." Senator Clinton Anderson of New Mexico said on the floor of the Senate, "I want to make clear that I am in favor of helping our British allies in every way possible. But in helping the British, we should be ever vigilant to protect real security. By 'real security' I mean really protecting military blueprints and not paper protection of ideas and other things not protectable."

Perhaps Senator Anderson's words were still ringing in Mr. Macmillan's ears when the Portland spy case broke. The way the case was handled reflected the desire to convince the United States that Great Britain was an ally to be trusted, not a negligent NATO partner that couldn't keep a secret.

The case was given the widest publicity and tried in open court. This in itself was intended to show no major leaks were involved. Great pains were taken to show that the information gathered by the spies was of relatively minor value. Sir Reginald Manningham-Buller, British Attorney General who prosecuted the case, said in his opening statement:

"Perhaps I should say that the nature of their [two of the defendants'] duties did not give them any access to atomic secrets or secrets about nuclear propulsion, and there is no ground for supposing they were able to obtain any such information or for supposing they communicated any such information."

Mr. Macmillan in the Commons echoed these reassurances, saying that "while it is obviously not in the public interest to reveal the amount of damage done, there is no evidence to suggest that the information compromised covered more than a relatively limited sector of the whole field of British naval weapons.

"There is no ground to suppose that any information belonging to the United States or to other NATO countries was compromised. There is no possibility of information concerning nuclear weapons or nuclear propulsion having been betrayed by these spies."

At the same time, the trial was used to show that British justice was not tolerant of spies. The harshness of the sentences seemed in part a cover-up for the security lapses and in part an intended deterrent. But as the defense pointed out at the trial, espionage is a crime where the deterrent factor seldom enters. The professional agent expects to be caught at some point, and time in prison is not spent reflecting upon the error of his ways. He does not consider himself a criminal, since he is serving his country, but a victim of bad luck and someone else's carelessness.

The sentences meted out to the five defendants of the Portland ring were much more severe than those given to spies like Alan Nunn May and Klaus Fuchs, who had been charged with transmitting atomic secrets to the Russians. There were contradictions between the allegations that these spies really hadn't done very much and the total of ninety-five years in prison they were given to share. Again, the sentences were intended mainly for export purposes and the defendants, guilty though they were, served as the pawns of foreign policy.

The usual "what went wrong" inquiry followed the trial, and the spy probe began sniffing around naval intelligence and MI5, British counterintelligence.

But the probe had not really begun when the Blake case, far graver in its implications, broke upon the British scene. The adjective "incredible" is weary from overuse, but in the case of George Blake it is warranted. Blake was convicted of espionage on May 3 in a closed trial that contrasted sharply with the open proceedings of the Portland case. He was sentenced to forty-two years (fourteen years on each of three counts of violating the Official Secrets Act), the longest term of imprisonment imposed in a British court in the twentieth century.

Blake was the prototype of the secret agent—the spy who attains a position of great responsibility in one country while working for another power. Blake had worked for M16, the arm of British intelligence engaged in espionage abroad, since 1948. Since 1951 he had been working for the Russians. The damage he did was great. He turned over the names of British agents working in Germany and behind the Iron Curtain, he gave the Russians the organizational plan and the names of the chiefs of M16, and through his information he was able to frustrate for years a number of British intelligence operations.

George Blake was thirty-eight at the time of his conviction. He was born in Holland, the son of a Dutch woman, Catherine Beyer Wellan, and an Egyptian Jew, Albert William Behar. His father was one of fourteen children of a prosperous merchant of Spanish-Jewish origin who had settled in Egypt. Mr. Behar obtained a British passport after serving in the British Army in World War I. He was a volatile, adventurous man who had spent five years of his youth in the French Foreign Legion and who cut himself off from his family when he married outside his faith. The marriage broke up in 1924, when George was two. The child seldom saw his father after that, and learned of his death in 1936. George continued to call himself Behar until he went to England in 1944. His mother and two sisters had fled Holland in 1940 and his mother was working as a companion for an elderly woman. It was during the war that she changed her name to Blake and George adopted this more English-sounding name.

Blake's mixed origins were the object of a sardonic remark by Prime Minister Macmillan, who noted that the entire case would have been avoided had Foreign Service regulations not been revamped. In the old days one had to have two British parents to qualify. This rule would not only have disqualified Blake, it would have barred Mr. Macmillan himself and Sir Winston Churchill, both of whom had American mothers.

In Blake's case, it was pointed out that since neither of his parents was of British stock and since he had spent his formative years outside England, he had never developed a sense of loyalty or patriotism toward the country which he picked for his unusual career. His early life had been restless and from his frequent travels had emerged no particular national attachments. Without geographical roots, he was vulnerable to doctrines which, like himself, were able to cross frontiers and take hold in many different lands. This was in any case the somewhat oversimplified clue given by his family to those trying to pierce the mystery of his conversion.

George lived and went to school in Holland until the age of thirteen, when one of his father's sisters, who had married a Cairo banker, took an interest in him. She offered to pay for his education if he would agree to come and live in Cairo with them. From 1935 to 1939, George left the measured sobriety of Dutch middle-class life for the opulence of prewar Egypt in a wealthy family. It was while at school in Egypt that George learned English. He always retained a slight but guttural accent which set him off from his Foreign Office colleagues as someone who did not have the usual background of public schools and English country life.

It was also while in Egypt that Blake first indulged a strong but hitherto suppressed bent for make-believe. His aunt bought him exotic costumes which he wore around the house, playing the part sometimes of a Lawrence of Arabia, sometimes of a British admiral. His family photograph albums are spotted with pictures of the adolescent Blake striking a pose in keeping with the costume he is wearing. His wife remembers that he enjoyed playing make-believe games with his sons. For instance, he would wrap a sheet around his body and pretend to be a monk, while dressing up his eldest son as a choirboy. Bach organ music would play in the background for mood.

In 1939, George returned to Rotterdam and entered a high school there. When the Germans invaded the Netherlands in 1940, he was

arrested as a British subject and interned. He escaped from the intern-
ment camp and joined the Dutch resistance shortly after his eighteenth birthday. For about a year he worked as a courier, relishing in
the perilous clandestinity of what were in effect his first espionage
assignments. Having learned that his mother and two sisters had
reached England safely, he decided in 1942 to join them. With a
forged passport, he made his way from Belgium into France, where
he was harbored by friendly Dominican monks. He ran the border
across the Pyrenees into Spain but was caught near Madrid by the
Guardia Civil. An arrangement having been reached with Spain in
1943 for the repatriation of British refugees, he was sent to Gibraltar
and from there to England. He enlisted in the Royal Navy but because
of his knowledge of German and Flemish he was loaned to an intelligence outfit.

His main task with the "Special Operations Department" was brief-
ing Dutch agents who were about to be parachuted behind German
lines. His work gained the attention of the Dutch Government, which
awarded him a knighthood in the Order of Nassau at the end of the
war.

Blake was "demobbed" (as the British say) from the Navy in
1947, but asked to stay on in civilian intelligence work. "In normal
times, he couldn't even have obtained a job as a London policeman,"
one commentator later wrote. These were not normal times, and
despite Blake's heteroclite background, he was accepted gladly in the
ranks of British intelligence. He brought the service a gift for languages, a wide experience in foreign lands, and the ability to be stationed abroad without being immediately spotted as British. His new
employers sent him to Downing College, Cambridge, for a Russian-
language course and he then joined the Foreign Office as an "unestablished" member. Unestablished members do not rise through the
regular channels but sometimes have far more important tasks to
perform than officers in the regular hierarchy. Blake's real bosses were
not the Foreign Office, however, but M16, which sent him from one
temporary assignment to another. His name never appeared on
Foreign Office lists and he was never officially promoted.

His first post was in Seoul as British vice-consul. He did his job
well, traveled widely across Korea and made Korean friends. In
1949 he warned his superiors that the North Koreans were building
up for an attack across the 38th parallel, but his information was

disregarded. The attack came in June, 1950. Blake was arrested at the legation in Seoul along with Sir Vivian Holt, the chief of mission. They were taken with other captured diplomats to the North Korean capital of Pyongyang and thrown into a prison compound. The next three years were the least pleasant but the most important of Blake's life.

Fellow prisoners commenting on Blake's captivity describe a man of great courage and energy, undaunted by physical hardship and untainted by the North Korean's crude but persistent brainwashing attempts.

He so effectively matched the dialectic of the North Korean instructor assigned to instill Marxism into the British prisoners that the instructor finally quit in disgust and was replaced by a more thick-skinned Soviet tutor.

He shared a nine-foot by nine-foot hovel with nine other British prisoners. In the winter they were taken out in the snow and beaten as a matter of routine. In the summer, the heat and the lice bred disease. Throughout the year, indoctrinators tried to stamp the Communist faith into the minds of the ill and weakened prisoners.

A fellow prisoner, Bishop Cecil Cooper, recalls that "Blake was a man of great energy. He helped keep us alive by his enthusiasm and his courage. Blake resisted the brainwashing fiercely, arguing with the political officers who were attempting to indoctrinate us. . . . He was a regular churchgoer, a fine chap and a very good diplomat."

Another fellow prisoner, the journalist Phillip Deane, insisted that Blake had not been brainwashed and was an unlikely recruit for Communism after beholding the "monstrous injustices" of the prison camp. "The torture of kindly old nuns, the imprisonment of a mother with her nine-month-old child, the crazy laughter of the 'death camp' commandant—Are we to believe that these things converted an intelligent, sensitive man like Blake, convincing him that Communism could establish a more just society?"

Mr. Deane remembers Blake as a harmless dreamer "with an endearing willingness to let his leg be pulled. He had Walter Mitty dreams, always seeing himself knighted or consecrated bishop for some service to the State or God; it was a game but it was quite seriously meant. Treason is hardly the road to pomp and circumstance."

But treason was admittedly the road for Blake, who in November, 1951, after seventeen months of captivity, went to his captors and calmly informed them that he had been converted to Communism. Fellow prisoners recall that about this time, they were to have been taken on a death march. The night before the scheduled march, Blake vanished from the compound. He was brought back the next day by the ruthless chief guard called "Tiger," and explained that he had been caught while trying to escape. His cellmates did not question the story but had inner reservations about it, for Blake boasted he had been given a good meal and cigarettes—hardly the treatment reserved for escapees. Blake's conversion made him eligible for liberation from the camp. It is a tribute to his remarkable single-mindedness that he elected to stay a prisoner to keep from arousing suspicions. He remained in the camp another fifteen months. Perhaps one of the reasons for his exemplary conduct as praised by fellow prisoners is that he was there by choice and that his freedom depended only on himself. The secret knowledge that he was now working for his captors, and the spiritual satisfaction that must come with any ideological conversion, could easily have been interpreted as courage and determination. Also, in all fairness to Blake, it should be noted that he made three conditions at the time of his conversion: that he receive no privileges as a prisoner, that he receive no payment for the information he provided, and that he be absolved from reporting on his fellow prisoners.

Why did he do it? The explanation, as simple as it is unsatisfactory, was given by Lord Chief Justice, Lord Parker, who said, "To quote his own words, he resolved to join the Communist side in establishing what he believed on balance a more just society. What he did was to approach the Russians and volunteer to work for them."

Such a total ideological reversal in the midst of imprisonment brings to mind the fascinating book by Richard Condon, *The Manchurian Candidate*. The novel deals with an American prisoner of the Chinese Reds who is mesmerized through some Pavlovian hocus-pocus into becoming a Communist agent. His mind is controlled by a key phrase which unleashes him to do the bidding of his former captors; in the case of the novel, to assassinate the President of the United States.

It is so difficult to understand the mechanics of a decision like Blake's that one is tempted to give credence to occult techniques that can control men's minds. Perhaps the Russians understood him no better than the British agents who later had to investigate him, but his new employers were not about to look a gift horse of Blake's value in the mouth. In the long confession he made after his arrest, Blake admitted with complete candor that "there was not any official document of any importance to which I had access which was not passed to my Soviet contact."

In March, 1953, Blake and the other British prisoners were released and received a hero's welcome on their arrival in London. Photographs of the homecoming show the prisoners haggard but smiling, with Blake an impressive figure with his wavy hair and full beard. Blake was carefully screened by British intelligence. He was asked to write a full account of his prison camp experiences. His Korean memoirs aroused no suspicions and he was sent on a long leave after he reported to the Foreign Office in London. He waited two years before being given another foreign assignment, unremarkable years professionally but years that saw him become a family man. In October, 1954, he married one of the pool secretaries in the Foreign Office, the auburn-haired, delicately featured daughter of a retired Army officer. Blake had no close personal friends and his wife's brother filled in as best man at the wedding.

In April, 1955, Blake was sent to Berlin where he worked in the political branch of the British military government. His wife recalled in a series of articles written for the London *Sunday Telegraph* that he was doing a great deal of clandestine work, meeting contacts at strange hours and so on. She knew he was working in intelligence, she said, but never suspected that his real sympathies were with the Soviet Union. Looking back, she remembered that he sometimes expressed admiration for the Soviet system and for the way Soviet leaders outmaneuvered the West in several political crises. He read Russian books and had bookshelves full of works by Marx and Lenin. In 1956, when Burgess and Maclean defected, he asked: "What would you do if I went to Russia?" However, since he was a kind and thoughtful husband who was never stingy with household money and since a wife is not a political commissar, these details of Blake's personal life only took on significance after his arrest.

In addition, life in Berlin during the four years they spent there was pleasant for the Blakes. He was making a good salary and had plenty of leaves, which they spent in Italy and Yugoslavia. "The Firm," as British intelligence is known in Berlin, was pleased with his work. It is likely that the Russians made sure Blake was always well rated in the MI6 progress reports. Blake worked on a special Allied intelligence staff which gathered and evaluated agent reports from East Germany. What he was actually doing was giving away to the Russians the names of agents operating for the West. As part of his duties, Blake made frequent trips to East Germany, where it is believed he met his Soviet contact. According to a West Berlin newspaper, *B.Z.*, at least six German nationals working for Allied intelligence in East Germany were arrested as a result of Blake's intervention.

One of Blake's minor contacts in Berlin was a German named Horst Eitner. Blake knew Eitner as "Mickey" and Eitner knew Blake as a Dutchman named Max de Vries. Eitner had had a checkered career as an intelligence agent. He was living in East Germany when he first contacted British intelligence in 1950. Several years later he defected to the West and is said to have worked briefly for the Gehlen Organization.

In 1956, he was doing part-time agent work for the British, and to supplement his income he offered his services to Soviet intelligence for something like $25 a month. Eitner was the true double agent, working with equal conscientiousness and equal duplicity for both sides. If there had been other sides ready with regular paychecks, doubtless he would have worked for them as well. He photographed his Western contacts, taped their conversations and turned the results over to the Soviets. The information he gave the Allies and the Soviets was sometimes true, sometimes false.

During most of the four years Blake spent in Berlin, he worked with Eitner. He had a low opinion of the thirty-six-year-old German, however, and made him give up several contacts he considered unreliable. Eitner is believed to have discovered that Blake was working for the Soviets. This was another bit of useful information to be stored and unearthed at the proper time. The time came in 1960, when Eitner's wife gave him away to his Western superiors in a burst of spite over the attentions he was paying other women. Eitner was discreetly arrested in October. There were no press leaks. He was not tried until thirteen months later, when the Blake case was closed. Eitner was given a lenient, three-year sentence, purportedly because he had no police record. His wife, who had served as a sort of espionage "girl Friday," had been charged as an accessory but got off with an eight-month suspended sentence. Clearly, Eitner had been able to make the most at his closed trial of the flotsam and jetsam he had picked up on both sides of the Iron Curtain, including the real identity and function of his amiable Dutch contact de Vries.

Blake left Berlin in early 1959 and apparently was not informed a year later when Eitner was arrested. He had been told he was to go to the Foreign Office's Middle East College of Arabic Studies in Beirut to prepare for an intelligence assignment in an Arab country (the time he had spent in Egypt had been duly noted by his superiors), but he did not leave until September, 1960. The school was in Shemlan, twenty miles away from Beirut, and Blake, his wife, and their two young sons settled into a leisurely life marked for him by a pleasant schedule of morning and afternoon classes. It was at this time that some rather startling reports on George Blake began to arrive at MI6 headquarters in London.

There was the information provided by Eitner, which in view of the doubtful reliability of the source was cause for suspicion but not condemnation of Blake. There was a bad slip made by Blake himself, who, having learned that the Portland spies were being investigated, held several meetings with a known Soviet agent in Beirut to pass on the information. He was seen at one of these meetings by a security officer at the British Embassy. Finally, in March, 1961, there was the defection of Colonel Anthony Alster, Vice-Minister of the Interior in the Polish Government. Alster had been the effective head of the Polish secret police (Z-2). He was in charge of Polish agents engaged in "Westwork" and had personally met Blake several times. The fifty-four-year-old Polish defector was of Jewish origin and reportedly fled Poland after the Soviet Union announced a drive to purge the satellite governments of Jews. When Alster told what he knew about Blake, MI6 decided it was time for his recall (Alster gave a great deal of other valuable information to the British and as of February 1962 he had still not been surfaced). In April a telegram from the Foreign Office summoned Blake to London. The telegram suggested that he remain in Beirut until after the Easter break if that suited him. Blake, either from thoughtlessness or overconfidence, had no second thoughts about the abrupt recall which was interrupting his academic year. His superiors at MI6 spent an agonizing week in the fear that he would bolt, and as soon as he arrived in London he was arrested and held incommunicado.

Pre-trial hearings were held *in camera*. The first notice the press received about the case was the day of the trial, May 3. The trial itself was one of the shortest in the history of British courts. It lasted fifteen minutes, enough time for Blake to plead guilty and for the Lord Chief Justice to convict him. The courtroom in the Old Bailey was cleared, and the glass windows of the courtroom doors were shuttered with boards.

In the words of Attorney General Manningham-Buller, Blake had furnished the Soviet Union with "a mass of information so secret that I can tell your Lordship little about it in open court. . . . He had access to information of very great importance." The Attorney General added that "although he held a responsible position, his employment fortunately did not give him access to information relating to secret weapons or nuclear atomic weapons."

This again was an effort to reassure the United States that although Britain was riddled with spies, some of whom were working inside British intelligence, NATO secrets were safe.

When the Lord Chief Justice passed sentence, he pointed out that the information communicated by Blake had not been "of a scientific nature [but] was clearly of the utmost importance to that power [the Soviet Union] and has rendered much of this country's efforts completely useless. . . . Your case is akin to treason."

Blake left the trial in a state of shock and was hospitalized. Later he appealed his sentence and the appeal was denied. The day after the trial, Mr. Macmillan took the floor in the House of Commons and combined reassurances with promises that security in England would be tightened. Mr. Macmillan confessed that he was as perplexed as the average man about Blake. "Although he no doubt underwent a certain amount of ill treatment, in common with the others who were interned by the Chinese, he was subject to none of the brainwashing which military prisoners suffered. After his release and after having been subjected to a very thorough security vetting [checkup], Blake was employed for a period with the British military government in Berlin and subsequently attached for a time to the Foreign Office in London. His case is unusual because he gave every outward evidence of being a loyal government employee."

Mr. Macmillan further admitted that he knew of no foolproof method for catching spies who change allegiances and are able to conceal their conversion skillfully. "Blake received no money for his services," he said. "He was never at any time a member of the Communist Party, or any of its affiliated organizations. What he did was done as the result of a conversion to a genuine belief in the Communist system. In these circumstances, suspicion would not easily be aroused in relation to a man who had served his country well for some eight years, who gave every appearance of leading a normal and respectable life, but who had decided to betray his country for ideological reasons. Indeed, having agreed to work for the Russians, he was careful not to arouse suspicion and to conceal his conversion to Communism."

It was not easy for the Government to disregard the damage done by the Blake case, especially when it was disclosed that the British press had been asked to exercise voluntary censorship in the case. There is a long-established system in Great Britain that when national security is menaced, the newspapers play along with the Government to suppress information. The system is implemented by the so-called "D" notices, which are sent out by the Government to editors, asking them not to print certain information. These official requests for secrecy are approved by a board of twenty newspaper and television executives known as the Services Press and Broadcasting Committee. Two "D" notices were sent out in the Blake case, one asking editors to suppress mention of Blake's link with MI6, the other asking that foreign reports to that effect not be reprinted.

The British press was willing to agree to the first request, but when it saw that American and French newspapers used the information, they charged the government departments with trying to conceal their own shortcomings. Foreign newspapers, sold freely in London, were carrying the reports they had been asked to suppress.

These two spy cases, coming within two months of each other, sparked a complete reappraisal of the British security system, and investigations are still going on to trace the ramifications of the Portland ring and the strange conversion of George Blake.

*   *   *

One thing could be said for Harry Houghton, the slight, weak-chinned clerk who acted as "bag man" in the Portland spy ring—he was never the victim of an ideological motive. Rather he was the product of the twin scourges of the lower middle class—stupidity and cupidity. He was one of those sad little people who go stumbling through life at the mercy of their own pettiness.

There is one redeeming factor in his pathetic biography, one trivial grace—He was a choirboy in the cathedral in his home town of Lincoln, about 120 miles north of London. At the age of sixteen, he ran away from home and joined the Navy. Through a talent for flattering his superiors and browbeating his inferiors he rose to the rank of master at arms, or chief petty officer. During the war, he kept his head down and stayed out of the line of fire.

Through no fault of his own, he emerged the holder of the Africa Star, European and Burmese Theater Medals, the General Service Medal, the Atlantic Star, and a long service and good conduct pension. He had been assigned to merchant cruisers that ran the 1942 Malta convoy and subsequent convoys to Russia, and at war's end he found himself in India in charge of discipline in a rest camp for former prisoners.

In later years, Harry liked to regale the patrons of his favorite pub, the Old Elm Tree, near his home in Weymouth, with vivid accounts of the war years. Before ordering a round of bitter, he would intone: "When I was torpedoed by the Jerries in '42," or, "When I was serving on a gunboat in the Gulf of Bothnia"—to the mild amusement of his cronies who knew that their paunchy drinking companion with the pointed nose and crimson-veined cheeks had never touched water in twenty-three years of Navy life.

When Harry was demobilized in 1945, he joined the civil service and was promoted from temporary to full-time clerk. After clerking four years for the Navy in the small channel town of Gosport, he was assigned to the staff of the naval attaché in Warsaw, Captain Nigel Austen, who remembers him mainly for his drunkenness. Captain Austen said he was notorious at embassy parties and that once he found him completely gone "in broad daylight in the streets of Warsaw."

Despite his drinking, it was in Warsaw that Harry discovered his true vocation. There was a thriving black market in antibiotics at the time; penicillin and the other new wonder drugs were easier to handle and worth more than gold ingots.

Harry found an entree into this lucrative sideline through a young Polish woman named Christina, whom he met at a party given by a British Embassy official. His wife Peggy had gone back to England after a series of bitter quarrels over his drinking and he was living the gay bachelor life. Christina was attractive and responsive to Harry's broad humor and Yorkshire accent.

When he began taking her out, Christina warned him that "any time we meet it will have to be done with the utmost secrecy because if I am seen talking to a Britisher or any Westerner, I'll be carried off to Mugatal [secret police prison in Warsaw]." Harry took precautions in keeping with the risks and put a bedside lamp on his window sill as an all-clear sign for Christina to come to his apartment.

Christina also introduced Harry to some of the most prosperous citizens of satellite Poland, who were not above dabbling in private enterprise to make ends meet. Through the diplomatic valise and a favorable exchange rate, Harry became the pivot of a black market ring in wonder drugs. He was paid in care of a London bank, and between 1949 and 1951 his account grew to 4,000 pounds (roughly $11,000).

At the time, the pound was worth 11.7 zlotys but the embassy rate was 30. As Harry explained at his trial, "If we bought anything in England and we sold it in Poland for Polish money we made a terrific amount of profit."

Even after Harry had left Poland, he kept in touch with Christina and sent her cosmetics unavailable behind the Iron Curtain. "Occasionally I would send her a Max Factor lipstick and I think it is Coty face powder. On two occasions I had a letter of thanks."

What Harry didn't know was that his black market activities were being carried out with the knowledge and encouragement of the Soviet and Polish secret police.

Harry had fallen prey to techniques that have since became familiar through the testimony of Pawel Monat, a colonel in Z-II (Polish intelligence) who defected to the United States in 1959. Colonel Monat gave the following testimony to a Senate subcommittee on June 13, 1960:

Q. How does Z-II recruit its agents?
A. In several ways. In carrying out its mission against Western forces, Z-II also attempts to recruit civilian and military visitors to Poland. . . . The official diplomatic representatives responsible for issuing visas prepare lists of all visa applicants and make these lists available to the Z-II representatives there. The lists are forwarded to Z-II headquarters in Warsaw where appropriate action is

taken for possible recruitment. The method of cultivating and approaching visitors varies in each case. Z-II may not necessarily approach a foreign visitor while he is still in Poland: rather Z-II might decide to wait until the visitor has returned to his own country. It is also possible that some of the persons recruited as a result of trips to Poland would assume the status of sleeper agents until such time as Z-II desires to activate them.

This was the technique used on Harry while he was piling up pounds in his London bank from the proceeds of his penicillin transactions. Z-II had a file on him from the moment he left London to take his minor clerical post in Warsaw. When he left Warsaw, they had two levers of influence: one, the correspondence and receipts proving his black market activity; two, his liaison with Christina, who could if the need arose nag Harry with a paternity suit.

The foresight Z-II showed in Harry's case was remarkable, for after he was sent home to England for repeated drunkenness he obtained a job at the Underwater Weapons Establishment at the Portland naval base. From 1951 to 1957 he worked as a clerk at the naval base and was given a security classification in spite of his lamentable record.

The Portland naval base is a sprawling amalgam of docks, shipyards, research and test facilities, administration buildings, and secret naval installations which employs upward of 20,000 persons. Since 1958, it has been devoted almost solely to submarine and anti-submarine research.

The North Atlantic Treaty Organization, which parcels out to member nations the military tasks to which they are best suited, gave the Royal Navy the job of building up NATO's underwater defense program, and all the work of detecting and destroying enemy submarines was centered at Portland.

The British atomic submarine, the *Dreadnought,* was also being built at Portland with an American atomic plant. The key difference between the Polaris-equipped American atomic subs and the *Dreadnought,* however, was that the British sub was designed as an "anti-submarine submarine." The Russians have a fleet of 350 or 400 conventionally powered subs and are building three atomic subs. The *Dreadnought* was conceived as a deterrent to Soviet atomic subs which would escape detection through the usual methods.

Thus, the *Dreadnought,* the first of which is to be commissioned in early 1962, will be equipped with some of the devices being tested at Portland. These devices include:

A *sniffer apparatus,* which can "smell out" submarines by capting unseen diesel fumes.

Ice eyes, a sound-detection device that detects gaps in the ice through which snorkel subs can place their breathing tubes. It also contains navigation equipment that permits the subs to check on their position even when traveling under ice. The *Finwhale* and the *Amphion,* two experimental and nonatomic British submarines, are said to be already equipped with these devices.

Asdic sets, sonar devices used since the end of World War II. Their range for sending supersonic waves through the water to detect subs was said to be six miles at the end of the war and is now reported to be five times as great. The asdic set is not a foolproof detection device, for there are special paints that protect submarines against supersonic rays, paints that the Germans had already used in World War II. Nonetheless, the Russians, according to a British naval expert, "still don't have effective asdic sets" and this was one of the main things they were after at Portland.

The top-secret anti-submarine device they were most interested in, however, is one against which there is no defense. This is a device which registers slight changes in the gravitational field, a sort of pendulum that can be installed in low-flying helicopters to detect the slightest changes in the gravitational pull. Thus it works at any depth and there is no way to parry its effect. There are strong reasons for believing that this "absolute" anti-submarine device was part of the information handed over by the Portland ring to the Russians.

Going back to the testimony of Colonel Monat, we find that Polish intelligence, or Z-II, had a specific mission of collecting information about NATO forces. "Z-II has a special mission," he said in his testimony, "to collect information about all NATO forces throughout the world. There is even a special section in the reports branch which is responsible for evaluating, collecting, and disseminating all intelligence about NATO forces wherever they might be stationed."

Thus, Harry Houghton's assignment to the Portland base was one that Z-II approved completely. In 1951, when he started work there, all anti-sub work had not yet been concentrated at the base. In fact, the concentration was not accomplished until one year after he had been transferred to the auxiliary repair unit at Portland as a clerk.

He had been shifted from the sensitive Underwater Weapons Establishment, not because of suspected espionage activities, not because of his drunkenness, but because his work was unsatisfactory.

There were two incidents connected with Houghton's employment that illustrate the amazing laxity of security at Portland. When he was transferred to the repair unit, it was learned that he had never been given a security check. Commander Stuart Erskine Crewe-Read, a retired destroyer commander who served as the only security officer at Portland ("my requests for help seem to have got lost somewhere between here and the Admiralty"), lamely explained that Houghton had not been checked because "his job was not sufficiently important, it takes six weeks to vet a man, and it would be an impossible job if each man and woman on this base had to be checked with our present manpower resources." Also, it took six months to obtain Houghton's transfer under a civil service system seemingly designed to protect incompetents and guard sinecures. This in spite of the fact that Houghton was on probation with the civil service through his accumulated inadequacies.

In May, 1958, his wife went to see the probation officer in Bournemouth in a vengeful mood. She charged that he habitually brought home classified documents taken from the naval base. She regaled the probation officer with snatches of family life. "He's always boasting how he's going to get even with the Admiralty," she said.

The probation officer, a cautious type, never passed on his report to Naval intelligence "because it sounded like a novel and I was afraid the laws of slander would be invoked if I recommended an investigation."

It is interesting to note that British laws of defamation are so severe in the protection of the individual from slander that they provide no immunity for allegations made in the course of an official investigation. In the United States, such allegations are privileged if they are made without malice in the course of official business to qualified persons and become the subject of an official report.

Thanks to these security lapses, Houghton was able to hang on at Portland in spite of his shortcomings and the denunciations of his wife, who divorced him not long after and remarried a Royal Air Force corporal stationed in the Far East.

During Houghton's tenure at Portland, his drab clerk's life was seasoned by a slow-moving romance with a co-worker. In a neighboring office at the Portland base there was a temporary clerk, forty-six-year-old Ethel Elizabeth Gee, who could serve as the prototype of the British spinster. Of humble origins (her father had been a blacksmith), she nonetheless received a genteel upbringing at a private school. She did her bit during the war years, was turned down when she tried to enlist in the WRENs and took a defense job inspecting small parts at the Folland Aircraft plant in Hamble. She joined the Underwater Detection Establishment in Portland in 1950 as a temporary clerk, as did Houghton, and worked there unperturbed up to the time of her arrest.

Miss Gee had the kind of birdlike English looks which consists of clear skin, good teeth and a fragile bone structure and which hardens in later years into a fossil-like version of youth.

Shy, colorless, plain, she lived in a small cottage in Portland with an eighty-year-old mother, an invalid aunt, and a seventy-six-year-old uncle. "You might say she lived a rather dull life in the West Country," her lawyer commented in one of the trial's understatements. She did have two diversions, however: badminton and petitpoint.

She was, in keeping with her upbringing, a very proper person and a conservative. During her trial testimony, she described a transportation strike as "disgusting" and when questioned about the stencils she had to use in her work at Portland, there was this exchange: Q—Are they dirty things? A—Oh, shocking.

Harry Houghton and Elizabeth Gee struck up an acquaintance because they both lived in the Portland area. It was a very casual office friendship, with Harry picking her up and driving her home from work. They had known each other for five years before they started going out on "dates."

In 1958, the relationship was cemented when Harry moved into a trailer near Portland which he had bought with 200 pounds borrowed from Miss Gee. By this time he was no longer living with his wife.

The courtship included visits to Miss Gee's family, Sunday lunch with the eighty-year-old mother, weekend trips to Bournemouth (a popular resort about thirty miles east of Portland) and trips to London for the theater or an afternoon on the town.

Miss Gee liked Harry's bonhomie, his free spending, and his vast circle of acquaintances, which enlarged her own social horizons. "Almost everywhere he goes he knows people," she said, "while I am probably a rather shy person and I do not look forward to meeting people."

Harry was waiting for his divorce and Miss Gee was waiting for the old people she had charge of to leave for a better world. "I would have married him had conditions been different at home," she said.

In 1959, Harry bought a cottage in Portland for 9,000 pounds ($25,000) and Miss Gee helped decorate it. Her influence could be felt in the fifty cactus plants that decorated the imitation Tudor cottage, and in the "perennial" Christmas tree that stood in all seasons on a side table in the drawing room. "We were working on the cottage and just hoping that things would straighten out and we could get married," she said.

The sensationalist London press tried hard, but in vain, to transform Harry and Elizabeth's practical, common-sense arrangement into a fiery romance. The degree of passion can be measured by this exchange at the trial: Q—Needless to say, there was no other love in your life. A (Miss Gee)—No, I hardly had time for that.

Patrick O'Donovan, who sat in on the Secrets trial for the London *Observer*, wrote that "hers was a sad little story. Her life had been a dim one and suddenly there was a man friend and money. There were frequent trips to town, for a show and a night at the Cumberland Hotel. There were evenings out in the saloon bar where she could sip her whisky and ginger ale as often as she wished. And above all there was that ultimate pleasure—shopping."

Although Miss Gee was a minor cog at the Portland base, she had been given a security check and had signed the Official Secrets Act, which specifies:

> I undertake not to divulge any information gained by me as a result of my employment to any unauthorised person either civilian or member of Her Majesty's Forces, verbally or in writing, without the previous sanction of the Admiralty. I understand that these provisions apply not only during the period of my employment but also after employment with the Admiralty has ceased.

Miss Gee had started at Portland as a clerk in the stores section and was transferred in 1955 to the drawing-office section. There she worked with two other civil servants and had the rank of clerical assistant, the lowest grade in that type of work. Her weekly salary was eleven pounds, eleven shillings and sixpence before taxes (about $30). Her job was filing "test pamphlets," the result of tests made on Navy equipment. Many of the pamphlets were classified and stencils were kept in a storeroom in the back of her office. When an order came in, Miss Gee put the stencil in the OUT tray and a typist came to get it and run off copies. The pamphlets were often ordered by contractors who manufactured parts for Navy equipment and wanted to know the results of the tests. Other shipyards and qualified persons could also obtain copies of the highly technical pamphlets. Miss Gee kept lists of pamphlets in stock and filled orders. Pamphlets were sent by ordinary mail unless they were classified SECRET, in which case they required registered mailing. The defense pointed out at the trial that it would have been simple to pose as a supplier and obtain a pamphlet through the mail. It was all very routine for Miss Gee, with pamphlets coming in and pamphlets going out. She took little interest in their subject matter.

But by 1957, the surface routine of Elizabeth Gee's and Harry Houghton's lives had been badly shattered. In January, Harry received a telephone call at his Portland office from a man with news of Christina. "I knew this girl was trying to get over because she told me when she was in Poland," Harry said, "and the man said he had some information about her." A Sunday morning meeting in front of an art gallery was arranged, and Harry arrived promptly, hoping to hear that his former Warsaw playmate had escaped Poland. What he heard was just the opposite. From Christina the conversation passed to Harry's work at the Admiralty, in which the mysterious caller showed great interest.

"Can you get me any snippets of naval information?" he asked Harry, who replied with great propriety: "I can't do that. I am not allowed."

"Things will go badly with you and your wife if you don't," the man continued. He told Harry how future meetings would be arranged. Harry would get a promotional pamphlet on Hoover vacuum cleaners in the mail, meaning that he should come to a London tavern called the Tobyjug the first Saturday after receiving it.

Harry's reaction was not to report to the nearest police station that he had been asked by an enemy agent to spy on his country. It was to ask his foreign friend: "You have dragged me all the way up from Weymouth. What have I got out of this lot?" The man removed eight pounds from a billfold and told Harry: "That will do for expenses."

Harry said at his trial that he "toyed with the idea of reporting the conversation," but thought, Well, that's shook him off and that's that.

The first Hoover card didn't come until the following fall. Harry, rather from boredom than anything else ("I had nothing spoiling and I just went to see what was happening"), arrived at the Tobyjug armed with back copies of his local newspaper, the Hampshire *Telegraph and Post,* which carries a naval chronicle on its back page. The chronicle, called "Naval and Dockyard Notes," gives detailed information on ship movements, naval maneuvers, and naval personnel promotions and transfers.

"Can't you do better?" Harry's contact asked disgustedly. "That's all I can get without committing myself," Harry replied. The man renewed his threats that Harry and his wife were not beyond the purview of Iron Curtain justice. "That sort of thing doesn't happen in England," Harry said.

There ensued a high-level discussion on the efficiency of Soviet intimidation abroad. "Do you remember a man by the name of Petrov?" the man said. "He was in the Soviet Embassy in Australia. He went over to the West. But the Australians can't protect him. They are giving him two thousand pounds a year and still he is in fear of his life. Do you know that man is a drooling alcoholic? And that as soon as he goes, the Australian Government will be pleased about it?" (At last report, Vladimir Petrov and his wife Evdokia, who defected to the West in 1954, were still in Australia and still alive, though Mr. Petrov was admittedly giving the Australian authorities trouble with his drinking.)

Houghton countered with Trotsky, an ill-chosen example.

"We got him, didn't we?" the man said. "After twenty years, and he lived in a fortress almost, in Mexico, with bright lights on the place, armed guards and machine guns. We'll get you easy."

Houghton left the meeting somewhat shaken, and when he received another Hoover brochure in December, 1957, he decided to ignore it. Two months later (he was still living in his trailer), he was coming home from the pub one Friday evening about 11 when he was accosted by two men, Londoners by their accent. "Are you Houghton?" one asked. "Why didn't you go to London when you got the card?" the other asked.

"I'm not bloody well going there," Harry replied.

The men escorted Harry inside his trailer where they gave him a methodical and professional beating, with body blows that left his face unmarked. The two were London thugs hired by Z-II to do the job. They left with the warning that "your wife will get it as well if you're not careful." They were evidently not up on Harry's marital status, for he was no longer living with his wife.

Harry was too frighened to go to the police, he said. "I couldn't tell the doctor because I would have to tell him how I got it. I was not prepared to go to the police. I did not think they could do anything about it. I was first and foremost concerned with my personal safety. I thought I might lose my life."

After his beating, Harry received a six-month reprieve from Z-II, which did not send him another Hoover card until September, 1958. A message that came with the card told him to carry a newspaper in one hand and a glove in the other.

His initial contact at the Tobyjug had been replaced by an affable Balkan type who introduced himself as "Nicky." Harry had his usual copies of the Hampshire *Telegraph and Post* and some back copies of service periodicals. When Nicky said the stuff was useless, Houghton had a fit of temper about the beating he had been subjected to. Nicky laughed and said: "I don't know anything about that, it must have been a mistake. In any case, they weren't very subtle. There are other methods, such as booby traps on your gates and a parcel that goes off when you open it. Perhaps one day when you're having a cup of tea there'll be some poison in it."

Nicky gave Houghton a matchbox with a false bottom, which contained instructions for further meetings. Houghton was to mark OX in chalk on a wooden gate in a London park when he wanted to see Nicky. OX underscored with two lines meant a meeting at the Maypole tavern on the first Saturday in any month, and if he failed to show up by 8 P.M., the meeting was automatically carried over to the first Sunday of the month at 1 P.M. Houghton was to carry a copy of *Punch*.

Nicky wanted Harry to find out whether Portland was testing a device that could be towed behind a war vessel or any vessel so that the engine noise from the vessel could be transmitted to the device two miles astern, which would lead a listening submarine to fire at the device and miss the ship. He also wanted to know about homing torpedoes.

Harry knew nothing about either the device or homing torpedoes, but pocketed five pounds for his trouble with the promise of another meeting soon.

The next meeting was far from fruitful, with Harry sticking to back copies of newspapers and Nicky pressing him for information on the homing torpedoes and warning that "you have had a long time to find out. . . ." Harry, who had made no attempt to find out, claimed the information was unavailable.

When another card arrived in January, 1960, Harry ignored the summons because "I did not want to be at the beck and call of these people the whole time. I was making an effort in my own way to shake them off." By this time it had dawned on Harry that he was being used by foreign espionage agents and he had "every suspicion," he said at his trial, "that they were of the Eastern block—Czechs, Poles, or Russians."

Again his failure to turn up at a meeting resulted in quick punishment. The trailer beating was acted out again by a couple of hired thugs, this time in Harry's newly acquired cottage. After a series of well-administered kidney punches, Harry was told: "You've got a girl friend, Bunty [Miss Gee's nickname] now, haven't you? If you don't come over, she'll be the next one." Harry said he "hated anything coming to Miss Gee or my former wife and decided to be more compliant in the future."

The next day at the naval base, Miss Gee noticed Harry's downtrodden air and said, "My goodness, what is the matter with you?" Harry said he wasn't feeling well and went home early. He didn't dare see a doctor about the beating, he said, for fear it would be reported to the police.

In April another summons came and Harry responded "out of fear they would get at me through Miss Gee. I thought they could send her a parcel which might explode when opened up, or a booby trap. I thought some physical violence might come to her."

A third contact named John was at the Maypole tavern and berated Harry for supplying worthless information. "You work in a naval dockyard among ships," he said. "Why can't you do better?"

At his trial, Harry identified John from photographs as Vassily

Dojdalev, Second Secretary of the Polish Embassay in London. By the time the identification was made, however, Dojdalev had been transferred. In his meeting with Harry, the Polish diplomat-spy made a curious blunder. He told Harry that "in case of emergency, you can send a card to this address—16 Lancaster Road, London." Harry could with this information have gone to the police and become a hero instead of the villain he was in the dock.

But by this time, after having passed like a football among minor members of Z-II in London, he was ripe for a more important contact. It was at this point that he met the pivotal figure of the Portland spy ring.

Now, after two beatings and the conviction that worse would come to himself and Bunty if he did not follow orders, he was ready to be taken in hand by one of the Russian "executives" of the apparat. The co-operation between intelligence services of the Soviet Union and its satellites, as illustrated in Houghton's case, was described in Colonel Monat's testimony.

He said that "the methods used by Z-II are similar to those of Soviet military intelligence. This similarity, of course, is attributed to the direct control of Z-II by the Soviet Union between 1951 and 1956, and to the fact that Polish staff officers were given excellent training by the Soviets during this same period . . . between 1955 and 1956 the majority of Soviet officers assigned to Z-II were recalled to the Soviet Union. All positions of responsibility were filled by Polish professional military officers. Since then, Soviet control has been indirect rather than direct. There is now only a Soviet liaison officer assigned to Z-II, Commander Igor Amosow [former Assistant Naval Attaché to the Soviet Embassy in Washington who was declared *persona non grata* by the United States in 1954 for espionage activities].

"Through Amosow, the Soviets levy intelligence requirements on Z-II. In addition, copies of all reports are furnished to the GRU [Soviet military intelligence]; the Soviet services can force any of the satellite services, including Z-II, to concentrate their operations on certain geographical areas merely by levying on the services intelligence requirements pertaining to those areas. Information furnished by Z-II to the GRU is evaluated by the Soviets, and results of the evaluation are made known to Z-II. I believe Z-II contributes quite a bit of information to the GRU which the GRU has officially reported as being of enormous value."

The man who took Houghton in hand was one of the most important Soviet agents captured by the West since World War II, on a par with Colonel Rudolf Abel. His real identity was disclosed in November, 1961, by the FBI as Conon Molody, a thirty-eight-year-old Russian. Even his family knew only that he was in the West on a foreign mission, that letters were long in arriving because they had to be sent by microdot.

Molody was a commander in the GRU (Abel was a colonel in the GRU) and may have been the GRU Resident for Great Britain.

The police investigation, the evidence given at the Secrets trial, the information culled from his letters to his family in Russia and the reminiscences of his friends, give only a vague and skeletal outline of his espionage career.

From letters exchanged with his wife, Galyusha, we learn that his daughter Liza, twelve, is doing poorly at school. "For the first time in six years at school," his wife writes, "Liza brought home a school report with four 'threes' [three, in the Russian grading system, means passable], for geometry, algebra, English and Party training. The rest are fours [meaning good]. You cannot imagine how this upset me, considering that the institute [high school] is not far in the offing." Sometimes, she plays hooky: "Liza has got completely out of hand. Yesterday I was called to the school. She failed to attend the last two lessons, and was roaming about somewhere during these hours."

His son, Trofim, is about five and hasn't started school yet. He is a playful, mischievous child who "went alone in the lift and got stuck between the sixth and seventh floors clinging with his tiny hands to the net. Everybody in the entrance went to his rescue, and for two hours he went on crying and imploring 'get me out of here.' "

He is, in the words of his mother, "clever and sagacious" and asks "When is Daddy coming, and why has he gone away, and what a STUPID job Daddy has got."

The Molody family lives according to the high standard granted to Russia's secret service personnel. They have a modern apartment in one of the postwar residential suburbs of Moscow. Mrs. M has a nurse for the children while she fulfills her obligations as chairman of the Communist Party Cultural Commission for her community. This involves teaching and organizing holiday celebrations. They are waiting to have a telephone installed.

The children's nurse, a country girl brought to Moscow by her family, "is definitely not justifying her job." When Trofim got stuck in the elevator she "stood and slept dreaming" while the others organized the rescue.

Molody, though doing clandestine work in England at the time, was able to send his children Christmas presents in 1960. Trofim received a scale-model automobile that could be dismantled and Liza got a big Teddy bear which was christened "Mishka."

Galyusha, his wife, probably was a Czechoslovakian whom Molody met while on duty in Prague. She has a good voice and is often asked to sing at party gatherings and other festive occasions. She is a pretty, rather vain woman who pleads with her husband in a letter for "a white brocade dress, a tight-fitting one, and white shoes. I beg you to forgive me, but I would like to meet the New Year well. By the way, I'll be singing in two places. I beg you to carry out my request, my first and last one. I hope that you will not be angry, but I must sing and I would very much like to rise to the occasion."

To which Molody replied from London: "In respect of a white brocade dress—a very difficult matter. In other countries brocade is not worn. It may be assumed that it could be made on order, but to pass it on to you? And when? You must understand that a dress and shoes cannot be put in a pocket."

Galyusha also feels that her monthly allotment is insufficient and asks for 2,500 roubles more a month. This request was made in December, 1960, when the Soviet Union currency reform took place, so he answered: "I'll write this very day to V.M. [his superior at the Center] that 2,500 should be handed over to you (or more correctly 250 roubles—a few days ago I saw photographs of the new currency. To my taste, a considerable improvement)."

The frustration and loneliness of living in permanent disguise, the constant alienation from others because of his work, the inability to communicate except by subterfuge, could only be forgotten by Molody in his letters. A spy's letters to his family become his one remaining tie with his own identity, which explains the risks the Soviet take to see that their agents get letters from home.

The day of his arrest, Molody wrote his wife that "for the last twenty minutes I have been pacing my room and I simply cannot continue the letter. This is literally a case of 'I am weary I am sad, and there is no one to shake hands with' [words of a Russian poem]. I am not complaining. But even you cannot imagine how saddened I feel in general and especially at this moment. . . . I celebrated New Year's with a fellow baptized and punctually at midnight Moscow time we drank Stolichnaya [a brand of vodka] to all friends in the Union. We drank separate toasts to you and the children. I personally felt very sad this was the 8th New Year since 1954 which I celebrated without you. Some wise man said in the long ago 'such is life' . . . I'll be thirty-nine shortly. Is there much left? Jan. 7, 1961."

The letter never reached his wife and was in fact read later that day by Scotland Yard investigators, who saw a special significance in the last line. For the man they had arrested held a passport under the name Gordon Arnold Lonsdale. He was a Canadian subject, had a passport in good order, and was doing legitimate business in London. A check with Canadian authorities revealed that a Gordon Arnold Lonsdale had in fact been born in Cobalt, 250 miles northwest of Ottawa. Cobalt was once a boom town in the Canadian gold mine belt.

Lonsdale's father was a half-breed named Jack Emmanuel Lonsdale, and his mother was a Finnish immigrant named Alga Bousu. Her home was in Karelia, that part of Finland invaded by the Russians in 1940. The Lonsdales were married in 1920 and their son was born four years later. The couple separated and Mrs. Lonsdale went back to Finland and took young Gordon with her. He was sixteen when the war broke out and Karelia became a part of Russia. His physical characteristics were similar to those of Molody, who was short and dark, with the rubbery nose and high cheekbones of a Slav and a slightly Oriental cast to his eyes. Molody's face was undistinguished but lively, not handsome but attractive by its expressiveness. He could look like a satyr in an eighteenth-century etching, or he could assume the petulant expression of the bad boy who has just been punished. The only unalterable difference between Molody and his Canadian passport made out to Gordon Arnold Lonsdale was his age. The real Lonsdale had been born in 1924, which would have made him thirty-seven in 1961. Molody, as he admitted in his letter to Galyusha, was about to turn thirty-nine and wondered if there was much left.

It was in the war years that Lonsdale's passport changed hands. The real Lonsdale was in all likelihood a casualty of that confused period when Karelia was a battleground. His replacement had by this time been commissioned in the Red Navy, recognized as a talented prospect for "special" work, and trained in espionage techniques.

Another similarity between Molody and the real Lonsdale is that their early lives were equally hectic. Canadian-born Lonsdale went to Finland as a boy and was swallowed up by the chaos of Karelia in his teens. Molody, in a letter to his wife, wrote that "from the age of ten I have spent only ten years with my own people. . . . It all started as far back as 1932 when Mother decided to dispatch me to the nether regions. At the time she could not imagine of course all the consequences of this step, and I do not blame her." (The Russian word *tartaros* can be translated as nether regions or bowels of the earth.)

By the nether regions, Molody meant the United States. His mother had a sister in California, and she sent her eleven-year-old son to live with his aunt in 1933. For some reason, he pretended to be the son of his aunt and was enrolled under her name in a private school in Berkeley. He stayed in California until 1938, which explains his command of English and why he was such an attractive prospect for Soviet intelligence. In 1954, Molody returned to the Western Hemisphere as a clandestine passenger aboard a Soviet grain freighter that landed at Vancouver. He was using the name Gordon Arnold Lonsdale.

It took several months for Lonsdale to build up his identity. He took out the papers one can get without being questioned too closely —a driver's license, a Young Men's Christian Association membership card, various professional cards after he had started working as a salesman. He moved to Toronto, asked for a birth certificate at City Hall, and obtained his sterling, bona fide, gilt-lined Canadian passport with the help of his birth certificate.

In February, 1955, Lonsdale took a bus across the Canadian border to Niagara Falls. After taking in the sights, he went to New York, where he contacted either the legal Soviet espionage network (members of consulate or United Nations staffs with active roles as agents) or the illegal network headed by Colonel Abel. The FBI was able to trace his movements through the leads provided by the discovery of the Portland ring.

It was from New York early in the spring of 1955 that Lonsdale sailed for Britain aboard the liner *America*. There is a striking parallel between Lonsdale's five years as a spy in Britain and Abel's eight years of undetected espionage work in the United States. Abel posed as a painter and the pose absorbed him. He spent most of his time in his artist's studio, and his friends were painters. He could talk shop endlessly and haunted museums. Those who have seen his work insist he was a gifted artist.

Lonsdale posed as an entrepreneur, a free-wheeling businessman full of money-making schemes, the finest distillation of a capitalist society. His friends remember Lonsdale the *bon vivant;* Lonsdale the ladies' man; Lonsdale the financial wizard, who played the market and read the *Financial Times* every morning with his breakfast.

Actually, his business deals met with mixed success, but not for want of effort. This espionage agent for Communist Russia became a typical small-time capitalist; on weekdays he was regulated by the "what's in it for me" and "how to turn a dollar" philosophy, while on weekends he directed his spy network for the cause of Marxism-Leninism.

During the spy trial, the London papers carried a daily defendants' list which described Lonsdale as a "company director," a far more appropriate title than "spy" or "secret agent." He was, in fact, but a weekend spy who did his best to compartmentalize the two conflicting aspects of his life. One of the few times the compartments overlapped may have been the day of his arrest. A large amount of money was found on his person (215 pounds and $300), which was presumed to have been a payoff for Miss Gee and Houghton. His business associates insist, however, that the money was a down payment for two tons of Spearmint chewing gum that Lonsdale was supposed to buy.

For his chosen field was the vending machine business. Lonsdale, a facile and practiced liar, was fond of regaling his cronies with accounts of the golden age of the vending machine business in the United States, when rival gangs fought over territories and imposed the machines on frightened barkeeps. "I was shot at once," he said, "and mark my words, it'll get as bad over here."

It was some time after arriving in London that Lonsdale made his first business venture. In 1955, he had checked in at the Overseas Club on St. James Street, which provides rooms at twelve shillings a night ($1.75) to visitors from far lands. Shortly afterward he moved into a furnished flat in a residential hotel called the White House in the Regent's Park section of London. He moved out after neighbors complained that he was bringing girls up, had a succession of other flats, moved back into the White House in the fall of 1960 and was living there at the time of his arrest.

Lonsdale passed himself off as a Canadian sent by his government to study at London University's School of Oriental Languages. He was on a grant to study Chinese, he said, because the Canadian Government foresaw the lifting of the trade ban with Red China. He had a rich fund of Canadian reminiscences. He said his Canadian father and Finnish mother had separated when he was a child (this much was true of the real Lonsdale) and his father had arranged for a Chinese family in San Francisco to care for him. His father, a man of means, had left him a large estate in Vancouver, which explained the steady stream of dollars he received at the American Express. He had worked as a cook in a labor camp in northern Canada, he had been a gold prospector, a long haul driver, a soda jerk, a gas station attendant. He had seen the country. In World War II he had been a conscientious objector. He wove a wife and a child into this richly textured legend. "My wife nagged me so much I almost killed her with a kitchen knife," he admitted to his business friends. "I walked out on her but I've got to give her fifty dollars a week support for the kid." Lonsdale added that his unhappy childhood and experience with marriage had left him faithless and misanthropic.

In 1956, Lonsdale spotted an advertisement in a London evening newspaper: A vending machine company offered investors a route for a small down payment. He did not reach an agreement with the company but was directed to another firm that handled jukeboxes. He paid a deposit on five Minstrel brand jukeboxes and started on his route to try to place them in taverns and coffeehouses. Lonsdale took a more and more active part in the business and decided he wanted to expand. He invested through his contacts in a syndicate called Peckham Automatics Limited and became managing director. One of his associates recalls that he was a bear for work, "opened the place up in the morning [his office at 163 Rye Lane] and closed it down at night. You could tell the time by Gordon." Lonsdale attached one condition to his working schedule—he was to have weekends free.

Having invested in the company and been named managing director, he bought a Ford station wagon and appointed himself director of export sales. He pushed the export side of the business and had his associates beaming when he announced that he had obtained a $300,-000 order for bubble gum machines in Milan. A factory was tooled up for the order, the machines were made ready for delivery, but the deal folded. It was Lonsdale's first major business setback. The company declared bankruptcy and Lonsdale and his associates took the loss philosophically.

After Lonsdale's espionage activities were revealed in the Secrets trial, one of his former co-directors, Peter Ayres, began brooding about the bankruptcy action and the Milan order and grew convinced he had been cheated. "The business was a sound and growing one when Lonsdale appeared on the scene," he said.

"Our failure appeared straightforward and for reasons that were apparent at the time. But since Lonsdale's conviction I have learned a number of things I did not know before. These things are beginning to tie up. I now suspect there was more in our failure than met the eye at the time."

Mr. Ayres promised to take action against Lonsdale, whom he suspected of still holding interests in various companies though he was in jail and of retaining his company directorships by proxy.

Rebecca West, who commented on the Secrets trial in the *Sunday Telegraph,* deplored the Government's negligence in failing to investigate his business mismanagement:

> Is it really too much to ask, that the authorities might show some interest in a director responsible for the bankruptcy of a company who was also not a British subject? It is surely not an excessive demand. There are, after all, fewer than 3,000 bankruptcies a year. Moreover, it is relevant that Soviet agents, according to those who have studied their ways, have two favourite ways of covering up their financial transactions. One is by buying land which then changes hands several times, with someone along the line suddenly taking a large profit; the other is buying a firm and going bankrupt, which produces an illusion of indigence useful to those who have money for which they cannot account, and affords a smoke-screen for jiggery-pokery.

The bankruptcy action was followed by one of Lonsdale's mysterious absences. He told his cronies he was going to Canada to raise money for further investments. He even managed to send postcards and letters postmarked Vancouver, a measure of the Soviet espionage network's breadth and organization. Actually he was on home leave in Moscow.

He came back to London "a changed man," his friends said. Doubtless the time spent with Party officials had impressed him with the urgency of his mission and he was determined to spend more time on undercover work at the expense of his business interests.

His good intentions faded fast, and in August, 1959, he paid 1,000 pounds for a directorship in the Master Switch Co., which was manufacturing a device for car and truck dashboards that locked the hood, the trunk and the doors automatically. The device had just been patented, and there were all the administrative and production problems of a growing business to which Lonsdale could apply his inexhaustible energies.

In March of 1960, he and his two associates set up a stand displaying their security switch at the Ninth International Exhibition for Inventors in Brussels. There were some fifty countries represented at the fair, and one of Lonsdale's partners pointed to a man standing behind a neighboring booth, a man of decided Slavic appearance. "Say, Gordon, he looks just like you," the associate said. Lonsdale, instead of being embarrassed, walked over to the man, who was a Finn, introduced himself, and they spent long hours together.

After the fair, Lonsdale went on another "European trip," returned to London in October, took a flat at the White House, and was arrested January 7, 1961.

In his personal life, this remarkable man was a curious mixture of caution and recklessness. He had an obsession about paying bills on time, about getting his taxes in and his insurance premiums paid. In 1959 he was in anguish because he hadn't received his road-tax bill (if you own a car in England you pay a yearly road tax of 12 pounds, 10 shillings—about $35). He was a hypochondriac who always carried orange-flavored halibut-oil tablets in a pocket and had his bathroom cabinet stocked with patent medicines.

He was careful about the bank account he had opened in 1957 and was considered such a good client that the bank at one time granted him overdraft facilities of 2,500 pounds (about $7,000). The bank was not taking a risk on Lonsdale, who had securities to the full amount in his account at the time plus 500 pounds in cash.

At the same time, he was not above smuggling cameras into England after each of his foreign trips, and he boasted that the laxity of British customs had earned him tidy sums. It did not occur to him that he was leaving himself open to exposure.

His propensity for the opposite sex nourished the vulgarity of the London press. In what may go down as a record for bad taste, one journal published an interview with pictures the gist of which was: "I was Gordon Lonsdale's mistress when my husband was out of town." More than one of Gordon's former girl friends came out of the woodwork to exploit their lover's notoriety. Each of the interviews was in the same vein: "I never suspected . . . he was so considerate . . . always the life of the party. . . . I'll always have a place in my heart for him."

Those who knew him well confirm that it is hard to exaggerate the amount of time and attention he spent on women. There were periods when his current girl friend moved in with him, hardly regulation for a spy. But then he picked the type of woman who doesn't go looking through drawers. He practically had squatter's rights at a hostel for young women who have come to London seeking work as domestic help, an associate recalls. And the stories about Lonsdale's conquests seem inexhaustible: "Remember when Gordon picked up those two Italian girls who were hitchhiking and took them for an all-day visit to the British Museum and an all-night visit to his flat?"

"Remember that Belgian girl who left her husband and followed Gordon around Europe? Remember the night he brought a bottle of gin and a bottle of orange and roast chicken for dinner at his flat with two Yugoslavian girls . . ." and so on.

His associates remember Lonsdale fondly. To them, he was a happy-go-lucky Canadian who wore "off-the-peg" clothes that would make a London tailor cringe, who always "stood his round," and who could be depended upon in a pinch.

One of his former partners had a nasty car accident in 1960—he struck another car while driving drunk. The next day, Lonsdale took photographs of the damage to both cars and turned up at London Sessions Court at his friend's trial to testify on his behalf. The friend got off with a three-year suspended sentence, and Lonsdale said disgustedly outside court: "If that's a sample of British justice, I never want to see the inside of a court again."

With a full schedule of business and social activities, where did Lonsdale find the time for spying?

He found that he could do it on weekends, keep up his contacts, arrange to have information transmitted, and keep his agents in line. In the summer of 1960, then, it was Lonsdale's turn to move in on Houghton and take him over. On a Saturday in June, Lonsdale drove

out to Houghton's cottage in Weymouth and introduced himself as
"Alex Johnson, the American Naval Attaché."

"I've just spent the day in Portland on duty," Lonsdale said, "and
some mutual friends suggested I drop by for a chat."

Houghton recalled that Lonsdale "was talking as though he knew
all about the American Navy and the subject got around to asdic sets.
It was not a direct question—did I know anything about asdic sets?—
it was a negative way. He was trying to convince me that I knew about
asdic sets and submarines."

The conversation turned to music and the ballet. "I have a friend
who's very fond of the ballet," Houghton said, "and we've been thinking of getting tickets to the Bolshoi if any are available." Lonsdale
promised to get tickets for July 9 and a meeting was arranged for that
date.

Later in the evening, mulling over his conversation with "the
American Naval Attaché," Houghton said, "the penny dropped." He
realized Johnson was a part of the same ring that had been after him
since 1957. Still, the prospects of the Bolshoi were pleasing and
Houghton decided not to pass up the chance.

That decision was regrettable for Houghton, for by this time the
sluggish British security system had begun to move and he was under
suspicion. Ironically, it was after Houghton was accused of something
he had nothing to do with that he became a suspect. In March, 1960,
a photographer at the Portland Underwater Weapons Establishment
reported to Admiralty Constable Fred Hosking that he had received
an anonymous letter. The letter, scrawled with a brush in tracing ink
on a single sheet of dockyard note paper, bore the words "you dirty
Jew" and had a black swastika daubed in one corner. The photographer,
who was not a Jew, told Hosking the only employee at Portland who
bore him a grudge was Harry Houghton. A few days later, the photographer's head of department received an anonymous letter on the
same kind of paper charging that the photographer was using the
Navy's photographic material for his own use.

Hosking investigated Houghton, who was absolved in the case of
the anonymous letters. The inquiry nonetheless revealed some puzzling
bits and pieces of Houghton's life. Here was a junior-grade civil
servant who was living like the Lord of the Admiralty. The cost and
refurbishing of his cottage had totaled 9,000 pounds, which is awfully

high in suburban England; he had just become the proud owner of a Renault Dauphine; he was one of the heaviest spenders at the Old Elm Tree pub; he entertained often and well; he made frequent trips to London; and he had a salary of roughly fifteen pounds a week ($40). While the investigation was going on, one of Houghton's neighbors made a report that jibed with Constable Hosking's findings on Houghton's free spending and limited means.

Constable Hosking told Scotland Yard about Houghton, and Scotland Yard turned the case over to the Special Branch of its Criminal Investigation Department, which is responsible for national security cases, protecting the Royal family and V.I.P.'s, and keeping tabs on political subversives and known extremists.

At about the same time that Lonsdale, posing as an American naval attaché, knocked on the rustic oaken door of Houghton's cottage, the Special Branch people began their investigation and surveillance. The dark patches they turned up in Houghton's record warranted bringing in MI5.

MI5 is the fifth, or counterespionage branch of Military Intelligence. It was created in 1910 as one of the Army's service departments, but has since expanded far beyond a Military Intelligence function until it corresponds somewhat to the Federal Bureau of Investigation in the United States. Like the FBI, it is mainly concerned with internal subversion and is called in on any violation of the Official Secrets Act. Also like the FBI, it is responsible to the Attorney General, although the information it gathers is collated with that of other intelligence groups and made available to the Joint Intelligence Bureau, which reports once a week to the Ministry of Defense. It is staffed mainly by civilians, which makes its title something of a misnomer.

MI5 makes a fetish of secrecy. The identities of its estimated 1,500 employees, including its chief, are not known.

Its headquarters too are supposedly secret, although every Londoner who lives around Mayfair knows that the massive eight-story office building on Curzon Street called Leconfield House is home base for Britain's spycatchers.

Unlike the FBI, MI5 is purely an investigatory agency and has no police powers. It cannot search a house and it cannot make an arrest. Thus any major security investigation is two-pronged, with the Scotland Yard Special Branch people implementing the findings of MI5.

After their night at the Bolshoi, another meeting between Houghton

and Lonsdale was set up for August 6. They met in front of the
Old Vic Theater and went from there to Steve's, a nearby café. A
couple of MI5 agents were tagging along behind and worked so close
to their quarry that they overheard snatches of conversation at the
café. The case of William H. Martin and Bernon F. Mitchell, the two
National Security Agency mathematicians who defected to Russia,
broke in Washington on August 5, and was splashed all over London's
August 6 front pages. Lonsdale and Houghton quite naturally discussed the case. "Do you really think they've gone over?" Houghton
asked incredulously. Lonsdale assured him that they had.

The MI5 agent who overheard the conversation testified at the
trial that he was sitting back to back with Houghton and that although
"I could not see him, I could feel as he leaned away from my back.
The café tables were very close together."

Turning to business, Lonsdale said: "You seem to have plenty in
your attaché case."

"Yes," Houghton replied with high good humor, "I have more than
my sleeping and shaving gear."

Lonsdale: "We can arrange these meetings if you would like to put
them in your book."

Houghton: "Yes, they will take some remembering."

Lonsdale: "These will be the first Saturday in each month, especially
the first Saturday in October and November. The driver will sit in a
car in the area. I don't know where. I am ninety per cent sure I
will be there. We will use an interpreter. You will have to find him."

At the end of the talk, Houghton was heard to say: "I don't want
paying now."

This incriminating bit of small talk did not satisfy MI5, which made
no move to apprehend the two. They left the café and went into a
telephone booth together. This maneuver was explained by Houghton
at the trial. "My trousers were slipping and I wanted to adjust them,"
he said. As it turned out, the "fat package" Lonsdale was rubbing
his hands over contained nothing but newspapers.

In October, Houghton received another summons through the mail
and went to the Maypole tavern, where he met one of his Polish contacts, John. "Did you bring anything?" John asked. "No," replied
Houghton.

Harry had previously mentioned that he had some Navy friends
posted in Gibraltar, and John asked him: "Can you find out whether

or not it is a fact that from the African coast to the Straits of Gibraltar is a series of listening posts, meaning that if any submarine passes through the Straits would there be anything with which they could listen in at Gibraltar, and by the pulses of their engines detect the submarine? We can pay for a holiday to Gibraltar for you so you can see your friends and ferret out the information."

"I can't do it," Houghton replied. "I don't know these people well enough. They're only shipwrights, a painter, and an electrician. They wouldn't know about all that. Besides, I don't want a holiday right now."

"How is Miss Gee getting on?" John asked suddenly. "Is she still as lovely as ever?" Then added ominously, "You had better get some stuff for us soon. You are only a small man. They can't look after you day and night. Who do you think you are?"

At this point, Harry decided the best thing to do was break off his relationship with Bunty. But since he could offer no reason for his change of heart, he vacillated. He also renewed a halfhearted attempt he had made the year before to get a transfer from Portland. He had his eye on a vacancy in Bridport, where they needed a harbor master, but he was told he was too old for the job.

The crucial meeting between Harry, Bunty, and Lonsdale took place on December 10 in the gardens around London's Festival Hall. Harry finally agreed to get some solid information in return for an undisclosed sum. Lonsdale gave him a camera and told him to photograph the basic handbook of the Royal Navy, *Particulars of War Vessels.* This is a large, 412-page illustrated book with the designs and specifications of every ship used by the Royal Navy, including the then uncommissioned nuclear submarine *Dreadnought* and other advanced types of warships. Each copy has on its outside cover the word SECRET in large black print, and the notice: *This book is invariably to be kept locked up when not in use and is not to be taken outside the ship or establishment from which it is issued without the express permission of the commanding officer.*

Harry also promised to take pictures of Admiralty fleet orders and get the series of test pamphlets on asdic sets from Miss Gee, who apparently viewed the entire proceedings with typical feminine ingenuousness. She took Lonsdale, who "chewed gum and had a typical American accent," at face value.

Instead of seeing a Russian spy, she saw a brash American "who thought he knew better ways of doing things than the British knew and wanted to prove it." When Lonsdale gave her a list of twelve questions and asked her to find the answers, she admitted the questions "did not make sense to me."

The twelve questions, had she been able to answer them, "would have given a complete picture of our current anti-submarine plans, plus research and development," the prosecutor said at the trial. Some of the questions dealt with the construction and installation of hydrophones and radiators in submarines and warships, details on high-speed cruising, and the work being done with asdic sets.

That evening, in Harry's cottage, she copied the questions on some notepaper while Harry "was preparing sandwiches and potting his cacti," and burned the original. Harry and Bunty studied the questions together, he said, and "we both had a good laugh. We took the whole thing as a joke, as something funny and something we couldn't understand at all."

They had a month to get the information before the next meeting, scheduled for January 7. It was no problem for Miss Gee to take the pamphlets from her office. She planned to give them to Harry on Friday and have them back by Monday. Apparently, security at Portland was a five-day-a-week affair, and there were never any security checks on weekends. Even on working days, there were seldom spot checks of employees at the gates, and Miss Gee knew she could walk out of the base with her handbag bulging with classified documents without the slightest risk.

Harry had a tougher job. He managed to lock himself up in an office with his miniature camera and photograph pages 181 to 412 of *Particulars of War Vessels,* the whole last half of the book. He claimed at his trial that he deliberately put the camera out of focus so that the printed specifications could not be read. The thirty photographs he took of the atomic submarine *Dreadnought* were, he said, "made each so that it would not intermarry and form a working composite picture. I wanted them to be a jigsaw puzzle no one could put together."

The prosecution said he was simply a poor photographer who had done the best he could.

Although much of the material in *Particulars of War Vessels* had been released to the press, Houghton's photographs, and particularly his series on the *Dreadnought,* contained details which were still classified. There was no information in the book on the U.S.-made atomic plant, however.

He also took twenty-nine photographs of eight separate Admiralty fleet orders, dealing with all aspects of Navy life, including the treatment of venereal disease on Her Majesty's ships, the general type of medical treatment given sailors, and lists of naval personnel, promotions and transfers. He apparently chose these haphazardly as he ran across them, though he was careful to point out in his own defense that he had picked those of least value to a potential enemy. For good measure, he threw in an outdated map of the Portland base.

The seven test pamphlets Miss Gee sneaked out of her office dealt with asdic sets, and although only one was marked CONFIDENTIAL (the British security classification system is *restricted, confidential, secret,* and *top secret*), "collectively they were of undoubted marked value to a potential enemy," the prosecutor said.

As for the list of twelve questions Lonsdale had given Miss Gee, she said she did some research among the papers and documents in the department but "couldn't make any sense out of them." Since she had been working on an asdic project in the first week of January, she took seven pamphlets that were lying on her desk, put them in an Admiralty official envelope, put the envelope under her arm, and walked out. She had written the word *keep* against three pamphlet numbers on a list. "I was meaning Mr. Houghton should not give them all back to me on Monday morning," she explained. "I did not wish to take back an odd bundle then. I thought he was going to read them or find out any information that was more useful."

Miss Gee turned over the pamphlets to Houghton on January 6 and he took four of them ("so it would not be too bulky a package," he said) and wrapped them with the roll of undeveloped film he had taken. Saturday morning, they set out for London by train because the roads were icy. Miss Gee had the parcel in a straw shopping bag. They reached London at 3 P.M. after some shopping in Salisbury, went to a market near Waterloo Station and returned to the station at 4:30 P.M.

They were walking down Waterloo Road near the Old Vic when Lonsdale came up from behind and fell in step between them. He took the shopping bag from Miss Gee, who said, "We have had adventures on British Railways. The line was washed away and we had to go round Basingstoke to get to Waterloo."

Detective Superintendent George Smith of Scotland Yard's Special Branch heard the tail end of her explanation as he walked up from behind, passed, turned around and faced them and said, with a formality befitting the occasion: "You are under arrest. I am a police officer." Half a dozen Scotland Yard and MI5 agents surrounded the trio. Miss Gee, describing the arrest, said, "We were absolutely swooped on. At that time, I could not imagine what it was. I thought they were Teddy boys. Mr. Smith stood out. I could not imagine how one gentleman came to be mixed up with a lot of Teddy boys. There was so much noise I could not hear a word. I did not know who they were."

Miss Gee was indignant in the car on the way to Scotland Yard and asked the policewoman sitting beside her: "Just what is this?"

"There was a gentleman in the car with a microphone talking about lock, stock, and barrel," she said. "It did not mean much to me."

At Scotland Yard, Lonsdale spoke for the first time to say that "to any questions that you might ask me, my answer is 'no,' so you need not trouble to ask." Lonsdale was carrying $300 and 215 pounds on his person and had two driving licenses, one issued in Vancouver and the other in London.

Police found 16 pounds and two day-return tickets from Waterloo to Salisbury on Houghton. When Superintendent Smith told Harry he was being detained under the official Secrets Act, he broke down and said, "I've been a bloody fool." Smith asked him who Lonsdale was and Harry replied, "Your guess is as good as mine." Harry wanted to know how much money had been found on Lonsdale's person.

Miss Gee, who kept insisting that "I have done nothing wrong," had twenty-seven pounds in her handbag. Her weekly pay check was a little over ten pounds, but as she explained later, she had inherited some money when her father died and had invested it wisely.

Superintendent Smith put in a full day that January 7. After questioning Lonsdale, Houghton, and Miss Gee in Scotland Yard, he went to Ruislip, a suburban community in Middlesex, twenty miles west of London. He drove past a statue to the memory of fallen Polish airmen just outside Ruislip and wound over side streets until he reached Cranley Drive, a quiet dead-end street of two-family houses with small front lawns and uniformly appalling architecture. The last house on the left, 45 Cranley Drive, was a one-family bungalow in artificial Tudor, whitewashed, and with apparent beams. A yard-high brick wall and a wrought-iron gate set off a carefully clipped lawn, trimmed hedges, a magnolia tree and flowering cherry. To the right of the lawn a roadway led to a small garage that could not have fitted a standard American car. The neat, postcard bungalow was soon to become a Ruislip landmark. Another landmark was the Third United States Air Force Headquarters, about a mile away from the bungalow.

At about 7 P.M. Superintendent Smith rang the bell at Number 45. A tall, white-haired man in shirt sleeves answered and Smith said, "I am a police officer and am making certain inquiries. Can I see you?" The white-haired man took the detective into a lounge where the walls were lined with books. A square-faced, large-boned woman rose as they entered and started to leave, but Smith said, "I would like to see your wife as well."

The tenants of the cozy bungalow were Peter John Kroger, fifty, and his wife, Helen Joyce Kroger, forty-seven. They traveled on New Zealand passports and listed their occupation as antiquarian book dealers. They had been under surveillance by MI5 and Scotland Yard ever since Lonsdale had been trailed to their home in the fall of 1960.

The real identity of the Krogers was discovered through a routine fingerprint check with the FBI. The prints matched those of two American Communists recruited by the Soviet espionage network after World War II and linked with the Rosenberg apparat in New York. The Krogers were identified as Morris and Lona Cohen, both longtime Communists who had been forced to flee the United States in 1950 when the Rosenberg atom spy ring was dismantled.

The Cohens' biography follows the classic line of American Communists who left the Party to do underground work for Russia. Morris Cohen grew up in the Bronx, the son of Russian-Jewish immigrants who ran a vegetable store. In 1924, he went to James Monroe High School in his neighborhood and made the football team. The chunky two-hundred-pounder is still remembered as a hard-hitting guard and in 1927 the team was undefeated. Cohen acquired the nickname "Unc" because of his friendly concern for the welfare of his teammates. He acted like "everybody's uncle," with a surfeit of good fellowship and team spirit. In the classroom he was less brilliant and squeaked through with a passing average, not enough to get into a good college.

"Unc" Cohen won a football scholarship at Mississippi State University, where they had no language requirements, but dropped football after a year because he injured his knee.

He attached himself to the team as a student trainer and was so popular he was asked to stay after graduation. He went to the University of Illinois for his master's degree but did not graduate. In 1937, he obtained a passport under the assumed name of Israel Altman, signed an affidavit that he did not intend to use the passport for travel to Spain, and promptly joined the Abraham Lincoln Brigade in Madrid. By that time his sympathies were open, and he told a former teacher that he was going to Spain to fight with the Communists. He participated for a year in the chaotic civil war and returned to the United States in 1938.

He was deeply committed to Communism. He worked for Amtorg, the Soviet trade bureau in New York and a front for Soviet agents. In 1939, he filled in as a guard in the Russian pavilion of the New York World's Fair. He made no effort to conceal his party affiliations and his militant role. A union official in New York, Benny Gottesman, recalls that Cohen tried to recruit Communist Party members among the waiters' and waitresses' union. He also sought recruits to study at the Jefferson School of Social Sciences, an admittedly Communist institution on West 13th Street in New York.

Mr. Gottesman said, "One time I contributed five dollars to a celebration for a union official. Later, Cohen brought me a receipt and said I had become a member of the Abraham Lincoln Brigade. One day I said to Cohen, 'Why you dirty Red, what about the nonaggression pact the Russians have signed with the Nazis?' He answered, 'My Uncle Joe is very smart. He'll smoke his pipe and he'll watch.' Cohen was smart, educated, well dressed. He was always smiling. You could never make him mad no matter what you said to him or what you called him."

In 1940, according to Joseph "Doc" Weidman, his old high school coach, Cohen "was a substitute elementary schoolteacher in Manhattan. I don't know where it was, but it must have been a poor neighborhood, because he called me and asked if I could lend him some baseballs, footballs and bats. He was always interested in kids playing sports."

About this time Cohen started courting Lona Teresa Petka, the daughter of Polish immigrants. She was authoritative, determined, and held the same ideas as Cohen. She had been born in Adams, Massachusetts, and had run away from home at the age of fourteen. When she met Cohen she was working as a governess with a family named Winston at 1125 Park Avenue in New York. They were married in Norwich, Connecticut, on July 13, 1941. Cohen continued his substitute teaching job and his wife did part-time work in a public library. Six months after Pearl Harbor he was inducted and assigned to the Quartermaster Corps. For two years he served as a cook in Alaska and Canada, and in 1944 he was sent to England with a detachment of U.S. troops. He was demobilized in November, 1945. Mrs. Cohen worked during the war years as a shop steward in a Long Island defense plant.

It was at the end of the war that the Cohens went underground. The resident Soviet spy for the United States was Jack Soble, the neurotic Lithuanian-born son of a prosperous pig bristle manufacturer who had been pressed into espionage by the Russians partly through threats against his family and partly through his own vacillating character. Soble and his wife Myra, a strong-willed autocratic type like Lona Cohen, entered the United States in 1940 as refugees and had set up their ring by 1947.

It is believed that Soble and his wife recruited the Cohens, who were used in a minor capacity with the Rosenberg atom spy ring.

Soble, who had fallen out of favor with the Center in Moscow through his frequent trips to Europe, his squandering of espionage funds, and his inability to obtain any valuable information, probably lost control of the Cohens around 1949 and they were passed on to a new contact. It is doubtful whether their new contact was Abel. Abel arrived in the United States on a forged passport from Canada in 1948, and traveled around the country for more than a year before settling in New York. The Soviet illegal services are extremely slow-moving, and it may have been three or four years before Abel was in control of the network he inherited from the Sobles.

It came out in the Old Bailey trial that the Cohens had met Abel in 1948. The couple moved to a low-rent apartment at 178 E. 71st Street and "it appears," according to Detective Superintendent Smith, "that early in 1950 the Cohens gave a dinner party at which [Abel] was introduced as a wealthy English businessman." Detective Smith said Abel used the name "Milton." Milton is an Anglicized version of Emil and it is entirely possible that at a social gathering where he was unlikely to see the guests again he passed himself off as a British businessman rather than his usual alias of Emil Goldfus, the painter.

The Cohens' move to an East side neighborhood coincided with a resumption of Morris Cohen's teaching career. He was teaching fourth and fifth graders in a public school on Lexington Avenue and 96th Street.

At the same time, he had taken the Board of Education exams to become a full-fledged high school teacher. His co-teachers at the public school remember him as "quiet, dignified," a good natural teacher who lacked experience.

The results of the Board of Education exams, posted in the summer of 1950, showed that Cohen had placed first in the junior high school list and third in the high school roll. Cohen never found out how well he had done, for in August he and his wife disappeared.

The Cohens made their getaway as the Rosenberg ring was crumbling. Klaus Fuchs' arrest in England in February, 1950, had exposed the Rosenbergs. Julius and Ethel Rosenberg knew the FBI was closing in and they were preparing their escape that summer. Morton Sobell, a minor member of the ring, fled to Mexico and was arrested there. David Greenglass, Ethel Rosenberg's brother, was told by Julius to get ready to flee. Greenglass, however, was disenchanted with Communism and had no intention of leaving. This attitude was confirmed after the following conversation with Rosenberg one day in June, 1950: "Do you think we will beat the FBI?" Rosenberg asked.

"I don't know."

"Well, you know, if I get word that it is too hot, we will just take off and leave the children and the women [Greenglass and Rosenberg each had two children]."

"Two women and four children? We are going to leave them and go? Will we ever be reunited with them?"

"Well, I don't know . . . The Russians send in division after division against a position and they will all be killed, and they won't bat an eyelash as long as something is being done to gain their end."

Rosenberg then told Greenglass that he had already arranged for the escape of several other agents in the ring. A few days after their conversation Greenglass was arrested and led the FBI to the Rosenbergs.

Practically on the same day Greenglass was arrested, the Cohens closed their bank accounts and cashed their savings bonds. In August, Cohen resigned from his teaching job and told friends he was going to the West Coast for a stint as a screen writer. (The Screen Writer's

Guild in Hollywood has no record of his having worked in that capacity.) The Cohens' departure from their New York apartment was so hurried that Lona Cohen left behind her jewelry, her cosmetics and toilet articles, and most of her clothes.

After escaping the FBI net that closed in on the Rosenberg ring, the Cohens turned up in Austria. Under the name of Kroger, Cohen wrote the New Zealand Embassy in Paris and asked for passports for himself and his wife. Using false birth certificates and a marriage license in the name of a couple who had been New Zealand citizens but were long since dead, they obtained passports and entered Great Britain in 1954.

There, for the first time since the end of World War II, the Cohens (or Krogers) could breathe easy. They faded into the anonymity of British suburbia, bought a cottage like thousands of other cottages, and lived quiet, seemingly dull lives.

In August of 1955, Kroger set up his cover as an antiquarian book dealer specializing in Americana. He had a small shop on the Strand, attended book auctions assiduously and advertised in the weekly trade journal *Critique: Americana—from the North Pole to the South Pole —want lists and reports always welcome.*

He was a member in good standing of the Antiquarian Booksellers Society and the National Book League. Other book dealers said he was a dabbler who bid on all types of books, but rarely over fifty or sixty pounds. Kroger said most of his clients were abroad, and he often traveled to Paris or Geneva with a few books in his briefcase. The books contained tiny microdot messages concealed in the bindings. In 1956, he gave up his shop and conducted his business from his home. In Ruislip, where the Krogers had bought a bungalow for 5,000 pounds from a retired policeman, they were popular with their neighbors. Mrs. Kroger gave parties for children, took pictures of family groups, and made herself generally popular. She was a hard drinker and impressed acquaintances as a bustling, restless woman, the opposite of the quiet, bookish Kroger, with his ready smile and his fondness for athletics. Kroger was an active member of the Antiquarian Book Dealers' cricket team and his wife took pictures of him, bat in hand. He exercised in the back yard of the Ruislip bungalow every day with bar bells.

But beneath the veneer of the friendly suburban couple, the Krogers were the most dangerous of the five arrested in the Secrets case. Lonsdale was a Russian and was working for his own country. Houghton and Miss Gee were but dimly aware of their involvement and did not look beyond their growing hoard of pound notes.

But the Krogers were agents who had renounced their country and were bound by the ties of international Communism. It is doubtful that they ever went to Russia, but to Lonsdale they were "fellow baptized." They were veteran agents who had been hounded halfway around the world, had changed their name and their nationality several times, and had been cornered into the fanaticism that Rebecca West described after observing them at their trial:

> Wherever one met them, it would have been obvious that they were engaged in some ferocious struggle with reality, from which they were trying to force an admission that it was at some point quite different from what was generally supposed.
> It might have been that they were the more puritanic type of nudist, who thought it wrong and unnatural to wear clothes; they might have believed that the earth was flat; or they might have spoken with the dead at seances. Though by luck of the draw their form of dissent was Communism, they held this most secular faith so intensely that it gave them distinction of a religious sort.

When Detective Smith rapped on the bungalow door and began asking his questions, there was an immediate awareness on the Krogers' part that the time for settling many long-standing accounts had come round. Still, for the sake of form, there was a brief period of cat-and-mouse.

"I would like you to tell me the name and address of the gentleman who comes and stays with you each weekend, particularly the first Saturday of each month. He arrives about a quarter past seven," Smith said.

Kroger scratched his chin and appeared perplexed. "Well, we have lots of friends." They rattled off names, but did not include Lonsdale.

Smith told them they were under arrest and Mrs. Kroger asked if she could stoke the boiler before leaving the cottage. Smith acquiesced but asked first to see a handbag she was clutching. She was reluctant to let go of the bag and there was a brief tug of war. Smith pulled on the flap and a white envelope fell to the ground. The envelope contained a letter written in Russian by Lonsdale to his wife, which Mrs. Kroger was to reduce to microdot size and send concealed in a book or magazine to Moscow via Paris. A further search of the bag disclosed: three microdots on a glass slide, for convenience in reading them under a microscope—the microdots were letters from Lonsdale's wife and children; a list of eight London street names used for meetings; and a sheet of paper in six-figure code.

"After the envelope had been taken from her," Smith said, "Mrs. Kroger showed no further interest in stoking the boiler."

It took Scotland Yard and MI5 nine days to search the Cranley Drive bungalow, which was later described as "the hub and the bank of the spy ring." The inventory included all the familiar devices students of Soviet espionage have come to know so well. Working from the outside in, there was a burglar-proof mortise lock on front and back doors, and bolted locking devices on all the ground-floor windows. These fortresslike security measures could be justified by Kroger's bookselling activities. He had some rare books in his home, which also served as an office, and police found a letter from the company that had insured his books for 2,750 pounds suggesting that he obtain the locking devices.

In the ground-floor bedroom on the left there was a microscope on a chest of drawers, with a slide identical to the one found in Mrs. Kroger's bag. There were forty-nine feet of electric cord with a plug on one end and a bulb on the other in a laundry hamper. In a black handbag there were 200 pounds in 5-pound notes, and hidden behind some books there were two forged New Zealand passports issued in Paris in 1954. In one of the chest's drawers was a metal hip flask with a concealed compartment on either side. One compartment contained iron oxide, useful for sprinkling on magnetic tape to read Morse code messages. In the drawer of a dressing table, a mauve flashlight was found to contain a fake battery. Inside a Bible on the chest of drawers there was a piece of cellophane coated with a substance sensitive to light, which could have been used as a kind of homemade film to make microdots.

Passing from the bedroom to the front room, the police found another concealed compartment in a Ronson table lighter. The space in the bowl of the lighter contained two film negatives, signal plans for radio communication.

One signal plan had three columns indicating the date, time, and frequency for broadcasts to Moscow, another listed the call signs for broadcasts on the first and third Sunday of each month. The call signs were names of Russian towns and rivers. A third signal plan listed Morse call signs for Monday broadcasts, and the last had column heads in Russian.

The lighter also contained six rolls of one-time pads, the cipher pads made famous in 1957 when Abel was found to have used them. The one-time-pad system makes it impossible for the code to be broken, since it is only used once and there is neither recurrence nor frequency. The pads in the lighter were coated with potassium permanganate so that they would ignite when exposed to the slightest heat.

Also in the front room there was a short-wave radio with a headset plugged into the back, which operated on high-frequency bands. A tape recorder could be plugged into the radio. And in a black bag at the back of the house there was a Pratkina camera in a leather case, which belonged to Lonsdale.

On the next, or loft floor, there was a bathroom that could be used as a darkroom. A large board fitted over the top of the bathtub and black painted boards fitted over the windows with catches. In a tin of face powder a hidden cavity contained a microdot reader, a tiny telescope with a slot at one end where the microdot is inserted. Next to the bathroom, there was an attic where Kroger, a health and exercise enthusiast, kept apples. He also kept a seventy-four-foot-long aerial and, hidden under the insulation fiber in the roof, $2,563 in cash, $230 in traveler's checks, and ten pounds in British traveler's checks.

At the trial, the Krogers' lawyer made a desperate attempt to convince the jury that the long-cord aerial was used in the loft "to turn over or look at the rotten apples."

The last room the police searched was the kitchen. A refrigerator on casters was rolled away, and they found a trap door under the linoleum carpet. There was a rubble-filled space a yard deep under the trap door. Under the rubble there was a concrete slab, and under the slab there was a board. Removing the board, police found a hole containing five bags wrapped in plastic, a linen bag, a paper bag, and a green tray. One bag contained a wireless transmitter capable of broadcasting direct to Moscow. Not a commercial make, it had an aerial in its lid and an earth wire. It featured an automatic playing device using magnetic tape. This made possible high-speed transmission, for the message could be taped, and the tape plugged into the wireless and played at high speed.

In the brown paper bag were a roll of film with the words "twelve frames exposed" written on it, two Minox film reloads, and $6,000 in twenties.

As the prosecution said at the trial, "This innocent-looking suburban house, with no external wireless aerial, not even a television aerial, in which the Krogers had lived since 1956, was in my submission quite clearly a high-powered wireless station capable of transmitting and receiving direct from Moscow, full of equipment required for making and reading microdots and also code pads for coding messages. I would suggest that here one has the hub of a spy ring and also possibly, in view of the money found there, the bank of a spy ring."

Having broken the "hub" of the spy ring, Scotland Yard made two moves to carry the investigation further. The first was to keep the arrests secret so that they could attempt to establish radio contact with Moscow by using the signal charts they had found. There were leaks and the arrests were known the following day, but on January 9, two days after the arrests, they tuned in on the Monday frequency at 12:30 A.M. and heard the right call sign at the right frequency. At 12:45 A.M. they again heard the call signs for four minutes. Direction findings showed that the signals had been transmitted from the Moscow area. On Wednesday, January 18, they again listened in and again heard the call signals. Why the Russians would still keep up radio contact after it had been announced around the world that the spies had been arrested was never satisfactorily explained, and the argument was used to advantage by the defense.

The second move made by Scotland Yard was to plant evidence uncovered in the Krogers' house to see who would come to get it. The police, on top of everything previously listed, had found a leather writing case in which were secreted Canadian passports with fake names and pictures of the Krogers. The passports, purportedly issued in Canada in 1956, were made out to Thomas James Wilson, a storekeeper, and Miss Mary Jane Smith, a secretary. Each contained a slip of paper explaining the meaning of the visa stamps on it and detailing the immigration procedure in Canada and England. Police also planted some fake book ends which contained $4,000.

A few days later, a representative of Stanley & Co., the law firm handling Lonsdale's "estate," obtained permission to go through the house. He found a number of photographs of the Krogers which he sold to newspapers under the orders of the solicitors. He also stumbled on the leather writing case and the book ends and turned them over to Scotland Yard.

The lawyer's representative, Michael Holbrooke-Bowers, had been a business acquaintance and friend of Lonsdale when both were in the vending business. "I found the writing case in the right-hand drawer of a bedroom dressing table," he said. "I noticed it made a crinkling sound, which I thought to be money. I made a small incision, so as not to do a great deal of damage. I noticed a type of coat of arms. I investigated further and found two passports." Then he found the money in the book ends. Because "I was shocked and did not know what to do with it," he said, he waited three days before turning it over to the police.

Lonsdale's sixth-floor studio apartment in the White House was also crammed with the paraphernalia of the professional spy.

His Royal typewriter matched the typed code messages found in Kroger's study. A belt on a pair of pants hanging in the closet had a secret money compartment holding fifteen $20 bills. A box of talcum powder concealed a microdot reader and three pieces of film, while radio signal plans were in a phony flashlight battery.

One of the most exotic hiding places ever conceived was Lonsdale's Chinese scrolls, one above his bed and the other folded on top of a cupboard. As was explained at the trial, "If you pass a pin between certain threads on the end of the roller you come to a pin hole, and the pin has been left in to avoid the difficulty of finding the hole. If you press the pin it releases a catch and then you can unscrew the end of the pin hole and you will see that the hole of this drum is hollow and this is made with a very fine screw and a very light metal so you have a cavity." There was $1,800 tightly rolled in the scroll above his bed.

A search of Houghton's cottage in Weymouth revealed an Exacto camera, a matchbox with a false bottom, an inventory of test pamphlets marked KEEP or GONE, 500 pounds in bonds in a locked box under the staircase, and 650 pounds in mildewed one-pound and ten-shilling notes in a tin in the garden shed. The only thing found in poor Miss Gee's home was the list of twelve topics Lonsdale had given her and which she did not understand.

The five members of the spy ring went on trial in March in the Old Bailey's number one court, the same court where Alan Nunn May and Klaus Fuchs were tried and convicted of espionage. The British press dubbed the case "the Secrets trial" and avidly recorded the proceedings during the eight days it took to convict the defendants.

It was as much of a showcase trial as the British would permit themselves. The aim was to give the whole case a full airing, let most of the goblins out, and try to cover up security lapses and stolen secrets with the publicized dismantling of the spy ring, the thoroughness of Scotland Yard and MI5, and stiff punishment for the defendants.

If the defendants had been charged under the Official Secrets Act, as were Fuchs and May, they could have received no more than a fourteen-year prison sentence. But they were indicted on a conspiracy charge, which read that "between the 14th of April, 1960, and the 7th of January, 1961, they conspired together and with other persons unknown for purposes prejudicial to the safety or interest of the state to communicate to other persons information which might be directly or indirectly useful to an enemy." Conspiracy in England is a common law offense and there is no statutory limit on the sentence.

The trial, which opened March 14, was prosecuted by Britain's Attorney General, Sir Reginald Manningham-Buller, a name that begs the nickname "sir bullying manner," which the press did not overlook. Sir Manningham-Buller tried hard to overcome the inherent dullness of the proceedings as well as his own tendency to fastidious rhetoric. Eight days is unusually long for a trial in England, and there were few high points in the courtroom drama of five cogs in the Soviet espionage machine whose guilt was transparent from the start.

Thirty witnesses were paraded in and out to add a bit of mortar to the formidable wall of evidence already built up, and there were 120 exhibits ranging from the Chinese scrolls to the shopping bag. MI5 agents from A through T (they testify without giving their names and are referred to by letter) took the stand with their inventories of surveillance.

They were brought in from a special room in the corner of the court and vanished after taking the stand, so they could not be photographed, drawn, or otherwise identified.

The number one court in the Central Criminal Court building (Old Bailey) is lined with light oak and has an opaque skylight. The prisoners were in a glass-enclosed dock across from the dais where the judge sits. Behind the prisoner's dock there is room for about 100 spectators in the gallery and it was filled to capacity every day. The all-male jury sat in its box across from a bleachers-type arrangement with long wooden desks for the attorneys in their black robes and tatty wigs.

The hero of the trial was Lonsdale and the villain was Houghton. Observers found it difficult to conceive, now that he had been exposed, how anyone could take Lonsdale for anything but a Slav. Even his English had heavy Slavic intonations betraying that it was not his first language. When he opened his mouth at the trial he looked and sounded exactly what he was: a Russian who had been trained to pretend he was a Canadian. At the same time, he demonstrated the qualities of a thorough professional. He maintained a debonair detachment to the trial and showed up daily in the dock with a paperback edition of a nineteenth-century spy novel, *The Lotus and the Wind,* which he read when things got dull.

Rebecca West, in one of her Sunday articles, found him attractive thanks to "a suggestion of physical self-respect which was surviving in difficult circumstances. After weeks in prison he looked as if he could have walked out of the Old Bailey to the nearest tennis court and played a good hard game."

Whether by accident or design, Lonsdale found exactly the right tone to appeal to his British audience. He satisfied the Englishman's love for the sportsman and the good loser by making a statement in mid-trial taking the blame and absolving the Krogers. When he had finished you could almost pick up a few "hear hears" and "good shows" in the Old Bailey. He said, in his thick but musical accent:

> I am making this statement because I am anxious that Mr. and Mrs. Kroger should not suffer from what I have done by putting my property in their house. . . . The Krogers knew I lived in a very small service flat in a residential hotel where many members of the staff had passkeys to my flat. I used this as an excuse to keep some of my property at their home. . . . I gave Mrs. Kroger as a private present the cigarette lighter and a pair of wood book ends, which appeared to be ordinary household articles. As you have seen, these articles had secret compartments which contained various objects produced here in evidence. A cursory examination will show that even the signal plans were a reserve duplicate set of plans found at my flat. . . . I even used the Krogers' bathroom as a darkroom. Some of the chemicals in the house belonged to me. At one time I was conducting some experiments in microphotography, and the strip of cellophane exhibited here was a result of these experiments. . . .

While the Krogers were away I constructed the hiding place found in the foundations of the house and deposited there the radio transmitter. . . . I knew that if the contents of the hiding place were discovered I would land the Krogers in very serious trouble. I decided to obtain false passports which could be offered if such an event took place.

I took photographs of Mr. and Mrs. Kroger and inserted them in the passports. The passports were concealed in a leather writing pad and concealed by me at their home. If the police had checked the transmitter and the passports and so on for fingerprints, they would have found no fingerprints of the Krogers.

On Saturday, January 7—that is, on the day of our arrest—I was out shopping with Mrs. Kroger. She bought a quilt and cloth. The salesman gave me the delivery notes. When I got home I discovered I had forgotten to hand them over to Mrs. Kroger and decided to put them away for safekeeping. While shopping I gave Mrs. Kroger a large envelope and asked her to take it to her house. It contained my business correspondence, and I did not want to take it with me to a party I had to attend that evening. I realize it is too late to make any amends now, but I feel the least I can do under the circumstances is to accept full responsibility for my actions irrespective of the consequences to me personally.

Who could listen to this plea without immediately recalling the hero of *A Tale of Two Cities* and his "this is a far, far better thing that I do now than I have ever done"?

Kroger then made a statement corroborating Lonsdale's fanciful fabrications. In a dry and weary voice he explained that "since I invariably awoke earlier than my wife, I made a habit of listening to the morning news on the wireless with the earphones, not wishing to disturb her sleep" (this might have appealed to women jurors, but there were none).

Mrs. Kroger chimed in that Lonsdale was an old family friend who was "most helpful in the house—bringing in the coal, helping me with the dishes, even going shopping—and on several occasions he helped me with my photography."

Whereas Lonsdale had sacrificed himself in an attempt to save two of his codefendants and "fellow baptized," Houghton tried to save his own skin by turning Queen's evidence.

On the day following his arrest, Houghton requested an interview with Detective Superintendent Smith (by now known as "Moonraker"

Smith) from his jail cell in Brixton Prison. Houghton, according to Smith, "wanted to strike a bargain with me not to appear here [in court] but to turn Queen's evidence . . . he wanted to give information that I could place before the proper authorities whereby instead of standing trial here he could give evidence against the other four prisoners. I told him I could not have that."

Houghton had told Smith that he would help identify photographs of Russians and Poles who had been in diplomatic posts in Great Britain and who also worked for the secret services. Some of his contacts had been Iron Curtain officials, he said, who might still be working in Great Britain under the cover of diplomatic immunity. Houghton's proposal having been turned down, he joined his cohorts in the prisoner's dock.

The defense attorneys' closing speeches were almost apologetic in the face of the overwhelming evidence. W. M. F. Hudson, attorney for Lonsdale, managed to sow one seed of doubt when he pointed out in reference to the signals intercepted by MI5 from Moscow several days after the arrest that "I suppose stupidity exists everywhere, but is it not fair comment to submit to you, whatever one's personal feelings about the abilities of the Russians, that if this man was a Russian spy, whoever was responsible for his activities, whoever was his chief of staff, or whatever it is, would know in a matter of moments that this man had been arrested?

"We know that spies exist on both sides of this unhappy world and one assumes that spies are relatively intelligent and efficient and it seems incredible that his staff would continue to send out a message which, if he was a Russian spy, they would know that the British security service would be only too anxious to pick up and use as evidence that he was in fact a spy."

This argument, whatever doubts it raised, failed to impress the jury, which went out at 2:33 P.M. on March 23 and returned with a guilty verdict at 4 P.M.

The sentences administered by the Lord Chief Justice Parker were stiff—a total of ninety-five years, the most severe collective sentence dealt in a British peacetime court. Lonsdale received the lion's share, twenty-five years, because, as Lord Parker told him:

"You are clearly a professional spy. It is a dangerous career and one in which you must be prepared, as you no doubt are, to suffer if and when you are caught. Moreover, I take the view in this case that yours, so far as the activities of the five of you are concerned, was the directing mind."

The Krogers' sentence was twenty years apiece, because "You are both in this up to the hilt—you are professional spies, the only distinction I can see between you and Lonsdale is that, if I am right, yours was not the directing mind or minds and you are older than he is."

Houghton got off with fifteen years since "You are now fifty-six—not a very young fifty-six—and it is against all our principles that a sentence should be given which might involve your dying in prison. But for that I would give you a longer sentence."

As for Miss Gee, who also got fifteen years, Lord Parker told her: "I am quite unable to think it a possibility that you did what you did out of some blind infatuation for Houghton. Having heard you, and having watched your demeanor in the dock and in the witness box, I am inclined to think yours was the stronger character of the two. I think you acted for greed."

In addition to their sentences, the defendants had to pay 4,000 pounds of court costs that totaled 5,100 pounds.

The sentences, when compared to the ten years handed Alan Nunn May and the fourteen years to Klaus Fuchs, both of whom betrayed atomic secrets, seemed unusually severe. All five defendants appealed and all five had their appeals denied on May 9. Again Houghton made an attempt to obtain special treatment when his appeal came up. His lawyer introduced in court a handwritten "confession" which gave information about others who had been involved in the ring.

The lawyer said, "Houghton is entitled to believe that in that document he has done as much for his country as previously he did against it." The justice presiding over the appeals court replied after perusing it that "the document should certainly be kept in custody."

Another mitigating argument Houghton brought up was that he had been approached in prison before the trial by two fellow prisoners who offered him 5,000 pounds and a small business in Dublin if he would not go into the witness box and mention a certain name. Houghton claimed he refused the offer, at the peril of life and limb.

An interesting point in the appeals hearing was the argument used by Lonsdale's counsel. He acknowledged that Lonsdale was a member of the Soviet secret service and that consequently "his conduct was not stamped with dishonor. There was no element of treachery in his case.

He did what he was required to do and came to this country as a matter of obedience to the allegiance which he owed. Thus, any element of deterrence, a prime reason for prison sentences," was wasted in Lonsdale's case. "When he gets out," his counsel said, "he will waste very little time in this country. Nor will a deterrent operate on the minds of those who organize spying enterprises."

The three appeals judges refused to be swayed by the problem of the deterrent power of punishment in the case of professional spies, and all sentences were upheld. Houghton, Kroger and Lonsdale were packed off to Wormwood Scrubbs. Houghton was given a job in the prison's canvas shop where mailbags are manufactured, and Kroger and Lonsdale were put to work in the tailor's shop. The ladies went to Holloway Prison for Women.

XI. "I Like Treason but Not Traitors"

—OCTAVIUS CAESAR

HᴵˢᵀᴼᴿY has always had its Abels and Lonsdales, and turn-coats—though less common—were not unknown in the past; but the tortured figure of the defector has risen to such prominence in the Cold War that a major function of Russian and American espionage networks is to encourage the discontented to "change systems." A man turns his back on his country, his work and his family, literally casts his slough, and puts on a new set of beliefs, principles and duties, ready-made and sometimes ill-fitting. There is a steady stream of defectors in both directions and colonies of turncoats are part of the scene in cities like Moscow and Washington.

Defection today has become many things—a way to solve personal problems, an alternative to suicide, a cure for neurosis, a relief from emptiness and the "suction of the absurd," and mixed with all of these, an ideological decision. And the range of defectors stretches from famous scientists and high-ranking intelligence agents to mental patients, tourists, simple seamen and ballet dancers.

There is a willful ambivalence in the West's attitude toward defectors. We describe Russians defecting to the West as heroes and Americans defecting to the East as traitors. This reflects the naïve

336

conviction that the former have risen out of hell to bathe in a hallowed light while the latter have sunk to the depths of evil.

It is not easy to understand why someone would want to leave a free society and accept the strictures of the Iron Curtain. We feel the person must be unbalanced, or desperately beset by insoluble pressures. On the other hand, we consider it quite normal that a Russian aspires to escape from his country and come to the United States, where he may live in freedom.

It would be closer to the truth to say that man in whatever society tends to consider the order he lives in as natural. Usually, it is the only order he has known. He is surrounded by the familiar and accepts things that would shock a visitor from another society. At its worst, this condition could be compared to "Charlie Chaplin in the Gold Rush, bustling about in a shack poised precariously on the edge of a cliff" (Czeslaw Milosz in *The Captive Mind*). A Russian is convinced by propaganda that things in the West are no better than at home. There is rarely a qualitative choice in defection, a departure for a dream world. Defection is more often a desperate gesture than a selective process. Only through despair or revulsion can the defector, whether Russian or American, surmount the accumulation of propaganda in his system:

> The propaganda to which he [the Russian] is subjected tries by every means to prove that Nazism and Americanism are identical in that they are the products of the same economic conditions. He believes this propaganda only slightly less than the average American believes the journalists who assure him that Hitlerism and Stalinism are one and the same.*

When William H. Martin and Bernon F. Mitchell defected in August, 1960, President Eisenhower chose to voice personally the nation's indignation and said the traitors deserved to be shot. They had fled behind the Iron Curtain with valuable information on the National Security Agency. When Peter Deriabin, an officer in the KGB, defected to the West in 1954, he was kept undercover by the CIA for five years, so vital was the information he brought over. And when he was surfaced, he was wreathed in the clichés of the defecting hero: He had "chosen freedom," he had "thumbed his nose at the

* Czeslaw Milosz, *The Captive Mind* (New York: Alfred A. Knopf, 1953).

Communist dictators," and so on. Basically, he had done exactly the same thing as Martin and Mitchell—betrayed his country, left behind a family which would undoubtedly suffer from his action (something Martin and Mitchell didn't have to worry about), and brought secret information as the price of admission to the West. Privately, CIA officials admit that Deriabin was prompted by opportunism, not ideology, and that many other important defectors have practical reasons for their change of heart. They are in trouble with Moscow, their family life is a mess, they brood about lack of advancement—all the reasons that might drive a man to drink now can also drive him to defection.

This is not to underrate the revulsion to the Communist system that seizes defectors. Time after time defectors describe the growing awareness of lies and gradual disgust that drove Czeslaw Milosz to write:

> My own decision proceeded, not from the functioning of the reasoning mind, but from a revolt of the stomach. A man may persuade himself, by the most logical reasoning, that he will greatly benefit his health by swallowing live frogs; and thus rationally convinced, he may swallow a first frog, then the second; but at the third his stomach will revolt. In the same way, the growing influence of doctrine on my ways of thinking came up against the resistance of my whole nature.

The terrible thing is that today people on both sides have to swallow live frogs, and the squeamish on both sides are revolted. It was shock at CIA methods that helped prompt Martin and Mitchell to treason. And rather than a question of good and evil, we should see defection as a human problem, a sickness of our time.

The intelligence value of defectors is enormous. The CIA concedes that it has obtained far more information about Soviet intelligence organizations from defecting Russian agents than from its own operatives. The Russians, on the other hand, were given a detailed description of the National Security Agency, as well as the Russian codes that had been broken, by Martin and Mitchell. Besides the acquired intelligence, defectors are always good for a week or two of propaganda. Each side makes much of dissatisfaction in the other camp. Techniques are similar—accounts of the defections appear in newspapers and the defectors themselves appear on television. Their adjustment to a new life is followed closely in the press.

An American diplomat who served a recent tour of duty in Moscow remembers his surprise one winter day when he took his family ice skating. The paths in Moscow's Gorki Park had been flooded and frozen into mile-long trails. There were wooden shacks to change in, and the diplomat was surprised to hear English spoken nearby as he was lacing his skates. He turned and recognized a group of American defectors. Other Americans in Moscow have reported seeing defectors in Moscow public places. They are said to band together under the leadership of the two deans of English-speaking defectors, Guy Burgess and Donald MacLean.

Burgess and MacLean provide the simplest explanation for defection—defection by necessity. They fled while British intelligence was looking into their political background. They have been in Moscow since 1951, and reports on their activities dribble in from Westerners passing through Russia.

MacLean's two sons, Fergus and Donald, are sent in the summer to a children's camp on the Sea of Izov, close to Crimea and Russia's South Coast. They are Russian Boy Scouts (Pioneers). MacLean and Burgess both work for the English Department of a Soviet Government publishing house. Burgess is the more communicative of the two former Cambridgeans, who were recruited by Soviet intelligence when they entered the Foreign Service. When Randolph Churchill visited Russia in 1959 he had a drink with Burgess, who turned up in blazer and old school tie. In 1957, an American lawyer named William W. Goodman was at the Moscow opera and the man next to him introduced himself as Burgess. They chatted during intermissions. Burgess seemed relaxed and calm. "They do well by eggheads in Moscow," he confided.

Last October, Burgess crashed a party given in honor of a departing correspondent for the Agence France-Presse. Burgess said he wanted to go back to Britain to see his ailing mother, Mrs. Eva Bassett. He freely discussed his years in Moscow and said mysteriously that "it comes to everybody to feel he has made a mistake," but added, "I'm more happy after ten years than I was after five years." When he left the party, which had been attended by practically every newspaperman in Moscow, he said with a kind of perverse satisfaction: "Oh, God, I suppose this will make world headlines again." MacLean is less flamboyant than his fellow defector and lives quietly with his Chicago-born wife, Melinda.

Another example of defection under threat of arrest is that of the Sterns. Martha Dodd Stern, daughter of one-time Ambassador to Germany William E. Dodd, and her husband, Alfred Stern, millionaire stockbroker, fled to Mexico in 1957 after being identified as members of the Jack Soble apparat in New York. They refused to answer subpoenas to appear before a grand jury investigating the Soble case and were fined $25,000 apiece for contempt of court. They were indicted on espionage and conspiracy charges in September, 1957. By that time, they had made their way from Amsterdam to Prague with fake Paraguayan passports.

There is a honeymoon period for arriving defectors. The Sterns were feted all over Russia and taken on guided tours. Visitors to Yasnaya Polyana, Tolstoy's estate 80 miles south of Moscow, can see their names prominently placed in the guest book. They spent a weekend there as guests of honor. But the bloom soon wore off and the Sterns finally settled in Prague. Martha Stern, the couple's guiding spirit, was rebuffed in attempts to work on the propaganda magazine *Czechoslovak Life*. She wrote the chief editor criticizing the English-language edition's style and presentation and offering to improve it, and was told in effect: "We already have a managing editor, a defector with thirty years' experience." The couple has since dropped into an obscurity burdened by the abiding thought that must haunt all defectors: *You can't go home again.*

The motives of those who defect freely are more mysterious and we will study the cases of American defectors who provide a cross section of types, origins, and motives. These Americans of widely divergent personalities and backgrounds have one thing in common: they fled the United States for the Soviet Union. If we cannot exhaust the enigma of why they did it, since their own reasons are tentative and obscure, we can at least examine the mechanics of their defections.

The Mystic: Professor Alexander Kasem-Beg taught Russian language and literature courses at Connecticut College for Women. He had lived in the United States since the twenties and he and his two children were American citizens. He was active in one of the many groups of Soviet exiles that sprang up in the twenties and thirties. He wrote articles for the Russian Orthodox Church magazine, gave talks on world affairs and was a favorite with the students.

In 1956, he asked for leave to be treated for a serious eye ailment in Switzerland. He left in August, and a month later the college received a letter postmarked Switzerland saying he was too ill to return. A doctor's certificate was enclosed. Not long after, his arrival in Moscow was announced in *Pravda*. Dr. Kasem-Beg followed the traditional pattern of writing anti-American articles. There was an extraordinary debate in *Pravda* on culture in the United States, with the professor denouncing the lack of it and with Communist writer Ilya Ehrenberg defending it. Later, Dr. Kasem-Beg told some American visitors in Moscow that he had "come home to die."

The Romantic: Robert E. Webster, a thirty-year-old plastics technician for the Rand Development Corporation of Cleveland, Ohio, went to Russia in August, 1959, to prepare his company's exhibit at the Moscow fair. Webster, a devout Quaker, left his wife of eight years and his two children at home in Pennsylvania. His Moscow exhibit, an abstract-shaped plastic swimming pool, was a great success, and Webster was praised by the company president, Dr. H. J. Rand.

In October, when the fair was being dismantled and the American exhibitors were going home, Webster wrote Dr. Rand that he was staying in Moscow. "I've examined both systems and decided that I like it here and want to live here," he said. "I'm doing this for ideological reasons." Other Americans who had worked alongside Webster at the fair knew better. His reason for staying behind was a restaurant waitress named Vera. The Russians needed a good plastics technician for a new plant in Leningrad, and with Vera's assistance they in effect hired the gullible Webster away from Rand. The honeymoon lasted about a year, and in 1960 Webster began writing his wife and children "hope to see you soon" postcards. In early 1961, he applied at the American Embassy for re-entry papers. The Embassy told him that since he had renounced his citizenship and taken out Soviet papers, the only way back was through the Russian immigration quota. Webster is still waiting for his quota number to come up.

The Introvert: Bruce Davis attended many schools as a youth. Teachers remembered him as a boy who did not mix. Fellow students described him as "a pill." He came to Asbury Park High School in 1954 as a transfer student from a California school. In his class book he described his ambition as "getting a college degree and returning to the West Coast." After two years in the Marines, he enrolled in an electrical engineering course at Arizona State University but switched to foreign service studies after flunking the course. He finally quit the university altogether and joined the Army. But the Army didn't live up to his expectations either, and in August, 1960, he went AWOL from his mortar company at Bad Kissingen and crossed the border into East Germany.

Two months later, the Soviet Embassy in Washington released the following statement signed by Davis:

> On August 19 I left my unit of the United States Army and crossed the border from West Germany into East Germany for the purpose of seeking political asylum. I am twenty-four. I was born and grew up in the United States of America. I had seen active service for four years and nine months and came to my decision after two years of deliberation.
>
> Since the end of World War II, the American press has been playing up in all ways the Cold War and the Iron Curtain which the Socialist countries were purported to have raised. In this way the notion was created in the U.S.A. that the blame for a third World War could rest only with the Socialist countries. These often repeated declarations of the American press aroused my doubts. The question invariably suggested itself as to how the Soviet Union, the country which had suffered the most in World War II, could prepare a new war. At the very time the American public was being made to believe that we Americans seek peace, I could see for myself, while in the Army, that actually we are seeking to extend the might of our Army.

In two months in the Soviet Union, Davis had evidently learned to take Russian dictation.

The Fellow Traveler: Morris Block was one of the group of American students who went to Red China in 1957, in defiance of the State Department, after attending a youth festival in Moscow, where he had singled himself out as an excitable party-line doctrinaire. When the delegates were interviewed by CBS correspondent Daniel Schorr, they were asked whether they approved the Soviet Union's methods in Hungary. One replied that there were many in the group who disapproved of the Soviet stand. At this point, Block broke in and shouted, "Liar, liar, don't you know Schorr wants to start a counterrevolution?"

The high-strung Block had his passport canceled when he came back from Red China in 1957. In January, 1958, the House Un-American Activities Committee called him to testify at a hearing on the activities of the group. When his passport was introduced as evidence, Block walked over to the table where it lay, picked it up, and put it in his pocket.

He refused to return it; the court was not empowered to take it from him forcefully, but declared him in contempt. Soon afterward, Block used his passport to go to Europe, and August, 1959, found him in Moscow, beyond the reach of the passport office and Congressional committees. He is presently in the Black Sea port of Odessa working as a shipfitter.

The Plant: Vladimir Sloboda was one of the many members of the Soviet secret police who were launched toward the West after the war under cover of displaced persons seeking asylum. It was impossible to weed out the "sleepers" from the real D.P.'s during this chaotic period, and many agents found their way to the United States or Canada under the auspices of a philanthropic group or an international organization.

Sloboda was a native of Lvov region of Poland, which was attached to the Ukrainian Republic in 1939 in one of the periodic gerrymanderings of the Polish territory. He came out of Poland into Germany in 1953, carrying a small cardboard suitcase and no papers, and took one of the solutions offered able-bodied male D.P.'s: he joined the U.S. Army in Brement. Because of his knowledge of Polish and Russian, he was assigned to a military intelligence group in Fort Bragg, North Carolina. He helped train "goon squads"— paramilitary units taught commando tactics for eventual action behind the Iron Curtain. In 1958, having fulfilled his five-year residency requirement, he became a United States citizen. Transferred to an intelligence group in Germany, he was made a deputy chief of section with the rank of specialist fifth class (sergeant).

In August, 1960, he left his unit, his wife, his three children, and fled to East Germany. Hailed as a hero by *Izvestia,* he soon became a

Soviet television personality. His appearances were broadcast all over Europe by Radio Moscow. He described the U-2 flights and the networks for smuggling agents into East Berlin. "Most agents recruited by the CIA are under great pressure of blackmail, threats, and bribery," he said.

He denounced U.S. military personnel as spies and named intelligence units. In an article in *Pravda,* he wrote:

> I know that there is an extensive, ramified network of the American intelligence service in West Germany. The activities of all the American and foreign intelligence agencies are directed and coordinated by the CIA, which has its European headquarters at Frankfurt am Main. The numerous subdivisions of the CIA are scattered throughout West Germany and are often camouflaged as military units.
>
> The biggest U.S. military intelligence groups are the 513th Reconnaissance group, the 66th Reconnaissance group, and the 532d Reconnaissance Battalion of the 7th Army. These groups have several thousand professional agents, and their strength is constantly increasing. Colonel Franz H. Ross is chief of the 513th unit of the American military intelligence at Oberursel in West Germany. He is in charge of the numerous branches of the 513th Reconnaissance group in nearly all the big cities of West Germany and in West Berlin.

If usual Soviet procedure was followed, Sloboda has been reintegrated into the ranks of the secret police with back pay and the rank of major or colonel after eight years of foreign service.

The Scientist: In December, 1956, a Ukrainian-born scientist whose parents and brother had been slain by the Communists in Poland, and who had gained renown in the missile field in the United States, defected to the Soviet Union. He had information on the two intercontinental ballistic missiles, Titan and Atlas; he was one of the foremost authorities on aerial photography and probably knew something about U-2 overflights, which were starting at the time he defected; and he had worked at the Alamogordo testing ground where the first atom bomb exploded.

His case is typical of what one is tempted to call "the scientist's syndrome": the conviction that science is a law unto itself, above ethics and religion. Today the scientist, like the artist of the Renaissance, will sometimes work for the prince who gives him the best working conditions, just as a Leonardo could leave his native Florence for Rome and the patronage of the Medicis.

Professor Orest Stephen Makar worked in Russia until 1949, stayed in the United States until 1956, and then went back to Russia. Admittedly a-political, he was concerned only with what the system had to offer the scientist: "While following scientific literature in my own field, I found that science is being taken very seriously over there and that the best conditions for scientific-research work exist in the Soviet Union. That is why I want to continue my work there," he explained.

Professor Makar came to the United States as a refugee in 1949 with his wife, Alexandra. He was a native of Nove-Misto in Western Ukraine, which had once been Polish, and he was fluent in Ukrainian, Serbian, Polish, and German. Not English unfortunately, for after obtaining a teaching job at the University of St. Louis, he was dismissed on the grounds that his work was unsatisfactory. Before teaching, he had worked at the White Sands missile proving grounds in New Mexico for eight months, had served as a mathematics consultant and general physicist for the Air Force and the Army, and was sent to Alamogordo. At White Sands he had access to classified information, but resigned from his research work "for personal reasons" before the security check was finished.

An invitation to attend an international conference on photogrammetry in Stockholm in the summer of 1956 gave him the opportunity for defection. He left with his wife and wrote his friends that he was staying in Stockholm for a series of lectures. He went to the Soviet Embassy, asked for asylum, and "they more than met me halfway." Today he is teaching at the Lvov Polytechnic Institute, in Western Ukraine, his land of origin.

Was there a measure of hurt pride in his defection when he compared the honors heaped on Russian scientists with the shabby treatment he received at the hands of American university authorities? In the Soviet Union the title "scientist" automatically confers rights, privileges, and a high position in a curiously stratified society. In public places in Moscow, scientists go to the head of the line, they don't have to queue up—the state gives them *dachas,* modern apartments, chauffeur-driven cars, tax privileges, incentive prizes, and all the other amenities that liberate the mind for research. In the morass of American university life, the scientist must compete on many levels, at deans' teas and in the lab, before his students and before trustees. There is no privileged status, and advancement is not automatic—Professor Makar learned that even a scientist can get a pink slip.

Coupled with these attractions is the scientist's conviction that he is indispensable. The smug understatement "they more than met me halfway" reflects the prima donna side of today's scientist, aware that his talents are sought by both sides. He has become a latter-day mercenary who sells his knowledge not for money but for the cause of science and ideal working conditions. Given his modern lab and his competent assistants, why should he care whether the equipment is Russian- or American-made? Does science have a flag?

The nature of scientific work divides men from reality. There was the case of Hans Ertel, vice-president of East Germany's Academy of Science and one of the world's four leading authorities in the field of theoretical meteorology, who was sent to jail for fifteen months in March, 1960, for setting up a cheap chiseling scheme. For seven years he had posed as a resident of West Berlin who worked in East Berlin. This allowed him to convert his East German marks for West German marks at a one-for-one exchange, while the free exchange was four East for one West. Over the seven-year period he bilked the West Berlin Government of about $15,000. His explanation: "Thirty years of life in the abstract sphere of natural sciences made me lose my grip on reality."

When respected scientists behave like petty thieves, we should not be too surprised that they change political systems like body linen.

From Klaus Fuchs and Bruno Pontecorvo to William H. Martin and Bernon F. Mitchell, a parade of scientists and mathematicians have gone East in the conviction that the cause of science was better served behind the Iron Curtain. How can a closed society where the individual cannot shake off the oppressive presence of the state even in his most routine occupations provide freedom for its scientists?

In Russia, the scientist and the artist are outside society. It has been this way ever since the Bolsheviks took power and ruled that although it would take years to correct existing social injustices, in the fields of arts and sciences it could be done right away. Privileged groups were born with the Communist regime and formed a kind of upper class to which the masses could aspire without envy. Workers live on a subsistence level while researchers, engineers, mathematicians, physicists and chemists skim the cream after they have proven in the ruthlessly competitive educational system that they will be able to contribute to Soviet might and Soviet glory.

Science takes the place of religion in this scheme of things, and scientists are given the opportunity for untrammeled meditation that the Church reserves for its contemplative orders. Russia's most emphatic claims are that its scientists are the best scientists, that its technological intelligentsia is unmatched. The thread of Soviet claims to scientific inventions "stolen by the West" runs much farther back than the early days of Communist regime. The *Large Soviet Encyclopedia* says, for instance:

> In the eighteenth century a self-taught man, Kulibin, constructed bridges with remarkable mechanical qualities; the mechanic Polzunov invented the steam-engine; in the nineteenth century a member of the Russian Academy, Yakob, created galvanoplastics and built the first motorboats; engineer Yablochkov was the inventor of arc lamps, and Lodygin of the incandescent electric lamp; Popov invented and was the first to use the radio receiver; N. E. Zhukovski was the greatest creator of the theory of air flights.

With this kind of a tradition to live up to, where unschooled peasants are said to be responsible for the four or five outstanding inventions of the modern age, the Soviet system depends mightily on its men of science. They are given free rein and are not confined by dogma. They are liberated from the obligations of artists and writers, who are only privileged as long as they comply with the Party line. There is an anti-Party art and an anti-Party literature, but how can there be an anti-Party science? The scientists are able to accept the offerings of the state without a crisis of conscience. They may have to appear at an occasional Party function, but the papers they read and the speeches they make are outside Marxist-Leninist doctrine. They are by the nature of their vocation essentially unrestricted.

In addition, there is a vast amount of scientific exchange going on today between East and West. Scientists in the United States hear about programs in Russia, who is doing what, the difficulty (or facility) of getting pure research accepted, and the invasion (or lack of it) of the scientist's private life for security reasons. More and more scientific congresses are attended by Soviet scientists and provide a forum for comparing science and the scientist in the two systems and also a possible breeding ground for defection. There is a solidarity among scientists that transcends national boundaries and provides an outstanding example of the Marxist principle that the bonds between the same class in different countries can be stronger than the bonds between different classes in the same countries. Marx had the workers in mind, but the scientists have come closer to proving him right.

For whom does the American scientist feel a greater affinity: the CIA employee who gives him a lie-detector test, the company official who refuses to budget a pure research project because it can't be translated in terms of a new product, the university dean who fires a teacher because he didn't publish, or the Soviet scientist he meets at an international conference and who is working on a similar project? With the migrations of the last fifteen years, the affinity is sometimes more than professional. At a recent scientific congress in Geneva, for instance, a Soviet and an American scientist began chatting and finally exchanged addresses. They were both named Reinhart. They were both originally from Leipzig. They were second cousins. The Russian had recently visited their eighty-year-old aunt in the East German city. At some point these two men, with similar backgrounds and training, had taken different forks in the road.

American scientists often point to the amount of pure research being done in the Soviet Union. (One-third of all research is in the applied science or technical field, two-thirds in theoretical or fundamental research.) There is a story, perhaps apocryphal, showing that no scheme is too weird to be accepted by the Soviet Government and alloted funds—a celebrated Soviet scientist is reportedly working on an engine that will use the passage of time as energy. He goes on with his research despite critical articles in *Pravda* that this type of "science-fiction" hurts the prestige of the Soviet Union.

Such stories pain American scientists who must sell their projects to private business or the Government. They depend on trustees or the legislature for the handling of funds and deal with men too result-conscious to be open-minded about certain types of research.

There is one American scientist who gets his way by calling his superiors long distance and saying, for instance: "What are they doing with our atomic project? Oh, they don't want it. Well, we'll sell it to the Russians."

The fear that the Russians will get something through the wrong decision of a government official is a major incentive for American scientific programs. It was not so long ago that Admiral Rickover said in a commencement speech at Annapolis that if he told the Government the Russians were sending a man to hell, he would immediately be given a blank check so he could get his man there first.

On the other hand, there are Russian scientists who fled to the West because they had private eccentricities unacceptable to Soviet society. One Hungarian physicist liked to hold seances and communicate with the dead. This was deemed unworthy of a scientist in a popular democracy. He is now working for a well-known company in the United States where he is encouraged to hold all the seances he likes; the company offered to supply the necessary equipment.

Generally speaking, however, the flow of defecting scientists runs West-East, thanks to the lure of the Soviet Union as the best of all possible worlds for men of science. Things are very different with another privileged Russian group—intelligence and military personnel. "We have a list as long as your arm of Soviet intelligence agents who came to us loaded down with information," a CIA man said. "Some of them we haven't even surfaced yet."

These are men who live in luxury in Moscow, with all the privileges mentioned previously for artists and scientists. They also live in fear and revulsion. The next purge is always around the corner and nothing is more bereft of security than a Soviet intelligence officer's job. The nature of their work makes them privy to the state's corruption. As professional eavesdroppers with dossiers on important political figures, they are silent witnesses to the orgies, the graft, and the Byzantine maneuvering in high places characteristic of every Soviet regime since Ivan the Terrible.

Thus the secret police breeds its own defectors, who may have qualms about going West but who, since they have access to classified information, have a more sophisticated image of the capitalist society.

Alexander Orlov, an NKVD official who headed Soviet operations in the Spanish civil war and who defected to the United States in 1938, has described the uncertainty of Soviet intelligence officers that leads to defection. Before a Senate subcommittee, he testified that "when they started their work, they honestly served their country —they were good patriots. But through decades of assassination of innocent people, of liquidations by Stalin of every MVD officer who knew his criminal secrets . . . there has been created an atmosphere so that each of the intelligence officers at one time or another, usually during periodical purges, would be happy to quit and to start his life anew. They say that the life span of aviators is very short; but the life span of MVD officers is the shortest of all."

Orlov recalled that he defected when he saw all his chiefs being executed in purges. He had a distinguished record of intelligence work: commander of guerrilla detachments during the Russian revolution, Red Army chief of counterintelligence, chief of department in the NKVD, and *éminence grise* to the Spanish Republicans in 1936 —still he did not feel beyond the reach of purges. "I received an order to send my assistant to Russia, an assistant who was decorated by Stalin personally, and who had carried out great feats. He was invited to Russia to report on the Spanish civil war. One month passed, and we did not receive a single letter from him. My other assistants would converge and say, 'Something must have happened —he was an honest fellow, what do you think?' They were gloomy, all of them."

Orlov's turn came next: "I received a telegram instructing me to go to Belgium and board a ship, ostensibly for a secret conference where a top member of the Party would be waiting for me. Two of my assistants talked to me privately. One of them said: 'I do not like that telegram.' I asked him: 'What do you think; what conference could there be?' He did not answer me, and looked away. He was afraid to talk, but at the same time wanted me to feel that—and he said: 'Why didn't he come here to Spain to talk with you?' "

Taking the hint, Orlov, whose mother was still in Russia, wrote Stalin that if anything happened to her or to himself, he would publish his memoirs. "To show forcefully enough to Stalin that I meant business, I, in spite of the protests of my wife, attached to that letter a whole list of Stalin's crimes, with some of the expressions which he himself had used in secret conferences when he was forging the evidence against the leaders of the revolution during the Moscow trials."

Having mailed the letter, Orlov fled with his wife in July, 1938, from Spain to Canada, and thence to the United States. He stayed underground for fifteen years. "In 1953, I came to the conclusion that our mothers could no longer be alive, because so many years have passed, and I decided to take the chance and submitted my manuscript while Stalin was still alive."

The same sort of panic seized many intelligence officials when Lavrenti Beria, head of the secret police, was arrested in 1953 and executed. A purge of "Beria's men" continued over the next two years. About eleven leaders in the KGB were executed and many more were sent to labor camps or given long prison terms.

It is not a coincidence that a rash of important intelligence officials defected during this period: Yuri Rastorov, Second Secretary of the Soviet mission in Japan and a lieutenant colonel in the KGB, defected in January 1954. In February, Peter Deriabin, a section head in the KGB, defected in Vienna; in April, Vladimir Petrov and his wife asked for asylum in Australia. He was a cipher clerk at the Soviet Embassy and an MVD official. She was assigned to operational espionage work under the MVD Resident. Also in February, Nikolai Khokhlov, a captain in the MVD whose chiefs had been purged as Beria men, defected in Berlin.

The circumstances of the Petrovs' defection are enlightening. Vladimir Petrov, whose real name is Shorokhov, joined the OGPU in 1933 as a cipher clerk. In 1942 he was posted to the Soviet Embassy in Stockholm, as a cover for his intelligence work with what had become the MVD. In 1951, he was transferred to the embassy in Canberra. He was appointed temporary MVD resident soon after arriving, and kept the position until his defection. In 1929, Petrov had adopted the name Proletarsky in a fit of Communist fervor and later changed it to the more mundane Petrov. His wife had been a member of military intelligence for seven years when they married in 1940. In Stockholm she was typist to the MVD resident and went under the name "Tamara." By 1951, she had the rank of captain in the MVD. Her overt post was that of embassy accountant and secretary to the Ambassador. Her real work was MVD cipher clerk when her husband became temporary Resident.

As the Royal Commission Report on Espionage pointed out, Petrov made some heavy sacrifices upon defecting:

> It meant leaving a service which was his very life in which he
> had risen to a comparatively high rank and was enjoying a very good

salary. He was forfeiting not only his salary but substantial savings in cash and public bonds in Moscow. He was forsaking forever his native land, for which he had great affection. He was, he believed, breaking his marriage ties, and about to face life alone in a new country with the certainty of being branded a traitor and incurring the hatred of the Soviet Government . . . which would cloud his life with the constant apprehension of retribution.

Mr. Petrov's decision sounds almost heroic until we examine the reasons that compelled him to bolt his job, his wife, and his country. After Beria was arrested, the Petrovs were caught in an uncertain position at the embassy. The Soviet Ambassador sent reports to Moscow accusing the Petrovs of seeking to form a pro-Beria group among embassy officials. However pro-Beria Petrov may have been when Beria was in power, it was not in his nature to remain loyal to a man who had been executed for reasons of state. The Ambassador's charges were a convenient device for getting rid of a cumbersome MVD agent. The Ambassador was backed up in the power play by the commercial attaché, who was also the representative of the Central Committee of the Soviet Communist Party. Petrov had an office spy who told him about the adverse reports being sent to Moscow.

When a new ambassador arrived, Petrov curried his favor, but in vain, and the adverse reports continued. Mrs. Petrov was relieved of her cover duties as accountant and secretary and her salary was cut.

A special meeting of the embassy staff was called to criticize the Petrovs' pro-Beria heresies. Trouble reached its peak in April, 1954, when the Ambassador filed an official complaint that Petrov had dealt with a secret document in a manner contrary to the administrative regulation. Petrov had seen it happen to others too often and he knew that on this petty technical charge he could be recalled to the Soviet Union and imprisoned.

"With the increasing tension in the embassy," the Royal Commission report said, "Petrov had guardedly broached to Mrs. Petrov the question of leaving the Soviet service and seeking political asylum, but she had not responded. She had an intense feeling of loyalty to Russia and to the Russian people. Moreover, unlike Petrov, she had close relatives living in the USSR; and she had cause to fear for their fate if she left her post."

Petrov made another effort to convince his wife through a Soviet friend who was instrumental in his defection and who was in reality an Australian agent. The friend, Dr. Bialoguski, came to the Petrovs' home, expressed indignation at the shabby treatment they were getting at the embassy, and suggested that the couple defect. Mrs. Petrov furiously upbraided Dr. Bialoguski for making such an "indecent proposal" and said that neither she nor her husband would think of leaving Russia. She gave the impression her husband would follow her decision. After his wife's tirade, Petrov made up his mind to save his skin even if she did not want to save hers.

When orders came from the Center in Moscow that some letters to which he had access be burned and a certificate of destruction be signed by himself and his wife, he hid the letters and told his wife they had been destroyed. He also filched some MVD documents, so that he would be provided with information to turn over to Australian authorities if he decided to defect. Through Dr. Bialoguski, Petrov secretly met the deputy director for security in Australia. He was told he would have to sign an application for political asylum and that a special fund could be drawn upon to help provide for his future. When Petrov showed signs of reluctance, the Australian made a cash offer of 5,000 pounds.

The security officer had the money in a briefcase, opened it, and shook out the bills on a table. Here was an ideology Petrov could understand, and he made up his mind to leave the embassy. On April 3, Petrov told his wife he was going away on business for three days. He went to the Sydney airport, where he turned himself over to the Australian authorities and exchanged the 5,000 pounds for the documents he had stolen from the embassy. He was driven to a house outside town and kept there undercover.

When Petrov failed to return, the Ambassador ordered his wife to be placed under house arrest at the embassy. The Australian Department of External Affairs wrote the Soviet Ambassador in protest and enclosed a letter from Petrov asking to see his wife; the Department offered to arrange the meeting. The Ambassador showed the letters to Mrs. Petrov and prevailed on her to write in reply "I am afraid to fall into a trap."

On April 19, the slight, blond woman was driven to Mascot Airport under guard of two couriers. By this time she had become a *cause célèbre* in the Australian press and a hysterical crowd at the airport screamed at her not to return to Russia because she would surely be killed. She spent the night on the plane, filled with fear and uncertainty. The Royal Commission Report says:

> Although Mrs. Petrov was an alien and an employee of a foreign embassy, she, like any other person in Australia, was entitled to the protection of our law against unlawful restraint. The Australian Government was concerned to see that she was not being forcibly taken from Australia against her will, and in consequence, the captain of the aircraft was asked to discover her wishes and Mr. Leydin, the Acting Administrator of the Northern Territory, was instructed at midnight to interview her on her arrival at Darwin Airport [a stopover en route to Moscow]. The captain spoke to her on the flight and radioed to Canberra that he had formed the impression that she desired to stay in Australia but was afraid, and that she had told him that her guards were armed.

When the plane landed at Darwin, the Soviet guards were disarmed after a brief scuffle. The Australian administrator found Mrs. Petrov distraught and still uncertain—she believed her husband was dead, she was afraid harm would come to her relatives if she stayed behind, she was suspicious of a trap, she could not understand what had happened.

Minutes before the plane was to take off for Moscow, Petrov in Sydney reached his wife over the phone. He told her he was well, had been forced to leave the embassy because of the campaign against him, and that if she went back to Russia she would be disposed of. The hulking guards hovered behind her, listening to the conversation.

Mrs. Petrov asked to see the Australian administrator away from the guards and said: "I will stay." The plane took off for Russia with the two guards and the pilot. Whatever nobility there was in the couple's defection came from Mrs. Petrov, who was torn between love of a country, concern for her relatives, and duty to her husband.

If Mrs. Petrov had chosen to return to Russia, it is likely she would have been done away with. An example of a defector who did return is that of Anatole Barzov, who in 1948 took an airplane from the Soviet base in Kolomaya with his friend Peter Pirogov and flew to the American zone of Austria. After four months of on-the-spot interrogation they obtained permission to go to the United States. At the time of the defection, *Pravda* explained their absence by saying they had been forced to land in the American zone because they ran short of fuel.

Once in the United States, both men were contacted by the Soviet Embassy and promised a safe return to Russia. Alexander Panyushkin was Soviet Ambassador at the time and was also NKVD Resident for the United States. One of the most redoubtable Soviet agents ever to work in the United States, Panyushkin persuaded Barzov that although he had committed a crime against the state, he would be given only a two-year sentence if he returned. If he could prevail upon Pirogov to come with him, the sentence would be suspended.

Barzov had left behind a wife and four-year-old son. He was convinced that Panyushkin's offer was sincere. He approached Pirogov, showed him the passport the Soviet Embassy had given him, and said there was another ready for him. He wanted to know why Pirogov wouldn't return with him.

Pirogov said: "I have signed a contract to write a book and got from them a big amount of money; and therefore I cannot return to the Soviet Union until I have paid this debt."

"I am writing too," Barzov replied, "but I will write a book which will be much better than any books which emigrants wrote here in America about Russia."

"Don't worry about your book," Pirogov said. "They will write it for you. You will sign your name and after six months, the author will not be alive. They will kill you."

"Well, after five or ten years, you will be there too," Barzov said. "I will be free, but you will take the place in jail where I'm going now."

Barzov opened a pack of Kazebek (Russian) cigarettes, and Pirogov said, "I've got my own," and pulled out an American brand. "You think that is already yours," Barzov said derisively, "you qualify yourself already as an American?"

"No," said Pirogov, "I am still not American, but I am trying."

"Nonsense," Barzov said.

Barzov went home and was never heard from again. Vladimir Petrov, the Australian defector, wrote in his book *Empire of Fear*:*

> One day in 1950 at MVD headquarters in Moscow, my colleague Igolkin, who worked in the American section of the SK [Soviet Kolony, whose duties are reporting to the Moscow Center on the conduct of Soviet officials] department, told me of Barzov's return

* Vladimir Petrov, *Empire of Fear* (London: A. Deutsch, 1956).

and said he was interrogating him in his cell at Taganskaya Prison. Igolkin had a series of interviews with Barzov, who supplied a mass of valuable information. He was talking freely and was describing every detail of his experiences in American hands, in hope of working his passage back to pardon and of being permitted at least to see his wife and son again. As Igolkin described it to me, "Each time I go to see him he looks at me like a dog that wags its tail and gazes at you in the hope of a bone." They kept Barzov about eight months in prison because he had so much interesting information to supply and because so many senior MVD officers wanted to check up on various points in his story.

Of course, no one told him that he had been sentenced to death while he was still in America. When they had finished with him they shot him without letting him see his wife and son again.

Captain Nikolai Ferdorovich Artamonov is an outstanding example of a Soviet defector who was not under any kind of threat but escaped to the West when overpowered by a feeling that the Communist system could not work. Captain Artamonov had a vested interest in the system he abandoned. When he defected at the age of thirty-one, he was one of the most brilliant officers in the Red Navy. He had been given command of a Baltic fleet destroyer when he was twenty-seven, and had been singled out in articles in *Red Star* and *Soviet Navy*. The articles praised his outstanding performance and leadership, his competence in anti-submarine training, and his ability for propagandizing Party decisions among his men.

His destroyer was one of two in the Baltic fleet chosen for an official visit to Copenhagen. He defected in June, 1959, while in Gdynia, Poland, training Indonesians in destroyer operations.

In testimony before the House Un-American Activities Committee, Captain Artamonov explained, "I did not come to the United States because of any connection with foreign intelligence, for I had none. Nor did I make this move because of threats of repercussions for something I had done—for there were none. On the contrary, I was given a favored treatment by the Soviet authorities and had a bright future ahead of me—having been publicly described as one of the brilliant young career officers of the Soviet Navy. My defection was also not prompted by the prospect of greater material gain or security or an easy life, for I gave up what promised to be a successful career in the Soviet Union to come here. In a very true sense, I am here because of the Kremlin's policies."

The objection one might make to defectors who leave their families behind have no bearing on the captain's case. He was unmarried, his parents were dead, and he had no brothers or sisters.

His was a model of Communist upbringing. As a child, he belonged to the Pioneers, Soviet-style Boy Scouts, graduated to the Komsomol, the Young Communist League, and became a Communist Party member at the age of twenty-one. "To use Soviet political-agitation language," he said, "I was a one hundred per cent Soviet citizen of the new generation unmarred by capitalist birthmarks, uncorrupted by depraved bourgeois imperialist ideology, and unbought by capitalist money."

Artamonov was living in Leningrad, where his father worked as a mechanic. "In the Pioneers," he said, "I was taught to be ever vigilant, that enemies were all about; if necessary, I should denounce even my own father. I witnessed arrests and noted that people whom I had known disappeared into the torture chambers of the NKVD, but in my immaturity I was pleased that our motherland was being made more powerful through this crushing of the 'enemy of the people.'"

After finishing elementary school, Artamonov, who dreamed of becoming a naval officer, volunteered for the naval school in Vasilevsky Island off Leningrad. From the secondary naval school he went to the Frunze higher naval school, Russia's best.

He was marked by "the strong national pride of all Soviets early in World War II, at times mixed with bitterness for our suffering. In spite of the hard times caused by the blockade of Leningrad and our evacuation from the city, I never once doubted the policies of Stalin and our Government. My friends and I were prepared to do anything for our motherland and our leader."

Curiously, the first seeds of doubt were sown by the two-year course in Marxism and Leninism the captain had to take at Frunze. He felt that "the Soviet system was constructed without valid foundations and that there was a great breach between the theory of Soviet Communism and its practice as we saw it every day. Still I sought to justify things by lame analyses of the country's current needs."

There was one incident he could not justify—the 1956 Hungarian uprising. "It gave rise to the conviction that the Government's foreign policy statements were untrue. They showed the aggressive character of that policy." Captain Artamonov was also perturbed about an article that appeared in 1955 in the journal *Voyennaya Mysl* (*Military Thought*) under the signature of Marshal Pavel Rotmistrov. The journal is available only to the officer corps of the Soviet Armed Forces and the article dealt with the advantages of a surprise attack on the West. It said in part:

> Sudden attack involving the use of atomic and hydrogen weapons and other modern means of warfare assumes at present new forms and is capable of leading to considerably greater results than in the past war. It can be stated directly that under conditions in which atomic and hydrogen weapons are used the surprise is one of the decisive factors in achieving success not only in a battle and in operation, but in the war as a whole. In some cases a sudden attack involving a massive use of new weapons may result in the rapid collapse of a state, the ability of which to resist is low due to inherent defects of its social and economic structure as well as its unfavorable geographical position.
>
> The duty of the Soviet Armed Forces is not to allow a sudden attack of the enemy upon our country . . . and to deal the enemy counterblows or even preventive surprise blows of a great destructive force. For this purpose the Soviet Army and Navy have at their disposal all necessary means.

This philosophy made Captain Artamonov doubt the system's validity all the more. "In 1957," he said, "my illusions about internal policies were shattered when Khrushchev praised Marshal Zhukov as a war hero and in three months' time fired him. I asked myself: Do the internal and especially the external policies conform with the interests of my people? The answer was: No!"

This model product of Soviet youth movements and military academies built up his own rationale, after asking himself: "Where is my place, and what am I to do? Should I pursue the 'brilliant' career promised me as a naval officer?

"Should I keep on saying things which I myself do not believe to be true, things which I know are absolute lies? Should I keep on spreading ideologies which I do not share, which I detest? Should I keep on helping the Kremlin to accumulate more and more power, to deceive my people, to dominate my people; and help the Kremlin to perpetrate crimes on an international scale?"

The answer came on a summer day in 1959, when the captain doffed his uniform and escaped from Poland to seek asylum in the West. He had received no encouragement from any agency or individual in the West. Thanks to his commission, he had traveled more widely than most Russians, but, like any defector, he was leaving the known for the unknown. In other cases, defections have been arranged through a Western intelligence agency or anti-Communist group, not always with happy results.

Nikolai Khokhlov is one who has good reason for regretting his defection to the West, since through the bungling of Allied intelligence, he sacrificed his wife and small child, who are today in a Siberian labor camp.

Khokhlov was an artistic whistler in a vaudeville show when he was recruited by the NKVD in 1941. He was a captain at the time of his defection in 1954. He had been sent on one successful and one unsuccessful assassination mission and it was the order to embark on a third such mission which led to his defection. He too was upset by the upheaval in the secret services that followed Beria's demise, even though he was too low in the hierarchy to be affected by it.

In his book *In the Name of Conscience*,* Khokhlov writes that "the life of intelligence officers that summer of 1953 was full of fear and rumors. Nobody knew what the 'investigation' of the Beria case would bring, nor what could happen within twenty-four hours to one service or another, or to one person or another."

Khokhlov's revulsion came when he was ordered to go to West Germany and supervise the assassination of Georgi Okolovich, a leader in the anti-Communist Association of Russian Solidarists, known as NTS (Nesyom Tiranam Smert, or "we bring death to the tyrants"). Khokhlov knew what would happen if he declined the assignment: "It did not mean that the three of us—Yana [his wife], Alyushka [his daughter] and I—would be physically destroyed. Reprisals would be taken probably only against me. I would be transferred to some provincial town, or even arrested and exiled. The family would be informed that I had perished in the performance of some government mission and ordered to keep silent."

Khokhlov's wife, who had remained a devout Russian Orthodox

* Nikolai Khokhlov, *In the Name of Conscience* (New York: David McKay, 1959).

despite warnings that it was unheard of for the wife of a secret police official to be seen in church, told her husband that if he went through with the assassination "our life together will collapse hopelessly and irreparably." As Khokhlov was preparing Okolovich's murder with the help of two paid German assassins, he studied the NTS dossier in the MVD files and became convinced the organization could help solve his dilemma. The power of the anti-Communist group was exaggerated in the files, which described vast networks inside and outside the Soviet Union preying on the Communist state. Khokhlov believed he could go to Okolovich, present his case, turn himself over, and the NTS could subsequently arrange for the escape of his wife and child.

Unlike some other Soviet defectors, Khokhlov had a genuine concern for his family's welfare. It never crossed his mind that by going to Okolovich he might be placing himself in a situation where he would be unable to return to the Soviet Union and unable to get his wife and daughter out. His first meeting with Okolovich in Frankfurt was a bitter disappointment. The NTS leader told him candidly that "it seems to me you are under the influence of a myth, a myth which has apparently been created by the MVD itself. We're not so almighty. On the contrary, technically we are rather weak. Why should I deceive you? What you're asking of us is definitely beyond our power to cope with."

Okolovich said he could put Khokhlov in touch with some "connections, foreigners with a head on their shoulders and a sense of decency." He gave Khokhlov the choice of British, French or American intervention and Khokhlov showed the traditional Soviet suspicion of the British. "Not the British," he said. "My impression is that in the name of the British Empire they could cheat us or even betray us. As to the French, I don't know whether they could handle it."

It was agreed that Okolovich would get in touch with the Americans (in this case the CIC) and report the result to Khokhlov at another meeting. Okolovich said that at the second meeting he would bring Dr. Vladimir Poremsky, the head of NTS, but no one else. When Okolovich went to CIC with the news that he had a captain in the MVD ready to defect, the entire matter was taken out of his hands. It was decided to capture Khokhlov at the next meeting.

By the time Khokhlov realized he was the victim of a double cross it was too late. He slipped into the front seat of the car driven by

Okolovich, near the opera house. In the back seat was Poremsky. The car stopped. "I must apologize," Okolovich said. "Things took a turn so that I've been compelled to invite the Americans already, today. They're here, not far . . . I don't know whether this suits you or not. If it doesn't, say so." Whatever Khokhlov might have said would have been academic, for at that moment a CIC man came up to the car and got in. The car drove off, followed by a CIC car.

Khokhlov was submitted to a harsh interrogation by CIC agents, who at times showed hostility and suspicion for his motives. "I don't understand why you came here," one said. When Khokhlov tried to explain his dissatisfaction with the Soviet regime, another interjected: "Are you trying to say the Russians are discontented with bolshevism?" Okolovich whispered apologetically: "If you had said 'no' on the square, I would have darted forward in the car. You think we wouldn't have gotten away? We would. Poremsky and I planned it that way."

At a second meeting with the CIC, Khokhlov was introduced to one of the "bosses," who was distinguished from the operating agents by his ignorance of the Russian language and his arrogance. He demanded that Khokhlov show him the Austrian "cover" passport he had been given for his mission. At the end of the meeting, he said: "I want to keep your Austrian passport. Give it to me, please." Khokhlov was dumfounded and was about to express his anger when Okolovich intervened and he was allowed to keep it.

The next meeting took place without the presence of Okolovich and Poremsky. As a lesson in how to mismanage an important defection, it is matchless. If the procedure as related by Khokhlov is standard, one can only be amazed that the number of defections remains so high.

It was the same high-ranking CIC officer (named Leonard) who asked Khokhlov to tell his story from the start. When Khokhlov had finished, Leonard took him into another room, closed the door and said, "Look here . . . enough of that nonsense. Now tell me who you really are! Tell me anything you want to—except that you're a captain of Soviet intelligence."

"Well! That's really good," replied Khokhlov. "Who am I then, in your opinion?"

"I don't know. That's why I'm asking. Maybe a journalist. Maybe just a crackpot." Khokhlov was arrested, mugged, fingerprinted, and given the third degree. He was taken to a nearby "high-class concentration camp" where military intelligence kept defectors who were being questioned and filtered.

To make himself believed, Khokhlov had to turn in the two German agents with whom he had been sent on his mission and reveal the hiding place for the murder weapon—an ingenious gun disguised as a cigarette case, concealed in a car battery. His ordeal had just begun, however, as he worked to get his family out of the Soviet Union. Questioning continued, and Khokhlov was considered such big game that British and French intelligence were let in on the operation and two CIA men flew in from Washington to handle the affair. After a month of questioning, Khokhlov was informed that his "political trustworthiness" had been established. Moscow was not alarmed by Khokhlov's failure to carry out his mission, since he kept in touch with his Vienna contact regularly and gave reasons for his inability to reach his target.

After having been double-crossed into the hands of Western intelligence, Khokhlov was double-crossed into sacrificing his family. The higher echelons decided the Khokhlov case should be released to the world as a victory of West over East and that Khokhlov should hold a press conference announcing his defection. Such a conference meant automatic imprisonment for his wife and child. Khokhlov was given the reassurance that the American Ambassador in Moscow himself would drive up to his Moscow residence as the press conference was being broadcast, give his wife a letter explaining what had happened, and offer her asylum in the embassy. After repeated guarantees that the plan had been approved, Khokhlov agreed to face reporters and photographers. Effort was made to keep from him the language of the press release, which he insisted on seeing. It was full of inaccuracies and absurdities ("his wife, an active enemy of the Soviet regime" was one of the phrases that made Khokhlov blanch).

After the much publicized press conference, two days of anxious waiting for news of his family passed, and on the third day a CIA official told him simply, "Nobody went to your family in Moscow. I don't know why. It looks like at the last moment they got cold feet." Khokhlov never found out whether the orders were not sent or whether they were not acted on in Moscow. For him, the uncertainty was over. He had defected, but the price had been high. All the reassuring phrases that his wife was now a symbol for the free world, that there were international organizations which could arrange her rescue, and that the Russians would not dare touch her while there was so much publicity about the case, could not erase the terrible conviction that he was responsible for the imprisonment or death of his wife and child by having entrusted himself into the hands of Western intelligence.

Khokhlov has since his defection been active in the clandestine operations of the NTS and makes his home in Switzerland. He has had no direct news of his family but has heard from others that they are paying for his defection in a Siberian labor camp.

Khokhlov's book was distributed by the NTS through the Soviet Union, but one can only wonder whether the over-all effect was not to discourage potential defectors since it portrays so strikingly the ineptness of Western intelligence in such dealings. On the one hand we have, as defector Igor Gouzenko said in 1957, the fact that "there are Communist-sickened Russian officials and agents who yearn for an opportunity to break for freedom and to carry with them vital documents, evidence of Kremlin-directed espionage against the West, as I did in 1945." On the other, we have Khokhlov's tragic misadventure, an example of coercion, broken promises, and callousness. It would probably not be very reassuring for Mr. Okolovich if Khokhlov were asked what his choice would be if he had it to do all over again.

The Western position toward Eastern defectors is full of contradictions. In Washington, defection is officially praised as an escape to freedom, an excellent solution for the enslaved peoples of the Soviet Union and the satellites. The House Un-American Activities Committees' pamphlet "Patterns of Communist Espionage" suggests a four-point program to make defections more attractive and safer.

1. Defectors should be offered immunity from prosecution for past espionage offenses. Statutes of limitation do not apply to espionage, and a spy or diplomat who has broken espionage laws and wants to defect could be prosecuted as soon as he chooses freedom. A prison term is hardly an inducement to defection.

2. Defectors should not be bribed. Alexander Orlov pointed out that "offering any money to a man of that kind would not be good because people who come to a decision, when they have to break with their country, with their families, with their past which they cherished

for many years, their participation in the civil war, in the Party, and in the revolution, they will not be moved by money. They would feel insulted. They do not want to feel that they are regarded as traitors, and they do not want to be traitors in their own eyes."

Although they should not be bribed, they should be given guarantees that they will be secure financially. When Petrov was offered 5,000 pounds, the Australians insisted it was not a bribe. This is largely a matter of semantics. The defector must be given money at the same time he is told he is not being bribed. As the pamphlet points out, "the Communist-diplomat-MVD agent who chooses freedom here, loses everything except the clothes on his back and such money as he may have in his pockets. He must start life anew in a strange country whose customs and language he often does not know."

3. Defectors should be given permanent residence in the United States. Facing severe immigration laws and quotas, the defector is theoretically in the position of becoming a man without a country as soon as he flees the West. He tells what he knows about Soviet espionage activity and then faces the possibility of expulsion from the United States.

4. Defectors must be promised that their lives will be protected. Men who have lived most of their adult lives with the intimate knowledge of the Soviet secret police's thoroughness, know they are not safe from kidnaping and assassination.

This enthusiasm to abet defection has more than strictly humanitarian motives. The occasional KGB or GRU agent who defects provides Western intelligence with some of its most reliable information and forces the Soviet camp to reappraise many of its intelligence programs and relocate its agents.

But American officials working in West Germany who have gained a firsthand knowledge of the defector question hold the opposite view. They point out that defections are not helpful to the West for three major reasons. First, for every defection that is valuable from an intelligence standpoint, there are several hundred which provide no useful information. Yet all must be relocated and processed. The lot of the average defector is not a happy one. The vast majority of escapes from the Iron Curtain countries are made from Poland and Czechoslovakia into West Germany. Here is what happens to defectors unless they are important regime officials, eligible for preferred treatment:

They are usually picked up by Bavarian border police. Western intelligence services are notified and they are questioned at length by the CIC and by French and British military intelligence. Then Voice of America, Radio Liberation, and Radio Free Europe have a crack at them to learn about trends and changes behind the Iron Curtain. After this brief honeymoon, when the defector is treated with consideration because he has something to deliver, he is relegated to the status of cattle. Having made his application for asylum, he is detained in a "high-class concentration camp," the Federal Collection Point for Foreigners in Zirndorf, near Nürnberg. Since 25 per cent of West Germany's population is made up of refugees, asylum is not given with good grace. The West Germans rather cantankerously feel they have enough of a refugee problem of their own without having to bother with defectors from the Soviet Union and its satellites. Refugees from East Germany are not considered defectors—in the official view, they have simply moved from one part of the country to the other, like moving from Nebraska to California, and are automatically conferred West German citizenship.

The others come under the Geneva Convention, which specifies that political asylum may be granted to those who left their country because of fear of persecution or imprisonment for political reasons. Many left because of human, not political, problems and do not qualify for asylum. Even those who qualify must wait in the camp with their families while their case is processed. In the interim period, they have no legal status. Technically, they cannot work, marry, or travel. The bureaucratic absurdities of defection forbid even that they die until their case is processed.

If asylum is refused or if the defector cannot be absorbed by the West German economy, he must wait in the camp until he has acquired two years' residence in West Germany. Then he can migrate to countries that welcome inexpensive labor. The limbo of the camp (every year West German reformers campaign to put an end to it and every year promises are made for the following year) is a cheerless welcome for those who have "chosen freedom," and it is little wonder that the redefection rate is high. After rotting in a camp for a year or so, the defector sometimes prefers to return to a certain prison term in his country of origin.

This brings us to the second reason why defection is not encouraged by the allies in West Germany. A redefector scores an important propaganda point for the East and brings back intelligence. Upon returning he is put on the radio and describes the horror of the West, the camps, the endless waiting, the poor living conditions. His distaste is genuine, and his words have the weight of sincerity, a rare quality on the regime radio. After he has been squeezed of his propaganda value he is sent to a work camp, to prison, or is relocated in one of the Soviet Union's underdeveloped regions.

The third reason that makes defection a mixed blessing in the Western view is that dissatisfied persons are far more useful if they stay behind the Iron Curtain than if they defect. The most vigorous elements of protest in the Soviet Union and the satellites can build up some form of effective action. They can prompt changes in the regime or plot uprisings.

They can act as chafing agents that create internal difficulties for the regime. All these advantages are lost once they defect. This problem is acute in West Germany, where many responsible leaders view the refugee rate from the East with alarm. They see East Germany becoming a nation of "yes-men" with all the virile elements defecting to the West. Their hopes for a united Germany fade with each new arrival of refugees.

Thus rather than an official defector program for the United States and allied governments, there are contradictory positions in Washington and at the points where defections occur. The ideological pap we are fed at home nourishes us with the belief that defection should be promoted as a kind of individual's right to self-determination. The hard facts of defection, however, are that it creates more problems than it solves, both for the defector and for the country to which he defects. Since there is no working program, those defectors of substance whose passage to the West scores an important point in the Cold War are at the mercy of the human equation. In some cases the defection is successful, thanks to the patience and intelligence of diplomatic or secret service officials, while other cases are bungled through inept handling.

In 1959, Burma, a neutral sensitive about antagonizing the Soviet Union, was the scene of two spectacular defections, one a tragic failure, the other a success. The failure came first but did not deter the second defector.

When Mikhail I. Stryguine was assigned as military attaché to Rangoon in 1957, his wife and fourteen-year-old daughter were not allowed to join him. This is traditionally the first sign that one has come under a cloud. It serves notice on the diplomat that his family may be used as hostages in case he should be planning to defect. The mechanics are not overtly harsh. Stryguine was probably told something like this: "You won't be gone long—your daughter is nearly through her schooling and you want her to finish her Soviet education, so let her stay in school and leave your wife here to look after her."

As Alexander Orlov pointed out, the man who has been sent abroad without his family becomes anxious and ineffective in his work. He knows he is not trusted any more. Two things are possible:

> Either he writes that he cannot work here, he wants to go back, and his work slackens—and it is not the same thing. You cannot send a man to risk his life and at the same time show him he is not trusted. So they send him his wife and they send him his children. Some of them who still have their families in Russia won't exchange the safety and lives of the members of their family for a doubtful future in the United States. They just continue, they return to the MVD in Moscow, and just take a chance that sometime, somehow, not everyone will be killed, not everyone is liquidated.

Colonel Stryguine, a silent, sunken-faced man who resembled Frank Sinatra, was overcome by anxiety. He was a battle-scarred veteran who had joined the Red Army at the age of seventeen and been promoted in combat so that he was a full colonel at the age of thirty-one.

He had spent two years as a liaison officer with American troops in Frankfurt, and the nature of his assignment was enough to make him fall under the suspicion of the MVD. He had seen something of the West, he had liked the open friendliness and willingness to compromise of the American officers he worked with, he matched what he had seen in his Frankfurt tour of duty with what he read in the Soviet military journals and general publications. The seeds of doubt were fertilized by the lack of faith of his superiors. After two years in Rangoon, his wife and daughter were still in Moscow.

Stryguine's inability to concentrate on his work brought him official rebukes. On April 28, he was severely criticized at a Soviet Embassy Communist Party meeting. He admitted his mistakes, and explained that he was the victim of heart trouble and had already asked for a transfer to Moscow. He asked the Party members to pardon him. His hysterical defense annoyed the Soviet Ambassador, who remarked, "He is promising to change his attitude and improve his work, but he is behaving like a woman."

Three hours after the party meeting, Colonel Stryguine, obsessed by doubt and anxiety, tried to take his life. He was found unconscious by a houseboy at his home on Inya Road, and the embassy was notified according to standard procedure. Russian security men rushed to his home and reluctantly allowed him to be taken to the Rangoon Hospital, where his stomach was pumped and he was found to be suffering from an overdose of sleeping tablets.

Security men in civilian dress stood guard over his hospital bed. Stryguine was delirious. When he became coherent the next day, the guards began to berate him and call him a traitor.

"I'm not the traitor," Stryguine screamed, "it's you fellows who are. Why don't you speak English so everyone can hear what you're saying?" He pleaded for help to the nurse who came to take his temperature. "Don't you understand?" he said in anguish. "I have a fourteen-year-old daughter in Russia."

That night, Stryguine made his desperate break for asylum. Taking advantage of a moment of inattention on the part of his two Soviet goons, he leaped out of bed and through the window of his first-floor hospital room. Stumbling across the courtyard, he yelled hoarsely in English: "Help, the Burmese army, help, the Burmese army." He found his way to the guardroom, but the soldiers there were too surprised to take swift action, and by the time they had summoned the officer on duty, Stryguine had been overpowered by his Soviet guards.

Back in the hospital, the guards explained to doctors that Stryguine was the victim of a nervous breakdown. The doctors ignored Stryguine's request that they summon the chief of Burmese intelligence, even though he had given them the telephone number. The Russian guards doped Stryguine into unconsciousness and carried him back to the Soviet Embassy.

There were brief accounts of the wild hospital escape attempt in the Rangoon newspapers the next day, but no action was taken.

Several days later, a commercial Chinese Communist plane out of Kunming landed at Rangoon Airport at 6 A.M. Nine black limousines drove to the plane's landing strip and circled it. Five men stepped out of each of eight cars. Out of the ninth emerged a sagging figure unable to walk, who was loaded into the plane like a duffle bag. Reporters and photographers who tried to approach Stryguine were blocked by the goons.

The operation had been arranged through close collaboration with the Chinese Communists, and Stryguine was accompanied on the plane by the Chinese military attaché. His fate has not been disclosed.

In contrast to Colonel Stryguine's dramatic failure, Aleksandr Yurievich Kasnakheyev successfully defected the following month with calm deliberation and diplomatic propriety. In his case there were no unpleasant airport scenes, no scuffling on hospital grounds, and no jumping out of windows. His was a model defection. According to Arnold Beichman, who covered the story for the *Christian Science Monitor*, the defection had a tremendous effect on Burmese public opinion. "That a Soviet diplomat was willing, after living in Burma for a total of two years, to break with his government is something which is still a major topic of conversation here," he wrote. Kasnakheyev was a junior officer at the embassy and also an intelligence agent.

An editorial in the Rangoon *Guardian* commented:

> What is most damning to the Soviet cause and prestige is that Kasnakheyev is a man in his twenties, and till recently he has known nothing but the best the Soviet system could offer. That he decided to give up all these official favors and turn on his lifetime training at the first contact with various aspects of human freedom in Burma is a blow that Soviet propaganda will not be able to recover from in this part of the world.

Who was this young and privileged member of the Soviet "new class" who defected several months after being given an important promotion and one month after an embassy colleague had illustrated the price of defection's failure?

Kasnakheyev had a privileged background that corresponded to upper middle class in Western society. One might say that "his folks were well off." He could afford the luxury in his youth of dropping out of school and becoming a *"Stilyaga"*—the Soviet version of a Teddy boy or a hipster.

The Stilyagi show their contempt for the regime by adopting eccentric dress, giving up their studies, and imitating their conception of American teen-agers. They imitate America to protest against the dullness and uniformity of Soviet life. Under Stalin any such "decadent" behavior on the part of zoot-suited, duck-tailed youths would have been repressed by mass deportations to labor camps. Under Khrushchev the only protest to this golden youth protected by influential parents are articles in the Soviet press. The magazine *Soviet Culture* wrote:

> The Stilyagi form only a part of disoriented youth, but it is the most spectacular part, and so far authority has been able to do nothing about them, although they parade themselves publicly with all their flaunting eccentricities: the long draped jackets in loud checks of yellow or green, the painted "American tie," patch pocket, padded shoulders, turned-back cuffs, peg-top trousers, and—pride of the whole outfit—yellow or light tan shoes, with thick crepe soles, worn a size too big so that they turn up at the toe. Their haircuts are works of art, and they favor sideburns. They spend their evenings in bars and billiard saloons, or dancing where dancing may be had. You can see them any night in any Soviet hotel that has a dance band; but they prefer dancing to hoarded records of American jazz. And with them are girl Stilyagi, whose skirts are stretched over their figures to the point of indecency. They wear slit skirts. Their lips are painted with bright colors. In the summer they wear sandals. They do their hair in the style of "fashionable" cinema actresses.

And as Edward Crankshaw wrote in *Life Without Stalin*:

> They like calling towns and streets by their revolutionary names: Petrograd for Leningrad, Tsaritsyn for Stalingrad, neither of which are at all well thought of. They call Gorki Street in Moscow "Broadway." "Good evening ladies and gentlemen!" they call out on meeting their friends if there is only one lady and gentleman present. There is no nonsense about "Comrade"; "Hello Mister" is preferred. Kopeks are cents; rubles are dollars.

Kasnakheyev's mother was a nurse who received a doctor's degree in 1941 but never practiced, and his father was an electronics specialist with the Radio Institute of the Academy of Science. He was an only child, another characteristic of the new class. As Kasnakheyev testified before the Senate internal security subcommittee: "I myself have no aquaintances or friends in Moscow who have three or four children. I never saw such a family. I can state that thirty per cent of the city population can afford to have two children; fifty per cent can afford to have only one child; and twenty per cent can't afford to have even one child. . . . About eighty per cent of the Great Russian population is living in cities under the conditions I have already described. The Great Russian population constituted fifty per cent of the population of the Soviet Union in 1919. Nowadays it is estimated to be no more than thirty per cent."

It was halfway through high school that Kasnakheyev made his first open show of discontent with the regime by joining a group of Stilyagi. As he explains it, his group was made up of "Soviet youths ranging from juvenile delinquents and criminals to intellectual nonconformists."

To him, joining the group meant "a basic expression of opposition to the regime, an expression of the disillusionment of youth, of the conditions they live in, disillusionment with the teachings of the party and with the knowledge that they were only slaves of the Communist regime."

Reason prevailed, and after his brief Stilyagi fling, Kasnakheyev went back to school in the fall. The next organization he joined was different in character. The Komsomol is a youth organization which recruits 90 per cent of Soviet students. Kasnakheyev had applied for admission to the Chinese Department of Moscow's Oriental Institute and had to join the Komsomol as a condition of admission. "It was a necessity of life," he said, "as compulsory as being a citizen of the USSR. If you are a citizen you can't avoid being a member of the Komsomol as a youth because it is dangerous otherwise."

Membership involved attendance at meetings and work as a political agitator at election time. "I was given several houses which I had to visit at least once a week, keep a list of voters, give them lectures on the Soviet Government policies and decisions, to assure that all of them came to elections and voted. As a rule the voters were passive and showed no interest in the elections. When they come to the polls, at least fifty per cent of the voters don't know for whom they are going to vote though there is only one candidate."

After three years in the Oriental Institute, Kasnakheyev gained admission on the basis of his excellent scholastic and Komsomol record to the International Relations Institute, Soviet Foreign Office school.

There he studied Burmese and passed a state examination as a specialist in Eastern affairs in 1956. With his knowledge of Burmese, normal Foreign Office practice would have been to send him to Africa or South America, but no, he was sent to Burma in early 1957. By that time he had been married and divorced, and left his former wife and their small son behind.

From March to December, Kasnakheyev completed his area and language training in Rangoon. Back in Moscow, he made a good impression on his Soviet superiors and was sent back to the Rangoon Embassy as information officer.

On the day before his scheduled departure for Rangoon, he was invited for a drink at the Hotel Moscow by two diplomats who had formerly served in Burma. "We are from the political intelligence service," they disclosed, "and we have chosen you to work for us."

"It was not a proposal," Kasnakheyev recalled, "it was an order. There was no way for me to refuse. They just acknowledged that I had been chosen because of my knowledge of Burma and the Burmese language. I was given a paper to sign which was an oath that I would keep dead silence about all secrets given to me; that I would do my best to fulfill obligations assigned to me. I was told that if I revealed willingly or unwillingly any state secrets, I would be ready to meet any sort of punishment, including death. I was ordered not to reveal my participation in work for Soviet intelligence to other members of the embassy, even to the Ambassador himself."

Kasnakheyev arrived in Rangoon with the cover of a low-grade diplomat. He was an information officer, "the smallest, lowest diplomatic rank. It has nothing in common with the press." His covert duties were to translate from Burmese into Russian material obtained by Soviet intelligence; to meet Burmese politicians, obtain information about the political parties, and attempt to recruit Soviet agents among them; to cultivate members of foreign missions in Burma, including American diplomats; and to keep an eye on the behavior and morality of other Soviet citizens.

The bonds between Kasnakheyev and the Soviet regime began to loosen when he realized that his nationality did not make him universally loved by the Burmese. He found it difficult to cultivate them. He was met with suspicion, not admiration.

"Many people openly refused to have anything in common with me," he said. When he traveled to a small river town with three Burmese whose friendship he had won, "we were looking for a house to spend two or three nights. We were admitted to the house of the local river pilot. He returned the next day and asked who I was and where I was from and learned that I was from the Soviet Embassy."

"Take your things and get out," the Burmese told Kasnakheyev. Others speaking among themselves and not knowing he could understand Burmese said, "These Soviet troublemakers, they're all spies."

Kasnakheyev's description of the cool reception the Russians received in Burma and the blunders they made might go under the heading of "The Ugly Russian." He showed that the blunders and half-measures of Americans in the Far East, as described in *The Ugly American,* were easily matched by the Soviets. Some specific criticism in *The Ugly American* to which Kasnakheyev gave the Soviet side:

Americans are sent on assignment without knowing the language: "I was the only member of the staff in the Soviet Embassy in Rangoon that could read and speak the native language. Nobody else in the embassy could do it."

Americans don't fraternize with the natives: "The whole system of the Soviet foreign service is such that it prevents people from fraternizing, making good contacts, and working with the native population. Of course the members of the embassy were ordered to make friends with the local population . . . but at the same time they were instructed not to go so far in these fraternizations as to become intimate with their Burmese contacts. Warnings were constantly repeated not to trust anyone."

Americans can't meet the natives at their own level: "As a rule, [the Soviet Embassy position] implied that the country was poor, nothing was interesting, the people were lazy, poor and superstitious." When a Burmese student in Moscow married a Russian girl, "the Ambassador was enraged and referred to the girl as a prostitute . . . because she had married a native of an inferior nation."

Americans don't try to adjust to the customs of the country, while the Russians win people over with their understanding of and compliance with national custom: "I myself was present at a talk between high Soviet officials and a group of influential monks in Burma in Mandalay, the center for Burmese Buddhists. The Soviet delegation was accompanied by the Soviet Ambassador. When the Soviet officials arrived at the Pagoda, they were invited to sit. On the advice of the Ambassador they refused. They were offered some food, which they also refused to eat because it was not good for Soviet stomachs. A member of the Burmese Parliament later mentioned the incident to the Ambassador, who replied with irritation: 'What for we will be sitting? In Russia, when we want to show our respect to somebody, we stand.' "

Perhaps Kasnakheyev himself was the Russian counterpart of *The Ugly American,* the man who understood the country and tried to counteract the blunders of others. He grew to love Burma and its people. "I spent practically all my free time with my Burmese friends. The working day in the Soviet Embassy in Rangoon was from 8 A.M. to 2 P.M. After that, I usually started a completely new life. I visited my friends. They often invited me to their homes. I adjusted to the Burmese way of life to a considerable degree. Sometimes Burmese told me they forgot I was a foreigner. I hated being in the Soviet Embassy, the whole atmosphere there was tense and unfriendly. My real life started only when I was with my Burmese friends.

"I made many very good and even intimate friends among the Burmese. I believed in them and they were very sympathetic toward me. Several of my friends knew about my plans to defect for five months before I acted. I practically put my life in their hands and they didn't betray me."

Kasnakheyev became known as a "Burmese-lover" in Soviet circles in Rangoon. Professor Garshkov, who had been sent to Burma on a United Nations mission, reported to Moscow that the young diplomat had become infected by capitalist surroundings and was behaving suspiciously. Since Kasnakheyev had an intelligence assignment that made frequent contacts with the Burmese necessary, Moscow disregarded the reports.

After two years, Kasnakheyev realized that the only logical outcome for his growing distaste with everything Soviet and his admiration for the Burmese was defection. He was planning to defect to Burmese authorities, but Colonel Stryguine's mishap made him reconsider. He realized that "my step couldn't be effective if handled by the Burmese Government."

Kasnakheyev handled his defection with intelligence and calm. On June 23, he drove to the center of Rangoon. Instead of going to the American Embassy, he went to the United States Information Service library, which is in a large office building. His visit to the building was unlikely to draw attention. He told the American librarian that he wanted to talk to someone at the embassy, and a political officer came over. The political officer proceeded cautiously, naturally worried about the possibility of a frame-up that would make the United States look bad in neutralist Burma. Kasnakheyev's halting English had a ring of truth, and a meeting was arranged at the same place on the following day.

At a second meeting, Kasnakheyev said he was willing to renounce his Soviet citizenship in return for asylum. He expressed qualms about retaliation against his parents and his estranged wife and two-year-old son. He said, however, that his father's privileged position in the Soviet hierarchy would make him immune from any action, and the fact that he was divorced would probably protect his former wife and child.

Kasnakheyev was then taken for questioning by a CIA officer at an undisclosed place. The CIA officer had to give his approval before the defection could be arranged. Kasnakheyev was to be taken to the American Embassy, but a diplomatic contretemps held up the defection. It happened that the American Ambassador, Walter P. McConaughy, was receiving the Soviet Ambassador, Alexei Shilborin. Mr. Shilborin was paying a farewell call prior to reassignment.

The vision of the Soviet Ambassador exchanging amenities in the American Embassy's reception room while a defecting member of his staff was being whisked through the back door was repugnant to American sense of protocol. American officials kept Kasnakheyev under wraps until they received word that the Soviet Ambassador's visit was over. Then the twenty-seven-year-old defector was given a room on the top floor of the embassy. He stayed there until his departure for Washington five days later.

The American Ambassador immediately notified the Burmese Government of the defection and a formal announcement was made to the press on the evening of June 26. The inevitable press conference was held on the 27th, and Kasnakheyev fluently answered the questions of newsmen in Burmese.

Kasnakheyev spent his time at the embassy writing a statement explaining his defection and a curriculum *vitae*. He was given some clothes, since he had defected with only what he had on, read magazines and newspapers, and was shown the embassy library of films.

A request from the Burmese Foreign Ministry to question the youthful defector was granted by Ambassador McConaughy. On the day of his departure for Washington, he was taken to Rangoon's National Defense College for the questioning, which lasted from noon to 4 P.M. An offer from Burmese Foreign Minister U Chan Htoon Aung to the Soviet Ambassador to see Kasnakheyev before his departure was turned down.

From the National Defense College, Kasnakheyev was driven to Rangoon Airport in an American Embassy limousine under Burmese military escort. On the ramp of the United States Air Force C-130, he posed for photographs in the summer heat. Smiling, he placed his hands on his waist and pointedly looked at a group from the Soviet Embassy that was taking pictures.

The contrast with Colonel Stryguine's forced flight a month earlier was striking. Kasnakheyev walked up the ramp and into the plane alone. There were no goons roughing up photographers, no officials with syringes in their pockets to dope a reluctant traveler into submission, no armed escort to watch over him during the flight.

When we behold such clear examples of a flight from oppression to liberty, how can we explain the reverse? Is it a flight from liberty to oppression? Do defectors from the Soviet Union think straight while defectors from the United States think twisted? The two most intriguing cases involving American defectors occurred at the beginning and at the end of what has been referred to as "a low, dishonest decade."

XII. Flights from Freedom

THE names Noel Field, William H. Martin and Bernon F. Mitchell continue to inspire more questions than answers.

Three dates sum up the saga of Noel Field: In May, 1949, after a distinguished career in the State Department, the League of Nations, and the Office of Strategic Services, he disappeared behind the Iron Curtain with his wife Herta; in October of the same year, he was taken to Budapest, arrested as a *provocateur* and a spy, and jailed with his wife for five years; in November, 1954, upon his release from the AVH (Hungarian secret police) prison, he asked for asylum in Hungary rather than return to the United States.

Field lived through the postwar Hungarian purge trials—his testimony was instrumental in the conviction and execution of Laslo Rajk, one-time Hungarian Foreign Minister. He was a witness to the fabrication and injustice of a trial staged to wipe out anti-Nazi Hungarian leaders he had helped as an OSS agent—the group Moscow referred to as the "Spanish nobility" of the satellites, whose heorism and national pride led to their liquidation.

Field lived through the 1956 Hungarian uprising and emerged from that tragic and bloody period still paying lip service to the satellite government. Described by his many friends as an idealist, a deeply religious man, a noble and selfless individual, he came out of a Hungarian prison to attain heights of hypocrisy and nonsense in a public statement that read in part: "I am grateful to enjoy the advantages of witnessing and experiencing in practice the building of socialism in Hungary. I was dreaming of that in prison and the dream now has been realized."

And he could add with an almost dreamlike naïveté: "I did not turn my back on my own country. I am and always will be an American." That was in late 1956. A year and a half earlier, the State Department, after observing Field's mysterious Odyssey for a number of years, finally decided to strip him of his citizenship and withdraw United States protection from him.

He stands out as an untarnished example of the true believer. While the Hungarian uprising shook the foundations of world Communism, Field, brought up in the liberal American traditions and steeped in the humane aspirations of the League of Nations, displayed a doctrinaire callousness to prove that no event could shake his faith.

His is one of the few cases of a Western Communist who saw at close quarters the flaws in the system and was not revolted. After all the intellectuals who attested to "the God that failed," after the Communists disillusioned by the Nazi-Soviet pact and nauseated by the repression of the Hungarian revolt, here was one who saw the God that failed and kept his faith, who witnessed totalitarian horror and overcame his nausea.

Czeslaw Milosz described the fundamental difference between the hardened Communist who has lived all his life in the system and the squeamish Western Communist who must be fed on illusions to keep believing.

> [The Eastern Communist] has served perhaps three years behind the walls of prisons or slave labor camps. He was not broken; he did not lost his faith. Wherever trees are being chopped down, splinters must fall.
>
> The fact that he, and many of his fellow-inmates, were innocent, proves nothing. It is better to condemn twenty innocent people than to release a single evildoer. To endure this trial successfully is a source of moral strength for him, and of esteem from his comrades in the party. Having learned the workings of the machinery behind the scene, he knows the country of socialism to be a vale of tears, and a gnashing of teeth. Nevertheless, the belief in historical necessity and the vision of the fruits of tomorrow persuade him that the harsh reality of the present—even extended over many years—is unimportant.
>
> [In contrast to this abnegation, the Western Communist] is directed

above all towards the injustices of the system in which he lives. He is filled with a noble indignation against what is going on here and with a longing for what is going on there, in the land from which his companion has come. His companion looks at him benevolently, and his words fulfill all expectation . . . but the moral indignation and enthusiasm of the other are for him unattainable luxuries in the sphere of moral comfort. If the other knew, if he had undergone the same trials, what would his faith be like?

Experience has proven that those from the West cannot hold up nervously under the strain of a protracted stay in the center. The dose is too strong for them. They may be extremely useful as missionaries among the pagans, or when their countries are invaded by liberating armies . . . but the Western Communist needs a vision of a golden age that is already being realized on earth.*

Noel Field is one of the few who made the transition from the Western to the Eastern Communist. He could say, as in the poem by Ezra Pound: "We who have gone beyond our dreams of living— we have passed through."

For years, the Field case was one of the great mysteries of the Cold War. In 1949, Noel Field went to Czechoslovakia where he had been promised a teaching job. He had been out of work for two years after being relieved of his duties with the Unitarian Service Committee. He registered at Prague's Palace Hotel. On the night of May 12, he walked out of his room and vanished. The following day a mysterious wire arrived at the hotel from Vienna explaining that someone would drop by to pick up his bags and pay his bill. His wife Herta, who was in Geneva, went looking for him. She too disappeared. His brother Herman was also engulfed by the Iron Curtain when he went to search for the missing couple. There were strong family ties in the Field family, and Noel's sister, Dr. Elsie Field Doob, left her husband and her practice in Urbana, Illinois, to comb Europe for traces of her two brothers and her sister-in-law. She found nothing in Western Europe and was persuaded not to go behind the Iron Curtain. When she returned to the United States she was ruled heir to Field's estate, which amounted to about $60,000.

The missing Fields were still among the living. They were in Hungarian and Polish prisons for five and a half years. All three were released by the Imre Nagy government in 1954, but only Herman

* *Loc. cit.*

asked to go home. He had lost thirty pounds, had a glazed look and a haggard body.

Noel and Herta moved from prison to a spacious villa in Budapest's suburban Gellert Hill, the scene of some of the bloodiest fighting during the Hungarian revolt. There they were photographed by the local information office to show that time spent in prison had not been too wearing. The photograph shows a tall, aristocratic-looking man, with long and wavy gray hair and a Barrymore profile, looking into the horizon. He is dressed with the studied neglect that indicates true elegance. His eyes are out of focus and probably filled with the visions that come with a perpetual state of grace. His wife's eyes are directed at him, in sharp focus. Her hair is in a bun, she is wearing an Eton collar and a tie and looks like one of the resident mistresses in the German movie *Mädchen in Uniform*.

Noel Field's public statements on his release from prison dissipated the mystery of his whereabouts but not the mystery of his motives. In June, 1957, in a 900-word statement broadcast by Radio Budapest, he denounced the United Nations report on Hungary as "slanderous falsehoods interspersed at best with misleading half-truth." He defended Communist Hungary's refusal to admit the U.N. investigating committee, rejoiced in the Communist triumph over the freedom fighters, and predicted that the whole world would eventually go Communist.

"Neither four hundred nor four thousand pages of dubious testimony by one hundred times the number of defectors," he said, "can hamper the forward march of Hungary and other countries of the Socialist camp along the highroad toward Communism, which all other nations will ultimately follow in their own manner and their own good time."

The beginning of the road to Communism for Noel Field was London, where he was born in 1904, son of a Brooklyn-born zoologist. Noel grew up in Zurich, where his father published a scientific magazine. He was the eldest of three children. He went to the United States for the first time in 1922 to matriculate at Harvard, and was graduated in three years *cum laude*. On the traditional European tour that followed graduation, Field met a German girl, Herta Katherina Vieser, and brought her back to the United States as his wife.

Field entered the foreign service in 1926 and served there ten years. When he quit in 1936, he was chief of the State Department's Division of European Affairs. One of his good State Department friends was Laurence Duggan. Field was upset when Duggan died mysteriously (he jumped or was pushed out of a window) in the middle of an investigation of his pro-Communist leanings. "It's really a shame," he said. "God knows people are being put to death."

Another Washington friend was Hede Massing, confessed recruiting agent for a Soviet apparat and first wife of East German Communist Gerhart Eisler. In her book *This Deception* she recalls that she met the Fields in 1934. Mrs. Massing's husband Paul had published his experiences in a German concentration camp in the Communist magazine *New Masses,* and the Fields wanted to meet the author.

Mrs. Massing recognized in Field a liberal of the thirties toying with Marxism. She was told by her superiors to develop Field as a possible agent and they formed "an intensive relationship from the very start. It became so intimate and genuine on both sides that I did not always know where 'business' ended and friendship began . . . gradually I became almost a member of the family and stayed at their house during my visits to Washington." Field's growing pro-Communism had a juvenile and romantic quality. One night he took Mrs. Massing to the Lincoln Memorial. He climbed the steps, stood under Lincoln's contemplative bronze face, and sang the Communist hymn, the Internationale, in Russian. Following this musical statement of faith, Mrs. Massing appealed to Field to help Russia with information and documents. Field was reluctant, not because he was squeamish about betraying his country, but because like a popular debutante at a coming-out party, he was being fought over by several apparats. Field told Mrs. Massing that he felt the other apparat would be more "congenial."

At a dinner at the Field's home, Mrs. Massing and her rival squabbled over who would get Field. Mrs. Massing pulled rank and said her Soviet superior wanted Field in her apparat. Not long after joining Mrs. Massing's group, Field left the State Department for the League of Nations. The League corresponded to his idealized vision of saving mankind, it preserved him from the difficult decision of turning over classified information to Russia, and it allowed him to believe that he would be more useful to the Party in the long run.

Since he had worked for three years on the State Department's League of Nations desk, Field had no trouble obtaining work with the

League in Geneva. He remained there until the League was dissolved in 1940, serving in the disarmament section and on a mission to assist the evacuation of foreign troops from Spain in 1938 and 1939.

Sources agree that upon reaching Geneva, Field became a part of a vast apparat directed by General Walter Krivitsky, chief of Soviet military intelligence for Western Europe. Krivitsky was working under the cover of a relief organization called the Centrale Sanitaire Suisse, which sent food packages to underprivileged families. He defected to the West in 1939 and was brought to Washington to testify before American authorities. He was shot to death in his hotel room by members of the Spetsburo (terrorist) branch of the Soviet secret police.

Isaac Don Levine, an authority on Soviet affairs, wrote that Krivitsky told him in 1939 that Noel Field was one of his Geneva sources. Whittaker Chambers wrote in *Witness* that "I had wondered why the parallel apparatus would let Noel Field leave the State Department. It was Gen. Krivitsky who first told me that Noel Field had left the State Department on the order from his apparatus to work for Krivitsky."

When the Fields went to Spain in 1938 to help in the evacuation of foreign troops, their lives became linked with that of Erica Glaser, a young German-Jewish girl they befriended and who after Noel Field's defection went behind the Iron Curtain looking for him. She was arrested, condemned to die, sent to the notorious Vorkuta camp in Siberia, and finally reprieved in 1955.

Dr. Glaser, Erica's father, was a Pomeranian Jew who fled Germany for Spain when the Nazis began their persecutions in the thirties. When the Spanish civil war broke out, the Glasers could not go home and Dr. Glaser was recruited by a Loyalist medical unit. When the Loyalist units were purged of foreigners, he was transferred to a Communist-controlled International Brigade, where he served until the end of the war in 1939. Erica, sixteen at the time, took a nursing course and served in Loyalist hospitals, as did her mother.

Noel Field visited the hospital where Dr. Glaser was working and they continued to meet socially. Erica was suffering from typhoid fever at the time and did not meet the Fields. She was separated from her family, which was evacuated northward with other foreigners and temporarily resettled in a Pyrenees border town. When she was well, Erica set out to find her parents. At the border village, a letter from the Fields was waiting for her. The Fields, who were childless, wanted to adopt Erica sight unseen and take her to the United States.

Erica found her parents, who were reluctant to let her go, in a filthy, crowded refugee camp. They were able to make their way to Paris thanks to the Fields. Erica was too old for adoption, but she joined the Fields in Geneva and was enrolled at a girls' school there. Her French was too weak to keep up and she moved to Zurich, where she lived in a roominghouse and studied at a German-language school. In 1941, Field, who had found work as European director of the Unitarian Service Committee, went to unoccupied France and regularly sent Erica money.

Erica had been prepared to hate the Fields before she met them, simply because he was a member of the Disarmament Commission, which she blamed for her parents' misfortunes. "I hated her," she added, "because for me she was a society lady visiting poor Spaniards, and being so sorry about it. You know, the charity type."

When she joined them in Geneva, "I didn't like being shown around like a special horse or something. Therefore, I didn't like the Fields. But I came to like them very much when I got to know them. They were both very, very nice to me, and very friendly. Herta had a very good heart, and was very kind. As for Noel, I always felt everthing he did or said, he thought about for at least a day beforehand. You know, he couldn't make up his mind very quickly. He was not the impulsive type at all."

Erica noticed that although Mrs. Field admired and loved her husband very much, she often seemed the dominant partner. She was more practical, also more impulsive than her husband, who seemed above all else "a humanitarian, an idealist in every sense of the word."

It was through the Fields that Erica became a Communist and a secret agent. In 1940, Noel Field introduced her to a German Communist and she agreed to take part in some minor missions in Switzerland. Twice during the war she was held by Swiss police investigating Communist circles and twice she was released. In 1942, the Fields returned from the South of France to Geneva and Erica came to study at the University of Geneva. All three lived in an all-female boardinghouse where Noel Field was allowed to stay by special arrangement.

In the war years, Field had a multi-faceted role in which he acted as an OSS agent and used his position with the Unitarians to help his

Communist friends. Allen Dulles has confirmed that Field worked as a money courier and liaison man between the OSS and Communist groups that were being used for resistance work. Field, with his long-time residence in Switzerland and his Communist contacts, was an invaluable agent in the marriage of convenience between American intelligence and Communist groups. While the Fields were in southern France, Dulles used him to forward about $10,000 to French resistance groups.

In Geneva, Field continued to receive reports from his Communist contacts on resistance in France. "I remember that Field got illegal reports from France into Switzerland," Erica recalled. "They were brought over by all sorts of contact people, some people completely unknown, who did this border work. We never knew their names. We didn't even know who they were in normal life; all this was written up on very thin paper. And I read some of it. Noel Field told me that he was going to take these things up to Allen Dulles. He also showed them to Communists."

Field recruited Erica in the OSS operations. She worked with two German Communists along a stretch of Franco-Swiss border to smuggle Germans out of France, put them on trains, and see that they were fed. The smuggling operation was run jointly by the German Communist Party and the OSS and some of those smuggled out were OSS personnel.

Field was so involved with OSS operations that Soviet dossiers later made public described him as a "possible American spy who cultivates Communist contacts." Field's final action as an OSS agent was a meeting with Dulles in Berne in 1945, where he proposed a plan for the reorganization of Germany. Field suggested the creation of a "West German Committee" that would be made up of anti-Fascist resistance leaders. He saw the committee as eventually becoming Germany's reconstruction government with American backing. Dulles sent Field to Paris to expose his plan to Arthur M. Schlesinger, who was then in the OSS. Schlesinger saw through the Communist-sponsored plan. "Field's project involved the extension to Western Europe of the operations of the Moscow-controlled Free Germany Committee," he later wrote. "In my judgment, Field acted like a Communist agent."

Active though he was as a secret agent during the war, Field also got a lot of mileage out of the Unitarians. He supervised rescue operations through Spain and Portgual under Unitarian auspices. He filled the relief offices with Communist personnel, and many of the refugees who made their way to the United States subscribed to another faith than Unitarianism.

Leo Bauer, a well-known German Communist who operated in Switzerland during the war, would go to Field and say, "Now look, so-and-so and such-and-such should be helped. What can you do for them?" This was a period when the Gestapo was asking the Swiss to extradite German Communists, and Bauer was anxious to get the leaders to safety in the United States and Mexico. Bauer in return helped Field with money transfers from Switzerland to France. Bauer served as adviser to Field on refugees most deserving of assistance from the Unitarian Service Committee. As it happened, according to Erica, Field "helped mainly Communists . . . he liked to help Communists because they were most of the political cases."

Field overstepped himself with his kindly and politically myopic employers in backing his secretary, Herta Tempi, an open Communist Party member. He defended her when the Unitarians questioned the wisdom of her employment in the Service Committee.

Another dispute took place between Field and the Unitarians when Field expressed in a letter his "consternation" that the USC was planning to work with the Ukrainian American Relief Committee. Field claimed the Ukrainians "represented in the public mind a force little less reactionary than Nazism itself . . . they have been the center of anti-Soviet agitation."

The Unitarians' reputation would be ruined if they co-operated with the Ukrainians, Field said; "all our friends will turn away from us in disgust." Field suggested that instead, the USC should give additional funds to train Yugoslav and Polish refugees so they could go back and rebuild their countries. Field added that he was opposed to helping Lithuanian refugees (who were strongly anti-Communist).

In 1946, the Unitarian Central Committee in Boston began to receive information that Field was playing favorites with Communists. Dr. Raymond Bragg, a prominent Unitarian minister, went on a fact-finding trip to Europe where he "was able to get no information that Field was a Communist or following the Communist Party line. There was evidence that many of the people who were being helped were Communists, but you could say that was understandable since they were the ones who needed the most help. They were the poorer people and also probably had been the most active against the collaborationists."

Following the inconclusive Bragg trip, a special committee went to Europe and told Field the rumors that were being spread about his work. Field denied their foundation and defended his wartime and postwar refugee work. He put on a good show and impressed the committee members, who nonetheless decided that "he had to go; his continued employment was detrimental to the operations of the Service Committee and detrimental to the high respect and reputation of the Unitarian denomination."

Field and his wife returned to New York and he started job hunting, writing his friend Alger Hiss for help. Field had gone to Hiss before for help in finding work. In 1940, before Field landed the Unitarian job, Hiss recommended him for a post as assistant to Francis B. Sayre, then United States High Commissioner to the Philippines. Hiss was careful to point out in his letter of recommendation that Field's name had been mentioned by J. B. Matthews in testimony before the Dies committee. The pertinent testimony was as follows:

> Q. Did you know he [Field] was a member of the Communist Party?
> A. I knew inasmuch as he freely discussed the matter with me on many occasions during my year of residence here [Washington, 1928]. I had known him before he became a member of the staff of the State Department, when he was engaged in radical activities as a student in Boston in the early postwar years.

Hiss commented on the basis of a State Department investigation of Field at the time: "It seems clear that Mr. Matthews' charges are irresponsible and without foundation in fact." Hiss added that Field was "obviously a talented man, is an expert draftsman, and has a brilliant and flexible mind." Despite the endorsements, Field did not get the job in the Philippines, and this time also, Hiss failed to find work for his friend.

The Fields spent two aimless years in New York, he looking for work in a desultory fashion, she taking odd jobs to keep the family ledger in the black. It was apparently during those two years that Field, chafing over what he imagined to be the injustices of a reactionary society, formed the plan of living in an Iron Curtain country, where he would be better appreciated. He was in his mid-forties, had served in many fields of government work, and now found himself come full circle—without a job, without prospects, and discouraged by life in postwar America.

In April, 1949, he was sent by a front group as an observer to a Communist World Peace Congress in Paris. There he ran into Erica Glaser again, who had become Erica Wallach through her marriage to an American soldier. Because of her Communist past (she had broken with the Party after the war) the couple was not allowed to enter the United States, and Erica worked irregularly while her husband studied on the G.I. Bill. Mrs. Wallach was at the Congress writing résumés of speeches and translating them into German.

She saw a great deal of Field, who told her he was going to Prague to try for a teaching job there. He left in May and his wife went to Geneva until he could summon her. Erica heard a few days later from Field, who said everything was fine in Prague. Although the Fields' departure from the United States alarmed no one at the time, it is believed that the timing was a result of the Hiss case.

After Whittaker Chambers' sensational revelations, Hiss appeared before a Federal Grand Jury in 1948 and denied he had ever given Chambers original State Department documents. To anyone deeply involved in the Hiss case, the grand jury appearance was a warning buzzer. Andrew Marton, an Associated Press reporter in Hungary who met Field during his Budapest trial, indicated Field's involvement in the Hiss case before a Senate subcommittee: "I don't think there is any doubt why he [Noel Field] didn't come back," Marton said. "He knew perfectly well that he was involved in the Hiss case . . . that is what he said. It was obvious why he preferred to remain in Hungary."

The Hiss case seems an undeniable factor in Field's defection, though Field did not realize at the time that he was in effect making a choice between an American and a Hungarian prison. Noel's disappearance in Prague started the chain reaction of vanishing Fields. His brother Herman went looking for him and vanished between Prague and Warsaw. Mrs. Field, still in Geneva, went to the United States consul in Prague. A few days later she disappeared.

In the spring of 1950, Erica Glaser Wallach went looking for the Fields out of a sense of devotion and obligation. She made her way to Berlin where she sought out one of her wartime German Communist contacts who had known Field well. The man was in East Berlin and she went to find him there, taking a terrible risk since she had left the Party herself and was on the blacklist. As she tells the story, she walked into the Communist Party building in East Berlin and was told her man was in Thuringia. She was allowed to leave the building "and I was already figuring out in my mind, I thought, My God, I made it. I'm going to get out." She was thirsty and stopped to get a lemonade at a street stand. She took the first sip "when I heard steps behind me. And then I knew that was the end. I didn't even turn around. And after a second, somebody just put a hand on my shoulder and said 'Criminal Police. Would you please come around the corner with me?'"

Mrs. Wallach's devotion to her friends cost five years of her life. She was held in the East Berlin Schumann Strasse Prison for eight months; was transferred to the Russian-policed Karlshorst Prison for four months; went from there to the Hohen Schoenhausen Prison until September 1952; then back to Karlshorst; in December she was taken to the Liechtenberg Prison in Germany, tried, convicted of espionage, and sentenced to death. Sent to Moscow for execution, she was held in a death cell for six months. After Stalin's death her sentence was commuted to fifteen years in the Vorkuta labor camp in far eastern Siberia. Until December, 1954, she worked on railroad construction at Vorkuta; was sent to Abes, a camp near Vorkuta, for several months; then to Lubyanka political prison in Moscow; then back to Abes. In 1955, without warning, she was told her case was under revision and several weeks later she was freed. She went back to West Germany in October, 1955, and was able to join her husband in the United States. Wallach had not heard from his wife until she arrived at Vorkuta, where the penal system allows the inmates to write their families.

Mrs. Wallach had shown unusual courage throughout her confinement. She refused to admit any espionage activity even though it cost her months of solitary confinement, and she had the temerity to plead guilty "with pleasure" to the charge of "defamation against the Soviet Union and propaganda in favor of the United States of America."

For two years, Mrs. Wallach resisted the rich repertoire of physical and mental tortures designed to prompt a false confession, and she probably owes her release to her remarkable fortitude.

While Mrs. Wallach was undergoing solitary confinement, exposure to cold, threats, uncertainty, undernourishment, alternating periods of kindness and harshness, and the isolation that breeds despair, Noel Field was receiving privileged treatment in his Budapest prison.

Field had picked an unfortunate time to defect. The Tito split in Yugoslavia had brought swift repression in other satellite countries. It happened that Field knew some of those being purged in Hungary and the Communists saw his potential value as a co-operative witness and shanghaied him in Prague.

Field's part in the Budapest trials was described by Joseph Swiatlo, who was deputy chief of the Polish Security Service when he defected in 1953. Swiatlo said in testimony before a House committee that Field followed the usual pattern of forced witnesses: "The arrested man agrees to testify to what he was told by the officer. If he refuses he will never even appear at the trial as a witness. His testimony nevertheless will be procured and will be given during the trial as written by him, although he didn't write it.

"For instance, I spoke to Field—Noel Field—an American citizen who was arrested in Budapest. In the trial of Rajk, a prominent Communist leader, it was stated during the trial that Noel Field confessed that he himself was an American agent, and that Rajk was his agent, his informer; that Rajk worked for Noel Field. Well, Field personally told me, first, he was never an agent of the American Government; and secondly, he learned for the first time that he was an agent of the American Government in prison from the officer who was conducting his investigation. This is why Field did not appear at Rajk's trial—he wouldn't confess. This is why his written testimonies were procured, but he didn't appear himself."

Andrew Marton agreed in his testimony that "Field first refused to co-operate, but he was broken in no time in the usual way, and later, when he learned in prison that the number three man in the Rajk case had been sentenced to death on the grounds of his testimony, he wanted to withdraw his testimony but it was too late. The man was hanged."

Field's willingness to serve his captors as a "good Communist" had a bearing on his sentence. In addition, accounts of the purge trials in the press had mentioned Field, and the Western world learned of his whereabouts after nearly a year's silence. In 1952, Field did a repeat performance in the trial of Rudolph Slansky in Czechoslovakia.

In 1954, Noel, Herta, and Herman Field were released with an official announcement that "the charges against them have not been vindicated."

Field and his wife disdained an indemnity and Field pointedly wrote a statement that appeared in the Hungarian Communist newspaper *Szabad Nep*. There he declared that "although I have been one of many victims of false accusations and illegal persecutions, I remain sympathetic to Socialism. I am not sorry for my decision to stay and work in this country where I suffered so much and where I got such sincere and generous amends." The statement was published not long before the Hungarian uprising. After Soviet troops had quelled the uprising with wholesale slaughter, Field cropped up again in print. For the first time since his defection, he had agreed to see Western newsmen. His message for them was that he was convinced the puppet government of Janos Kadar had "saved Hungary from a white terror and was acting in the people's interest." The words did not catch in his mouth. He spoke them with the fervent clarity of a humanitarian idealist of thirty years' standing.

William H. Martin and Bernon F. Mitchell represent a new generation of defectors. Field was a civil servant, they were scientists. Field was steeped in Marxism, they were admittedly apolitical (Mitchell flunked courses in the history of civilization at two different colleges). Field defected partly because he was implicated in an espionage case (Alger Hiss) and partly because he felt he would be received like a hero behind the Iron Curtain. Martin and Mitchell were under no pressure to flee and knew next to nothing about the Soviet Union. Fields' was essentially a political defection that could be explained up to a point, theirs was a neurotic defection that defied analysis.

IT CAN HAPPEN HERE, the headlines read when the two junior mathematicians for the National Security Agency turned up in Moscow in August, 1960. How was it that these two men, with backgrounds as all-American as "apple pie and Momism" (in the words of a magazine), and who had been stamped "approved" for the most sensitive kind of government work, could appear suddenly at a Moscow press conference and give the detailed organizational setup and the function of an agency so secret that its recruiting pamphlet describes it only as dealing with "communications"?

Martin and Mitchell displayed the puritanical disenchantment of militants who suddenly learn that their team has been fighting dirty. "The United States Government secretly manipulates money and military supplies to bring about the overthrow of unfriendly governments," they revealed to the world. "It pays code clerks of friendly embassies to get information to break their codes. The National Security Agency gathers communications intelligence from almost all nations of the world, friendly and unfriendly, for use by the Government."

The two young men (Mitchell was thirty-one and Martin twenty-nine at the time of their defection) gave the impression that they had been outraged by the immoral practices of United States intelligence. Like a husband who thought his wife above suspicion only to discover her infidelities, they had decided that divorce was the only solution. Such a fragile sense of the realities of life made the defection seem slightly unreal.

The Government itself had trouble believing in it. The two cipher experts, close friends since the Navy, had gone to Mexico on a two-week vacation that began June 25. They told NSA security officers that they were driving to the West Coast and then violated the rule requiring that employees clear trips outside the United States. They bought one-way plane tickets to Mexico City. They checked into a second-class hotel under assumed names and changed hotels the next day. From Mexico they flew to Cuba and stayed in Havana for four days, waiting for their Communist contact. On July 4, it is believed, they were picked up by a Soviet trawler refueling in Havana, which carried them to a Soviet harbor.

The investigation that followed revealed that in late 1959 they had made an initial unauthorized trip to Cuba and Mexico, indicating that their defection may have been planned long in advance.

The official reaction was shock, so that no word of the defection was given to the press until more than a month after it had occurred. It was on August 5 that the nation learned from the Defense Department that "two junior mathematicians of the National Security Agency appear to have gone behind the Iron Curtain."

The official announcements were deliberately misleading. The Pentagon said the information available to the two in their work "could in no way be prejudicial to the security of the United States communications. They had no access to classified documents about American weapons and defense plans."

Like dust swept under a carpet, the case was covered up and even today many details are being kept secret. While the public was told the defection was nothing to worry about, Pentagon sources said privately that the Martin and Mitchell defection was as staggering in its implications to intelligence as Pearl Harbor was to the military. They compared the defection to Klaus Fuchs' delivery to the Russians of atom bomb secrets.

In the NSA itself, the 10,000 employees (figures graciously supplied by Martin and Mitchell) were put on double shifts and worked around the clock to repair the damage the mathematicians had done. For their work had been deciphering Soviet codes and the codes of allied nations, which the NSA systematically breaks. And when the story came out in the September 6 Moscow press conference, cryptographers all over the world began devising new codes to test the mettle of the NSA code breakers. For some time the NSA was said to be "working blind" as its computers strove to keep up with the new ciphers that were pouring into their monitors.

But perhaps more important than the front-row seats the defectors had given the Russians on the vast and vital code-breaking agency, there was the human problem. What were the defectors' motives?

The first and most obvious answer was their homosexuality. The public was shocked to learn that practicing homosexuals could run the gantlet of security clearance without having their perversion discovered.

In this sense, the case closely paralleled the defection of British diplomats Guy Burgess and Donald Maclean, who were known to have carried on a homosexual relationship since their student days at Cambridge.

Martin and Mitchell's homosexuality was seized upon with relish in certain quarters as the all-embracing answer to the defection. Congressional investigations looked into the laxity of NSA security, which allowed "perverts" to infiltrate its sacrosanct ranks. Rep. Francis E. Walter, chairman of the House Committee on Un-American Activities, said his committee's investigation had shown that "additional homosexuals are employed at NSA, that the agency has dismissed a number of employees since our investigation began, and that some security regulations have not been strictly observed at the supersecret NSA."

According to NSA employees, Martin and Mitchell's homosexuality was an open secret in their circle of acquaintances. When their presence in Moscow became known, the unsavory joke circulating in Fort Meade was that "they didn't defect. They went on their honeymoon."

In Mitchell's case, records of his security clearance interviews show that he admitted "abnormal sex practices at the age of nineteen" (this euphemism refers to experiments with chickens and cats). It was felt that juvenile experiments that were not repeated and that were freely admitted were not sufficient grounds to bar Mitchell from employment at NSA. Since the rest of his clearance, including a lie-detector test, showed no signs of aberration or instability, his deviation was written off as a youthful error. What did not come out in the clearance tests was that neither Martin nor Mitchell had shown an interest in women in their youth. When Mitchell was in high school in his home town of Eureka, California, he was considered "backward with girls"—he never went to dances or on dates, and at an age where youths spend more evenings in the back seat of a car than at home with books, his main interest was still his chemistry set. In college and in the Navy, he was also known for his indifference to the opposite sex. It was only after his employment at NSA and during a year when Martin was away on a fellowship for graduate work at the University of Illinois that he was known to have had an affair, a brief liaison with a married woman. The woman finally decided to return to her husband, a government worker posted in Greece, and Mitchell was upset by the decision. He told his parents he was in love and complained to his mother about the unhappy end of the affair.

Martin was remembered in his home town of Ellensburg, Washington, as a youth whose arrogance and fastidious style of dress contrasted with his acute shyness with girls. When he was at NSA, however, he bragged about women he picked up in Washington bars, and once complained in a way that showed he was pleased with himself that he had been rolled by a B-girl.

Thus neither man appears to have been exclusively homosexual. Yet the investigation that followed their defection unearthed examples of their own relationship. In a motel in Laurel, Maryland, where Martin lived after returning from his graduate fellowship, a number of incriminating photographs were found. Mitchell was a physical culture faddist who worked out with bar bells and was proud of his athletic physique. Many photographs show him in the muscle-flexed contortions made popular by magazines for "men," hunched like a discus thrower to show his back muscles or flexing his biceps in the "Atlas-holding-up-the-world" position. Other pictures apparently taken as delayed action shots by the amateur photographers showed them together and separately in nude poses.

A more sophisticated notion of the implications of homosexuality on defection was provided by Dr. Clarence Schilt, a Bethesda, Maryland, psychiatrist who unwittingly became one of the authorities on the defection. In June, 1960, a man Dr. Schilt had treated previously for minor physical ailments came to his office at the Silver Springs Medical Center and said he needed psychiatric treatment. The man was Mitchell, and Dr. Schilt knew him as an employee of the National Security Agency.

Mitchell said he did not want to be treated as a patient but that he wished to discuss certain theories he had concerning sex, theories he considered so important he felt they should be submitted to a psychiatric journal. Dr. Schilt agreed to see Mitchell on that basis and there followed three one-hour interviews.

Dr. Schilt did not realize it at the time, but the meetings had a Faustian quality. Mitchell was contemplating defection and wanted to test his ideas and have them confronted. He chose Dr. Schilt for a dialogue where the real but concealed issue was not Mitchell's need for psychiatric care but his decision to defect. From the first meeting, Mitchell showed obvious signs of emotional strain. He sought assurances that the office was not bugged and that the conversations would not be taped.

He began by discussing his own life, and showed that he was versed in psychiatric terminology and literature. He thought of himself as a superior being above man-made laws, who had created his own order and his own set of principles. One way of affirming this superiority, he said, was his great sexual freedom and his absence of guilt feelings.

He had affairs with men and women, he said, and felt equally at ease in both cases. He mentioned no specific involvements and Martin's name never came up. But he made it clear that his bisexual escapades were freely and lucidly undertaken.

He was knowledgeable about the origins of his homosexuality. He explained that his mother was too protective and his father, a successful trial lawyer, was too domineering. He was never close to his father, he said, and disliked the values he represented. He did not want to emulate his father and was jealous of his two brothers, who were much closer to their parents. He was at the same time envious and contemptuous of his family. He mocked their religious convictions and upset his strongly Episcopalian parents by calling himself an agnostic. He argued the existence of God with Dr. Schilt and held that if there were a God he would not allow the world's present chaos. He did not, however, discuss politics or any specific events. At his third and final session with Dr. Schilt, he said mysteriously: "Maybe I'll see you again and maybe I won't." Less than a month later he was en route to the Soviet Union.

Viewing the defection with the hindsight of his conversations with Mitchell, Dr. Schilt is convinced that the NSA employees followed the classic homosexual pattern. The usual reason given for the danger of homosexuals in government work is that their perversion makes them vulnerable to blackmail. They might give away government secrets under threat of exposure. Dr. Schilt, however, sees this risk as far less important than the homosexual's own nature. Citing Mitchell as an example, Dr. Schilt points to the pattern of absence of guilt feelings and the sense of belonging to a higher order of mankind above authority and morality.

"The danger of the homosexual in government work," he explains, "is that he has a blunted moral sense—there is a defect in his conscience. He does not choose to be cured. He feels himself to be a member of a third and misunderstood sex. To men like this, the loyalty oath means nothing. They feel that law is a matter of convenience. Mitchell's intellectual arrogance was evident in that he felt no need to justify his attitude. Justification of course would have implied that he was wrong or capable of being wrong."

Running parallel to the homosexual's disdain for the established order is the pattern of rebellion against authority which is always a repetition of rebellion against family. This too was illustrated by Mitchell, who admitted his resentment toward his father. (When his father was questioned about the defection, he described his son as a brilliant but politically naïve scientist "who had no knowledge whatever of political things. That sort of thing was not his dish. He is qualified as a mathematician but not as a political observer.")

"Mitchell didn't want to grow up to be like Dad," Dr. Schilt says.

"He didn't admire Dad. So he turned to his mother. The pattern started in youth. Mitchell was the child who's called a sissie, who plays with dolls. He consciously avoided taking part in activities where his brothers excelled. [One was a college football star who became a stockbroker, the other was active in college dramatics and the debating team and became a member of his father's law firm.] Mitchell certainly took satisfaction in the disgrace he caused his family. In this sense his defection was a form of suicide. Suicide is a way of getting even, of punishing those around us by the embarrassment and anguish of our death."

"The suicide basically is saying: See what you've forced me to do. In a less drastic but no less final way, Mitchell was saying the same thing when he defected. His parents were branded as the parents of a traitor. His behavior was bound to reflect on them and on the way he was brought up. They automatically shared his guilt. The homosexual by his withdrawal from society is striving for the same effect."

The silver thread that ran from Mitchell to his mother led in Dr. Schilt's view from homosexuality to defection. Dr. Schilt added that nothing in Mitchell's appearance gave away his homosexuality. He was not effeminate. His stride was athletic (he practiced swimming and tennis and had daily bouts with the bar bells), he was tall and lean, with dark hair and regular features. He wore glasses, and his expression ranged from deference to disdain to petulance. Dr. Schilt did not consider Mitchell's problems unique. At the same time he was treating half a dozen government workers, including a Marine sergeant, for homosexuality. He saw no need to report his conversations with Mitchell to the security people.

Martin's homosexuality seems to have been less constant. The announcement of his marriage to a Soviet girl was made indirectly at the end of a press conference the two gave in Moscow in December, 1960. A brief glimpse into Martin's new-found domestic bliss was given when he stated: "My wife is also going to do scientific work. She is a wonderful Soviet girl, an excellent housekeeper, and I am very happy with her." One of Martin's bitterest complaints about the American way of life, according to his friends, was the American woman's lack of femininity and grace. It took him only three months to find a mate in the Soviet Union and make his application at the brand-new palace of weddings.

Next to the pair's homosexuality, it was their intelligence that puzzled investigators. Both were highly regarded junior mathematicians in the $9,000-a-year salary bracket, with top security clearance.

In 1959, Martin was the only NSA employee to receive a full-time academic scholarship. The scholarship was based on the excellence of his work, and he was the holder of letters of praise from Dr. Kullback, Director of Research and Development at NSA, and from Pentagon officers. Mitchell had recently been selected to work in the mathematical research division because he had received one of the highest scores in a competitive exam in the field of probability and statistics. Mitchell was also president and team captain of the NSA chess team.

Of the two, Martin had the higher I.Q. He finished high school in two years and took part in many extracurricular activities. His high school principal had been so impressed with him that she gave him a test to see if he could skip high school altogether and enter the University of Chicago's accelerated program for gifted youths. Other high school advisers felt that Martin had the intelligence but not the maturity for the program and offered him the compromise solution of a two-year high school course. After high school, Martin spent two years at the Central Washington College of Education and joined the Navy in 1951. Former college acquaintances remember a Prussian arrogance over his intellectual accomplishments that made him contemptuous of those he could defeat in argument or at the chessboard and standoffish to those whose intellects he did not feel equal to his own. He flaunted his agnosticism and once berated Catholic friends for keeping religious literature in their homes, saying: "You should know better. Don't you know that all religion is superstition?"

Mitchell was a child math prodigy but displayed sustained indifference for all other academic fields so that he ended the first year at the California Institute of Technology with a C-plus average, against a student average of B. As a youth he shunned team sports and spent most of his free time devising chemistry experiments. He once astonished his mother by reading Galileo's experiments, proving them to himself and announcing one day, "You know, Galileo was right about the truncated pyramid." In high school in his northern California home town of Eureka, he was anathema to his teachers. He refused to study non-science courses and pompously announced his resignation when his math teacher could not explain the Einstein theory to his satisfaction. He transferred to a larger high school in nearby Del Norte. Like Martin, Mitchell stayed in college only briefly, and then joined the Navy, knowing he was about to be drafted anyway.

The two had much in common when they met as cryptographers at the Navy base at Yokosuka, Japan. Both were from upper middle class backgrounds in small and unimpeachably American towns. Both were brought up in congenial, close-knit families (Martin was the eldest of three and Mitchell the youngest of three) whose values they held in contempt. Both were of far-above-average intelligence but were diffident and ungregarious with their classmates in school. Both displayed a pointed indifference to girls in their formative years. Both were attracted to the lofty, formal, and impersonal world of science and both had a gift for mathematics. Their personal tastes were also similar, including a fondness for chess and reading the works of noted psychologists like Freud and Jung. Their friendship was the natural result of these numerous affinities.

Martin and Mitchell showed that high intelligence is not a deterrent to defection. In their December press conference, they fought back against a third element that was often mentioned in analyzing their motives—that they were unbalanced mentally.

"Government officials sought refuge by leveling petty personal accusations against us in order to attempt to undermine the credulity of our statements," Martin said. "Some of the letters we received from the United States indicate that these attempts were not completely successful and that many people were sincerely interested in the issues involved."

"The Defense Department," Mitchell chimed in, "stated among other things that we were not in full possession of our mental faculties. A claim of this sort could only come from people who are unacquainted with the qualities required of a mathematician working in the field of cryptanalysis."

Despite their disclaimers, several psychiatrists questioned about the case feel certain that the defection followed a pattern of neurotic behavior. According to this view, the pressures of society and the special work they were doing upset a balance that was fragile at best. As one psychiatrist said: "Society places today fantastic demands and goals on individuals. We send our sons to the Boy Scouts —what do they have to do there? Win merit badges. The pattern continues through life, we have to fulfill our duties, keep abreast, read this, read that, it's an impossible task. Everywhere the pressures assail us." Sensitive, withdrawn personalities like Martin and Mitchell probably could not cope with even routine pressures, and yet by the nature of their work they were assailed with a whole set of new pressures.

First, because they were doing secret work. Employees for "spook" agencies are always conscious of the secretiveness of their work. They must always be careful not to make a slip. The normal end of the day banter on "what happened at the office" is forbidden. They can't go home and have their wife ask: "What did you do today at the office?" and answer: "Oh, I cracked the new Russian code and found out they're planning to attack South Viet Nam on Tuesday." There is none of the outer-directed satisfaction that most people get in their work. The man in the sensitive agency must keep his accomplishments to himself and is never identified with any achievement.

There are added frustrations in cryptographic work, stemming from what psychiatrists call "the syndrome of the labyrinth." This is caused by the pressures of code breaking, where failure leads to obsession. This kind of thing is not as acute today as when Lord Tweedsmuir, one of the most celebrated chiefs of British intelligence, described a cryptographer who could not break a German code and feverishly drew the portrait of his vis-à-vis, who had devised the code he could not break—he saw him sometimes as an implacable Teutonic warrior, sometimes as a malevolently beautiful and pitiless woman. Herbert O. Yardley, who created the American Black Chamber after World War I, began in later life to see codes everywhere—in telephone books, Shakespearean sonnets, and lottery results. At NSA, pressures of this kind are absorbed by computers, which do most of the work, but code breaking is still taxing for the employees and there is a high rate of nervous breakdowns.

Indications of Martin and Mitchell's neurotic personalities came out in their obsession with what they considered unethical American practices, although they felt not a twinge of guilt about their own unusual personal life. In the course of their work they had learned that the United States was decoding the messages of its Allies as well as its enemies, that attempts had been made to subvert employees of friendly powers to engage in espionage work, and that the U-2 program was successfully violating the air space of the Soviet Union. Many of the 10,000 employees of the NSA knew all this, and it may have struck them with varying degrees of distaste. Caught up in their work as they were, however, and convinced that the Cold War could not be fought according to the Marquis of Queensbury rules, they went on with their jobs and were not gnawed by feelings that they were working on the side of the devil. Most intelligent adults are sophisticated enough to balance the evils done in both camps and come up with a fairly reassuring balance sheet. Not so Martin and Mitchell. A sense of outrage and lost innocence led them to the office of an Ohio Democrat, Representative Wayne L. Hayes. They picked Mr. Hayes because he was a member of the House Foreign Affairs Committee and had publicly expressed concern over the violation of Soviet air space by American planes.

Martin and Mitchell felt they were being very courageous in taking their protests to the Congressman. They faced ten years in prison or a $10,000 fine by revealing some of the inner workings of their agency. They saw Mr. Hayes in February, 1959, gave their names and their function and asked that their visit remain confidential. As Mitchell said in his December 1960 press conference: "We told him about the true nature of the espionage overflights and discussed the possible international complications that might result."

"Hayes expressed the opinion that perhaps Congress should make an investigation of this matter," Martin went on, "but that what he could do would depend mainly on the reaction of his seniors in Congress. We asked Mr. Hayes to treat our visit in the strictest confidence, because if what we related to him had become known to the Federal Government we might have been sentenced to ten years in prison or a $10,000 fine. For months we vainly waited for an answer or at least a phone call from Hayes in compensation for the risk we had taken. It gradually became apparent that Mr. Hayes either could not or chose not to do anything about the matter. Some people reproach us for the way in which we left. But if we had made an attempt to request permission to change our citizenship through normal channels, we would have in all probability not been allowed to do so. Such an attempt would, I suppose, have resulted in our imprisonment."

A list of the practices that shocked Martin and Mitchell include: "I would like to convince some of the U.S. Allies, namely, Italy, Turkey, and Uruguay, if they are interested, how their secret communications were read by the U.S. Government. This could be done by describing their enciphering machines and cryptographic procedures." (Mitchell in a Moscow press conference.)

"In the summer of 1955, an American Neptune military plane was attacked when it violated the Soviet Far Eastern border. The plane was heavily damaged but managed to fly away. It crashed upon landing outside Soviet borders. Ships are also employed for spying. In the autumn of 1959, an American hydrographic ship, the *Maury,* was sent to collect intelligence concerning the location of Soviet radar stations on the Caucasian shore and in the Transcaucasus. It was sent into the Black Sea."

The defectors also said intelligence flights were being conducted as early as 1952 and 1953, that NSA monitor stations based abroad in friendly countries include those countries in their deciphering work, and that "the U.S. Government secretly manipulates money and military supplies to bring about the overthrow of unfriendly governments."

It is ironic that two men employed in an agency whose main duty was to collect information about the Soviet Union and other Communist nations appear to have been shocked by the methods used by their own people and unaware of the methods used by the other side. They were like a man with a pair of binoculars who knows all about the principle of magnification but has never troubled to look through them. They were as naïve about the Iron Curtain espionage techniques as they were well informed about their own government's clandestine activities.

Several psychiatrists questioned interpreted this naïveté as a form of neurotic behavior. "Martin and Mitchell," said one, "were guilty about the wrong things. They were like the man who makes a point of stepping on every crack in the pavement and if he misses one goes back and walks over it again. Or the man who climbs stairs a certain way and climbs them over if he misses. The same man will be homosexual or compulsively unfaithful to his wife and will feel no guilt at all about it."

It was this unbalanced sense of outrage at the unpleasant necessities of the Cold War that seems to have determined the action of Martin and Mitchell. In a twisted way, these men whom President Eisenhower described angrily as "self-confessed traitors" thought of themselves as patriots. In some ways their departure seems to have been hasty. Mitchell left behind $7,000 worth of belongings, including a new car.

This intrigued his parents, who described him as "very frugal. Although he was making $9,000 a year he always called home collect. When he returned from a vacation in Cuba he could talk of nothing but the joy of first-class hotels at $8 a day." In a more important way, however, the departure was deliberate. The two left a copy of a statement which they gave in Moscow in a safe deposit box in a Laurel, Maryland, bank. The statement was evidently designed to alert the American people to the dangers of practices carried on by intelligence agencies.

In a later statement, the pair emphasized that they were not Communists, and explained that they were good Americans working for the cause of peace. "I am not a Communist and neither is Bernon," Martin said. "But certain practices I see here, certain governmental and economic practices, seem better than their counterparts in the USA. In the Soviet Union I have not met anyone who advocated war. I feel that the Soviet Union and the Soviet Government are sincerely interested in avoiding war. I don't see any reason why the peoples of the United States and the USSR should not be on friendly terms with one another. Here in the Soviet Union Mr. Mitchell and I have decided to devote ourselves to work of a peaceful nature in the area of mathematics."

As efforts had been made to explain away the defection because of their homosexuality (which was a cause of but not a reason for their act) Martin and Mitchell were branded now as Communists in certain quarters in another attempt at a pat, clear-cut motivation. Chairman Walter of the House Un-American Activities Committee said, "Martin, while studying at the University of Illinois during the academic year prior to his defection, was an associate of at least one known Communist and a number of known leftists. Most of you, I am sure, read the statement these two men made at their press conference in Moscow.

"If you are at all familiar with the Soviet Communist propaganda you know this statement was just packed with it. In commenting on this statement, one person interviewed by our committee said, 'It sounds just like Martin.' Even while employed by the NSA, Martin apparently did not attempt to cover up his feelings about either the United States or the Soviet Union."

However, apart from this very tenuous association at the University of Illinois, investigators were unable to unearth any proof that either man had ever been remotely connected with Communism. The NSA security clearance, which follows past political affiliations more closely than early personal life, gave both a clean slate on "leftist leanings." Much was made also of the pair's connection with Washington's Chess Club Divan. It was said they met their Soviet contact over the chessboard. Actually, according to club president, George Thomas, Russians and other Iron Curtain nationals who have tried to join the club have been turned down.

The question of security clearance acutely embarrassed Washington officialdom. It illustrated security weaknesses that had already been exposed in 1955 by the Hoover Commission Task Force on Intelligence Activities. It had been pointed out that "one flaw in the present system seems to be the absence of a general plan for a periodic review of the security status of every person after employment in intelligence activities, to guard against the possibility that some employee who was completely dependable and honorable when starting work might have changed character, fallen from grace, or succumbed to alien blandishments or some personal weakness such as strong drink or sexual perversion."

Perhaps a review would have prevented the defectors' action. Even with this periodic security check, however, psychiatrists say you can no more prevent defection than you can prevent infection in a hospital, and you can no more select sure-fire security risks than you can select drivers who won't have accidents. (Ask the insurance companies how successful they are in that field.) The intelligence community in Washington is so vast and hires so many that the danger of defection and other infractions to security is always present. If security standards were applied to the letter, it would be impossible to fill jobs. As one psychiatrist put it: "If all those who have ever been guilty of abnormal sex acts (homosexuality, sodomy, group masturbation or Don Juanism/nymphomania) were turned down, they couldn't fill one tenth of their job needs." Thus security officers and psychiatrists look for patterns that still persist rather than youthful experiments or the results of drunken brawls. If ten individuals are checked for a job and eventually are narrowed to two, the chances are a choice will have to be made between a man "who admits that when he goes to a convention every two years he tears off a piece with the boys, while the other has kept a girl friend for five years on the side without his wife knowing. Which one do you pick?" Periodic security checks may be useful but are no solution. As one authority put it, "People have to be audited regularly, just like auditing books, and yet it's just as bad to make them feel they are under constant surveillance. Oversecurity creates bad working conditions and low morale."

Sensitive agencies all have a number of employees who show signs of cracking. Often, instead of firing them, they risk the danger of keeping an unstable employee rather than letting him loose. Perhaps Martin and Mitchell were under this kind of observation.

Shortly after the defection, the head of NSA, General Samford, retired for reasons of health. He was replaced by Admiral Laurence H. Frost, former head of naval intelligence. The abrupt retirement following an incident that indicated serious security weaknesses belied the official Pentagon attitude that the defections were unimportant. Pulling chestnuts from the fire, NSA counsel J. Vincent Burke said: "They can cause no damage to the security of our own communications . . . but they can assist the Soviets in their efforts to render secure the Soviet communications activities."

Lieutenant General Joseph F. Carroll, Inspector General of the Air Force, was assigned to head a probe into how Martin and Mitchell made contact with the Russians and fled to the Soviet Union. The results have not been made public. Two Congressional committees also launched investigations of the case but had issued no reports as of February, 1962.

The consternation in official circles was matched in the defectors' families, who clearly had no idea of the ferment going on in the two men's minds. Even as Martin and Mitchell were exhibited like new arrivals at the zoo in Moscow's House of Journalism, the statements of their fathers to reporters echoed with the pathos of disbelief, like the man who says when told a friend is dead: "But I saw him alive this morning."

"He called me from Washington on Father's Day," Martin's father mumbled when told of his son's defection.

"His friends called him The Professor because he loved to teach," Mitchell's father recalled. "He loved to explain things to children and elderly people. When I asked him about classified matters, he would say: 'Sorry, Dad, but that is top secret.'"

Now that the secret was out, there remained some explaining to do.

XIII. Diplomats, Soldiers, and Espionage

D IPLOMATIC historians will remember the Cold War as the era of *persona non grata*. Between 1947 and 1961, at least seventeen American diplomats serving in Moscow were expelled, while at least thirteen Soviet diplomats in Washington and ten Russians working at the United Nations were ordered out of the United States.*

This periodic banishment of accredited officials reflects an awareness of the concept of legal espionage by the United States and Russia. Working parallel to the undercover agents are the "polite" or "legal" networks. These "spies in striped pants" gather intelligence under the halo of diplomatic immunity and at the risk of being sent home as "undesirables."

The Soviet Union's legal network is so vast that its entire diplomatic corps seems like a "cover" for the intelligence setup. Ambassadors sometimes take orders from clerks, and "special" missions are given priority over normal diplomatic functions. As a special committee of the American Bar Association pointed out in 1958, "Diplomatic recognition is essential to Communist subversion. The Communist espionage apparatus needs the diplomatic immunity of its embassies and consulates to set up spy centers. It needs the un-

* See Appendix for lists of Russian diplomats expelled from the United States and Americans expelled from the USSR between 1947 and September, 1961.

405

broken seal of the diplomatic pouch to transmit orders to its spies and couriers and to receive back their reports and microfilmed documents."

The legal network performs three vital functions for Russian espionage: it acts as a link with illegal agents (Abel and Judy Coplon both had diplomat contacts in New York); it collects information on its own; and it tries to recruit illegal agents. The pattern, as described by defecting Soviet diplomats in Washington, Ottawa, Sydney, London, and Tokyo, is remarkably consistent.

The CIA's legal network is far more limited in scope and manpower. Every important American Embassy and consulate has its quota of CIA men who are given a "cover" rank but whose work escapes diplomatic discipline. The CIA "legal" operative reports directly to Washington. His job, like his Soviet counterpart, is to recruit illegal agents, build up contacts with nongovernment forces in the country, and collect information through sources not available to the regular embassy staff.

The Australian Royal Commission on Espionage in 1955 defined the advantages and disadvantages of "legal" versus "illegal" networks:

> The "Legal Apparatus" operates from a base (the embassy) which is immune from visitation and search by officials of the country where it is situated; its communications with its Moscow Center enjoy the cover of a diplomatic bag and are thus safe and quick; and its resident and such of its cadre workers or collaborators as enjoy diplomatic status are immune from arrest and search. Also, they have wide opportunities of meeting and associating with fellow diplomats and persons holding high positions who may be in possession of confidential information. On the other hand, an embassy official may attract the attention of counterespionage services.
>
> An "Illegal Apparatus" has not the advantages which diplomatic cover gives to a "Legal Apparatus," but those who work in it are less likely to attract the attention of counterespionage services and its operations will not be automatically disrupted by war or by breaking off of diplomatic relations. . . . Care is taken to keep the "Legal" and "Illegal" organizations separate as far as possible from one another. . . . The Legal resident and his apparatus may be called upon to assist, however, in setting up an "Illegal Apparatus," more especially by assisting the entry of illegal workers into the target country.

One major difference between Soviet and American legal networks is that Russian diplomats working for intelligence must keep their role secret even from their co-workers, while CIA men in embassies and consulates are often officially registered as such with the foreign country to which they are posted. The identity of the CIA man in a given embassy is an open secret, not only among his colleagues, but among the American colony and in official circles. With Russian intelligence, things are different.

Aleksandr Kasnakheyev testified, several months after his defection, to a Senate subcommittee in Washington that he was a low-ranking employee with special duties. There was this exchange:

> Q. You had two jobs. One was your cover job as a lower grade diplomat, and the other was your job as an intelligence agent.
>
> A. Yes.
>
> Q. Were you told not to reveal your intelligence activities to other Soviet officials?
>
> A. I was ordered not to reveal my participation in work for Soviet intelligence to other members of the Soviet Embassy, even to the Ambassador himself.

Another difference between legal networks of East and West is that the Soviet structure of intelligence is more clearly defined. Inside a given embassy there may be a GRU (military intelligence) apparat and a KGB apparat which might handle security matters inside the embassy and the recruitment of Soviet sympathizers. Each of these apparats works separately and has its own staff within the embassy, and it has happened that a KGB official with the rank of clerk had enough real power to have one of his superiors removed and sent back to Russia.

The American intelligence setup in embassies is more flexible and less overpowering. Many of the American diplomats expelled from Russia were military attachés who were not CIA men but who collected intelligence as part of their assignment. Where a diplomat's normal work ends and espionage begins is a thin line to draw, and the Russians have a narrow conception of what an accredited official should be allowed to see and do.

In a sense, every diplomat is an accredited spy sent to gather information on the country where he is posted. The intelligence function of diplomats has been recognized through history. In Napoleon's correspondence, for instance, there is the following comment on the nomination of a Captain de Lagrange as Second Secretary to the French Embassy in Vienna:

> My intention is that M. de Lagrange keep an exact count of the strength of Austrian regiments and the places where they are stationed, and that he keep in his office a filing cabinet with an index card for each regiment; and that he change the position of the cards according to the troop movements.

Soviet wariness of foreign diplomats is a reflection on their own traditions. The Russian military attaché to Napoleonic France, Colonel Czernitcheff, was tried and convicted of attempting to subvert an employee of the French Defense Ministry to obtain information about the Russian campaign. In 1914, the Russian military attaché in Berlin, Colonel von Basarow, was thrown out of Germany after he obtained from the secretary of a German general the fortification plans of Prussia.

The United States is no latecomer to these methods either. In 1890, a Captain Borup, the American naval attaché in Paris, was caught buying restricted documents from an official of the French admiralty.

As a result governments must decide where to draw the line on a diplomat's conduct. The Russians frankly equate diplomacy and espionage. In an age that is becoming ever more conscious of security, what once would have been considered perfectly routine and legitimate has become grounds for expulsion. For an American diplomat in the Soviet Union, being declared *persona non grata* is an occupational hazard.

In this period of arms race and Cold War, the military attachés get special attention from counterespionage services. We have come a long way since the time when military attachés in Bismarck's Germany followed the maneuvers of the Imperial Army on horseback. Before World War II, military attachés were loaded down by governments with useful material. They were invited to air shows, artillery displays, made friends with their fellow officers and had access to military journals. Today, in Russia, according to an American diplomat, "a military attaché can be declared a spy if he happens to look out a train window at the wrong time." Of the seventeen American diplomats expelled by the Soviet Union since 1947, thirteen were on the staffs of military, air, or naval attachés.

To understand how the legal networks function, however, we must compare working conditions for American diplomats in Moscow and Soviet diplomats in Washington. To begin with, all personnel in Soviet embassies abroad is made up of Soviet nationals, from the Ambassador to the chambermaids. On the other hand, most of the clerical and domestic help in U.S. embassies are foreign nationals.

As of July, 1960, the number of Soviet officials (and their families) in the United States was 660. The number of American officials (and their families) in the Soviet Union was 195. The Soviet officials include correspondents of Soviet newspapers and radio stations, the Intourist representatives and several other categories that come under the nonofficial category in the American listing.

The breakdown of the personnel of the two embassies as of July 1960 is as follows:

U.S. Embassy in Moscow total: 195 Americans, including 56 Department of State, 17 on the Army attaché staff, 9 on the Naval attaché staff, 12 on the Air attaché staff, and 101 dependents; and 93 Soviet nationals in clerical or service posts.

Soviet Embassy in Washington total: 271 Russians, including 101 accredited officers and employees and 170 dependents. (Not to mention the staffs of satellite countries, who work closely with the Russians.)

The overriding reason for not staffing the U.S. Embassy in Moscow entirely with American personnel is financial. It is not feasible to bring over domestic and clerical help who would have to be paid American salaries when help can be found in Moscow. Instead of an American chauffeur at $6,000 a year, one can get a Russian chauffeur for 2,000 rubles a year. Also, the Americans would want to bring their families. Russia is considered a hardship assignment, and Americans have trouble adapting to the standard of living. The Russians make an effort to provide adequate housing for U.S. diplomats but it is usually not on a par with what they are accustomed to.

The principal argument against hiring Soviet nationals is the danger of a security breach. It is common knowledge that the clerical help at the American Embassy report regularly to the Russian secret police and that some are high-ranking counterespionage agents. But the

State Department insists that there has never been a security breach in the embassy, and the position on hired help doubling as spies is: "They're agents, we know they're agents, and they know we know they're agents."

Since everyone knows that servants provided for embassy personnel are more interested in looking under the bed than making it, a habit of caution must be built up.

All classified documents are kept on the top three floors of the chancery, which was remodeled by American workmen to make sure it was not "bugged." There are always Marine guards at the door and the "need to know" principle prevails. Looking on the bright side, a former counselor to Moscow said, "In periods of deep freeze, the Russian employees are the only link we have with the Russian people."

It is in fact a two-way street: the Russians report to their superiors on what the inside of the embassy looks like, what working habits are, and what the assistant military attaché said about his boss. But in return they can also provide (often without knowing it) a great deal of useful information, particularly in periods such as right after the war, when Stalin's hostility toward the West was so great that embassy officials were virtually boycotted.

There is a Soviet government office, formerly called Burobin, which deals with all the "housekeeping" details for foreign officials. They find apartments, domestic help, language teachers, and take a deep and sincere interest in how the foreign official is getting on in Russia. The control exercised over those allowed to deal with foreigners sometimes verges on the absurd. Roy Essoyan, an Associated Press correspondent in Moscow, recalled in an article that after waiting three days for his phone to be repaired, he contacted the telephone company and was told the repairman had not been cleared to work for foreigners.

Another visitor to Russia, Dr. Nicholas Nyaradi, the last non-Communist finance minister of Hungary, wrote in a book called *My Ringside Seat in Moscow** about his experiences in 1947. Dr. Nyaradi had been invited to dinner by Ambassador Walter Bedell Smith. The next day he saw a Soviet general who "amazed me by giving a letter-perfect report on the night's entertainment—who was there, what we had worn, what we had said—word for word—what we had to

---

* Dr. Nicholas Nyaradi, *My Ringside Seat in Moscow* (New York: Thomas Y. Crowell, 1952).

eat and drink, and how much. 'It's a shame,' the general said, pouring me a glass of cognac from a glittering Waterford decanter, 'that General Smith, the Ambassador of the richest country on earth, must use a cheap white-enameled tin pitcher for his drinks!"

Where servants cannot go, there are other familiar techniques. Western diplomats operate on the assumption that telephones are tapped, rooms are wired, and they are followed. Rear Admiral Leslie Stevens, Naval attaché from 1947 to 1949, wrote in his book *Russian Assignment*:*

> There have been too many cases of wiring for sound for one to feel comfortable even when there are no Russians about. One feels safe in talking only in the presence of noise, or when one is outdoors. It would be naïve and foolish for a foreigner to fail to observe these precautions, whether or not he believes in their absolute necessity under all circumstances.

Henry Cabot Lodge, former U.S. Ambassador to the United Nations, confirmed that Admiral Stevens' warning should still be in force. He said in an interview that on a recent trip to Moscow, he and Ambassador Llewellyn Thompson went into the middle of Red Square for their private conversations. Inside the embassy, they spoke "for the mikes," and Mr. Lodge was amused by the thought that all their "on the record" conversations were duly recorded, printed in six copies, and labeled "top secret" for the use of various Soviet intelligence agencies.

It was also Mr. Lodge who on the floor of the United Nations exhibited the American eagle emblem that had been "bugged" by the Russians. The eagle, a gift from the Russians to Ambassador Averell Harriman, had a special wireless device that picked up conversations inside the living room where it had been hung. The subterfuge was discovered several years later in a thorough check of the embassy for concealed devices.

Phone taps are routine—Westerners learn to speak on the phone for the benefit of the silent eavesdropper. Anyone who checks carefully can hear distinct "beeps" on the line. If he wants to test further, he can do what *Herald Tribune* correspondent to Moscow Tom Lambert did while there was still censorship on news dispatches. He

* Rear Admiral Leslie Stevens, *Russian Assignment* (New York: Harper and Brothers, 1953).

called his office, gave the first ten words of his story, and was cut off. A moment later, an engaging female voice chided him in perfect English: "Mr. Lambert, you know you're not meant to give anything with news content over the phone."

Since Khrushchev's rise to power, and varying with the ups and downs of Soviet-American relationships (ranging from the spirit of Camp David to Soviet anger over the U-2), surveillance of Western diplomats has been relaxed. Under Stalin, diplomats were submitted to round-the-clock police surveillance, instituted during the war as "protection," as a courtesy in troubled times to help diplomats get through the crowds, know where to go in air raids, and keep from getting lost in the spider's web design of Moscow. Stalin's golden rule was that there should be three members of the secret police assigned to watch every foreign official.

Admiral Stevens ridiculed the "protection" excuse in the account of an attaché who "one night came out on the street to find the tires stripped from his car and the thieves hard at work on the instrument board. Across the street, the Soviet car which always followed him was parked, and its plainclothesmen were sitting in it, idly watching the scene. Needless to say, he got no satisfaction from them or from his complaints at police headquarters, beyond the doubtful satisfaction of throwing the protective theory back in their teeth."

Total surveillance was abolished in 1954, after becoming the subject of hundreds of jokes and anecdotes: One diplomat was walking in a wooded district on the outskirts of Moscow when he noticed a tail following and hiding behind trees. The temperature was subfreezing and the tail had a heavy coat and a cap with flaps. Apparently thinking he could elude detection by subtle disguises, the tail would appear from behind one tree with his cap on and the flaps down. Five minutes later, he had taken the cap off. Ten trees after that, he had the cap on and the flaps up. And so the game continued. American diplomats were told to ignore the tail or *"slezhka,"* for any other attitude leads to suspicion.

Surveillance today is still efficient but more discreet. Militia men stand guard outside the embassy and record who comes in and who goes out. There are also militia men in front of embassy residences. The concierges in every building where a foreigner lives are paid by the KGB to clock the foreigners in and out. Entertainment tickets purchased through a special bureau are another form of control. The police know what performance foreigners are attending, at what date, and with how many guests.

What often strikes American diplomats is the obviousness of Soviet surveillance. Mail not sent through diplomatic pouch via the American Embassy in Helsinki is opened, and the Russian censors use an inferior grade of paste to put the envelope flap back in place.

Travel restrictions have also been relaxed under Khrushchev. "It used to be," an American diplomat said, "that if you wanted to go somewhere outside of Moscow, they told you: 'There is no train.'" Travel could be arranged through the Government, which provided the diplomat with the necessary documents to stay at a hotel, eat in a restaurant, and get gas for his car if he had one at the few and far between Russian service stations. Getting a full tank of gas is one of the details of daily life that is certain to be reported to the secret police.

In 1959, fifty-three regulations for travel by foreign diplomats were removed, but spur-of-the-moment trips are still difficult and any trip farther than twenty-five miles outside Moscow must be planned with all the care of an archaeological expedition.

If one has a car, it must perforce be driven by a Russian chauffeur. It is almost impossible for a non-Russian to obtain a driver's license. Since there are few service stations, less qualified mechanics, and almost no privately owned cars, the Government reasons that the man who wants to have and drive his own car must be able to put it together and take it apart. The test for a driver's license includes a nomenclature examination in which the applicant must rattle off the parts of a standard Soviet car in Russian. By dint of hard work, the foreign diplomat might pass on the third or fourth try, but the examiner can always flunk him if he likes.

The practical part of the test was recently done away with. This was another insurmountable obstacle for the average driver. In the past, the examiner handed the applicant a screwdriver, showed him a Soviet car with the hood up, and asked him to tune the engine, fix the carburetors, and so on. Most diplomats were worn down by this kind of treatment and accepted the services of a Russian chauffeur with weary relief.

In addition to the inherent difficulties of travel, there are parts of the Soviet Union closed to foreigners for security reasons. These travel restrictions were first imposed in 1941, and were tightened in

1947 so that even today almost one-third of Russia remains closed.

In 1955, the American State Department decided to apply reciprocal restrictions and closed about one-third of the United States to Soviet diplomats. The State Department has periodically proposed abolition of closed areas in both countries, but its notes have received no reply. The State Department has also found reason to complain that its diplomats were prevented from visiting open areas on the grounds that they were temporarily closed.

The most recent American proposal for an end on travel bans, in January, 1961, went unanswered. At the same time, changes were made in closed areas in the United States to balance changes on closed areas in the Soviet Union. Some major cities in the United States now closed to Russian nationals are St. Louis, Houston, Phoenix, Cincinnati, Milwaukee, and Wichita. In December, 1961, the State Department reopened the question by easing restrictions on Communist newsmen working at the United Nations.

Working in this muddle of restrictions, diplomats and intelligence agents using diplomatic cover find themselves thwarted in efforts to obtain the most innocent information. The Soviet Government, perhaps judging others by its own standards, considers that a diplomat's job by definition is espionage. Low-ranking officers find themselves the object of special surveillance because the Russians reason they have been planted by the CIA, as they themselves plant colonels in the KGB under clerical cover.

Two examples of the Soviet mania for secrecy are the lack of any railroad timetables or recent telephone books. In railroad stations, train arrivals and departures are announced on a blackboard and then erased. Anyone wanting to know the train schedule from Ormsk to Sverdlovsk would be asked: "Why do you want to know?" The Russians reason that train schedules can be used by military intelligence.

When Russian troops moved into Berlin at the end of World War II, they found a heavily annotated copy of a Moscow telephone book in German intelligence headquarters. They were so shocked that their telephone books had been used to advantage by the Germans that they didn't print another until 1953. Then they printed so few copies that it has become a collector's item, and as of 1961 it has not been brought up to date.

The telephone book is in itself a gem of circumspection. It lists the Central Committee of the Communist Party—a vast organism with multiple branches—under one number without subsections. It fails to list foreign embassies in any of its four sections: Government Organizations, Party Organizations, Dwelling Houses and Private Subscribers. In the Dwelling Houses section, buildings are listed by street and number, and unaccountable jumps in the numbers are explained by the failure to list buildings where foreigners live.

To make up for this lack of printed information, large Russian cities have information kiosks where a person may write a question in Russian, pay a few kopeks, and get an answer from the employee on duty. This is the way to find out where someone lives, what their phone number is and so on. It also enables the secret police to keep track of who is asking for what. This attitude of all-embracing paternalism is not meant to prevent you from getting the information, it simply enables the authorities to keep up to date about what is being sought.

To hamper diplomats they suspect of spying, the Russians go beyond refusing information. Bold attempts to frame diplomats who were doing too good a job or were suspected of being intelligence agents are sporadically made. Major General Richard Hilton, a former military attaché in Moscow, tells that he was once stopped in Gorki Park and held on a charge of trying to photograph a factory. "Why don't you search me and see if I have a camera?" he asked the police. "We can't do that, because you have diplomatic immunity," was the reply. The accusation was followed in typical fashion by a letter to *Pravda* from four factory workers who said they were eyewitnesses and added that Hilton had been wearing an old sheepskin coat.

This detail amused Hilton, who indeed had such a coat, but had not been wearing it on the day of his seizure. It was an indication of the thoroughness of the Soviet secret police dossier, which even had a list (supplied by a maid) of his clothes.

Another obvious frame-up cited in the 1959 House Committee on Un-American Activities' Report, "Patterns of Communist Espionage," tells of the U.S. embassy official in an Iron Curtain country who planned a Sunday afternoon drive with his family into the countryside of the Red nation in which he was stationed. As required by law, he informed the appropriate officials of the Red government of his plans and made known to them the route he planned to follow in his drive.

"When Sunday arrived, he took off with his family for what he thought would be a routine, uneventful, and pleasant drive. When he was about halfway to his destination, he encountered a detour sign which he naturally followed. It led to another and then another, all of which he followed—until suddenly he found himself at the entrance gate of a military airfield.

"As soon as he stopped his car he was surrounded by guards who hustled him off to a nearby plane. There pictures of him were taken, 'proving' that he had been caught in the act of spying."

The diplomat was declared *persona non grata* and recalled to the United States.

John A. Baker, a Second Secretary of the American Embassy in Moscow, obtained permission in 1956 to take a lecture course in Soviet medieval history at Moscow University. When the Hungarian uprising broke in 1956, the freeze was on again and standards changed. Baker had struck up friendships with Soviet students. He invited them to his apartment, met them at restaurants and skating rinks. These inoffensive activities became a source of embarrassment to Soviet officials at a time when the Kremlin was adopting a tough line toward the United States.

In May, 1958, he was declared *persona non grata* for "systematically violating the norms of behavior for diplomatic representatives." At the time, Baker was on leave in London with his wife and a small child, and he did not return to the Soviet Union.

A booklet on "U.S. Espionage and Subversion Against Russia," published by the Soviet Information Bureau in 1960, charged that "during his stay in the Soviet Union Second Secretary of the U.S. Embassy in Moscow, John Baker and other secret agents made a large number of trips across the Soviet Union, during which they actively collected military, economic and political intelligence. To facilitate his espionage activities, Baker passed himself off to Soviet citizens as a Soviet army officer, as a Czech and as an American studying in Moscow University."

The gullibility of the Russian people is put to the test by the charge that an American attaché could pass himself off as a Soviet army officer.

The booklet continues that "Baker was permitted to attend lectures at the History Department of Moscow University. In his conversations with other students Baker slandered Soviet life viciously, and statements to that effect were addressed to the Chancellor of the University by a number of students."

Baker's comment on his expulsion was: "I can only conclude that my attempt to develop better understanding of the Soviet Union through friendships with its citizens is considered by the Soviets as a 'violation of the norms of diplomatic behavior.' "

By far the most extraordinary case of an American diplomat in Moscow is that of Russell A. Langelle, who was in charge of security at the embassy from 1957 to 1959. The trouble with Langelle was that he did his job too well. He ferreted out Soviet attempts to penetrate the embassy, reported cases of attempts to subvert American personnel, and fired a number of Soviet employees at the embassy who were obviously KGB agents. Before the 1959 visit of Vice-President Richard Nixon, he thwarted attempts to "bug" the embassy. His ability at circumventing the Russians on their own ground led to a KGB directive that he should be removed.

The Soviet scheme, improbable as it may sound, involved kidnaping Langelle, trying to recruit him as a double agent, and failing that, banning him from the Soviet Union on espionage charges. Langelle was a thirty-seven-year-old former advertising account executive who had served in Vienna for two years before being assigned to Russia.

On October 16, 1959, his wife said she needed the car for shopping and he took the bus to the embassy.

He alighted at 9 A.M. at the stop on the corner of Chaikovskovo (Tchaikovsky) Street and Vorovskovo Street, in plain sight of the American Embassy, about a block down on Tchaikovsky Street. Five men grabbed him gangland style and heaved him into a waiting black ZIM limousine. He was taken to a KGB building, where he showed his diplomatic card to the general mirth of his captors.

He was asked to remove his topcoat and hat. The man who searched the coat took out a notebook which Langelle said he had never seen before and used a chemical solution to bring out invisible ink on the pages. During a two-hour interrogation, Langelle was first told that he would be arrested for espionage and his career would be ruined by the bad publicity. He was told that the notebook found in his topcoat contained state secrets. He was threatened with imprisonment following revocation of his diplomatic immunity. He was threatened with physical violence against himself and his family.

His interrogators then gave up menaces for cajolery, and he was offered a "gentleman's agreement"—no charges would be pressed if he gave the Russians information. He was offered cash payments in either dollars or rubles, and the Russians also promised to give him information that would lead to promotion. Langelle remained insensitive to these enticements and was driven to another point close to the embassy, where he was allowed to leave the car.

The following day, *Pravda* said Langelle had been caught giving 20,000 rubles and material for making secret ink to an agent on the bus. Bus riders had seen the transaction, seized Langelle, and handed him over to the authorities, the article said.

Langelle was given three days to leave Russia, and another embassy staff member, attaché George P. Winters, was accused as Langelle's accomplice and also declared *persona non grata*. Winters was described in virulent terms in *Pravda* as wearing "the black coat, striped trousers, and starched collar and cuffs of the diplomat, which for him was a camouflage like the skin of some poisonous snake."

Another danger for the Western diplomat in Moscow is the use of women agents. Under Stalin, diplomatic personnel was systematically subjected to the advances of the *Mozhnos* or "permitted girls," women recruited and trained by the secret police to seduce Western officials and report the "pillow talk" to their superiors.

This sort of thing was described in *I Spied for Stalin,* a book by Nora Murray, a Russian woman who eventually married one of the diplomats she had been sent to seduce. Mrs. Murray had a room at the Hotel Metropole and was told to contact specific Western diplomats. Her first effort was with a British attaché and she was told: "You will talk to him about the weather, horses and sport generally. Englishmen love to talk about such subjects. Then lead the conversation to discover if he has any pet subjects. But no political discussions."

At the initial meeting, the diplomat told her: "Listen, I know you are one of the *Mozhno* girls who work for the NKVD."

After Stalin's death, the systematic use of *Mozhnos* in Moscow was abolished, although the secret police still kept lists of available women for this type of work as well as dossiers on the foibles of Western diplomats.

State Department officials today attach little importance to the dangers of the *Mozhnos*. They point out that diplomats sent to Iron Curtain countries are specially recruited and excellent security risks, and that they are briefed on precedents and techniques. In addition, the State Department has a standing rule that only married persons accompanied by their families may be posted to Iron Curtain embassies. Nonetheless, the Mata Haris are still in circulation and still get results, even from supposedly sophisticated diplomats with a healthy family life. Some of the temptations diplomats are likely to find strewn in their paths have been listed in the Congressional report, "Patterns of Communist Espionage." According to the report, "official U.S. representatives who have to travel overnight by train in Communist-controlled countries quite frequently run into an odd situation. When they enter the compartment of their train, they find it already occupied by an attractive woman who claims the compartment is hers—and produces a ticket to prove it. The conductor is called to settle the difficulty. Before the solution is worked out, the woman invariably indicates to the American official that to avoid further inconvenience and difficulty, she is willing to share the sleeping quarters with him."

In June, 1961, a career diplomat with an outstanding record was brought back from Poland where he was serving as Second Secretary and arrested in Washington on espionage charges. The diplomat, Irving Chambers Scarbeck, had fallen prey to the manifest blandishments of a Polish blonde and had given her secret information. Scarbeck had access to the embassy code room and to a wealth of classified embassy reports. He met the girl in January and his behavior quickly drew the suspicion of State Department security men, who kept him under surveillance until May, when he was whisked out of Poland for arrest. Scarbeck, at forty-one, was married and the father of four children. He had joined the Foreign Service in 1956 after serving as a staff officer for the United States Commissioner to Germany; in 1959 he had won the State Department's Meritorious Service Award for work in student exchange programs. Cases such as this reveal that although the use of *Mozhnos* is no longer systematic, the Soviet Union and the satellites still use trained women agents, sometimes successfully.

Men are not the only victims in romantic involvements that lead to espionage and defection. One of the best-known cases was that of

Annabelle Bucar, who defected from the Moscow Embassy in 1948 to marry Konstantin Lapshin, a tenor of the Moscow Operatic Theater. Although Mr. Lapshin was not a member of the secret police, he was doubtless encouraged in his affection and the marriage was an espionage as well as a romantic coup.

Miss Bucar was a strapping blonde of Croatian origin who had been brought up in a mining town near Pittsburgh. Admiral Leslie Stevens, then naval attaché, remembers that she gave the impression of "being a rather earthy person who would be apt to be more interested in men than in their ideologies."

She left the embassy to marry the singer and settled down to the life of a Moscow housewife. She told her friends, "I am seeking my happiness in him rather than anything else." The price of that happiness was a publicized switch in loyalties. In a letter appearing under her signature in Soviet newspapers, she renounced her American citizenship and said the Soviet Union was the only country that could give ordinary people happiness.

In 1952, she wrote a book called *The Truth About American Diplomats*, which denounced the embassy as a hotbed of spies. The book was a primitive mixture of outraged homilies, pious recriminations, and twopenny morality, channeled through the Soviet propaganda mill. She wrote that under Ambassador Walter Bedell Smith, "I found myself in the front line of a spying organization," and that Smith had been appointed "after a long career in military intelligence work for the express purpose of organizing a vast espionage nest."

Some of the examples of "espionage" she gave, however, would seem to an objective observer within the bounds of diplomatic propriety. Counselor Elbridge Durbrow, "a double-faced intriguer, sometimes went so far as to insist that embassy employees write down anecdotes they happened to hear from Soviet acquaintances in the city and present them as memos."

Ambassador Smith "made it the duty of all embassy employees to establish brief contacts with Soviet citizens, to talk with them on various aspects of Soviet life, and prepare lengthy, detailed memorandums on all the information they gathered, important or unimportant."

Miss Bucar's book did well. It was serialized in *Pravda*. It became the basis for a movie called *Farewell America*. The movie was made into a play called *The House on the Lane*. Miss Bucar prospered, and when an old friend from Pittsburgh dropped in on her in 1958, she was working as an announcer for Radio Moscow's American section. At forty-eight, she had grown stout and complained of high blood pressure and a heart condition.

Today she lives in a modern, four-room apartment (one room is used by her mother-in-law), and is the proud possessor of a piano, a television set with a twelve-inch screen, and a five-passenger brown Pobeda car.

Another annoying feature of diplomatic life in Moscow is the inconsistency of the Soviet attitude. The American Embassy was once on Mokhovaya Street, close to the Kremlin. Stalin lived in the Kremlin and it annoyed him to have the Stars and Stripes so close by. He let it be known that the American Embassy would have to move farther away from the Kremlin's walls. A suitable building was found on Tchaikovsky Street and renovated at great expense after a battle in Congress for funds. After Stalin's death in 1953 there was a relaxation of tension, and the Russians told the American Ambassador he could stay where he was.

By that time funds had been voted, and the Ambassador did not have the courage to explain the intricacies of Russian reasoning to Congress. The changes were carried through, and the remodeling was done under American supervision to lessen the chances of "bugs."

The Russians also changed their minds about the book display that was part of the United States exhibit at the 1959 Moscow fair. The books had been cleared by the authorities, but when the police noticed their popularity, they regretted their largesse and pulled out a considerable number of the titles.

Thus, despite periods of *détente,* the Western diplomat in Russia works under twin handicaps of hostility and suspicion. In some cases, expulsion is an admitted retaliatory measure for the expulsion of a Soviet diplomat. Shortly after Valentin Gubitchev was arrested as the contact man for Judy Coplon and removed from his post at the United Nations Secretariat, the Moscow *Literary Gazette* wrote: "[His arrest] gives Russia the right either to demand satisfaction from the United States or adopt reprisal measures against American citizens or diplomats."

In August, 1960, Colonel Carl Watkins Miller, military attaché in the American Embassy in Budapest, was expelled by the Hungarian satellite government in avowed retaliation for the expulsion of a Hungarian attaché. The Hungarian note to the American Embassy said curtly: *Miller is being declared* persona non grata *in consequence of action taken against our attaché in Washington, Mr. Laszlo.*

Sometimes retaliation is not admitted, but is obvious. In October, 1960, Igor Melekh, a member of the United Nations Secretariat, was arrested in New York and charged with trying to steal defense secrets. Less than a month later, an assistant air attaché in Moscow, Major Irving R. McDonald, was given forty-eight hours to leave Moscow. He was not officially charged with any offense. The charges made in the Moscow press said that he had entered restricted areas containing military installations. The thirty-four-year-old attaché noted that "during my entire time of nineteen months in the Soviet Union, my activities were consistent with my position as an assistant air attaché diplomatically accredited in and by the Soviet Union as a military observer."

Since diplomatic procedure for a government is to withdraw any envoy declared *persona non grata* notwithstanding the validity of the charge, McDonald, his wife and his two children complied with the forty-eight-hour order.

The expulsion of Air Attaché Colonel Edwin M. Kirton in August, 1960, points up another difference in attitudes. *TRUD,* the propaganda organ of Soviet trade unions, wrote indignantly that Colonel Kirton had made thirty-seven trips to eighty-three cities in the Soviet Union in 1959 and eighteen trips to thirty-four cities in the first four months of 1960. This, according to *TRUD,* was enough to brand him as a spy, since "it is impossible that Kirton and his staff were interested in the landscape and historical monuments of our country." Kirton expressed surprise at the charges and said: "I have traveled widely in the Soviet Union in my two years here, but I had no ulterior motives."

Colonel Kirton was also charged by the Russians with using special cameras to photograph military objectives, which is getting closer to the usual definition of espionage, but these charges were never subjected to the burden of proof. They were published in the Moscow newspapers, but never pressed.

Some of the other charges made against American diplomats in the Russian booklet "Caught In the Act" were:

Made regular trips across Soviet territory collecting intelligence data . . . manhandled Soviet citizens who obstructed them in their reconnaissance intentions . . . covertly photographed defense installations . . . tried to trespass on the territory of military installations and munitions factories and also used a special spy camera.

The booklet offers what purports to be "a photo showing employees of the U.S. Embassy in the USSR on the roof of the embassy building in Moscow, taking pictures of Soviet military aircraft during a fly-past (1953)." In the picture four men wearing American-style clothes are on the roof of a building and gazing at the sky. One is taking a picture with a telescopic lens, another is looking through binoculars, and a third has a camera hanging around his neck.

Whatever the validity of the Soviet charges, it is a fact that the Western diplomat in Moscow is handicapped by the closed and security-conscious society. He knows from sixteen years of Cold War that his expulsion from the Soviet Union needs only the flimsiest reason.

In contrast, the Iron Curtain diplomats in Washington live according to the law of the land, and consequently are under few overt restrictions. They are limited in travel by the reciprocal bans. And they are under surveillance by the FBI. The former keeps dossiers on all Iron Curtain diplomats and carries on spot checks. Any unusual activity or wanderlust on the part of a diplomat merits extended surveillance.

However, there are similarities in American and Communist "legal" networks. Both try to recruit agents among civilians. Frank Tisler, Czechoslovakian military and air attaché who defected to the West in 1959, testified before a Congressional committee in May, 1960, that "my cover as a military and air attaché accredited to the United States furnished a legal reason for my being in the United States and being assigned to the Czechoslovak Embassy in Washington, D.C. This legal reason enabled me to meet and develop contacts with other foreign diplomats who were accredited to the United States. It also provided me with a valid reason for being interested in military developments in the United States. In this cover position I was to interest myself in military matters, but at the same time these cover duties were not to detract from my real mission.

"This mission called for me to attempt personally to recruit American citizens to act as agents, and in their agent capacities, to furnish me with intelligence on classified materials related to United States military developments."

The annals of Soviet diplomats expelled from the United States are full of examples of crude attempts to recruit Americans as agents. One can see from these attempts that the success of Soviet espionage is based on determination rather than subtlety.

Here are three cases taken at random to illustrate Soviet diplomats at work recruiting:

Captain Boris Fedorovich Gladkov was named naval adviser to the Military Staff Committee of the United Nations in December, 1953. In January, 1955, he met a sales engineer for a New York City marine engineering firm at a cocktail party, cultivated him, and held a series of meetings with him. He told the engineer he was willing to pay high prices for information on marine engine design and operation and the power plants of American vessels. The meetings continued on a regular basis through June, 1956, and Gladkov paid $1,550 for two unclassified publications on marine boilers which he could easily have obtained free had he called the manufacturer.

The engineer notified the FBI and after several months of surveillance, Gladkov was declared *persona non grata* by the Department of State for "activities which were highly improper and incompatible" with his status as a U.N. delegation member. He left July 12, 1956.

Nikolai Ivanovich Kurochkin was named Third Secretary of the Soviet Embassy in Washington in April, 1956. That fall, Charles T. Beaumet, a reporter for the *National Guardsman* and a free-lance magazine writer, called the Soviet Embassy seeking statistics on hosiery production in the Soviet Union.

Kurochkin, who was one of the nine secretaries at the embassy, gave Beaumet the information and said he too was doing some writing. He was writing for Soviet military journals, he said, and if Beaumet could get him training and field manuals of the United States Army he would share with him the proceeds of the articles. Beaumet turned over unclassified material and was paid $450. He declined to give Kurochkin two classified manuals the diplomat had sought.

Beaumet went to the FBI, resigned from the *National Guardsman,* and continued seeing his Russian contact on the advice of the federal agents. He gave Kurochkin material through military liaison channels, including high school and college army training manuals. In June,

1958, the Department of State advised Kurochkin that he was *persona non grata,* and he left five days later.

Vadim Kirilyuk was named as a political officer in the United Nations Secretariat in September, 1958. In April, 1959, an American citizen in Mexico City got in touch with the Soviet Embassy there about the possibility of obtaining a scholarship in a Russian university. The Russians were interested when they learned that the American had worked with cryptographic machines in the Army.

They told him he could easily get a scholarship if he went to New York and contacted Kirilyuk. The two met five times, and Kirilyuk tried to persuade the American to get a job with the National Security Agency, the top-secret coding and decoding center. He also asked for data concerning cryptographic machines. The American lived in Springfield, Massachusetts, and when Kirilyuk was spotted making frequent out-of-town trips, he was put under FBI surveillance. Agents called on his contact in Springfield, who co-operated, and the matter was brought to the attention of the U.N. Secretary General. Kirilyuk, as a member of the Secretariat, did not have diplomatic immunity and could have been prosecuted, but he benefited from foreign policy considerations: Soviet Premier Khrushchev was in the United States at the time and it was felt that prosecuting a Soviet U.N. official might sour the visit. Kirilyuk and his family were asked to leave the country and did so in January, 1960.

Against these three examples of Soviet attempts at recruitment, here is one American attempt—probably the right proportion.

Lieutenant Robert Dreher was an assistant naval attaché at the American Embassy in Moscow in 1948, serving under Ambassador Walter Bedell Smith and Naval Attaché Rear Admiral Leslie Stevens. The thirty-two-year-old native of Oil City, Pennsylvania, was arrested by the Soviet secret police April 23. He was charged with obtaining unauthorized information from a Russian national, and was declared *persona non grata,* shortly before his two-year tour would normally have ended.

The details of the case appeared in *Pravda,* where facts are at the service of propaganda and "the good of the state," but in this unusual case an American Embassy official told the Associated Press that "most details in the newspaper *Pravda* were essentially correct."

The story was that Dreher, before coming to Moscow, had been posted in Odessa. There he had made friends with a customs official.

Curiously enough, when Dreher was transferred to Moscow, the customs official followed. On the day of his arrest, Dreher had gone to the Moscow customshouse at the request of the Russian in connection with the shipment of embassy property from Odessa.

Dreher, in civilian clothes, was talking to the Russian customsman and taking notes when the two were seized by secret police. They hurriedly tried to hide certain papers, *Pravda* said, and when a security officer seized several sheets of paper lying on a table, Dreher tried to tear them out of his hands and began to beat him. The customs official's notebook reportedly contained secret military information and other papers. He was charged with "going beyond the bounds of government business" and his fate was not disclosed.

As for Dreher, he was detained for several hours, asked to sign a confession, which he refused to do, and the incident was reported by the Soviet Foreign Office to Ambassador Smith. According to *Pravda,* Smith said in an interview with Soviet Foreign Minister Andrei Vishinsky, "In the future I'll ask the State Department to send to Moscow more intelligent and careful persons, who are able to keep their tongues between their teeth." Smith allegedly admitted that Dreher had been receiving military information.

The activity of the legal network of the Soviet Union in the United States also centers on the recruitment of naïve or fellow-traveling Americans and the pressuring of former Soviet citizens. The first such postwar case in the United States involved Jacob M. Lomakin, who was Consul General in New York. Lomakin was expelled on the personal order of President Truman in 1948 for planning the kidnaping of Mrs. Stepanovna Kasenkina, a consulate employee who had defected. She made a much-celebrated escape by jumping out the window of the consulate and Lomakin demanded her return to Russia. It was he who returned, however, after Mr. Truman's ire had been aroused. Lomakin died in 1958 while serving as a counselor to the Soviet Embassy in Peiping (a hardship assignment).

In many cases, the Soviet diplomat builds up a contact with an American and asks him for unclassified information he could get himself as the first step of recruitment. Some of the charges pressed against Soviet diplomats seem just as silly as those aired in Moscow newspapers against Americans, since the real crime is one of intention. Soviet diplomats have been expelled because they tried to obtain an electronic device that was commercially available or a map any mapmaker would have been happy to sell them.

In other cases, the Soviet attempts to get information are so crude they become burlesque. Here is the short and happy career of Yuri Krylov in the United States, according to the FBI "Exposé of Soviet Espionage," prepared in May, 1960:

> Krylov entered the United States May 4, 1955, as Assistant Soviet Military Attaché . . . In April, 1956, Krylov was introduced to the manager of a Washington electronics supply house. Through the Washingtonian, who co-operated with the Federal Bureau of Investigation, Krylov purchased hard-to-get electronic equipment. In August of 1955, Krylov contacted an employee of the Atomic Energy Commission and attempted to obtain from him information concerning the technical aspects of nuclear power. In December, 1955, he contacted a former commissioner of the Atomic Energy Commission in an effort to develop information concerning atomic energy for space heating. In February, 1956, he attempted to purchase 26 unclassified films on peacetime atomic energy.
>
> In February, 1956, he endeavored to join the Society of American Military Engineers and to subscribe to the publication *The Military Engineer* which contained information concerning United States fortifications.
>
> On January 14, 1957, the Department of State declared Krylov *persona non grata* as a result of his activities. He departed the United States January 26, 1957.

In another case, Maksim Martynov, a U.N. delegation member, tried to subvert a high-ranking Army officer in 1954. Eugeni Zaostrovtsev, a second secretary, tried to subvert a State Department foreign service officer in training. One can almost imagine one of these determined diplomats walking up to the White House to ask the President for classified information.

Then there are the intriguing cases of Soviet clerks and chauffeurs with responsibilities far above their station. Vladmir Mikheev was a translator clerk in the Soviet Embassy in Washington with a large expense account for entertaining Americans. In a matter of months, three government employees reported he had approached them seeking information. To Sidney Hatkin, an Air Force statistician under suspension as a security risk, Mikheev posed as a student. He invited Hatkin for nights on the town with liberal quantities of small talk and vodka martinis. Hatkin reported him and was reinstated in his job. Mikheev, with his "Russian Rotarian" bonhomie, next contacted Richard S. Cutter, an employee at the Armed Forces medical library, and said he wanted help on writing a dissertation on American military history from the Civil War to the present. Cutter reported him. Mikheev's third strike was Robert W. Davis, a historian at the Armed Forces Pathology Institute. He took Davis and his wife to dinner and tipped a dime on a $16 check. Davis gave the waitress a dollar and apologized that "my friend doesn't understand American ways."

Davis said Mikheev was a sort of Russian low-comedy type, "crude and boorish in his social habits," and with "a bland, kowtowing manner, except when someone asked him a question he didn't like. Then he became like a wild animal." Davis reported him and he was declared *persona non grata* in June, 1956.

Vasiliy Molev, who was contact man for Boris Morros, was a lowly chauffeur at the Soviet consulate in New York. On a previous tour of duty, he had served as property custodian at the embassy in Washington.

There are indications that the State Department is getting on to clerk-spy gambit. In 1958, Nikolai Gvozdev was refused entry into the United States as a delegate to the 51st general conference at Los Angeles of the International Aeronautical Federation. The dossier of this aeronautical specialist showed that in 1954 he had been posted as a chauffeur at the Soviet Embassy in Washington.

The Soviet legal network has also concentrated on obtaining aerial photographs of strategic areas. Since 1955, Soviet citizens have been forbidden to take photographs of military areas, defense plants, seaports, or to take any photographs at all from planes.

The man who was in charge of gathering aerial photographs was Pyotr Y. Ezhov, who had the added distinction of being a dead ringer for former Vice-President Richard Nixon. Ezhov, a third secretary at the Soviet Embassy, had the same heavy jaw and prominent nose, the same height and the same curly black hair as Mr. Nixon. He was often stopped on the street for autographs.

Ezhov recruited a free-lance aerial photographer to take pictures of the Eastern seaboard. The Russians paid more than $1,000 for the pictures and offered to pay for flying lessons and a private plane so that the photographer could carry out "systematic aerial reconnaissance." In this case as in so many others, the photographer was in touch with the FBI, and Ezhov was declared *persona non grata* July 22, 1960.

To draw this comparison of Western and Iron Curtain diplomats to a close, it is evident that both sides are indulging in activities that draw the disapproval of the host governments. Both have gone beyond the restrictions imposed by the security-conscious governments in attempts to ferret out intelligence and build up contacts with nationals. Both have independent intelligence agents within the embassy framework. The difference between the Soviet Union and the United States in this respect is one of degree, not of kind. The Russians are bolder, have a far greater number of "legal" agents, and benefit from the freedom of movement and accessibility of information in a democratic society. The Americans are at the mercy of the capricious but all-powerful Soviet security network and still are able to obtain information the Russians are trying to keep secret, and perhaps even recruit Soviet nationals.

Cases involving Iron Curtain diplomats in the FBI files show that "recruits" usually get in touch with federal agents and help in the investigation that leads to the expulsion of the envoy. The number of investigations is an indication that Americans are not so easily duped. In another area where the Soviets make systematic attempts to subvert Americans, however, the results are less encouraging. The armed forces, particularly the occupation forces in Germany, have a checkered record in their contacts with the Russians.

At the lowest level, it is a matter of deserting to East Germany to avoid punishment or as the result of a drunken spree. This was so common at one time that the East Germans were disgustedly sending the American soldiers back. They had more than they could handle. Thus Sergeant James Bissonette, a thirty-eight-year-old native of Grand Rapids, Michigan, defected in November, 1954, because he was in trouble with his unit and was about to lose his sergeant's stripes. He asked the Russians for asylum, and was told they "didn't want to bother with small fry." Bissonette went back West and was sentenced to three years for desertion.

In fact those who make the mistake of border-running usually regret it. In May, 1954, Sergeant William J. Smallwood, thirty-one, of Beattyville, Kentucky, wandered drunkenly over the East German border where he was seized by Soviet guards. He was thrown into an East German prison which he described as "the worst place I have ever seen or heard of. I was thrown in a cell two yards wide by four yards with six other prisoners. There was no toilet, no heat, no light, no work, no letters, no cigarettes, no soap. They starved me until I was so weak I could hardly stand." Smallwood escaped and was glad to serve two years for desertion in a comfortable West German jail.

Yet the germs of subversion attack soldiers of all ranks. The following cases provide a panorama of subversion and attempted subversion from private to general.

Private Robert D. Blevens of Omaha, Nebraska, had been in Berlin only a month when he was involved in a drunken barroom dispute with some German nationals and was arrested by the military police. The time was February, 1952, and U.S. commanding officers had been told to crack down on misbehaving GIs who were giving the occupation forces a bad name.

Blevens, a twenty-nine-year-old regular army private, was charged with being drunk and disorderly. The day after the soldier's arrest, his commanding officer visited him in the stockade and told him he would probably be court-martialed. The high-strung Blevens exploded and shouted: "I might as well be in the Russian Army as in an American stockade."

Blevens wasn't bluffing. When his German girl friend, Ingrid Janek, came to see him, he asked her to find out how he would be treated in East Germany. She came back a few days later and told him "you'll be treated like a king."

That was enough for Blevens, and on February 13 he escaped with Ingrid to the East zone. In East Berlin, the couple checked in at the Intourist Hotel and Blevens changed into civilian clothes. Soon representatives of the East German State Security Service, the Russian-controlled secret police, were at his door and politely asked the couple to come with them to Potsdam, where persons seeking asylum in East Germany are processed.

In Potsdam, Blevens met Colonel Karpov, a bibulous, expansive Russian who bragged that he was "in control of all foreigners coming into East Germany." Karpov's Russian aides searched Blevens, and found among his papers a card from the public information office in Japan. Thanks to the card, they mistook Blevens for a journalist, and he encouraged the mistake. He built himself up as a specialist of long years' experience in the public information field.

Blevens was treated with respect. He was asked to write articles for East German newspapers. His first articles were so poor they had to be completely rewritten, but then Blevens discovered a library in Potsdam that he used for source material. He submitted an article that he had copied word for word from an English translation of Gorki. The Russians were impressed; Karpov told him that was "very good work."

Blevens and Ingrid were sent to Bautzen, a town sixty miles south of Berlin, near the Polish and Czechoslovakian borders. There the Russians and East Germans operate a "faith school" for defectors. Hundreds of allied soldiers have been processed in Bautzen and are taught by Communist instructors the history of the Party, comparative social science, and the evils of capitalism. At the same time, Bautzen serves as a "little America," where Soviet spy trainees pick up American speech mannerisms, physical attitudes, and slang expressions. Most of the Bautzen defectors are confined to a camp that is part of the school and take jobs around town between classes. Almost all American military defectors from West Germany wind up there, like the island in *Pinocchio* where all the self-indulgent little boys were turned into donkeys.

But Blevens and Ingrid were given a suite at the Stadt Bautzen and were provided with passes for travel anywhere in East Germany. Because they had favored conditions, they were told: "If anyone asks you, say you are Russians."

Blevens was introduced to a "John Peet," an English defector who was assigned to help him with his articles. Together they wrote a defector's column for East German journals.

Then Karpov came to Bautzen and told Blevens and Ingrid they were going back to Berlin. A furnished apartment was waiting for them in a respectable residential neighborhood. Karpov showed them around the apartment, helped them unpack, and had a good dinner with the right wines sent up. After dinner, he rubbed his hands and said, "Well, now the fun is over, it's time to go to work."

Karpov explained that the apartment was more than a love nest. From now on, he said, Ingrid would lure American GIs to the apartment, and Blevens would talk them into defecting to the East. "All you have to do is tell them how well you were treated," the colonel said. When he left, Blevens and Ingrid discussed this new development in their love life. Blevens felt he was getting in too deep and had vague notions that what he was being asked to do might qualify as treason.

He told Ingrid he would turn himself in to the Americans and they would "give me a break" when they heard his story. Blevens surrendered the next day and found himself back where he had started—in the stockade. Once imprisoned, he had a change of heart. He had surrendered in April, and in May he again escaped. He later explained that he wanted to "capture someone and do a little bargaining so I could clear my name."

Back in the East zone among his Communist contacts, he was sent to Karlherst and put to work in an office copying documents in English. One night, he stayed late and filched a report from the files. The document's absence was noticed the next day, someone remembered that Blevens had stayed in the office afterhours, and he was arrested and sent to jail in Dresden. Blevens had a chance to compare the penal systems of East Germany and the American Army. In the Dresden jail, he was severely beaten and forced to sign a confession that he was an anti-Communist counterspy. He was told that he would be put on trial and would probably be shot. Instead, he was sent back to the Bautzen school in August. There were many other Americans at the school, and he learned from one of them the identity of a counterintelligence agent working as a proctor at the school. Blevens approached this man, named Glockenstein, and paid him to go to West Berlin and contact American intelligence on his behalf. He told Glockenstein that he wanted to be recruited as an intelligence agent working for the West. Glockenstein was supposed to be back in three days. When he didn't show up, Blevens went to see Mrs. Glockenstein and asked for her help. She arranged a pass for him with Glockenstein's name and Blevens' description, and he made it back to the French zone of Berlin, where he was picked up in a routine check by French police.

Turned over to the Americans, Blevens was the first American soldier to be tried under the Smith Act, which forbids consorting to advocate the overthrow of the American Government. He was charged with affiliating himself with the East German State Security Service, described as a "Communist gestapo."

Blevens' behavior at the trial was curious. On one hand he tried to excuse his behavior by telling of his efforts to join American intelligence and working as a double agent. On the other hand, he refused to disclose details of what he had seen and been through in the East zone. "The confinement officer has been after me for the last four months to get me to talk and I won't do it," he told his court-martial judges. Blevens was given one of the stiffest sentences an Army private in Germany ever got—thirteen years.

In March, 1952, one month after Blevens deserted, another U.S. Army private disappeared under similar circumstances. Robert W. Dorey, twenty-year-old native of Somerville, Massachusetts, was facing court-martial for the theft of $134 from another soldier's footlocker. Like Blevens, Dorey made his way to East Germany and approached East German police in the village of Granassee. He asked to be taken to Russian authorities and granted asylum.

Taken to Weimar and Potsdam for questioning, he was given civilian clothes, money, and other items. He seemed eager to please the Russians, and agreed to take Soviet agents back to West Germany and show them his barracks. With the kind of luck usually reserved for sleepwalkers and drunkards, Dorey brazenly returned to his old barracks in Phillipstahl in the company of three MVD agents and took them for a tour of the ammunition and gasoline storage dumps and other installations. He used his uniform for entry to the various installations the Russians wanted to visit, saluting briskly at each guard post. Dorey and his Russian friends stayed in West Germany from April 23-26, and also visited military bases at Frankfurt am Main and Obersul.

Dorey went back to Potsdam with the MVD and settled down to a writing career for *Pravda* and the East German newspapers. The articles followed the usual line, denouncing the Army and the Government.

In July, he was taken for indoctrination at the Bautzen school and given his identification papers, which restricted him to the town. He took the regular courses with the other defectors and was given a job in a bakery. Dorey began to tire of life in the People's Democracy. In August he made the first of many escape attempts, but found that leaving Bautzen was not as easy as getting out of stockade. He was given a new job in the Lowa auto works, which were carefully guarded. In the next few months he was jailed five times, four times for trying to escape and once for theft.

Sent back to the Bautzen school for further indoctrination, he attended a lecture in which a Soviet army major advocated the overthrow of the United States Government by a workers' revolution. At the end of the lecture, the students were asked to sign a petition endorsing the revolution. Dorey ducked out before his turn to sign came.

He continued to attend the propaganda classes and put in for overtime at the auto works. Finally, in August, 1953, he had saved enough money for another escape attempt. He bribed a Bautzen resident into buying a train ticket to Berlin, boarded the train undetected, and surrendered to U.S. authorities in West Berlin.

Court-martialed in November, Dorey said in his behalf that he had acted under threats and pressures. He too was convicted of violating the Smith Act and was sentenced to fifteen years, but the sentence was later reduced to three years.

Master Sergeant Roy Rhodes, thirty-four, found that Moscow did not agree with him. It was cold, it was grim, it was definitely not a "fun" town. He didn't like his job, either. Playing chauffeur to diplomats wasn't his idea of Army life. He was lonely. He missed his wife and two-year-old daughter. After nine years in the Signal Corps, with training and experience as a code clerk, he had drawn a hardship assignment. He looked after the motor pool with the help of two Russian mechanics, Vassily and Ivan. Much of the time he chauffered the embassy's military attachés.

May in Moscow was like January in Sergeant Rhodes' home state of Oklahoma. There was no one to talk to. His family and friends were at his base, Fort Huachuca, Arizona. The Russian mechanics who repaired the embassy vehicles didn't seem too bright and couldn't speak English.

Sergeant Rhodes, a tall, rawboned man with jug ears and a glass jaw, did two things to improve his condition: he applied for visas for his wife and daughter so they could join him; he took advantage of the liberal liquor allowance at the embassy commissary. On this he was agreed with a good many Russians: vodka took the edge off the Moscow winter and made time go by far more painlessly.

On Christmas Eve, 1951, Rhodes received the news that his wife and daughter had been granted visas and were on their way. It was a day to celebrate, Rhodes had a few drinks at lunchtime and went back to the garage two miles away from the embassy, feeling an overwhelming friendliness toward everyone. As he later explained it in his own inarticulate way:

"On arriving back to the garage, the two Russian nationals, mechanics that worked for me there in the garage, I believe, as I can recall it, I decided that they should have a drink with me, and so one drink led to another, and apparently it went on all afternoon. At three-thirty or four P.M., I suppose, something like that, the youngest mechanic's girl friend had his car that day, and she came up to the garage to pick him up, and there was still some of the vodka left that we had been drinking in the afternoon, so I said: 'Why don't you bring your girl in for a drink?' And when she came in there was a girl with her, and I had never seen the girl before. So we had a few more drinks from what was left of the vodka, as I can recall it, and I don't know who suggested it, that maybe we should have dinner that night, but maybe I did.

"I just can't recall exactly how it got started, but we left the garage in his car with the two girls and I know we made a trip to I guess it was his apartment. I never was inside of it. I don't know what was on the inside of this building. But anyway he was gone fifteen or twenty minutes. He cleaned up and changed his clothes and came back to the car, and the four of us went to a hotel in Moscow and the party just rolled on through the night, and I know that I was dancing, drinking, and eating with these people and I have no recollection of leaving the hotel in any way, shape, or form. I don't know, possibly I passed out there and they had to carry me out. I know I woke up the next morning in bed with this girl in what I had taken to be her room."

Rhodes reported for duty at the garage nursing a hangover and the two mechanics kidded him good-naturedly about the night before. The sergeant had forgotten the incident when, about a month and a half later, the young mechanic told him the girl he had spent the night with wanted another date with him.

A meeting was arranged, and the fun-loving sergeant found himself involved in a classic scene. The girl was there, looking forlorn, and a man introduced as her brother was there, looking indignant; a kindly go-between who called himself Bob Day and spoke fluent English with an American accent, was also there. Bob Day threw his arm around Rhodes' shoulders and explained the situation, man-to-man. "You're in trouble, Sarge," he said. "This girl is pregnant. When she has her kid and names you as the father, they won't give you a visa to leave the country. You'll be the father of a Russian national. You'll be stuck here."

Rhodes swallowed the story. With his wife due in Moscow any day and an Army court-martial hanging over his head, he was desperate to cover up his escapade. The smooth-talking Bob Day told Rhodes it was a very simple matter to settle. "Why don't you work for us?" he asked. "That would square things."

"But I don't have any information," Rhodes demurred. Bob Day explained that he would only have to tell about his own background, training, family life, and work at the embassy. This Rhodes readily agreed to do.

Although he would probably have been astounded to be referred to as one, Rhodes was now a spy in the service of the Russians, a valuable inside man who could tell them harmless gossip about the personal lives of the embassy staff that would be correlated and edited to become essential intelligence data. Conversations overheard while driving embassy staff, rumors about the sex lives and personal idiosyncrasies of the staff, the habits of the State Department and military personnel, all this was recounted by Rhodes. He held a total of fifteen meetings with the Russians between the start of 1952 and June, 1953, when he was sent back to the United States. The friendly Bob Day was present at the meetings held in various Moscow apartments, as were high-ranking Soviet officers in uniform and MVD men in mufti.

At the first meeting, Rhodes said, he was asked "a lot of specific questions and I gave specific answers." Searching his memory for information tidbits, Rhodes recalled a trip he made as chauffeur for the air attaché. They drove out in civilian clothes to a guided missile factory not far from Moscow and the air attaché took photographs of the factory, Rhodes told the Russians. Bob Day was pleased and slipped some rubles into Rhodes' pocket as he left. Rhodes estimates that he received a total of about $3,000 in the fifteen meetings. He was naïve enough to give the Russians signed receipts after each visit, as though he had been a landlord collecting rents.

At the next meeting, Rhodes was shown a camera no bigger than a book of matches: "They told me to take it back to the embassy, stating that if I did not have time to read documents in the embassy I could photograph them and bring the negatives back to the Soviets." Rhodes was urged to take photographs in the office of the same air attaché with whom he had driven to the missile factory. His ready sense of self-preservation kept him from accepting such a hazardous mission, but he continued to supply information on embassy mores and schedules.

At all the meetings, Rhodes said, an atmosphere of cordiality prevailed. He was treated like a respected comrade-at-arms, the vodka flowed freely, and there was always a bundle of rubles in his pocket when he left. Occasionally, there were other parties with other girls, orgies worthy of the Boyards, but he never saw the first girl again, the one whose Russian child he had purportedly sired.

When Rhodes found out that he was being transferred to an Army base in San Luis Obispo, California, that summer, he tipped off his Russian cronies. "About the last three meetings prior to my leaving Moscow, they had drilled into me instructions for making a contact in the United States," Rhodes said. "They had requested that I continue to co-operate with them in the United States and I had agreed to do so feeling that I was in it by this time up to my neck. I could see no other way out."

Rhodes was given the code name "Quebec" and told that if Soviet agents in the United States did not contact him within a year, he should get in touch with them. This was the method he was to use: Clip articles critical of the Communist economy from *The New York Times* and send three in the mail to the Soviet Embassy in Washington with a question mark in red crayon drawn on the articles. Do the same thing on the same day three weeks running. On the fourth week, same day, be in front of a certain movie theater in Mexico City, smoking a pipe. Rhodes was to ask his contact for a match, and the box of matches would contain directions for the next contact. Rhodes promised to keep in touch. Shortly before his departure, he was involved in a driving accident while drunk, but the Moscow police did not press charges. His Soviet contact told him: "That could have cost you a lot of money," and reminded him that he was expected to continue working for the Russians once he was home.

When Rhodes left Moscow in June, 1953, he thought he was leaving a bad dream. He had no intention of persisting in espionage activities. He spent about six months in San Luis Obispo, then was transferred to Fort Monmouth, New Jersey. The Russians knew he was in New Jersey, for the "Quebec" message sent to Abel said that he could be found "in Red Bank, N.J., where he owns three garages. The garage work is being done by his wife." Rhodes and his wife had in fact settled in Red Bank, at 55 Linden Place, but did not operate any garages.

By the time Abel received the Quebec message, instructing him to recruit Rhodes for espionage work, the sergeant had again been transferred, this time to his permanent base in Fort Huachuca. It was there that his tour of duty was completed and he was honorably discharged on November 17, 1955. Rhodes had no trade, wasn't particularly fond of hard work; there was only one thing left to do— he re-enlisted. He had a good Army record, and in January, 1956, he went back to Fort Monmouth, where he received top-security clearance for access to secret information in his work as a Signal Corps code clerk.

In June of 1957, Rhodes received a visit from the FBI, which had identified him through the Quebec message. "Tell us about your espionage activities for the Soviet Government," a federal agent asked. Rhodes seemed somehow relieved and said: "I wondered when somebody was going to ask me about that."

Rhodes testified at the Abel trial in the fall of 1957 in Brooklyn Federal Court. After he had told his story, Abel's counsel, James B. Donovan, gave him a rough half hour of cross-examination and pictured Rhodes as an irresponsible drunk:

Q. What did you drink?
A. Whisky, vodka, almost anything you want to name.
Q. In what quantities did you drink these liquors?
A. They weren't moderate.
Q. Is it not true that for the last two months of your stay in Moscow you were drunk every day?
A. I believe that is right—yes, sir.

Rhodes further admitted under cross-examination that besides espionage, he had delved in the black market in rubles during his Moscow stay. When he was picked up by the FBI, he had a bank account of $19,000, which he explained was his "sergeant's savings."

Donovan's efforts to impair the credibility of the sergeant did not help his client, but it did add a few touches to the portrait of one of the most lackluster military specimens ever to pass muster.

In a matter-of-fact Washington court-martial in February, 1958, Rhodes said in his defense: "I feel now that my involvement in this whole situation was due to either being scared to death or riding the middle of the line as I have just stated or possibly due to the fact that they had offered me more money than I ever had offered to me in my whole life."

The candor of a soldier who could admit that he had turned traitor for "sex, vodka, and rubles" did not help. Rhodes was sentenced to five years at hard labor, forfeiture of pay and a dishonorable discharge. When his wife heard the news, she said, "I'm shocked. I kind of thought he would be released." Others were shocked at the lightness of the sentence.

In the spring of 1957, Captain George H. French, thirty-six years of age, reached what is generally called the end of one's rope. French was a World War II hero who had flown thirty-two combat missions from England as pilot or navigator in a B-17. He had won the Distinguished Flying Cross with clusters for dropping bombs on the German Ministry of Munitions in Berlin. The explosion was so powerful that it rocked his plane in mid-air. Reaching the Korean war toward its end, he flew five combat missions in B-29s, destroying key North Korean supply dumps.

With his boyish face and crew-cut hair, Captain French was the prototype of the dashing airman. He was flying planes in combat while youths of his age back home still had to ask their fathers' permission for the family car. He was known as a good pilot, liked the risk and excitement of combat and was considerate and friendly with his crew and fellow pilots.

The captain was an old married man. He met his wife in 1942 while taking flight training in Alabama. Like quite a few others, he had signed up the day after Pearl Harbor. By 1956, he had three daughters. His wife thought he should leave the Air Force and become a company man with a ranch house in suburbia. He tried, between wars, and sold insurance for Metropolitan. But he received his call back to active duty in 1950 with undisguised relief.

After Korea, Captain French had the problem of every other combat veteran home from the wars—adjusting to a life that can be plotted as precisely as a navigator's chart. Most of his Air Force cronies found jobs as salesmen, or went to law school on the GI Bill, and a few who had the right contacts became commercial pilots.

But he stayed in. There is a sense of futility that plagues a peacetime army and weakens its best men. There were no more bombs to drop. French had to go back to school, learn about the new weapons that had been invented while he was using the old, learn about the new strategies that had been developed in his absence. It was all pretty dull, and French had never liked school. He had been an average student at Edison Technical High School in his home town of Mount Vernon, New York. His favorite subjects were gymnastics and football. The war had taken care of the decision about college.

French had always liked to gamble; he became a devotee of an institution scorned by wives, the Saturday night poker game. He threw himself into gambling as he had thrown himself into flying. He was soon playing two or three times a week for high stakes. He wasn't a good player, and his losses piled up.

He began to drink too much. The muscles he had built up lifting weights turned to fat. The circle tightened. He borrowed from banks, kept losing at poker, drank more, and borrowed from his father to make his bank payments. His father, a building superintendent in Mount Vernon, lent him $2,000. When he asked for $1,800 more, his father pulled the purse strings.

Temporary escape came with a new assignment. In December, 1956, French was sent to Ramey Air Force Base in Puerto Rico as a bombardier on a B-36 crew. It was no ordinary B-36—it was geared to carry atomic payloads. French was cleared for access to the atomic data he needed to do his job. Again he went to school, attending the special weapons classes that taught him how an atom bomb is handled and dropped.

French was the kind of man who can take the heat of combat but breaks under the continued pressure of a personal problem. The more debts he piled up, the more drinking he did, and the more convinced he became that there was no way out through ordinary channels. His pay and allowances came to $803.88 a month and his debts had soared to $8,000.

Reasoning with the maturity of a ten-year-old, he hatched a scheme so fantastic and naïve that one could only expect to find its like in the pages of a comic book or an afternoon radio serial.

He asked for leave to visit his family in Mount Vernon and flew to New York City from San Juan on April 3. He moved into Room 1877 of the Hotel New Yorker, Eighth Avenue and 34th Street, after checking a package in a railroad locker at Pennsylvania Station. Then he went on a two-day drunk.

On April 5, he took a train to Washington, D.C. He looked up the address of the Soviet Embassy in the telephone book and went there late that night. The embassy is a tall white brick building set back thirty feet from the sidewalk at 1125 16th Street, one block north of the Statler Hotel. A low box hedge runs along the sidewalk, separating it from the embassy lawn. In the back of the building a large garden is set off by a high brick wall, a twelve-foot-high spiked wrought-iron fence, and a steel-covered door with a circular peephole. The street side runs parallel to the sidewalk and also has a high fence flush to the lawn.

Just before midnight, French strode across the lawn and up to the fence. He took a letter out of his pocket, wrapped it in a newspaper to weight it, and flung it over the fence. He saw it land on the other side, hurried back to Union Station, and took the first train to New York.

The letter said:

> *To whom it may concern*—I believe that I can furnish you with valuable information.
>
> This information consists of some diagrams of weapons and other information.
>
> I wish to sell this information for $25,000 cash.
>
> The utmost secrecy must be taken because I am a member of the United States Air Force.
>
> I can be contacted at Room #1877, Hotel New Yorker, New York City.
>
> Send someone familiar with modern Air Force weapons to discuss this matter.
>
> This letter will serve as an introduction.
>
> I urge you again to observe secrecy as I will be liable to the severest penalty.
>
> (Signed) A U.S. AIR FORCE CAPTAIN

How a sane man could realize the implications of such an act and still carry it out is perplexing. When his wife was told the story, she said that "his mind must have snapped." Yet the letter was terse and precise, its phrasing was as lucid as the scheme was absurd.

The only comment the Air Force later made viewed the incident from a practical point of view. "His price wasn't high," an Air Force spokesman said, "considering what he had to sell."

The Air Force captain had placed on the espionage market documents explaining the handling of nuclear payloads, and information on how to fuse the bomb. It is likely that the Soviets already had information of this type in 1957, but had the letter been picked up by a member of the Soviet Embassy staff, as intended by French, it would have been manna from the skies. Not so much for what French had for sale, but for what he would have been able to get once he was firmly in the hands of the KGB.

As it happened, it was an FBI man who picked up the small packet from the embassy garden. This was planning, not coincidence. French had long been under the scrutiny of Air Force intelligence. His debts, his drinking, and his depressions had come to the attention of security officers in a periodic check of airmen with access to restricted data. When he went on leave, he was trailed by members of the Air Force security police, the Office of Special Investigation. When the trail led to Washington the FBI was called in.

As soon as French was out of sight, an FBI man and an OSI man went up to the fence and retrieved the letter from the garden.

The following day, French was nervously pacing his hotel room when there was a knock on the door. Two men entered, identified themselves by showing the letter, and asked, "What have you got for us?"

"Where's the money?" French demanded. "This has got to be strictly cash."

There followed a pathetic scene as French dickered with two FBI men over the mode of payment. To prove he was on the level, French displayed drawings he had made and memos on the type of information he could provide. He was all over the agents in his eagerness to conclude the deal. They kept trying to obtain the information without paying, and he kept insisting on cash.

When the game had lasted long enough, the federal agents identified themselves. French collapsed on the bed, moaning, "I knew it, this is it." He admitted everything and gave the agents the key to his railroad locker, in which they found six documents stolen from Air Force files. Three were stamped CONFIDENTIAL and three were RESTRICTED DATA.

In his oral confession to the FBI, French showed the kind of thinking that had given birth to his spy scheme. "I don't feel morally guilty because my original intent was a suicide plan with subsequent capture of Russian agents," he explained. French seemed to be absorbed by a fantasy world made up of cloak-and-dagger heroics, melodramatic sacrifices, and special codes of honor. He had felt above everything else the moral obligation to pay his gambling debts, he said. He admitted, in a moment of perception, that "my conduct was, to put it mildly, unbecoming an officer and a gentleman."

At his court-martial at the Barksdale Air Force base near Shreveport, Louisiana, French pleaded not guilty. He was charged with violating Article 13 of the Uniform Code of Military Justice, which forbids attempts to communicate with foreign powers on matters of defense. The court-martial judges were three generals, two colonels, and two lieutenant colonels.

French denied the charges, said he was "all mixed up." His defense was transparent, and on September 20, he was dishonorably discharged and given a stiff sentence—hard labor for life.

The case had been kept out of the papers until after sentencing. The headlines dubbed him "the poker-playing bombardier." French had written his wife that he was ill and had been admitted to the Shreveport military hospital. When his case and conviction became publicly known, he called his father in Mount Vernon and told him: "Don't believe what you hear about me." He told his wife the same thing.

In February, 1959, the Military Court of Appeals recognized that French's act, though reckless and immature beyond belief, was not the act of a professional spy or a traitor. In effect, it was the same type of offense that came up every day in court-martials, where money was the only object: stealing, selling government property, gambling with loaded dice, and the like. His sentence was reduced to ten years.

It is not easily conceivable that men trained in the disciplines and ideals of one of the military academies and promoted to the responsibilities of high command could turn their backs on everything they represent. The border-running and impulsive escapism so prevalent in the lower ranks do not find their way into the rarefied atmosphere of men groomed for command. The instability and blunted sense of duty of a Captain French are defects that prevent professional military men from attaining high rank.

However, the number of stars on a uniform does not deter the Russians from preying on an officer. Some high-ranking officers who seemed friendly to Russia have been approached, while the weakness of others has been exploited with varying degrees of success.

Brigadier General Phillip R. Faymonville was one of those who was approached and remained loyal. A 1912 graduate of West Point, he first went to Russia as a young officer on a military mission to Siberia.

As one of the few American officers who had seen the Soviet Union he came to be known as something of an authority on Soviet affairs. To establish this growing reputation, he studied the language and became a reader of Soviet military publications. He kept up his contacts in the Soviet Union, and his interest in Russian affairs became so intense that his West Point cronies nicknamed him "the Bolshevik."

In 1934, on the recommendation of Ambassador William C. Bullitt, who said "he knows more about Russia and the Russian language than any other officer in the United States Army," Faymonville was named the first military attaché to Moscow. He was one of Moscow's most popular diplomats, and he sent Washington glowing reports on Russian military strength. He found that some of his old friends had been liquidated in the purges, but he made new ones, and his esteem for the Russians did not fade.

Faymonville's reports caused some eyebrow-raising in Washington, and when he wrote that "the Russians are the greatest warriors the world has ever seen," the State Department queried his superior for an explanation. Alexander Kirk, who was then serving as Chargé d'Affaires in Moscow, replied that "you can't talk to Faymonville about Russia any more than you can talk to a man about his mother."

Those who did try to talk to Faymonville about Russia, like his assistant, Colonel Frank B. Hayne, found that the discussions always grew highly emotional, with the temperamental Faymonville taking to his bed for several days to recover from the controversy.

Faymonville served as military attaché until 1939, and the irony of his Moscow tour is that for all the glowing adjectives that spiced his official reports, his appraisal of Soviet military strength was more accurate than those of his confreres who tended to downgrade the Red Army. Faymonville, describing the Russian build-up of heavy artillery, tanks and other mobile units, and pointing up the Russian tradition of desperate fighting to protect their own soil, was one of the few men who saw Russia as a military power to be reckoned with.

Faymonville's value as a military expert was recognized and he was again sent to the Soviet Union in 1941, as a member of the Special War Supplies Mission, which co-ordinated U.S. lend-lease to Russia. This assignment only lasted a year. In his zeal to help Russia obtain war supplies to fight the Second Front, General Faymonville quarreled with War Department officials and military attachés. To demonstrate his sympathy with the Russians, Faymonville became a regular contributor to the Moscow blood bank.

MVD officers who had been told of Faymonville's sympathies by some of his Russian friends got in touch with the general and tried to recruit him to their service, using the tried and true arguments that helping Russia is helping the cause of world peace, and that allies cannot work too closely. For all his friendship toward Russia, Faymonville had the good sense to refuse the MVD's advances categorically. Feelers kept coming out to him in the form of invitations, flattery, and offers of decorations, but there was no response.

It was not the MVD's recruitment attempt, which only became publicly known years later, that ended Faymonville's lend-lease trip. Complaints that he was impossible to work with and "knew it all" were streaming into the State Department, and in 1942 he was recalled without an explanation and given an assignment far removed from any controversy, in an Army training camp in the Southwest.

There Faymonville spent the remaining years of his Army career, a man who had understood the Russian military better than most, but whose emotional affinity for Russia and the Russians had marred a brilliant military career. He retired in 1948 at the age of sixty and went back to his home, San Francisco.

When Yuri Rastorov, a Soviet intelligence officer who defected to the West in 1954, testified before a Senate committee, Faymonville's name cropped up. Rastorov confirmed that Faymonville had been tagged as a possible recruit by the MVD because of his "abnormal behavior," but had rebuffed their advances.

At Fort Meade, Maryland, in July, 1952, a major general was court-martialed, suspended from command for six months, and reprimanded by seven of his peers. It was the first time since the Civil War that an officer of his rank had undergone the indignity of a court-martial.

The General, Robert W. Grow, was found guilty of two charges and acquitted of a third charge which was never made public. He was found guilty of improperly recording classified military information and failing to safeguard properly classified military information.

In one of the most embarrassing espionage coups perpetrated against the West in the Cold War this general, who had served for two years as military attaché in Moscow, had his diary stolen by Soviet spies. His loyalty was never in doubt. He was a fierce anti-

Communist and favored waging a preventive war to crush the Eastern bloc.

Perhaps he considered himself a superb military theoretician whose thoughts had to be noted for posterity. For years he had indulged in the vanity of keeping a daily diary, which in itself is a dubious practice for a high-ranking officer entrusted with a wealth of confidential information. In wartime, there is a ban on diary writing for officers in the American Army. After the Grow incident, military intelligence urged that the ban be enforced as long as Cold War conditions prevail.

Iowa-born, General Grow was an expansive, opinionated man who established a brilliant record as Commander of the Sixth Armored Division in Europe during World War II. He was assigned to a postwar mission in Iran and from there was posted to Moscow in 1950 with the diplomatic rank of military attaché.

No two more dissimilar military attachés to Moscow could possibly have been found than Faymonville, with his emotional attachment to Russia as a country and the Russians as a people, and Grow, with his omnivorous craving to beat the Russians and his obsession with the inevitability of war.

In June, 1951, Grow attended a top-secret military conference at Frankfurt am Main. He was chairman of the committee on the use of special weapons. The conference itself was devoted to the study of targets, strategic objectives, and vulnerable spots in the Soviet Union, to which Grow brought information gleaned in his two years as military attaché.

Most of the conference members were staying in a requisitioned hotel renamed the Victory Guest House. Two of the hotel employees were in the pay of the East Germans and it was no problem for them one afternoon to photostat Grow's diary, which he had negligently left in his room while attending the conference. When he returned, it was exactly where he had left it, waiting for him to make his latest entry. But the two hotel employees had disappeared. Not much attention was paid to their departure at the time.

In January, 1952, a book appeared in East Germany entitled *On the Path to War*. Its author was a turncoat English major named Richard Squires who had defected to East Germany in 1947. Unassumingly buried in the book's sixth chapter were handwritten excerpts from Grow's diary, undeniably genuine reproductions of an American general's private thoughts. Shortly after the book's publication, the Moscow *Literary Gazette* launched a propaganda barrage blaming a bellicose military clique of American officers for preparing a war against the Soviet Union. It was a perfectly planned and executed coup, and Grow's literary aspirations led to a swift court-martial.

Through the pages of his diary, Grow emerges first of all as a military attaché who put Soviet strictures on foreign diplomats to an almost daily test. On December 1, 1950, he was detained by Russian police while taking photographs of the bridge across the Velikaya River, and was forced to give up his film. The following spring, he was stopped while trying to enter a district near Moscow where a military camp was stationed.

He worked at locating Soviet military targets, military units, anti-aircraft batteries, industrial installations, and transportation centers. This was his job, and he was competent at it. To the Russians, he seemed a dangerous spy. His diary shows that information of all sorts interested him:

> *April 16, 1950:* The Tolstoi Museum was closed today, but this did not bother us at all, because we had no intention of going there. I have taken down many license numbers of military cars, and have seen a few military installations on the road.
>
> *May 23, 1950:* Rostov is a beautiful city located on the high northwestern bank of the Don. The bridge here is the best target in the South of Russia.
>
> *Feb. 15, 1950:* Turnall and I made a thorough examination of industrial districts in the northern part of the city.
>
> *Jan. 12, 1950:* Spent the entire afternoon with Turnall and Abel exploring the southeastern part of the city along new streets. Found no AAA positions, but some good data concerning the terrain.
>
> *Jan. 28, 1950:* Up at 10 o'clock and breakfast; then rode on the metro to the "B" ring and walked around in the neighborhood of the Frunze Academy. Discovered nothing new, but there are a few horses being kept in the old cavalry stables.

Grow also exchanged information with other military attachés, and his published diary compromised a number of allied nations whose attachés had matched Grow's eagerness to nose out Soviet secrets. He mentioned close contacts with attachés of Britain, Canada, Turkey, and Greece.

Some of the diary excerpts read: "Pope [on the British Embassy staff] dropped by and we had a lengthy conversation concerning the military strength of the Soviet Union. I received a report from Col. Guimond and Major Bush concerning their trip to Tiflis and found it a very informative and useful document."

Again, "Pope dropped by—he insists that we have not seen all positions. Quite right, but we discovered four that he had not seen himself." [There was a healthy rivalry between military attachés that was matched by an exchange of information.] "Pope gave us information about AAA of Leningrad and confirmed our own observation here.

"Sgourdeous, the Greek, likewise longs for a decisive war. He is one of the fighters among the Europeans."

Grow's position on "a decisive war" was the most damaging element in his diary, and the one that provided propaganda fodder for the Russians. Grow was trying to interest General Walter Bedell Smith, one-time Ambassador to Russia and then head of the Central Intelligence Agency, in the merits of preventive war.

He wrote in his diary:

> Got a letter from George King who had been showing my letters to Smith who is interested. I am urging action on preparation for after the next war, which is where we have failed before. He says Smith is interested but there is little action. He also feels that this is a very critical year.

At the Frankfurt conference, he recorded, he represented a "tough" line that he tried to sell to the State Department. He wrote:

> The conference was devoted to a general discussion of Soviet intentions by the groups working on the paper. Freers presented the cautious State Department view that there was nothing going to happen. Barbour thought our paper should be like the one a year ago as there had been no change of importance. I threw a minor bombshell by reading our paper which definitely estimated action this year or before July 1952 by all forms of warfare, including Europe. It was backed up by capabilities and reasons. The paper was accepted as sound and worthy of serious consideration. I admitted it was "a probable" and not necessarily "the most probable" line. Troan backed me up well. I think the State Department will now agree that the situation is not the same as a year ago.

And he adds:

> I started a study on an estimate Barbour wants this week on Soviet intentions—particular reference to the military. Typed notes all evening—sort of thinking out loud. My conclusion pretty close to: This is the year. They can't afford to let the balance tip in our favor. They must have European industry to compete with us—or destroy us—not a simple task.

Grow also made some damaging remarks in his diary along the lines of: "We must hit with blows below the belt. This war cannot be fought according to Marquis of Queensbury rules."

Grow's faith in his European allies was mixed. He wrote on February 5, 1951, that "the Europeans are so timid and the British businessmen are afraid of losing Hong Kong. The French are also reneging."

Not all of the diary was devoted to Grow's thoughts on war and peace and the information he had culled in Russia. He was an inveterate gambler and kept accurate accounts of his gains and losses in Friday night high-stake poker games.

He grumbled about his ambassador, as many diplomats doubtless do, but seldom in writing. He was serving under Alan Kirk, a retired admiral, and he felt that Ambassador Kirk had singled him out for unfair treatment. In his diary, he rages that he was given smaller housing accommodations for himself, his wife, and his two children, than another embassy staff member with the same size family. He complains that the Ambassador criticized him for small mistakes. On April 14, 1951, he wrote: "The Kirks do not seem to be able to behave naturally and at the same time to appear as leaders of the mission." And referring to a cutting remark made by Mrs. Grow to the Ambassador, the general writes: "She really gave it to him."

The contents of the diary were never disputed in Washington after they had appeared in East Germany. Efforts were made to tone down the story and court-martial Grow without having the press find out. But the story broke and the general's indiscretions became a matter of public record.

Grow was the victim of his own carelessness and could never be accused of being "soft" on Russia. So, in all espionage cases involving the American military from general to private, the motive was not political or ideological. There is one case, however, where ideology was important and which shows how the Russians can use even the most bizarre weaknesses to their advantage. This case involves an American general who allegedly helped the Russians because he was an Irish patriot. It happened in 1932, and the general died before he could be prosecuted, but it is important to note today for it shows to what extent responsible leaders can be duped into working against their country.

The case of this general who served the Russians while believing he was helping the Irish was first mentioned by Whittaker Chambers. Chambers' charges were investigated by the Attorney General's office and substantiated, but the names of the principals were never disclosed. According to Chambers, the general gave the Russians the blueprints of the Chrystie tank, which was unmatched in its day for speed and maneuverability.

Chambers writes:

> The Soviet apparatus discovered that an army officer with access to secret tank material was also an Irish patriot. He was in touch with the IRA, which was then fighting the British. The fourth section [of the GRU] decided to secure this officer as a source. In London, representatives of the Soviet underground made contact with an underground group of the IRA. The Russians undertook to send two submarines loaded with machine guns and other arms for the IRA to the West coast of Ireland. In repayment, the IRA agreed that the American Army officer, whom I shall call General O'Gordon, would regularly turn over to Soviet agents in the United States material relating to the Chrystie tank. . . .
>
> In the United States, the deal was clinched by a politician in Queens (whose name I know). General O'Gordon, a man in advanced middle age, was introduced to a Soviet underground contact. The general agreed to take home on weekends the secret tank material. He would turn it over to Soviet agents who would have it microfilmed and return it in time for the general to replace it in the Army's files early Monday morning.*

Chambers added that the general said: "I am glad to help the IRA but I would not do a thing to help those god-damn Rooshians."

He continued:

> There was one hitch. One afternoon the Army called up the general and asked him to return at once a document which for some reason was needed. The general was momentarily embarrassed because none

* Whittaker Chambers, *Witness* (New York: Random House, 1952).

of the tank documents were in his possession. They were being microfilmed and he did not know where they were.

The moral of the story was that the Russians got the tank blueprints, the IRA never received its promised shipment of arms, and the fiery general who loved the Irish died from drinking too much cognac.

Russian methods vary in sophistication, but the principle is always to exploit an individual's discovered flaw. An officer with money problems, with women problems, is always likely to be approached. In West Berlin, a vital Soviet espionage center, there was the case of Colonel Patrick Hayes, forty-eight, bald, flabby, and watery eyed. Hayes was an Air Force colonel assigned to the inspector general's special investigations wing, an intelligence unit supervising the defense of West Berlin against the threat of Soviet attack. It was remarkable that Hayes, as a senior intelligence officer, had never heard of the *Mozhnos*.

Twenty-four-year-old Imgard Margarette Schmidt was trained at the so-called Dance and Gymnastics School in East Germany near the Czechoslovakian border. In this "school" girls ranging in age from nineteen to twenty-six are trained as secretaries, interpreters, barmaids or dance hall hostesses for a period of three months.

Miss Schmidt was trained as a secretary before she was sent to West Berlin. The tall and striking brunette had been recruited at the University of Halle in East Germany, where she was doing graduate work in languages. She agreed to work for the Russians in exchange for better treatment for her fiancé, who had been jailed for political activity.

In West Berlin, she was given enough money to keep up with the international set made up of diplomats, officers, officials, and the more daring elements of German society. She dressed fashionably, wore expensive jewelry, and built up her contacts as she was seen in the right places with the right people. In 1953 she met Colonel Hayes at a party and soon afterward became his mistress. Hayes was a gullible, hail-fellow-well-met type who did not suspect that the attractive Imgard, who was half his age, was granting her favors for anything but his natural charm.

Out of gratitude, he obtained a job for Imgard as a secretary in his own intelligence outfit. She was working in the Order of Battle Section of Military Intelligence, which is responsible for keeping track of Soviet troops through all available sources, including informants from East Germany. She was so openly curious about papers lying on other people's desks that she was dismissed several months later. She had a strong hold on Hayes, for instead of investigating her, he got her another secretarial job, this time at the Templehof Air Force Base.

For almost a year, she transmitted to her Soviet contact information about the Order of Battle Section and the Air Force base, and reports on the duties of Hayes and another American she was seeing, a civilian working for an intelligence unit in West Berlin. Growing bolder when she saw how easy it was, she approached a German national at Templehof and tried to pressure him into giving counter-intelligence information. Instead, he reported her to his superiors and she was placed under surveillance. Less than a month later, she was arrested as she tried to leave West Berlin with confidential documents taken from the base on her person.

She was tried by the American High Commission and sentenced to five years in prison after pleading guilty to collecting and passing American Intelligence data from West Berlin to the Russians in East Berlin.

Not long after, Hayes and his wife were shipped home and on June 17, 1955, the colonel was quietly given an "other than honorable" discharge and forfeited his retirement pay for the next twelve years. The reason given by the Air Force was that he had "shown poor judgment."

XIV. Germany: In the Eye of the Hurricane

AGENTS, defectors, "magic," and subversion all meet head-on in Germany, whose East-West division makes it the battleground of the secret war.

Bypassing the cathedrals and the castles on the Rhine, a visitor to Germany today can make a new kind of tour, learning as he does so of the country's extraordinary postwar boom in espionage. The showpiece, of course, is West Berlin, in many ways a Trojan Horse under permanent menace of engulfment.

High points of this guided cloak-and-dagger tour would be the sites of the proliferating intelligence networks in East and West Germany; a visit with well-known spies in semiretirement; the tour could end in Karlsruhe, a manufacturing center just over the border from France, where a federal tribunal handles a growing backlog of espionage cases with an indifference and dispatch that could only be matched by a New York traffic court.

In Munich, a sight not to be missed would be an innocent-looking compound in the suburb of Pullach. Behind the ten-foot-high concrete wall stands the headquarters of the Federal Intelligence Service, a euphemism for the 5,000-man-strong espionage organization headed by "the Gray General," Reinhard Gehlen.

In Frankfurt's modern I. G. Farben building, offices under the name of Department of Army Detachment mask one of the CIA headquarters for West Germany. In Munich, the CIA is known as

453

the Special Detachment, and in other centers such as Stuttgart and
Berlin it calls itself simply U.S. mission. The national headquarters
for the Defense of the Constitution, West Germany's FBI-like counterintelligence agency, with its political police and its specialists in
Soviet affairs, is in Ehrenfeld, a suburb of Cologne.

Also in Cologne, in a dingy apartment building at 271 Suelzberger-
strasse, one could look in on Otto John, one-time head of the Defense
of the Constitution, who defected to East Germany in July, 1954,
and came back West in December, 1955. He was tried for treason
in 1956, sentenced to four years of hard labor, and was released for
good behavior in 1958. He is now trying to obtain a re-trial on the
basis of new evidence.

Moving on to Berlin, there is a profusion of organizations engaged
in clandestine work. West Berlin has been dubbed "the new Tangiers,"
where secret military information, a forged passport, a gun disguised
as a cigarette case, or a microscope concealed in a fountain pen can
be bought or sold as easily as the morning paper. Also for sale are
the services of agents, for either side, and often both. West Berlin,
represented as a bulwark against Communism, a gallant advance
post in the Cold War, is actually more like a sponge, oozing and
absorbing elements from East and West. The hardening of positions
in recent months has slowed the flow of agents and information.
Before the East Germans built their Chinese wall, passage from one
zone to the next was unimpeded save for irregular and ineffective
controls. Going from East to West, from Mr. Ulbricht's jail to the
free world, was as simple as going from the East to the West side of
New York City. There was no language problem, no adjustment to
new customs. It was ideal for spies.

There were hidden motives for the most innocent activity. A visit
in the East zone to see relatives, daily commuting for those who
worked in the West and lived in the East, mailing a letter from one
zone to another, having a friendly chat with a Vopo at the Friedrich-
strasse (East zone) subway station—these and many other innocent
acts could reap vital information.

With false papers, CIA-directed agents were sent through the
Brandenberg Gate on the first lap of a secret journey that was to take
them deep into the Soviet Union. Scores of agents came into East
Berlin to prompt doctors and other professional men to defect to the
West. Before the wall was built, West Berlin was known as "a kidnap

town," where East German goons could drag a victim across the line to the complete indifference of passers-by, inured by long years of submission to an abnormal situation, like New Yorkers passively watching a teen-age gang fight or a mugging.

In East Berlin's Lichtenberg sector, the buildings that were once the Third Reich's Ministry of Finance today hold what former Secretary of State Christian Herter once called "the heaviest concentration of subversive and espionage activity in the world"—the East German Ministry for State Security (MfS). Not far away, in Berlin's Karlshorst enclave, the Soviet KGB has taken over Saint Antonius Hospital and installed a staff of more than 800. The Soviet GRU houses its staff of 250 in Wunsdorf, a small town near Berlin, and has four branch offices staffed by at least 25 Soviet officers each.

East Germany is crawling with special espionage bureaus, such as the courier service at Beyerstrasse 7 in Potsdam, where about fifty young men and women are trained for operations in the Western zone. They have a fleet of Western-make cars, mainly Mercedes-Benz and Opels, with forged license plates, some of them diplomatic plates. A device that permits the driver to change license plates while the car is in motion is a feature not found on factory models.

Pushing further east to Dresden, the tour would include a visit to the East German Central Institute for Nuclear Physics, where atom spy Klaus Fuchs was given the job of deputy director when he was released from his British prison.

All over East Germany, branch offices of the Ministry for State Security and front organizations of every description are at work directing espionage efforts against West Germany and West Berlin, efforts which the West does its best to match.

Such massive penetration was bound to produce results. It is because of the Eastern espionage effort and its successes that West Germany has been called NATO's weakest security link. The NATO allies share military and political secrets, which time and time again have been leaked to the East through the espionage open door of West Germany. The fact that one out of five West Germans has relatives behind the Iron Curtain, the thousands of refugees who have created a floating population that constitutes a major security risk, the political instability of Germany over the last twenty years which has worn thin the meaning of loyalty, the necessity on the part of many German officials to suit their political ideologies to changing times, all these have made West Germany the most vulnerable of all Western allies to espionage.

It has become so customary for spies to be found in high places that two significant espionage arrests in December, 1961, created hardly a flurry. Yet the arrests showed:

1.   That Soviet intelligence had penetrated the supposedly security-proof Gehlen Organization. Heinz Felfe worked on the Gehlen Soviet desk where he collated reports from agents behind the Iron Curtain. He was a senior official working at Gehlen headquarters outside Munich and he was arrested December 13 and charged with suspicion of treasonable activities. Felfe reportedly confessed that he had penetrated the Gehlen Organization for the Russians out of ideological conviction. He said he had been a Communist for many years.

2. That Soviet intelligence had infiltrated the NATO command. Arrested forty-eight hours before Felfe was Wehrmacht Colonel Carl Otto von Hinckeldey, a regular officer since 1937 who had important NATO functions and who had been granted the so-called NATO "cosmic clearance" which gave him access to all NATO documents. The colonel was arrested on suspicion of turning over classified documents to the Russians.

It was not the first time that prominent West Germans had betrayed allied secrets to the West. Possibly the most important espionage case discovered in postwar West Germany broke in the fall of 1960. On October 28, Alfred Frenzel, a respected Social Democratic member of the West German parliament, was arrested by agents of the Defense for the Constitution in the parliament (Bundestag) building in Bonn. Frenzel, a native of the Sudeten, which was annexed by Germany in 1938 and returned to Czechoslovakia in 1945, had been a deputy since 1953 for the district of Augsburg in southern Bavaria. Through his zealous Party work he had risen to be deputy chairman for his district. In the Bundestag he served on two key committees. Through his chairmanship of the Restitution Committee, which settles war-damage claims, he was in contact with refugees and East Germans; through his membership on the Defense Committee, he had access to the secret military information which Defense Minister Franz-Josef Strauss reported to parliament.

One can imagine the furor the arrest of a prominent American Congressman in the Capitol building on espionage charges would create. The Frenzel case was that kind of a sensation. Parliamentary immunity did not protect him, for under German law it cannot be invoked if a deputy is arrested within twenty-four hours of committing a crime.

The sixty-one-year-old Frenzel had been observed the day before giving information to his Communist contact. In a near state of shock, Frenzel signed a full confession and resigned his seat in parliament with a letter to the speaker that he was "not worthy to serve."

His story was pathetically symptomatic of postwar turbulence in Central Europe. Born in a working-class family in the Sudeten, he drifted toward Communism in his student days and became a member of the Czechoslovak Communist Party in the twenties. He was made cashier for his district but was forced to leave the party in shame after he was exposed as an embezzler of the party funds he was meant to safekeep.

In the thirties he emigrated to England and served during World War II in the Royal Air Force as a cook. He left a young daughter behind in Czechoslovakia. Moving to West Germany after the war, he first ran for political office in 1953. In the course of a bitter campaign, a political opponent revived the old embezzlement offense of the thirties and also charged that Frenzel had lied about his former Communist ties when he joined the Social Democrat Party. Frenzel sued his opponent for libel and swore under oath that the charges were untrue. He won the election and rose swiftly in the Party ranks.

In 1956, the East Germans became interested in Frenzel's political success. Using the classic blackmail technique and the argument that his daughter in Prague would be better off if he co-operated, they put Frenzel in touch with the Czechoslovak apparat in Bonn.

From 1956 up to his arrest, Frenzel met with his Czech contact thirty-nine times, and divulged military secrets and information on the refugee problem, which he knew well. He was paid for his trouble and received in all 27,000 Deutsche marks (nearly $7,000). In a four-day trial held behind closed doors, Frenzel gave a list of the secrets he had sold to Communist agents. He was sentenced to fifteen years in jail, the maximum sentence under the peacetime treason charge. The case was a blow to his party and to the relations between the executive and legislative branches of government. It was a handicap for Willy Brandt, who ran for election in the fall of 1961 on the Social Democratic ticket against Chancellor Adenauer.

One of the complaints Brandt had made against the Adenauer Government was that it did not give parliament enough information on defense matters. The Frenzel case was an excellent reason for the members of the Adenauer cabinet to cast doubt on the parliament's trustworthiness, and to continue to withhold sensitive information.

The Frenzel case had a curious aftermath. In December, 1961, two Czech agents who had been arrested with Frenzel and sentenced one to six and the other to five years in prison, were exchanged by the Bonn Government for three Nazi generals convicted by a Czech wartime court. Spy exchanges had often been discussed, as in the plan to trade U-2 pilot Francis Gary Powers for Soviet spy Colonel Rudolf Abel, but had never been carried out. The exchange of convicted spies for convicted war criminals was an unprecedented Cold War move. Perhaps the Bonn Government felt it was getting the best of the bargain. It was receiving three generals whose death sentences had been commuted to life imprisonment for a major and a captain in Czech military intelligence who were serving much lighter sentences. The generals were seventy-one-year-old Rudolf Toussaint, who had been Wehrmacht plenipotentiary in Nazi-occupied Czechoslovakia; Ernst Hitzegrad, seventy-three, one-time police commander in the area; and a division commander Richard Schmidt, sixty-seven. The two Czechs turned over by the Germans to the Czech Red Cross were Major Jindrich Augustin and a captain known under the alias of Ernst Langer. They had been Frenzel's Bonn contacts.

In April, 1961, the West German Minister of the Interior summed up before the Bundestag what the massive East German espionage effort meant in terms of money and manpower. Gerhard Schröder, who was later to become Foreign Minister in Adenauer's coalition government, said there were roughly 16,000 Communist agents active in West Germany. He said the Pankow regime was spending $125,000,000 a year in "Westwork," the Communist term for espionage.

He quoted a Soviet official who explained espionage directed against West Germany in these terms: "The espionage organizations of the Soviet bloc have no clear missions of information-gathering. Their task consists rather in altering the political situation in West Germany in such a way that the unification of Germany can be made possible in the Communist sense. Behind the information-gathering are the preparations for the overthrow of the regime. There is no element in the state, whether economic, political, or cultural, that must not be a target for spying and subversion."

Dr. Schröder added that between 1950 and 1960, 2,500 agents had been caught in West Germany, and 2,186 had been convicted on treason charges; 19,000 more had confessed to espionage missions and were not prosecuted.

Dr. Schröder knew whereof he spoke. Weeks before he delivered the speech, a clerk in his own ministry had been caught stealing top-secret documents and turning them over to East German agents. The minister ordered new security checks throughout his ministry. The clerk admitted under questioning that his only motive had been to add to his low salary. He was getting ridiculously low sums for the secrets he stole, $20 or $30 for each document.

To describe in detail the espionage activities of East Germany, the Government in 1959 published a white book entitled *East Berlin, Propaganda and Subversion Center,* and a black book called *Eastern Underground Activity against West Berlin.* Not to be outdone, the East Germans followed up with a white book of their own, called *Espionage in West Berlin,* in which they listed twenty-four espionage organizations operating out of West Berlin, with specific charges against each group.

In a memorandum on the Berlin question in 1959, the East German Foreign Ministry wrote that "at present more than sixty bureaus of foreign secret services and organizations of agents and spies exist on West Berlin territory."

Thus it appears that in Germany, and more particularly Berlin, espionage is being conducted on a massive scale by both camps. A scale model of the secret war between Eastern and Western blocs is fought with ruthless vehemence. All the symptoms observed on the large scale are present—the charges and countercharges; the denunciation of tactics and goals; the mutual use of "dirty tricks"; the indignation to territorial violations. Statements of outrage by East and West German governments often sound so much alike they can be interchanged.

For instance:

"The activity of these organizations is aided by the fact that an open frontier and unhindered traffic exist between West Berlin and the democratic part of Berlin: This makes it easier to funnel agents and saboteurs into the German Democratic Republic and the other socialist states." (East German memorandum on Berlin in February, 1959.)

"West Berlin, owing to its geographical position and political situation, seems to be a target of particular importance for subversive operations." (West German black book, April, 1959.)

East and West complain about violations of the common border and the ease with which agents are infiltrated. The West charges that one-third of the refugees into West Berlin are agents. The East countercharges that a number of organizations are specialized in conducting defection campaigns in East Berlin.

One of these is the League of Free Jurists, founded in 1949 with CIA subsidies. With its staff of eighty based in Berlin, the league offers free information to East Germans. Those who come to their headquarters at Limastrasse 29 in Berlin-Zehlendorf are told how they can defect and what job possibilities there are. They are also questioned about developments in East Germany and may be passed on to other agencies for further questioning. Through its contacts, particularly with lawyers in East Germany, the League of Free Jurists obtains data on secret trials, new laws and legal procedures, and other matters kept from the East German public. It also collects data on violations of treaty agreements by the East Germans.

A measure of the Free Jurists' effectiveness has been the abduction of two of its leaders by the East Germans. In 1952 Dr. Walter Linse was kidnaped on his way to work and dragged across the border. When General Lemuel Mathewson of the American zone command protested to the Soviet Control Commission for Berlin, the Russians denied knowing anything about the kidnaping. Several weeks later, a sensational spy trial started in East Germany. The seven defendants were charged with being agents for the Free Jurists. The star witness for the prosecution was Ruth Schramm, who had been Dr. Linse's secretary and defected to the East. Two of the defendants were sentenced to life imprisonment, the five others were given heavy prison terms. The Linse mystery was never cleared up. His successor, Ernst Tillich, said he was in Lichtenberg Prison in the East zone. In June, 1960, the Associated Press reported that Dr. Linse had died in a Soviet prison in 1953, but several days later the wire service sent out a correction—it was not the same man.

In 1957, forty-year-old Dr. Erwin Neumann disappeared while sailing on the Wannsee. Investigation revealed that the Free Jurists' chief had gone to the East zone to pick up a fellow sailing enthusiast. This unidentified friend, according to security police, was an East German agent who had lured the good doctor into dangerous territory. Witnesses reported that on the morning of his disappearance, they saw an East German gunboat conspicuously near the spot where he was to pick up his friend. Dr. Neumann was not heard from again.

Some of the strongest attacks of the East Germans against a Western group were directed against the Kampfgruppe gegen Unmenschlichkeit (Fighting Group against Inhumanity). West German officials change the subject when the Kampfgruppe is mentioned. It attracted so much criticism that it was dissolved in 1959.

The organization was set up in 1948 to support political prisoners and their families. It reportedly received funds through the CIA and later through the private fund-raising agency that finances Radio Free Europe, Crusade for Freedom. The Kampfgruppe soon took its name seriously and sent commandos into the Eastern zone on various missions, from sending up propaganda balloons to blowing up a bridge.

Some of the crimes the Kampfgruppe has been accused of by the East Germans tax credulity. In one case, East German security police investigated the strange deaths of 7,000 cows in a co-operative dairy near Fürstenberg. They allegedly found a Kampfgruppe agent working in a plant that made wire to bale corn fodder. The wire was coated with a rustproof and waterproof wax, and the agent, according to the East Germans, poisoned this coating so that when the cows ate the corn they died a horrible death.

Other crimes attributed to the Kampfgruppe:

1951: Agents set fire to outdoor stands of the State Trade Organizations in East Berlin; they added soap to powdered milk destined for East German schools; they short-circuited the electric plant at Eberswalde.

1952: Convicted Kampfgruppe agent Johann Burianek attempted to blow up a railroad bridge near the town of Erkner; agents sabotaged gas stations along national highways; destroyed air pressure hoses on freight trains; derailed diesels in railroad yards; put sand in the turbine of a factory, bringing it to a standstill; and more than 500 phosphorus bombs were distributed among agents.

1953: Agents burned twelve cars in a freight train in the Wustermark station.

1955: Agents set fire to an East Berlin radio station.

1958: Two agents blew up the bridge at the Baltic Sea resort of Herringsdorf; other agents set fire to a tile-producing factory in Fürstenwalde; an attempt was made to blow up the six-span bridge at Weimar.

Some of these charges were made by the East German regime, most of them were published in West German newspapers and magazines, including the popular weekly *Der Spiegel*. It appears that one of the main tasks of the Kampfgruppe was to try and cripple the East German economy. After several agents were caught in 1955, the Hamburg magazine *Der Stern* wrote that "the leaders of the Kampfgruppe have turned it into a spy center. Refugees and young idealists are pressed into service for espionage and sabotage. They lose the best years of their lives in prison because of these senseless undertakings."

Another favorite target for Communist propaganda and provocation is the NTS (Narodno-Troudoyov Soyouz or National Alliance of Russian Solidarists). This group of anti-Communist Russians is remarkable for two reasons:

It is the only organization that systematically penetrates the Soviet Union. A recent MVD directive on Western espionage described NTS as a "very dangerous organization . . . the only one operating on Soviet soil."

It is not a product of the Cold War, but was founded in 1930 with the aim of overthrowing the Soviet regime. Since then, it has been infiltrating the Soviet Union with agents and literature and its experience has proved indispensable to Western intelligence.

NTS headquarters is a combined office and printing press in Frankfurt am Main. It also has a training camp in Bad Godesberg where volunteers are trained for the perilous mission of penetrating the Soviet Union with the help of CIA instructors and equipment.

The position of NTS is complex. It is not an intelligence but a revolutionary organization. It is committed to the overthrow of the Soviet Communist regime by forceful means. With its limited resources, this is like knocking over an elephant with a fly swatter. Privately, Western intelligence officials scoff at the organization and describe its leaders as "dreamers" or "hotheads." However, since they are virtually the only ones who have succeeded in penetrating the Iron Curtain and since they continue to undertake such missions, the CIA and other Western intelligence groups humor them. Conversely, the

NTS knows its aims are not those of Western intelligence but co-operates with the agencies in exchange for equipment and subsidies. The relationship is unofficial and cynical. NTS men carry out espionage missions on the side while they pursue their ideal of revolution. Western intelligence keeps the organization solvent while deriding its goals.

The man in charge of NTS secret operations is Georgi Okolovich, chairman of the executive bureau. Although in his sixties his face is almost boyish, with bright blue eyes and a lock of hair that falls over his brow. Stocky and barrel-chested, he looks like one of those Russians who live to be one hundred and fifty and attribute their longevity to vodka and cigars. Okolovich has led the picaresque life of an old revolutionary, highlighted by two clandestine trips into Stalinist Russia. Attempts on his life are made regularly; the most recent was the sensational case of Captain Nikolai Khokhlov, who was sent to assassinate him in 1954 and defected instead.

Okolovich cringes when the NTS is referred to as an *émigré* group. He recalls Napoleon's aphorism that "an *émigré* is a man who had forgotten nothing and learned nothing." The members of NTS have forgotten nothing but have learned a great deal in their years of exile, he feels. The number of members is confidential, perhaps because it is not very large. There is an "Active Committee" of 100 members, most of them in Frankfurt, although NTS has an important West Berlin bureau.

Since the Communist line is to attack the group as "pawns in American hands" and "tools of the CIA," Okolovich tries to tone down any association with allied intelligence. Privately, he admits that "we work with all the secret services. We are the allies of everyone who is against Communism." He denies, however, that NTS agents are spies. "The men we send into the Soviet Union," he says, "are forbidden to carry out any intelligence work. It would conflict with their revolutionary mission." The job of the NTS agent is to spread the gospel of revolution like a Jehovah's Witness diffusing warnings of Armageddon from door to door.

NTS no longer uses American equipment, but buys what it needs from the Germans. The organization is understandably discreet about its budget, mentioning only that it comes from "private" sources.

Above all else, NTS strives to keep clear of domination by other groups. "Our people are not for sale to intelligence services," Okolovich says. "We are caught in a cross-fire between Soviet efforts to discredit us by labeling us foreigners and American stooges, and Western interests with which we are only in partial agreement."

If the NTS had its way, it would attack the Soviet Union tomorrow. Its leaders claim that the only way to avoid a nuclear world war is to overthrow the Communist regime. They believe that the majority of the Soviet people would rise up against the regime once the battle begins. Okolovich sees a terrifying civil war shaking Russia to its foundations, with the regime using atom bombs against its own people. The only ones faithful to the Government would be the handful of rulers who have a vested interest in it. NTS remains ready "to support every earthquake," and considers any less forceful position "soft" and unrealistic.

While waiting for the revolution to begin, it sends its agents into the Soviet Union via West Berlin, East Germany, and Poland or Czechoslovakia. The agents set up "molecular" cells which carry on propaganda activity and wait in readiness for the cataclysm to begin. The cells do not communicate, but learn of one another's existence through the NTS symbol, St. Vladimir's pitchfork. This crudely drawn trident is sometimes seen on the side of a building or a wall in a Soviet city, along with the NTS slogan: *Nesem Tiranam Smert* (Death to the Tyrants).

Nikolai Khokhlov said in testimony before a Congressional committee in 1954 that "the NTS have their own cells within the ranks of the Soviet Army and in the Soviet Union. For liaison, NTS sends a large number of couriers regularly who cross the frontier and go to both the territory of the Soviet Union and the people's democracies . . . the NTS uses the same revolutionary methods by which the Communist Party itself came into power, namely the molecular method of revolution." (Penetration is discussed in greater detail in the chapter on CIA techniques.)

It sends propaganda into the Soviet Union by balloon, by floating waterproof packages downriver, by handing pamphlets to Soviet garrisons in East Germany, and by other methods. Since Stalin's death in 1953, NTS estimates that it has sent more than 100,000,000 pamphlets and magazines into the Soviet Union. Its publishing company Possev puts out a weekly and other periodicals, including *Za Rossiou* (*For Russia*), and *Nacy Dni* (*Our Days*). It also publishes forged copies of *Pravda* and *Izvestia*.

Its radio station, Free Russia, broadcasts ten hours a day, but West German authorities occasionally silence the station after vigorous Soviet protests. In 1958, East German raiders time-bombed the building where the technicians and their families live, in Sprendlingen, near Frankfurt. There were no victims, but the building was destroyed.

The NTS contacts many of the increasing number of Soviet visitors to the West. It sends its agents to congresses and exhibits where the Soviets have delegations. Close to 8,000 Soviet tourists went to the Brussels Fair in 1958, thousands more attended a youth festival in Vienna last year. Many of them go back to the Soviet Union knowing what NTS is. Some even agree to take back NTS literature and distribute it. When Red Navy units visited the Scandinavian countries in 1956, NTS contacted 1,230 Soviet officers and sailors: 385 were indifferent; 700 showed interest in the movement and accepted its publications; 110 expressed active disapproval of the regime and promised active support of NTS (according to an NTS poll).

When Molotov was Soviet delegate at a Geneva four-power conference, an NTS agent took his picture, which was published in *Possev* with the caption:

> *This photo of Molotov was taken by a special* Possev *correspondent from a distance of sixteen feet. Noiseless bullets that the Soviets supplied to Capt. Khokhlov penetrate two feet of cotton at a distance of thirty feet. We do not know what Molotov's relative density is, but we wonder what his chief of security Borzov was thinking about and what he is being paid for?*

In 1956, an NTS official found himself on the same Berlin-Bonn plane as Soviet Ambassador Valerian Zorin, who was returning from the Communist Party Congress. The two men talked politics during the two-hour flight and their photograph was published in *Possev*.

Claims of NTS propaganda and penetration are substantiated and even sometimes exaggerated in the Communist press. *Literatournaya Gazeta* said in March, 1957:

> In March, 1955, NTS printed 14,000,000 tracts, sent by balloon from the German Federal Republic, in the direction of the East . . . it has been established that NTS sent into Eastern Europe not only tracts, but also secret agents. Its daily task is infiltrating the state organisms of the socialist republics.

Izvestia in September, 1960, warned all Soviets traveling in the West that "in Europe there are groups who will try to give you political propaganda. This happened especially during the Rome Olympics when Soviet athletes received tracts printed on the official stationery of the Italian Olympic Committee."

A member of the Soviet delegation at the United Nations said in December, 1959, that "many groups like the NTS have found asylum on American territory. They are anti-Soviet criminals and it seems that the United States is spending a great deal of money to assist those who work against the Soviet regime."

If all the Soviets did was complain in the press and on the floor of the General Assembly, the NTS could breathe easier. But they supplement their indignation with assassination attempts, kidnapings, and bombings. The most recent act of violence was on July 18, 1961, when a bomb was thrown into the courtyard of the NTS Frankfurt headquarters, shattering the windows and damaging some of the printing equipment. The bomb left a crater in the concrete courtyard three feet in diameter and one foot deep.

In December, 1958, a former Hitler youth member named Wolfgang Wildprett was hired by the East German Ministry for State Security to assassinate Dr. Vladimir Poremsky, president of NTS. Wildprett, a black marketeer and small-time gangster, was given a dagger, an automatic, photographs of his victim, and a down payment of 500 marks ($125), with the promise of 20,000 marks if he succeeded. He got cold feet and turned himself in.

Nikolai Khokhlov also balked when he was sent to kill Okolovich, and today he is one of the most active members of NTS. Two successful operations against NTS members were the kidnapings of Valeri Tremmel in Austria and Dr. Alexander Trushnovich in West Berlin in 1954. Tremmel was drugged by Soviet agents, removed to the Soviet sector, and never seen again.

The Trushnovich case is still controversial. He was a member of the NTS council and had volunteered to be chief of the Berlin office. A long-time member of NTS, he was preparing for a lecture tour of the United States at the time of his kidnaping. On April 13, 1954, he was lured into a trap by an Eastern agent named Heinz Glaeske, who had gained his confidence by helping him arrange meetings with Soviet refugees.

He was subdued in Glaeske's apartment, thrown into a car waiting outside, and carried to East Berlin. Glaeske disappeared, and a few days later his wife also vanished. Police found traces of struggle in Glaeske's apartment, and bloodstains on the floor.

Several days later, the East German news agency announced that Dr. Trushnovich had defected to the East. An article headlined WHY I BROKE WITH THE PAST said that "after many trips throughout Europe, I became convinced there was no future for *émigré* organizations. These organizations are obliged to offer their services to Western intelligence to survive. Their members are used for espionage, subversion, and diversion."

The article said that a school for Soviet *émigrés* which Dr. Trushnovich had created in West Germany had been turned into a spy school. The NTS, the article said, was riddled with American agents acting as watchdogs. The East German news agency also announced that Glaeske had been arrested as an American agent.

All this was denounced as fabrication by the doctor's family and the NTS, but the controversy kept raging. While petitions were signed for his release and rewards were offered, the West German newspaper *Die Welt* wrote that Trushnovich was a double agent who had worked for Moscow since the founding of the NTS.

The NTS believes today that Trushnovich was badly hurt in the struggle to subdue him and died on his way to East Berlin. It is noted that he had been seriously wounded in World War I and had a silver plate in his head. A blow on the head could easily have killed him. The NTS points out that he did not go through the routine of the traditional defector's press conference in East Berlin. After the single article published under his name, he was never heard from again.

Aside from openly "aggressive" organizations like the Kampfgruppe and the NTS, there are a number of Western agencies whose job it is to collect and diffuse information behind the Iron Curtain. To the spy-conscious East Germans these are simply more espionage organizations.

It is not easy to distinguish when an operation such as a newsletter on East Germany becomes espionage. Nor can a border line be easily drawn where radio broadcasts begin to advocate subversion. Faced with the broad issues of the Cold War, the struggle between democracy and totalitarianism, we tend to lose a sense for nuances— to the East, these are pure espionage outfits; to the West, they are legitimate radio and press operations. Actually, they are a little of both.

The most important of these agencies are Information Bureau West, Radio in the American Sector (RIAS), Radio Free Europe (RFE), and Radio Liberty. All are ostensibly concerned with information, yet all have a political line, deal in the Berlin "refugee trade" and receive funds from "confidential" (*i.e.,* Western intelligence) sources.

Information Bureau West is a private news agency dealing exclusively with East Germany. It operates from a black, fenced-off two-story house in a wooded suburb of Berlin, with no identifying marks. Its workers have pseudonyms and it receives office supplies and mail at a drop with a front name. These elaborate security measures are mainly due to East German threats against employees and other measures of intimidation.

IBW gets much of its information from secret sources in East Germany and from refugees. The 150 clients for its daily newsletter read like a "Who's Who" of the West German Government, press, and secret services. Through a middleman, IBW buys every available East German publication, from high school newspapers to house organs for factories. Through the same middleman, the East German Government obtains the IBW newsletter. The agency interviews selected refugees at the Marienfelde camp. Through these efforts, IBW has built up one of the best-stocked archives on East Germany, government archives not excluded. An entire room is stocked with 90,000 filing cards on important East Germans, detailing their past affiliations and present careers.

The agency is able to ferret out signs of discontent and other information the Pankow regime is trying to keep secret. In June, 1961, IBW learned that fifty workers in the Lev electronic plant in Henningsdorf had sent a letter of protest to Walter Ulbricht about the lack of consumer goods. The letter was destroyed before it reached Ulbricht, and some of the fifty were arrested. Others fled to West Germany.

In 1958, fifty-eight students from the University of Jena were given heavy prison terms in secret trials. Their crime? They had sent East German boss, Walter Ulbricht, a petition calling for free elections. There was not a word about the trials in the East German press until IBW revealed their existence.

IBW receives funds from the Ministry for Pan-German affairs. It has secret contacts with East Germans. On these two counts, the

East German Government brands it an espionage organization. Helmuth Bohlmann and Elizabeth Rapp, who head the fact-finding agency, are accused by the East of being former propaganda officials of Goebbels'. In reality the two directors are themselves refugees from the East. After World War II, they both worked for the East German press agency, the Allgemeiner Deutscher Nachrichtendienst. In 1949, they left in disgust when the agency refused to print the results of a referendum which had been overwhelmingly defeated despite the trick phrasing of the question: "Are you in favor of a lasting peace— if you are, vote for so and so." The director of the agency told Bohlmann and Miss Rapp that "we're not here to publish news, but to make propaganda." They fled to West Germany and founded IBW, which is dedicated to the exposure of Eastern propaganda. The East Germans charge that IBW disseminates false information. An East Berlin agent who gave IBW false reports was quoted as saying: "I realized Bohlmann and Rapp were eager to receive reports of every kind whether verified or not, and also that the Western press lived on such reports. I began to disorient Bohlmann. I gave the impression I had received a secret report concerning the state secretariat for high schools. This communication was received with interest and Rapp did not even ask to what extent it was true."

In the Englishgarten, a park in the center of Munich, a compound of prefabricated buildings houses Radio Free Europe, which broadcasts news and "special" programs to satellite countries (not to the Soviet Union).

Through its twenty-eight transmitters in Germany and Portugal, Radio Free Europe beams to Poland, Hungary, Czechoslovakia, Rumania and Bulgaria (Albania does not have enough radio sets to make broadcasts there worth while). With a budget of $11,000,000 a year, much of it gifts from large corporations such as Esso, Ford, and General Motors, and with a staff of 1,200 in Munich alone, the radio station is as large as a good-sized government agency.

Its programs to the satellites, emphasizing whatever can make the puppet regimes look bad, are broken down in the following way: 17 per cent straight news, 20 per cent commentary (the commercial), 7 per cent Western press review, with the balance consisting of features, music, and programs for specific groups (housewives, factory workers, students, etc.).

Twice in its eleven-year career, Radio Free Europe has been in serious trouble. In 1956, it was charged with acting as a kind of cheerleader in the Hungarian revolution, promising American aid and calling on the freedom fighters to continue their heroic struggle. This is a black eye from which RFE has never fully recovered and some people still refer to the organization as "the ones who caused the Hungarian revolution."

RFE officials explain that the revolution in the fall of 1956 caught them by surprise and that their only role during the uprising was to monitor the Hungarian radio taken over by the freedom fighters and rebroadcast it throughout Hungary. They kept up their usual programs of news and commentary, and reported on the simultaneous Suez crisis. RFE cites two reasons for public belief that it promised to aid the Hungarian revolt. First, radio Leipzig went "black" at that time and broadcast as Radio Free Europe, purposely misguiding the Hungarian rebels. Second, there was an unfortunate deletion from the text of an interview of three freedom fighters carried by major wire services. At the interview in Bonn, the three were asked: "Is it true that radio broadcasts promised the freedom fighters United States military aid?" The answer was yes. But the next question and answer were deleted from the dispatches. They were: "Are you sure it was Radio Free Europe?" "No, of course I'm not sure."

Since Radio Free Europe is a private American organization operating on West German soil, its alleged involvement in the Hungarian uprising strained its relations with the West German Government. To vindicate itself, RFE sent tapes of all its broadcasts during the revolution, more than three miles of tape, to the West German Government and to the Council of Europe in Strasbourg.

RFE was not given a complete bill of health and was induced to fire members of its staff who had, it was felt, gone too far in giving moral support to the revolution. Chancellor Adenauer, after studying the tapes, said reports of promised help to the Hungarian people were not based on fact. He added, however, that some "remarks" broadcast by the station had been open to misinterpretation.

RFE's second black eye was administered by U.S. Ambassador to Poland Jacob Beam in the summer of 1959. Ambassador Beam asked the State Department to induce RFE to cease its Polish broadcasts, which he said hampered him in his work. He said that since he had no control over the propaganda content of the broadcasts, he was often at cross purposes with the RFE "line." He suggested his relations with Polish officials would be less strained and more purposeful if RFE stayed off his territory. When Secretary of State Christian A. Herter was asked to comment on the request, he sidestepped gracefully by saying he had the utmost confidence in and respect for Ambassador Beam's ability, and also knew the effective and necessary work Radio Free Europe was doing.

Since these two incidents reflecting a rather aggressive line of propaganda, Radio Free Europe has gone out of its way to describe its basic dogma thus: Russian rule in the satellites will end through gradual changes and the fractionalist tendencies of Communism. We do not advocate revolution, but we want to prepare these countries for change and at the same time keep alive the interest of exiles in their own countries.

One indication of RFE's effectiveness is the tremendous jamming operation conducted against its broadcasts. Since the RFE network began competing with state-controlled radios, more than 2,000 jamming transmitters have been installed in the satellite countries, at a cost of $225,000,000. This is more than twice the total budget of RFE since its founding. Despite the jamming, RFE gets through by using several frequencies, especially at night, when jamming is less effective.

As other examples of its usefulness, RFE claims the following "exclusives": In 1956, it broadcast Khrushchev's "secret" speech for three and a half days to make sure all the satellites would get it. It also broadcast the text of Djilas' *The New Class,* which had been suppressed behind the Iron Curtain. When the workers of Poznan rose against the Polish regime in 1956, RFE told the other satellites. When Joseph Swiatlo defected from the Polish secret police, he taped 100 hours of interviews with RFE, describing secret police methods and aims—RFE claims that following the broadcasts of the interviews, there were improvements in the treatment of political prisoners in Poland. RFE broadcast the full United Nations report on Hungary, which had been distorted in the regime press. In 1958, the Rumanian regime passed a new criminal code, making unauthorized contact with foreigners punishable by death. The code was not published, so that Rumanians could be arrested and convicted without knowing they had broken a law. RFE obtained the text of the code and broadcast it in Rumania. The Rumanian radio announced later that the code had been published and was available.

Another way of judging RFE is through attacks in the satellite press. A recent exhibit in Budapest on "Espionage Against the Hungarian People's Republic" includes mention of a Mrs. Angyal, "who was condemned to death and hanged for sending spy reports to Radio Free Europe." In Poland, the Party organ *Tygodnik Demokratyczny* claimed in its March 8, 1961 issue that RFE was used as a source of information by espionage organizations that train spies to penetrate the Iron Curtain.

The charges that RFE is a spy organization are based on its questioning of Iron Curtain refugees and its monitoring of thirty-five satellite radio stations. RFE has about fifteen advance posts on the periphery of the satellite countries, from Stockholm to Istanbul, and their job is to obtain information about the puppet regimes. Employees of RFE who defected to their satellite countries of origin said they had carried out espionage assignments for the network. Like all the other private or semiofficial anti-Communist agencies in West Germany, RFE is a target for East German provocation. The East Germans single out American agencies in the hope of making them unpopular with the West German regime that harbors them. Front organizations such as the League for German Purity call German employees of RFE and jibe: "Why don't you find honest work instead of staying with that spy group?" Tetrahedron nails are sprinkled over the Englischgarten yard to give cars flat tires and prompt RFE to ask for police protection. In December, 1959, the salt cellars of the RFE cafeteria were spiked with atropine, a belladonna extract. The *provocateurs* apparently wanted to kill no one, for they could have used strychnine instead with lethal results. In this case, many employees were violently sick, the police were called, and one policeman remarked: "Why are things like this always happening to you people?"

RIAS (Radio in the American Sector) and Radio Liberty perform functions similar to RFE for East Germany and the Soviet Union, respectively. Radio Liberty operates out of Munich in a building near the airfield where Chamberlain landed in 1938. It broadcasts in Russian and sixteen other languages spoken in the Soviet Socialist Republics. The programs are beamed into the Soviet Union from West and East—tapes are flown to Formosa for broadcast there. The staff is made up of 150 Soviet *émigrés* who know the mentality and needs of their listeners. Like Radio Free Europe, Radio Liberty gets through despite jamming and is attacked in the Soviet press as a front for American intelligence. Also like RFE, it questions Soviet defectors and has access to "special" information. Since it was founded in 1953, two of Radio Liberty's *émigré* announcers have been murdered by KGB agents. Recently, the network changed its name from Radio Liberation to its present designation, feeling that "liberation" might be too aggressive a word.

It states that its objective is to inform the Soviets about what they don't know through their own media or what they get distorted. The goal is not to advocate overthrow of the regime but to prompt the Russians themselves to put pressure on their Government for better conditions and liberal institutions. Radio Liberty gets about a dozen letters a week from its Soviet listeners and learns from recent defectors that its broadcasts get through. Some letters approve and plead for help from the regime's oppression. Others are mixed in approval, like the engineer in Leningrad who wrote: "I listen to your broadcasts and would like to object to your stand of opposition to the aspirations of the Soviet people."

RIAS comes in for special attack from the East Germans since it is directed specifically against them. Based in Berlin-Schöneberg, it is said to be under the direct control of the CIA and the CIC. The East German Government published what claimed to be a request from the RIAS director to have refugees on call at certain times for questioning by a CIC man. The memo, dated March 2, 1955, and signed G. A. Ewing, was addressed "to all interviewers in the policy department," and said: "The CIC representative Mr. Meissemer will be at your disposal in the future every Thursday and Friday. We beg you to make appointments on both those days for refugees from the Soviet occupation zone who should be introduced to him."

Another organization with "twilight" activities is the Ministry for Pan-German affairs (Bundesministerium fur Gesamtdeutsche Fragen), which handles, among other things, the refugee problem. In 1958, the West German newspaper *Spandauer Volksblatt* revealed a quarrel going on within the ministry on the use of funds. Minister Lemmer wanted to stop subsidizing secret organizations but ran up against the opposition of his deputy Franz Thedieck, who enlisted the support of Secretary of State Dr. Hans Globke. The subsidies were kept up.

The outright espionage agencies in West Germany are the Gehlen group and the CIA. Reinhard Gehlen, alias Herr Doktor, alias Mr. Schneider, alias the Gray General, is the most mysterious public official in West Germany. Now fifty-eight, he has not been photographed since 1944, when he was a youthful-looking lieutenant general, with close-set eyes, rather pointed ears, and the self-satisfied air Hitler's generals were wont to assume.

Today, according to those who have seen him recently, his hair has grayed and he is heavier. He wears a pencil-line mustache and his manner is courteous but diffident. A lifelong professional soldier who joined the Reichswehr in 1920, Gehlen has been a foe of Communism and a specialist on Soviet affairs ever since he was transferred from France to the Eastern front when the Russian war broke out in 1941. A year later, he had risen to become intelligence chief for the front. The East Germans charge that he was a Nazi and a leader of the "foreign army of the East," a ragged group of Soviet deserters and other non-German anti-Communists. Gehlen says he never joined the Nazi Party. His intelligence reports predicting the 1944 Soviet offensive made him suspicious to Hitler, even after the reports had proved accurate. With laudable foresight, Gehlen saw the end ahead and stored fifty cases of priceless documents in Bavaria. When the Allied invasion came, he turned himself in to United States forces and offered to set up an anti-Communist intelligence agency with his files and some of his former staff. The Gehlen organization mushroomed and was given headquarters outside Munich. When West Germany became a sovereign state in 1955, Adenauer took Gehlen under his wing.

Today, his "Federal Intelligence Service" is said to have 5,000 full-time employees, another 5,000 "occasional" agents, and a yearly budget of $10,000,000. Two of his most-talked-about feats are: Dismantling the Czech apparat setup in West Germany in 1948; and planting an agent in Walter Ulbricht's cabinet, who was brought back safely when the East Germans caught on. Gehlen's main function is foreign espionage but he also works closely with the Defense of the Constitution West German counterespionage agency in ferreting out Eastern agents. Many Eastern spies are simply trying to make a little extra money on the side, and Gehlen has been successful in using them as double agents. His primary mission has been described by Daniel De Luce of the Associated Press as: "To identify and locate at all times the forward Soviet and satellite armed forces.

This is fundamental to Allied security, including 400,000 American, British, and French troops outposting West Germany."

Gehlen is the undisputed boss of West German intelligence. One of the reasons Dr. Otto John defected to East Berlin in July, 1954, was that he had lost a power struggle with Gehlen. Adenauer, upset by reports of John's drinking and erratic behavior, sided with Gehlen in the quarrel between the two intelligence chiefs (John headed the Defense of the Constitution). When John visited the United States in early July, 1954, he was given no encouragement from Allen Dulles. Gehlen was Dulles' man. It was only a matter of weeks after his return from the United States that John fled to East Berlin, charging that the West German Government was riddled with former Nazis. The removal of General Trudeau from G-2 in 1955 further consolidated Gehlen's position.

Gehlen's headquarters in Pullach is called the "General Direction." He also has a number of field offices throughout Germany, which use such cover names as "South German Industrial Organization." His foreign residences are patterned after the Communist espionage cells he knows so well. Residents work in small operational groups, with the ruling principle that no agent knows the work of another or enough about him to give him away under questioning. From time to time, defendants in East German espionage trials have admitted being Gehlen agents. In 1954, seven were convicted for stealing patents and documents from an electrical plant. A fifteen-point Gehlen directive for agents was purportedly found by East German security police. The directive outlined espionage targets, such as troop movements and aerial and harbor installations. Gehlen's tentacles are said to reach into friendly countries and he is reported to have agents as far afield as Rome and Paris.

The CIA, which considers its West German operation with special fondness, still flushes with pride when the celebrated story of the Berlin tunnel is told.

It was while studying a map of Berlin in 1955 that a CIA official noticed that a section of the American zone boundary was only 300 yards away from the main telephone line of the Soviet military head-quarters. Shortly afterward, a new radar control station was built just over the border from the Soviet zone. The control station was a cover for some very literal underground work. The CIA had decided to dig a tunnel leading to the Soviet telephone line and to tap the wire. The scheme was bold, and initially successful. The tunnel was a masterpiece of construction. A man six feet tall could stand almost upright in it. It was air-conditioned and soundproof, had indirect fluorescent lighting, a telephone switchboard, and three master cables that tapped the Soviet wires. The most modern monitoring equipment was set up for about twenty yards along the tunnel wall.

The tunnel ran 500 yards from the radar station under a cemetery in the Alt-Glienicke section of East Berlin and stopped under Schönefeld Road, along both sides of which Soviet military headquarters had their underground telephone cables.

The wire tap went on for nearly a year, controlling about sixty Soviet military telephone lines. The information obtained was incalculable. The control room, manned around the clock, was protected by heavy iron doors. On the doors, signs in Russian and German warned: ENTRANCE FORBIDDEN—by order of the commander in chief of Soviet troops in Germany. None of the equipment used was of American make. Beyond the control room, at the border point between East and West Berlin, there was a barbed-wire fence to make it appear that the Russians had built the tunnel. In April, 1956, men of the Soviet signal corps checking the telephone wires discovered the tunnel. According to the East German press agency, three Americans were working in it at the time but managed to escape. In their haste, they left the lights and the monitors on.

The CIA in West Germany has access to the findings of other intelligence organizations. It acts as a "super-spook" that skims the cream off the intelligence product of the other groups. It handles the most important defectors, masterminds the most important schemes, contacts the most valuable agents.

The CIC's main task is finding Communist agents in U.S. military installations, such as clerical or kitchen help, and helping to sift agents who come to West Berlin as refugees. Agents thus found are turned over to the CIA for possible use as double agents. Army intelligence in West Germany also has an operational espionage group, the mysterious Field Operations Intelligence (FOI). But CIA crowns all other agencies and takes over any case it chooses to handle. Some intelligence officials in West Germany complain that too often CIC is commanded by officers who have no intelligence experience. The story is told of a colonel plugging for his first star who was given a CIC command. At his first staff meeting, a main topic under discussion concerned the activities of the CIA, known as Department of Army Detachment, or more commonly DAD. The colonel listened thoughtfully, nodded at appropriate times, and whispered to his aide as the meeting broke up: "Who the hell is Dad?"

German counterintelligence is handled by the Defense of the Constitution, which fights Communist infiltration and espionage (the Communist Party is illegal in West Germany). There are 400 agents working directly on counterespionage and they are in liaison with the police of the Federal Republic's eleven districts, with Gehlen, and with German military intelligence. There are also special judicial officers attached to the Attorney General's office. The Defense of the Constitution has come under attack as a political police force and in February, 1959, Minister of the Interior Schröder seized an issue of the magazine *Der Stern* which contained an article called "Who Protects Us From the Protector?"

Infiltration from East to West Germany is so easily accomplished and front groups are so numerous that the Defense of the Constitution is an overtaxed agency. Dr. Schröder recently charged that a political party, the German Peace Union, was a Communist front, and the party sued him for libel. The case is pending. The Frenzel case showed that infiltration could reach high into government circles.

German post offices seize more than a million pieces of subversive mail sent from East Germany every month, but it is estimated that this is only a tenth of what gets through. Propaganda is mailed in unmarked envelopes often postmarked West Berlin. Addresses and return addresses are taken from the West Berlin telephone book, which sows confusion whether the addressee or the returnee gets the letter. The literature is directed at special groups. Soldiers are sent a magazine called *Barracks* denouncing Defense Minister Strauss' "militaristic" policies and making a broad pacifist appeal to the conscripts. Teachers get newsletters from fellow teachers in East Germany. One hundred and eighty different publications are directed at the working classes, showing the East's determination to infiltrate the trade unions. Workers' delegations are invited to East Berlin and taken through a modern plant (for exhibit only) on a tour that ends with an intimate, heart-to-heart chat with the factory director. Dr. Schröder, in a recent speech in the Bundestag, said Communist subversion in West Germany was unrivaled in history and that the number of front organizations was increasing.

Espionage and provocation centers in East Germany have grown to such importance that the subject was given detailed treatment in a State Department document released in November, 1961. The 21-page document, which is worth quoting extensively, said in part:

> The East German regime's Ministry for State Security (MfS), acting at the behest of the Soviet Union, is responsible for a massive program of kidnaping, murder, subversion and propaganda, as well as for the conventional brand of espionage.
>
> Since the end of the war, West Berlin and West German authorities have counted 255 cases of successful kidnaping, at least 143 planned or attempted kidnapings and six assassination attempts by East German agents.
>
> The recruiting of Communist spies and informers is done by a wide variety of methods in both West Germany and the Soviet Zone, including the threat of reprisals against relatives in the Soviet Zone. Extortion, bribes, various forms of coercion and pressure are standard practices. Since it frequently resorts to criminal techniques, the MfS has also released many inmates of Soviet Zone prisons who have in turn agreed to act as agents.
>
> From its headquarters on Normannenstrasse in East Berlin, the MfS carries out these subsidiary activities through "specialists" among its 16,000 Communist agents operating inside West Germany. This has been confirmed by defected Communist German agents. Behind this network are some 22,000 staff officers of the MfS, 5,000 police officers and some 3,000 hard-core functionaries of the German Communist party in the Soviet Zone.
>
> Of the 16,000 spies, more than 5,000 reside within West Germany and transmit their reports to the Soviet Zone while the remainder maintain their residence in the Zone but are periodically dispatched to the West on special espionage missions. In 1959 alone, 2,802 agents were caught in West Germany.
>
> The missions assigned these agents are predominantly of a military and political nature. About 25 percent of all missions are directed against the West German State of North Rhine-Westphalia where the Ruhr industry and the seat of the Federal Government are located.
>
> The second most important area is West Berlin where more than 16 percent of all German Communist agents operate. From August 30, 1951, until February 15, 1960, 590 persons were convicted of espionage and related felonies in West Berlin.
>
> According to the testimony of defectors and other reports filtering

out of the Zone, the MfS has a staff of 22,000. Moscow pulls the controlling strings through a hard core of German Communists who acquired Soviet citizenship during the war.

The first head of MfS, when it was established in April, 1950, was Wilhelm Zaisser, with Erich Mielke as his deputy.

After years as deputy, Erich Mielke was finally elevated to MfS chief in 1957. Mielke had joined the German Communist party in the 1920's. On August 9, 1931 he shot two unsuspecting Berlin police captains in the back. To escape prosecution, he fled to the Soviet Union where he, too, became a Soviet citizen.

During the Spanish Civil War Mielke was a captain with Communist forces and afterwards went to France where he remained during World War II. He returned to Germany in 1945 with the Soviet Army after an absence of 14 years. Mielke went into secret police work with training visits to the Soviet Union. He continues as top man of the MfS, despite the double murder charge against him.

The chief of the MfS, whoever he happens to be, is in turn subject to the control, supervision and exploitation of an "Advisors Section" of the USSR's Committee of State Security (KGB), permanently assigned to East Germany.

The MfS is organized into departments which, besides carrying on espionage work outside of the Soviet Zone, also infiltrate into every aspect of human life within Communist controlled Germany. Main Department I, for example, insures the "reliability" of members of the Soviet Zone's armed forces. It has almost 900 agents scattered throughout the military forces. The agents' main task is to recruit officers and enlisted men to spy upon each other.

Espionage in the west is conducted by Main Department II. There are over 800 master spies at its headquarters in East Berlin who recruit and control thousands of agents abroad, mostly in West Germany.

One subdivision of Main Department II is the Department of Harbors. Established in 1958, its activities encompass spying on all harbor installations in West Germany and other NATO countries, recruiting agents, and taking photographs of NATO fleet units.

Another division is a new Department "R," created early in 1960. It conducts operations against the Allied Military Missions assigned in the East German capital. One section recruits and directs agents who reside or work near these missions. Another section follows Allied personnel on all trips, while a third has the responsibility of harassment actions against the Allied Missions.

Main Department III is responsible for spying upon all economic activities inside the Soviet Zone. Its major job is enforcing production and work quotas. It prosecutes such "crimes" as frequent illness of workers, unauthorized leaves and complaints about shortages. Recently Main Department III has been busy enforcing the collectivization of agriculture.

At present there is no Main Department IV. It was "re-organized" out of business and its functions combined with those of another department in a characteristic reshuffling which keeps the pressures even on the oppressors themselves.

Main Department V is charged with maintaining a constant security and "loyalty" surveillance of all Soviet Zone officials and civil servants. Also among its duties is control of all religious organizations through harassment and intimidation.

The MfS also has a bodyguard unit of no less than 6300 men for the specific purpose of protecting the German Communist leaders from their own people.

On the outskirts of East Berlin is the Soviet Zone regime's harmless-sounding "School of Administration." Actually, according to graduates of this school who have defected to the West, it is the School for Spies of the Main Administration for Intelligence (HVA) of the Soviet-directed East German Ministry for State Security.

The HVA, the elite foreign intelligence arm of the Soviet Zone Communists, is charged with the responsibility of creating the espionage apparatus and acquiring information in West Germany and elsewhere.

The School for Spies is under the direct supervision of Lt. Cols. Rudi Bartonek and Willy Woehl but it receives the closest attention and guidance from the head of the HVA itself, General Markus "Mischa" Wolf.

The 40 student-candidates in the one-year course are hand-picked by a special HVA committee. Roughly half of them come to the school with previous experience.

All students receive fictitious names and identity documents and are forbidden, under heavy penalty, to reveal their true identity, even to each other.

Classes run six days a week from 8 AM to 6:30 PM with a lunch break. Sunday mornings there are compulsory sports. Sunday afternoon is "free," if there is no homework. Lights are out at 11 PM.

The first six months are given over to political indoctrination and knowledge of foreign countries. Dialectical materialism; history of the Communist Party of the Soviet Union; the class structure of foreign countries; and the strength of their respective Communist Parties are some of the subjects covered.

Particular emphasis is placed on West German political parties—their personnel, structure, outlook and internal dissensions; the structure of the Federal German Government—especially its security services, Ministries of Defense, Foreign Affairs, All-German Affairs and the Federal Chancellery; the West German Army and its relations with NATO, CENTO and SEATO pact countries.

The second half-year of study is devoted to practical subjects, such as audio-surveillance and the use of audio equipment, lock-picking and making copies of keys. The students have to prepare two dead drops (places of concealment and pick-up of intelligence material), which are filled and serviced by other students. They have to prepare and carry through two meeting plans in East Berlin using an experienced HVA officer to play the part of a secret agent. They have to take and develop clandestine photographs of secret installations.

To prepare for work in cultured circles, the students are lectured on etiquette, literature, architecture and religion. During the entire year there is regular instruction in English, photography, driving, military training, sports and hand-to-hand fighting.

At the completion of the course the students are taken across the border for a trip through West Germany. The purposes are to allow the students to become acquainted with the targets they will be working on; to give them some background knowledge of the area so they will be able to instruct their agents; to give them some familiarity with the target area so they will be able to estimate the validity of their agents' reports and provide tighter control.

Each year, roughly half the students—about 20—are sent forth to be Resident Agents—Soviet Zone spymasters actually living in West Germany—with the responsibility of establishing and supervising a network of sub-agents.

Since 1955, when the school was opened, roughly 120 master spies, each with a number of locally recruited assistants, have been sent out of East Berlin.

The HVA has a staff of 800 and since its foundation in 1956, has controlled an estimated 20,000 agents in West Germany. Most of these agents are active and are directed by radio according to traditional methods. A "sleeper" network has also been set up, however, and is under orders to go into action only in case of war, like the famed Soviet-organized *"Rote Kapelle"* (Red Chapel) of World War II. West German monitors regularly pick up code messages for agents broadcast between regular programs over East

German radio stations such as Berliner Rundfunk. Other messages are taped and broadcast at high speeds to sound like static. The agent retapes the message and plays it at the proper speed.

Many of the sleeper agents were sent in as refugees and have become a part of West German society, taking jobs or even government positions. Many are students, who take up key subjects that will allow them later to apply for sensitive government work. Agents who get factory jobs infiltrate the trade unions. Some German officials fear that infiltration by agents has been so intense that they could paralyze West Germany with strikes, riots, and sabotage if the situation became critical enough. Others doubt the loyalty of these thousands of agents, who after years of life in West Germany have probably begun to neglect their espionage missions.

Some insight into East German espionage work was provided in December, 1961, when a member of the Ministry for State Security who worked in the United States section defected. The importance of Lieutenant Guenther Maennel's defection was such that it was compared to George Blake's conversion to Communism. In newspaper interviews which only skimmed the surface of the information he is giving to West German intelligence, the twenty-eight-year-old defector said women were used in penetration attempts of United States, British, and French embassies in Bonn. He indicated that penetration through subverting German women employees at the embassies had been successful in all except the British Embassy. He said the MfS had been less successful in attempts to subvert American tourists on visits to East Germany. It turned out that they had come to witness Communism in action not out of sympathy but because they were opposed to it.

Some of Lieutenant Maennel's most interesting revelations concerned East German techniques for forging Western passports. The passports of Western visitors are often secretly photostated at border points, he said. The passport is held as long as fifteen minutes behind glazed windows, providing ample time for the photostats to be made. "If I wanted to give an agent a West German identity," he said, "it was easy, because we could make up West German passports easily. I would fill out a requisition form and take it along to Section 6. I'd say I needed a passport for a dark-haired man going bald in front, aged about forty-five, selling sewing machines for a Rhineland company but born on the North Sea, married with one or more children.

They'd flip through the files and pretty soon I'd have it, and all of it would be about a man who really existed somewhere in West Germany." Lieutenant Maennel said that in most cases of agent recruitment, ideology did not enter into account.

The same is true of agents recruited by the HVA, who are won over with bribes or pressured with blackmail. The techniques most often used are outlined in the West Berlin black book.

East German agents are more often recruited by the HVA with blackmail and bribes than with ideological persuasion. The techniques most often used are outlined in the West Berlin black book.

1. *The potential agent who has committed a criminal offense or who is made to believe he has committed one is offered suspension from prosecution in exchange for agent's work.*

A buxom and attractive young woman recently came to the photographic studio of Herbert Reppin (although he lives in East Berlin, his studio was in West Berlin). With a mixture of timidity and brazenness, she explained that her boy friend, an East German army officer, had been transferred far from Berlin and that he wanted some pictures of her in the nude. Reppin at first hesitated—caution is a habit with Berliners—but finally agreed when the girl offered a good price.

A week later, HVA agents broke into Reppin's home and arrested him. They produced the pictures and told him the "pornography" could bring a stiff jail sentence. If he agreed to carry out a "special" mission, however, the negatives would be destroyed and he would be handsomely paid.

Reppin was given forged West German papers in the name of Kurt Lange, and in the next few months he toured the Federal Republic, sending several hundred shots of sixty-two different subjects: automobiles, subway stations, police headquarters, private houses where anti-Communist militants live, meeting places, and the like. His quest took him to Munich, Würzburg, Hamburg, Frankfurt, and Bonn. By the time he was arrested, he had been paid nearly $1,000 for his photographs, which he sent by courier through West Berlin.

2. *Refugees in West Germany are told harm will come to their relatives in the East if they do not co-operate.*

Ilse Pohl, a nursemaid employed in West Germany, was alarmed one evening to receive a telegram that her mother in East Germany was gravely ill. She took the first train to Glauchau, a small town about sixty miles southwest of Dresden, and found her mother in perfect health and fine spirits. Since she had made the trip, she decided to stay a few days. The following night, she was dragged from her mother's home by HVA militia and questioned about her work in West Germany at the Kommadantura. An HVA colonel expressed concern for her mother's welfare and invited her to work for the organization. She agreed.

3. *The prospective agent is threatened with personal reprisals.*

Hans Neumeier, a thirty-seven-year-old West Berlin customs official, was driving through East Germany on a honeymoon trip to the North Sea. He was stopped by HVA agents and questioned. They told him they would allow him to continue on his journey with his bride if he agreed in writing to meet an East German agent in West Berlin at a certain date. Several months later, he received a telephone call from a woman with a soft, seductive voice. He ignored it. Then he received a threatening letter reminding him of his promise. He tore the letter up. About fifteen months later, his wife received an anonymous letter charging that he had committed adultery and including a photograph of a nude woman.

4. *Prisoners serving sentences are promised parole in exchange for co-operation.*

A political prisoner was serving eight years in the dreaded Soviet-run prison of Lichtenberg on a charge of incitement to boycott and war. He was transferred to an HVA workshop, where he remained for four years. He was offered release from prison if he would undertake espionage missions in West Germany. When he accepted, a jailbreak was staged to supply him with a convincing cover story.

Two other East German organizations deal in extensive "Westwork." Military Intelligence (Verwaltung für Koodinierung or VFK), has a staff of 500 officers and a mission to gather intelligence on Western forces stationed in West Berlin and on NATO troops in West Germany. It works closely with the Soviet GRU, whose men go to its training school at Klietz on Elbe for German language courses. The school has the cover name of School of Languages of the Ministry of Defense, and the courses last a year and a half. The VFK has special laboratories where forged documents are manufactured and invisible ink and other chemicals are made.

The East zone Free German Trade Unions (FDGB) also have an independent foreign espionage apparat. They gather economic information through their agents planted in West German factories and conduct infiltration of Western trade unions. Under the cover of trade unionism, the FDGB recruits agents in all aspects of West German economic life, from banks to steel mills.

A vast research and technical production center is operated by the Ministry for State Security in East Berlin (Freienwalderstrasse 12). This is actually a prison camp where the inmates are Western scientists and technicians who have been put to work devising espionage equipment. The center produces microcameras, invisible ink, tiny microphones, wire-tapping equipment, drugs, forged passports, and forged rubber stamps. The head of the Documents Forgery Department is an old-time Communist named Richard Quast, who made his first forged passport in an apartment in Berlin's Kaiser-Allee in the early 1930's.

Quast, at that time, conducted the largest Pass-apparat ever unearthed. In 1932, because of Hitler's rise, 600 German Communist leaders were told to prepare to go underground. With seven artists under his orders, Quast received stolen blank passports from half a dozen countries and turned out masterful forgeries for them. Genuine German passports were falsified, with pages removed and visas inserted. Quast, whose apparat nickname was "Abel," maintained agencies all over Europe and had about thirty "branch offices" in Germany. In its heyday the Pass-apparat had close to a thousand German Communists working under its orders. The police in 1932 raided the main workshop and found 2,000 rubber stamps, 600 passport blanks, 807 passport photographs, and 700 police forms. Quast fled to Prague and turned up later in Paris and Mexico City. He came back to Germany (East) in 1947 and went back to his old profession.

Other old-time apparat members and Rote Kapelle veterans with thirty years' experience in illegality help devise some ingenious spy devices which the West German security police sometimes stumble upon. Recently, a delivery truck with a revolving roof ventilator was parked outside Berlin headquarters of the Social Democrat Party. Police became suspicious when it remained there for a long time, and found a camera concealed in the ventilator which was photographing everyone entering and leaving the building. Microcameras have been found hidden in wrist watches and cigarette lighters—winding the watch or flicking the wheel of the lighter snaps the shutter. Tiny tape recorders, found clamped to the wall of a house, were sensitive enough to record the conversations going on inside.

The technical center also produces methods of destruction. One agent arrested in West Berlin had a blowpipe disguised as a cigarette lighter. It contained three tubes of crystalline curare, of which 0.025 grams is enough to kill a man. In another case, an agent had a box of twenty miniature chocolate cognac bottles, each attractively tinsel wrapped. One of the candies contained cognac, the others were drugged. The agent offered a candy to his victim and ate the non-drugged candy to allay her fears.

All these techniques may seem too farfetched to belong outside a cloak-and-dagger novel, but to German security officers they have become almost mundane. And the West Berlin figures on abductions from 1945 to 1958 prove that drugs and violence are used with success—there were sixty-three successful abductions in that period from West to East Berlin, four of them with the aid of narcotics, the rest by use of force.

East and West German espionage setups both have what could be called "malicious mischief departments." Dedicated to spreading confusion and fostering demoralization, hundreds of misleading letters and newspaper ads are thought up by these practical jokers of espionage.

An East Berlin youth, for instance, received an official-looking letter with a Ministry of the Interior letterhead saying: "You are herewith ordered to appear at the above-mentioned draft office for the purpose of an interview concerning your service in the National People's Army. Bring your identification papers. Carfare will be provided. In case you can't come, send an explanation." The same letter had been sent to over a thousand youths, many of whom showed up on the appointed day to the total confusion of the draft office, which had no idea what it was all about and had to deal with an angry horde clamoring for carfare.

In West Berlin, the neighbors of a police officer received an anonymous letter stating in part: "Beneath his air of propriety, he is an evil and licentious man. He has made false proposals of marriage, has induced his mistresses into espionage, and has persuaded some of his women friends to have abortions."

In East Berlin, a Communist Party worker received this invitation:

Having been recommended for your role in the national front, you are invited to attend a meeting on the first of the year for the National People's Army in the culture hall of our ministry. It is our wish to celebrate with you the first anniversary of our National People's Army. Your presence will testify to the firm bonds between the militants and their people's army as well as the unshakable will to ensure the peace and success of our socialist society.

Hundreds of happy militants arrived for the first-of-the-year party only to be turned back from the ministry by stern-faced and uncomprehending guards. The militants thought this was a strange reward for their zeal.

A classified ad in a West Berlin newspaper said there was an important sale of furniture and office equipment on the premises of the League of Free Jurists. Bargain hunters arrived in droves and the Free Jurists spent the better part of the day explaining it was all a mistake.

The campaign of misinformation and malice, anonymous letters and forged invitations, continues daily. One of the lowest tricks was the letter sent to refugees from the East at Marienfelde camp announcing that the senate had voted a Christmas gift of 50 marks per refugee.

Almost all West Berlin government workers have received anonymous letters at one time or another. The case of a couple working for the Association of Political Refugees is typical. The husband got a letter warning him to "keep a close watch on your wife because there are goings on with her boss that overstep normal business relations." The wife meanwhile found a message in the mail asking "what right have you got pumping unsuspecting people for information in this mean fashion? I can assure you of one thing: I'll see that you are well known and well avoided because that's what you deserve, you underhanded bitch."

This paper war helps to keep tension up in both German camps. Thus Germany today in its tragic division serves as the advance post for the intelligence services of the two blocks and has become what one official mournfully described as "a nation of spies."

XV. The Future of Espionage

WHAT is the future of espionage? This question leads to a series of others.

1. *How has espionage changed over the years?* Espionage is a curious mixture of the old and the new. Techniques such as invisible ink and hidden compartments have been in use for thousands of years. Gordon Lonsdale's hollowed-out scrolls could easily have been used by a spy for one of the pre-Christian Chinese empires.

The spy still faces what Churchill called "the well-known forfeit" if he is caught. He can still be seen chewing valiantly on indigestible secret papers as the security forces close in. He is still told that suicide is preferable to capture (not for him but for his country). And he still depends on what he hears and what he sees. The Chinese military theorist Sun Tzu said that observation was the only sure way to learn the enemy's dispositions. Twenty-five centuries later, Compton Mackenzie agreed that the only reliable intelligence was obtained "in the field." There have been obvious improvements in transmissions and communications. The day when Andrew Jackson could carry the strategy for an entire Indian campaign in his head is gone. Radio, radar, magnetic tape, airplanes, IBM computers, and a multitude of other technical achievements have added a new dimension to the spy's shadowy world. But all these simply assist the basic element—the human spy.

The real change in espionage has come about through what scientists call a quantum jump—not an improvement of an existing method, but a complete rethinking of the problem. Such a quantum jump has been made with the "spy in the sky" satellite, which photographs enemy territory while in orbital flight. The SAMOS (satellite and missile observation system) was first launched successfully on January 3, 1961, at Point Arguelle, California. The date is a historic one in the annals of espionage, and may make the secret agent as obsolete as the halberd.

For Samos can from its astral perch take photographs with the detail that a human eye can see at 100 feet. Samos is invulnerable and completely reliable. It sends its rolls of film earthward by capsule and also transmits what it sees by television circuit. It could theoretically photograph the entire land mass of the Soviet Union, showing road traffic and troop concentration. It is a permanent peephole into the enemy camp. As *The New York Times* said in October, 1960, when a Samos launching failed to achieve orbit because of a faulty disconnect that damaged the second stage: "In the military community, the Samos project is considered of consummate importance."

Here is what Samos is and what Samos does: It is a 5-ton satellite launched by an Atlas rocket. The huge Atlas rocket is 77 feet high and weighs 262,000 pounds. The second stage containing the instrument package is cigar-shaped and measures 22 feet. Samos has a north-south orbit 300 miles above the earth which it takes 95 minutes to circle. It has Eastman Kodak and Ansco cameras so sensitive they can snap detailed pictures by starlight. The photographs are as good as those taken by the U-2 planes, and Samos can reach many areas beyond the U-2's range. The photographs are automatically developed on board. Samos tilts so that its nose section is always pointed toward the earth. Two of its present limitations are that its transmitters operate only twenty days and that the fuel supply for the jets that keep its cameras pointed earthward is limited.

Samos has a sister satellite, Midas, which carries infrared detection equipment that issues warnings when missiles leave their launching pad. When the Midas and Samos systems are perfected (several of both types of satellites are already being tested in orbit, but the Pentagon is closemouthed about the project), Midas satellites will give half-hour advance warnings about missile attacks instead of the quarter-hour now provided by radar and Distant Early Warning (DEW) systems. And Samos will report troop concentrations and other suspect activity through its camera eye aimed at the Soviet Union. The CIA knows the Russians are working on similar projects and that their electronic espionage is making swift advances. The day is foreseen when both blocs will have a necklace of spy satellites girding the globe and keeping watch over possible aggression.

Another change has to do with the function of espionage. Collecting intelligence with one hand, the spy today is told to encourage subversion and defection with the other. Intelligence organizations today spearhead ideological warfare and battle for men's convictions. The CIA bases its hopes on dissatisfaction in the Soviet Union that prompts important intelligence officers and other government officials to abandon the regime. It is also attracted by the seductive but dangerous belief in the essential fractionalism of Communism. An alumnus of the Matthausen concentration camp recalls that the interned Communists in a matter of months had managed to form an anti-Party group and were constantly quarreling among themselves with doctrinaire fervor. These scissions, divisions, and quarrels are encouraged by the CIA wherever they arise, on both sides of the Iron Curtain. The hope that the Communist regime will collapse through inner divisions and purges is nourished fondly by every Western intelligence expert. The Soviets, on the other hand, use—as they have been using for forty years—the promise of Communism to recruit and hold their agents. They too consider psychological warfare as part of their espionage duties. And they foment dissension in the Western camp, as they did when they convinced the French Government for a brief period that the CIA was mixed up in the Algiers *Putsch*.

2. *Has the romance gone out of espionage?* Some of the stories this writer picked up in his research show that the aura of glamour still glimmers about the imperiled head of the international spy.

One of the most amusing reasons given for the success of the British in espionage is that they are a nation of hobbyists. In what other country could you find on emergency notice a man to lead you through a mountain trail in the Peloponnesus because he went on hikes there one vacation? Or a man who knew every inch of a French beach because he'd hunted for seashells there?

One of the most absorbing reasons given for Spanish-American friendship is the purported existence of a huge subterranean lake under Minorca, one of the Balearic Islands. The United States, according to this theory, wants to build a submarine base and atomic shelter in the cavernous lake, which would be matched only by the French-held Bizerte submarine base in Tunisia. A reason for friendship between the Turks and the Americans is said to be that the Turks have agreed to stop archeological digs that were too close to military bases.

One of the most chilling thoughts of the Cold War: Observers of the Khrushchev-Kennedy encounter in Vienna noticed that after their long first session Kennedy emerged looking pale and drawn, as though he had been badly frightened. This was attributed to his back injury which had begun to nag him in Paris and had grown tremendously painful by the time he reached Vienna. Others, however, recalled these words of Khrushchev at the 1958 Communist Party Congress: "What our scientists have in their briefcases is so horrible I can't even mention it." Was he thinking of the neutron bomb, or had Soviet scientists accomplished a quantum jump and come up with the "absolute weapon"—not a bigger or more destructive bomb but a completely new method of destruction, as remote from a bomb as a bomb is from a cudgel? Something along the lines of an electronic weapon that can invert the roles of electrical conductors and insulators.

The insulators become conductors. This could electrocute everyone driving a car, using a telephone or any other electrical appliance. Did Khrushchev tell Kennedy he had the absolute weapon? It sounds like the farfetched chimera of a science fiction writer, but anyone who has spent time in the dubious company of intelligence officials and "special" agents in Geneva, Washington, and Berlin hears this kind of "information" daily.

3. *Are the huge espionage networks that engulf billions of dollars, jeopardize the lives of many men, and add to international tension, worth the trouble?*

Basically, espionage is like armament. As long as the other camp is conducting total espionage and sending wave upon wave of agents to steal military secrets and foment subversion, the threat must be met. Why did we resume testing atom bombs? Because the Soviet Government did. Why do we have such a powerful intelligence service? Because the Soviets have. At this level, a novel "businessman's theory" of espionage is sometimes expressed: That it is possible to obtain almost any secret information, as long as one is willing to pay. Thus, if the Western camp can come up with an intelligence product of equal quality at a lower cost, it is winning the intelligence battle. Total espionage is sometimes defended as contributing to great expense in the opposite camp while cutting its own production costs.

The West can also cite the preventive nature of its intelligence. Western powers need to be warned against the menace of surprise attack. Troop movements behind the Iron Curtain, missile strength, air bases, secret weapons, and many other factors must be known to gain an accurate picture of the Soviet Union's intentions in the Cold War. The Soviets, with their mania for suspicion and residual fears from other wars, reason along much the same lines. Here, too, intelligence is like armament. We stockpile for eventual defense. All manner of aggression is committed in the name of preventive measures. The great change in Western intelligence has come through the CIA's rationale that it must meet the crusading spirit of the Communist world. The CIA has embarked on a number of crusades in the past decade, some of which blocked the advance of Communism (Guatemala), while others assisted that advance (Cuba). In other nations where the CIA's sometimes heavy hand was felt, the battle is still being waged (Iran).

No one but President Kennedy, his cabinet and his advisers are in a position to know what the CIA's balance sheet is. Perhaps the intelligence successes under Allen Dulles' aegis were so overwhelming that the President is willing to forgive several fiascos of Cuba's proportion (particularly since he had a hand in the Cuba failure). Soon after he was elected, Mr. Kennedy agreed that Dulles could retire after overseeing the CIA's transfer from the Foggy Bottom compound to its sparkling new headquarters in Virginia. The choice of a successor first centered on Fowler Hamilton, a New York lawyer. But Hamilton was lukewarm about accepting the assignment, and said that in any case he would not serve longer than President Kennedy's first term. This ruled him out on the Dulles principle that an intelligence chief must be a career man and assure the continuity of the silent service.

The job was also offered to Arthur H. Dean, chief American negotiator at the atomic test-ban meetings in Geneva. Dean had impressed President Kennedy with his knowledge of Soviet atomic strength. He turned down the offer, however, replying in effect that "I was trained as a lawyer and I'm used to dealing openly with the truth. I'm afraid the CIA would be a little too rough for me." When the President asked him to think it over, Dean replied with characteristic forthrightness: "I won't even think it over one half hour."

On September 27, President Kennedy announced at the Naval War College in Newport, Rhode Island, that he had found his man. He said:

> I have asked Mr. John McCone to accept the responsibility of being the director of the Central Intelligence Agency and chairman of the Joint Intelligence Board, and have asked him to assume the responsibility later in the fall. . . . He will come, in about two weeks, and work with Mr. Dulles and in November will assume the responsibility.
>
> I know of no man who is a more courageous, selfless public servant that Mr. Allen Dulles and I therefore, in expressing pleasure at having secured the services of Mr. McCone, want to express my profound regret that at the age of sixty-eight, after ten years in this responsibility, Mr. Dulles should be retiring. He has agreed to continue to serve as a consultant to me on intelligence matters, and therefore his long experience will be available to the people of this country.

As it happened, the President was flanked by Dulles and McCone at the war college, and each said a few words to mark the occasion. Thus, Dulles had rounded out the decade as intelligence chief. He would stay around to break McCone in on the CIA routine. He actually retired on Nov. 29 and was given the National Security Medal on that date by President Kennedy. He plans to draw on ten years of extraordinary memories to write a book on intelligence, both good and bad.

John Alex McCone has all the requirements needed to head the CIA but one—he has not had one iota of intelligence experience. In his favor can be mentioned that:

He is fifty-nine years old, of strong and healthy constitution, and can be expected to last a good ten years in the job, like his predecessor.

He is a Republican who is serving in his second Democratic administration (he served on President Truman's Air Policy Commission in 1947-48 and as Under Secretary of the Air Force in 1950-51) and is popular with Democratic Congressmen. He is at the same time a personal friend of Dwight Eisenhower and Richard Nixon.

He is a Cold War warrior who will never be accused of being soft on Russia. As chairman of the Atomic Energy Commission from mid-58 to January, 1961, he fought the nuclear test ban and told scientists who favored the ban that "your statement is obviously designed to instill fear in the misinformed . . . you have apparently been taken in by Soviet propaganda." When the ban was in force, he repeatedly accused the Soviet Union of conducting secret underground tests. He has visited the Soviet Union in his atomic energy capacity and nurses no delusions about the nature of the Cold War. Ten years ago, when he was Air Force Under Secretary, he urged a $2,000,000,000-a-year missile program. (His appointment was opposed by neutralist groups who charged that McCone would carry on the CIA's tradition of "aggressive Cold War" in foreign countries.)

He is described as having "a slide-rule mind." He obtained his engineering degree at the University of California, became vice-president of a steel company at the age of thirty-two, ran the huge California Shipbuilding Corporation during World War II. Under his hard-driving leadership, the company turned out 467 ships worth $1,000,000,000.

At a time when the CIA is still licking its wounds and subject to extensive reorganization, he is known as a stubborn and determined boss who runs a tight shop. At the same time, he won a reputation as a skillful politician when he healed partisan rifts in the Joint Congressional Committee on Atomic Energy. Representative Chet Holifield, chairman of the committee, said that "he did the miraculous and achieved a harmonious commission, something we badly needed."

Although he lacks the formal intelligence training that made Dulles the ideal CIA chief, he is prepared for the increasing scientific nature of espionage. His name was first mentioned as a possible successor to Dulles when the Soviets resumed nuclear testing September 1, 1961. McCone's knowledge of Soviet atomic strength is a prime requisite for modern intelligence.

Despite these references, there were those who wondered why a man described in *The New York Times* as "an engineering production man at heart" should be chosen to head one of the nation's largest, most vital, and most specialized agencies. Did it mean a downgrading of the CIA? Apparently not. President Kennedy said pointedly in announcing McCone's appointment that he was "concerned that this agency should continue to serve as an effective instrument of our country's policy."

McCone had evidently been chosen primarily for his steadfast toughness where the Soviet Union is concerned. It was held unlikely that he would be less powerful a figure in the Administration than Dulles. Indeed it seemed that the CIA, like a star batter being considered for a trade, had recovered from its spring slump. According to oral reports made to President Kennedy by a special three-man investigation board consisting of Robert Kennedy, General Maxwell Taylor, and Admiral Arleigh Burke, there will be changes made within the CIA to separate intelligence-gathering from operational functions. This will help the CIA lose its Messianic quality. It will no longer be able to advocate the coup it has been asked to prepare. But this will probably not alter the policy of clandestine interference in the affairs of states menaced by Communist take-overs. The CIA budget is likely to keep growing, as is the size of the intelligence estimate placed daily on the President's desk.

The Soviet Government has recently paid homage to the need for total espionage. At the Congress of Writers in Moscow in the spring of 1961, the importance of espionage was underlined. The writers were chided for the lack of espionage literature in the Soviet Union while in the West there was an abundance of cloak-and-dagger books pitting the valiant and resourceful CIA agent against the ponderous villain of the KGB.

The writers set to work turning out potboilers about iron-willed Communist spies who stole state secrets and made off with the enigmatic blonde in the last chapter. The books read like carbon copies of the Western espionage thrillers. This is only one facet of the continued importance attached to the secret war in Soviet Russia. Other signs are the vigilance campaign and the increasing number of articles in the Soviet press dealing with espionage. These include factual "case histories" of Soviet spies at work against the Nazis in World War II, and build up a public image of the spy as a hero protecting the Soviet people from invasion.

4. *How can the effectiveness of total espionage be evaluated?*

Some critics of cold-war espionage claim that both East and West intelligence organizations are hopelessly incompetent and useless. There are four sets of objections. The first is that very few secrets are really worth stealing today. The scientific level of both societies is such that it is less trouble to develop a new weapon oneself than to steal it from your enemy. The belief that the Russians stole the atom bomb from the United States during World War II has been discredited by all responsible sources. Troop movements are monitored by radar and tracking stations. Cryptographic computers today can break any code. Code departments of intelligence services are now reportedly trying to use little-known dialects as the only way to get unbreakable code messages through. Thus, the NSA is said to recruit Navajo Indians and form codes based on their dialect, a spoken language for which very few texts exist. The only way the Russians could break it would be supposedly to find a Navajo to work for them. The Soviet code bureaus in turn use little-known Russian dialects.

A second level of criticism is that the "illegal" agent who leads a shadowy existence under a "cover" identity is not really worth a great deal in peacetime. Those who were caught, like Colonel Abel and Gordon Lonsdale, did not send any sensational revelations to the Center in Moscow. Alexander Foote pointed out in his *Handbook for Spies* that the average spy's "real difficulties are concerned with the practice of his trade. The setting up of his transmitters, the obtaining of funds, and the arrangement of his rendezvous. The irritating administrative details occupy a disproportionate portion of his waking life."

In other words, there is not much time left for espionage. It is a feat to have an "illegal" agent in enemy territory, but once that feat is accomplished, there is perhaps little for him to do. Malcolm Muggeridge, expressing similar sentiments in *The New Statesman,* compared the "illegal" agent to the professional seducer "who engages in various stratagems and deceptions. These in time come to seem an end in themselves, quite irrespective of their purpose. He finds himself so busily engaged in clandestine correspondence, keeping mysterious assignations, inventing cover stories and alibis, that he has neither time, energy nor inclination to avail himself of the opportunity these activities are ostensibly intended to procure."

Other faults of the "illegal" agents are either that their enthusiasm falters or that it becomes excessive. The spy can, like Jack Soble, onetime Soviet resident in the United States, devote much more time and interest to his cover (the bristle business in Soble's case) than to reporting to Moscow. As Boris Morros said, Soble was more interested in "milking Moscow of its espionage funds and expense money" than anything else. Or he can, like Graham Greene's Man in Havana invent entire networks of agents and sends his "center" the model of a new weapon which he has designed himself from a streamlined vacuum cleaner.

In peacetime, it is doubtful whether illegal agents can obtain information that is inaccessible through public or diplomatic channels. This is less true in the Soviet Union, where public sources are meager and where a cross-country drive can provide intelligence enough to keep the Soviet Union desk at the CIA busy for days.

The kind of person attached to intelligence work is another source of criticism. The reasons one is drawn into espionage are not always laudable. The mythomaniac, the neurotic, the flamboyant braggart, the compulsive mystifier, the permanent adolescent and other unsavory types seem to find their way unerringly into intelligence organizations.

Many of them do well, despite their quirks and flaws, and there are some highly responsible officials at the CIA who undergo more or less permanent psychoanalysis. As Muggeridge wrote:

> The basic weakness of all intelligence services lies in their personnel, who tend to be immature. A *fantaisiste* like Guy Burgess, for instance, is bound to drift into intelligence work and to thrive at it. But for his fortunate withdrawal to Moscow, he might quite easily have become very high up in MI6, if not its actual head. His temperament was exactly right—flamboyant, untruthful, gregarious, and energetic. Intelligence services are unfortunate in that the more suitable a person seems to be for recruitment to them, the more disastrous he is likely to prove. Blake was perfect. He had every requisite qualification, and by virtue of this, was the more apt to prove unreliable. Petrov, by Soviet standards, was an almost identical case.

There is still room for these grandiloquent and unscrupulous types in today's intelligence services, although the large number of people employed leads also to quite opposite personnel problems. Recently, at a Washington cocktail party, a mousy, unassuming little man was asked by his hostess what his job was. "I'm in the CIA," he replied softly. "That must be terribly exciting," the dowager gushed. "I'm afraid not," the little man said with a sigh. "I'm fiscal." Thousands of employees working for intelligence today carry out exactly the same kind of dull clerical or administrative tasks they might have in any large office. The only difference is that they can't talk about their job. This too can lead to psychological disorders, acute dissatisfaction, and resignations.

For intelligence officers to be unable to distinguish clearly between truth and falsehood seems a contradiction in terms, like a violin without strings. Yet this criticism has been addressed not only to the individual official, but to the entire Soviet Union espionage organization. It was George F. Kennan who wrote in *Russia, the Atom, and the West:* *

> I have been asked hundreds of times in recent years how it could be that men of such native intelligence as the Soviet leaders, commanding so elaborate and costly a network of intelligence-gathering agencies, could be anything else but excellently informed about ourselves and everything having to do with us. I should like to suggest an answer to this question.

Kennan noted that intelligence analysis breaks down in Soviet hands "because over all these forty years the Communist Party has made it impossible for the people who collect information to accompany that information with any really objective analysis of the nature of Western society."

> Some of the fictions dearest and most basic to Russian Communist views of itself would be jeopardized at every turn by that sort of analysis . . . the Soviet leaders find themselves committed to a badly distorted image of the outside world . . . their habitual carelessness about the truth has tended to obliterate in their minds the distinctions between what they do believe and what they merely find it convenient to say.
>
> Forty years of intellectual opportunism have wrought a strange corruption of the Communist mind, rendering it incapable of distinguishing sharply between fact and fiction in a single segment of its experience, namely in its relationship to any external competitive power. The Russian Communists have always been characterized by their extraordinary ability to cultivate falsehood as a deliberate weapon of policy.

* George F. Kennan, *Russia, the Atom and the West* (New York: Atlantic Monthly Press, 1953).

This systematic distortion of the truth is perhaps the basic weakness of Soviet intelligence. Reviewing the CIA's brief history, we find an agency that has adopted many of the methods of Soviet intelligence, an agency that has become notorious through aggressive coups and sensational failures. How can we draw encouragement from this kind of record? Encouragement can be found in the discussion and analysis provoked by the coups and failures and in the process of change to guard against a repetition of mistakes. The criticism leveled against the CIA was eminently healthy. The dangerous similarity of methods and goals between Soviet and American intelligence was brought into the open. The tension between democratic principle and the need for an effective intelligence service was restored.

This is the first paradox: that totalitarian techniques can be used to protect democratic institutions. The second paradox is that democracy is like the Moslem religion, which accepts Jesus Christ as one of its saints, alongside Allah. Democracy has power of assimilation great enough to withstand inner contradictions and apparent absurdities. We live in a society where Bertrand Russell goes to jail and James Hoffa flouts the courts, where Congressmen complain about a few thousand dollars spent by a State Department-sponsored theatrical tour while millions are being quietly earmarked for the overthrow of a Latin-American government. What can we salvage from these contradictions to counter the steely core of the Soviet police state, with its despotic inflexibility and its rule through fear? Another kind of strength, which can stand almost any amount of bending and battering and which, like the India rubber man, always holds together because of its very shapelessness. The CIA is considered a kind of freak in a democratic society, but it is allowed to exist (under increasing control, one hopes) because it has proved its necessity. The Soviet intelligence system, on the other hand, is the core of the regime and its disappearance could lead to the end of the Communist dictatorship in the Soviet Union as we have known it for forty years.

Epilogue

THE professional Soviet spy and the U-2 pilot met for the first time at a white line that marks the halfway point of an old iron-girder bridge leading from West Berlin to Potsdam in the East Zone. It was a strange confrontation that seemed at first to be some sort of showdown between two rival gangs. Hands in pockets, their hatbrims pulled low, two small groups of men moved cautiously across the Glienicke Bridge, which was renamed "Bridge of Unity" in overhasty praise of Soviet-American alliance in 1945. The man leading the group on the Berlin side was stooped. He wore clothes of American cut, a topcoat and a snapbrim Fedora. The taller, huskier man at the head of the other group wore a Russian fur hat and trousers with wide bottoms. In the gray light of morning, the men stood around at the center of the bridge, shuffling from one foot to the other, their breath frosting. After a twenty-minute wait, a whispered command was given. The man in Russian clothes strode to the Western side of the bridge and was clapped on the back by one of the civilians, who told him: "You're home." The man in Western clothes quietly joined the Soviet plainclothesmen on the Potsdam side.

The scene was banal, and yet it marks what is perhaps the most dramatic exchange of spies in modern history. Powers and Abel were "blown agents" and as such, beyond the help of their governments. Abel, loyal to his profession, had refused to bargain with the authorities who arrested him. He remained mute throughout his trial although he knew his appearance on the witness stand would inspire leniency. As he told his lawyer, he had made his peace with himself and was prepared to spend the rest of his life in prison, serving his thirty-year sentence.

Powers was trained as a pilot but caught as a spy. Because of his lack of training and his own weakness of character, his behavior was unheroic. Where Abel had been silent, he was voluble. Where Abel had done nothing to influence the jury, Powers did everything to have his sentence mitigated. The only common element in their cases was that the CIA refused to recognize that Powers existed just as the GRU failed to acknowledge Abel as one of their employees.

Many factors worked against an exchange of the two men. The Soviet Union claims it has no spies. Only imperialist powers carry out espionage. But the swap of Abel for Powers would reverberate all over the world. It would be impossible to keep the news from Soviet public opinion. The embarrassment caused by Powers' return would be even greater. Should Powers be hailed as a hero or condemned as a traitor? Should he be given a ticker-tape parade up Broadway or the ten years in jail to which he is liable for betraying his CIA oath?

James B. Donovan, who as Abel's lawyer was the key figure in the exchange, ran into opposition when he first broached its possibility. This was under the Eisenhower Administration, and the Administration, which was responsible for the U-2 program, was not enthusiastic about receiving the man responsible for its exposure. The suggestion for the swap had been made through Soviet channels, and there was no resistance to the move on the Soviet side. But wherever Donovan turned in Washington, he was met with temporization and equivocation.

It was in June, 1960, that Powers' father had written Donovan suggesting "a swap for my boy." Through Donovan, Abel told the elder Powers to write his family in East Germany. In the fall of 1960, Donovan received a letter with an East German postmark signed *Hellen Abel,* asking for clemency for her husband.

The appeal was referred to Attorney General William P. Rogers, who advised that the matter be held over for the incoming Kennedy Administration. In early 1961, Reed Cozart, pardon attorney for the Justice Department, ruled there were insufficient grounds for a pardon. The correspondence continued between Donovan and Mrs. Abel, however, and they explored the chances of an exchange. Attorney General Robert F. Kennedy and President Kennedy were familiar with the progress being made. Moreover, the President, whose Administration had not been linked with the U-2 program, felt the exchange would be helpful in relieving international tension.

In the fall of 1961, Donovan was given the go-ahead to negotiate the exchange in East Germany. In East Berlin and Leipzig, he met with Soviet officials and showed them a letter from Cozart indicating that Abel's sentence could be commuted "under proper circumstances." Donovan, though he was acting in a private capacity as

Abel's lawyer, was in effect an ambassador without portfolio charged with a delicate and important government mission. He found the Russians willing to make the exchange and willing even to throw in with Powers another American held as a spy behind the Iron Curtain —twenty-eight-year-old Frederic L. Pryor.

After about two weeks of negotiation, Donovan let the President know that the exchange had been firmly agreed upon. The President signed a commutation for Abel which was to become effective when Powers was in American hands. In complete secrecy, Abel was whisked out of his Atlanta jail cell and flown to Fort Dix, New Jersey, for the first lap of a trip that would probably take him back to the Soviet Union. At the same time, Powers was being taken from his cell in Vladimir Prison outside Moscow.

The exchange added another dimension to the mystery of Abel's identity. In the letters from his family which were brought out at the trial in 1957, his wife signed "Ilya" and his daughter "Evelyn" or "Evernya." But the letters from East Germany were signed "Hellen." Also, the trial letters described the life of Abel's family in the Soviet Union, their dacha, their servants, their television set, and the rest of the comfort limited to the ruling class. Was it his wife who was writing from East Germany, and if so, how did she get there? Abel spoke fluent German and had served on the German front during World War II. German-speaking friends he made as a spy in New York said he could have passed for a German easily. Abel's German connections and his own real name (Abel is a common *nom de guerre* among Communist spies) remained one of the loose ends of this extraordinary case.

Powers also had some explaining to do, and was due to appear before a CIA board of inquiry soon after his return to the United States. The State Department, however, said he would probably not have to stand trial and barred the possibility that all he would have gained from his trip was a transfer from a Soviet to an American prison.

Powers' release was not given great importance in the Soviet press and Abel's recovery was not mentioned at all. A Soviet radio announcement said: "The Praesidium of the Supreme Soviet, having considered the plea of the relatives of Francis Gary Powers, the American pilot sentenced in the U.S.S.R., and taking into consideration his acknowledgment of having committed the most severe crime, and also being guided by the desire for an improvement in relations between the U.S.S.R. and the U.S.A., has adopted a decision giving mercy to Powers and handing him over."

Pravda's announcement was even more cursory. The liberation of Powers was listed on an inside page as one of several decrees. More space was given to another decree awarding the title of "People's Artist" to V. F. Ryndin, the husband of ballet dancer Galina Ulanova.

According to Associated Press correspondents in Moscow, Russian citizens would not believe it when the correspondents told them Powers had been exchanged for a Russian spy. "There aren't any Russian spies," was the usual reply. Others said they had never heard of Abel. Yet his trial did not go completely unreported in the Soviet press. In November, 1957, the Moscow *Literary Gazette* described it as a frame-up. It seemed, however, that the Soviet regime had, initially at least, been successful in keeping the terms of Powers' release from the Soviet people.

In the United States, when the traditional homecoming ceremonies with the proud parents and smiling wife were over, there were some who thought President Kennedy had struck a poor bargain and some who thought Powers should have been brought home in handcuffs. William Tompkins, who prosecuted Abel, said: "Abel was a real professional and a genius in the field of intelligence, but Powers was just a pilot." An angrier comment came from John Wickers, an American Legion official, who said: "I view the exchange with astonishment and disgust. Powers was a cowardly American who evidently valued his own skin far more than the welfare of the nation that was paying him handsomely."

In the final analysis, the U-2 case had at first struck a severe blow at Soviet-American relations by scuttling the summit meeting, but then had contributed to a Cold War thaw through the Abel-Powers exchange. The principle implicitly recognized by Premier Khrushchev and Presidents Eisenhower and Kennedy was that espionage is an organic branch of foreign relations and foreign policy, similar to diplomatic exchanges and summit conferences.

APPENDIX

List of American diplomats expelled from the Soviet Union between 1947 and 1961:

1947: Lt. Robert Dreher, Assistant Naval Attaché

1954: Lt. Col. Howard Felchlin, Assistant Military Attaché and Maj. Walter Mc Kinney, Assistant Air Attaché

1955: Lt. Col. John Benson, Capt. William Stroud, and Capt. Walter Mule, all Assistant Military Attachés

1957: Martin S. Bowe Jr., Second Secretary; Maj. Hubert Tansey, Assistant Military Attaché; Capt. Charles Stockell; and Capt. Paul Uffelman, Assistant Air Attachés; Lt. William Lewis, Assistant Naval Attaché

1958: John Baker, Second Secretary

1959: David E. Mark, First Secretary and Russell A. Langelle, Security Officer

1960: Col. Edwin M. Kirton, Air Attaché; George P. Winters and Maj. Irving T. Mc Donald Jr., Assistant Air Attachés

(There were also fifteen representations made by the Soviet Union about American diplomats in Moscow that did not lead to expulsion).

List of Soviet diplomats expelled from the United States between 1948 and 1961:

United Nations	Soviet Embassy and Consulates
1952: Nikolia Svortsov, Assistant to Undersecretary Constanin Zinchenko	1948: Jacob M. Lomakin, Soviet Consul General in New York
1954: Alexander Kovalek, Second Secretary of Soviet delegation	1953: Yuri V. Novikov, Second Secretary
1955: Col. Maksim Martynov, member of the Military Staff Committee	1954: Lt. Col. Leonid Pivnev, Assistant Air Attaché; Commander Igor Amosov.
1956: Konstantin Ekimov, First Secretary of Soviet delegation	1956: Col. Ivan A. Bubchikov, Assistant Military Attaché
	1957: Maj. Yuri Krylov, Assistant

UNITED NATIONS	SOVIET EMBASSY AND CONSULATES
1956: Aleksandr K. Guryanov, employee of Soviet UN delegation; Capt. Boris F. Gladkov, member of Military Staff Committee; Viktor I. Petrov, UN translator; Rostislav Shapovalov, Second Secretary of Soviet delegation 1957: N. Vladimir Grusha, First Secretary of Soviet delegation 1959: Kirill S. Doronkin, UN secretariat member	Military Attaché; Gennadi F. Mashkantsev, Second Secretary; Vasily M. Molev, Embassy chauffeur 1958: Nikolay I. Kurochin, Third Secretary 1959: Eugeni A. Zaostrovtsev, Second Secretary 1960: Valentin M. Ivanov, First Secretary; Vladimir F. Glinsky, Assistant Naval Attaché; Peter Y. Ezhov, Third Secretary

Two Soviet members of the United Nations secretariat were prosecuted for espionage: Valentin Gubitchev, who was convicted but released by order of the Attorney General and allowed to return to Russia, and Igor Melekh, who was indicted but never tried, and allowed to return to Russia by order of Attorney General Robert Kennedy.

With respect to using the United Nations as a base for Soviet espionage, it is interesting to note the paradox of Soviet representation in the United Nations Secretariat, where recruitment is based partly on geographic distribution. The Soviet Union complains that it is underrepresented, but often when a post opens it has no candidates to offer for it. Thus a member of the Soviet delegation said in October, 1960, before a General Assembly committee that "of 1,170 officials selected under the principle of geographical distribution, 800, or about 65 per cent, were citizens of the United States and of its allies in military blocs, while the Soviet Union and other socialist countries had only 84 officials, or about 7 per cent." He added that of posts at the Under Secretary level (28), the Socialist countries had only one.

He omitted to mention that the highest-ranking Soviet Secretariat member the UN ever had, left under a cloud in 1952. He was Constantin Zinchenko, one of eight Assistant Secretary Generals who served directly under Trygve Lie and was in charge of Security Council affairs. It was he who arranged to have Valentin Gubitchev posted at the UN so he could act as courier for Judy Coplon. When he became aware that he was the object of an FBI investigation, he left for Russia with two years still to run in his contract and cabled that he was too ill to return. He left behind a now famous anecdote: A reporter once told him that anyone could walk into the Capitol in Washington and yell "Down with the American President" but that "you couldn't do that in the Kremlin."

"I could quite freely walk into the Kremlin and shout 'Down with the American President,' " Zinchenko replied.

Despite their shabby record of extracurricular activity, the UN tries to comply with Russian requests for Secretariat jobs when they have a candidate.

In this way, their underrepresentation becomes an asset, since the Soviet Union is able to post its nationals at the UN on short notice and give its operatives a valuable cover for their espionage assignments.

Dag Hammarskjold was well aware of this use of the UN Secretariat by the Soviet Union, and emphasized in a speech before the fifth committee of the General Assembly in October 1960 that Soviet demands for geographical representation were at variance with the charter. Of the three factors named in the charter, "efficiency, competence, and integrity," he said he would put integrity first. This meant that "United Nations officials, in the performance of their duties, should be loyal only to the United Nations." The Secretary-General added, in apparent reference to Iron Curtain countries, that it was difficult to increase recruitment among groups "who only too frequently retired, resigned, or were perhaps withdrawn after a short time and without pre-warning."

In the case of UN Secretariat members accused of espionage, the Soviets have twice been rebuffed on the principle of diplomatic immunity. In the case of Gubitchev as in the case of Igor Melekh, it was ruled that they could not claim diplomatic immunity, since they had automatically given up diplomatic protection by working for the international organization.

Members of the Soviet delegation at the UN, however, are also a source of trouble. In 1947, Sergei N. Koudriatzev, a member of the UN delegation, was identified by one of his former subordinates as a member of the GRU. In his long career in the legal network, he had been involved in the Gouzenko atomic spy case in Canada. He was recalled to the Soviet Union, but turned up recently as Ambassador to Cuba.

Index